THE
LYLE
OFFICIAL
ANTIQUES
REVIEW 1991

WHERE CAN YOU BUY A PERFECT REPLICA OF AN ANTIQUE WHICH IS INDISTINGUISHABLE FROM THE ORIGINAL?

Often at Auctions, sometimes in fashionable antique shops and at British Antique Replicas in Burgess Hill near Brighton where they have discarded 1990's machinery and production line methods in favour of 18th Century hand made craftsmanship. It is unlikely that there is any other group of highly skilled mastercraftsmen displaying 18th Century skills of cabinetry, marquetry, carving, French polishing, metal work, marble masonry, desk top leather lining, upholstery and hide colouring under one roof. Prospective buyers of Antiques and Perfect Replicas are invited to visit their workshops where they can view 18th Century skills practised today. Visit the showrooms and see if you can endorse the Company's claims that they make the finest Replica Antique furniture in the world today at a fraction of the price of the original. The Company supply every conceivable design of the 18th and 19th Centuries for the Drawing, Dining Room, Office and Boardroom.

ANTIQUE SECTION MEMBER

LAPADA
Registered Member

MEMBER

THERE ARE MANY ANTIQUE

… few, if any, who are as quality conscious as Norman Lefton, Chairman and Managing Director of British Antique Exporters Ltd. of Burgess Hill, Nr. Brighton, Sussex.

Nearly thirty years' experience of shipping goods to all parts of the globe have confirmed his original belief that the way to build clients' confidence in his services is to supply them only with goods which are in first class saleable condition. To this end, he employs a cottage industry staff of over 50, from highly skilled antique restorers, polishers and packers to representative buyers and executives.

Through their knowledgeable hands passes each piece of furniture before it leaves the B.A.E. warehouses, ensuring that the overseas buyer will only receive the best and most saleable merchandise for their particular market. This attention to detail is obvious on a visit to the Burgess Hill showrooms where potential customers can view what must be the most varied assortment of Georgian, Victorian, Edwardian and 1930s furniture in the UK. One cannot fail to be impressed by, not only the varied range of merchandise, but also the fact that each piece is in showroom condition awaiting shipment.

As one would expect, packing is considered somewhat of an art at

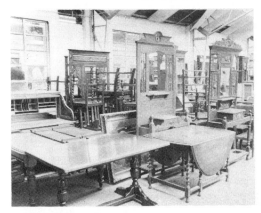

B.A.E. and the manager in charge of the works ensures that each piece will reach its final destination in the condition a customer would wish. B.A.E. set a very high standard and, as a further means of improving each container load, their customer/container liaison dept, invites each customer to return detailed information on the

BRITISH ANTIQUE EXPORTERS LTD,
SCHOOL CLOSE, QUEEN ELIZABETH AVENUE,
BURGESS HILL, WEST SUSSEX RH15 9RX, ENGLAND.
Telephone BURGESS HILL (04 44) 245577.
Fax (04 44) 232014.
Members of L.A.P.A.D.A. and Guild of Master Craftsmen

SHIPPERS IN BRITAIN BUT...

£10,000 container will immediately it is unpacked at its final destination realise in the region of £15,000 to £20,000 for our clients selling the goods on a quick wholesale turnover basis."

When visiting the warehouses various container loads can be seen in the course of completion. The intending buyer can then judge for himself which type of container load would be best suited to his market. In an average 20-foot container B.A.E. put approximately 75 to 100 pieces carefully selected to suit the particular destination. There are always at least 10 outstanding or unusual items in each shipment, but every piece included looks as though it has something special about it.

B.A.E. have opened several new showrooms based at its 15,000 square feet headquarters in Burgess Hill which is 15 minutes away from Gatwick Airport, 7 miles from Brighton and 39 miles from London on a direct rail link, (only 40 minutes journey), the Company is ideally situated to ship containers to all parts of the world. The showrooms, restoration and packing departments are open to overseas buyers and no visit to purchase antiques for re-sale in other countries is complete without a visit to their Burgess Hill premises where a welcome is always found.

saleability of each piece in the container, thereby ensuring successful future shipments.

This feedback of information is the all important factor which guarantees the profitability of future containers. "By this method" Mr. Lefton explains, "we have established that an average

BRITISH ANTIQUE EXPORTERS LTD,
SCHOOL CLOSE, QUEEN ELIZABETH AVENUE,
BURGESS HILL, WEST SUSSEX RH15 9RX, ENGLAND.
Telephone BURGESS HILL (04 44) 245577.
Fax (04 44) 232014.
Members of L.A.P.A.D.A. and Guild of Master Craftsmen

While every care has been taken in the compiling of information contained in this volume, the publishers cannot accept any liability for loss, financial or otherwise, incurred by reliance placed on the information herein.

All prices quoted in this book are obtained from a variety of auctions in various countries during the twelve months prior to publication and are converted to dollars at the rate of exchange prevalent at the time of sale.

The publishers wish to express their sincere thanks to the following for their involvement and assistance in the production of this volume:

EELIN McIVOR (Sub Editor)
NICKY FAIRBURN (Art Editor)
ANNETTE CURTIS
TRACEY BLACK
LOUISE SCOTT-JONES
CATRIONA McKINVEN
GILLIAN EASTON
DONNA BONAR
JACQUELINE LEDDY
FRANK BURRELL
JAMES BROWN
EILEEN BURRELL
RICHARD SCOTT
FIONA RUNCIMAN

Cover Illustrations
Front: Pair of 19th century German nodding figures 'Grandma and Grandpa'
 19th century Masons Ironstone jug
 Pair of 18th century plated chocolate pots
 Doulton character jug Touchstone, issued 1936 - 1960
Spine: 19th century Saffordshire jug in the form of a standing figure of Nelson
 30. 5 cm high
Back: Early 19th century parquetry two division tea caddy with ivory keyplate
 W H Kerr & Co Worcester Parian figure of Shakespeare reclining against a tree
 Home Sweet Home Bargeware treacle glazed tea pot 30 cm high

A CIP catalogue record for this book is available from the British Library.

ISBN 86248 - 134 - 1

Copyright © Lyle Publications MCMXC
Glenmayne, Galashiels, Scotland.

Printed and bound in Great Britain by
Butler & Tanner Ltd, Frome and London

THE
LYLE
OFFICIAL
ANTIQUES
REVIEW 1991

COMPILED & EDITED BY
TONY CURTIS

be guided by

LYLE

Erotic Antiques

1001 Antiques worth a Fortune (which not a lot of people know about)

LYLE PRICE GUIDE TO DOULTON

THE LYLE OFFICIAL ARTS REVIEW 1991

The Price Guide to Paintings

Tony Curtis

THE LYLE OFFICIAL ANTIQUES REVIEW 1991

Over 1 million copies sold

The Price Guide to Antiques

Tony Curtis

ANTIQUE DEALERS POCKET BOOK

Popular ANTIQUES *and their Values*

Popular ANTIQUES *and their Values 1800-1875*

Introduction

This year over 100,000 Antique Dealers and Collectors will make full and profitable use of their Lyle Official Antiques Review. They know that only in this one volume will they find the widest possible variety of goods — illustrated, described and given a current market value to assist them to BUY RIGHT AND SELL RIGHT throughout the year of issue.

They know, too, that by building a collection of these immensely valuable volumes year by year, they will equip themselves with an unparalleled reference library of facts, figures and illustrations which, properly used, cannot fail to help them keep one step ahead of the market.

In its twenty one years of publication, Lyle has gone from strength to strength and has become without doubt the pre-eminent book of reference for the antique trade throughout the world. Each of its fact filled pages are packed with precisely the kind of profitable information the professional Dealer needs — including descriptions, illustrations and values of thousands and thousands of individual items carefully selected to give a representative picture of the current market in antiques and collectibles — and remember all values are prices actually paid, based on accurate sales records in the twelve months prior to publication from the best established and most highly respected auction houses and retail outlets in Europe and America.

This is THE book for the Professional Antiques Dealer. 'The Lyle Book' — we've even heard it called 'The Dealer's Bible'.

Compiled and published afresh each year, the Lyle Official Antiques Review is the most comprehensive up-to-date antiques price guide available. THIS COULD BE YOUR WISEST INVESTMENT OF THE YEAR!

Tony Curtis

PERIODS

TUDOR PERIOD	1485 - 1603
ELIZABETHAN PERIOD ..	1558 - 1603
INIGO JONES	1572 - 1652
JACOBEAN PERIOD	1603 - 1688
STUART PERIOD	1603 - 1714
A. C. BOULLE	1642 - 1732
LOUIS XIV PERIOD	1643 - 1715
GRINLING GIBBONS	1648 - 1726
CROMWELLIAN PERIOD ..	1649 - 1660
CAROLEAN PERIOD	1660 - 1685
WILLIAM KENT	1684 - 1748
WILLIAM & MARY PERIOD	1689 - 1702
QUEEN ANNE PERIOD ..	1702 - 1714
GEORGIAN PERIOD	1714 - 1820
T. CHIPPENDALE	1715 - 1762
LOUIS XV PERIOD	1723 - 1774
A. HEPPLEWHITE	1727 - 1788
ADAM PERIOD	1728 - 1792
ANGELICA KAUFMANN ..	1741 - 1807
T. SHERATON	1751 - 1806
LOUIS XVI	1774 - 1793
T. SHEARER	(circa) 1780
REGENCY PERIOD	1800 - 1830
EMPIRE PERIOD	1804 - 1815
VICTORIAN PERIOD	1837 - 1901
EDWARDIAN PERIOD	1901 - 1910

MONARCHS

HENRY IV	1399 - 1413
HENRY V	1413 - 1422
HENRY VI	1422 - 1461
EDWARD IV	1461 - 1483
EDWARD V	1483 - 1483
RICHARD III	1483 - 1485
HENRY VII	1485 - 1509
HENRY VIII	1509 - 1547
EDWARD VI	1547 - 1553
MARY	1553 - 1558
ELIZABETH	1558 - 1603
JAMES I	1603 - 1625
CHARLES I	1625 - 1649
COMMONWEALTH ..	1649 - 1660
CHARLES II	1660 - 1685
JAMES II	1685 - 1689
WILLIAM & MARY ..	1689 - 1695
WILLIAM III	1695 - 1702
ANNE	1702 - 1714
GEORGE I	1714 - 1727
GEORGE II	1727 - 1760
GEORGE III	1760 - 1820
GEORGE IV	1820 - 1830
WILLIAM IV	1830 - 1837
VICTORIA	1837 - 1901
EDWARD VII	1901 - 1910

CONTENTS

Acknowledgements

A.J. Cobern, The Grosvener Sales Rooms, 93b Eastbank Street, Southport, PR8 1DG.
Abbotts Auction Rooms, The Auction Rooms, Campsea Ashe, Woodbridge, Suffolk.
Allen & Harris, St. Johns Place, Whiteladies Road, Clifton, Bristol BS8 2ST.
Anderson & Garland, Marlborough House, Marlborough Crescent, Newcastle upon Tyne, NE1 4EE.
Andrew Hartley Fine Arts, Victoria Hall, Little Lane, Ilkley.
Antique Collectors Club & Co. Ltd., 5 Church Street, Woodbridge, Suffolk, IP12 1DS.
Aucktionsverket Jakobsgatan, 10 103-25 Stockholm, Sweden.
Auction Team Koln, Postfach 501168 D 5000 Koln 50, West Germany.
Auktionshaus Arnold, Bleichstr 42, 6000 Frankfurt/M 1, West Germany.
Bearnes, Rainbow Avenue Road, Torquay, TQ2 5TG.
Biddle & Webb, Ladywood Middleway, Birmingham, B16 OPP
Black Horse Agencies, 18 Guy Street, Leamington Spa.
Boardman Fine Art Auctioneers, Station Road Corner, Haverhill, Suffolk, CB9 OEY.
Bonhams, Montpelier Street, Knightsbridge, London, SW7 1HH.
British Antique Exporters, Queen Elizabeth Avenue, Burgess Hill, Sussex.
Central Motor Auctions, Barfield House, Britannia Road, Morley, Leeds, LS27 ONH.
Christie's (International) SA, 8 Place de la Taconnerie, 1204 Geneva, Switzerland.
Christie's (Monaco) S.A.M., Park Place, 98000 Monte Carlo, Monaco.
Christie's Scotland, 164-166 Bath Street, Glasgow, G2 4TG.
Christie's South Kensington Ltd., 85 Old Brompton Road, London SW7 3LD.
Christie's, 8 Kings Street, London, SW1Y 6QT.
Christie's, 219 East 67th Street, New York, NY 10021, USA.
Christie's, 502 Park Avenue, New York, NY 10022, USA.
Christie's, Cornelis Schuystraat 57, 1071 JG, Amsterdam, Netherlands.
Christies S.A.Roma, 114 Piazza Navona 00186, Roma.
Christies Swire, 1202 Alexandra House, 16-20 Charter Road, Hong Kong.
Clifford Dann, 20/21 High Street, Lewes, Sussex.
Cooper Hirst Auctions, The Granary Saleroom, Victoria Road, Chelmsford, Essex, CM2 6LH.
Cooper Hirst, Goldlay House, Parkway, Chelmsford, Essex, CM27 PR.
D.M. Nesbit & Co., 7 Clarendon Road, Southsea, Hampshire, PO5 2ED.
David Lay, The Penzance Auction House, Alverton, Penzance, Cornwall, TR18 4KE.
Dee & Atkinson, The Exchange Saleroom, Driffield, North Humberside, YO25 7LJ.
Derek Roberts Antiques, 24-25 Shipbourne Road, Tonbridge, Kent, TN10 3DN.
Diamond Mills & Co., 117 Hamilton Road, Felixstowe, Suffolk.
Downer Ross, Charter House, 426 Avebury Boulevard Central, Milton Keynes, MK9 2HS.
Du Mouchelles Art Galleries Co., 409 E. Jefferson Avenue, Detroit, Michigan 48226, USA.
Duncan McAlpine, Stateside Comics plc, 125 East Barnett Road, London EN4 8RF.
Duncan Vincent, Fine Art and Chattel Auctioneers, 105 London Street, Reading, RG1 4LF.
Duran Sala de Artes yubastas, Serrano 12 28001 Madrid.
E.W. Banks, Welbeck House, High Street, Guildford, Surrey, GU1 3JF.
Fellows & Son, Augusta House, 19 Augusta St., Hockley, Birmingham.
Finarte, 20121 Milano, Via Manzoni 38, Italy.
G.A. Key, Aylsham Salesroom, Palmers Lane, Aylsham, Norfolk, NR11 6EH.
G.A. Property Services, Canterbury Auction Galleries, Canterbury.
G.E. Sworder & Son, Northgate End Salerooms, 15 Northgate End, Bishop Stortford, Herts.
Galerie Moderne, 3 Rue du Parnasse Bruxelles, Belgium.
Galerie Moderne, 10 Rue du Parnasse 1060 Bruxelles, Belgium.
Galevie Koller, Rämistr 8, CH 8024, Zürich, Switzerland.
Geering & Colyer (Black Horse Agencies), Highgate Hawkhurst, Kent, TD18 4AD.
Giles Haywood, The Auction House, St Johns Road, Stourbridge, West Midlands, DY8 1EW.
Greaves, Son & Pilcher, 71 Church Road, Hove, East Sussex, BN3 2GL.
H. Spencer & Son, 1 St. James Row, Sheffield, S. Yorks, S11 XZ.
H.Y. Duke & Son, 40 South Street, Dorchester, Dorset.
Halifax Property Services, 53 High Street, Tenterden, Kent.
Halifax Property, 15 Cattle Market, Sandwich, Kent, CT13 9AW.
Hamptons Fine Art, 93 High Street, Godalming, Surrey.
Hanseatisches Auktionshaus für Historica, Never Wall 75, 2000 Hamburg 36, West Germany.
Hanswedell & Nolte, D-2000 Hamburg 13, Pöseldorfer Weg 1, West Germany.
Heatheringtons Nationwide Anglia, The Amersham Auction Rooms, 125 Station Road, Amersham, Bucks.
Henry Spencer & Sons, 20 The Square, Retford, Nottinghamshire, DN22 6DJ.

CHAIR BACKS

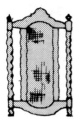 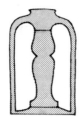 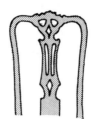 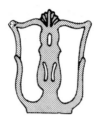 

| 1660 | 1705 | 1745 | 1745 | 1750 |
| Charles II | Queen Anne | Chippendale | Chippendale | Georgian |

 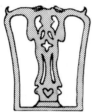 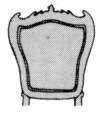 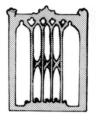 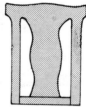

| 1750 | 1750 | 1760 | 1760 | 1760 |
| Hepplewhite | Chippendale | French Rococo | Gothic | Splat back |

  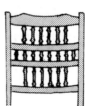  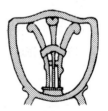

| 1770 | 1785 | 1785 | 1785 | 1790 |
| Chippendale ladder back | Windsor wheel back | Lancashire spindle back | Lancashire ladder back | Shield and feathers |

  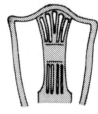 

| 1795 | 1795 | 1795 | 1795 | 1810 |
| Shield back | Hepplewhite | Hepplewhite camel back | Hepplewhite | Late Georgian bar back |

CHAIR BACKS

1810
Thomas Hope
'X' frame

1810
Regency
rope back

1815
Regency

1815
Regency
cane back

1820
Regency

1820
Empire

1820
Regency
bar back

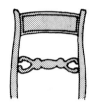

1825
Regency
bar back

1830
Regency
bar back

1830
bar back

1830
William IV
bar back

1830
William IV

1835
Lath back

1840
Victorian
balloon back

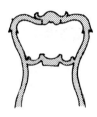

1845
Victorian

1845
Victorian
bar back

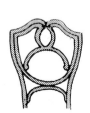

1850
Victorian

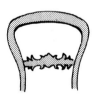

1860
Victorian

1870
Victorian

1875
Cane back

LEGS

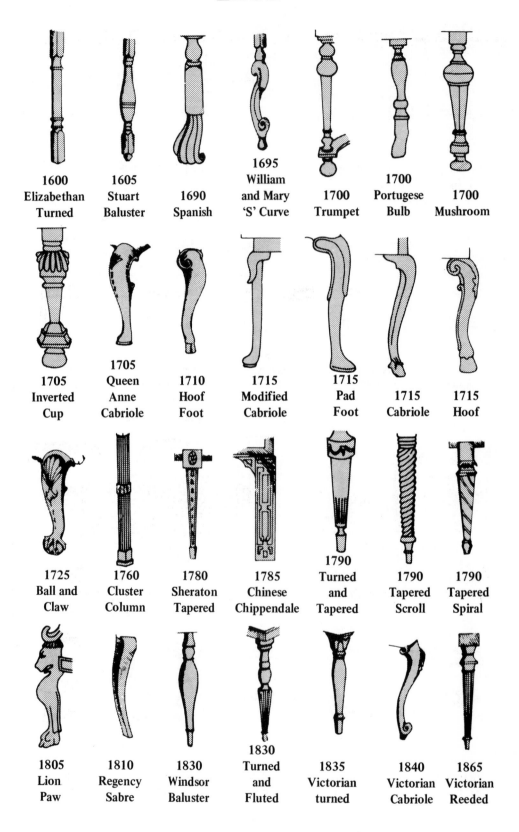

1600
Elizabethan
Turned

1605
Stuart
Baluster

1690
Spanish

1695
William
and Mary
'S' Curve

1700
Trumpet

1700
Portugese
Bulb

1700
Mushroom

1705
Inverted
Cup

1705
Queen
Anne
Cabriole

1710
Hoof
Foot

1715
Modified
Cabriole

1715
Pad
Foot

1715
Cabriole

1715
Hoof

1725
Ball and
Claw

1760
Cluster
Column

1780
Sheraton
Tapered

1785
Chinese
Chippendale

1790
Turned
and
Tapered

1790
Tapered
Scroll

1790
Tapered
Spiral

1805
Lion
Paw

1810
Regency
Sabre

1830
Windsor
Baluster

1830
Turned
and
Fluted

1835
Victorian
turned

1840
Victorian
Cabriole

1865
Victorian
Reeded

22

FEET

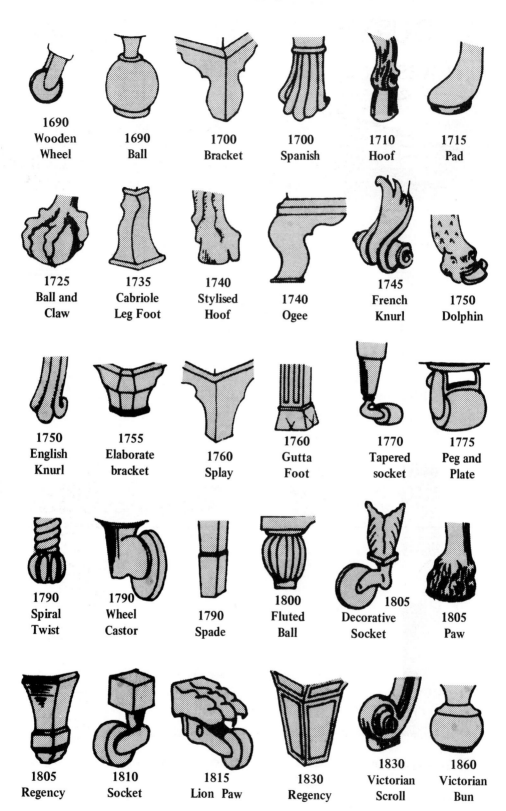

1690
Wooden
Wheel

1690
Ball

1700
Bracket

1700
Spanish

1710
Hoof

1715
Pad

1725
Ball and
Claw

1735
Cabriole
Leg Foot

1740
Stylised
Hoof

1740
Ogee

1745
French
Knurl

1750
Dolphin

1750
English
Knurl

1755
Elaborate
bracket

1760
Splay

1760
Gutta
Foot

1770
Tapered
socket

1775
Peg and
Plate

1790
Spiral
Twist

1790
Wheel
Castor

1790
Spade

1800
Fluted
Ball

1805
Decorative
Socket

1805
Paw

1805
Regency

1810
Socket

1815
Lion Paw

1830
Regency

1830
Victorian
Scroll

1860
Victorian
Bun

HANDLES

1550
Tudor
drop

1560
Early
Stuart
loop

1570
Early
Stuart
loop

1620
Early
Stuart
loop

1660
Stuart
drop

1680
Stuart
drop

1690
William &
Mary solid
backplate

1700
William &
Mary split
tail

1700
Queen Anne
solid back

1705
Queen Anne
ring

1710
Queen Anne
loop

1720
Early
Georgian
pierced

1720
Early
Georgian
brass drop

1730
Cut away
backplate

1740
Georgian
plain brass
loop

1750
Georgian
shield drop

1755
French
style

1760
Rococo
style

1765
Chinese
style

1770
Georgian
ring

1780
Late Georgian
stamped

1790
Late Georgian
stamped

1810
Regency
knob

1820
Regency
lions mask

1825
Campaign

1840
Early
Victorian
porcelain

1850
Victorian
reeded

1880
Porcelain or
wood knob

1890
Late Victorian
loop

1910
Art
Nouveau

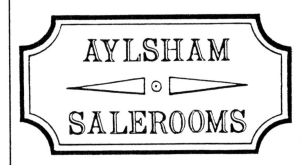

PEDIMENTS

1690
Swell frieze

1700
Queen Anne

1705
Double arch

1705
Queen Anne

1710
Triple arch

1715
Broken circular

1720
Cavetto

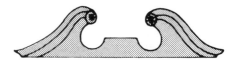

1730
Swan neck

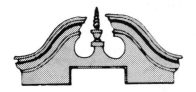

1740
Banner top

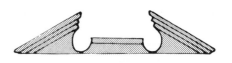

1740
Broken arch

1750
Dentil cornice

1755
Fret cut

HALIFAX ESTATE AGENCIES LTD.

PRINCIPAL SALEROOM

RETFORD - 20 The Square, Retford, Nottinghamshire, DN22 6BX. (0777) 708633

REGIONAL SALEROOMS

NANTWICH - Victoria Gallery, Market Street, Nantwich, Cheshire, CW5 5DG.
     (0270) 623878
ROSS-ON-WYE - The Georgian Rooms, Old Gloucester Road, Ross-on-Wye,
     Herefordshire, HR9 5PB. (0989) 762227
CARMARTHEN - 19 King Street, Carmarthen, Dyfed, SA31 1BH. (0267) 233456

OFFICES

ALTRINCHAM - 22 Railway Street, Altrincham, Cheshire, WA14 2RE. (061) 929 0101
BRISTOL - 18-20 The Mall, Clifton, Bristol, BS8 4DR. (0272) 738083
CAMBRIDGE - 65 Regent Street, Cambridge, CB2 1AB. (0223) 327592
HARROGATE - 1 Princes Square, Harrogate, North Yorkshire, HG1 1ND. (0423) 500566
LINCOLN - 42 Silver Street, Lincoln, LN2 1TA. (0522) 536666
LONDON - 69 Walton Street, Knightsbridge, London, SW3 2HT. (071) 584 0920
LYTHAM ST ANNES - 21 St Annes Road West, Lytham St Annes, Lancashire, FY8 1SB
     (0253) 712224
NOTTINGHAM - 4 Regent Street, Nottingham, NG1 5BQ. (0602) 5088335
SHEFFIELD - 1 St James' Row, Sheffield, S1 1WZ. (0742) 728728
SHREWSBURY - 10 High Street, Shrewsbury, Shropshire, SY1 1SP. (0743) 272183
YORK - Bell Hall, Escrick, York, YO4 6HL. (0904) 87531

FINE ART AUCTIONEERS and VALUERS

Regular Specialist Sales held monthly.
Individual or Subscription Catalogues and Full Auction Programmes available;
for details contact the saleroom concerned.

Valuations carried out for open market, insurance, capital gains tax and
probate purposes.

REGISTRY OF DESIGNS

BELOW ARE ILLUSTRATED THE TWO FORM OF 'REGISTRY OF DESIGN' MARK USED BETWEEN THE YEARS OF 1842 to 1883.

DATE AND LETTER CODE USED 1842 to 1883

EXAMPLE: An article produced between 1842 and 1867 would bear the following marks. (Example for the 12th of November 1852).

CLASS OF GOODS
YEAR
MONTH
DAY
BUNDLE

EXAMPLE: An article produced between 1868 and 1883 would bear the following marks. (Example the 22nd of October 1875).

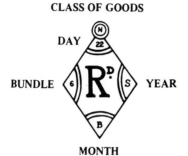

CLASS OF GOODS
DAY
BUNDLE
YEAR
MONTH

1842	X	63	G
43	H	64	N
44	C	65	W
45	A	66	Q
46	I	67	T
47	F	68	X
48	U	69	H
49	S	70	O
50	V	71	A
51	P	72	I
52	D	73	F
53	Y	74	U
54	J	75	S
55	E	76	V
56	L	77	P
57	K	78	D
58	B	79	Y
59	M	80	J
60	Z	81	E
61	R	82	L
62	O	83	K

January	C	July	I
February	G	August	R
March	W	September	D
April	H	October	B
May	E	November	K
June	M	December	A

CHINESE DYNASTIES   REIGN PERIODS

Shang	1766 – 1123 BC
Zhou	1122 – 249 BC
Warring States	403 – 221 BC
Qin	221 – 207 BC
Han	206 BC – AD 220
6 Dynasties	317 – 589
Sui	590 – 618
Tang	618 – 906
5 Dynasties	907 – 960
Liao	907 – 1125
Song	960 – 1279
Jin	1115 – 1234
Yuan	1260 – 1368
Ming	1368 – 1644
Qing	1644 – 1911

MING

Hongwu	1368 – 1398	*Hongzhi*	1488 – 1505
Jianwen	1399 – 1402	*Zhengde*	1506 – 1521
Yongle	1403 – 1424	*Jiajing*	1522 – 1566
Hongxi	1425	*Longqing*	1567 – 1572
Xuande	1426 – 1435	*Wanli*	1573 – 1620
Zhengtong	1436 – 1449	*Taichang*	1620
Jingtai	1450 – 1456	*Tianqi*	1621 – 1627
Tianshun	1457 – 1464	*Chongzheng*	1628 – 1644
Chenghua	1465 – 1487		

QING

Shunzhi	1644 – 1662	*Daoguang*	1821 – 1850
Kangxi	1662 – 1722	*Xianfeng*	1851 – 1861
Yongzheng	1723 – 1735	*Tongzhi*	1862 – 1874
Qianlong	1736 – 1795	*Guangxu*	1875 – 1908
Jiali	1796 – 1820	*Xuantong*	1908 – 1911

Fourth and foremost

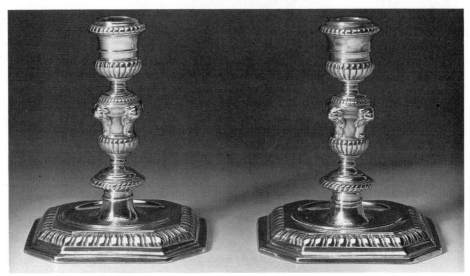

This fine pair of William and Mary cast table candlesticks fetched £16,500 last December at one of Bonhams regular monthly sales of English & Continental Silver & Plate.

B onhams are the fourth largest auction house, but in recent years the fastest growing. We have come to the fore as the saleroom where *everyone* receives special treatment.

Bonhams are almost two hundred years old and our Knightsbridge premises are perhaps the most attractive purpose-built salerooms in London.

There is even a wine bar and coffee shop for the use of Bonhams visitors, and our innovative Bonhamcard offers useful privileges to regular customers.

We open to suit your convenience, including evening and Sunday viewings.

You will find a very wide range of sales at Bonhams. We are pioneers in frames and Lalique glass, and in the vanguard of the contemporary ceramics market.

Our Theme sales, linked to special occasions throughout the year such as Crufts, the Chelsea Flower Show and Cowes Week, always attract special attention from collectors.

Our Chelsea salerooms offer less valuable items, and specialise in the new collecting areas, while Bonhams West Country, in Honiton, has opened a gateway to the London auction market in South Devon.

Buying, selling or browsing, you will always find a friendly welcome at Bonhams.

BONHAMS

KNIGHTSBRIDGE & CHELSEA

Montpelier Street, London SW7 IHH
Telephone: 071-584 9161   Fax: 071-589 4072

65-69 Lots Road, London SW10 0RN
Telephone: 071-351 7111   Fax: 071-351 7754

ANTIQUES
REVIEW

L ooking back over the past twelve months, the general consensus amongst those engaged in the buying and selling of antiques seems to be that it has been a period of ongoing expansion, with the emphasis on steady development rather than any great changes. There have, of course, been many surprises, and records have been broken in just about every branch of the business. These, however, have tended to be one-offs, and, rather than indicating any headlong take-off in prices, have on the contrary proved almost self-limiting. Of this, more anon.

So, what's been selling and who has been buying it? From just about every quarter come reports of the widening gap between the prices fetched by first quality items and more mediocre examples. Buyers are, it seems, becoming ever more discerning and unwilling to settle for second best. Unfortunately, quality pieces are becoming harder and harder to find. With the current state of the property market, fewer people are willing (or able!) to sell their houses and so there is a decrease in the flow of the items released for sale. Indeed, many now prefer to extend and upgrade their existing property, so in fact may be actively looking for additional pieces to fill the space thus gained. One suburban London auctioneer was also heard to bemoan the mild winter and the warmer weather in general. Not through any concern about the Greenhouse Effect, you understand."It's just that people aren't dying as they used to do during the cold spells!" so, again, there are fewer house clearances and a dwindling supply of goods for sale.

Nowhere is the search for quality so pronounced as in the furniture field. The year saw the all-time record for the sale of a single piece, the Nicholas Brown desk and bookcase. Christie's New York in fact devoted a sale entirely to it. Nor did it disappoint, coming in at

$12,100,000, beating the previous record by more than $9 million. The desk was in all senses a one-off, a perfect example of one of the rarest forms of American furniture. It had remained in the Brown family since it was made in the late

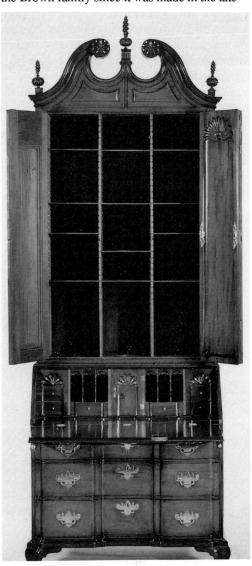

The Nicholas Brown desk and bookcase. (Christie's New York) $12,100,000

33

18th century, and thus held a special appeal to the combined grounds of American history, craftsmanship and heritage. In the UK too quality furniture performed well, with Alderman Beckford's commode, attributed to the 18th century cabinet maker John Channon, becoming the most expensive item of English furniture ever sold at £1.1 million.

Even more spectacular was the price paid for the Badminton cabinet, made in Florence in the early 18th century to the orders of the Duke of Beaufort, which obtained the staggering sum of £7.8m plus 10 per cent premium at Christie's in London.

In more general terms, Georgian furniture, .especially good carved pieces, continues to sell well, as do Edwardian and good Art Nouveau examples. Dining room furniture seems to be particularly in demand, perhaps, again, because people are doing more entertaining at home.

With regard to materials, pine, except for good Georgian examples, is perhaps not so highly favoured as previously, while country oak will do very much better, by all accounts, in the west country than it will in London.

A late 18th century French marquetry secretaire a abattant, 3ft. wide. (Greenslades) $2,635 £1,550

An interesting French provincial oak commode, the serpentine front with three drawers, 4ft. 4½in. wide. (Greenslades) $4,505 £2,650

A George II statuary white, fleur- de-peche, breche-violette and sienna
marble chimney piece, 58in. wide. (Christie's) $88,000 £55,000

Continental furniture has remained fairly
steady, with the exception of giltwood and
tapestry suites. In the past, these had proved
very popular with Arab and Italian buyers, but,
as often happens, simply too many came on the
market, with a resultant slump in the prices they
would fetch.

Architectural antiques have been selling
particularly well in recent years, and this trend
shows no signs of abating. Christie's South
Kensington report an excellent market for good
marble fireplaces, while at King Street a pair of
white marble urns on pedestals, the Hope vasi-
cippi, exceeded all expectations to fetch £93,000.
On the other hand, many people see a moral
dilemma in taking such pieces from their original
sites, and one or two court actions are pending
which could prove to be interesting test cases.
When you've furnished the house, it's time to
start on the garden, and garden furniture of all
kinds is enjoying a boom. London in particular
seems to be very garden-conscious at present,
and according to a spokesman for Lots Road
Galleries people are buying anything 'from
Coadestone to concrete'. Cast iron benches too
are doing very well. On the negative side, the
high prices commanded by good garden
statuary make it a particularly tempting target
for thieves, and, by reason of its usual position,
a fairly easy one too.

One of a pair of white marble urns on pedestals
by Thomas Hope, 82in. high, circa 1800.
(Christie's) $149,600 £93,500

Set of six Regency mahogany dining chairs with X pattern back rests, on fluted tapering supports, together with a matching carver. (Greenslades) $5,550   £3,000

Price £4.95, over 2000 photographs.

A Victorian burr walnut pedestal card table, the fold over swivel top raised on an octagonal baluster pillar. (Greenslades) $2,220   £1,200

A Victorian mahogany pedestal writing desk, the centre writing slope opening to reveal a fitted interior, 5ft wide. (Greenslades) $2,125   £1,250

A superb blue and white Ming Palace bowl, finely painted with a musk mallow and central medallion with a flower head, 5¾in. diam. (Christie's) $1,312,364 £815,133

A large Chinese vase decorated with famille rose enamels, 23in. high. (Greenslades)
$544 £320

Turning to ceramics, most ranges seem to be fairly buoyant. In the field of Oriental ceramics, the prices fetched by good kakiemon and Imari pieces have continued to rise. Chinese blue and white and Ming pieces are becoming very expensive with £1 million bids not unheard of at some Hong Kong sales. Jitters about the future of the colony certainly do not seem to have affected sales of Oriental works of art held there!

As far as Continental ceramics are concerned, the market has been steady and fairly unspectacular, with dealers in both pottery and porcelain reporting no difficulty in finding buyers for good and unusual pieces. It is finding the pieces themselves that often presents the problem. Meissen has been selling particularly readily, and while Dutch delft, German faience and stoneware and French faience have been less than consistent performers, Italian maiolica has been selling very well of late.

A Satsuma hexagonal Koro, the cover with a Dog of Fo surmount. (Greenslades)
$2,465 £1,450

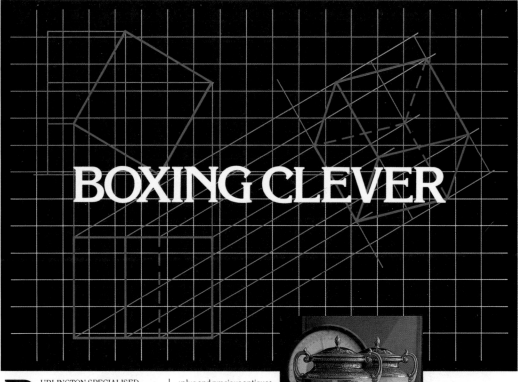

Finally coming home to domestic products, there have been some interesting developments recently. Many auction houses report a strong Continental, in particular Italian, interest in English ceramics. Some old favourites have, inevitably perhaps, performed less well. There seems for example to be a declining market for Doulton mask jugs just at present, and it may be too that the vogue for Clarice Cliff has finally passed its peak. The west country auctioneers, Michael Newman, held a sale recently where about 130 lots of Clarice Cliff were up for grabs. Two Bizarre Fantasque pieces did well enough, coming out just over estimate, but the middle quality £200–£800 range attracted much less interest and such items have certainly dropped considerably in value over the last few months. 'New' potters seem set to rise in the wake of this possibly setting star. At the same sale late 19th and early 20th century pieces by Maling and Watcombe did very well, while Christie's South Ken. for the first time devoted an entire sale to Poole pottery in February. Perhaps unsurprisingly, there was a high proportion of private buyers among the bidders, and bidding overall was cautious. At the end of the day, however, only four pieces remained unsold, and most attracted thoroughly respectable prices. It remains to be seen whether Poole will take off into the stratosphere in the same way as CC did before.

Bonhams, too, continue to hold their specialist sales of contemporary ceramics, with Hans Coper, Lucie Rie and Bernard Leach as the big names, but attended by a galaxy of other talents who may rise to become just as desireable. Certainly interest in this field shows no signs of abating.

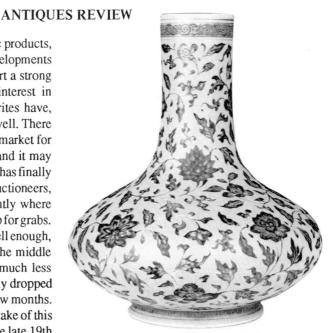

A fine and rare underglaze blue, yellow - ground vase, 8in. high. (Christie's) $690,814 £429,077

A 1930's novelty three piece pottery tea set. (Greenslades) $148 £80

A Crown Derby oval soup tureen, cover and stand decorated with flowers on a speckled green ground. (Greenslades) $422 £240

'The McCallum', a large Kingsware character jug made for D & J. McCallum Whisky Distillers, circa 1930. (Abridge Auctions) $2,320   £1,450

A Castelli large dish painted in the Grue workshop, the centre with the Mystic Marriage of St. Catherine, early 18th century. (Christie's) $44,275   £27,500

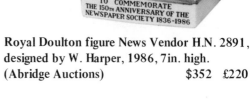

A Royal Doulton 'Master of Foxhounds' presentation jug. (Greenslades) $775   £470

Royal Doulton figure News Vendor H.N. 2891, designed by W. Harper, 1986, 7in. high. (Abridge Auctions) $352   £220

Royal Doulton figure Hostess of Williamsburg H.N. 2209, designed by M. Davies, 7¼in. high. (Abridge Auctions) $112 £70

A rare Burleighware wall plaque with a design of a galleon in full sail by Charlotte Rhead. (Michael Newman) $1,550 £940

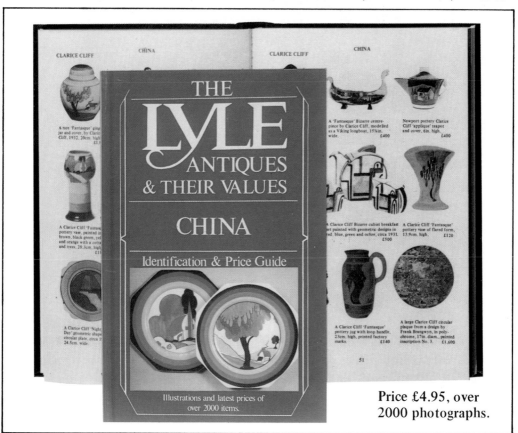

Price £4.95, over 2000 photographs.

Do you have a £2,400 biscuit tin? What about a bird-cage for £16,500, or a pair of high heeled shoes worth £8,000?

This book is certain to intrigue and fascinate, with over 3,000 illustrations and prices of just the sort of collectable which is possibly pushed out of sight and forgotten until now!

Price £7.95, over 3000 photographs.

A Staffordshire cheese dish, the cover modelled as a bullocks' head. (Greenslades) $185 £100

19th century Blackamoor wearing a wide brimmed straw hat, 2ft 4½ in. high. (Greenslades) $1,672 £950

Clarice Cliff Bizarre Fantasque vase in the Farmhouse pattern. (Michael Newman) $2,640 £1,600

George III silver tea service by Robert Peppin, London 1818, 39ozs. (Greenslades) $884 £520

In the field of silver, word is that there are still lots of bargains to be found, and that in particular functional items such as knives and forks may well be undervalued at this time. Fine traditional pieces are always in demand, but perhaps a more recent development has been a surge of interest in Arts and Crafts silver. Omar Ramsden seems to be the name to conjure with here and his work, in which a strong Arts and Crafts influence is often combined with aspects of Art Nouveau, is typical of the kind of objects which are attracting increasing attention. At a Phillips sale in Leeds in March, a fruit bowl by Ramsden, dated 1938, sold for £10,700 against an estimate of £2000–£3000. Then, in the G.A. Salerooms in Canterbury in April, a 29oz dish of quatrefoil shape, also dated 1938 and chastely estimated at £900–£1200 finally sold for £11,000. Definitely one to watch!

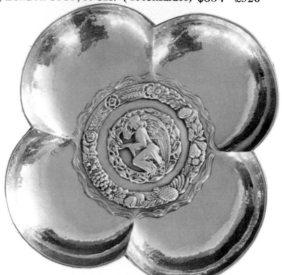

Omar Ramsden silver dish of quatrefoil shape, dated 1938, 29ozs. (G. A. Canterbury Auction Galleries) £11,000

An early Victorian four piece silver tea and coffee service by George Burrows and Richard Pearce, London 1845, 65ozs. (Greenslades) $2,380 £1,400

46

Price £4.95, over 2000 photographs.

George II silver lidded quart tankard, London 1749, Richard Gurney and Co, 30ozs. (Greenslades) $2,035 £1,100

Popular **ANTIQUES** *and their Values*
1800-1875

These two books make it easy for those either buying, selling or merely interested in the value of pieces in their own home, to identify and have a knowledge of the price the Antiques Dealer is likely to pay for a piece in average condition.

Price £7.95

The items shown are, on the whole, representative of the middle section of the market, with the addition of a few rare pieces, which, although not to be found in every corner shop, command such surprisingly high prices as to make their inclusion of interest to the reader.

Popular **ANTIQUES** *and their Values*
1875-1950

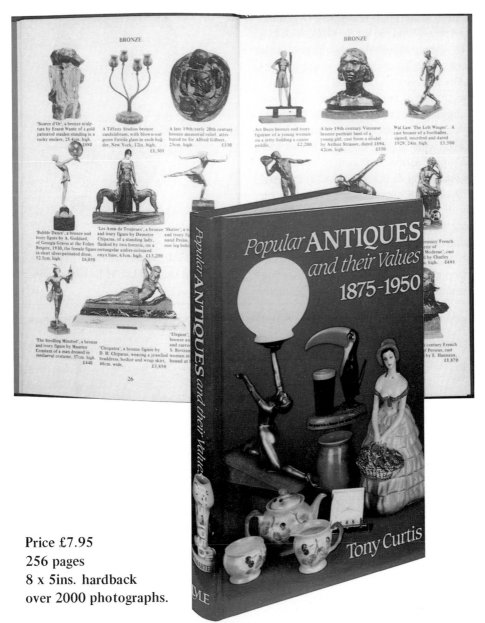

The Art Nouveau style is also currently in vogue when it comes to glass, with a strong interest in European, especially French, Art Glass on both sides of the Atlantic. Skinner Inc. in the USA sold a charming example of English Cameo Glass by an unknown artist for $26,400, while in Switzerland Habsburg Feldman achieved an all-time record for Galle with two massive vases, reportedly the largest ever produced by the Nancy factory, which sold for an equally massive Sfr. 929,500.

Toys are just as popular as ever, so it's still worth digging out your old Dinkys. Tin-plate examples are now fetching better and better prices even when in poor shape. G. E. Sworder of Bishops Stortford, recently sold a 4" clockwork model of Mickey Mouse, battered and with one arm missing, for £1300. Diecast models, though still very healthy, are tending to level out somewhat. It's significant that even comparatively recent toys will now fetch good money, with 50's and 60's robots in particular now creeping into four figures. New collecting fields are also emerging, such as paper toys.

English Cameo glass portrait vase reminiscent of Eve in the Garden of Eden. (Skinner Inc.) $26,400

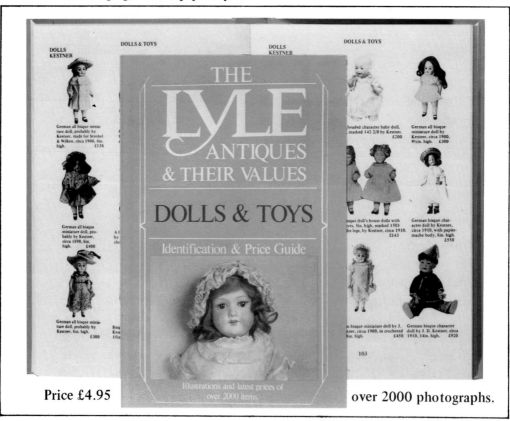

Price £4.95   over 2000 photographs.

Tin plate clockwork 'Mickey Mouse' barrel
organ toy, German, circa 1930, possibly
Distler, 8¼in. high. (G. E. Sworder & Sons)
$2,210   £1,300

Christie's South Ken. for example, sold a set of
Victorian hand coloured theatre figures for
£4,697. The great excitement of the year in
Toyland, however, has got to be Sotheby's
teddy bear, which beat last year's record breaking
Alfonzo, romantic history and all, by a staggering
£43,000. Let anyone who may still be tempted
to rush along to the nearest saleroom with their
own furry friend think again however. This
must be the all-time one-off – it seems that it just
so happened that two agents were sent along to
the saleroom on that particular day with
instructions to 'bag that bear', at any cost. The
final cost was, in fact £55,000, and the market
has been so flooded since by people trying to
cash in on this non-existent boom, that it has
suffered considerably in consequence.

'Skirolf', a clockwork tin plate figure by
E. P. Lehmann, No. 781, 18.7cm high.
(Lawrence Fine Art) $2,150   £1,265

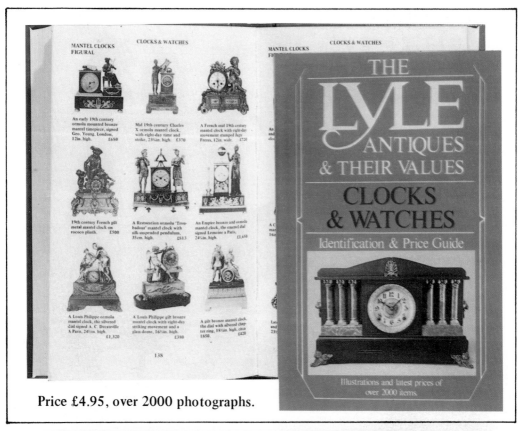

Price £4.95, over 2000 photographs.

19th century French porcelain and gilt clock garniture. (Greenslades) $3,060 £1,800

An orrery clock made by J. T. Castel,
Conseiller Secretaire to Louis XVI.
(Christie's)   £550,000

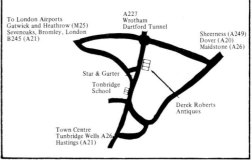

One of the most noticeable trends in recent times is the development of the 'Lifestyle' market, and this has had an effect on many different branches of the trade. People, or those with the money to do so, at any rate, are buying things, be it cameras, cars or watches, to flaunt as an indication of their style of living. Cameras are a case in point, with particular interest being shown by the Italians and Germans. Christie's, for example, sold a Leica 35mm platinum R6 camera in a lizardskin case to an Italian buyer for £26,400. It was a brand new model made to celebrate 75 years of Leica cameras. Watches too can be used for a similar purpose. Those by Patek Philippe, Rolex and Cartier are especially popular, though modern examples by The International Watch Co. are also doing well. It was a Patek Philippe no. 198103 platinum moonphase watch which broke the record recently when it sold at Sotheby's to a Japanese buyer for £308,000. The price it fetched is particularly interesting, given that, when new in 1935, it had remained unsold for some considerable time at Philippe's Paris showroom. Originally in a tonneau case it had been recased in platinum at the request of the eventual purchaser and finally sold on 4 December of that year for Sfr. 1135.

Jewellery is another obvious 'lifestyle' buy. Coloured diamonds are a new collectable moving ahead strongly. Though they are often very small, they attract big prices per carat. Emeralds are also popular, while vertu pieces by such as Faberge continue to be much sought after.

Then there are sporting goods, with 'Golfiana' having perhaps the highest profile. Phillips, Sotheby's and Christie's all now hold annual sales of golfing memorabilia timed to coincide with the British Open. The interest is world wide, with old clubs and 'featheries' particularly in demand to grace the walls of new club houses as far apart as Kyoto and Kansas City. Phillips Chester have become especially well-known for their specialist golfing sales.

For the upwardly mobile, interior design is obviously a priority, even if it comes at second hand. Lots Road report a ready market for lined, modern curtains, and recently sold a set in apricot silk, about eight years old, with a designer label, for £2,000.

The Harcourt emeralds sold by Christie's for £1,870,000, a record price for a piece of emerald jewellery.

Toshusai Sharaku, portrait of the actor Sakata Hangaro III sold at Christie's, New York for $462,000, a record price for a Japanese print.

This down to earth publication deals with the vast range of collectable items which do not always fall into the recognised category of antiques. Compiled with the close co-operation of collectors in many specialised fields this book contains information and prices on a diverse range of subjects from corkscrews, fishing reels and walking sticks to thimbles, ship's figureheads and prams. With over 3,000 photographs, descriptions and the latest prices — this book could be your wisest investment.

Price £7.95, over 3000 photographs.

John Wallace (George Pipeshank) Saturday Morning, Reiss Golf Club, Wick, Caithness, dated 1895, watercolour, 36.5 x 54.5cms. (Phillips Edinburgh) $45,900 £27,000

A golden beechwood headed play club by A. Munro, 41in. shaft. (Phillips Edinburgh)
$7,140 £4,200

A good feather ball by J. Gourlay, the ink written weight 28. (Phillips Edinburgh)
$13,600 £8,000

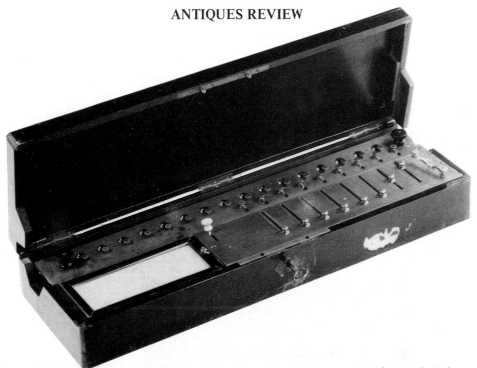

The World's first calculating machine produced in series, Arithometer by Thomas de Colmar, circa 1850. (Auction Team Koeln) $4,400   £2,670

Price £4.95   over 2000 photographs.

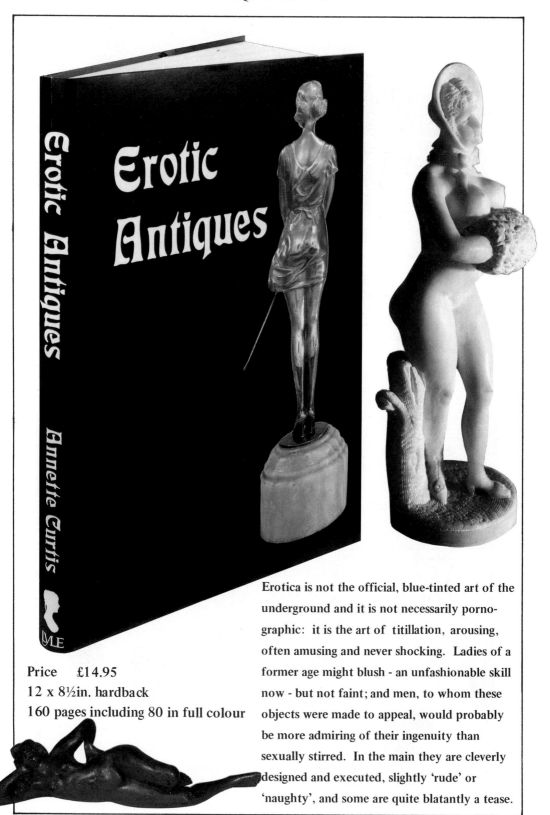

Price   £14.95
12 x 8½in. hardback
160 pages including 80 in full colour

Erotica is not the official, blue-tinted art of the underground and it is not necessarily pornographic: it is the art of titillation, arousing, often amusing and never shocking. Ladies of a former age might blush - an unfashionable skill now - but not faint; and men, to whom these objects were made to appeal, would probably be more admiring of their ingenuity than sexually stirred. In the main they are cleverly designed and executed, slightly 'rude' or 'naughty', and some are quite blatantly a tease.

A stuffed pike naturalistically mounted, caught by M. Goulding on the River Nidd, 18lbs. (Greenslades)   £986   £580

George III walnut and parcel gilt wall mirror with cherub surmount, 4ft. 3in. high. (Greenslades) $6,460   £3,800

'Ayouta', a 1920's Chiparus figure of a dancing girl in cold painted bronze and ivory, 11¾in. high. (William H. Brown) $4,420   £2,600

ANTIQUE DEALERS
POCKET BOOK

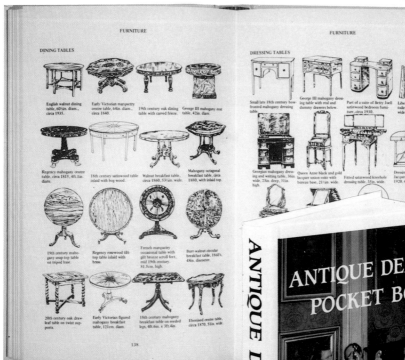

Price £7.95, over 3500 illustrations.

Instant recognition and dating of thousands of antiques is possible with this clear and comprehensive pocket manual. Over 3,500 illustrations, not only of expensive objects, but especially the day-to-day items which make up the bulk of the antiques market.

THE pocket book to make inter-trade reference simple between dealers and their clients.

But the lifestyle ad. par excellence must be the Classic car, and it seems that Monaco (where else?) is coming to be its central marketplace. The record still stands at £5.5 million for a Bugatti Royale sold by Christie's, but estimates of up to £9 million were put forward for two Ferraris due to be sold by Christie's and Sotheby's respectively in May. Alas, perhaps again there are just too many being offered for sale, for the results were very disappointing with many lots withdrawn. If you can't afford the Ferrari itself, however, how about just the engine? The auction house of Finarte in Milan sold this Ferrari 312 T5. engine for £100,000, making it surely the ultimate spare part!

Automobilia in general is one of the fastest growing auction departments, and for those with less money to spend, just about everything to do with the car is now collectable. Motoring related art is perhaps worth looking at as a long-term investment, and both Bonhams and Onslows hold sales of more reasonably priced automobilia.

It is perhaps inevitable that the age of technology is now providing its own range of thoroughly collectable antiques, and Cologne is now becoming a centre for some interesting auctions of such items. At sales held by Uwe Breker's Auction Team Koln you can buy everything from blowlamps to vacuum cleaners, from toasters to telephones. They're all collectable now, and generating such an international interest that sections for some of the more popular categories have been introduced in this edition. The doyens of this range are, however, office antiques, and a new record was recently set when a rare American Morris typewriter dated from 1885 fetched a whopping DM 37,950 (£13,500).

So, what's tipped to rise in the near future? Bonham's, ever innovative, have recently held highly successful sales devoted to such subjects as scent bottles and fountain pens (another candidate for 'lifestyle' antiques?). Games machines are another lively area generating a lot of nostalgic interest. Also tipped to rise are

Ferrari type T5. engine, 1980 complete with cast iron display stand, which can be rotated, and the original aluminium packing case used by the Ferrari Racing Team. (Finarte) $170,000   £100,000

A rare American Morris Index Typewriter, circa 1885. (Auction Team Koeln)
$22,300   £13,500

books, especially those with coloured plates, and there seems to be a trend in general towards the illustrative arts and artwork. Cartoons, for example, even comparatively modern ones, are fetching big money, with five anti-German cartoons commissioned by MI5 from Tom Purvis selling at Onslow's recently for £1,400.

The rise of such new fields may be a result of antiques in the traditional sense becoming so much more expensive. People want to collect, and they can only collect what they can afford. On the other hand, it may simply be that perceptions of what is genuinely worth collecting are broadening all the time. Whatever the cause, items which a few years ago would have been looked upon as distinctly 'wacky', are steadily coming into the fold of what is considered quite conventional, and auctioneers are assisting this rite of passage by willingly including such ranges in their normal sales. Among the new collectables, there is something to catch the fancy of just about everyone, and while the traditional ranges have lost none of their timeless appeal, the constant broadening of scope for collecting has made the field of 'antiques' in general of more direct, personal interest to many more people than ever before.

EELIN McIVOR

Norwegian wall telephone with decorative cast iron back plate by Aktieselskabet Elektrisk Bureau Kristiania, Oslo, circa 1890. (Auction Team Koeln) $1,722   £1,031

1001 Antiques worth a Fortune

1001, Antiques worth a Fortune (which not a lot of people know about)

Tony Curtis

Price £14.95
448 pages - 96 in colour

£22,857

When a doll with a blonde horsehair wig and bright pink rouged cheeks sells for £71,500, when an American comic featuring Superman sells for £25,000 and when a weather-vane shaped like a locomotive sells for £115,625 it is definitely worth taking a second look in your local auction rooms or in the nearby antiques shop or even at the next car boot sale for, featured in this book, there are a thousand and one antiques worth a fortune just waiting to be found — which not a lot of people know about.

ANTIQUES
REVIEW 1991

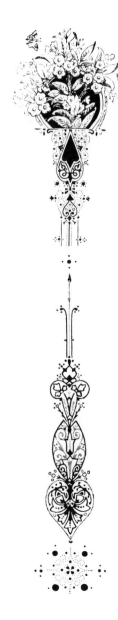

THE Lyle Official Antiques Review is compiled and published with completely fresh information annually, enabling you to begin each new year with an up-to-date knowledge of the current trends, together with the verified values of antiques of all descriptions.

We have endeavoured to obtain a balance between the more expensive collector's items and those which, although not in their true sense antiques, are handled daily by the antiques trade.

The illustrations and prices in the following sections have been arranged to make it easy for the reader to assess the period and value of all items with speed.

You will find illustrations for almost every category of antique and curio, together with a corresponding price collated during the last twelve months, from the auction rooms and retail outlets of the major trading countries.

When dealing with the more popular trade pieces, in some instances, a calculation of an average price has been estimated from the varying accounts researched.

As regards prices, when 'one of a pair' is given in the description the price quoted is for a pair and so that we can make maximum use of the available space it is generally considered that one illustration is sufficient.

It will be noted that in some descriptions taken directly from sales catalogues originating from many different countries, terms such as bureau, secretary and davenport are used in a broader sense than is customary, but in all cases the term used is self explanatory.

A Mercedes Euklid Model 29 adding machine, 1934. (Auction Team Koeln) $223 £141

A German Scribola chain drive adding machine with printer, in original box, 1922. (Auction Team Koeln) $1,156 £709

An early German Archimedes Model C tiered platen adding machine, by Reinhold Poethig, Glashuette/Sachsen, 1912. (Auction Team Koeln) $1,156 £709

An early German Archimedes Model C tiered platen adding machine with ten inputs, by Reinhold Poethig, Glashuette/ Sachsen, 1912. (Auction Team Koeln) $1,284 £788

The famous Swiss Millionaer adding machine, made by Hans W. Egli, Zurich, in fine wooden box with purpose made sloping wooden desk, 1895. (Auction Team Koeln) $3,852 £2,363

A German Adix nine key adder with in line reading and carry ten facility, in velvet case, 1903. (Auction Team Koeln) $963 £591

A German Walther Model RMKZ16 variable wheel adding machine, circa 1930. (Auction Team Koeln) $142 £87

An American Calcumeter linear adding machine with eight control settings, made by H. N. Morse, Trenton, N.J., USA, with instructions, 1901. (Auction Team Koeln) $931 £571

A very rare American Duco rapid adding machine with large honeycomb wheels and nine settings, 1909. (Auction Team Koeln) $706 £433

A 1909 Burroughs Klasse/3 Pike, American printout adding machine with full case, originally produced in 1904 by Pike, New Jersey and distributed after 1909 by Burroughs. (Auction Team Koeln) $385 £236

A Swiss Madas tiered platen adding machine with nine inputs and in original tin cover, 1908. (Auction Team Koeln) $1,284 £788

A Curta Model 1 adding machine with original tin case and box, 1948. (Auction Team Koeln) $417 £256

Reports adding machine in black bakelite casing, with box (not original), circa 1955. (Auction Team Koeln) $321 £197

A Sun adding machine, by Taylor's Typewriter Co., with stylus and fitted case, 8½in. long. (Christie's S. Ken) $271 £165

A very early American Webb's Adder, double plate, with carry ten facility, 1868. (Auction Team Koeln) $706 £433

An American Gem chain adding machine, with original pen and in black velvet case, 1904. (Auction Team Koeln) $385 £236

A rare Fax Klein seven setting adding machine of previously unknown rack type, for addition and subtraction, circa 1930. (Auction Team Koeln) $1,219 £748

An Exact (Addi 7) rare export version of the Addi 7 (Lipsia) adding machine, with original box, 1930. (Auction Team Koeln) $164 £104

'Strike Out Foreign Competition by Buying England's Glory Matches', tinplate sign with original frame, 54 x 75cm. (Onslow's) $978 £600

Lithographed sheet metal trade sign, National Carbon Company, Cleveland, Ohio, early 20th century, 26¼in. high. (Skinner Inc.) $425 £261

'Hudson's Soap Liverpool to York in 11 Hours', advertisement on linen, 75 x 100cm., framed. (Onslow's) $456 £280

'Keating's Powder Kills Bugs Fleas Beetles Moths Tins 6d and 1/-', showcard, 46 x 31cm. (Onslow's) $326 £200

A painted resin figure of a young girl holding a large ice cream cone, with black lettering *Ice Cream With a Facchino Cone It's Lovely,* 21in. high. (Christie's S. Ken) $51 £33

'Three Nuns Tobacco' golf clubs, showcard. (Onslow's) $106 £65

A golfer mascot, circa 1960, 39cm. high. (Auction Team Koeln) $131 £83

'Wills' Gold Flake', mirror, 48 x 38cm., framed. (Onslow's) $73 £45

A photographic electric advertising lamp with decorated shade *Travel with a Kodak* and *Remember with a Kodak,* 13½in. high, mid 1920s. (Christie's S. Ken) $448 £275

'Dreadnowt Razor Blade Vending Machine', enamelled advertising exterior, wall mounting, 52cm. high. (Onslow's) $440 £270

Original Coca Cola refrigerator, with original handle, circa 1959. (Auction Team Koeln)
                        $232   £139

Two Coca Cola trays, circa 1958. (Auction Team Koeln)
                        $47 £29

'Coleman's Mustard By Appointment to HM The King', mirror, 54 x 38cm., framed. (Onslow's) $114 £70

A painted plaster advertising figure of a young girl wearing a petticoat, with a plastic sign for *Sparwick Underwear,* 21½in. high. (Christie's S. Ken)
                        $154 £99

Van Jones, 'Players Please', girl and dalmations showcard. (Onslow's) $33 £20

An original Coca Cola fridge, circa 1959, with original handle and base. (Auction Team Koeln) $316 £195

Norman Wilkinson, 'Players Medium', Yacht Race Burnham showcard. (Onslow's) $90 £55

A Schucoscope foot x-ray machine, circa 1955. (Auction Team Koeln) $283 £175

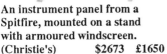

An instrument panel from a Spitfire, mounted on a stand with armoured windscreen.
(Christie's) $2673 £1650

A chromium plated cocktail shaker in the form of an airship with spirit measures contained in the base, German, 1920s, 30.5cm. high.
(Christie's S. Ken) $1,057 £682

Saunders Roe, a rare publicity book for the 'London' flying-boat, colour cover, photos, text, 31 pages.
(Christie's) $107 £66

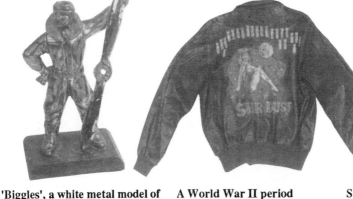

'Biggles', a white metal model of an anti-war period pilot in flying suit with helmet and goggles, 10³/₄in. high.
(Christie's) $802 £495

A World War II period U.S.A.A.F. issue leather flying jacket, size 44, painted with the insignia of a B-29.
(Christie's) $1782 £1100

S F Cody FRMS of Texas USA Inventor of the Famous War Kite, pub by Allen & Sons, double crown.
(Onslow's) $412 £250

Aero Club du Rhone et du Sud-Est 13eme. Grand Prix, 1924, lithograph in colours, backed on linen, 63 x 47in.
(Christie's) $2317 £1430

A four-bladed laminated mahogany propeller with brass tips, stamped 'DARROO MOTOR ENG CO LTD LONDON', 94in. diam.
(Christie's) $1960 £1210

Leconnu (j): La Navigation Aérienne, 6 edn., Paris, 1913, original cloth, gilt.
(Christie's) $168 £104

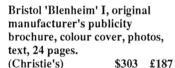

Bristol 'Blenheim' I, original manufacturer's publicity brochure, colour cover, photos, text, 24 pages.
(Christie's) $303 £187

A rare continental silver cigarette case inscribed on the gilded interior, and signed Fokker, dated Berlin Jan 1919, in original pouch, 3³/₄in. long.
(Christie's) $4633 £2860

A 1931 Schneider Trophy Contest Official Souvenir Programme. (Christie's S. Ken)
$290 £187

A 'R.A.F. issue' leather flying helmet, oxygen mask and goggles, on dummy head.
(Christie's) $392 £242

A Second World War R.A.F. fur-lined flying jacket, size 2, by D.G.L. London, with matching trousers, size 7.
(Christie's) $2317 £1430

A Japanese fighter pilot's coat, c. 1942.
(Christie's) $802 £495

R.A.F. Display, Hendon, seventeen programmes, 1921 to 1937.
(Christie's) $392 £242

A Royal Flying Corps pilot's No. 1 jacket, with label by Simpson & Son, pilot's wings, lapel badges, buttons and rank badges.
(Christie's) $1069 £660

Bristol 'Bulldog' Mk IV, original publicity booklet, colour cover, photos, text, 16 pages, 1st Edition, 1930.
(Christie's) $214 £132

71

Sud Aviation SO. 1221-S Djinn, FR145
(military serial number) built in September
1960 and entered service with ALAT that
year.
(Christie's) $30294 £18700

North American B-25J (NA 82) Mk. 3
Mitchell, G-BKXW (N9089Z) is not airworthy,
but is believed reasonably complete, no log
books exist.
(Christie's) $80190 £49500

Fokker DR I Replica, N5523V is perhaps the
earliest replica Dr I made in the U.S.A. built in
California circa 1958 for film use.
(Christie's) $23166 £14300

De Haviland DH. 110 Sea Vixen FAW. 2 (TT),
G-VIXN, was one of the last Sea Vixens
produced, coming off the Hawarden
production line in 1965 as XS587, operational
career was with 899 Squadron, operating from
R.N.A.S. Yeovilton and H.M.S. Eagle.
(Christie's) $17820 £11000

Moraine-Saulnier MS733 'Alcyon', F-BLYA,
the fuselage bears manufacturers plates
inscribed Rebuilt 1960 at Chateaudun.
(Christie's) $6772 £4180

Max Holste MH1521M 'Broussard', G-BJGW,
serial number 92, manufactured in 1957 at
Rheims, April, 1964.
(Christie's) $39204 £24200

Sopwith Tri-Plane Replica, G-PENY was built
in 1988 by J. S. Penny using modern materials
to externally resemble the original machine
but with the fuselage widened to carry two
persons side by side in the cockpit.
(Christie's) $35640 £22000

Focke-Wulf Fw 44J Stieglitz, D-EFUR was
built by Focke-Wulf in Bremen in 1936 to the
order of the Swedish Air Force, entering
service as an Sk-12 trainer, setial Fv 617, in
that year.
(Christie's) $71280 £44000

Boeing Stearman PT-13D-BW, G-BRTK was built asa Model E75 PT-13D at Wichita in 1942 as 42-17786 for the U.S.A.A.F., powered by Lycoming R680-17, from a run of 1,018.
(Christie's) $83754   £51700

Morane-Saulnier M.S. 733 'Alcyon', F-BLXV offered for sale fitted with the up-rated Patez 6D02 power plant rated at 240 h.p. coupled to a three-bladed propeller.
(Christie's) $31185   £19250

De Havilland DH. 104 Devon C.2/2, G-BLRB was part of the initial batch of Devons ordered for the R.A.F. and was taken on charge on November 15, 1948.
(Christie's) $32967   £20350

Marcel Dassault MD 312 'Flamant', F-AZEN offered here fully equipped in the basic communications role with accommodation for two pilots and a navigator, with up to eight removable seats for passengers.
(Christie's) $53460   £33000

Nord 1002 Pingouin II, LV-RIE built at Les Mureaux in June 1947, towards the end of the production run of the type.
(Christie's) $15147   £9350

Cessna 195 B, N 4461 C, built in 1953, in excellent, almost concours, condition having had one owner prior to the vendor for the previous 15 years.
(Christie's) $80190   £49500

Hawker Fury Replica, G-BKBB built to the order of the late the Hon. Patrick Lindsay, constructed as near as practical to the original by Westwards Airways Ltd. 1984–1988.
(Christie's) $320760   £198000

Bucker Bu 133C Jungmeister, D-EHVP was built for the Swiss Air Force as U-91 in 1938, it was civilianised as HB-MIW and imported into Great Britain and registered as G-AYSJ in February 1971.
(Christie's) $106920   £66000

A 19th century alabaster tazza, with a moulded rim raised on a turned base, the wreath carved loop handles with lion mask terminals, 14in. wide.
(Christie's S. Ken.) $998   £605

A giltmetal-mounted alabaster tazza, the pierced handles mounted with confronting silver plate portrait medallions of Roman style on spreading base, third quarter 19th Century, 18in. diam.
(Christie's) $1122 £660

A 19th century alabaster bust of a young lady in pre-Raphaelite headdress, signed E. Fiaschi, 50in. high.
(Sworders) $1551   £940

A pair of late 19th century Italian alabaster seated putti, one reading an alphabet book, the other writing *Canova,* 43cm. and 41cm. high.
(Christie's London) $3,010 £1,870

German alabaster figure of a woman, Ernst Seger, late 19th century, nude figure supported on a tree stump, 31in. high.
(Skinner Inc.) $900 £552

A pair of Italian alabaster ewers with zoomorphic spouts and exotic bird handles with stop-fluted baluster bodies, late 19th century, 33¼in. high.
(Christie's) $2274   £1430

A fine carved alabaster figure of a girl, scantily clad, her arms upraised, with an infant putto at her feet, 69cm. high.
(Henry Spencer) $550 £360

A sculpted alabaster model of a snarling lion with inset glass eyes, its head turned to dexter, on a naturalistic rocky base, 22in. long.
(Christie's S. Ken.) $908   £550

An alabaster bust of Romanlady, signed G. Besji, (repaired).
(Cobern) $718   £460

A Woodlands buckskin bag, the surface covered with a geometric design in dark and light blue, red and white beads, 16cm. high. (Phillips London) $72 £45

Miniature decorated covered storage basket, North East American Indian, late 19th century, 3in. high. (Skinner Inc.) $2,800 £1,657

Handled burl bowl, North American Indian, Plains, 19th century, with shaped ends and carved handles, 14¼in. long. (Skinner Inc.) $2,600 £1,538

Painted two pocket splint wall basket, Northeast Woodland Indians, mid 19th century, the high back with hanging bracket, 26in. high. (Skinner Inc.) $2,000 £1,290

A North American Indian beadwork boy's shirt, possibly Blackfeet, decorated with geometric designs in multicoloured and metallic beads, 60 x 60cm. (Phillips London) $4,186 £2,600

Three pocket wall basket, North East American Indian, 19th century, wooden hanging loop above four graduated pockets, traces of red stain, 30in. high. (Skinner Inc.) $2,100 £1,243

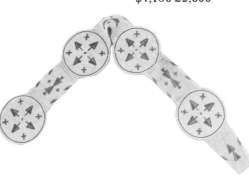

An unusual Naskape moose skin pouch, decorated with imprinted geometric designs in red paint, 50 x 28cm., 19th century. (Phillips London) $10,465 £6,500

A Blackfeet blanket strip, comprising a broad band bordered in pink, linking four discs covered with concentric circles, 1.70cm. long. (Phillips London) $3,703 £2,300

A Cree black stroud octopus bag, decorated in multicoloured glass beads, with a tree bearing exotic flowers, fruits and leaves, 46.5cm. high. (Phillips London) $2,592 £1,610

Detective Comics No. 35,
January 1940.
$10,000 £6,000

Batman No. 1.
$25,000 £15,000

The Amazing Spiderman.
$675   £400

Superman. $20,000 £12,000

Teenage Mutant Ninja Turtles.
$300   £175

Detective Comics No. 31,
September 1938.
$10,000 £6,000

Detective Comics No. 29,
June 1939. $10,000 £6,000

Detective Comics No. 38.
$16,500 £10,000

Iron Man and Sub Mariner.
$125   £75

(Duncan McAlpine - Stateside Comics P.L.C.)

Batman No. 2, Summer Issue.
$6,750 £4,000

The Incredible Hulk.
$200 £125

The Fantastic Four.
$1,100 £650

Detective Comics No. 33,
November 1939.
$13,000 £8,000

Lois Lane. $750 £450

Detective Comics No. 27, May
1939. $50,000 £30,000

Green Lantern. $750 £450

Action Comics No. 1, June
1938. $40,000 £25,000

Giant Size X-Men. $40 £95

(Duncan McAlpine - Stateside Comics P.L.C.)

AMUSEMENT MACHINES

Pointsettia, U.S.A., circa
1929. (Costa/Bates)
$830 £500

Matrimonial Bureau,
U.K., circa 1930.
(Costa/Bates) $664 £400

Bursting Cherry, U.S.A.,
circa 1938. (Costa/Bates)
$788 £475

Answerite, U.K. circa
1948. (Costa/Bates)
$373 £225

Ding a Bell, U.K. circa
1959. (Costa/Bates)
$373 £225

Try Your Grip, U.K.,
circa 1955.
(Costa/Bates) $249 £150

Sports, U.K. circa 1910.
(Costa/Bates) $1,245 £750

Roulomint, Germany, 1956.
(Costa/Bates) $141 £85

3 Ball 7 Win, U.K. circa
1962. (Costa/Bates)
$415 £250

Gapwin, U.K., circa 1962.
(Costa/Bates) $415 £250

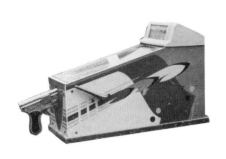

Flyover, U.K., circa 1962.
(Costa/Bates) $415 £250

Be a Sport, U.K., circa
1958. (Costa/Bates)
$415 £250

Nulli Secundus, U.K.,
circa 1910. (Costa/
Bates) $1,660 £1,000

Bajazzo, Germany,
circa 1920 (Costa/
Bates) $747 £450

A Greek bronze fragment of a hydria or stamnos depicting a satyr carrying a maenad aloft, 14cm. high, second half of 4th century B.C. (Phillips London) $8,855 £5,500

Chinese straw glazed pottery guardian figure, Sui Dynasty, 589-617A.D., standing in full armour, 12in. high. (Skinner Inc.) $2,100 £1,338

An Attic red figure shallow stemmed kylix, the interior medallion framing two standing youths, repaired and restored, 28.5cm. diam. across handles, 530-510 B.C. (Phillips London) $3,703 £2,300

A bright blue glaze composition Royal Ushabti of Queen Henttaway, adorotress of Hathor, 12cm. high, 21st Dynasty, from Deir el Bahri. (Phillips London) $2,093 £1,300

Pair of Chinese pottery figures of musicians, Tang Dynasty, one holding cymbals, traces of white slip decoration, 7in. high. (Skinner Inc.) $2,100 £1,338

An unusual Fiji wood club, the intricately incised grip squaring towards the butt, 93cm. high. (Phillips London) $1,046 £650

An Amlash pottery vessel in the shape of a bull, the head, a detachable cover for the mouth of the vessel, 32.5cm. high, 1st millennium B.C. (Phillips London) $5,635 £3,500

A large copper figure of a standing bearded man, both hands held before him, from Lebanon (Sidon), beginning of 2nd millennium B.C., 39cm. high. (Phillips London) $19,320 £12,000

Etruscan lidded urn, 6th century BC, possibly from Chiusi, Italy, decorated with battle scene from Etruscan mythology, 40 x 34cm. (Auktionshaus Arnold) $883 £573

A Greek bronze equestrian group, 4cm. high, Geometric Period, 8th century B.C. (Phillips London) $547 £340

A Hittite bronze figure of a man with simple bird-like features, the right hand extended, 17cm. high, 2000-1500 B.C. (Phillips London) $483 £300

A Greek marble relief of a mounted warrior, 24 x 25cm. 5th century B.C., split across bottom left hand corner. (Phillips London) $1,207 £750

A Hittite pottery horse rhyton, the cylindrical neck of the vessel on its back, the two spouts at its front hooves, 26cm. high, 2000-1500 B.C. (Phillips London) $17,710 £11,000

A black granite male head, 12.7cm. high, 26th Dynasty to Ptolemaic Period. (Phillips London) $8,372 £5,200

A Boeotian terracotta figure of a dog, carrying a puppy in its mouth, 16.5cm. long, 6th century B.C. (Phillips London) $966 £600

Chinese pottery tomb figure of a horse, Tang Dynasty, 618-906 A.D., covered in brown glaze (extensively restored), 13in. high. (Skinner Inc.) $8,000 £5,096

Pair of Chinese pottery male tomb figures, Tang Dynasty, traces of red, black and white slip decoration, 11in. high. (Skinner Inc.) $1,700 £1,083

An Elamite grey steatite standing male figure, the robe decorated with incised designs, 14.2cm. high, 3rd millennium B.C. (Phillips London) $11,270 £7,000

ARMOUR

A good composite late 16th century Almain Collar, hinged gorgot with key-hole fastening stud, medial ridge to front plate.
(Wallis & Wallis) $1361   £825

One of a pair of finger gauntlets, pointed cuffs with roped borders, roped knuckle plates, probably German, early 17th century.
(Phillips) $858   £520

A scarce WWI tank driver's face mask, leather covered, chamois lined, mail chin guard.
(Wallis & Wallis) $297   £180

A Victorian Household Cavalry Officer's breast and backplates, of steel with brass riverts and edging.
(Phillips) $1485   £900

A rare pair of Italian vambraces, each comprising a tubular upper-cannon made in two parts linked by a recessed turning joint, early 16th century, 18¼ in. long.
(Christie's S. Ken.)$9982   £6050

An etched Italian Infantry half-armour, comprising Spanish morion, gorget of two plates pivoted together at the side, cuirass with peasecod breast plate, probably Milanese, circa 1580. (Christie's S. Ken)
$34,760   £22,000

An iron circular shield (target), made in one piece, and comprising a main domed central section within a wide flat border, early 17th century, probably Spanish, 22¼in. diam.
(Christie's S. Ken.)$7260   £4400

A composite Italian armour, comprising close-helmet with one-piece skull, high roped comb, brass plume-holders, comprehensively circe 1570.
(Christie's S. Ken.)$6534   £3960

An etched and gilt pommel plate from a saddle, the upper edges bordered by narrow flanges, probably French, circa 1570, 8in. high.
(Christie's S. Ken.) $726   £440

A rare Italian breast-plate, of slightly flattened form with low medial ridge, bold angular turn at the neck, early 16th century, 30½ in. high.
(Christie's S. Ken.) $8349   £5060

A rare late 16th century German elbow gauntlet, 13in, long arm plate with medial ridge, open at back and secured by leather straps and 4 buckles.
(Wallis & Wallis) $660   £400

A rare German gothic breast-plate made in two parts (associated), joined by a central screw, late 15th century, 21in. high.
(Christie's S. Ken.) $8167   £4950

An armour in 16th century style, comprising close-helmet with two-piece pointed skull, pivoted visor and upper and lower bevors.
(Christie's S. Ken.) $5082   £3080

A pair of German gauntlets, of bright steel, each comprising a flared boxed cuff made in two pieces, roped turned borders with narrow recessed band and central cusp, late 16th century, 11in. (Christie's S. Ken)
$4,171 £2,640

An English Civil War period breastplate, distinct medial ridge, turned over edges, flared narrow skirt, twin studs for securing straps.
(Wallis & Wallis) $495   £300

A good 18 cavity brass gang mould c. 1800 for casting graduated balls from 120 bore to 12 bore.
(Wallis & Wallis) $124   £75

An attractive 19th century Indian all metal shield dhal, 13¾ in. finely damascened in silver and gold scrollwork.
(Wallis & Wallis) $462   £280

A good heavy early 19th century Moro cuirass, composed of shaped brass plates linked together by thick brass mail.
(Wallis & Wallis) $742   £450

BADGES

A rare OR's cap badge of a militia Bn The N Staffordshire Regt (as 678), with lugs.
(Wallis & Wallis) $49   £30

An OR's darkened glengarry badge of the 1st Midlothian Rifle Vols.
(Wallis & Wallis) $82   £50

An officers silver cap badge of The Middlesex Regt, HM B'ham 1926.
(Wallis & Wallis) $107   £65

A Vic OR's helmet plate of the 2nd Vol Bn The Manchester Regt.
(Wallis & Wallis) $115   £70

A Vic officers silver plated Maltese Cross pouch belt badge of the 4th Lancashire Rifle Vols.
(Wallis & Wallis) $190   £115

A Vic OR's WM helmet plate of the 8th Lancashire Rifle Vols.
(Wallis & Wallis) $115   £70

A good Vic OR's WM glengarry badge of the 10th Lanark R.V. (Glasgow Highlanders).
(Wallis & Wallis) $247   £150

A Geo oval silver plated shoulder belt plate, with impressed crown over 'GR' cypher.
(Wallis & Wallis) $181   £110

A Vic officers silver plated pouch belt badge of the Central Provinces Police (India).
(Wallis & Wallis) $74   £45

BADGES

A scarce NCO's WM arm badge of the Northumberland Hussars (Cox 1303), with cloth backing.
(Wallis & Wallis) $107   £65

A good officers 'Sterling' cap badge of the King's Dragoon Guards, 1st Pattern (734).
(Wallis & Wallis) $140   £85

A scarce cap badge of the 249th CEF.
(Wallis & Wallis) $58   £35

A post 1902 officers silver plated helmet plate of the 1st Vol Bn The York & Lancaster Regt.
(Wallis & Wallis) $165   £100

A scarce Vic OR's WM helmet plate of the Second Middlesex Artillery (Vols).
(Wallis & Wallis) $107   £65

A post 1902 officers gilt and silver plated helmet plate of The Royal Irish Regt.
(Wallis & Wallis) $214   £130

An officers fur cap grenade badge of The R Inniskilling Fusiliers.
(Wallis & Wallis) $107   £65

A rare French Revolutionary period officer's gorget, of brass with applied silvered trophy of arms and flags, the centre with royalist fleur-de-lys and crown, circa 1789-92. (Phillips London) $1,360 £800

A silver colour belt badge of the 1st Bn The L North Lancashire Regt.
(Wallis & Wallis) $99   £60

BADGES

A rare OR's cap badge of a Militia Bn The Middlesex Regt design as for regular bns. (Wallis & Wallis) $74 £45

An OR's WM cap of the 2nd VB The S Lancashire Regt. (Wallis & Wallis) $66 £40

A good officers silver, gilt and enamel star cap badge of the Kings Dragoon Guards, 1918. (Wallis & Wallis) $247 £150

An OR's brass Maltese Cross helmet plate of the 38th Middlesex (Artists) Rifle Vols. (Wallis & Wallis) $91 £55

A scarce 1902 officers helmet plate of The 7th City of London Regt. (Wallis & Wallis) $256 £155

An officer's early 19th century rectangular gilt shoulder belt plate of the Southwark (Princess Charlotte's Infantry) Volunteers. (Christie's S. Ken) $589 £385

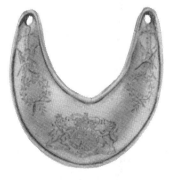

A scarce post 1902 OR's WM glengarry badge of the 2nd Vol Bn The Highland Light Infantry. (Wallis & Wallis) $173 £105

A Georgian officer's gorget of silver, engraved with pre-1801 Royal Arms, the shoulders engraved with a helmet and trophy of arms. (Phillips London) $714 £420

A Vic OR's WM glengarry badge of the 1st West York Administrative Battalion. (Wallis & Wallis) $99 £60

CASED SETS

A Colt 1849 model pocket percussion revolver, the blued sighted barrel engraved *Sam Colt* in gothic script on the top flat, in original American mahogany case lined in blued velvet with accessories including 'eagle and shield' flask, 9in. (Christie's S. Ken)
$4,519 £2,860

A self cocking six shot percussion pepperbox revolver with case hardened fluted barrels, in original lined and fitted brass bound mahogany case with trade label and accessories including three way copper flask, by B. Cogswell, 224 Strand, London, London proof marks, circa 1850, 9½in. (Christie's S. Ken)
$5,214 £3,300

A fine 40-bore D.B. percussion sporting rifle with browned twist barrels leaf sighted to 250 yards and rifled for a belted ball, in original fitted oak case lined with red felt with trade label and accessories, by J. Purdey, 314½ Oxford Street, London, London proof marks, 30in. barrels. (Christie's S. Ken)
$8,169 £5,170

A 120-bore Beaumont-Adams double action percussion revolver, with blued octagonal sighted rifled barrel stamped *L.A.C.*, in original lined and fitted oak case with accessories including bullet mould, London proof marks, 10in. (Christie's S. Ken) $1,564 £990

A good and very desireable cased 65 bore 4 barrelled boxlock sidehammer 'turnover' travelling pistol by W. Parker, London, 8½in., twist barrels 3½in., London proved, platinum safety plugs, ribs engraved 'W. Parker Maker to his Majesty Holborn'. (Wallis & Wallis) $5032 £3050

CASED SETS

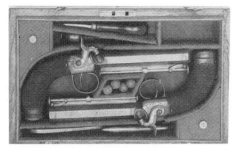

A good 5 shot cased 120 bore double action percussion revolver by W. Gallyon of Cambridge, 7¹/₂in. mirror blued octagonal barrel 3in., Birmingham proved, engraved W Gallyon Cambridge with foliate and border on top strap.
(Wallis & Wallis) $1138   £690

A pair of percussion box lock belt pistols with octagonal sighted barrels signed in full on the top flat and rifled with eight grooves, foliate engraved breeches and tangs, foliate engraved bolted actions, by E. & W. Bond, 45 Cornhill, London, London proof marks, circa 1840, 9¼in. (Christie's S. Ken)
$2,086 £1,320

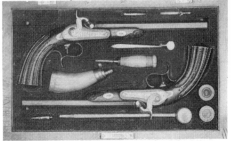

A very good and desireable cased 70 bore 4 barrelled boxlock sidehammer 'turnover' travelling pistol by H. Tatham, London, 8¹/₂in., barrels 3¹/₂in., London proved, platinum safety plugs, ribs engraved 'London' steel ramrod retained by spring clip.
(Wallis & Wallis) $3712   £2250

A fine pair of flintlock duelling pistols with heavy rebrowned octagonal polygroove rifled barrels signed in full on the top flats, in original lined and fitted mahogany case, with trade label and accessories including red leather covered flask, by John Manton & Son, 15in. (Christie's S. Ken) $14,773 £9,350

A scarce 20-shot pinfire revolver, 13cm. sighted barrel, frame engraved with foliage against a stippled ground and signed J. Chaineux.
(Phillips) $3465   £2100

A pair of Belgian percussion rifled target pistols with browned octagonal sighted barrels inscribed *A cier* on the top flats, adjustable back sights, foliate engraved tangs, the locks and mounts decorated en suite, Liege proof marks, circa 1850, 15½in. (Christie's S. Ken) $2,781 £1,760

DAGGERS

A good ivory mounted Kindjal, 39cm. triple fullered blade, the ivory hilt
and scabbard carved with foliage, scrolls and geometric patterns imitating
silver niello decoration.
(Phillips) $4125   £2500

An old Tibetan Ritual dagger, spatulate iron blade 7in. with copper tip
edge mount of stylised flames, blade issuing from Dragon's mouth and
with brass hilt with thunderbolt pommel emblem.
(Wallis & Wallis) $91   £55

An attractive Indo Persian copper gilt mounted dagger Pesh kabz c. 1800,
18in., recurved 'T' section blade $9^3/_4$ in. with thickened armour piercing
tip.
(Wallis & Wallis) $297   £180

A fine left hand dagger with tapering blade of flattened hollow diamond section with
rectangular ricasso, iron hilt comprising straight quillons widening slightly towards the
rounded tips, late 16th century, $17\frac{3}{4}$in. (Christie's S. Ken) $13,904 £8,800

A good Geo officers dirk, shallow diamond section polished blade $8^1/_4$ in.,
foliate chiselled copper gilt crosspiece and lion's head pommel, turned tall
ivory grip.
(Wallis & Wallis) $346   £210

A rare Swiss (Holbein) dagger with double edged blade of flattened diamond section, in
gilt bronze mounted scabbard covered in leather, the front cast and pierced with the
Death of Virginia, late 16th Century, $15\frac{1}{2}$in. (Christie's S. Ken) $4,171 £2,640

A Scottish Highland dirk with straight fullered single edged blade (some pitting) back
edged towards the point, brass mounted root wood handle carved with interlace, early
18th century, $15\frac{1}{2}$in. (Christie's S. Ken) $1,390 £880

DAGGERS

An attractive Spanish ivory hilted dagger d 1859, 12½in., straight single edged tapered blade 7½in. with single fuller, deeply etched with scrolling foliage.
(Wallis & Wallis) $106   £64

A 2nd Pattern FS fighting knife, blade 6½in. etched with label 'Wilkinson Sword, etc', and within scrolls 'Hand Forged by Tom Beasley, the Famous Sword Smith'.
(Wallis & Wallis) $198   £120

An unusual and attractive polychrome enamelled Balkan dagger jambiya, curved double edged blade 10¼in. chiselled with 3 standing figures and a goat, silver damascened at forte with scrolls and foliage.
(Wallis & Wallis) $122   £74

A Nazi Army officers dagger, by Eickhorn, blade retains most original polish, plated hilt, orange grip, in its plated sheath with original hanging straps.
(Wallis & Wallis) $214   £130

A good 19th century Romantic period 'Satanic' ritual dagger, 11¾in., straight bi fullered shallow diamond section blade 7in. cast and chased brass hilt and sheath.
(Wallis & Wallis) $264   £160

A Scottish silver mounted dirk with tapering hollow ground single edged blade back edged towards the point and with incised device on each face, the blade of the by-knife (tip missing) stamped *Paton* on one side, circa 1745, 18¾in. (Christie's S. Ken)
$1,564 £990

A silver mounted Scottish dress dirk with signed partly hollow ground single edged blade, stamped *McLeod*, circa 1830, and a silver mounted sgian dubh, with fullered single edged blade, early 19th century, 17in. and 8½in. (Christie's S. Ken) $1,043 £660

HELMETS

A Victorian officer's shako of the 31st Regiment, blue cloth body with two gold lace bands to top. (Phillips London) $534 £340

A cocked hat worn by Mussolini for Court dress, black fur with gold bullion tassels fore and aft, gilt button to right side. (Phillips London) $7,222 £4,600

An officer's 1869 pattern blue cloth shako of the Worcestershire Militia trimmed with silver lace. (Christie's S. Ken) $437 £286

An Albert pattern officer's helmet of the 2nd Dragoon Guards, gilt brass skull and fittings, including front plate with *VR* cypher. (Phillips London) $1,099 £700

A rare and interesting helmet probably made for an officer of an Indian light cavalry unit in the 1850s. (Christie's S. Ken) $538 £352

An officer's shako of the Cameronians (Scottish Rifles) of dark green cloth trimmed with black braid bearing black bugle horn badge. (Christie's S. Ken) $504 £330

A post-1902 officer's blue cloth helmet of the Lincolnshire Regiment, with gilt fittings including front plate, spike, rose bosses and leather backed chin chain. (Phillips London) $502 £320

A lobster tailed pot, the one piece hemispherical ribbed skull with separate ring shaped finial, probably German, second quarter of the 17th century, 11in. high. (Christie's S. Ken) $956 £605

An 1871 pattern officer's helmet of the 2nd Dragoon Guards, gilt brass skull, silver, gilt and enamel front plate, rosette bosses. (Phillips London) $1,334 £850

HELMETS

An Imperial German officer's busby of the 1st Leib Hussars, with applied silver skull and crossbones badge to the front. (Phillips London) $1,491 £950

A dress fez worn by Mussolini as First Honorary Corporal of the MVSN, with large gold bullion embroidered eagle and fasces to front. (Phillips London) $69,080 £44,000

A fine leather helmet of a Land-wehr officer of Bavarian Artil-lery with square peak, gilt fittings including ball ornaments and chinscales. (Christie's S. Ken) $757 £495

A French Second Republic shako, with copper front plate, painted tricolour cockade, silver lace top band. (Phillips London) $408 £260

A French Cuirassiers trooper's helmet of steel with brass crest and with black mane and red horsehair tuft and 10in. red hackle plume. (Christie's S. Ken) $471 £308

A trooper's Victorian lance cap of the 9th (Queen's Royal) Lancers, of black patent leather with black/dark blue cloth sides. (Christie's S. Ken) $471 £308

A Victorian Other Ranks' helmet of the 2nd West York-shire Yeomanry, steel skull with brass fittings, black horse-hair plume. (Phillips London) $910 £580

An officer's fine scarlet topped Victorian lance cap (chapka) of the 12th (Prince of Wales's Royal) Lancers, with scarlet feather plume with gilt socket. (Christie's S. Ken) $3,029 £1,980

An officer's helmet of the Hertfordshire Yeomanry, silvered skull with gilt fittings, circa 1870. (Phillips London) $1,491 £950

HELMETS

Painted leather fire helmet, Cairns & Brothers makers, New York, dated *1852,* painted red with gilt highlights, 9½in. high. (Skinner. Inc.) $900 £533

A scarce Nazi Waffen SS officers fur cap, field grey cloth crown, fur flaps and front.
(Wallis & Wallis) $660   £400

A Nazi Police shako, field green cloth covered body, black fibre imitation leather crown, neck guard and peak, leather lining stamped 'Pol 1937'.
(Wallis & Wallis) $239   £145

A rare French burgonet, of blackened steel, the robust two-piece skull with high roped comb, third quarter of the 16th century, 11³/₄in. high.
(Christie's S. Ken.)$6897   £4180

A Persian chiselled and damascened steel kulah khud, the skull cut with twelve petal shaped panels and fitted with three plume holders damascened in gold with invocations to Allah, 19th century, 10in. high.
(Christie's S. Ken)
    $5,562   £3,520

A scarce Victorian officer's helmet of the 1st Huntingdonshire (or Duke of Manchester's) Mounted Rifles, leather skull and peaks.
(Wallis & Wallis) $907   £550

A Victorian Life Guards Officer's helmet, silver plated skull with gilt plate applied with garter star in silver.
(Phillips) $4950   £3000

A German closed burgonet from a black and white armour (polished bright), comprising one-piece skull with prominent roped comb, mid-16th century, 10¹/₂in. high.
(Christie's S. Ken.)$3993   £2420

A 19th century Austrian cavalry troopers black leather helmet, raised ribs to skull, black and white wool comb.
(Wallis & Wallis) $4290   £2600

HELMETS

A scarce WWI R Naval Volunteers Captains uniform, comprising: peaked cap, 2 double breated tunics and frock coat.
(Wallis & Wallis) $214   £130

An English Civil War period pikeman's pot, two piece skull with raised comb, rivetted border.
(Wallis & Wallis) $949   £575

A scarce Bavarian Paymaster officer's Pickelhaube, leather backed chiscales and mounts, both cockades, silk and leather lining.
(Wallis & Wallis) $990   £600

A troopers helmet of the 4th (Royal Irish) Dragoon Guards, brass skull, ear to ear wreath, leather backed chinchain and rosettes.
(Wallis & Wallis) $1072   £650

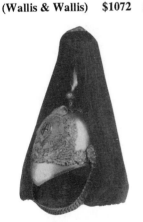

A post-1902 Royal Horse Guards Officer's helmet, silver plated skull with copper gilt plate applied with garter star in silver.
(Phillips) $2310   £1400

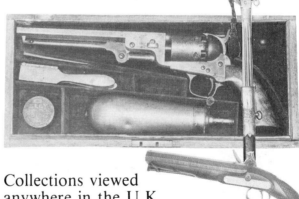

MEDALS

South Africa 1877–9, bar 1878–9
(564 Pte G Wright 80th Foot).
(Wallis & Wallis) $264   £160

Four: D.C.M. Geo V military
bust second type, MM Geo V
military bust, BWM and
Victory, D.C.M. London Gazette
16.1.1919.
(Wallis & Wallis) $709   £430

The King's Police Medal, Geo V
issue, (Edward Victor Collins,
Commr of Police, Gold Coast).
(Wallis & Wallis) $256   £155

M.G.S. 1793, 4 bars Busaco,
Fuentes D'Onor, Cuidad
Rodrigo, Badajoz (Peter Fisher,
95th Foot).
(Wallis & Wallis) $528   £320

Three: Scottish Police Visit to
Scotland 1903, Scottish Police
Coronation 1911, Special
Constabulary Faithful Service
Geo VI.
(Wallis & Wallis) $107   £65

South Africa 1853 (impressed
Chas Hogg 74th Regt).
(Wallis & Wallis) $239   £145

The Royal Victorian Order
Members badge of the 4th Class.
(Wallis & Wallis) $247   £150

Three: Crimea 3 bars Alma, Bal,
Seb; Indian Mutiny 1 bar
Lucklow; Turkish Crimea
Sardinian issue.
(Wallis & Wallis) $594   £360

Q.S.A. 4 bars C.c., Wepener,
Trans, Witte. (3408 Pte E A
Hulseberg Cape M.R.), and
details of the siege of Wepener
are included.
(Wallis & Wallis) $335   £215

MEDALS

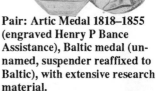

Pair; China 1900 no bar (Pte W
Burns, Shanghai Vols); Shanghai
Volunteer Corps Long Service
medal.
(Wallis & Wallis) $511   £310

West Germany: Order of Merit
of the Federal German Republic,
contained in fitted gilt embossed
'Steinhauer & Luck
Ludenscheid' case.
(Wallis & Wallis) $429   £260

Pair: Artic Medal 1818–1855
(engraved Henry P Bance
Assistance), Baltic medal (un-
named, suspender reaffixed to
Baltic), with extensive research
material.
(Wallis & Wallis) $528   £320

An interesting Volunteer Rifles
gold medal, Obverse 'Presented
by Captain Wingate to the
Partick Volunteer Rifles (33rd
Lanarkshire) 1860'.
(Wallis & Wallis) $643   £390

Four: M.C. Geo V (reverse
engraved Lieut F.W. Rivett
R.G.A. 3.6.19), Mons Star,
BWM, Victory.
(Wallis & Wallis) $313   £190

Turkey Order of Mejidie, breast
badge in gold, silver and enamel,
diam 59mm.
(Wallis & Wallis) $148   £90

Order of the Bath, military
division KCB neck badge in gilt
and enamels.
(Wallis & Wallis) $594   £360

Pair: M.V.O. 4th Class,
Territorial Decoration Geo V
issue (reverse engraved Lieut
Col Donald A Matheson T.D.)
(Wallis & Wallis) $256   £155

Victoria Empress of India medal
1877 (un-named as issued), in
case of issue.
(Wallis & Wallis) $396   £240

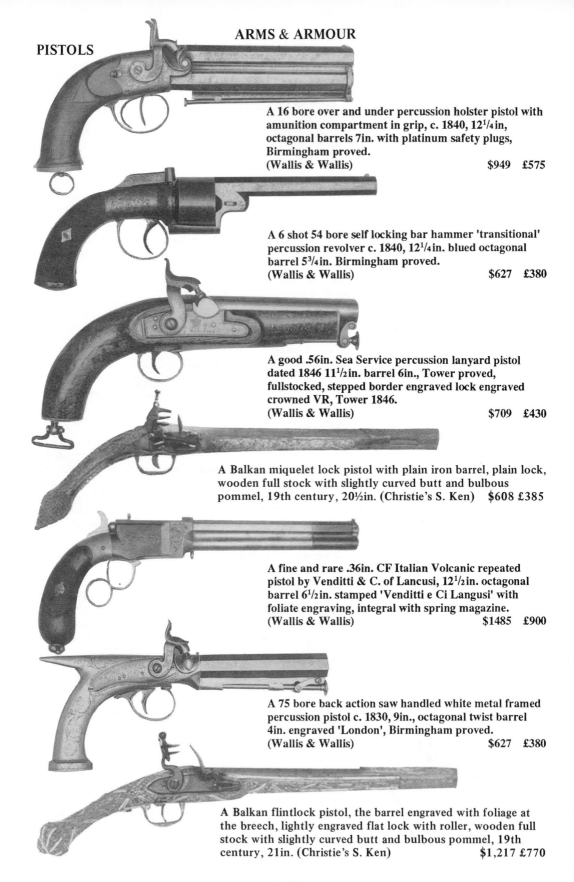

A 16 bore over and under percussion holster pistol with amunition compartment in grip, c. 1840, 12^{1}/$_{4}$in, octagonal barrels 7in. with platinum safety plugs, Birmingham proved.
(Wallis & Wallis) $949   £575

A 6 shot 54 bore self locking bar hammer 'transitional' percussion revolver c. 1840, 12^{1}/$_{4}$in. blued octagonal barrel 5^{3}/$_{4}$in. Birmingham proved.
(Wallis & Wallis) $627   £380

A good .56in. Sea Service percussion lanyard pistol dated 1846 11^{1}/$_{2}$in. barrel 6in., Tower proved, fullstocked, stepped border engraved lock engraved crowned VR, Tower 1846.
(Wallis & Wallis) $709   £430

A Balkan miquelet lock pistol with plain iron barrel, plain lock, wooden full stock with slightly curved butt and bulbous pommel, 19th century, 20^{1}/$_{2}$in. (Christie's S. Ken) $608 £385

A fine and rare .36in. CF Italian Volcanic repeated pistol by Venditti & C. of Lancusi, 12^{1}/$_{2}$in. octagonal barrel 6^{1}/$_{2}$in. stamped 'Venditti e Ci Langusi' with foliate engraving, integral with spring magazine.
(Wallis & Wallis) $1485   £900

A 75 bore back action saw handled white metal framed percussion pistol c. 1830, 9in., octagonal twist barrel 4in. engraved 'London', Birmingham proved.
(Wallis & Wallis) $627   £380

A Balkan flintlock pistol, the barrel engraved with foliage at the breech, lightly engraved flat lock with roller, wooden full stock with slightly curved butt and bulbous pommel, 19th century, 21in. (Christie's S. Ken) $1,217 £770

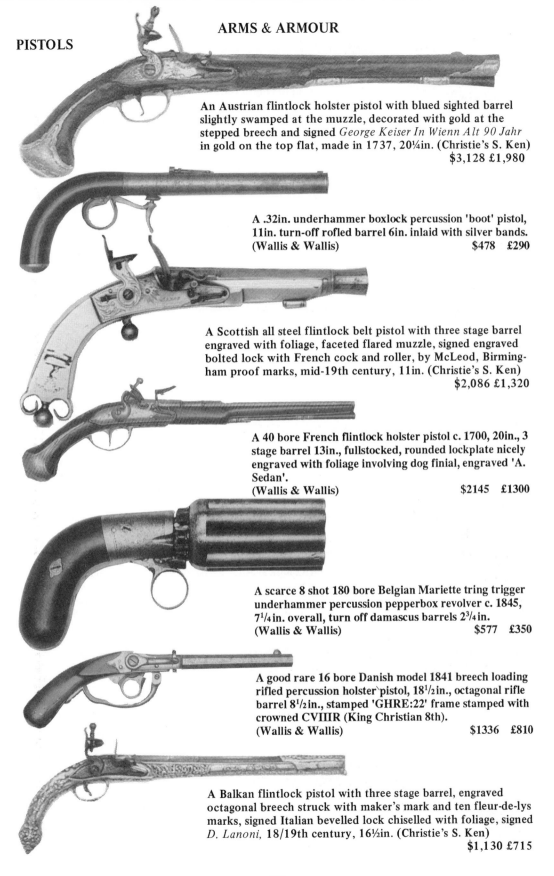

An Austrian flintlock holster pistol with blued sighted barrel slightly swamped at the muzzle, decorated with gold at the stepped breech and signed *George Keiser In Wienn Alt 90 Jahr* in gold on the top flat, made in 1737, 20¼in. (Christie's S. Ken) $3,128 £1,980

A .32in. underhammer boxlock percussion 'boot' pistol, 11in. turn-off rofled barrel 6in. inlaid with silver bands. (Wallis & Wallis) $478 £290

A Scottish all steel flintlock belt pistol with three stage barrel engraved with foliage, faceted flared muzzle, signed engraved bolted lock with French cock and roller, by McLeod, Birmingham proof marks, mid-19th century, 11in. (Christie's S. Ken) $2,086 £1,320

A 40 bore French flintlock holster pistol c. 1700, 20in., 3 stage barrel 13in., fullstocked, rounded lockplate nicely engraved with foliage involving dog finial, engraved 'A. Sedan'. (Wallis & Wallis) $2145 £1300

A scarce 8 shot 180 bore Belgian Mariette tring trigger underhammer percussion pepperbox revolver c. 1845, 7¼in. overall, turn off damascus barrels 2¾in. (Wallis & Wallis) $577 £350

A good rare 16 bore Danish model 1841 breech loading rifled percussion holster pistol, 18½in., octagonal rifle barrel 8½in., stamped 'GHRE:22' frame stamped with crowned CVIIIR (King Christian 8th). (Wallis & Wallis) $1336 £810

A Balkan flintlock pistol with three stage barrel, engraved octagonal breech struck with maker's mark and ten fleur-de-lys marks, signed Italian bevelled lock chiselled with foliage, signed *D. Lanoni*, 18/19th century, 16½in. (Christie's S. Ken) $1,130 £715

An unusual Flemish flintlock sporting gun with two stage
etched twist barrel slightly swamped at the muzzle and
profusely decorated over its entire length with etched and gilt
cabbalistic script, unsigned, early 18th century, 44½in. barrel.
(Christie's S. Ken) $8,342 £5,280

A good scarce 10 bore Brown Bess New Land pattern flintlock
musket with 42in. barrel, 58in., browned barrel 42in. Tower
proved.
(Wallis & Wallis) $3382   £2050

A scarce .704in. Brunswick military percussion rifle dated 1865,
46in., barrel 30in., Tower proved, two leaf rearsight, bayonet bar
at muzzle.
(Wallis & Wallis) $1056   £640

A scarce and interesting Belgian combination 6 shot 8mm double
action pinfire revolver/sidearm, c. 1870, 27in. overall, fullered
blade 20in., round barrel 3³/₄in., Liège proved, the frame
stamped 'G.G. & F Brevetes'.
(Wallis & Wallis) $1526   £925

A good 52 bore Westley Richards patent breech loading 'monkey
tail' percussion carbine no. 1117 36in., blued barrel 20in. to
breech, engraved Whitworth Patent, Birmingham proved.
(Wallis & Wallis) $1237   £750

An Italian flintlock sporting gun with long two stage sighted
barrel, octagonal breech with gold filled maker's stamp and
signed *Benedetto Picinardo,* the lock signed *Francesco Donati,*
circa 1730-40, 46in. barrel. (Christie's S. Ken) $869 £550

A scarce 20 bore Princes Patent breech loading rifled percussion
carbine by R.S. Garden No. G571, 40¹/₂in., browned stepped
twist round barrel 24in.
(Wallis & Wallis) $1650   £1000

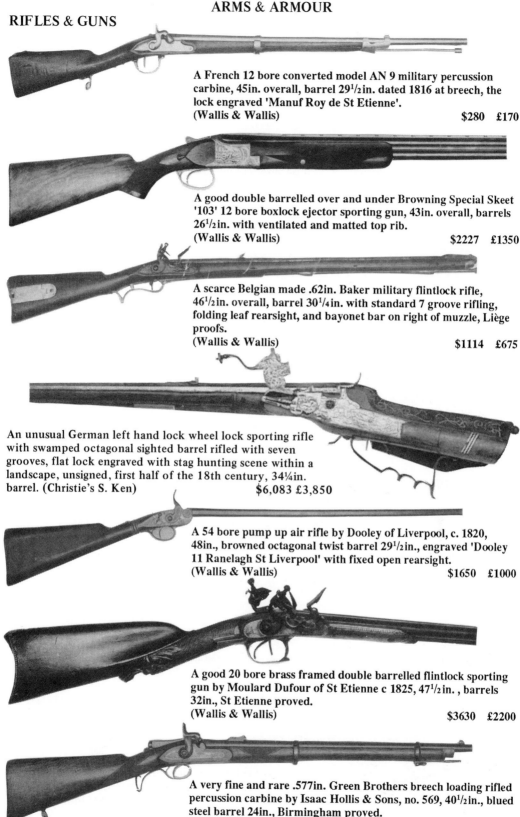

A French 12 bore converted model AN 9 military percussion carbine, 45in. overall, barrel 29½in. dated 1816 at breech, the lock engraved 'Manuf Roy de St Etienne'.
(Wallis & Wallis) $280   £170

A good double barrelled over and under Browning Special Skeet '103' 12 bore boxlock ejector sporting gun, 43in. overall, barrels 26½in. with ventilated and matted top rib.
(Wallis & Wallis) $2227   £1350

A scarce Belgian made .62in. Baker military flintlock rifle, 46½in. overall, barrel 30¼in. with standard 7 groove rifling, folding leaf rearsight, and bayonet bar on right of muzzle, Liège proofs.
(Wallis & Wallis) $1114   £675

An unusual German left hand lock wheel lock sporting rifle with swamped octagonal sighted barrel rifled with seven grooves, flat lock engraved with stag hunting scene within a landscape, unsigned, first half of the 18th century, 34¼in. barrel. (Christie's S. Ken) $6,083 £3,850

A 54 bore pump up air rifle by Dooley of Liverpool, c. 1820, 48in., browned octagonal twist barrel 29½in., engraved 'Dooley 11 Ranelagh St Liverpool' with fixed open rearsight.
(Wallis & Wallis) $1650   £1000

A good 20 bore brass framed double barrelled flintlock sporting gun by Moulard Dufour of St Etienne c 1825, 47½in. , barrels 32in., St Etienne proved.
(Wallis & Wallis) $3630   £2200

A very fine and rare .577in. Green Brothers breech loading rifled percussion carbine by Isaac Hollis & Sons, no. 569, 40½in., blued steel barrel 24in., Birmingham proved.
(Wallis & Wallis) $1320   £800

101

SWORDS

A rare silver hilted small sword for a child, the blade (seized in scabbard) of flattened hollow triangular section, in original leather covered scabbard, Britannia standard silver mark, 1697-1719, 19½in. blade. (Christie's S. Ken) $2,086 £1,320

A Spanish silver gilt hilted court sword with narrow single edged hollow ground blade double edged towards the point, silver marks and Barcelona assay mark, early 19th century, 32in. blade. (Christie's S. Ken) $695 £440

A German or Austrian hunting sword, the curved single edged hollow ground blade (tip broken) etched with suns, moons and stars, in recovered leather scabbard with brass locket and chape en suite with the quillons, circa 1750, 19¾in. blade. (Christie's S. Ken) $730 £462

A fine and rare Neapolitan cup hilt rapier with long slender blade of hollow diamond section changing to diamond section towards the point, signed *Fecit Lavrentivs Palvmbo De Napoli*, circa 1660, 44¼in. blade. (Christie's S. Ken) $13,904 £8,800

An English hanger, the curved single edge blade with two broad fullers on each face, in original leather covered wooden scabbard (slightly damaged) with gilt iron locket and chape chased with rococo strapwork and trophies, circa 1750, 21in. blade. (Christie's S. Ken) $1,130 £715

A French silver mounted hunting sword with broad single edged blade double edged at the point and etched and gilt at the forte with cabalistic signs, in original leather scabbard (damaged and repaired) with silver mounts, Paris discharge marks for 1768-74, 24in. blade. (Christie's S. Ken) $1,217 £770

An English basket hilted broadsword with tapering fullered double edged blade of flattened hexagonal section changing to diamond section towards the point, Irish basket hilt of blackened iron, circa 1610-20, 37¼in. blade. (Christie's S. Ken) $1,912 £1,210

SWORDS

A silver mounted sasa-no-maru-mon efu-no-dachi, the blade honzukuri and torii-zori with
full length wide and narrow grooves, ihorimune and chugissaki with itame hada, choji-
midare hamon of nioi, midare-komi boshi and o-suriage nakago with three mekugi-ana,
unsigned, circa 1500, 53.8cm.long. (Christie's London) $6,952 £4,400

An Imperial German Infantry Officer's presentation sword,
84cm. double fullered blade by Ed. Schultze, Hoflieferant,
Potsdam, etched and gilt for half its length with scrolls and
inscription.
(Phillips) $3135   £1900

A fine Edward VII officer's mameluke levee sword of the XIth
(Prince Alberts Own) Hussars, curved blade 32in. by 'Henry
Wilkinson, Pall Mall', retaining virtually all original polish.
(Wallis & Wallis) $3465   £2100

A very fine daisho, in shirasaya with handachi koshirae fitted with tsunagi; the katana
blade, honzukuri and torii-zori with full length grooves, signed *Bizen Kuni ju Osafune
Tadamitsu* and dated *Eisho shichinen* (1510), 66.4cm. long, the handachi shakudo-
nanako-ji fittings decorated in gilt takazogan with chrysanthemum leaves and flowers and
scrolling tendrils. (Christie's London) $52,140 £33,000

A fine Italian knightly sword with broad sharply tapering double edged blade of flattened
hexagonal section changing to flattened diamond section towards the point, circa 1400,
32in. blade. (Christie's S. Ken) $17,380 £11,000

A late 18th century Turkish gold damascened sword yataghan,
recurved single edged blade 23¹/₂in., nicely ribbed back edge,
sides gold damascened with foliate cartouches.
(Wallis & Wallis) $429   £260

A Singhalese gold and silver mounted kastana with short slightly curved single edged
blade struck with a mark on one side at the forte, the hilt comprising knuckle guard and
downturned quillons each terminating in a dragon's head, 23¾in. (Christie's S. Ken)
$1,912 £1,210

TSUBAS

A circular iron tsuba, ikizukashi with copper and gilt detail, a peasant loaded with brushwood holding two oxen by their tethers, signed *Nagato Hagi ju Kawaji Gonnojo Tomokane saku,* early 19th century, 8.3cm. (Christie's London) $6,604 £4,180

A Mokkogata Nerikawa tsuba decorated in roironuri and gold hiramakie with two swallows flying above waterfalls, inscribed *Zeshin,* 7.8cm. (Christie's London) $1,738 £1,100

An irregular shaped iron tsuba, flowering plum tree in yosukashi with slight engraved and gilt detail, unsigned, Hayashi school of Higo, early 18th century, 8.1cm. (Christie's London) $869 £550

An oval Sentoku Migakiji Tsuba decorated in iroe takazogan with a part of a rats procession, signed Jogetsusai Hiroyoshi, first half 19th century, 6.7cm. (Christie's) $918 £550

An oval sentoku ishimeji tsuba, aoi leaves in yosukashi, engraved detail, unsigned, 19th century, 7.3cm. (Christie's London) $1,390 £880

An oval iron migakiji tsuba, Haichu no Fuji or Fuji reflected in a sake cup representing the elixir of life, signed *Shinoda Hisakatsu,* 19th century. (Christie's London) $4,171 £2,640

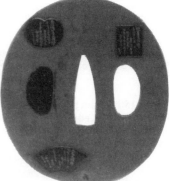

A shakudo-nanakoji gilt rimmed aoigata tsuba decorated in iroe takazogan with aki-no-nanakusa, unsigned, Mino-Goto school, 17th century, 6.7cm. (Christie's London) $729 £462

A circular iron tsuba, tree peony seedlings in yosukashi, signed *Inshu ju Suruga saku,* 18th century, 8cm. (Christie's London) $1,564 £990

An oval Sentoku Migakiji Tsuba inlaid in gilt sujizogan with eighteen poems by the Rokkasen, 19th century, 7.2cm. (Christie's) $1653 £990

TSUBAS

An oval iron Tsuchimeji Tsuba decorated in takazogan and nunomezogan with crabs of various sizes among reeds, signed Shoami, 19th century, 7.4cm.
(Christie's) $4041 £2420

A mokkogata shakudo-nanakoji tsuba, horses and autumn plants in copper, gilt and shakudo takazogan, inscribed *Ganshoshi Nagatsune,* late 18th century, 6.8cm. (Christie's London) $1,425 £902

An aorigata iron tsuba with fine amida yasurime, Daruma in katakiribori, his eyes in gilt hirazogan, signed *Shumin* (Someya family), 19th century, 8.2cm. (Christie's London) $2,085 £1,320

A rare Namban Tsuba based on the shape of a European small-sword guard, carved and pierced with interlaced tendrils, unsigned, Nagasaki work, 18th century, 7.5cm.
(Christie's) $2204 £1320

A fine aorigata iron tsuba, a dancing crane (tsuru-maru) above breaking waves in yosu-kashi, unsigned, Higo school, style of Nishigaki Kanshiro, 18th century, 6.7cm. (Christie's London) $729 £462

A rounded rectangular shibuichi-migakiji tsuba decorated in iroe takazogan with five passengers in a ferry-boat, signed *Yokodo Nobuyoshi,* (1850), 6.5cm. (Christie's London) $4,171 £2,640

A circular iron Heianjo Tsuba decorated in Shinchu takazogan with children's toys, unsigned, 17th century, 8.2cm.
(Christie's) $826 £495

A fine shakudo hari-ishime aorigata tsuba, a Bodhisattva in a precipitous landscape, gilt detail, unsigned, 19th century, 6.3cm. (Christie's London) $869 £550

A circular iron Tsuba decorated in hikone-bori with men cutting scouring-rush, signed Kofu Hikone ju Soheishi Nyudo Soten sei, 18th century, 8.1cm.
(Christie's) $2204 £1320

UNIFORMS

A rare Georgian officer's coatee, of the 57th Regiment, scarlet with yellow facings, together with an oval gilt shoulder belt plate. (Phillips London)
$1,491 £950

A Captain's dress uniform of the 6th Duke of Connaught's Royal Canadian Hussars, comprising brown fur busby, in its japanned tin, dark blue tunic with gold bullion frogging and decoration. (Phillips) $1452   £880

A good, rare officers uniform, c. 1835, of the Royal Perthshire Militia comprising scarlet coatee, double breasted with 2 lines of 10 buttons in pairs, pair epaulettes, blue cloth with silver thistle embroidery solid cresents. (Wallis & Wallis) $1006   £610

A post 1902 Lieutenants full dress scarlet tunic of the 16th (The Queens) Lancers, blue facings and plastron, collar badges, gilt lace trim, shoulder cords.
(Wallis & Wallis) $1171   £710

A rare WWI Lieutenants khaki uniform of the Womens Royal Air Force, comprising peaked soft cap, tunic, ankle length skirt with twin pockets.
(Wallis & Wallis) $874   £530

A good post 1902 Colonel's full dress scarlet doublet of The Royal Scots Fusiliers, blue facings, gilt lace and braid trim, shoulder cords, embroidered collar grenades with solid thistles.
(Wallis & Wallis) $891   £540

UNIFORMS

A Victorian officer's coatee
of the 10th Madras Native
Infantry, scarlet with red
facings, gold lace decoration to
collar and cuffs. (Phillips
London) $345 £220

A good Leicestershire Yeomanry
Squadron Quarter Master
Sergeants uniform, c. 1910
comprising: blue peaked cap,
blue jacket with scarlet facings,
pair of blue overalls, pair of
Wellington boots, pair of gloves,
and a scarlet mess waistcoat.
(Wallis & Wallis) $610   £370

A complete Vic 1876 Pattern
uniform of a Lieutenant of the
City of London comprising:
cocked hat, peaked cap, scarlet
tunic, court sword, pair shoes
with box spurs and trees.
(Wallis & Wallis) $990   £600

A Vic Major's full dress blue
tunic of the 1st Punjab Cavalry,
scarlet facings, gilt lace, cord
and braid trim, including heavy
cuff ornaments.
(Wallis & Wallis) $1237   £750

The Victorian coatee and
epaulettes of an officer of the
Yeomen of the Guard, the
coatee scarlet with rich gold
embroidery. (Christie's S. Ken)
                    $706 £462

A good complete WWII
Subaltern's khaki SD uniform of
the Auxiliary Training Service,
comprising: baize cloth peaked
cap, tunic and belt, 2 ties, skirt,
together with details of the
wearer's service.
(Wallis & Wallis) $792   £480

Sir Arthur Sullivan, the autographed full score of Sullivan's Symphony in E (The Irish), with extensive passages deleted, numerous overlays and autographed revisions to the score, copyright, 1902 by Novello & Co. Ltd/11434.
(Phillips London) $26,010 £17,000

Two political campaign pamphlets for the North West Manchester By-Election, 1906(?) each illustrated with a portrait photograph of Winston Churchill, one signed and inscribed *Winston S. Churchill 24 Ap. 1906(?).* (Christie's S. Ken) $1,201   £770

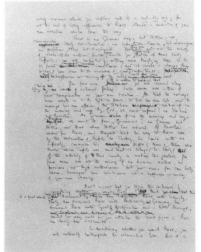

A. A. Milne autograph manuscript of his anti-war polemic *Peace with Honour: An enquiry into the War Convention,* revised throughout, dated May 1942. (Phillips London)
$4,056   £2,600

A rare German Third Reich citation for the Oak Leaves to the Knight's Cross of the Iron Cross, awarded to Major Gustav Pressler, bearing hand written *Hitler* signature.
(Phillips London) $2,637   £1,680

Identity cards carried by Mussolini, comprising that of Commandante Generale MVSN, with photo of Mussolini, card of the Associazione Nazionale Combattenti 1945, a card of the Presidenza Nazionale of the Opera and a card of the Istituto Nazionale Di Cultura Fascista. (Phillips London)
$9,734   £6,200

Felix Mendelssohn Bartholdy, the manuscript full score of Elijah, annotated throughout by Mendelssohn, sent by him in instalments from Leipzig to London, 1846, and used by the organist, Henry Gauntlett. (Phillips London) $134,640 £88,000

D. H. Lawrence's annotated copy of Bertrand Russell's Philosophical Essays, given to him by Lady Ottoline Morrell, inscribed by her in pencil on the fly-leaf *DHL from OM/1915*, 1910. (Phillips London) $6,864 £4,400

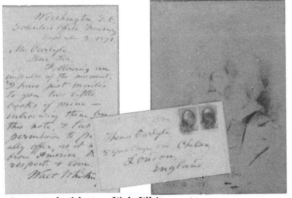

Autographed letter, Walt Whitman to Thomas Carlyle, signed and dated *September 3, 1872.* (Skinner Inc.) $1,300 £798

Oscar Wilde autograph letter signed, confessing himself *very anxious to have the privilege of being present at the dinner to be given in honour of my friend Mr Henry Irving on the 4th July,* probably May 1883. (Phillips London) $2,262 £1,450

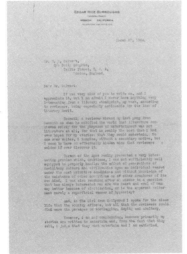

Fine typed letter signed by Edgar Rice Burroughs, about *Tarzan* and the craft of fiction, to W. K. Calvert of the Daily Graphic, two page, slight paper-clip stain, Tarzania Ranch, California, 27 March 1924. (Phillips London) $1,794 £1,150

A fine document signed by Queen Victoria, printed on vellum in English and Samoan, seven page, Great Seal (cracked) attached by silver thread tassels, Windsor Castle, 26 February 1880. (Phillips London) $1,326 £850

A painted tinplate clockwork musical Puss-in-Boots playing cello, the mechanism operating bowing right arm, probably Martin (one ear missing, spike loose), 9in. high.
(Christie's S. Ken.) $1270 £770

A bisque headed clockwork musical automaton pianist, with closed smiling mouth and fixed blue eyes, by Phali-bois, circa 1885, 24in. high, with label giving the airs.
(Christie's S. Ken)$5,214 £3,300

A hand operated musical automaton of a violin player, the bisque head with light brown wool wig, in original red and white suit with wood hands, feet and violin, 7½in. high.
(Christie's S. Ken) $660 £418

Clown Equilibriste, a composition-headed musical automaton, modelled standing on a chair, with green and red wool wig, by Vichy, 21in. high.
(Christie's S. Ken.)$9075 £5500

A hand-operated musical automaton toy of a village scene, depicting a train travelling through tunnels, circa 1900 Erzegebirge, 12¼in. wide.
(Christie's S. Ken.) $1089 £660

A black composition headed musical automaton, modelled as a smiling man seated on a stool strumming a banjo, by G. Vichy circa 1900, 24in. high.
(Christie's S. Ken.)$7260 £4400

A German hand-operated musical automaton, of three wooden fur-covered cats, having a tea party, 19th century, ¼in. wide.
(Christie's) $1180 £715

French musical bird-in-cage automaton, late 19th century, feathered figure with mechanical beak, tail and head, 11in. high. (Robt. W. Skinner Inc.) $600 £366

A carved wooded headed electric automaton, modelled as a man reading the complete car modeller, inscribed David Secrett, 18½in. long.
(Christie's S. Ken.) $635 £385

Bentley 4½ Litre, catalogue No 30, including supercharged model, October 1929.
(Onslow's) $1204   £730

A chromium-plated and enamelled Brooklands 120mph badge the reverse stamped Mrs E M Thomas 29-9-28, won driving a Sunbeam.
(Onslow's) $3300   £2000

Mercedes-Benz Model SS, loosely inserted technical data and price list of standard bodies, 1929.
(Onslow's) $1237   £750

Hispano-Suiza, one of two laminated showcards related to aero engines and vehicles, each 32cm. x 18cm.
(Onslow's) $396   £240

Peugeot Revue, no's 1–52, bound in three volumes with covers and advertisements, 1923–1927.
(Onslow's) $3960   £2400

The Years Automobile Sport 1906 with the compliments of the Michelin Tyre Company Lyd, pub in England.
(Onslow's) $3960   £2400

A picnic service by Coracle for six settings, including two thermos flasks and copper spirit stove, in black vinyl covered case, 74cm. long.
(Onslow's) $2640   £1600

Schrader Tire Gauge Display Cabinet in the form of a giant tyre gauge, printed tin, 38cm. high.
(Onslow's) $379   £230

A fine picnic service for four settings by Coracle, with bone china cups and saucers, 61cm. long.
(Onslow's) $1155   £700

A finely detailed hallmarked sterling silver model of the Alfa Romeo Monza FYE 7 of 1933, by Theo Fennell, London, 1988, 42oz., 9½in. (Christie's Monaco) $11,309 £6,499

A Shell glass petrol globe, 44cm. high. (Christie's S. Ken) $256 £165

Minerva, a gilt and enamelled badge decorated with the profile of the goddess, 6.5cm. high. (Christie's S. Ken) $188 £121

Monaco, 19 mai 1957, by B. Minne, lithograph in colours, printed by Imp Adia, Nice, fold marks, 47 x 31in. (Christie's Monaco) $3,480 £2,000

Nuvolari, L'Asso della Velocita, a single issue, Anno 1, No. 4, 1933. (Christie's Monaco) $1,392 £800

Ferrari Yearbook, 1946-1966, signed and inscribed by Enzo Ferrari, Italian text. (Christie's Monaco) $2,958 £1,700

Beligond — Reims Trophee France Amerique, 3 & 4 Juillet 1965, original poster, 60 x 40cm. (Christie's S. Ken) $239 £154

A silver plated trophy cup presented to Peter Collins for his British Grand Prix victory at Silverstone, 1958, 20½in. high. (Christie's Monaco) $2,784 £1,600

Beligond — Rouen, Grand Prix de France, 10 Juillet 1966, original poster, 60 x 40cm. (Christie's S. Ken) $171 £110

Alfa Romeo rules pamphlet 6C 2500 Gran Turismo, Italian, French, English and German text, circa 1948. (Christie's Monaco) $383 £220

A Brooklands BARC badge, enamelled with two racing cars on the banking at Brooklands, 9.5cm. high. (Christie's S. Ken) $443 £286

A black leatherette picnic hamper, the fall front opening to fitted canework interior, 24in. wide. (Christie's London) $1,165 £715

Ferrari Yearbook, 1950, Italian text. (Christie's Monaco) $8,699 £4,999

Geo Ham, Side-Car Cross Et Motocross Montreuil, on linen, 123cm. x 119cm. (Onslow's) $297 £180

H Behel, Georges Richard Automobiles & Cycles, pub by Camis, on linen 186cm. x 120cm. (Onslow's) $990 £600

A pair of Lucas King of the Road Duplex self contained acetylene headlamps, with concave clear glass lenses, 7¼in. diam. (Christie's London) $3,944 £2,420

A JRDC badge enamelled with stylised Brooklands racing car, 9cm. high. (Christie's S. Ken) $938 £605

A pair of Marchal headlamps with clear glass lenses and bullseye, 10in. diam. (Christie's London) $1,613 £990

Fine early 19th century rosewood framed Banjo Barometer with mother of pearl inlaid surround, inscribed at base 'A Rizzi, London'.
(G.A. Key) $1110   £690

A George III mahogany bowfront stick barometer, the silvered dial signed W and J Gillbert London, 3ft. 3³/4 in. high.
(Phillips)$6930   £4200

A 19th century mahogany wheel barometer, the 8in. silvered dial signed J. Ronchetti Manchester, 3ft. 3in. high.
(Phillips) $627   £380

A George III mahogany bowfront stick barometer, the silvered dial signed Dollond London, 3ft. 1¹/2 in. high.
(Phillips)$4620   £2800

A 19th century mahogany stick barometer, the silvered dial signed Whitehurst and Son Derby, 3ft. 2in. high.
(Phillips) $1320   £800

A mahogany wheel barometer, the six inch silvered dial signed J. Abraham, Optician, Bath, 36¹/4 in.
(Lawrence Fine Art)
              $1543   £935

An early 19th century mahogany stick barometer of unusual design, the silvered dial with venier signed Adie & Son, Edinburgh, 39¹/4 in. high.
(Christie's S. Ken.)
              $2590   £1650

A mahogany wheel barometer with eight inch silvered dial, contained in a banjo shaped case, 39in.
(Lawrence Fine Art)
              $799   £484

A large rosewood wheel barometer, the 12in. dial signed *C. Heseltine, London,* in a banjo shaped case, 127cm. high. (Lawrence Fine Arts) $1,434 £880

A 19th century rosewood and cut brass inlaid marine barometer, the ivory dial signed E Wrench London, 3ft. 1in. high. (Phillips)$3465 £2100

A mahogany and chequered strung wheel barometer inlaid with fan ovals, dial signed Cha. Aiano, Fecit, 36^t/4in. high. (Christie's S. Ken.) $1036 £660

A 19th century mahogany stick barometer, the ivory dial signed T.B. Winter Newcastle, 3ft. 3in. high. (Phillips) $726 £440

A early 19th century mahogany and chequered strung stick barometer, the silvered dial signed P. Gally & Co., Fetchet, 38in. high. (Phillips) $1451 £924

A 19th century mahogany wheel barometer, with 10in. silvered dial, signed P. Riva Edinburgh, 3ft. 6^1/2in. high. (Phillips) $693 £420

An early 19th century ebony strubg bow front stick barometer, the silvered dial with venier signed John Lacken, Maidstone, 38^1/2in. high. (Christie's S. Ken.) $2763 £1760

A 19th century mahogany wheel barometer, with 10in. silvered dial, hygrometer, thermometer, 3ft. 4^1/2in. high. (Phillips) $759 £460

Nantucket basket, Massachusetts, second half 19th century, small bound oak rim above woven body, 4in. high. (Skinner Inc.) $950 £583

Small splint basket, 19th century, bent oak handle above the single bound oak rim, 8½in. high. (Skinner Inc.) $80 £52

Nantucket basket, Massachusetts, early 20th century, on a turned wooden base inscribed with concentric circles, 4in. high. (Skinner Inc.) $950 £583

A grape basket for the wine harvest, circa 1920. (Auction Team Koeln) $47 £30

Nantucket basket, Massachusetts, late 19th/early 20th century, bound oak rim above a deep sided circular woven rattan body, 6in. high. (Skinner Inc.) $2,100 £1,355

A mahogany octagonal waste paper basket with sides pierced with Chinese fretwork and handles, on bracket feet, 13¾in. high. (Christie's London) $1,972 £1,210

One of a pair of Edwardian satinwood wastepaper baskets painted with ribbons and roses, each with brass liner, 14in. diam. (Christie's London)
Two $3,896 £2,420

Oval Nantucket basket, Massachusetts, late 19th/early 20th century, double bound oak rim above a woven rattan body, 5in. high. (Skinner Inc.) $300 £194

Paint decorated covered storage basket, Northeast American Indian, 19th century, of circular form, 13¼in. high. (Skinner Inc.) $300 £184

BIRDCAGES

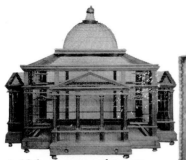

A 19th century mahogany birdcage of architectural form, modelled on Mereworth Castle, the front and side elevations each with a projecting Palladian portico, 89cm. square. (Phillips London) $7,956 £5,200

Wood and wire birdcage, America, late 19th/early 20th century, in the form of a two storey building (imperfections), 25 x 25in. (Skinner Inc.) $550 £355

An early 19th century painted wood birdcage in the form of a Georgian house, the recessed central section surmounted by a pediment inset with a timepiece, 89cm. wide. (Phillips London) $1,836 £1,200

BLOWLAMPS

A Wachthel system hand blowlamp with fuel container and pump in the handle, circa 1910. (Auction Team Koeln) $32 £20

A German jar shaped blowlamp by Eisenfuehr, Berlin, circa 1920. (Auction Team Koeln) $11 £7

A rod shaped blowlamp, circa 1930. (Auction Team Koeln) $35 £22

An early carbide powered blowlamp, circa 1920. (Auction Team Koeln) $3 £2

A heavy brass blow lamp stamped *E. H. Haehnel 261*, with fuel container and warming equipment, 1885. (Auction Team Koeln) $52 £33

An East German jar shaped blowlamp stamped *BAT DDR*, circa 1958. (Auction Team Koeln) $11 £7

A Victorian Bluejohn doorstop of domed shape surmounted by a knop. 5½in. high. (Christie's) $495 £300

A blue-john cup with turned stem and moulded circular foot, 4¾in. high. (Christie's London) $956 £605

A blue-john cup and saucer with domed cover, 4½in. wide. (Christie's) $510 £300

A Blue John goblet with girdle and domed circular base, in rich mauve and brown colouration, 19th century, 6³/₄in. high. (Lawrence Fine Arts) $2813 £1705

A pair of George IV ormolu bluejohn and white marble candlesticks with ribbed drip-pans and moulded pedestals with plinth bases, 9³/₄in. high. (Christie's) $12474 £7700

A George III blue-john urn on turned pedestal and black marble base, restorations, 11½in. high. (Christie's London) $2,316 £1,485

A blue-john urn with turned stem on black marble pedestal and square base, 19th century, 4½in. high. (Christie's London) $1,372 £880

A bluejohn chalice with turned tapering stem and spreading base with part of a printed label, 'J. Tenna No. 149, Minerralogist by Appointme', 7¹/₂in. high. (Christie's) $3858 £2310

A small tazza in Blue John, with moulded bowl resting on a turned pedestal, labelled 'H. Buxton, The Royal Museum, Matlock Bath', 6¹/₂in. tall. (Riddetts) $4537 £2750

BOOKS

Moth Minor sales literature with price list and specification, 1939. (Onslow's) $99 £60

Noel, E.B. & Clark, J.O.M., A History of Tennis, 2 volumes, Oxford University Press, 1924, original cloth in dust wrappers. (Woolley & Wallis) $1551 £940

The Royal and Ancient Game of Golf, published for Golf Illustrated Ltd., 1912, one of a limited subscribers edition of 900.
(Woolley & Wallis) $1485 £900

Dickens, Charles: All the Year Round, incorporating Household Words, 1859-1868, 20 volumes. (Phillips) $330 £200

Blunt, D.E., Elephant, printed and published by East Africa, London, 1933. Photographic illustrations.
(Woolley & Wallis) $660 £400

Dickens, Charles: Household Words, 19 volumes, 1850-1859. (Phillips) $1023 £620

John Dower: A New General Atlas of the World, folio, 1840, engraved title and 46 double-page maps. (Christie's S. Ken) $563 £352

119

F. Gerasch — Die Oestereich Armee, 11 hand-col. plates each 440 x 300mm., ½ red morocco, 1850. (Phillips London) $717 £440

Russian and German Uniforms, album containing 45 hand-col. lithos, Eckert & C. Weiss, 1835. (Phillips London) $1,200 £750

George Anson, Richard Walter and Benjamin Robins: A Voyage to the South Seas, By and for the Proprietors of the Yeovil Mercury, 1744, engraved frontispiece and 3 folding plates. (Christie's S. Ken) $1,144 £715

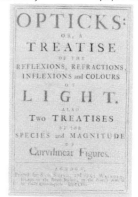

I. Owen and E. Bowen — Britannia Depicts or Ogilby Improv'd, first impression with King of Spain imprint on title page, 273 pp. of road maps. (Phillips London) $1,173 £720

H. Vernet and E. Lomi — Collection des Uniformes des Armees Francaises de 1791 a 1824, 2 vols. (Phillips London) $1,152 £720

Sir Isaac Newton — Opticks or, a Treatise of the Reflexions . . . and colours of Light, first edition, title printed in red and black, 19 folding plates, 1704. (Phillips London) $6,520 £4,000

L'Exposition Internationale des Arts Decoratifs Modernes a Turin 1902 (Exhibition catalogue), Darmstadt 1902. (Christie's London) $4,303 £2,640

Thomas Williamson — The European in India, 4to, by Edward Orme, 1813. (Christie's S. Ken) $322 £198

T. Jenner — A Book of the Names of all Parishes, Market Towns, Villages, Hamlets and smallest Places in England and Wales, printed title dated 1657. (Phillips London) $1,141 £700

T. Gardner — A Pocket Guide to the English Traveller, title in black and red, 100 double page road maps, London, 1719. (Phillips London) $1,874 £1,150

John Senex — An Actual Survey of all the Principal Roads of England and Wales, 2 vols, 100 double page strip maps, 1719. (Phillips London) $1,793 £1,100

Tegetmeier (William Bernard) — The Poultry Book, coloured lithographic title page and chromolithographic frontispiece and plate by Harrison Weir, 1867. (Henry Spencer) $198 £130

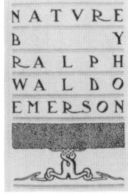

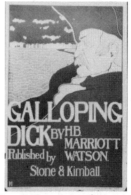

'Photographic Pleasures: popularly portrayed with pen and pencil', 1859, by Cuthbert Bede (Rev. Edward Bradley). (Christie's S. Ken) $430 £264

Nature by Ralph Waldo Emerson, published by the Roycrofters, East Aurora, New York, 1905, good condition. (Robt. W. Skinner Inc.) $250 £153

Frank Hazenplug (American, born 1873), Galloping Dick, 1896, publisher Stone and Kimball, Chicago, light staining, minor losses to margin. (Robt. W. Skinner Inc.) $350 £215

William Bligh — A Voyage to the South Seas . . . , 4to, for George Nicol, 1792, engraved portrait frontispiece. (Christie's S. Ken) $2,331 £1,430

Folly or Saintliness, /Jose Echegaray, Lamson Wolffe and Co., Boston and New York, 1895, signed A. Ethel Reed, in the matrix, sheet size 20¾ x 15in. (Skinner Inc.) $250 £154

J. White — Journal of a Voyage to New South Wales, 65 plates, hand coloured by Eleanor Parke Lewis, 1790. (Phillips London) $5,120 £3,200

A bronze model of a dove, its feather detail realistically rendered, unsigned, late 19th century, 25cm. long. (Christie's London) $4,171 £2,640

A bronze figure of the seated Abraham Lincoln, inscribed *Gutzon Borglum* and stamped *The Gorham Co. Founders Q501*, 21in., rich dark brown patina. (Christie's New York) $38,500 £25,163

A 19th century French animalier bronze figure of a lively retriever, 6in. high. (Christie's S. Ken) $549 £352

C. Marochetti — a bronze bust of Prince Albert, with a Roman toga across his shoulders, 40cm. high. (Henry Spencer) $596 £390

Coming Through the Rye, an important bronze equestrian group inscribed *Frederic Remington copyrighted 1902* and *Cire Perdue Cast. Roman Bronze Works N.Y. 1902* and *1*. (Christie's New York) $4,400,000 £2,784,810

T. Thornycroft, after Sir Frances Chantrey — a bronze bust of the young Queen Victoria, wearing robes and a coronet, 45cm. high. (Henry Spencer) $1,836 £1,200

Massive Japanese bronze garden lantern, 19th century, hexagonal domed roof with dragon heads at each corner, 77in. high. (Skinner Inc.) $6,250 £3,906

A pair of Napoleon III bronze and Siena marble campana urns, on square stepped plinths edged with a band of foliage, 17in. high. (Christie's London) $2,607 £1,650

Japanese bronze figure, late 19th century, characterisation of a Chinese general from the Warring States period, 16in. high. (Skinner Inc.) $1,200 £750

Austrian painted bronze figural group, late 19th century, after Franz Bergman, slave dealer auctioning nude young woman, 8½in. long. (Skinner Inc.) $600 £387

A pair of Hagenauer bronze Tennis figures, each one fashioned in sheet bronze as male tennis players wearing flannel trousers and adopting athletic poses, 22.4cm. high and 25.8cm. high respectively. (Phillips London)
$2,445 £1,500

A Hagenauer bronze, modelled as a sleek horse's head and neck, mounted on a rectangular bronze base, 31.5cm. long. (Phillips London) $1,467 £900

A 20th century English green patinated bronze figure of a naked young girl, signed and dated *Pibworth, 1923,* 25in. high. (Christie's S. Ken)
$707 £462

A pair of polychrome enamelled bronze andirons cast in low relief with a Royal coat-of-arms, the arched bases with domed bosses, 24in. high. (Christie's London) $4,089 £2,420

A wood and bronze cockerel, in the manner of Hagenauer, the stylised form having a wooden body and bronze face, 39.5cm. high. (Phillips London)
$261 £160

The Pioneer Woman, signed and dated *Bryant Baker 1927,* with copyright mark on base, 9in. high. (Skinner Inc.)
$700 £452

Dancers, a dark and silver patinated bronze group, both dancers wearing pointed caps, elaborate bodices and pantaloons, 10in. high. (Christie's S. Ken) $1,023 £660

Japanese bronze figure of Gama Sennin, late 19th century, standing with a frog riding his left shoulder and one on his walking stick, 13in. high. (Skinner Inc.) $600 £375

A 19th century French bronze figure of David, cast from a model by Marius Jean Antonin Mercie, inscribed *F. Barbedienne fondeur,* 73cm. high. (Christie's London) $3,542 £2,200

A 19th century French parcel gilt bronze figure of a recumbent Bacchante, supporting herself on her left hand, 34 x 65cm. (Christie's London) $1,948 £1,210

A 19th century cold painted spelter figure of a Moorish dancing girl, cast from a model by Louis Hottot, 78cm. high. (Christie's London) $2,302 £1,430

A large 19th century French bronze figure of Venus, shown standing naked to her waist holding an apple in her right hand, base stamped *Reductions Sauvage,* 103cm. high. (Christie's London) $3,542 £2,200

A 19th century French gilt bronze group of Jupiter and Hebe, cast from a model by Paul Dubois, 36 x 31cm. (Christie's London) $2,302 £1,430

A 19th century French bronze group of Le Genie de la Danse, cast from a model by Jean Baptiste Carpeaux, 104cm. high. (Christie's London) $19,481 £12,100

The Rejected Suitor, a gilt bronze and ivory figure, cast and carved from a model by Roland Paris, as a small bald headed man, 24.8cm. high. (Phillips London) $1,193 £780

Bronze and marble bust of a young woman, late 18th century, signed *D. Watrin* on back, in 16th century style costume, 21½in. high. (Skinner Inc.) $1,900 £1,226

A 19th century French bronze figure of Aphrodite, her right arm raised adjusting her robes, 18in. high. (Christie's S. Ken) $515 £330

A 19th century French bronze figure of a fisherboy, the base inscribed *Paris 1882, mon petit Charlot, M. de Vasselot,* 124cm. high. (Christie's London)

$8,855 £5,500

A bronze figure of a skier in a twisting posture on a naturalistic base above a variegated marble plinth, 12½in. long. (Christie's S. Ken) $787 £495

A 19th century gilt bronze bust of His Royal Highness The Duke of York, clad in classical mode, looking to dexter, 28.5cm. high. (Christie's London) $1,062 £660

A mid-19th century French silvered bronze figure of Sappho, cast by Victor Paillard from a model by Jean-Jacques Pradier, with foundry mark *V Paillard 1848,* 86cm. high. (Christie's London)

$106,260 £66,000

A silvered bronze figure of a dancer, cast from a model by Pierre Le Faguays, the young woman wearing a pleated dress with panelled skirt, 1920s, 65cm., overall height. (Bonhams) $2,324 £1,400

A 19th century French bronze bust of a demure young woman, wearing a diadem, signed and dated *E. Aizelin, 1870,* and stamped *F. Barbedienne, Fondeur,* 13½in. high. (Christie's S. Ken)

$589 £385

A 19th century French bronze group of two Bacchantes, after Clodion, the lightly draped nymphs shown dancing, 58cm. high. (Christie's London) $2,479 £1,540

An early 20th century Danish bronze equestrian group, cast from a model by Holger Wederkinch, of King Giorgios I, signed and dated 1913, 70cm. high overall. (Christie's London) $1,328 £825

A 19th century French bronze group of the infant Bacchus and Pan playing, after Clodion, on ormolu mounted green marble base, 25.5cm. high. (Christie's London) $797 £495

BRONZE

Japanese Fan Dancer, a cold painted bronze and ivory figure cast and carved from a model by Harders, 41.3cm. high. (Christie's London)
$7,531 £4,620

An Art Nouveau gilt bronze mounted ceramic vase by Charles Korschann, with a central gilded panel moulded with an Art Nouveau maiden, 65.3cm. high. (Christie's London) $19,723 £12,100

Sabre Dancer, a Viennese bronze figure of a scantily clad Oriental dancing girl in jewelled headdress, 55.5cm. high. (Christie's London)
$7,889 £4,840

The Cape, a gilt bronze and ivory figure cast and carved from a model by A. Gory, of a small child, 20.1cm. high. (Christie's London) $717 £440

A pair of Art Nouveau metal vases, each cast with the heads of three maidens with long hair, 42.5cm. high, indistinctly signed *Maurele?* (Phillips London) $424 £260

A Regency bronze statuette of George III wearing a wig and leaning on a stick in his right hand, incised *L. Gahagan June 1811,* 28cm. high. (Phillips London) $1,683 £1,100

Charleston Dancer, a cold painted bronze and ivory figure, cast and carved from a model by Ferdinand Preiss, as a slender female dancer wearing silvered tights, 43.5cm. high. (Phillips London)
$8,415 £5,500

The Sleep of Reason, cast from a model by Maurice Bouval, the dark patinated female figure, with eyes closed, her hair bedecked with flowers, 43.5cm. high. (Christie's London)
$3,227 £1,980

A late 19th century German bronze figure of Diana, cast from a model by Titze, the statuesque goddess shown standing naked, 20¾in. high overall. (Christie's S. Ken)
$785 £462

126

BRONZE

A bronze figure of Augustus, standing victorious after the battle of Actium, on cylindrical and square marble plinth base, 51cm. high. (Lawrence Fine Arts) $834 £528

Eastern Dancer, a bronze and ivory figure, cast and carved from a model by G. Schmidt-Cassel, on a black marble base, 37.6cm. high. (Christie's London) $12,551 £7,700

Silvia, cast from a model by Emmanuele Villanis, the green patinated Art Nouveau maiden mounted on a pedestal, 28cm. high. (Christie's London) $2,331 £1,430

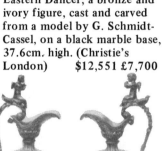

Sonny Boy, a bronze and ivory figure by Ferdinand Preiss of a schoolboy, his hands in his pockets, 20.5cm. high. (Christie's London) $3,765 £2,310

A pair of 19th century French bronze and parcel gilt ewers in the manner of Clodion, the handles with applied cherubs and birds, 16in. high. (Christie's S. Ken) $486 £286

Cabaret Girl, a cold painted bronze and ivory figure, cast and carved from a model by Ferdinand Preiss, as a slender female dancer, 38.5cm. high. (Phillips London) $6,732 £4,400

Tambourine Dancer, cast from a model by D. Simon, of a nude maiden dancing with a tambourine, 44cm. high. (Christie's London) $1,076 £660

The Dancer, an enamelled bronze and ivory figure, cast and carved from a model by Lorenzl, on green onyx pedestal, 27.4cm. high. (Christie's London) $2,510 £1,540

Athlete, a dark patinated bronze figure cast from a model by Bruno Zach, with impressed mark, 73.8cm. high. (Christie's London) $4,662 £2,860

BRONZE

An Austrian bronze of a foot-baller with his leg raised to kick a football, signed Fuchs, 13½in. high. (Christie's S. Ken) $787 £495

Tiffany Studios bronze book-ends, Buddhist pattern with seated deity above geometric platform, 6in. high. (Robt. W. Skinner Inc.) $375 £233

An Austrian erotic gilt bronze figure of a dancing girl, her skirt hinged to the front, 6in. high. (Christie's S. Ken) $280 £165

An Art Nouveau bronze vase, cast from a model by Louis Chalon, the top with icicle-like rim, 45.5cm. high. (Phillips London) $8,568 £5,600

An Art Deco cold painted and silvered bronze figure, the young woman wearing a brief skirt, with arms outstretched, lampholders suspended from her hands, overall height 48.5cm. (Bonhams) $4,316 £2,600

A 19th century Italian bronze figure of the graceful, naked Perseus, his left arm extended, draped in a cloak and holding the head of Medusa, 25in. high overall. (Christie's S. Ken) $1,294 £770

A large decorative figural bronze and cameo glass table lamp, the bronze base cast from a model by Bruno Zach. (Phillips London) $2,295 £1,500

French bronze figure of a pheasant, late 19th century, after Jules Moigniez, cast life-sized, 27½in. high. (Robt. W. Skinner Inc.) $1,200 £732

A 19th century German bronze figure of a young farm labourer holding a scythe, the naturalistic base signed H. Muller, 14in. high, on a marble stand. (Christie's S. Ken) $336 £209

A 19th century French bronze model of Cupid, holding a wreath and feather, on a later orb base, 9½in. high. (Christie's S. Ken) $598 £352

A bronze figure cast from a model by P. Rosanowski, of a grotesquely caricatured naked jester with Neanderthal physique, 7¼in. high. (Christie's S. Ken) $1,125 £660

A bronze bust of a smiling boy, his head turned to sinister, signed P. de Tavera, on a variegated marble base. (Christie's S. Ken) $332 £198

Actor with Mask, a bronze figure, cast from a model by Charles de Sousy Ricketts, R.A., it shows a muscular naked male resting on rockwork, 20cm. high. (Phillips London) $35,190 £23,000

A 19th century French bronze group, in the manner of Clodion, of a seated man playfully holding a bunch of grapes before a child, 14in. high. (Christie's S. Ken) $1,331 £792

An Art Deco bronze two dimensional sculpture, of a long haired woman dressed in sarong, supporting a hoop on the left hip, engraved initials ER, 25in. high. (Christie's S. Ken) $713 £418

A Russian bronze group of a Cossack shepherd on horseback, with the founder's mark of *Woerrffel, St Petersburg*, late 19th century, 49.5cm. high. (Lawrence Fine Arts) $5,562 £3,520

Adieu, a bronze and ivory figure, cast and carved from a model by Demetre Chiparus, as a Classical maiden in sandals, 35.5cm. high. (Phillips London) $2,295 £1,500

A bronze figure of The Tired Hunter, the horse standing saddled and bridled, signed *J. Willis Good*, late 19th century, 30.5cm. high. (Lawrence Fine Arts) $4,518 £2,860

A 19th century French parcel gilt bronze tazza, cast from a model by Beajault, the stem cast with a bust of Bacchus, 33cm. high. (Christie's London) $1,328 £825

A 19th century French bronze figure of the Cheval Turc, the rectangular base signed *Barye*, 19cm. high. (Christie's London) $4,604 £2,860

A magnificent 19th century French bronze parcel gilt and enamelled bust of La Juive d'Alger, by Charles-Henri-Joseph Cordier, signed and dated *Cordier 1863*. (Christie's London) $301,070 £187,000

A 19th century French bronze figure of David, cast from a model by Marius Jean Antonin Mercie, 1882, 48cm. high. (Christie's London) $2,479 £1,540

A pair of late 19th century German bronze statuettes of Victory and Justice, cast from models by Eichberg, 21cm. and 19cm. high. (Christie's London) $885 £550

A 19th century bronze figure of the pensive inventor, Ambroise Pare, in 16th century costume, signed *P. J. David*, with Barbedienne foundry stamp, 19in. high. (Christie's S. Ken) $757 £495

A 19th century French bronze bust of a lady, cast from a model by S. Salmson, in Louis XVI costume, 1873, 52cm. high. (Christie's London) $2,302 £1,430

A 19th century French bronze group of Venus and Cupid, cast from a model by Moreau, the goddess in classical dress, 32cm. high. (Christie's London) $1,417 £880

A late 19th century English bronze mask of Mary Swainson, cast from a model by Alphonse Legros, 30cm. high. (Christie's London) $2,302 £1,430

A 19th century French miniature bronze figure of a goat, cast from a model by Antoine-Louis Barye, shown grazing, 6 x 9.5cm. (Christie's London) $708 £440

A 20th century French bronze group of three running athletes, entitled Au But, cast from a model by Alfred Boucher, 32cm. high. (Christie's London) $2,479 £1,540

A 19th century French bronze model of the setter called Cora, cast from a model by Isidore Bonheur, 32 x 74cm. (Christie's London) $6,376 £3,960

A 19th century French bronze figure of Le Vainqueur au Combat de Coqs, cast from a model by Jean Alexandre Joseph Falguiere, with Thiebaut Freres foundry stamp, 80cm. high. (Christie's London) $3,896 £2,420

A pair of late 19th century Japanese bronze vases and liners, decorated in high relief with birds amongst leafy boughs, 51cm. high. (Henry Spencer) $1,825 £1,120

An early 20th century English bronze figure of Artemis, cast from a model by Hamo Thornycroft, the goddess shown striding forward, her hound at her side, cast 1912, 64cm. high. (Christie's London) $19,481 £12,100

An early 20th century French bronze bust of Beethoven, cast from a model by Pierre Felix Masseau, on a hardwood plinth, 27cm. high. (Christie's London) $2,656 £1,650

A 19th century French gilt bronze statuette of the Chef Gaulois, cast from a model by Emmanuel Fremiet, signed *E. Fremiet*, 39cm. high. (Christie's London) $1,416 £880

A 19th century French statuette of Milo of Croton, after Dumont, 77cm. high. (Christie's London) $3,187 £1,980

BRONZE

The Secret, cast from a model by Pierre Felix Fix-Masseau of a nude maiden in long robes and headdress, 61.5cm. high. (Christie's London)
$6,455 £3,960

An amusing German bronze group, cast from a model by Gustav Adolf Daumiller, as two naked children, the girl carrying a bouquet, 54.5cm. high. (Phillips London)
$4,401 £2,700

A gilt bronze figure, cast from a model by Alexandre Caron, as a naked young woman pondering one of her breasts, 37.5cm. high. (Phillips London)
$1,040 £680

An early 20th century gilt bronze and ivory group of a little girl and a baby snuggled-up in an armchair signed A. Croisy, 6¾in. high.
(Wooley & Wallis) $2480 £1550

A 19th century French bronze figure, after the antique, of the Venus de Milo, the base stamped F. Barbedienne, Fondeur, 18½in. high. (Christie's S. Ken)
$887 £528

A painted bronze and ivory figure, cast and carved from a model by Ferdinand Preiss, as a female skater wearing golden, short-skirted costume 23.5cm. high. (Phillips London)
$4,401 £2,700

A Lorenzl silvered bronze figure, the naked maiden in dancing pose, tip-toed upon one leg, 49.5cm. high, signed. (Lawrence Fine Arts)
$1,077 £682

A green patinated bronze group cast from a model by Amy Bitter as three naked children, 'See no evil, speak no evil, hear no evil', 25cm. high.
(Phillips) $3200 £2000

A stylish Art Deco bronze figure, cast from a model by Gilbert, as a naked girl with silvered body poised above a fluted bullet shaped base, 46cm. high. (Phillips London)
$1,956 £1,200

A 19th century French bronze figure of Pan, playing pipes, on a circular stepped base, with variegated marble stand, 12in. high. (Christie's S. Ken)
$251 £154

Towards the Unknown (Valkyrie), a cold painted bronze and ivory group, cast and carved from a model by Claire Jeanne Roberte Colinet, 31.5cm. high. (Phillips London)
$4,401 £2,700

The Torch Dancer, a painted bronze and ivory figure, cast and carved from a model by Ferdinand Preiss, as a bare-breasted girl wearing floral bloomers, 39cm. high. (Phillips London)
$9,780 £6,000

The Mandolin Player, a cold painted bronze and ivory figure, cast and carved from a model by Ferdinand Preiss, she wears a green silver blouse, green bloomers, fringed belt, golden tights and a top hat, 59cm. high. (Phillips London)
$14,344 £8,800

A pair of bronze vases decorated in iroe hirazogan and takazogan, with peacocks amongst the boughs of flowering trees, 19th century, 59cm. high. (Christie's London)
$10,775 £6,820

A 19th century bronze figure of a naked, seated youth, holding a pipe, signed *Vedres Mark,* 10½in. high. (Christie's S. Ken)
$303 £198

A brown patinated bronze figure cast from a model by Roell, of a naked young woman, 15in. high. (Christie's S. Ken)
$477 £308

A Bergman painted bronze figure, modelled as a bathing belle in one piece swimsuit and hair tied in a mobcap, 12.5cm. high. (Phillips London)
$522 £320

An amusing Bergman painted bronze group, modelled as an owl, with a seal which when pressed, parts the owl's body to reveal a naked female figure, 19.5cm. high, signed *Nam Greb.* (Phillips London) $2,690 £1,650

A Dutch cherry and ebonised bucket, the rippled tapering body on turned shaft and circular base with ball feet, mid-19th century, 15in. high. (Christie's London) $782 £495

A brass bound circular bucket with shaped handles and brass liner and shovel, 13¾in. diam. (Christie's London) $2,433 £1,540

A George III brass bound mahogany bucket of navette shape with brass liner and swing handle, 13in. wide. (Christie's London) $3,048 £1,870

Painted and decorated leather fire bucket, Nantucket Island, Massachusetts, dated 1847, the green ground decorated with black and yellow banding, 12in. high. (Skinner Inc.) $1,200 £774

A pair of Dutch fruitwood and ebonised buckets of ripple turned tapering outline, each with brass liner, 19th century, 14in. high. (Christie's London) $2,125 £1,320

An early leather fire bucket with copper studs and inscribed *Gemeinde Siddessen*, German, circa 1800. (Auction Team Koeln) $126 £78

A Georgian staved mahogany plate bucket, with two wide brass bands and overhead swing handle, 38cm. high. (Henry Spencer) $826 £540

One of a pair of George III brass bound mahogany buckets of navette shape, each with swing handle and liner, 12½in. wide. (Christie's London) Two $3,432 £2,200

A George III mahogany and brass bound plate bucket of coopered form with twin carrying handles, 41cm. high. (Phillips) $1072 £650

Mahogany, rosewood and ivory box, Nantucket, Massachusetts, 19th century, with turned ivory corner columns, 10in. wide. (Skinner Inc.) $1600 £976

A shagreen cutlery box of bow-fronted shape, the hinged lid enclosing a red velvet and metal thread interior, late 18th century, 8½in. wide. (Christie's London) $708 £440

Italian Pietra Dura Jewelery Box, 19th century, inlaid top above conforming case, inlaid throughout with floral swags, 5½in. high. (Skinner Inc) $800 £519

An early Victorian ivory, mother-of-pearl veneered and foliate cut tortoiseshell inlaid two division tea caddy, 8in. wide. (Christie's S. Ken.)$2087 £1265

A gilt metal kingwood, tulip-wood and parquetry jardiniere with metal liner, 19th century, 10in. square. (Christie's London) $834 £528

A red damask covered casket with domed hinged lid enclosing a later marbled paper interior, 12in. wide. (Christie's London) $106 £66

An attractive and unusual octagonal box, embellished in relief with panels of florets and foliage, set with amethyst cabochons and an ivory finial, 7.5cm. high, probably German. (Phillips London) $1,060 £650

Napoleon III Boulle and Ebonized Tantalus, c. 1880, brass foliate inlay on a red faux tortoiseshell ground (minor losses), 11in. high. (Skinner Inc) $1000 £649

Fruitwood pear-shaped tea caddy, probably England, early 19th century, with escutcheon and key, 6¾in. high. (Skinner Inc.) $1400 £854

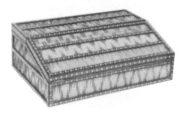

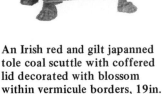

An Irish red and gilt japanned tole coal scuttle with coffered lid decorated with blossom within vermicule borders, 19in. wide. (Christie's London) $5,148 £3,300

Anglo/Indian ebony, ivory and quill lap desk, 19th century, opening to fitted interior inlaid with ivory elephant, foliage and inscription *Matura,* 14¾in. wide. (Skinner Inc.) $500 £307

A William IV rosewood sarcophagus shaped workbox, the hinged cover and front inlaid with foliate cut brass, 13½in. wide. (Christie's S. Ken) $377 £242

A George IV brass bound mahogany box of rectangular shape with hinged lid enclosing a cotton lined interior, 21in. wide. (Christie's London) $1,029 £660

A Regency tortoiseshell and ivory tea caddy of canted square form with hinged lid enclosing lined lidded compartment, 5in. high. (Christie's London) $2,152 £1,320

A Spanish walnut vargueno, inlaid with fruitwood lines and mounted with iron corners and hinges, 17th century, 24¾in. wide. (Christie's London) $5,205 £3,080

A North Italian ebony casket of 17th century style geometrically inlaid with brass lines, on bracket feet applied with repousse brass scrolls, 19th century, 14½in. wide. (Christie's London) $929 £550

An Anglo-Indian ivory and horn games box, the interior with backgammon board, with shakers, dice and draughts, early 19th century, 18in. wide. (Christie's London) $2,690 £1,650

A Regency gilt metal mounted red leather workbox with ribbed coffered rectangular lid, the interior lined with blue silk and blue paper, 10in. wide. (Christie's London) $1,043 £660

A Regency giltmetal mounted red leather casket, with ribbed scrolled ends and carrying handle, on foliate ball feet, 10in. wide. (Christie's London) $601 £385

A pair of early 19th century collectors mahogany cabinets, containing a collection of shells, fossils and hardstones, 80.5cm. wide. (Henry Spencer) $2,754 £1,800

A 19th century ebony and boulle rectangular encrier, surmounted by a machine turned and acanthus leaf chased handle, 13in. wide. (Christie's S. Ken) $480 £308

A late Victorian coromandel wood travelling dressing case for a lady, containing twelve various baguette and hobnail cut glass scent bottles and boxes, London, 1875/76, 33cm. long. (Henry Spencer) $1,344 £800

George III mahogany octagonal sewing box, late 18th century, banded and crossbanded in various woods. (Skinner Inc.) $1,100 £701

A 19th century Anglo-Indian sandalwood workbox, the interior with fitted and lidded compartments, on bun feet, 17in. wide. (Christie's S. Ken) $897 £550

A North Italian bone inlaid casket, with engraved pedimented borders engraved with terms, caryatids, classical masks, foliage and scrolls, 17th century, 14½in. wide. (Christie's London) $2,231 £1,320

A late Victorian oak decanter box in the form of a sentry box, signed Harry Payne, with a door to the side, 22in. high. (Christie's London) $3,048 £1,870

Early 19th century Anglo-Indian bone mounted sarcophagus shaped box, decorated with female figures, 11¼in. wide. (Phillips Manchester) $376 £200

An early 19th century bird's-eye maple and kingwood banded workbox of sarcophagus outline, with gilt metal lion ring handles, 9½in. wide. (Christie's S. Ken) $654 £385

A late Georgian mahogany work box with domed cover and swing carrying handle, 23cm. (Lawrence Fine Arts) $466 £286

Wallpaper covered hat box, S. M. Hurlbert's, Boston, Massachusetts, circa 1835, oval box covered with paper depicting Clayton's Ascension, 12in. high. (Skinner, Inc.) $1,300 £798

A German rectangular lacquer box containing four smaller boxes, Stobwasser's Fabrik, Brunswick, 22.5cm. (Lawrence Fine Arts) $9,609 £6,160

A Limoges enamelled box and cover designed by Camille Faure, covered with elaborate floral design in shades of blue and green, 16.8cm. diam. (Christie's London) $1,703 £1,045

A Victorian coromandel and brass bound sloping fronted stationery box, enclosing a leather lined and compartmented interior above a frieze drawer, 12½in. wide. (Christie's S. Ken) $523 £308

A Regency ivory, tortoiseshell veneered and pewter strung tea caddy of sarcophagus outline, on brass feet, 7in. wide. (Christie's S. Ken) $1,016 £605

A rare Jamaican tortoiseshell table cabinet with hinged cover and two doors, decorated with trees, flower, pineapple, alligator and figures, late 17th century, 18.5cm. high. (Lawrence Fine Arts) $9,385 £5,940

A Regency paper scroll work and chequer strung hexagonal single division tea caddy, 6½in. wide. (Christie's S. Ken) $511 £308

A Portuguese table cabinet, inlaid overall with bone in a delicate trailing leaf pattern, late 17th century, 34cm. (Lawrence Fine Arts) $1,390 £880

Rare miniature painted shaker box, Enfield, New Hampshire, dated *March 1836,* painted yellow, 7.3cm. (Skinner Inc.) $23,000 £14,110

Wallpaper covered wooden hat box, America, circa 1840, of oblong form, the fitted lid covered with Castles in Spain pattern, 11½in. high. (Skinner Inc.) $3,500 £2,147

A George III mahogany cutlery box, inlaid with chequered edging and the cover with an oval shell motif, 38cm. high. (Lawrence Fine Arts) $956 £605

An early 19th century tortoiseshell veneered and pewter strung bow fronted two division tea caddy with sunburst decoration, 7in. wide. (Christie's S. Ken) $1,478 £880

Diamond Dye advertising display box, with compartmented shelves. (Robt. W. Skinner Inc.) $700 £435

A George III mahogany decanter box, fitted with four glass decanters and a glass, each heightened in gilt, 9½in. high. (Christie's S. Ken) $561 £330

An early 19th century mahogany, rosewood, satinwood and yew wood three division tea caddy 12¾in. wide. (Christie's S. Ken) $730 £440

A George III mahogany serpentine fronted knife box, the sloping cover inlaid with an oval shell patera, on ogee bracket feet, 13in. high. (Christie's S. Ken) $561 £330

A tortoiseshell casket mounted with domed rectangular hinged top with handle, the interior lined with blue silk and fitted with compartments, 7½in. wide. (Christie's London) $720 £462

Painted and decorated dome top box, America, circa 1830, grain painted in brown over red and decorated with panels of leafage, 76.5cm. long. (Skinner Inc.) $850 £548

A French walnut and parcel gilt casket, the panelled rectangular top with an oval cartouche of a reclining female in a landscape, on sea-monster feet, redecorated, late 16th century, 20in. wide. (Christie's London) $2,417 £1,430

Regency rosewood tea caddy having marquetry inlay, sarcophagus formed top with indented sides, approx. 12in. wide. (G. A. Key) $605 £360

Pair of George III style mahogany knife boxes, with domed cover and turned finial, inlaid with chequered stringing, overall, 22½in. high. (Skinner Inc.) $700 £429

A Regency blonde tortoiseshell tea caddy with shaped rectangular domed top enclosing two lidded zinc lined compartments, 6½in. wide. (Christie's London) $446 £286

An Anglo-Indian micro mosaic ebony and ivory stationery box, the chamfered sloping rectangular lid enclosing a cedar divided interior, early 19th century, 8¼in. wide. (Christie's London) $858 £550

A fruitwood caddy in the form of a pear, with hinged lid, 19th century, 6½in. high. (Christie's London) $944 £605

A late Georgian mahogany cheese coaster, inlaid with flowers and outline stringing, length 41cm. (Osmond Tricks) $456 £280

A William IV parquetry work box inlaid in various woods, the interior with many accessories, 31cm. (Lawrence Fine Arts) $897 £550

A German walnut and marquetry box, the interior inlaid with fantastical architectural scenes, the flap inlaid with a drum, a lute, cards and dice, early 17th century, 18in. wide. (Christie's London) $3,824 £2,420

A Tunbridgeware rosewood writing slope, the double hinged top inlaid with a view of an abbey and a panel of roses, 14in. wide. (Christie's S. Ken) $1,109 £660

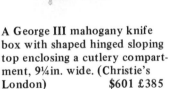

A George III mahogany knife box with shaped hinged sloping top enclosing a cutlery compartment, 9¼in. wide. (Christie's London) $601 £385

A Georgian tortoiseshell tea caddy, with sphere knop, the interior with two fitted compartments, 18cm. wide. (Henry Spencer) $765 £500

Four oval Shaker boxes, America, 19th century, each with fitted lid (minor imperfections). (Skinner Inc.) $3,100 £2,000

A gilt heightened tooled leather sloping fronted knife box, fitted with a pierced iron escutcheon plate, basically 18th century, 11¼in. high. (Christie's S. Ken) $480 £308

Anglo Indian bone sewing box, early 19th century. (Skinner Inc.) $1,100 £701

A Victorian brass bound and inlaid rosewood lady's dressing case, containing ten toilet jars and bottles bright cut with strapwork and stylised foliage, T. W., London, 1863, 12in. wide. (Christie's S. Ken) $2,227 £1,375

A Leica IIIc camera no. 376411 with a Leitz Summar 5cm. f.2 lens and Third Reich National Socialist insignia. (Christie's S. Ken)$1,496 £880

A Houghtons Ltd good Ticka watch camera with lens cap and swinging viewfinder. (Christie's S. Ken) $294 £176

A good and original Leica Ia camera no. 502 with a Leitz Elmax f.3.5 50mm. lens with double film cassette holder. (Christie's S. Ken) $8,976 £5,280

A half plate brass and mahogany Patent Ruby camera with a brass bound Thornton-Pickard-Beck Symmetrical lens. (Christie's S. Ken) $331 £198

A fine quarter plate Salex Tropical Reflex camera no. 8594, with polished wood body and brass fittings and with a Taylor-Hobson Cooke anastigmat 6in. f.3.9 lens. (Christie's S. Ken) $1,496 £880

A good 5 x 4in. Scovill Detective camera with a brass bound R. and J. Beck 5 x 4 rectilinear 7in. focus lens. (Christie's S. Ken) $698 £418

A Leica CL camera no.1430074 with a Leitz Summicron-C f.2 40mm. lens no. 2632004, camera body engraved 'DBP/US Pat. Mfg. in Japan for Leitz Wetzlar'. (Christie's S. Ken) $1,029 £605

A rare and good 4½ x 6cm. Simplex-Ernoflex camera no. O. 22696 with a Carl Zeiss Jena Tessar f.4.5 8cm. lens. (Christie's S. Ken) $882 £528

A fine and rare Amourette camera no. 4734 with a Meyer Trioplan f.6.3 3.5cm. lens. (Christie's S. Ken) $349 £209

A good Contax III camera with a Carl Zeiss Jena Sonnar f.1.5 5cm. lens. (Christie's S. Ken) $280 £165

A 2¾ x 3¼in. mahogany bodied wet plate camera with rising front, a brass bound A. Ross, London, lens, and one wet plate dark slide.. (Christie's S. Ken) $7,172 £4,400

A rare Seischab, Germany, 35mm. 'Esco' camera with a Steinheil Cassar f.6.3 3.5cm. lens set into a dial-set Pronto shutter. (Christie's S. Ken) $4,662 £2,860

A rare Pupille camera with an E. Leitz Wetzlar Elmar f.3.5 5cm. lens set into a Deckel shutter. (Christie's S. Ken) $374 £220

A rare 'Steineck ABC' wrist camera with a Steineck CL f.2.5 12.5mm. lens, brown wrist strap, all in a box. (Christie's S. Ken) $681 £418

Le Coultre Co., Switzerland, a Compass II camera with a CCL3B 35mm. f.3.5 anastigmat lens. (Christie's S. Ken) $524 £308

A Nagel, Stuttgart, Germany 127-film 'Pupille' camera with an E. Leitz, Wetzlar Elmar f.3.5 5cm. lens and with a rare Nagel coupled reflex viewfinder. (Christie's S. Ken) $986 £605

A good red dial Leica IIIf camera with a Leitz Summaron 3.5cm. f.3.5 lens and a SYOOM Leicavit rapid winder. (Christie's S. Ken)$1,028 £605

A 620-film 'Super Kodak Six-20' camera with an Eastman Kodak Co. Kodak Anastigmat Special f.3.5 100mm. lens. (Christie's S. Ken) $2,152 £1,320

A very rare and early 35mm. FED U.S.S.R. camera no. 241 with a Boomu f.3.5 50mm. lens no. 618, top plate engraved *'Boomu. No. 241. 1934r'.* (Christie's S. Ken) $1,056 £660

An 8 x 8in. mahogany wet plate camera with black square-cut bellows, brass locking clips and a sturdy brass handle. (Christie's S. Ken) $669 £418

An extremely rare, half frame Leica camera with an internally mounted Compur type leaf shutter, an upright format viewfinder and standard film rewind knob, body covered in red painted vulcanite and with a Leitz Elmar 3.5cm. f.3.5 lens. (Christie's S. Ken) $19,635 £11,550

A 35mm. mahogany cased, hand cranked, cinematographic camera with brass binding strips, two internal mahogany W.K. Co. Ltd (Williamson Kinematograph Co. Ltd) film magazines. (Christie's S. Ken) $1,345 £825

The American Camera Co, 2¼ x 2¼in. 'Demon' detective camera with lens, flap shutter, changing bag and unexposed plates all in maker's original box.(Christie's S. Ken) $1,076 £660

A good W. Butcher and Sons 3¼ x 4¼in. 'Royal Mail' camera with fifteen lenses mounted in five rows of three set into a simple shutter. (Christie's S. Ken) $2,152 £1,320

A good Shincho Seiki Co. Ltd., Darling-16 sub miniature camera with lens and internal film cassettes. (Christie's S. Ken) $551 £330

A good original box form 9 x 12cm. Anschutz camera no. 2 with wire frame finder, and a brass bound C. P. Goerz, Berlin, Extra Rapid-Lynkeioskop Serie C no. 1 lens. (Christie's S. Ken) $2,021 £1,210

A rare 6 x 6cm. Bayerflex twin lens reflex camera with a Laack Rathenow Pololyt anastigmat f.3.5 7.5cm. viewing lens. (Christie's S. Ken) $643 £385

A good Leica Ig camera no. 909554, with slow shutter speed dial. (Christie's S. Ken) $1,496 £880

A 45 x 107mm. 'Photo-Stereo-Binocle' camera with a pair of Goerz Doppel-anastigmat 75mm. lenses, in maker's original leather case. (Christie's S. Ken) $2,869 £1,760

A Leica IIIg camera no. 891046 with a Leitz Elmar 5cm. f.2.8 lens no. 1496866 in maker's leather ever ready case. (Christie's S. Ken) $1,496 £935

A 35mm. high polish platinum and karung leather covered 'Leica R6' camera no. 1750000 with a platinum and skin barrelled Leica Summilux f.1.4 50mm. lens. (Christie's S. Ken) $43,032 £26,400

A very good R. and J. Beck Ltd quarter plate Frena de luxe camera no. 9215 with tan skin covered body. (Christie's S. Ken) $1,378 £825

A good green chrome Leica Bundeseigentum M3 camera no. 927742, with chrome fittings and green leather covered body. (Christie's S. Ken) $3,553 £2,090

A very rare Thompson revolver camera no. 48, with a polished mahogany handle, lacquered brass body with upper rear mounted viewing tube. (Christie's S. Ken) $30,481 £18,700

A 'Heidoscop' stereo camera no. 7387 with a Carl Zeiss, Jena Sucher Triplet f.4.2 7.5cm. viewing lens. (Christie's S. Ken) $711 £418

A half plate brass and mahogany tailboard camera with a brass bound R. and J. Beck 5 x 4in. rectilinear 7in. focus lens. (Christie's S. Ken) $359 £220

A silver plated grinning cat mascot, the base marked *Rd No. 676202,* 4½in. high. (Christie's London) $932 £572

Archer, a Lalique frosted glass car mascot of disc form intaglio, moulded, with a kneeling naked male archer, 12.5cm. high. (Phillips London) $1,408 £920

A nickel plated policeman with right hand raised, the base stamped *Asprey,* 12cm. high. (Christie's S. Ken) $256 £165

A chromium plated head of a gun dog holding a grouse in its mouth, signed *Ch. Paillet,* 10cm. high. (Christie's S. Ken) $256 £165

Coq Nain, a Lalique glass cockerel, 8in. high. (Christie's London) $1,524 £935

A Red Ashay clear glass devil (slightly chipped), 5½in. high. (Christie's London) $394 £242

A bronze Spirit of Ecstasy showroom display, signed *Charles Sykes,* mounted on a circular marble base, 20½in. high. (Christie's London) $12,909 £7,920

A nickel plated little girl holding a teddy bear, 12.5cm. high. (Christie's S. Ken) $546 £352

A nickel plated ballroom dancing couple, the gentleman wearing tails and the lady wearing an ankle length ballgown, 13.5cm. high. (Christie's S. Ken) $171 £110

A chromium plated deer's head, 11.5cm. high. (Christie's S. Ken) $102 £66

Victoire, a polished, satin glass car mascot, moulded as a female head, mouth open to shout, moulded *R. Lalique France,* 26cm. long. (Bonhams) $6,640 £4,000

Tete de Belier, a Lalique glass ram's head, on chromium plated mount (base repaired), 4in. high. (Christie's London) $8,606 £5,280

A bronze showroom display of a graceful winged speed goddess, with hair streaming in the wind, her base inscribed *Susse Frs. Ed. Paris, Cire Perdue,* and signed *Ch. Soudant,* 21¼in. high. (Christie's London) $6,813 £4,180

A nickel plated Wills Sainte Claire flying goose, the base stamped *I. Florman 1923,* 4¾in. high. (Christie's London) $753 £462

A silvered bronze wind spirit, the crouching female figure with flowing hair and cloak, signed *Guiraud Riviere,* 7½in. high. (Christie's London) $5,020 £3,080

Vitesse, a Lalique car mascot in satin and clear glass, moulded as a naked maiden, 18.8cm. high. (Lawrence Fine Arts) $6,257 £3,960

Bouledogue a la Chaine, a nickel plated stylised bulldog straining on a chain, mounted on a marble plinth, 3¾in. high. (Christie's London) $537 £330

A nickel plated Spirit of Ecstasy mascot on a chromium plated radiator cap, 13.7cm. high. (Tennants) $343 £220

A silvered bronze car mascot cast from a model by Ferdinand Preiss, of a demonic satyr, 7in. long.
(Christie's S. Ken.) $1543 £935

'Cinq Chevaux', a Lalique glass Car Mascot, the model commissioned by Citroën in 1925, 11.5cm. high.
(Phillips) $4480 £2800

Levrier, a Lalique glass greyhound, moulded R Lalique France, 7¾in. long.
(Christie's) $3,227 £1,980

'Saint-Christophe', a Lalique glass Car Mascot of disc shape, intaglio-moulded on the reverse, 11.5cm. high.
(Phillips) $1408 £880

Coq Nain, a Lalique frosted and polished car mascot modelled as a cockerel, 8in. high. (Christie's S. Ken)
$853 £550

Grenouille, a Lalique glass car mascot, modelled as a small frog in crouched position, 6cm. high, signed R. Lalique, France,
(Phillips London)
$19,560 £12,000

Hirondelle, a Lalique glass car mascot, moulded as a swallow perched on a circular base, 14.8cm. high. (Phillips London)
$2,282 £1,400

Archer, a Lalique glass car mascot of disc shape, intaglio moulded on the reverse with a naked male archer kneeling with his bow, total height 15cm. (Phillips London)
$1,793 £1,100

'Grande Libellule', a Lalique glass Car Mascot, modelled as a large dragonfly resting on a circular base, 21cm. high.
(Phillips) $6400 £4000

CASH REGISTERS

A Berlin National Model 442X cash register with florid Art Nouveau decoration on the bronze casing, 1911. (Auction Team Koeln) $1,769 £1,092

A German National Model 642S cash register on wooden base with four control levers, decorated in the Art Nouveau style, circa 1910. (Auction Team Koeln) $885 £546

A National cash register for Dutch currency, circa 1900. (Auction Team Koeln)
   $877 £555

An early National Model 8 cash register for Dutch currency, *N. J. Creyghton* inscribed on the ornate casing, circa 1900. (Auction Team Koeln) $948 £585

A very decorative mahogany cash register by G. H. Glenhill & Sons Ltd., Halifax, Serial No. 79.103, circa 1885. (Auction Team Koeln) $771 £473

A richly decorated National Model 44 plated cash register for German currency up to 4.95 marks, Serial No. 255960, circa 1900. (Auction Team Koeln) $321 £197

A National cash register with richly decorated casing, 1924. (Auction Team Koeln)
   $2,337 £1,479

A National Model 313 cash register for German currency up to 2.95 marks, of narrow construction, Serial No. 690.423, circa 1910. (Auction Team Koeln) $258 £158

A National Model 442X cash register with richly decorated nickel casing with crank, for German currency to 99.99 marks and receipt dispenser, circa 1908. (Auction Team Koeln) $1,168 £721

A gilt metal eight light chandelier of inverted trumpet shape, hung with glass beads and faceted drops, 47in. high. (Christie's S. Ken) $1,614 £990

A Georgian crystal chandelier, the fluted baluster iron stem surmounted by a domed canopy hung with drops below a tulip shaped corona, 86cm. diam. (Phillips London) $11,016 £7,200

A gilt metal eighteen light chandelier with foliate scrolled branches, each supporting two nozzles hung with polychrome faceted drops, 26in. wide. (Christie's London) $1,239 £770

An ormolu twelve light chandelier with twin corona and French horn shaped spirally twisted branches, fitted for electricity, 48in. high. (Christie's London) $3,542 £2,200

A gilt metal and moulded glass basket shaped hanging lantern, with vitruvian scroll banding and flowerhead boss, 17in. high. (Christie's S. Ken) $897 £550

Bird's Nest, a Lalique chandelier, the hemispherical form comprising twelve radial segments suspended from a circular frame, 49cm. diam. (Christie's London) $3,227 £1,980

A French gilt metal six light chandelier, the scrolling branches emanating from a baluster column with applied drapery swags and suspension loop, 30in. high. (Christie's S. Ken) $538 £330

A 19th century bronze hall lantern, the cylindrical body inset with arched glass panels, 25in. high. (Christie's S. Ken) $1,165 £715

A North European brass twelve light chandelier with two tiers of scrolling branches, each with circular drip pan, 22in. high. (Christie's London) $1,208 £715

A brass twelve light chandelier, the twelve scrolling serpent branches in two tiers on a baluster shaft, 29in. high. (Christie's London) $1,115 £660

A Dutch style brass twelve light chandelier, the scrolling branches fitted with twin tiered nozzles and drip pans, 23½in. high. (Christie's S. Ken) $897 £550

An ormolu twelve light chandelier, the top corona mounted with crossed arrows, the scrolling foliate branches with drip pans, stamped *123EM,* 39in. high. (Christie's London) $3,188 £1,980

A Northern European brass chandelier with twelve scrolling branches interspersed with flowerheads, 19th century, 32in. high. (Christie's London) $2,231 £1,320

A Danish ormolu and cut glass six light chandelier with pierced overhanging corona hung with fillets and waterfall shaft, 47in. high. (Christie's London) $6,083 £3,850

An Art Nouveau brass six light chandelier, the circlet pierced with stylised flowers and whiplash motif, 102cm. high. (Christie's London) $986 £605

. 19th century twelve light chandelier from the Villa Meerholz, with drops, 90cm. high, partly damaged. (Auktionshaus Arnold) $1,325 £860

A French ormolu and bronze hanging ceiling light, modelled with the figure of a putti supporting a hobnail cut glass shade, 36in. high, overall. (Christie's S. Ken) $1,434 £880

A brass ten light chandelier, the ten scrolling serpent branches each with circular drip pan, 26in. high. (Christie's London) $2,974 £1,760

Navy blue Grueby pottery vase, Boston, circa 1910, impressed and artist initialled (glaze imperfection and bubble bursts), 5½in. high. (Skinner Inc.) $1,900 £1,173

Decorated marblehead pottery vase, Massachusetts, circa 1905, stamped with logo and incised with early *MP* mark, 5¾in. (Skinner Inc.) $1,600 £988

Flint enamel lion mantle ornament, Lyman Fenton and Co., Bennington, Vermont, circa 1849-1858, 9½in. high, 11in. long. (Skinner Inc.) $10,000 £6,135

Newcomb pottery carved vase, New Orleans, Louisiana, circa 1931, impressed *NC SY72,* 8½in. high. (Robt. W. Skinner Inc.) $2,600 £1,595

Eight Dedham pottery Birds in Potted Orange Tree plates, Massachusetts, early 20th century, 8in. diam. (Skinner Inc.) $1,700 £1,049

Roseville pottery jardiniere on stand, Zanesville, Ohio, early 20th century, listed as the Artcraft line, 24in. high. (Robt. W. Skinner Inc.) $375 £230

Grueby pottery vase, Boston, circa 1905, partial paper label and artists monogram *JE* (minor nicks), 12in. high. (Skinner Inc.) $2,300 £1,420

Vance/Avon faience pottery water pitcher, Tiltonville, Ohio, circa 1902; moulded relief decoration of hunt scene and grapes, 12½in. high. (Skinner Inc.) $180 £111

Teco pottery vase with four handles, Terra Cotta, Illinois, circa 1910, squat, impressed twice, 6½in. high. (Skinner Inc.) $1,300 £802

AMERICAN

Decorated marblehead pottery bowl, Massachusetts, circa 1905, squat shallow form, initialled *HT* for Hannah Tutt, 7½in. diam. (Robt. W. Skinner Inc.) $650 £399

Fulper pottery copper dust vase with two handles, Flemington, New Jersey, circa 1915, 6in. diam. (Robt. W. Skinner Inc.) $175 £107

Saturday Evening Girls pottery decorated bowl, Boston, 1912, artist initialled *S.G.* for Sara Galner, 10¾in. diam. (Robt. W. Skinner Inc.) $950 £583

Grotesque pottery jug, America, late 19th/early 20th century, carved into a devil-like mask, 19in. high. (Skinner Inc.) $600 £387

Porcelain pitcher, American China Manufactory, Philadelphia, circa 1830, each side decorated with floral bouquets, 9½in. high. (Skinner Inc.) $2,100 £1,288

Marblehead pottery experimental landscape vase, executed by Arthur E. Baggs, circa 1925, 7¼in. high. (Skinner Inc.) $3,200 £1,975

Dedham pottery crackleware vase, Dedham, Massachusetts, late 19th century, initialled *HCR,* for Hugh Robertson, (repair to neck) 9in. high. (Skinner Inc.) $1,700 £1,049

Vance faience vase with moulded mermaid decoration, Ohio, circa 1905, with repeating figures and fish (some chips and roughness), 12½in. high. (Skinner Inc.) $300 £184

A painted chalkware cat, Pennsylvania, mid 19th century, painted and decorated with red, yellow and black watercolour, 10¾in. high. (Christie s New York) $2,090 £1,314

ARITA

An Arita tokkuri decorated with four panels of two handled vases filled with chrysanthemums and peony, late 17th century, 22.5cm. high. (Christie's London)
$4,518 £2,860

A pair of Arita blue and white rectangular Sake bottles, the sides decorated with sprays of tree peony among rockwork, late 17th century, 13.5cm. high. (Christie's) $3674   £2200

A fine Arita blue and white hexagonal vase decorated with a ho-o bird perched on rockwork amongst peonies, chrysanthemums and other flowers, late 17th century, 61.5cm. high.(Christie's London)
$156,420 £99,000

A pair of rare and important Arita seated kirin enamelled in the Kakiemon style, with stylised fur markings (both with some restoration), late 17th century, 24cm. high. (Christie's London)
$86,900 £55,000

A rare Arita model of a seated horse following a Dutch delft original, its saddle cloth with flowers and foliage (ears slightly damaged), circa 1700, 18cm. long. (Christie's London)
$13,035 £8,250

A pair of rare Arita sake ewers modelled as minogame decorated in iron red enamel and gilt with panels on their backs of ho-o birds, late 17th century/early 18th century, 18.5cm. and 17cm. long. (Christie's London)
$11,297 £7,150

A pair of Arita blue and white trumpet shaped vases decorated with a continuous landscape with two figures walking across a bridge, late 17th century, 41cm. high. (Christie's London)
$11,297 £7,150

An Arita shallow dish modelled in the form of an uchiwa with a cloud shaped panel depicting a scholar and attendants, early 18th century, 19cm. long. (Christie's London)
$3,823 £2,420

An Arita blue and white oviform vase decorated with a continuous landscape of pavilions and other buildings amongst a rocky outcrop, late 17th century, 26.75cm. high. (Christie's London)
$5,214 £3,300

BELLEEK

One of a pair of Belleek salts modelled as sea-horses with mermaid tails recumbent on rectangular bases, 5in. long, late nineteenth century.
(Christie's S. Ken.)　$654　£385

A Belleek 9in. oval basket and cover in good condition.
(Phillips)　$1254　£760

A First Period Belleek Parian ware box and cover, modelled as a young boy wearing a souwester and waders, 16cm. wide.
(Spencer's)　$515　£320

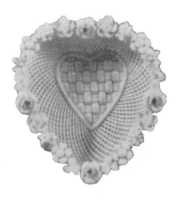

One of a pair of Belleek candleholders modelled each as a Putto supporting a sea-urchin on their heads.
(Christie's S. Ken.)　$1683　£990

A pair of rare First Period Belleek ice pails and covers, from the service ordered by the Prince of Wales, mark for 1868, 46cm. high.
(Allen & Harris)　$7084　£4400

Belleek heart form basket, floral design rim, four straw weave, 6in. wide.
(Du Mouchelles)　$200　£124

A rare Belleek satirical chamber pot, the base printed in black with a full face portrait of Gladstone, 16cm., first period mark and registration mark for 1877. (Phillips London)　$274 £170

A Belleek double Fish Vase with two open-mouthed entwined scaly fish supporting a central vase, 1st period printed and impressed marks, 30cm.
(Phillips)　$1155　£700

A Belleek circular plaque painted by E Sheerin with a view of Ballynahimch Connemara, 11¼in. diam.
(Christie's S. Ken.)　$524　£308

BERLIN

A Berlin figure of a putto emblematic of Plenty standing holding a gilt spirally moulded cornucopia of fruit, blue sceptre marks, 19th century, 7½in. high. (Christie's S. Ken) $287 £187

A large ormolu Berlin punch bowl and cover surmounted by a kneeling Bacchic boy holding a glass and a bottle, decorated with amusing scenes after Hogarth, 47.5cm. (Phillips London) $2,093 £1,300

A Berlin figure of a cooper standing at a barrel with his hammer raised, blue sceptre mark, circa 1780, 9.5cm. high. (Christie's Geneva) $282 £172

A Berlin oval plaque, painted with the head and shoulders of a nude sleeping woman, impressed sceptre and KPM marks, late 19th century, 22cm. high. (Christie's London) $974 £605

A Berlin table centre piece modelled as two maidens supporting a pierced shallow basket, blue sceptre and circular medallion mark, circa 1849-1870, 14¾in. high. (Christie's S. Ken) $677 £440

A Berlin porcelain circular wall plate, painted in sepia with a bare breasted Egyptianesque maiden, 40.5cm. diam. (Phillips London) $945 £580

A Berlin figure of Apollo, standing with an eagle at his side on a square base with canted corners, KPM mark, late 19th century, 9in. high. (damaged) (Christie's S. Ken) $237 £154

A fine rectangular plaque, possibly Berlin, painted with a horseman in military uniform, 14.5 x 17.2cm., impressed eagle mark. (Phillips London) $1,059 £650

A Berlin figural group of Ruhm and Zeit modelled as a classical maiden above an old man, blue sceptre and iron red KPM and globe mark, late 19th century, 16in. high. (Christie's S. Ken) $762 £495

BOW

A Bow figure of a new dancer of conventional type, modelled as a girl in plumed hat (restorations to one hand), circa 1762, 18.5cm. high. (Christie's London) $708 £440

A Bow partridge tureen and a cover, naturally modelled to the right on an oval basket-work nest, circa 1760, 12.5cm. wide. (Christie's London) $1,417 £880

A Bow figure from a set of the Seasons, emblematic of Summer, modelled as a girl in black and white hat, 12cm. (Phillips London) $741 £460

An extremely rare Bow figure of the Marquis of Granby from the engraving by Richard Houston after a painting by Sir Joshua Reynolds, 34.5cm. (Phillips London) $6,630 £3,900

A pair of large Bow white figures of a bagpiper and his companion, both on moulded scrolling bases, 27cm. and 26.5cm. (Phillips London) $4,347 £2,700

A Bow figure of a nun in pink lined black cowl and white habit, circa 1758, 14.5cm. high. (Christie's London) $885 £550

A Bow group of a dancing Turk and companion in blue and pink coats and flowered clothes (her right hand lacking), circa 1762, 20cm. high. (Christie's London) $1,151 £ 715

A Bow documentary cylindrical ink pot with a central circular well surrounded by five holes to the shoulder, painted by James Welsh, circa 1758, 9cm. diam. (Christie's London) $21,252 £13,200

A Bow white figure of Apollo by the Muses Modeller, the god scantily draped and with a laurel wreath in his hair, circa 1752, 17cm. high. (Christie's London) $3,542 £2,200

BRITISH

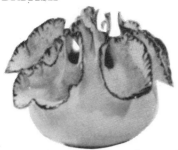

A porcelain pinched vase by Deirdre Burnett, covered in a white glaze with olive brown run and fluxed rim, impressed *DB,* 7.5cm. high. (Christie's London) **$129 £77**

A Plymouth cream jug, painted in underglaze faded sepia or blue with flowers, trees and rocks, 9cm. (Lawrence Fine Arts) **$660 £418**

A large English porcelain stirrup cup modelled as the head of a hound, his coat spotted in brown, 15cm. (Phillips London) **$547 £340**

A Pennington Liverpool ship bowl painted in blue with a ship in full sail, inscribed *Success to the Perseus, Capt. Gibson, 1790,* 25cm. (Phillips London) **$5,474 £3,400**

A creamware inscribed and dated swelling jug with flared foot and loop handle, painted in colours with a ploughman, perhaps Liverpool or Staffordshire, circa 1789, 25.5cm. high. (Christie's London) **$3,896 £2,420**

A Burslem ware ceramic wall plaque, the design attributed to Charlotte Rhead, decorated with stylised brown, and cream chrysanthemums with blue leaves and berries, 41cm. diam. (Phillips London) **$359 £220**

A Fowler's phrenology head, the cranium printed with the areas of the sentiments, the base with maker's label and title, 11¾in. high. (Christie's S. Ken) **$950 £605**

A creamware dated plate transfer printed by John Sadler with The Sailor's Return (minute rim chip at 1 o'clock), circa 1769, 24cm. diam. (Christie's London) **$2,834 £1,760**

A very rare small mug commemorating the birth of the Princess Royal, printed in black with ladies in waiting leading a horse drawn baby carriage, 6.3cm. (Phillips London) **$1,385 £860**

BRITISH

19th century pottery soup tureen and cover, by Turner, blue and white Willow pattern in the style of Nankin. (G. A. Key) $136 £80

James Hadley, a majolica ware model of an elephant carrying a howdah on its back, 22cm. (Phillips London) $676 £420

Newhall porcelain tea pot, oval panel shape with sprig flower decoration, complete with cover. (G. A. Key) $170 £100

An Aldermaston Pottery tin glazed earthenware dish, the white ground decorated in red and amber lustrous glaze with animals drinking in a landscape, 25.4cm. diam. (Christie's London) $296 £176

A large Castle Hedingham Essex jug, moulded in relief with Classical panels of chariot racing and the Muses, 30in. high. (Christie's S. Ken) $574 £352

The Clifton dish, a highly important slipware dish made at Clifton in Cumbria, press moulded and trailed in two tones of brown, 39.7cm. (Phillips London) $33,810 £21,000

A creamware baluster jug with grooved loop handle, the tortoiseshell ground applied with green swags of foliage, circa 1780, 16.5cm. high. (Christie's London) $619 £385

A very rare documentary toby jug of Fiddler type, inscribed *J. Marsh, Folley,* 27.5cm., the head a replacement made in bell metal. (Phillips London) $3,542 £2,200

An unusual ceramic and pewter inkwell, cast in the style of a Martin Brothers bird with the head forming the hinged cover, 4¼in. high. (Christie's S. Ken) $341 £220

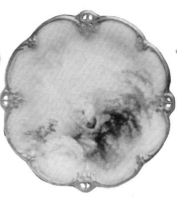

An English porcelain inkwell, cover and liner with dog's head quill holder, 6.5cm. (Phillips London) $179 £110

An English porcelain cream glazed basket modelled as a cat standing with its fore paws resting on the brim of a straw hat, possibly Brown Westhead Moore and Co Ltd. (Christie's S. Ken) $370 £242

An unusual Dutch decorated English creamware teapot and cover, painted on both sides with a lady and gentleman in 18th century costume, 12cm. (Phillips London) $935 £550

A Longton Hall vase of inverted baluster form with spreading neck and fluted base, the body painted in colours, 4¾in. high. (Christie's S. Ken) $352 £220

A wall plaque painted with two storks standing on the edge of a river, signed *W Powell,* 22.5cm., date code for 1910. (Phillips London) $1,445 £850

A Shelley nursery teapot by Hilda Cowham, modelled as a marquee and printed with two seated children reading, 5in. high. (Christie's S. Ken) $600 £352

A rare late 18th century creamware deer-head stirrup cup, decorated in brown and green streaky glazes, 12cm. long. (Henry Spencer) $1,606 £1,050

A Grimwades Cube lustre tea-pot, printed and painted with fairies, cobwebs and toadstools, printed factory mark, 4in. high. (Christie's S. Ken) $188 £110

A Charles Bourne beaded spill vase painted with floral sprays, on a scale blue ground, 11cm. (Phillips London) $326 £200

BRITISH

An interesting green glazed teapot and cover, moulded in relief with sprays of chrysanthemums and bell-like flowers, 14cm. (Phillips London) $6,800 £4,000

A white saltglaze basket and stand, pierced with a trellis design with flowerheads at the junctions on the exterior, 22.5cm. and 26cm. (Phillips London) $578 £340

An unusual Ault Pottery pouring vessel, designed by Christopher Dresser, of compressed globular shape with two pouring spouts, 28cm. wide. (Phillips London) $3,366 £2,200

A rare pierced jar and cover by M. J. Deacon, pierced with a scale pattern heightened in turquoise enamel, 13.5cm. (Phillips London) $277 £170

One of a rare pair of pate sur pate square plaques by Charles Noke, signed, decorated with portraits of a man and woman representing old age, 19 x 16.5cm. (Phillips London) Two $619 £380

An English blue ground majolica vase, the body painted with cherubs amongst clouds reversed with moulded lovers' trophies within moulded laurel and ribbon cartouches, circa 1860, 13in. high. (Christie's S. Ken) $508 £330

A Don Pottery Orange Jumper jug, the ovoid body printed and coloured with a figure of Mellish standing in profile, 18cm. (Phillips London) $952 £560

An unusual Victorian bargeman's pearlware smoking companion, the tobacco jar with an antique slavery portrait and a biblical reference, 38cm. high overall. (Henry Spencer) $337 £220

A Gray's Pottery Art Deco spherical lampbase, painted in colours with a stylised scene of golfers, 6in. high. (Christie's S. Ken) $1,313 £770

BRITISH

An English porcelain pot pourri basket and cover, with reserving panels painted with coloured flowers, 6.5cm. diam. (Phillips London) $195 £120

A Bodley rectangular tray, painted by Joseph Birbeck, with a cow, sheep and a goat in an extensive view in North Wales, 27.5cm. (Phillips London) $440 £270

An early 19th century English yellow ground tureen and cover, black printed with two children's scenes entitled *L'oiseau le* and *Le fit cheval,* 8in. diam. (Phillips Sevenoaks) $374 £220

A Longton Hall figure of a milkman with two pails, one on his head the other by his side, circa 1755, 27cm. high. (Christie's London) $4,427 £2,750

A pair of baluster vases painted with sheep in highland landscapes, signed *H. Davis,* 15cm., date codes for 1925. (Phillips London) $3,912 £2,400

A figure of a gentleman of George IIIs reign wearing a top hat and tails, by James Hadley, 20.5cm., date code for 1913. (Phillips London) $554 £340

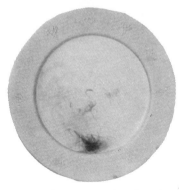

A plate, the centre painted with flamingos in a misty river landscape, signed *W. Powell,* 26cm., date code for 1912. (Phillips London) $896 £550

A Barumware triple handled pottery vase by C. H. Brannam incised and painted with aquatic scene, dated 1903, 13in. high. (Christie's S. Ken) $375 £220

A large plate, brightly decorated with an urn of flowers, coloured by and signed *E. Barker,* 27cm., 1933. (Phillips London) $587 £360

BRITISH

A Wade Heath novelty teapot as Donald Duck in blue sailors outfit, printed marks, circa 1935, 8in. wide. (Christie's S. Ken) $1,490 £968

An English porcelain tapering bough pot and cover with five apertures and four feet, 8in. high. (Christie's S. Ken) $915 £572

An attractive creamware tea-pot and cover, the body painted with an all over scale pattern in red and black, 14cm. probably Leeds. (Phillips London) $850 £500

Very fine Bretby pottery floor vase, with peasant girl figure by J. Barker, approx. 36in. high. (G. A. Key) $388 £250

A pair of Morrisware pottery vases decorated by George Cartlidge, of shouldered taper-ing cylindrical form, both with printed factory marks and artist's signature, 10¼in. high. (Christie's S. Ken) $844 £495

A figure of a French fisher girl standing barefoot and carrying a wicker basket, by James Hadley, 19cm., date code for 1918. (Phillips London) $147 £90

A plate, painted with a view of Tynemouth Priory, signed *H. Davis,* 23cm., date code for 1903. (Phillips London) $522 £320

An English porcelain tulip vase modelled as a red striped open yellow bloom, perhaps Spode, circa 1820, 15.5cm. high. (Christie's London) $3,187 £1,980

A rich Cauldon dessert plate, the shaped centre painted by Joseph Birbeck Snr., 21.5cm. (Phillips London) $358 £220

BRITISH

A creamware mug painted with a portrait of Lord Rodney wearing a green shirt and an inscription *Success to brave Rodney,* 12.5cm. (Phillips London) $306 £190

A Bates, Brown-Westhead and Moore parian bust of Apollo after a model by Delpech, Art Union stamp and dated 1861, 14in. high. (Christie's S. Ken) $508 £330

A rare Sabrina ware vase of pear shape, decorated with fish swimming among seaweed, 14cm., date code for 1931. (Phillips London) $195 £120

A Sabrina ware vase, painted with flamingos in a misty river landscape, signed *W. Powell,* 16.5cm., date code for 1910. (Phillips London) $277 £170

A pair of Royal Bonn slender baluster vases, each painted with a three quarter length portrait of a young lady, 14½in. high. (Both cracked) (Christie's S. Ken)$292 £187

An English porcelain pug dog seated on his haunches, with brown coat and black muzzle, perhaps Lowestoft or Derby, circa 1775, 9.5cm. high. (Christie's London) $1,505 £935

A Burmantofts faience vase, decorated in cobalt blue, turquoise, green and pink, on a white ground, 46.4cm. high. (Christie's London) $1,470 £902

A pearlware globular teapot and cover, printed with two circular panels of female archers, circa 1800, 7½in. wide. (Christie's S. Ken) $271 £176

A Crown Ducal shaped and ribbed two handled cylindrical vase decorated with a pattern by Charlotte Rhead, printed factory mark, 5½in. high. (Christie's S. Ken) $104 £61

BRITISH

Mochaware pitcher, England, 19th century, decorated with undulating lines in cream slip, (rim chips) 6¾in. high. (Skinner Inc.) $600 £368

A Longton Hall or West Pans teapot and cover of Meissen bullet shape with tau handle and grotesque spout, 8.5cm. (Phillips London) $886 £550

A Leeds creamware cylindrical teapot and cover, with floral terminals and spiral moulded spout, 12cm. (Phillips London) $2,737 £1,700

Mochaware pitcher, England, early 19th century, with four large brown, rust and white tobacco leaves, 9½in. high. (Skinner Inc.) $6,000 £3,681

Pair of George Jones & Sons crescent china vases with blue scale decoration with exotic birds in cartouches, 14in. (G. A. Key) $106 £65

A large S. Hancock & Sons Morrisware baluster vase, decorated with mauve and inky blue thistles on a greeny yellow ground, 32.9cm. high. (Christie's London) $1,663 £990

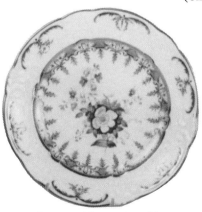

A well coloured traditional toby jug, the man seated holding a foaming brown jug on one knee, 25cm. (Phillips London) $1,127 £700

A Swansea plate painted by William Pollard with a wild rose and trailing blue flowers, red stencil mark, circa 1820, 20.5cm. diam. (Christie's London) $1,594 £990

A bisque figure of a cricketer with articulated head, modelled in the form of a cricket ball, inscribed *Hassall* on the base. (Christie's S. Ken) $42 £27

BRITISH

A large Carleton ware two handled punch bowl, moulded and painted on one side with King Henry VIII and Cardinal Wolsey on the other. (Bearne's) $579 £360

A Martin Brothers stoneware salt modelled on the corners with the heads of four comical horned beasts, 10cm. high. (Phillips) $352 £220

Liverpool creamware platter, Herculaneum pottery, circa 1800, transfer printed medallion of Liberty and Washington's tomb, 11¼in. wide. (Skinner Inc.) $4,300 £2,544

Mochaware pitcher, England, 19th century, blue decorated with light blue and white worming, 7in. high. (Skinner Inc.) $600 £355

James Hadley: a very large Cricklight figure of a Grecian water carrier holding an amphora, 79.5cm., date code for 1897. (Phillips London) $2,635 £1,550

A Davenport shaped oval two-handled foot bath, printed with the 'Mosque and Fisherman' pattern. (Christie's S. Ken) $2656 £1650

A Louis Wain ceramic animal model of a stylised dog with squared geometric features, coloured in green, red, black and blue, 13cm. high. (Phillips London) $717 £440

A Carter Stabler Adams pottery dish, possibly a design by Erna Manners, painted in mauve, green and blue with stylised leaves and scrolling tendrils, 37.8cm. diam. (Phillips) $288 £180

A George Jones majolica jug moulded in relief with panels of a pointer and its prey reversed with a fox hunting a rabbit, 1872, 10in. high. (Christie's S. Ken) $852 £550

BRITISH

A ceramic chamber pot with everted rim, decorated with a design by Christopher Dresser, printed in black, brown, beige and green, 23cm. diam. (Phillips) $416 £260

A Masons Ironstone foot bath and jug, printed in colours in Chinese style with vases and bowls of flowers among branches. (Lawrence Fine Arts) $2,781 £1,760

A Yorkshire pearlware model of a show horse, with an ochre and green saddle-cloth tied with a blue girth, circa 1800, 14.5cm. high. (Bearne's) $1937 £1250

An English Majolica model of an elephant standing on an oval rocky base, circa 1860, 7³/₄in. high. (Christie's S. Ken) $409 £264

English Pottery Toby Jug, probably Yorkshire, early 19th century, toby holding a cup in one hand and a pitcher in the other, 10¹/₄in. high. (Skinner Inc) $300 £197

Creamware Double-Tiered Sweetmeat Stand, England, 19th century, of Leeds type and formed as a seated figure of Flora above two groups of five shells, 10¹/₄in. high. (Skinner Inc) $450 £296

A creamware coffee pot and cover, brightly painted in iron-red, green, yellow and pink with a farmhouse on one side, 26.5cm. (Phillips London) $370 £230

Rare Mayer Creamware Oval Chestnut Basket with Cover and Underdish, England, c. 1800, moulded basketweave decoration, 10³/₄in. handle to handle. (Skinner Inc) $4600 £3026

An interesting small mug or coffee can, painted in underglaze blue with a central rock and tree, probably Vauxhall, 6cm. (Phillips) $998 £620

CANTON

Pair of Canton Blue and White Tea Caddies, China, mid 19th century, hexagonal shape, with lids, 6in. high.
(Skinner Inc) $5750   £3782

Canton blue and white porcelain charger, 19th century, circular scene with patterned banded borders, 16in. diam.
(Skinner Inc.) $600 £375

A pair of Canton vases, applied at the neck and shoulders with dragons and Buddhist lions, 61.8cm. high.
(Bearne's) $4025   £2500

CARDEW

A stoneware footed bowl by Michael Cardew, covered in a speckled mushroom coloured glaze with chocolate brown decoration of cross hatching and spiralling brushwork, 13.5cm. high. (Christie's London) $1,016 £605

A stoneware charger by Michael Cardew, covered in an oatmeal glaze, the interior with olive green glaze and combed waved bands through to oatmeal glaze, 34.3cm. diam.
(Christie's London) $739 £440

An earthenware jug by Michael Cardew, covered in a translucent brown glaze over a mottled lime green and olive brown glaze, 25.6cm. high.
(Christie's London) $259 £154

CAUGHLEY

A Caughley egg drainer, decorated in blue and white the Fisherman pattern, circa 1790, 3¹/₅ in. across handle.
(Wooley & Wallis) $288   £180

An important Caughley loving cup, printed in blue with a view of the Iron Bridge, 11.7cm.
(Phillips London)$5,705 £3,500

A good Caughley cabbage leaf mask jug, printed in blue with the Fisherman pattern, 23.5cm.
(Phillips London) $424 £260

CHELSEA

A Chelsea acanthus leaf moulded teapot and cover with bamboo moulded handle, incised triangle mark, circa 1745-49, 12cm. high. (Christie's London)
$38,962 £24,200

A rare Chelsea Kakiemon style leaf dish, with an exotic bird in display and another perched on a prunus branch, raised anchor period, 8½in. long. (Tennants) $6,552 £4,200

A Chelsea lozenge shaped spoon tray painted in the Kakiemon palette with the Quail Pattern, circa 1750, 14.5cm. wide. (Christie's London) $7,438 £4,620

A Chelsea mottled claret ground bucket shaped sugar bowl and cover painted with Oriental musicians, gold anchor mark, circa 1765, 11.5cm. diam. (Christie's London) $7,969 £4,950

Two Chelsea eel tureens and covers naturally modelled with their bodies curled, their tails forming the handles, circa 1755, 18.5cm. wide. (Christie's London)
$35,420 £22,000

A Chelsea mottled claret-ground oviform vase and cover with gilt loop handles, painted in the manner of Richard Askew with three putti, circa 1765, 30cm. high.
(Christie's London) $1496   £880

A Chelsea figure of a flautist, wearing a white beret, pink bodice and purple and yellow skirt, 15cm. (Phillips London)
$1,449 £900

A pair of Chelsea blue ground lobed tapering oviform vases and covers with pierced gilt scroll handles and finials, gold anchor marks, circa 1765, 32cm. high. (Christie's London)
$9,740 £6,050

Flower Seller, a Chelsea pottery figure by Charles Vyse, of a woman selling posies of violets and primroses from a basket, on wood base, Chelsea 1926, 29.7cm. high. (Christie's London) $554 £330

171

A good heart shaped dessert dish painted in blue with the Kang Hsi Lotus pattern, circa 1770, 26cm. (Phillips London) $680 £400

Late 19th century, Nankin porcelain dish with floral border and a design of a lakeland scene with a figure on a bridge, 15 x 12in. (G. A. Key) $374 £220

A fluted oval soup tureen and cover, enamelled with bouquets and sprays of flowers, 34cm., Ch'ien Lung. (Lawrence Fine Arts) $1,144 £715

Chinese porcelain charger with mahogany stand (chip on lip), 25½in. diam. (Skinner Inc.) $3,500 £2,229

A standing figure of Liu T'ungpin, wearing a robe chequered in blue, white and black, 23cm., K'ang Hsi, damaged. (Lawrence Fine Arts) $458 £286

A famille rose plate centrally painted with a lady in a chair breast feeding her child, Qianlong, 8¾in. diam. (Christie's S. Ken) $896 £550

A 19th century Chinese porcelain ginger jar and cover, all-over decorated with dragons, fishing boats, mountains, pagodas, flowers and leaves, 35cm. high. (Henry Spencer) $358 £220

Chinese Longquan celadon plate, Ming Dynasty, ribbed and floral incised decoration in centre, 13in. diam. (Skinner Inc.) $400 £255

A transitional mug, painted in underglaze blue with two children bringing gifts to a sage seated under a willow tree, 19cm. (Lawrence Fine Arts) $1,232 £770

172

CHINESE

Early 19th century Chinese Nankin porcelain decoration with Shi Shi dog and punt in a lake setting centre, 17 x 13in. (G. A. Key) $357 £210

Chinese export porcelain bowl, circa 1800, the exterior with scrolled reserves of Mandarin figures and birds, 11¼in. diam. (Skinner Inc.) $1,200 £750

An ormolu mounted Chinese crackle glazed celadon vase with twin lion mask and entwined drapery handles on spreading gadrooned base, 14in. wide. (Christie's London) $10,428 £6,600

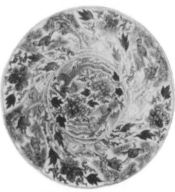

Chinese Doucai porcelain dish, late Ming Dynasty, raised on four bracket feet, central scene depicting a figure in an ox drawn cart, 7½in. wide. (Skinner Inc.) $1,000 £625

Chinese porcelain Clair de Lune vase, Qianlong, 18th century, glazed bottom, flaring neck, 8¾in. high. (Skinner Inc.) $400 £255

A Chinese moulded blue and white porcelain dish, the centre with phoenix and peony, leaf mark, Kangxi, 15¼in. diam. (Tennants) $592 £380

Chinese porcelain vase with Mandarin decoration, late 19th century, raised lizards to the collar, 25in. high. (Skinner Inc.) $700 £452

A pair of Chinese blue ground flattened hexagonal vases, gilt in the London studio of Thomas Baxter, circa 1802, about 28cm. high. (Christie's London) $1,063 £660

A triple gourd shape vase, decorated in underglaze blue, enamels and gold with flowering plants, 45cm., 18th century. (Lawrence Fine Arts) $1,496 £935

CHINESE

A Qianlong export mug, of cylindrical form, with entwined strap handle, decorated with scattered sprays of flowers, 14cm. high. (Henry Spencer) $424 £260

Chinese Famille Verte porcelain figure of Wenshu, 19th century, riding a lion, 15in. high. (Skinner Inc) $1400 £870

A blue and white baluster vase and matched cover, painted with a continuous scene of court figures, six character mark of Ch'êng-hau, K'ang-hsi, 15½in. high. (Lawrence Fine Arts) $1057 £682

A blue and white octagonal plate, painted in a vibrant blue with fruiting pomegranates, six character mark of Ch'êng-hau, K'ang-hsi, 10¼in. diam. (Lawrence Fine Arts) $255 £165

Chinese famille verte porcelain rouleau vase, 19th century, large rectangular reserves of a battle scene, 24in. high. (Skinner Inc.) $950 £594

A fine Ming Wucai square baluster jar painted on the body with scrolling underglaze-blue lotus below the eight Buddhist emblems, wood stand, fitted box, 18cm. high. (Christie'sLondon) $102960 £66000

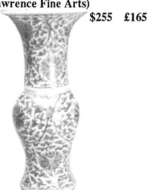

A blue and white Yen-Yen vase, painted overall with bold stylised peony blooms and foliage, blue double circle, K'ang-hsi, 17in. high. (Lawrence Fine Arts) $1534 £990

A pair of late 19th century famille verte baluster vases and covers, each painted with a horseman and attendants, 19½in. high. (Tennants) $1,326 £850

A blue and white ewer, of double gourd form, painted with a panel of a ferocious kylin, the reverse with a phoenix, late Ming, 9½in. high. (Lawrence Fine Arts) $2728 £1760

CLARICE CLIFF

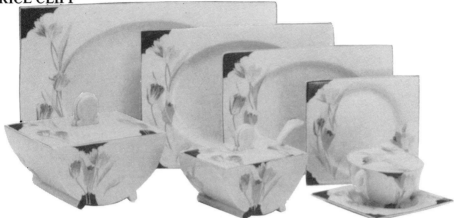

A unique Clarice Cliff pottery dinner service, each piece painted with tulips in bright enamel colours, comprising: two vegetable tureens, two sauce tureens, six graduated meat dishes, seven plates, 27cm., nine plates 23cm., twelve plates 18.5cm., and twelve two-handled covered bowls with stands. (Bearne's) $2978 £1850

A Clarice Cliff fantasque vase of globular form, painted with a balloon and orange-flash pattern, 14.8cm. high. (Bearne's) $449 £290

A Clarice Cliff Secrets pattern single handled 'Lotus' jug, painted in colours with two cottages on the slopes of a hill, 29.7cm. high. (Phillips London) $1,271 £780

CLARICE CLIFF

A Clarice Cliff tea set of Bonjour form painted with the 'Idyll' pattern within multi-coloured borders, teapot cover broken and re-stuck.
(Bearne's) $2557   £1650

A Clarice Cliff 'Age of Jazz' group, the two dimensional group modelled as a couple dancing the 'Tango', 18.7cm. high.
(Phillips) $2880   £1800

A graduated set of three Clarice Cliff pottery jugs, each painted with buildings on blue and orange hills, 18.4cm, 17cm and 16cm. high.
(Bearne's) $589   £380

A Clarice Cliff pottery vase of globular form, boldly painted with dots and geometric designs in orange, green and black on a yellow ground, 20.5cm. high.
(Bearne's) $1271   £820

A Clarice Cliff Sliced Circle pattern 'Lotus' jug, the vessel with twin handles and painted in bright colours, 29cm. high.
(Phillips London) $4,401 £2,700

A Clarice Cliff Biarritz plate, painted with the Idyll pattern, 23cm. diam.
(Bearne's) $708   £440

A Clarice Cliff Applique-Lucerne lotus jug, painted with an orange roofed chateau perched on the side of yellow and green hills, 29.5cm. high.
(Phillips London)$8,874 £5,800

CLARICE CLIFF

A Clarice Cliff jug of Lotus form
painted with the 'Melon' pattern
within orange, black and cream
bands, 29.5cm. high.
(Bearne's) $1550   £1000

A Clarice Cliff 'Idyll' shallow
circular powder bowl and cover,
incorporating the Tulip pattern,
15.5cm. diam.
(Bearne's) $338   £210

COALBROOKDALE

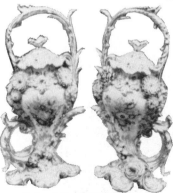

Pair of Coalbrookdale
porcelain covered potpourri,
mid-19th century, with
scrolled leaf handles, pierced
body and lid, 8in. high.
(Skinner Inc.) $1,500 £955

Coalbrookdale porcelain
handled ewer, mid 19th century, white ground with
applied flowers, leaves and
vines (minor flower and petal
damage), 8in. high. (Skinner
Inc.) $300 £191

Pair of Coalbrookdale
porcelain vases, mid-19th century, with handpainted floral
bouquet, accented in gilt,
(both handles showing breaks
and repair) 15½in. high.
(Skinner Inc.) $750 £478

COALPORT

A Coalport oval dish from the celebrated Animal service, painted with a proud lion, after Bewick, 28cm. (Phillips London) $489 £300

A Coalport jewelled ramshead vase and cover, the ovoid body with graduated turquoise beading, 19cm., 1909. (Phillips London) $570 £350

A Coalport miniature cabinet cup and saucer, painted by Edward Ball, signed, with scenes of San Stefano and Culloden Moor. (Phillips London) $391 £240

A Coalport miniature jewelled vase of shield shape, decorated with graduated turquoise and gilt jewelling, 9.5cm. (Phillips London) $138 £85

A pair of Coalport vases and covers in Sevres style, painted by William Cook, with ripe fruit and flowers, 37cm. (Phillips London) $1,548 £950

A Coalport teacup and saucer decorated in the studio of Thomas Baxter, circa 1805. (Christie's London) $425 £264

An important Coalport plate, the deep blue border reserved with the arms of the City of London, 1844, 26cm. (Phillips London) $1,304 £800

One of a pair of Coalport jewelled ewers with gilt scrolling handles, the ovoid bodies painted by Edward Ball, 24cm. (Phillips London)
Two $1,141 £700

A Coalport plate painted by J. N. Bradley, signed, with a golden pheasant, 24cm. (Phillips London) $244 £150

COALPORT

A Coalport bough pot and cover, after a Derby original, possibly by James Rouse, 18.5cm. (Phillips London) $521 £320

A rare Coalport table bell with gilt leaf finial, the flower panels framed in raised gold, 9cm. (Phillips London) $163 £100

Coalport style porcelain cream jug, early 19th century, blue ground, gilt leaf pattern with cartouches of flowers. (G. A. Key) $191 £120

An impressive Coalport two handled vase and cover, painted by John Plant, signed, with a view of Conway Castle, 36cm. (Phillips London) $1,385 £850

An impressive pair of Coalport vases and covers, decorated with alternating panels of flowers in a vase, 40cm. (Phillips London)$2,119 £1,300

A Coalport sponged pale blue ground urn shaped vase and cover, painted in the studio of Thomas Baxter, circa 1805, 27cm. high. (Christie's London) $797 £495

A Coalport plate, painted probably in London, with two Arabs standing by their donkeys, 21cm. (Phillips London) $106 £65

A Coalport flared flower pot and stand with gilt dolphin mask handles, decorated in the London studio of Thomas Baxter, circa 1805, 16.5cm. wide. (Christie's London) $974 £605

A Coalport pierced plate painted by Joshua Rushton, signed with a portrait of Lady Sarah Bunbury after Sir Joshua Reynolds, 23.5cm. (Phillips London) $805 £500

COPELAND

A Copeland Parian figure of a young girl entitled 'Young Englands Sister', after an original by G. Halse, 39.5cm. high.
(Bearne's) $177   £110

A Copeland bust of Juno, possibly after W Theed, in a coronet and with short ringlets, impressed mark, 20½in. high.
(Christie's S. Ken) $1735   £1078

Copeland, Parian porcelain bust 'The veiled bride', 14in. high.
(Riddetts) $2495   £1550

COPER

A stoneware Beaker by Hans Coper, bronze with white interior, impressed HC and LR seals, circa 1955, 4½in. high.
(Bonhams) $241   £150

An early stoneware shallow dish by Hans Coper, covered in a matt manganese glaze, the interior with carved abstract spiralling decoration through to a pitted translucent white glaze, circa 1950, 35.3cm. diam. (Christie's London)
$9,240 £5,500

A 'cup and disc' stoneware Form by Hans Coper, buff with dark brown disc, impressed HC seal, circa 1965. 4½in. high.
(Bonhams) $4186   £2600

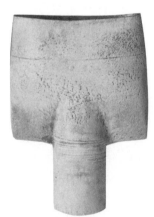

A Hans Coper stoneware vase of broad oviform on a tapering base, incised with panels of angled vertical lines, 29.1cm. high.
(Phillips) $4000   £2500

A stoneware Cup and Saucer by Hans Coper, white with brown edge to rim, circa 1956.
(Bonhams) $611   £380

A superb 'Spade' Form by Hans Coper, buff with textured surface and incised rings, circa 1965, 7¾in. high.
(Bonhams) $112670   £7000

CRESTED

Ornate German Grand Piano, 85mm. long. (Goss & Crested China Ltd) $28 £17

Carlton Drunkard By Lamp Post, 110mm. Fully coloured. (Goss & Crested China Ltd) $117 £70

Devonia Bagpipes, 118mm. long. (Goss & Crested China Ltd) $25 £15

Old Bill, Bruce Bairnsfather's cartoon character, 140mm. By Carlton. (Goss & Crested China Ltd) $209 £125

Cat With Bow, by Willow Art, 70mm. (Goss & Crested China Ltd) $30 £18

CRESTED

Fish tail field gun by Savoy, Southend on Sea crest (The Crested China Co.) $252 £150

Arcadian plum pudding bomb, Seaford crest (The Crested China Co.) $142 £85

Alpine gun by Grafton, Battersea crest. (The Crested China Co.) $924 £550

Jockey by Carlton, Great Yarmouth crest. (The Crested China Co.) $210 £125

Money box by Gemma, Bridlington crest. (The Crested China Co.) $40 £24

175 9.2 shell by Shelley, crest of Royal Artillery. (The Crested China Co.) $63 £38

Hastings Clock Tower, Sussex crest. (The Crested China Co.) $30 £18

Blackpool Tower by Shelley, Sussex crest. (The Crested China Co.) $26 £16

Withernsea lighthouse, Withernsea crest. (The Crested China Co.) $33 £20

Arcadian boy eating melon, Matlock Bath crest. (The Crested China Co.) $201 £120

Bathing belle, sitting with legs stretched out, by Carlton, 82mm., Deal crest. (The Crested China Co.) $235 £140

Cat on thistle by Willow, Penrith crest. (The Crested China Co.) $201 £120

CRESTED

A comical dog sitting playing the banjo, inscribed 'Some Band', by Carlton, Lewes crest. (The Crested China Co.) $92   £55

Water bottle by Aynsley, crest of 17th Lancers. (The Crested China Co.) $75   £45

Cat crouching, hind legs up, unmarked, Bournemouth crest. (The Crested China Co.) $70   £42

Bass by Savoy, Rochdale crest. (The Crested China Co.) $75   £45

Polar bear walking, neck stretched forward, by Savoy, See of Lichfield crest. (The Crested China Co.) $159 £95

Arcadian cat on yacht, Great Yarmouth Crest. (The Crested China Co.) $159 £95

Robinson & Leadbeater & Arcadian Kitchener, on square plinth. (The Crested China Co.) $142 £85

The Lincoln Imp by Grafton, 110mm., City of Lincoln crest. (The Crested China Co.) $36 £22

Hay war memorial by Wilton, Hay crest. (The China Crested Co.) $327 £195

Crich Stand war memorial, by Elite, no crest. (The Crested China Co.) $327 £195

A Shelley 235 motor coupe, Blackpool crest. (The Crested China Co.) $495 £295

Stylised goose, neck stretched upwards, by Willow, 145mm., Guildford crest. (The Crested China Co.) $92   £55

183

CRESTED

Baby Boy In Wash Bowl,
80mm. Long. By Arcadian.
(Goss & Crested China Ltd)
$100 £60

Box Gramophone, by Florentine, 55mm. (Goss & Crested
China Ltd) $30 £18

Girl On Beach Base, by Grafton
with some colouring, 75mm.
(Goss & Crested China Ltd)
$243 £145

Suffragette Handbell, 100mm.
(Goss & Crested China Ltd)
$92 £55

Willow Lancaster Castle
Gateway, 9mm. (Goss &
Crested China Ltd) $60 £36

Jovial Monk, by Carlton,
115mm. (Goss & Crested
China Ltd) $30 £18

Open Tourer EH139 by
Swan, 110mm. long.
(Goss & Crested China Ltd)
$75 £45

Shelley Bleriot Warplane,
150mm. long. (Goss &
Crested China Ltd) $25 £75

Sir Walter Scott's Chair, by
Willow, 80mm. (Goss &
Crested China Ltd) $15 £9

184

DE MORGAN

A William de Morgan red lustre charger, the white ground with ruby lustre decoration of startled antelope with band of elaborate geometric patterns to rim, 29.6cm. diam. (Christie's London) $647 £385

A William de Morgan Persian style pottery vase, early Fulham period, possibly painted by Halsey Ricardo, 25cm. high. (Phillips London) $6,520 £4,000

A William De Morgan ruby lustre wall plate, painted in the recessed centre with an eagle spreading its wings, 30.5cm. diam. (Phillips London) $1,102 £720

A William de Morgan two handled earthenware vase, decorated in the Isnik style in blue, turquoise and shades of green, 21.3cm. high. (Christie's London) $2,510 £1,540

A William de Morgan two handled baluster vase, decorated in green and purple with fruiting vines, the foot, handles and neck interior in turquoise, 27.3cm. high. (Christie's London) $2,218 £1,320

A William de Morgan ruby lustre vase, with cup neck and twin handles painted with a pelican and a crane against a background of scales, 19cm. high. (Phillips) $1920 £1200

A good William de Morgan 'Persian-style' circular wall plate, painted by Charles Passenger, depicting in the sunken centre, a pair of dolphins, encircled with stylised floral and scale borders, 43.5cm. diam. (Phillips) $8320 £5200

A William de Morgan Persian style pottery vase, Fulham period, painted by Jo Juster, 28.5cm. high. (Phillips London) $2,201 £1,350

A William de Morgan red lustre charger, the white ground decorated in shades of red with stylised birds and beasts amid floral patterns, 36.3cm. diam. (Christie's London) $4,066 £2,420

DE MORGAN

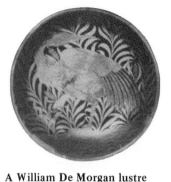

One of a pair of William de Morgan 'Persian-style' pottery bowls painted by Charles Passenger, signed 'W. de Morgan & Co', 17cm. diam. (Phillips) $660   £400

Two of a set of six William de Morgan 'Persian-style' pottery bowls painted either by Joe Juster or John Hersey, 11.5cm. diam. (Phillips) $1188   £720

A William De Morgan lustre dish painted by Charles Passenger, with a crane with blue silver, mauve and pale ruby amid silver and ruby lustre bulrushes, 28cm. diam. (Phillips London) $4,896 £3,200

A William de Morgan ruby lustre circular dish, painted with a pair of griffin-like creatures prowling in alternate directions, 36cm. diam. (Phillips) $4125   £2500

A William de Morgan vase, painted with white birds in flight against a deep blue ground, 19.5cm. high. (Phillips) $2880   £1800

A William de Morgan ruby lustre circular dish, painted by Fred Passenger with two birds of prey with their wings overlapping, 37cm. diam. (Phillips) $2805   £1700

A William de Morgan ruby lustre twin-handled oviform vase, painted with scaley carp swimming in alternative directions, 37cm. high. (Phillips) $3465   £2100

A William de Morgan circular plate, painted with a central griffin-like creature and bordered by a frieze of birds, 22cm. diam. (Phillips) $1248   £780

A William de Morgan 'Persian-style' vase and cover, painted with foliate fronds in turquoise, blue and pale-green against a white ground, 36cm. high. (Phillips) $7360   £4600

DELLA ROBBIA

A Della Robbia vase and cover, with incised decoration of yellow tulips against a blue sky, 19.5cm. high.
(Christie's) $717 £440

A Della Robbia bottle vase, designed by Charles Collis, with piped slip decoration of peaches and leaves covered in pink and turquoise glazes, 33.5cm. high.
(Christie's) $538 £330

A Della Robbia vase, decorated by Liza Wilkins, the incised decoration of horses' heads within cartouches, 35.6cm. high.
(Christie's) $538 £330

A Della Robbia two-handled vase, with incised and slip decoration of foliate designs within large cartouches and borders, 35.2cm. high.
(Christie's) $430 £264

A Della Robbia two-handled vase, of bulbous cylindrical form with knopped neck, with incised Della Robbia mark and decorator's signature Enid, 34.8cm. high.
(Christie's) $1165 £715

A Della Robbia two-handled vase, decorated by Annie Smith, of bulbous cylindrical form with knopped neck, dated 1895, 37.6cm. high.
(Christie's) $359 £220

A Della Robbia vase, with incised and slip decoration of two friezes of equestrian and Ancient Greek figures, 18.4cm. high.
(Christie's) $269 £165

A Della Robbia dish, with incised and slip decoration of a sea sprite riding a fish, covered with polychrome glaze, dated 1895, 26.2cm. diam.
(Christie's) $610 £374

A large Della Robbia two-handled bottle-vase and cover, decoration by Ruth Bare, date 1924, 53cm. high.
(Christie's) $628 £385

DELFT

A fine English delft political plate, the centre painted in blue with an allegory of Justice triumphing over Evil, 22.5cm., marked B in blue. (Phillips London) $2,550 £1,500

A Dutch Delft spittoon, the compressed globular body with spreading neck painted in blue, 18th century, 5in. diam. (Christie's S. Ken) $169 £110

A London delft dated blue and white two handled globular jar painted with winged putti and birds among shrubs, circa 1700, 19cm. wide. (Christie's London)
$1,417 £880

A Dutch Delft drug jar of shaped cylindrical form, painted in blue with a scrolling cartouche, inscribed Rob Samb, 18th century, 7¼in. high. (Christie's S. Ken) $271 £176

A pair of rare Dutch polychrome delft vases and covers, painted in blue with stags and does within yellow bordered panels, 32.5cm. (Phillips London) $3,230 £1,900

Dutch delft tile picture of a cat, late 18th century, mounted in a wood frame, 12½ x 17½in. (Skinner Inc.)
$2,200 £1,419

An English delft polychrome dish painted with a bird flanked by shrubs within a leaf garland border, circa 1750's, 7¾in. diam. (Christie's S. Ken) $406 £264

A large Dutch delft tobacco jar and tiered brass cover, the ovoid body painted in a rich blue with the name *Toskaanse* 30.5cm. (Phillips London)
$544 £320

A Lambeth delft polychrome plate painted with a cockerel, vase and flowering branches, circa 1740, 9in. diam. (Tennants) $312 £200

DELFT

A Liverpool delft rectangular flower brick painted in a Fazackerly palette with flowering shrubs and blue foliage, circa 1765, 13cm. long. (Christie's London) $3,365 £2,090

A London delft bowl painted in blue with a pine tree and fence, a manganese and green balloon floating above, 27cm. (Phillips London) $261 £160

An English delft blue and white deep bowl painted with flowers and grasses, Bristol or London, circa 1725, 35cm. diam. (Christie's London) $2,479 £1,540

An English delft blue dash tulip charger, the centre painted with a blue and yellow tulip and two buds, probably London, circa 1680, 35cm. diam. (Christie's London) $1,151 £715

A Dutch delft figure of a putto emblematic of Summer painted in blue, yellow and iron red, circa 1750, 40cm. high. (Christie's London) $1,345 £825

A large English delft blue dash Adam and Eve charger of flanged form, circa 1700, 35.9cm. diam. (Tennants) $1,092 £700

A delft blue and white oval Royal portrait plaque of Queen Anne, blue E mark to the reverse, probably London, circa 1705, 23cm. high. (Christie's London) $17,710 £11,000

A very impressive and dated English delft wassail bowl and two covers, the latter surmounted by a spice cup, 36cm. diam., overall height 53cm. (Phillips London) $40,800 £24,000

A London delft blue and white octagonal plate, the centre painted with an Oriental figure among rocks, circa 1685, 19cm. diam. (Christie's London) $496 £308

DELFT

A Liverpool delft plate, boldly painted in the Fazackerly palette with a spray of flowers by a fence, mid 18th century, 33.5cm. diam.
(Bearne's) $466   £290

A Dutch delft blue and white chamber-pot, the exterior painted with foliate lappets between medallions with flowers, animals and cockerels above monkeys and horses among rockwork, circa 1720, 33cm. wide.
(Christie's London) $1416   £880

A polychrome Liverpool delft plate attractively painted with a floral spray, circa 1770, 9in. diam. (Tennants)
    $249 £160

An English delft oviform dry drug jar, named in manganese for *Ther: Androm,* within a rectangular cartouche, 20cm.
(Phillips London) $644 £400

Pair of delft faience vases, painter's mark *MG,* 45cm. high. (Auktionshaus Arnold)
       $552 £358

Six of a set of forty-two Dutch delft tiles, painted in blue with a formal vase of flowers.
(Phillips London)
   Forty-two $886 £550

A London delft plate painted with a chrysanthemum and other flowers and the border with three flower sprays, circa 1750, 9in. diam.
(Christie's S. Ken) $255   £165

A Dutch delft candlestick, painted in dark blue with bands of flowers and stylised leaf scrolls, 16cm. (Phillips London) $741 £460

An English delft blue and white plate, the centre painted with a bird running among trees, probably London, circa 1770, 22.5cm. diam. (Christie's London) $354 £220

DELFT

A German Delft dish of silver shape, the centre painted with an animal running to the left within a border of tulips, early 18th century, 13½ in. diam. (Christie's S. Ken) $511 £330

A Dutch delft model of a cow, the animal painted in colours with garlands of flowers, yellow horns and blue features, circa 1750, 22cm. wide. (Christien's London) $1,278 £825

A very rare and interesting London delft pierced basket, attributed to Vauxhall, of circular shape supported on three bun feet, 26cm. (Phillips London) $7,406 £4,600

A Liverpool delft polychrome dish sketchily painted with a swan on a lake flanked by a willow tree, circa 1760, 33cm. diam. (Christie's London) $1,505 £935

A Dutch delft figure of Harlequin standing holding a blue hat, wearing a suit enriched with blue, yellow green and iron-red lozenges and dots, circa 1720, 23cm. high. (Christie's London) $4427 £2750

A Brislington royal portrait charger with a full face, half length portrait of James II, 33.5cm. (Phillips London) $5,780 £3,400

A Bristol delft polychrome plate painted with a bird in flight, flanked by manganese and iron red trees, circa 1740, 22.5cm. diam. (Christie's London) $1,063 £660

A rare London delft white flower vase, raised on a spreading circular foot, the wavy rim encircled by three cylindrical flower nozzles, 16.5cm., mid-17th century. (Phillips London) $4,991 £3,100

An early English Delft dish, probably Bristol, boldly painted with a tulip, four leaves on either side, late 17th century, cracked, 33cm. diam. (Bearne's) $775 £500

DERBY

A Derby plate, painted by Harry Hancock, signed, with a profusion of summer flowers in a basket, 22cm. (Phillips London) $652 £400

Pair of Derby porcelain wine coolers decorated in the Imari manner with heavy gilt handles and gilt designs, 19th century, 8in. (G. A. Key) $342 £210

A Derby group of a youth and girl, symbolic of Autumn, he carrying a bottle, she carrying a bunch of grapes, 20cm. (Lawrence Fine Arts) $4,048 £2,530

A Derby biscuit group of the two Graces adorning Pan with garlands of flowers, 31.5cm. (Phillips London) $1,191 £740

A pair of Derby Mansion House dwarfs, wearing brightly coloured striped and flowered clothes, Robt. Bloor & Co., circa 1830, 17.5 and 17cm. high. (Christie's London)$3,188 £1,980

A Derby group of dancers in 18th century costume, she in floral dress and he in turquoise coat, crossed swords mark, 6½in. high. (Christie's S. Ken) $1,346 £880

A Derby figure of a young lady in elaborate brightly painted 18th century costume, crossed swords marks, circa 1825, 10in. high. (Christie's S. Ken) $220 £143

A pair of Royal Crown Derby candlesticks, each baluster stem and candle sconce set on a shaped rectangular base moulded with dolphins, 1979, 26.5cm. high. (Bearne's) $644 £400

A Derby porcelain group 'The Dancers' after a Meissen original, late 18th century, slight restoration, 16.8cm. high (Bearne's) $1240 £800

DERBY

A Derby model of a stag at lodge in front of flower enclusted bocage, the white body dappled in brown, 17cm. (Phillips London) $1,288 £800

A Derby tea pot of quatrefoil outline, painted and gilt with birds and flowering plants in Chinese style, c. 1756, 17cm. high. (Lawrence Fine Arts) $358 £231

A Stevenson Hancock Derby figure of a Greenwich pensioner, the seated man in blue coat and yellow breeches, 5in. high. (Christie's S. Ken) $252 £165

A rare Derby chocolate pot and cover, painted in a deep blue with the Walk in the Garden pattern after Worcester, 23.5cm. (Phillips London) $3,220 £2,000

A pair of Derby candelabra figures of a shepherd seated playing the bagpipes, and a shepherdess playing the mandoline, 23cm. (Phillips London) $2,210 £1,300

A Derby crested tapering oviform mask jug with loop handle, Wm. Duesbury & Co., circa 1780, 23.5cm. high. (Christie's London) $1,151 £715

A Derby bocage group in the form of a seated young woman with a sheaf of corn and a sickle, late 18th century, 12.5cm. high. (Bearne's) $579 £360

A Derby botanical plate painted with a spirally moulded border gilt with foliage, Wm. Duesbury & Co., circa 1790, 21.5cm. diam. (Christie's London) $850 £528

A Derby porcelain figure representing justice, her eyes closed, a sword in one hand and scales in the other, late 18th century, 32.2cm. high. (Bearne's) $611 £380

DOULTON

A Royal Doulton plate, painted all over, by Joseph Birbeck Snr., with a covey of red grouse, 1907. (Phillips London) $358 £220

A Royal Doulton teapot with two figures of negro boys standing at the wicket, with comic captions: *Good for Fifty* and *I wasn't Out*, 4in. high. (Christie's S. Ken) $839 £528

A Doulton cabinet plate painted by Leslie Johnson, signed, with a naked maiden seated beside a woodland pool, 22.5cm., date code for 1901. (Phillips London) $749 £460

A Royal Doulton stoneware jar and cover, decorated by Eliza Simmance with pate-sur-pate geranium-like flowers on a textured ground, 29.5cm. high. (Bearne's) $713   £460

A large Royal Doulton two-handled loving cup produced to commemorate the Coronation of King George VI and Queen Elizabeth, 26.2cm. high. (Bearne's) $387   £250

One of a pair of Doulton stoneware silver mounted jugs, each of inverted baluster form, 1901, 8½in. high. (Tennants)   Two $296 £190

A Doulton stoneware baluster vase decorated by Mark Marshall, with an Art Nouveau design, 35.7cm. high. (Bearne's) $217   £140

Large Royal Doulton Slater patent vases, brown glazed with stylistic floral designs, 16in. high. (G. A. Key) $477 £300

Doulton Lambeth earthenware vase by Hannah Barlow, circa 1881/1910, the middle section incised with cattle, 12in. approx. (G. A. Key) $310   £190

DOULTON

A Royal Doulton figure entitled 'Maureen', H.N. 1770, withdrawn 1959.
(Bearne's) $289   £180

Large Royal Doulton pottery jardiniere by Hannah B. Barlow, with a middle band of Shetland ponies and cattle, approx. 12in. (G. A. Key) $652 £400

A Royal Doulton Holbein ware pottery vase, decorated by W. Nunn, in colours with two men seated drinking at a table, printed mark in green, 24cm. high. (Henry Spencer)
$321 £210

A Doulton stoneware jug, decorated by Hannah Barlow with cattle in an open landscape, impressed and incised marks, dated 1881, 24.4cm. high.
(Bearne's) $772   £480

Pair of Doulton Lambeth Slater patent pottery vases, with stylistic floral detail and jewel work, approx. 12in. (G. A. Key)
$248 £160

A Royal Doulton stoneware two-handled vase by Emily J. Partington, painted with foliage on a textured ground, 24.5cm. high.
(Bearne's) $131   £85

A Royal Doulton porcelain figure entitled 'Carpet Vendor', H.N. 76.
(Bearne's) $1240   £800

Royal Doulton stone glazed tankard, with raised hunting pattern and hallmarked silver rim, approx. 6in. (G. A. Key)
$78 £50

A Royal Doulton porcelain figure, entitled 'Suzette', H.N. 1696, withdrawn 1949
(Bearne's) $217   £135

DRESDEN

A Dresden group, Augustus III mounted on a rearing horse and wearing elaborate armour, 43cm. high. (Lawrence Fine Arts) $1,286 £814

A pair of Dresden five light candelabra, the stems modelled as three scantily draped putti holding floral garlands, blue crossed swords and star marks, late 19th century, 51cm. high. (Christie's London) $531 £330

A Dresden group of a huntsman in 18th century costume restraining two leaping hounds, 15in. high. (Christie's S. Ken) $968 £605

A Dresden large group, the central figure of a musician playing the flute and standing on high rockwork, incised numeral marks, circa 1880, 42cm. high. (Christie's London) $1,239 £770

A pair of late 19th century Dresden porcelain cabinet plates, decorated with 'The Virgin and Child' and 'The Assumption of Our Blessed Lady', after Murillo, 26.5cm. diam. (Spencer's) $1224 £720

Early 20th century Dresden porcelain vase and cover, white ground decorated with romantic figures and sprigs of flowers, 14in. high. (G. A. Key) $334 £210

A massive pair of Dresden yellow ground oviform vases and covers, reserved and painted with exotic birds, blue AR marks, circa 1900, 64cm. high. (Christie's London) $5,313 £3,300

A Dresden seated figure of Cupid pressing hearts in a press, on marbled circular base with gilt borders, 18.5cm. (Lawrence Fine Arts) $834 £528

A pair of Dresden China table lamps, 19th century in the form of rose encrusted urns supported by three putti. (Lots Road Galleries) $1191 £740

EUROPEAN

A Zurich figure of a sports-woman, a duck in her left hand, a rifle in her right, with a spaniel at her side, circa 1770, 20.5cm. high. (Christie's Geneva) $1,760 £1,073

Faience cow, Continental, 19th century, reclining figure on shaped marbleised base (repaired), 4¾in. high, 8in. long. (Skinner Inc.) $900 £552

A Robj porcelain jug, model-led as a rotund lady wearing a plum coloured dress, the spout modelled as an apron, 19.5cm. high. (Phillips London) $391 £240

One of an attractive pair of Austrian ewers, both painted on each side with panels of maidens in garden landscapes, 34.5cm. (Phillips London)
Two $2,576 £1,600

An amusing Goebels ceramic decanter set comprising: a decanter modelled as a young man and a set of six liqueur goblets each painted in colours with the head of a girl. (Phillips London) $619 £380

A Catalan coloured albarello painted in the workshop of Francisco Niculoso in the Deruta style, 17th century, 31cm. high. (Christie's London) $3,410 £2,200

A Continental figure of a crinoline lady in yellow dress and black lace shawl, painted mark L. Leyritz, 12¼in. high. (Christie's S. Ken) $85 £55

An Essevi ceramic wall mask, modelled as Columbine with a monkey perched on her wrist, 27cm. high. (Phillips London) $1,793 £1,100

A Galle style pottery cat, seated with free-standing forelegs, wearing a pale blue coat scattered with gilt flowers, 34.5cm. high. (Henry Spencer) $704 £460

EUROPEAN

A Holics tureen and cover, the ogee moulded and ribbed body and cover painted in manganese and blue with sprays of indianische Blumen, circa 1750, 31cm. wide. (Christie's Geneva) $1,970 £1,201

A Zurich figure of a young girl feeding chickens, her long skirt with alternating bands of cornflowers and berried foliage, circa 1775, 11.5cm. high. (Christie's London) $1,449 £935

A Continental majolica vase modelled as a playful poodle, lying on its back holding a brown simulated wooden bowl in its paws, second half of the 19th century, 34cm. wide. (Christie's London) $1,682 £1,045

A large Zsolnay lustre vase covered with a violet/plum lustre glaze with random spots of gold/green/amber hues, 45.5cm. high. (Phillips London) $1,040 £680

A Holics istoriato plate painted in colours in the Sienna style with Neptune standing in a shell chariot, HF and star mark, circa 1750, 25cm. diam. (Christie's London) $3,945 £2,420

A Wiener Kunstkeramische two handled vase of irregular form painted in pastel shades with a loosely defined fairytale scene, 19½in. high. (Christie's S. Ken) $281 £165

A Continental creamware figure of a cat on a rectangular green base, its fur sponged in black and yellow, 5½in. high. (Christie's S. Ken) $246 £154

An Ernst Wahliss Serapis Fayence earthenware figure, the semi nude young woman arching backwards, printed marks and applied paper label, circa 1911, 32cm. (Bonhams) $3,818 £2,300

A Zurich oval dish with pierced border, painted in colours with a parrot perching on a branch, incised Z, blue Z and two dots, circa 1770, 12.3cm. wide. (Christie's Geneva) $4,221 £2,574

EUROPEAN

A Vienna du Paquier large circular Jagd service dish finely painted in schwarzlot, with a putto seated on a stone bench feeding a buck, circa 1740, 37cm. diam. (Christie's Geneva) $19,700 £12,012

A Zurich ornithological teapot and a cover of bullet shape, painted in colours, one side with an owl and a woodpecker, the other with an eagle and a snipe, circa 1770, 17cm. wide. (Christie's Geneva) $3,096 £1,888

Teplitz pottery vase, Czechoslovakia, early 20th century, swollen form widening towards base, signed *Stillmacher Teplitz* and stamped, 8¼in. high. (Robt. W. Skinner Inc.) $400 £245

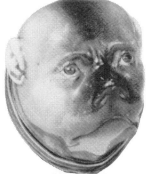

A Copenhagen snuff box and cover modelled as a pug's head, circa 1780, contemporary silver reeded mount, marked for Hamburg, 6cm. wide. (Christie's Geneva) $5,066 £3,089

A Robj spirit flask and stopper in the form of a Breton girl wearing national dress, 25.7cm. high. (Phillips London) $408 £250

An unusual Continental porcelain wall plate, the image based on a design by Alphonse Mucha for Sarah Bernhardt as La Samaritaine, 50cm. diam. (Phillips London) $796 £520

A fine Copenhagen botanical campana vase brilliantly painted with a broad register of specimen flowers, roses, dahlias, asters and lilies, blue wave mark, circa 1810, 43.5cm. high. (Christie's Geneva) $45,731 £27,885

A Metzler and Orltoff porcelain head and torso of a girl wearing a pale yellow scarf over her brown hair, 23.8cm. high. (Phillips London) $163 £100

A Copenhagen pale pink ground two handled oviform vase, painted with a view of a Royal residence, blue waved line mark, late 19th century, 26.5cm. high. (Christie's London) $850 £528

CHINA

EUROPEAN

A Royal Copenhagen porcelain vase of compressed shape, decorated with a slightly abstract frieze of lilies and foliage, 11.5cm. diam. (Phillips) **$256 £160**

Large Mettlach Stein, circa 1906, etched design depicting a man and woman beside a cask, signed *H. Schlitt*, 15½in. high. (Robt. W. Skinner Inc.) **$800 £488**

Italian Majolica Pottery Charger, 18th/19th century, bowled centre decorated with bakery scene, 19½in. diam. (Skinner Inc) **$5000 £3246**

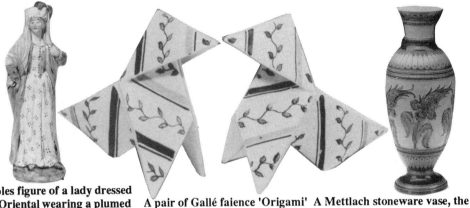

A Naples figure of a lady dressed as an Oriental wearing a plumed hat, yellow shawl and pink coat over a long dress with blue spots, circa 1790, 16cm. high. (Christie's London) **$12397 £7700**

A pair of Gallé faience 'Origami' models each as an abstract folded creature painted with yellow and blue bands, 8cm. high. (Phillips) **$576 £360**

A Mettlach stoneware vase, the ovoid body decorated with an encircling pattern of stylized flowers, 41.7cm. high. (Bearne's) **$248 £150**

A Mettlach salt glazed stoneware jardiniere, the continuous central band incised and decorated in colours with gnomes cavorting amongst blossoming branches, 23cm. diam. (Spencer's) **$644 £400**

A large pair of Turn porcelain figures of young women, each wearing a long dress, gathered at the waist, slight chipping, 62cm. high. (Bearne's) **$2,012 £1,350**

An Austrian porcelain circular plaque, painted with a woman and child reluctantly leaving house and family, 28.7cm. diam. (Bearne's) **$644 £400**

EUROPEAN

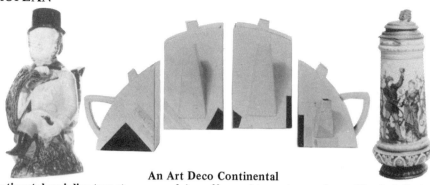

A Continental majolica teapot and cover in the form of a three legged man seated astride a tree stump, circa 1880, 10in. high. (Christie's S. Ken) $682   £440

An Art Deco Continental porcelain coffee and tea set comprising: two main pots and a sugar bowl and milk jug en suite. (Phillips London)
$408 £250

Large Mettlach Stein, circa 1898, etched decoration depicting lovers, signed *Warth*, pewter lid, 14½in. high. (Robt. W. Skinner Inc.) $750 £457

A Zsolnay lustre figural ewer possibly designed by Lajos Mack moulded around its circumference with three sinuous Art Nouveau maidens, 35cm. high.
(Phillips) $576   £360

A pair of Majolica blackamoor figures of a man and woman, each standing by a tree stump, damaged, 70cm. high.
(Bearne's) $1288   £800

A Dutch 'Distel' pottery vase and cover, decorated with slip-trailed tulips in colours, 33cm. high.
(Phillips) $736   £460

KPM Porcelain Plaque of a Young Woman, Berlin, late 19th century, hair bound at the top of her head, sceptre marks, 7³/₄in. high.
(Skinner Inc) $2800   £1818

Continental Porcelain Figure of a Bolognese Hunde, late 19th century, moulded in a shaggy manner, unmarked, 8³/₄in. high. (Skinner Inc) $700   £460

A Robj earthenware bowl and cover, formed as a Red Indian's head, with dark red glazed feather headdress, 20cm. high. (Christie's) $717   £440

FAMILLE ROSE

A Mandarin vase with trumpet neck, of large size, decorated in famille rose enamels with numerous groups of figures, 19th century, 64cm. (Lawrence Fine Arts) $1,320 £825

A pair of famille rose bough pots, of waisted octagonal form, decorated with groups of figures in panels, 19th century, 23cm. high.(Lawrence Fine Arts) $3,520 £2,200

A baluster vase and cover, decorated in famille rose enamels with flowers, 31cm., Ch'ien Lung. (Lawrence Fine Arts) $1,008 £638

FOLEY

A Foley Intarsio single handled jug, painted and enamelled in colours with two heralds blowing trumpets, printed factory mark, 11in. high. (Christie's S. Ken) $656 £385

A Foley Pastello twin handled vase of double gourd form printed and painted with rustic scene of house nestling in wooded landscape, 7in. high. (Christie's S. Ken) $750 £440

A Foley pastello solifleur, decorated with a cottage in a landscape in shades of blue, purple and yellow, 5in. high. (Christie's S. Ken) $205 £132

FRANKENTHAL

A Frankenthal figure of a Chinaman modelled by K. G. Lueck, seated on a fence wearing a broad brimmed hat, date code 77, 11.5cm. high. (Christie's London) $1,108 £715

A pair of Frankenthal figures of Oceanus and Thetis modelled by Konrad Link, the sea god standing extending his arm towards his companion, circa 1765, 28.5cm. and 24cm. high. (Christie's London) $93,775 £60,500

A Frankenthal figure of a sportswoman holding a gun, standing on a flat rococo scroll base enriched with gilding, 1776, 12.5cm. high. (Christie's London) $988 £638

FRENCH

A Robj porcelain decanter and stopper, the pear shaped decanter modelled as a Scotsman playing bagpipes, printed *Robj, Paris, Made in France*, 27cm. high. (Bonhams)
$199 £120

Rare Galle ceramic inkwell, figural depiction of an Oriental man and woman holding a flower decorated fabric between them, 17½in. long. (Robt. W. Skinner Inc.)
$2,000 £1,242

A St Clement faience figure of a beggar holding his hat before him, his cane in the crook of his arm, circa 1775, 17cm. high. (Christie's Geneva)
$1,970 £1,201

A French istoriato tazza painted with Diana and Acteon, the alarmed Diana and her attendants covering her with drapes, probably Nevers, last quarter of the 16th century, 28cm. diam. (Christie's London) $2,387 £1,540

A French faience figure of an Oriental lady standing in a classical pose, her long plaited hair tied by a blue top knot, circa 1730, possibly Nevers, 37cm. high. (Christie's London)
$6,813 £4,180

A Rouen a la corne shaped circular plate painted in high fired colours, red OD mark, circa 1750, 25cm. diam. (Christie's London)
$896 £550

A pair of French coloured biscuit figures of a gallant and companion, he holding a feathered hat, perhaps Gille Jeune, circa 1865, about 62cm. high. (Christie's London)
$1,593 £990

Six Chantilly Kakiemon pistol shaped knife handles, painted with a boy (four cracked), circa 1740, mounted with contemporary silver blades, impressed swan marks, the handles 8.5cm. long. (Christie's London) $1,875 £1,210

A pair of Samson figures of Autumn and Winter, on rococo bases highlighted in gilt, 14in. high. (Christie's S. Ken)
$574 £352

FRENCH

A St Clement bough pot, the bombe sides painted en camaieu with birds in landscape vignettes, circa 1785, 25.5cm. wide. (Christie's London) $1,255 £770

A Dagoty Paris ewer and basin, the ewer with matt blue ground, decorated in white relief with acanthus leaf borders and swan neck griffins, 31cm. high. (Phillips London) $4,629 £2,875

A St Cloud snuff box and cover modelled in the shape of a crouching cat, silver mounts with a decharge mark, circa 1735, 5.5cm. long. (Christie's London) $1,614 £990

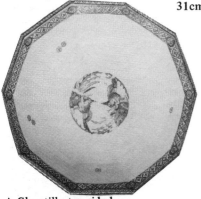

A Chantilly ten sided Kakiemon bowl, the interior with a roundel composed of two ho-ho birds, circa 1735, later French gilt metal mounts by A. Risler & Carre, Paris, 26cm. diam. (Christie's London) $2,216 £1,430

A French faience holy water stoup, painted in colours with St Louis kneeling before an altar in a landscape vignette, third quarter of the 18th century, probably Marseille 44cm. high. (Christie s London) $1,345 £825

A Nevers (Conrade) armorial blue and white tondino, the centre painted with a huntsman blowing a horn accompanied by his hound, circa 1680, 30cm. diam. (Christie's London) $1,620 £1,045

A Samson gilt metal mounted pot pourri vase and cover, painted with peasant figures in rural landscape vignettes, on a shaped square gilt metal base, late 19th century, 58cm. high. (Christie's London) $3,896 £2,420

A Paris porcelain plaque of Madame La Marquise de Rambouillet, painted by Dihl, the half length figure seated before a damask curtain, circa 1816, 20.5 x 15.5cm. (Christie's London) $3,069 £1,980

A French faience jug of fluted helmet shape on spreading foot painted in blue, (spout riveted) 8½in. high. (Christie's S. Ken) $152 £99

FRENCH

A French white soft paste model of an elephant, freestanding with long tusks and a curling trunk (one ear chipped, firing cracks to underside), circa 1750, probably Mennecy, 20cm. long. (Christie's London) $9,377 £6,050

A Vincennes sucrier and cover with flower finial (sucrier Bouret) painted in colours with scattered sprays of flowers, painter's mark *H* for Houry, 8.5cm. high. (Christie's London) $767 £495

A French coloured biscuit figure of a scantily draped young lady recumbent on a couch, 13in. wide (Christie's S. Ken) $151 £99

A blue and white charger, the centre with a roundel painted with Jacob meeting Rachel at the well, circa 1700, probably St Jean du Desert, 51cm. diam. (Christie's London) $6,820 £4,400

A French soft paste figure allegorical of Sight, the scantily clad youth seated on a rockwork base, circa 1750, possibly Orleans or Crepy en Valois, 15cm. high. (Christie's London) $717 £440

A Paris plate painted by Madame La Marechale de Lobau in sepia with an allegory of the artist supported by her muse, Cupid in attendance, circa 1810, 21cm. diam. (Christie's London) $1,023 £660

Clement Massier enamel decorated vase, Golfe-Juan, France, late 19th century, impressed and painted marks, 7¼in. (Skinner Inc.) $800 £494

Pair of faience pottery lions, France, 18th century, fanciful Oriental style, seated with open mouths, 11in. high. (Skinner Inc.) $1,600 £1,019

A French coloured bisque figure of a lady standing on a circular grassy base wearing 17th century costume, 16½in. high. (Christie's S. Ken) $387 £242

FRENCH

French Pottery Group of a Young Man and Woman, 19th century, both holding a moulded floral decorated trunk with a hat and umbrella placed on the cover, 12¼in. wide. (Skinner Inc) $200 £131

A Strasbourg bullet shape teapot and cover with crabstock spout and handle, Paul Hannong period, 1748-1754, 17cm. wide. (Christie's London) $3,227 £1,980

A Le Croisic fluted dish painted with a portrait bust of a Neo Classical figure, relief epsilon mark, circa 1730, 31.5cm. diam. (Christie's London) $574 £352

A Chantilly green ground two handled pot pourri, the waisted campana body applied with swags of flowers, circa 1750, 19cm. high. (Christie's London) $8,965 £5,500

Pair of Paris Porcelain Vases, late 19th century, pierced scrolled handles centred around a floral filled cartouche, 16¾in. high. (Skinner Inc) $700 £454

An Eastern French faience two handled ecuelle, cover and stand painted with sprays of fleurs chatironees with green branch handles, circa 1765, the stand 23cm. diam. (Christie's London) $1,193 £770

A Galle faience Origami model as an abstract folded creature painted with stylised cornflower sprays, 8cm. high. (Phillips London) $163 £100

Paris Porcelain Figural Desk Set, France, late 19th century, the cover modelled as three young girls, the oval base with mounted inkwell and sander, 8in. high. (Skinner Inc) $300 £197

A pair of French biscuit porcelain figures in the form of a man and woman, late 19th century, 42.5cm. high. (Bearne's) $547 £340

GERMAN

19th century porcelain comport by Potschappel, circa 1872, with a rococo stem supported by two young Cupids, approx. 18in. (G. A. Key)
$465 £300

A Bayreuth faience Hausmalerei famille rose baluster teapot and cover, painted in the manner of Adam Friedrich von Loewenfinck, in the delft dore style with indianische Blumen issuing from rocks, circa 1740, 18.5cm. wide. (Christie's London) $11,082 £7,150

A Carl Thieme Potschappel porcelain table centrepiece, the shaped base with an 18th century lady with two suitors, 55cm. high. (Henry Spencer)
$1,346 £880

A German faience dish, painted with a standing shepherd holding a lamb, 19th century, 12in. diam.
(Christie's S. Ken) $477   £308

A German porcelain rectangular plaque depicting Gretel and her companion reading a letter, late 19th century, 19.5cm x 14cm. (Bearne's) $387   £250

A Merkelbach stoneware bowl and cover, designed by Paul Wynand, of globular form on three feet, decorated with an all over design of scale like stippling, 28cm. high. (Phillips London) $261 £160

A Wurzburg Commedia dell' Arte figure of Bagolin, possibly modelled by Ferdinand Tietz, broken through at knees and repaired, circa 1770, 13cm. high. (Christie's London)
$3,751 £2,420

A pair of Thuringen oviform vases and covers, factory painted, blue mark on base with crown, 51cm. high. (Auktionshaus Arnold)
$662 £430

A Limbach bird nesting group, modelled as a boy climbing a tree and handing birds from a nest to his companion below, circa 1780, 20cm. high. (Christie's London)
$2,152 £1,320

GERMAN

A Boettger red Steinzeug hexagonal tea caddy and cover moulded with alternating panels of birds in trees issuing from terraces, circa 1715, 12.5cm. high. (Christie's Geneva) $42,214 £25,740

A Nymphenburg sucrier, cover and stand painted with a broad band of white and pink roses, on a black ground within gilt rims, circa 1770, the stand 14.5cm. diam. (Christie's London) $307 £198

A Furstenberg figure of Andromeda after a model by Desoches, seated on a rock to which she is chained by her wrist and ankle, circa 1774, 28.5cm. high. (Christie's London) $2,046 £1,320

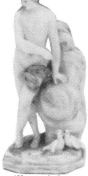

A German porcelain pierced tazza, with a military equestrian figure attended by a Moor, impressed numeral, 16¼in. high. (Christie's S. Ken) $616 £385

A pair of German porcelain figures of a youth and companion, wearing floral rustic costume, 17½in. high. (Christie's S. Ken) $549 £352

A Niderviller miniature group of Venus scantily clad in a puce cloth leaning against billowing cloud scrolls, circa 1780, 8.5cm. high. (Christie's Geneva) $317 £193

A North German dated blue and white rectangular tea caddy, the base inscribed *Fuls Spu Huls 1740* pewter mount and cover, 18cm. high. (Christie's London) $753 £462

An Ansbach arbour group of lovers, the lady seated holding a nosegay, her companion standing beside her, circa 1770, 25cm. high. (Christie's London) $20,460 £13,200

A German porcelain small rectangular plaque painted in colours with a mermaid and a youth seated on rocks, circa 1880, 2¾ x 2¼in. (Christie's S. Ken) $304 £198

GERMAN

A sugar box and cover, of flattened oval form, painted in sepia with a mounted sportsman surrounded by hounds, 12cm., German, circa 1740. (Lawrence Fine Arts)
$3,476 £2,200

A Nuernberg manganese ground writhen Birnkrug painted in underglaze blue with an oval rococo cartouche enclosing a flowering bush on a terrace, circa 1730, 25.5cm. high. (Christie's London)
$2,728 £1,760

A Frankenthal silver shape rococo sauceboat, painted in colours with scattered sprays of roses, chrysanthemums and deutsche Blumen, incised *PH*, for Paul Hannong, circa 1755, 24.5cm. wide. (Christie's Geneva)
$1,758 £1,072

A Hoechst group of Der Galante Gaertner modelled by Simon Feilner, the young aspirant bending forward and offering flowers to his companion, impressed *IH* and red wheel mark, circa 1755, 18cm. high. (Christie's Geneva)
$4,925 £3,003

A pair of Volkstedt groups of two children standing on high scroll moulded bases, 6in. high (slight damage to fingers). (Christie's S. Ken) $214 £132

One of a pair of German heart shaped vases on domed circular bases chased with scrolls and rocaille decoration, 6¾in. (Christie's S. Ken)
Two $561 £330

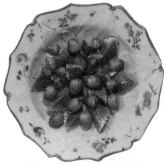

An Ansbach chinoiserie plate painted in colours with a Chinese pheasant perched on a branch, probably Johann Georg Forch, circa 1755, 24.5cm. diam. (Christie's Geneva)
$2,252 £1,373

A German faience hen tureen, naturalistically modelled as a roosting hen painted in manganese, yellow and blue, circa 1740, 22cm. wide. (Christie's London)
$1,434 £880

A German shaped circular trompe l'oeil plate moulded with leaves and applied with wild strawberries naturalistically coloured, circa 1765, 23cm. diam. (Christie's London) $3.227 £1,980

GERMAN

A Thuringian eye bath modelled as the head of a man wearing a yellow hat, last quarter of the 18th century, 8cm. long. (Christie's London) $753 £462

Potschappel porcelain cabinet cup and saucer by Carl Thieme, with a pink ground with a landscape decoration. (G. A. Key) $153 £90

An Erfurt cylindrical tankard painted with Harlequin holding his hat and slapstick, dancing on a blue mound before a fenced terrace, circa 1765, 26cm. high. (Christie's London) $2,387 £1,540

A Limbach group emblematic of Winter, he wearing a puce and blue hat, she with a puce and black hat, circa 1780, 16cm. high. (Christie's London) $1,165 £715

A KPM Berlin rectangular plaque painted Madonnina after Feruzzi signed with R. Dittrich named on reverse, 19th century, 10in. high x 7½in. wide. (Christie's S. Ken) $1,524 £990

A German porcelain group of four figures standing on a tiered rocky base, 13½in. high. (damage to extremities) (Christie's S. Ken) $378 £242

A Raeren brown saltglaze Krug, the waist moulded with arcades enclosing figures of soldiers, 17th century, contemporary pewter cover, 28cm. high. (Christie's London) $1,108 £715

A Ludwigsburg figure of a Tyrolean boy playing a pipe, standing on a shaped rectangular base (stick missing, damage to extremities), circa 1770, 10.5cm. high. (Christie's London) $477 £308

A Nymphenburg baluster coffee pot and domed cover painted in colours to both sides with birds roosting in trees and perching on terraces, indistinct incised mark, circa 1760, 23cm. high. (Christie's London) $3,586 £2,200

GOLDSCHEIDER

A Goldscheider figure of a woman in a long dress and hat, enamelled in shades of mauve, blue and black, 31.3cm. high. (Christie's London) $1,039 £638

A pair of Goldscheider pottery figures of negro children, each in a long dress carrying a broad brimmed hat, late 19th century, 25cm. high. (Bearne's) $563   £350

A Goldscheider figure of a dancing girl in bodice and split skirt which she holds out behind her, incised *1897*, 9½in. high. (Christie's S. Ken) $512 £330

A Goldscheider ceramic wall mask modelled as the face of a girl with orange lips, orange curly hair and one hand holding a green eye mask, 28.5cm. long. (Phillips London) $1,071 £700

An amusing Goldscheider painted group modelled as three young black boys each wearing short trousers, 56.5cm. high. (Phillips) $2400   £1500

A Goldscheider terracotta wall mask of a young girl with orange curls and green beret holding a Scottie dog to her cheek, 10in. high. (Christie's S. Ken) $563   £330

Parisienne, a Goldscheider polychrome ceramic figure modelled by H. Liedhoff, printed factory marks, 13¾in. high. (Christie's S. Ken) $713 £418

A Goldscheider polychrome ceramic group modelled by H. Perl, of a Spanish dancing couple, 16¼in. high. (Christie's S. Ken) $600 £352

A Goldscheider pottery figure of a batgirl, designed by Lorenzl, the ivory coloured girl walking with outstretched arms, designer's and maker's marks, 46.5cm. (Bonhams) $2,490 £1,500

GOSS

William Wordsworth's Home, Dove Cottage, Grasmere, 100mm. long. (Goss & Crested China Ltd) $837 £500

Whitby Pillion Stone, 70mm. long, with Arms of Knares—borough. (Goss & Crested China Ltd) $50 £30

Toby Jug, 100mm. Coloured, third period. (Goss & Crested China Ltd) $209 £125

First Period Dr. Keneally Spill And Match Holder, 190mm. high. (Goss & Crested China Ltd) $586 £350

The Sandbach Crosses, 260mm. high, made in three sections (Goss & Crested China Ltd) $2,512 £1,500

Lincoln Imp On Plinth, 115mm. First Period. (Goss & Crested China Ltd) $201 £120

A Goss Agent's Change Tray, 140mm. diam. (Goss & Crested China Ltd) $502 £300

Cyprus Mycenaean Vase, 90mm. diam. With International League Of Goss Collectors, issued in 1925. (Goss & Crested China Ltd) $209 £125

Cheshire Cat, 85mm. long. inscribed *'He Grins Like A Cheshire Cat Chewing Gravel'* (Goss & Crested China Ltd) $209 £125

GOSS

First period bust of The Veiled Bride, 270mm. (Goss & Crested China Ltd) $1,675 £1,000

Gibraltar Alcaraza, 70mm. high. (Goss & Crested China Ltd) $13 £8

St. Iltyd's Church Font, Llantwit Major, 90mm. high. Brown (Goss & Crested China Ltd) $837 £500

Bettws—Y—Coed Kettle, 75mm. high. (Goss & Crested China Ltd). $25 £15

Boulogne Sedan Chair, 70mm. (Goss & Crested China Ltd) $75 £45

HAMADA

A fine Slab Bottle by Shoji Hamada, tenmoku glaze with abstract design, circa 1960, 8in. high.
(Bonhams) $4830   £3000

A stoneware Bowl by Shoji Hamada, beige with olive brown vertical stripes and dark brown foliate decoration, 8in. diam.
(Bonhams) $2898   £1800

A rare hexagonal Vase by Shoji Hamada, tenmoku glaze with three floral motifs, circa 1958, 8in. high.
(Bonhams) $4830   £3000

HAN

Chinese painted pottery ding, Western Han Dynasty, with swirling red and white design, 6½in. high.
(Skinner Inc) $900   £559

A green-glazed pottery fortress tower, the four-storied tower with two balconies below a sloping tiled roof, Han Dynasty, 55cm. high.
(Christie's London) $12012   £7700

A grey pottery model of a mythical beast standing four-square, the thick tail curling upwards, Han Dynasty, 31cm. long.
(Christie's) $4356   £2640

Two grey pottery rectangular tomb bricks, one impressed to the centre with five parallel rows of lozenge-shaped panels, Han Dynasty, 92cm. x 38.5cm.
(Christie's London) $5148   £3300

A green-glazed red-pottery granary jar on three short bear feet, with ribbed mushroom-cap shoulder and short cylindrical neck, Han Dynasty, 25.5cm. high.
(Christie's London) $1407   £902

Chinese glazed pottery hill jar, Han style, conical cover with peaked terrain above cylindrical sides, 8½in. high.
(Skinner Inc) $1500   £931

HISPANO MORESQUE

A Hispano Moresque copper lustre dish with a central boss painted with lozenges enriched in blue, pierced for hanging, 16th/17th century, 39cm. diam. (Christie's London) $1,793 £1,100

A Hispano-Moresque copper lustre and blue albarello, painted all over with concentric bands of stylised foliage, late 15th century, 26.5cm. high. (Christie's London) $4,092 £2,640

An Hispano-Moresque copper-lustre dish with a raised central boss surrounded by stylised flowerheads and foliage, early 16th century, 40cm. diam. (Christie's London) $1151 £715

HOECHST

A Hoechst group of Die erlegte Taube, perhaps modelled by J. P. Melchior as a scantily draped youth, with a distressed maiden kneeling at his feet, circa 1770, 17.5cm. high. (Christie's London)$1,278 £825

A Hoechst milking group, modelled by J. P. Melchior, she milking a brown marked cow drinking from a pail, her companion holding it by a tether, circa 1770, 18.5cm. wide. (Christie's London) $2,557 £1,650

A Hoechst figure of Daphnis, modelled by J. P. Melchior, the nude god scantily draped in a yellow robe and holding a pipe in his raised right hand, circa 1775, 19.5cm. high. (Christie's London) $767 £495

A Hoechst figure of Winter, as a youth carrying a bundle of sticks on his shoulder, blue wheel mark, circa 1785, high. (Christie's London) $545 £352

Hoechst china cup and saucer, the cup with eared handle and perching birds of Paradise and gold rim, impressed blue mark, late 18th century. (Kunsthaus am Museum) $541 £311

A Höchst slender baluster coffee-pot and domed cover with rose finial, applied branch handle and leaf-moulded spout, circa 1755, 22.5cm. high. (Christie's London) $1151 £715

IMARI

Exceptional Imari Punch Bowl, Japan, 19th century, flying phoenix over a field of leafy vines and flowers to interior, 15in. diam.
(Skinner Inc) $3600   £2368

An Imari ormolu mounted garniture comprising a jar and cover and two everted rim vases, decorated with panels of pavilions beneath Mount Fuji, Genroku period, jar and cover 64.5cm. high, vases 43cm. high. (Christie's London)
$14,773 £9,350

An Imari hexagonal dish, the central roundel formed by iris sprays surrounded by two panels of lakeside landscapes, Genroku period, 40.5cm. diam. (Christie's London)
$4,345 £2,750

Good quality mid 19th century Imari plate with scalloped border and segmented decoration, 8in. diam.
(G.A. Key) $259   £110

An Imari square vase, painted with landscapes, buildings and flowering plants and rocks in alternate panels, 28cm., Ch'ien Lung. (Lawrence Fine Arts)
$880 £550

A large Imari charger painted with a fan shape panel containing warriors over-looking a river landscape, late 19th century, 62cm. diam.
(Bearne's) $1932   £1200

An Imari oviform vase decorated with a wide panel of ho-o birds amongst paulownia and peonies, the neck with iris sprays (restored), Genroku period, 42cm. high. (Christie's London) $3,128 £1,980

A very rare Ko-Imari shaped square mukozuke, the centre with a four-by-four square pattern, each panel containing various geometric designs, late 17th century, 14cm. square. (Christie's London)
$5,562 £3,520

A large Imari oviform jar decorated with two lobed panels alternately containing a pavilion nestling amongst rocks, Genroku period, wood cover 62cm. high. (Christie's London)
$10,428 £6,600

IMARI

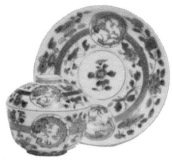

A rare Imari covered bowl and stand, each decorated with two roundels of coiled dragons dividing a narrow band of scrolling foliage, Genroku period, saucer 13.5cm. diam. (Christie's London) $1,390 £880

An Imari coffee urn on three shaped feet, with a moulded dragon head spout above the base, decorated with shaped panels of floral sprays, circa 1850, 30.2cm. high. (Christie's London) $4,866 £3,080

An Imari shallow bowl, painted in underglaze blue and enamelled in colours and gilt with a European warship, second half 18th century, hair cracks, 24cm. (Lawrence Fine Arts) $1,021 £638

An Imari porcelain plaque, of scalloped circular form, decorated with a phoenix perched on a branch, 56cm. diam. (Spencer's) $966 £600

A pair of Imari octagonal jars and covers, each decorated with shaped panels of cranes perched on branches and rocky outcrops, late 17th/early 18th century, 62cm. high. (Christie's London) $41,712 £26,400

Japanese Imari covered bowl, late 19th century, decorated overall with finely painted carp on a blue ground, 11in. diam. (Skinner Inc.) $1,200 £750

A foliate rimmed Imari rectangular dish, the central panel with kirin beneath branches of cherry blossom, the sides with floral panels, late 19th century, 30.5cm. long. (Christie's London) $695 £440

Imari porcelain floor vase, Japan, late 19th century, decorated with two panels of dancing geishas and irises, 36in. high. (Skinner Inc.) $1,800 £1,125

An Imari barber's bowl decorated with a vase of peonies and chrysanthemums on a veranda, the wide border with panels of pomegranates, Genroku period, 29.5cm. diam. (Christie's London) $3,128 £1,980

ITALIAN

A Casteldurante squat drug jar painted with the naked Fortune arising from the waves on the back of a dolphin, circa 1580, 23.5cm. wide. (Christie's London) $27,280 £17,600

A Deruta holy water stoup, the rococo scroll frame moulded with supporters, the pierced crest surmounted by a winged putto, early 17th century, 29cm. high. (Christie's London) $818 £528

A rare armorial wine pail, probably Savona, painted with a frieze of stylised birds, buildings and plants, 19cm. high. (Phillips London) $2,040 £1,200

A Castelli plate painted with two women washing clothes in the river, buildings and mountains in the background, 17th century, 18cm. diam. (Christie's London) $341 £220

A Palermo majolica albarello of waisted cylindrical form, painted with a yellow ground oval panel of a bishop saint, 17th century, 11½in. high. (Christie's S. Ken) $1,694 £1,100

A fine Urbino istoriato shallow tazza, painted with Aeneas setting off in a ship in his search for Italy, 26cm., mid-16th century. (Phillips London) $46,690 £29,000

A massive Montelupo armorial cistern, painted all over in green, yellow, manganese and brown with foliage sprays, stylised fruit and flowers and the arms of the Medicis, 16th/17th century, 47cm. high. (Christie's London) $16,197 £10,450

A Montelupo deep circular dish boldly painted in bright colours, with a moustached soldier holding a shield, 30cm. (Phillips London) $2,254 £1,400

A Deruta figural salt, the bowl supported by four three footed winged caryatids on a square pedestal with four claw feet, early 17th century, 15cm. high. (Christie's London) $3,069 £1,980

ITALIAN

An Italian majolica drug jar, the knopped cylindrical body on spreading foot painted in blue outlined in manganese, 18th century, 5¾in. high. (Christie's S. Ken) $372 £242

One of a pair of large Italian pottery circular dishes in the majolica style painted with classical figures, 24in. diam. (Christie's S. Ken)
Two $515 £330

A Southern Italian baluster pharmacy jar painted with a winged putto head above an empty scroll within an oval cartouche, 17th century, 31cm. high. (Christie's London) $2,216 £1,430

An Italian majolica dish, the centre inscribed Camilla B on a band within a roundel, 19th century, 9½in. diam. (broken and repaired) (Christie's S. Ken) $406 £264

An Italian majolica salt modelled as a figure of a woman standing at a table, 18th century, 8in. high. (Christie's S. Ken) $813 £528

A Pesaro istoriato tondo painted in colours after Sforza Marcantonio with the legend of Perseus and Andromeda, circa 1570, 25.5cm. diam. (Christie's London) $37,510 £24,200

An Italian majolica albarello of waisted cylindrical form on spreading foot painted in blue, 18th century, 8¼in. high. (Christie's S. Ken) $186 £121

An Urbino istoriato dish painted with Galatea being borne across the waves riding on the back of a scaly dolphin accompanied by putti and Cupid holding his bow, circa 1560, 32cm. diam. (Christie's London) $85,250 £55,000

A Montelupo wet drug jar, the flat handle and the spout painted green, the pharmacy sign of a crescent beneath the terminal of the handle, circa 1560, 25cm. high. (Christie's London) $2,387 £1,540

ITALIAN

A Tuscan trilobed jug with a strap handle, painted in yellow ochre and blue, (handle and rim restored) circa 1480, 15.5 cm. high. (Christie's London) $681 £418

An Italian moulded dish, the centre with a twin tailed mermaid holding a tail in each of her outstretched arms (rim chip, minor glaze flakes), late 17th/early 18th century, probably Angarano, 47cm. diam. (Christie's London) $5,115 £3,300

An Urbino pilgrim flask painted in the Patanazzi workshop, in colours with Actaeon surprising Diana at her bath and with Paris judging the goddesses Juno, Minerva and Venus being restrained by Cupid, circa 1580, 38cm. high. (Christie's London) $9,377 £6,050

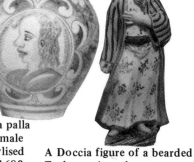

A Doccia white group of the Virgin and Child, modelled after Giovanni Battista Foggini, the mother suckling her infant, last quarter of the 18th century, 42cm. high. (Christie's London) $16,197 £10,450

A pair of Palermo vaso a palla painted in colours with male portrait busts within stylised scroll cartouches, circa 1680, 32cm. and 33cm. high. (Christie's London) $6,138 £3,960

A Doccia figure of a bearded Turk wearing a long puce and yellow striped coat over a blue and gilt flowered robe, circa 1765, 14cm. high. (Christie's London) $3,945 £2,420

A Deruta istoriato dish with Salome holding the head of John the Baptist before Herod, circa 1580, 34cm. diam. (Christie's London) $26,895 £16,500

A Sicilian Caltagirone albarello painted in colours with two portrait heads on yellow grounds, mid 17th century, 31.5cm. high. (Christie's London) $2,510 £1,540

A Bologna scrafiato dish, the centre with a profile of a young man with curly brown hair, 16th century, 24.5cm. diam. (Christie's London) $1,614 £990

ITALIAN

A Doccia slop bowl moulded con basso relievo istoriato with mythological figures and monuments in landscapes (foot-rim chip repaired), circa 1770, 15cm. diam. (Christie's London) $1,534 £990

A Milan (Clerici) partridge tureen and cover, the bird seated on a basket painted in colours, the plumage manganese, circa 1750, 17cm. wide. (Christie's London) $5,967 £3,850

A Le Nove two handled ecuelle cover and stand, painted in colours with scattered sprays of flowers, iron red star marks, circa 1770, the stand 22cm. diam. (Christie's London) $2,898 £1,870

A Doccia armorial beaker painted in colours with quartered arms on baroque mantling with rampant lion supporters, painted in the manner associated with Klinger, 1740-45, 7.5cm. high. (Christie's London) $1,345 £825

A pair of Savona faience figures of a gardener leaning on a watering can, his companion with a hurdy-gurdy, circa 1760, 20cm. high. (Christie's London) $3,751 £2,420

A Vezzi slender beaker painted in colours with a castle on an island, palm trees, flocks of birds and a long necked bird in flight, circa 1730, 8cm. high. (Christie's London) $3,410 £2,200

A Castelli scudella of circular form, painted in the Grue Workshop, with Saint Jerome holding a skull in one hand, 13.5cm. (Phillips London) $419 £260

A large Venetian Berretino albarello, painted with an elaborate scroll inscribed with the name of the contents *Mo Franda F,* 17th century, 34cm. high. (Christie's London) $4,662 £2,860

A Castelli armorial plate by Aurelio Grue, after a print from the Hunt Series by Antonio Tempesta, yellow and brown line rim, circa 1725, 29cm. diam. (Christie's London) $21,516 £13,200

JAPANESE

A Fukagawa Vase, the ovoid body painted in underglaze blue and grey with carp swimming amongst irises, 5¹/₂in. high. (Bonhams) $264 £160

A pair of Japanese porcelain faceted mugs brightly painted with flowers, foliage and exotic birds, 7.8cm. high. (Bearne's) $257 £160

A Satsuma type earthenware food warmer, the small globular pot with a pierced lid and elephant's mask handles, 8in. diam. (Lawrence Fine Arts) $261 £165

A Fukagawa Jar and Cover of ovoid shape, decorated in various coloured enamels with a continuous band of irises, 6¹/₂in. high. (Bonhams) $561 £340

A Ryozan compressed globular jar decorated in various coloured enamels and gilt with a continuous scene of gentry with attendants, fans and butterfly nets, signed *Dai Nihon Kyoto Ryozan,* late 19th century, 9cm. high. (Christie's London) $3,476 £2,200

One of a pair of early 19th century Japanese red stoneware baluser vases moulded with a twisting dragon chasing the pearl amongst clouds, 18in. high. (Michael Newman) $241 £150

A Kinkozan shallow dish decorated with a foliate shaped panel depicting children playing beside various ladies admiring chrysanthemums, signed *Kinkozan zo,* late 19th century, 21cm. diam. (Christie's London) $1,564 £990

A rare Japanese celadon double-gourd ewer decorated in Kiyomizu style enamels with branches of prunus blossom, 18th century, 7¹/₄in. high. (Bonhams) $1485 £900

A fine Japanese earthenware Saucer Dish, painted in coloured enamels and gilt with a shoal of carp enclosed by a swirling border, 4¹/₄in. diam. (Bonhams) $2475 £1500

KAKIEMON

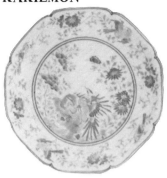

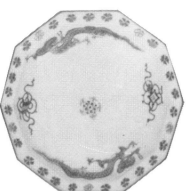

A foliate rimmed Kakiemon dish, the central roundel containing ho-o birds preening on a rocky outcrop, circa 1680, 15.2 cm. diam. (Christie's London) $5,214 £3,300

A Kakiemon model of a Bijin decorated in iron red, green, blue, yellow and black enamels (slight damage), circa 1680, 39.5 cm. high. (Christie's London) $52,140 £33,000

A rare Kakiemon decagonal saucer dish, the centre with a single floret surrounded by two dragons, late 17th century, 11 cm. diam. (Christie's London) $3,823 £2,420

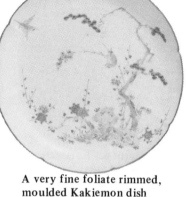

A Kakiemon type shallow dish decorated with a central roundel containing a village in a lakeside landscape, late 17th century, 25 cm. diam. (Christie's London) $6,604 £4,180

An important oviform Kakiemon vase decorated with three panels each containing figures standing beneath a parasol holding an uchiwa, circa 1680, 39 cm. high. (Christie's London)
$382,360 £242,000

A very fine foliate rimmed, moulded Kakiemon dish decorated with a bird in the bowing branches of bamboo, chocolate rim, circa 1680, 21.5 cm. diam. (Christie's London) $38,236 £24,200

KANGXI

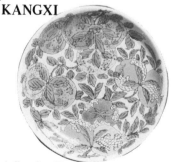

A fine famille verte 'Pomegranate' saucer-dish painted in bright enamels in aubergine, yellow and various tones of green with fruiting peach and pomegranate, encircled Kangxi six-character mark, 25 cm. diam. (Christie'sLondon)$102960 £66000

A blue and white brush-pot of cylindrical form painted with groups of scholars and attendants on a terrace, Kangxi, 18.5 cm. diam. (Christie's London)
                              $3775   £2420

A Kangxi porcelain vase, of inverted baluster form, painted in underglaze blue with a continuous rocky mountainous river landscape, 27.5 cm. high. (Henry Spencer) $179 £110

KUTANI

A late Kutani (Kaga ware) box and cover formed as a chest attended by three karako, signed *Takayama ga,* late 19th century, 25cm. high. (Christie's London) $4,866 £3,080

A Kutani Koro amusingly modelled in the form of a Shishi, the rounded body raised on four legs, the tail forming the handle, Meiji period, 7³/₄in. high. (Bonhams) $325 £200

A late Kutani moulded model of a pug dog playing with a brocade ball, its fur detail realistically rendered, mid-19th century, 25cm. long. (Christie's London) $1,738 £1,100

An important Ao-Kutani deep dish, with two fans interspersed on a ground of chrysanthemum flowerheads, late 17th century, 28cm. diam. (Christie's London) $62,568 £39,600

A Kutani elephant with tasselled saddling decorated with ho-o bird, carrying on its back an elaborate cage resting on an ornately fenced base, 19th century, 50cm. high. (Christie's London) $11,297 £7,150

A Kutani dish, painted with a dark purple dragon in a yellow sky, seal mark, 14½in. diam. (Lawrence Fine Arts) $634 £396

A pair of Kutani vases, painted on one side with figures and on the other with birds, 35.8cm. high. (Bearne's) $933 £580

A pair of hexagonal late Kutani (Kaga ware) vases decorated with six oval panels, surrounded by various designs including ho-o birds and clouds, late 19th century, 37cm. high. (Christie's London) $3,476 £2,200

A rare Kutani double gourd shaped bottle, the wide lower section with sprays of chrysanthemum amongst rockwork, circa 1670, 19.5cm. high. (Christie's London) $10,428 £6,600

LEACH

A stoneware Punch Bowl by Bernard Leach, with curved ridged conical lid and two handles, circa 1960, 12¹/₂in. wide.
(Bonhams) $515 £320

A porcelain preserve pot and cover decorated by Bernard Leach, covered in a mushroom glaze decorated with grey blue band with iron brown scrolling brushwork, 12cm. high.
(Christie's London) $517 £308

A fine stoneware lidded Bowl by Bernard Leach, with conical pagoda lid, impressed BL and St. Ives seals, circa 1967, 9in. diam.
(Bonhams) $5635 £3500

A large stoneware Bowl by Bernard Leach, the interior a celadon glaze with foliate painted decoration, circa 1960, 12¹/₄in. diam.
(Bonhams) $1690 £1050

A porcelain bottle vase by David Leach, covered in a mottled dark and chocolate brown glaze, two sides with combed decoration revealing glaze beneath, 26.7cm. high.
(Christie's London) $259 £154

A blue and white porcelain circular box and cover by Bernard Leach, the domed cover with cobalt blue bands and red enamelled birds, 7cm. high. (Christie's London) $2,218 £1,320

A rare porcelain Sake Bottle by Bernard Leach, with stopper, off-white with decoration of leaping fish in olive brown, circa 1960, 7¹/₂in. high.
(Bonhams) $1932 £1200

A porcelain Plate by Bernard Leach, blue and white with three fishes, circa 1958, (repair to rim), 7¹/₂in. diam.
(Bonhams) $1127 £700

A superb stoneware 'pilgrim' Bottle by Bernard Leach, tenmoku with orange markings, impressed BL and St. Ives seals, 14in. high.
(Bonhams) $6118 £3800

LENCI

A Lenci Art Deco ceramic figure, modelled as a girl wearing an orange hat, black jacket and black, white and grey chequered skirt, 37.5cm. high.
(Phillips) $3300   £2000

L Cacio Selle Colombe, a Lenci pottery figure modelled as a girl sitting with her floral and striped skirts spread out around her, 24.5cm. high. (Phillips London)
                    $945   £580

A Lenci ceramic figure of a young peasant woman wearing black skirt, maroon floral shirt and yellow print scarf, 12½in. high.
(Christie's) $1025   £638

A good Lenci ceramic group modelled as a mer-child holding a fish aloft, she kneels on the back of two open-mouthed fish, 51cm. high.
(Phillips) $4950   £3000

A Lenci ceramic group, modelled as a seated figure of a girl wearing a black dress, a coloured and patterned cape and a purple scarf, 34.8cm. high. (Phillips London)
                    $1,549 £950

A monumental Lenci ceramic figure, the stylised female nude standing on a rock, covered in a cream slip, 99.2cm. high. (Christie's London) $10,758 £6,600

A Lenci Art Deco ceramic figure with box and cover, moulded as the head, shoulders and torso of a young woman, 21.4cm. high. (Phillips London)
                    $1,793 £1,100

A Lenci polychrome ceramic figure of a mermaid and her baby astride a giant turtle, painted in shades of green and brown, 12¾in. high. (Christie's S. Ken) $2,157 £1,265

A Lenci ceramic head of stylised form, the hair and eye sockets painted in shades of blue and green, 14in. high.
(Christie's) $1593   £990

LINTHORPE

A Linthorpe Pottery double gourd vase, designed by Christopher Dresser, the red clay body overlaid with treacle brown glaze, 17.5cm. high. (Phillips London)$673 £440

A Linthorpe pottery bowl with electroplate cover, mount and swing handle, designed by Dr. Christopher Dresser, 5½in. diam.
(Christie's S. Ken) $177   £110

An Aesthetic movement vase, attributed to Linthorpe and a design by Christopher Dresser, with angular shoulders and short cylindrical neck, 26cm. high. (Phillips London)
$398 £260

A large Linthorpe Pottery vase designed by Christopher Dresser, of almost egg shape, covered with a brown, milky green, milky blue and amber glaze, 43.5cm. high. (Phillips London) $1,760 £1,150

A large Linthorpe twin-handled vase designed by Christopher Dresser of blauster form with tapering neck with angular loop handles, covered in dark brown glaze with pale green speckling, impressed Linthorpe 266, with indistinct designer's facsimile signature, 47cm. high.
(Phillips) $1312   £820

A Linthorpe twin-handled pottery vase designed by Christopher Dresser, the vessel of flattened oviform with bulbous neck, 20.8cm. high.
(Phillips) $149   £90

A Linthorpe pottery vase designed by Christopher Dresser, the vessel of oviform with tall cylindrical neck, entwined with raised spiralling decoration, 17.2cm. high.
(Phillips) $396   £240

A Linthorpe pottery vessel designed by Dr. Christopher Dresser, with vertical rows of raised beading, 7in. high.
(Christie's S. Ken) $850   £528

A Linthorpe earthenware jug, shouldered tapering form with flared neck, with facsimile signature *Chr. Dresser* 19.5cm. high. (Christie's London) $287 £176

227

LOWESTOFT

A Lowestoft blue and white leaf shaped pickle dish painted with trailing flowers, circa 1765, 11.5cm. long. (Christie's London) **$230 £143**

A Lowestoft 'Sparrow-Beak' cream jug painted in 'Curtis' style, with a bouquet of flowers, 9cm. (Phillips) **$515 £320**

A Lowestoft globular teapot and cover with ribbed loop handle, painted in Curtis style with bouquets of flowers, 15cm. (Phillips London) **$1,020 £600**

A Lowestoft blue and white baluster mug with scroll handle, painted with a three storey pagoda, circa 1765, 14.5cm. high. (Christie's London) **$495 £308**

A Lowestoft inscribed cylindrical mug, inscribed in black *A Trifle from Lowestoft*, circa 1790, 12cm. high. (Christie's London) **$4,250 £2,640**

A Lowestoft blue and white fluted baluster coffee pot and cover transfer printed with loose bouquets, circa 1780, 26.5cm. high. (Christie's London) **$1,593 £990**

A Lowestoft coffee can painted in blue with flowers, rockwork and a butterfly, 6.5cm. (Phillips) **$450 £280**

A Lowestoft 'Sparrow-Beak' cream jug painted with chioniserie figures of a lady and a boy seated by a bridge, 8.5cm. (Phillips) **$305 £190**

Lowestoft 'Sparrow-Beak' jug painted in 'Curtis' style with a bouquet in green, iron-red and purple, 9cm. high. (Phillips) **$386 £240**

LOWESTOFT

A Lowestoft polycrome sauce boat, moulded with fluting and floral panels, late 18th century, 14.8cm.
(Bearne's) $434 £270

A Lowestoft globular teapot and cover painted in a famille rose palette with a Curtis type pattern of bouquets, circa 1785, 16cm. high. (Christie's London) $672 £418

A Lowestoft blue and white pierced oval two handled basket, transfer printed with The Pinecone and Foliage Pattern, circa 1780, 24cm. wide. (Christie's London)
$850 £528

A Lowestoft blue and white moulded globular jug with cylindrical neck and loop handle, painted with Orientals at discussion, circa 1765, 26cm. high. (Christie's London)
$3,010 £1,870

An unrecorded Lowestoft ship bowl inscribed *Success To The Cruizer Cutter/Henry Major Master,* 27cm. (Phillips London) $3,910 £2,300

A Lowestoft blue and white cylindrical mug transfer printed with an Oriental crossing a bridge, circa 1780, 14.5cm. high. (Christie's London)
$708 £440

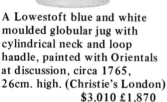

A Lowestoft circular sugar bowl and flat cover painted with scattered cornflowers, circa 1795, 11.5cm. diam. (Christie's London)
$1,771 £1,100

A Lowestoft figure of a putto, his brown hair tied in a top-knot, a puce scarf trailing from his shoulder, circa 1770, 13.5cm. high. (Christie's London) $3,010 £1,870

A Lowestoft blue and white fluted junket dish painted in a pale blue with trailing flowering branches, circa 1765, 22.5cm. diam. (Christie's London) $743 £462

LUCIE RIE

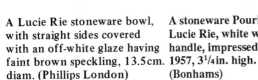

A Lucie Rie stoneware bowl, with straight sides covered with an off-white glaze having faint brown speckling, 13.5cm. diam. (Phillips London) $2,678 £1,750

A stoneware Pouring Vessel by Lucie Rie, white with pulled handle, impressed LR seal, circa 1957, $3^{1}/_{4}$in. high. (Bonhams) $644 £400

A stoneware Cream Pot by Lucie Rie, covered in an unusual yellow glaze with running bronze rim, circa 1960, $2^{3}/_{4}$in. high. (Bonhams) $724 £450

A rare porcelain Bowl by Lucie Rie, the white glazed exterior inlaid with small brown circles each with a dot, circa 1968, 5in. diam. (Bonhams) $6118 £3800

An exceptionally fine bronze porcelain Vase by Lucie Rie, with reddish brown shoulder and inner rim, LR seal, circa 1972, $9^{1}/_{2}$in. high. (Bonhams) $4508 £2800

A rare porcelain Bowl by Lucie Rie, bronze with a sloping white band inlaid with diagonal lines, circa 1958, $4^{3}/_{8}$in. diam. (Bonhams) $2898 £1800

A fine stoneware flared bowl by Lucie Rie, covered in a pale lemon, olive green and speckled pink spiral glaze, impressed LR seal, circa 1960, 32cm. diam. (Christie's London) $10,164 £6,050

A stoneware Salad Bowl by Lucie Rie, white with speckling and unglazed ring within, circa 1955, $9^{1}/_{2}$in. wide. (Bonhams) $1127 £700

A fine porcelain golden bronze Bowl by Lucie Rie, the deep terracotta foot and well surrounded by a circular ring of turquoise, circa 1986, $9^{1}/_{4}$in. diam. (Bonhams) $7245 £4500

MARTINWARE

An unusual Martin Brothers stoneware twin handled loving cup, with twin snake handles and incise-decorated with winged griffins having foliate tails in browns and beige. (Phillips London) $490 £320

A small Martin Brothers stone ware bird having pinkish brown, green and blue plumage, 17.5cm. high. (Phillips London) $3,366 £2,200

A Martin Brothers stoneware double face jug, each side of the globular vessel modelled in high relief with a grinning visage, 16.5cm. high. (Phillips London) $1,102 £720

A Martin Brothers John Barley-corn jug, the ovoid body modelled with grinning face, 18cm. high, incised mark and 6-1911. (Lawrence Fine Arts) $880 £550

A Martinware grotesque bird tobacco jar, the detachable head with long drooping beak, the incised plumage decorated in typical shades of brown and blue, 11in. high (excl. stand). (Christie's S. Ken) $10,503 £6,160

A Martin Brothers stoneware vase, painted with grotesque fish, eels, a starfish and aquatic foliage in browns, white, black and blue, 21.5cm. high. (Phillips London) $949 £620

A Martin Brothers stoneware vase, decorated with white clematis and marguerites on a dark brown ground, 1889, 21.4cm. high. (Christie's London) $430 £264

A Martin Brothers stoneware vase, painted in browns, white, black and blue with grotesque fish, an eel, a crab and a jelly-fish, 23cm. high. (Phillips London) $918 £600

A Martin Brothers stoneware double face jug, with a broad spout and overhead loop handle, 19.5cm. high, signed *Martin Bros., London & Southall.* (Phillips London) $3,060 £2,000

MEISSEN

A Meissen model of a carthorse by J. J. Kaendler, standing on a flower encrusted base and tree trunk support, 20cm. (Phillips London) $1,360 £800

A Meissen blue and white chinoiserie rectangular tea caddy painted with birds in flight above flowering plants and rocks, circa 1730, 10.5cm. high. (Christie's London) $538 £330

A rare Meissen model of Count Bruhl's Tailor, modelled by J. J. Kaendler, the tailor seated astride the goat, 15cm. (Phillips London) $7,140 £4,200

A Meissen chinoiserie salt from the Bruhlsche plat de menage modelled by J. J. Kaendler as a laughing Chinaman, crossed swords mark, circa 1737, gilt metal cover, 19cm. high. (Christie's London) $12,551 £7,700

A Meissen plate, the white centre painted with damsons, cobnuts, redcurrants and flowers, 26.5cm. (Phillips London) $1,530 £900

A rare late Meissen group of two naked young boys playing together on a scroll base, 13cm. (Phillips London) $544 £320

A late Meissen bottle shaped vase, the alternate panels finely painted in purple and red monochrome with coastal scenes, 19.5cm. (Phillips London) $1,054 £620

Two Meissen blackamoor sweetmeats, the male figure with a feathered skirt and headdress, the female wearing a yellow and puce skirt, crossed swords marks, circa 1760 and 1765, 17.5cm. and 20cm. high. (Christie's London) $2,869 £1,760

A fine Meissen milk jug and cover, painted within two panels with merchants on a quayside, probably by C. F. Herold, 21cm., crossed swords mark. (Phillips London) $7,820 £4,600

MEISSEN

A Meissen Bergleute two handled ecuelle and cover painted by Bonaventura Gottlieb Hauer with four vignettes of miners at various activities, circa 1745, 20cm. wide. (Christie's London)
$26,895 £16,500

A Meissen group of the Hand Kiss modelled by J. J. Kaendler, on a flat base encrusted with flowers (extensively damaged and repaired), circa 1740, 22cm. wide. (Christie's London)
$8,069 £4,950

A Meissen gelbe Lowe two handled oval tureen and cover, the scrolling handles and knop moulded with acanthus leaves, Pressnummer 26 to base and cover, circa 1740 35cm. wide. (Christie's London) $3,048 £1,870

A Meissen figure of an ape modelled by Johann Gottlieb Kirchner, seated on a rocky base, crossed swords mark, circa 1735, 25cm. high. (Christie's London)
$19,723 £12,100

A Vienna porcelain snuff box, the interior of the lid finely painted with two gentlemen seated out-of-doors at a table, drinking wine, 9cm. (Phillips London) $1,445 £850

A Meissen figure of a Moor restraining a horse, modelled by J. J. Kaendler (repair to the Moor, base and horse's fetlocks and ears), circa 1755, 23cm. high. (Christie's London)
$3,945 £2,420

A Meissen Monatsbecher representing the month of November, painted in colours with mounted huntsmen and dogs chasing a hare, Pressnummer 24, circa 1745, 7.5cm. high. (Christie's London)
$5,738 £3,520

A pair of late Meissen figures of cupids, one holding his thumbs to his nose to cock a snoot, 20cm. (Phillips London)
$1,275 £750

A Meissen powder purple ground milk jug and cover with bud finial painted in colours with Watteau figures, crossed swords mark, circa 1745, 14cm. high. (Christie's London) $1,972 £1,210

233

MEISSEN

A Meissen group emblematic of Water, modelled as Neptune and Venus scantily clad in puce and yellow flowered robes, crossed swords mark, circa 1750, 16.5cm. wide. (Christie's London) $682 £440

A Meissen turquoise ground quatrefoil teapot and cover with a wishbone handle, painted in Purpurmalerei with theatrical figures and women in landscapes, circa 1735, 17cm. wide. (Christie's London) $1,705 £1,100

A Meissen figure of a recumbent lion, modelled by J. J. Kaendler, painted with a brown coat, traces of crossed swords mark, circa 1745, 22cm. wide. (Christie's London) $2,046 £1,320

19th century Meissen Zwiebelmuster centrepiece, 39cm. high. (Auktionshaus Arnold) $1,435 £932

A set of twelve Meissen Kakiemon knives and forks painted with two birds perched on a branch, circa 1735, silver tines and blades, the handles 7cm. long. (Christie's London) $13,640 £8,800

A Meissen figure of a bagpipe player modelled by J. J. Kaendler, in green and yellow waistcoat and pink cloak with yellow stockings, circa 1740, 23cm. high. (Christie's London) $3,069 £1,980

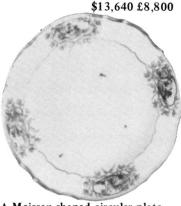

A fine Meissen chinoiserie arbour group modelled by Reinicke, the young lovers seated closely together, 18.5cm. crossed swords mark, circa 1755. (Phillips London) $4,347 £2,700

A Meissen shaped circular plate moulded with Gotzkowsky erhabene Blumen, the rim painted in colours with four quatrefoil cartouches, circa 1738, 23.5cm. diam. (Christie's London) $1,449 £935

A Meissen baluster coffee pot and domed cover, painted with fruiting vine and cut peaches, roses, a pear, wild strawberries and a butterfly, 22.5cm. (Christie's London) $2,557 £1,650

MEISSEN

A late Meissen group of three dogs, one a pug standing with black face and paws and wearing a green collar, 21cm. (Phillips London)
$1,771 £1,100

A Meissen Flaeschenhalter from the Swan service modelled by J. J. Kaendler and J. F. Eberlein for Count Bruehl, circa 1740, 24cm. wide. (Christie's London)
$64,790 £41,800

A late Meissen group after the painting by Francois Boucher entitled *Pensent-ils au raisin?* 19.4cm. (Phillips London)
$708 £440

A rare Meissen figure of a cellist, dressed in a puce striped jacket, yellow waistcoat and puce breeches, 12.5cm. (Phillips London)
$644 £400

A pair of Meissen models of doves modelled by J. J. Kaendler, the naturalistically modelled and coloured birds sitting on shaped round bases, circa 1745, both about 16cm. wide. (Christie's Geneva)
$9,146 £5,577

A Meissen candlestick from the Swan service modelled by J. F. Eberlein and J. J. Kaendler, for Count Bruehl, and his wife Anna von Kolowrat Kratkowska, circa 1739, 24cm. high. (Christie's Geneva)
$52,767 £32,175

19th century, Meissen porcelain group of two putti, 17cm. high, restored. (Auktionshaus Arnold)
$414 £269

A Meissen circular dish from the Red Dragon service, painted in orange and gold, circa 1740, 29.5cm. diam. (Christie's London)
$3,751 £2,420

A Meissen gardening group, the central figure standing on high rockwork before a tree stump, blue crossed swords and incised numeral marks, late 19th century, 29cm. high. (Christie's London)
$3,896 £2,420

MEISSEN

Meissen porcelain dish of early 19th century period, cartouches of flowers to the border with romantic figure designs to the centre, 16 x 11in. (G. A. Key) $340 £200

A Vienna teabowl and saucer painted in the style of Dannhofer with chinoiserie figures, one training a dog and the other a bird. (Phillips London) $884 £520

A Meissen oval bowl pierced with scrolls and with ram mask handles and four paw feet, cancelled blue crossed swords, circa 1880, 15in. across. (Christie's S. Ken) $1,101 £715

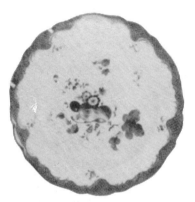

A good Dot period Meissen porcelain plate, painted in colours with a spray of flowers and fruit, 24cm. diam. (Henry Spencer) $214 £140

A Meissen armorial saucer for the Italian market, painted in colours with the arms of the Foscari, Dreher's mark of Meinert, circa 1740. (Christie's Geneva) $2,673 £1,630

A Meissen model of Harlequin Alarmed, modelled by J. J. Kaendler, faint blue mark to base, the porcelain circa 1740, the decoration later, 16.5cm. high. (Christie's London) $8,965 £5,500

A Meissen rectangular Bergleute teacaddy and cover painted in the manner of B. G. Hauer, faint crossed swords mark, circa 1738, 12.5cm. high. (Christie's Geneva) $3,870 £2,360

A Meissen chinoiserie two handled beaker, one side painted with an alchemist experimenting, the other with a woman on a terrace, circa 1725. (Christie's Geneva) $3,377 £2,059

A Meissen figure depicting an itinerant magic lantern show-man in 18th century costume, carrying a magic lantern on his back, 6in. high. (Christie's S. Ken) $986 £605

MEISSEN

A Meissen shaped oval bombe snuff box painted in colours with figures conversing on quaysides before Venetian palaces, circa 1740, 7.5cm. wide. (Christie's Geneva) $11,257 £6,864

A Meissen portrait bust of Princess Marie Zepherine de Bourbon modelled by J. J. Kaendler, crossed swords mark, circa 1755, 25cm. high. (Christie's Geneva) $13,368 £8,151

A Meissen chinoiserie teapot and cover with gilt pinecone finial, bird's head spout and shell and scroll handle painted with Chinese figures, circa 1740, 18cm. wide. (Christie's Geneva) $4,574 £2,789

One of two Meissen figures of Cupid kneeling beside a target centred with a pink heart, 8½in. high. (Christie's S. Ken) Two $1,101 £715

A Meissen rectangular snuff box painted by Christian Friedrich Herold, with early European scenes within slightly recessed cartouches, circa 1732, 7.5cm. wide. (Christie's Geneva) $45,731 £27,885

A Meissen figure of a lady holding a letter in her right hand, her left hand in a feather muff, blue crossed swords and incised and impressed numerals, circa 1880, 8½in. high. (Christie's S. Ken) $592 £385

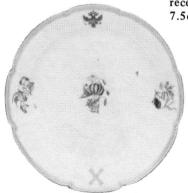

A Meissen armorial dish from the St Andrew the First Called service moulded with Gotzkowsky erhabene Blumen and painted with sprays of Holzschnitt lilies, circa 1742, 28cm. diam. (Christie's Geneva) $9,146 £5,577

A Meissen figure of a wheelwright from the Handwerker modelled by J. J. Kaendler and P. Reinicke, circa 1750, 21.5cm. high. (Christie's London) $1,972 £1,210

A Meissen circular powder box and cover, painted in colours with scattered tight sprays of deutsche Blumen, circa 1760, with chased copper gilt mounts, 8cm. diam. (Christie's Geneva) $1,760 £1,073

MEISSEN

Meissen Figure of the Cocoa Maker, Germany, second half 19th century, depicting a child sitting by a table making cocoa in a cup, 4in. high.
(Skinner Inc) $400   £263

A set of ten Meissen Kakiemon knives and forks painted with two birds perched on a branch and flowering chrysanthemum sprays, circa 1735, silver tines and blades, the handles 7cm. long. (Christie's Geneva)
$6,332 £3,861

Meissen 'Motto Child' Figure, Germany, late 19th century, with nude figure standing over a cage, 4½in. high.
(Skinner Inc) $475   £312

Meissen Figure of a Girl, Germany, second half of 19th century, elegantly clad in a soft pink floral dress, 5½in. high.
(Skinner Inc) $750   £493

Meissen baluster vase, with double serpentine handles applied with acanthus leaf mouldings, on tapering oval base, moulded on gilt relief, circa 1900, sword mark, 39cm. high. (Kunsthaus am Museum)
$1,296 £745

Meissen Gardener Group, 19th century, two female and one male figure in full enamel colours, all on rocky modelled base, 8¼in. high.
(Skinner Inc) $1500   £986

Meissen Group of a Lady Reading Beneath a Tree, Germany, late 19th century, a small nude boy at her side, (chips), 10¼in. high.
(Skinner Inc) $500   £329

A Meissen figure of Hofnarr Froehlich modelled by J. J. Kaendler, the portly figure standing on an octagonal shaped base, 1739, 24.5cm. high. (Christie's London)
$7,161 £4,620

Meissen Shepherd Lovers Group, Germany, second half of 19th century, the couple seated beneath a tree holding hands, 9in. high.
(Skinner Inc) $600   £394

MEISSEN

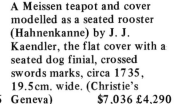

Meissen china group of a child kneeling beside a puppy drinking milk, 9cm. high, sword mark, 1905. (Kunsthaus am Museum) $595 £342

Meissen Oval-Shaped Tureen and Cover, Germany, 19th century, with gilded and moulded leaf-shape handles, finial of a young girl simply draped, 14³/₄in. handle to handle.
(Skinner Inc) $800 £526

A Meissen teapot and cover modelled as a seated rooster (Hahnenkanne) by J. J. Kaendler, the flat cover with a seated dog finial, crossed swords marks, circa 1735, 19.5cm. wide. (Christie's Geneva) $7,036 £4,290

Meissen Figure Group of 'The Apple Pickers', Germany, late 19th century, depicting a man and woman under an apple tree, apples, 10¹/₄in. high.
(Skinner Inc) $1000 £657

Meissen Group of Cybele, Germany, late 19th century, goddess modelled wearing a crown and seated on the back of a lion, 9in. high.
(Skinner Inc) $1400 £921

Rare Meissen Bust of a Child, Germany, late 19th century, a draping of grapes and vines over the shoulders and about the head, 10in. high.
(Skinner Inc) $1200 £789

A Meissen figure of a fish seller modelled by J. J. Kaendler, holding a large orange tailed carp in her arms, circa 1745, 19.5cm. high. (Christie's London) $3,410 £2,200

Meissen Group 'Silenus on a Donkey', late 19th century, on an oval moulded base, a nude child holding the donkey's tail, crossed swords mark, (chip), 8in. high.
(Skinner Inc) $1300 £855

A Meissen figure of an egg seller modelled by J. J. Kaendler standing offering an egg from a basket over her left arm, circa 1745, 18cm. high. (Christie's London) $3,069 £1,980

MINTON

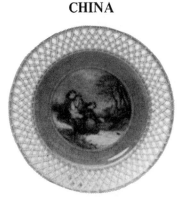

One of a pair of Minton Art Pottery Studio pilgrim vases painted with portraits of young girls, 20cm., 1871. (Phillips London)   Two $522 £320

A Minton plate with pierced gilt border, painted by James Rouse, depicting three children and a robin, 25cm., 1871. (Phillips London) $619 £380

One of an impressive pair of Minton vases in Sevres style, painted with scenes of rustic lovers, after Boucher, within scrolling tooled gold borders, 31cm. (Phillips London)
        Two $1,059 £650

A large Mintons art pottery circular wall plate by William Stephen Coleman painted in naturalistic colours with a pubescent young girl depicting an allegory of Leda and the Swan, 49.5cm. diam.
(Phillips) $6080   £3800

A magnificent Minton pate sur pate vase by Louis Marc Solon, of Greek amphora shape, 56cm., gold mark and date code for 1886. (Phillips London) $1,548 £950

A rare and interesting Minton majolica ware Lindsay platter, probably painted by Thomas Allen, the oval centre painted in bright colours with Venus kneeling in a shell boat, 46cm. (Phillips London) $676 £420

A Minton rectangular plaque by Louis Solon, signed, decorated with Cupid stealing flowers from a basket held by a maiden, 19 x 10.5cm. (Phillips London) $619 £380

A pair of brightly coloured Minton figure candlesticks, the candlestick columns in green with gilt bulrushes, 21.5cm. (Phillips London) $2,415 £1,500

Art Nouveau Minton majolica glazed jardiniere and stand, with stylistic blue flowers and green foliage, 36in. in height overall. (G. A. Key)$1,223 £750

CHINA

MINTON

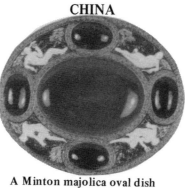

A large and important Minton majolica wine cooler and cover, moulded in low relief with military scenes below fox's masks and drapery, 64cm. (Phillips London) $8,211 £5,100

A Minton majolica oval dish with green glazed depressed centre, the border moulded in relief with reclining Classical nude figures, impressed date code for 1856, 38cm. wide. (Christie's London) $796 £495

A rare Minton figure of Lord Byron, wearing a claret coloured jacket and blue striped trousers on a rectangular base, 15.5cm. (Phillips London) $644 £400

A Mintons ceramic charger, the beige glazed ground decorated with painted floral reserves in turquoise and charcoal, 43.4cm. diam. (Christie's London) $554 £330

A Minton model of a cat wearing a black collar and sponged in green and yellow (ears restored), circa 1830, 12.5cm. high. (Christie's London) $531 £330

Minton porcelain plate painted by Joseph Smith, inscribed *The Bohemian Wax Wing* on the back, circa 1846. (G. A. Key) $134 £80

One of a pair of Minton pot pourri vases, each side painted with a circular landscape panel framed in gold on a pink ground, 13cm. (Phillips London) Two $1,060 £650

A Minton blue ground pate sur pate tapering oviform vase, decorated in white relief by L. Solon, with a nymph in a diaphanous dress, date code for 1893, 40cm. high. (Christie's London) $5,313 £3,300

A Minton majolica jardiniere and stand, the pink glazed basketweave moulded sides decorated in relief, date code for 1870, 21cm. high. (Christie's London) $1,594 £990

MOORCROFT

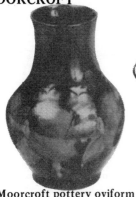

A Moorcroft pottery oviform vase with short cylindrical neck, decorated in the Pomegranate pattern of fruit and foliage, 6½in. high. (Christie's S. Ken) $356 £209

A Moorcroft pottery bowl, decorated in the Claremont toadstool pattern, on a mottled green ground, 27cm. diam. (Bonhams) $465 £280

A Moorcroft Cornflower pattern three handled cylindrical vase, with white piped decoration of cornflowers, covered in a yellow, blue and green glaze against a cream ground, 19cm. high. (Christie's London) $2,218 £1,320

A Moorcroft Pomegranate pattern tall cylindrical vase, with white piped decoration of fruit and berries, covered in puce, blue, green and amber glaze, circa 1914, 27.7cm. high. (Christie's London) $1,201 £715

A Moorcroft Hazeldene pattern bowl with incurved rim, decorated in the centre with a large central tree and smaller trees at the side, 24cm. diam. (Phillips London) $489 £300

A Moorcroft tall cup shaped vase, incised with horizontal bands, the green piped decoration of scrolling leaves, covered in a blue and white glaze, 26.4cm. high. (Christie's London) $1,109 £660

A Moorcroft Florian ware Lilac pattern baluster vase, with white piped decoration of lilac branches, covered in a pale and dark blue glaze with splashes of crimson, circa 1900, 30.2cm. high. (Christie's London) $3,511 £2,090

A Moorcroft Chrysanthemum pattern urn shaped vase, the white piped decoration of chrysanthemums amongst scrolling foliage, covered in a puce, green and amber glaze, 1913, 21.6cm. high. (Christie's London) $2,772 £1,650

A Moorcroft baluster vase, the green piped decoration of poppies in scrolling leaf cartouches, covered in pale green and blue glaze, circa 1935, 20.9cm. high. (Christie's London) $702 £418

MOORCROFT

A Moorcroft Eventide pattern two handled vase, with green piped decoration of tall trees before distant mountains, covered in an amber, green, crimson and inky blue glaze, circa 1925, 21.2cm. high. (Christie's London)
$3,326 £1,980

A Moorcroft pottery vase, painted in the Pomegranate pattern with a frieze of fruit and foliage, impressed marks, 31.5cm. (Bonhams) $282 £170

A Moorcroft Claremont jardiniere decorated with large mushrooms, painted in clear colours of maroon, yellow, green and blue, 24.8cm. high. (Phillips London)
$1,935 £1,265

A slender Moorcroft late Florian ware baluster vase tube lined with flowers and foliage of curvilinear design, 10¼in. high. (Christie's S. Ken)
$788 £462

A pair of Tudric Moorcroft candlesticks, each with blue ground pottery stem decorated with pansies, circa 1930. (Tennants) $592 £380

A Moorcroft Eventide Landscape pattern dish, with green piped decoration of trees in hilly landscape, covered in amber, crimson, green and blue glaze, circa 1925, 27.5cm. diam. (Christie's London)
$2,033 £1,210

A Moorcroft pottery shallow bowl, decorated with the Orchid pattern on an inky blue ground, signature in blue, 22cm. diam. (Henry Spencer)
$275 £180

A Moorcroft pottery tazza, decorated in the Pomegranate pattern of tube lined fruit and foliage, mounted on a Tudric pewter base, 8½in. high. (Christie's S. Ken) $375 £220

A Macintyre Moorcroft pottery amphora, decorated in autumnal colours with flowers, circa 1900, 11.8cm. high. (Tennants) $858 £550

PEARLWARE

A dated Staffordshire Pearlware globular jug, inscribed 'Samuall Piggott 1799' and flanked by the farmer's arms, 7¼in. high. (Christie's S. Ken) $176 £110

A pearlware show horse with docked tail and brown sponging, Yorkshire or Scottish, circa 1810, 18cm. long. (Christie's London) $4,958 £3,080

A Staffordshire pearlware yelow-ground Bacchus jug, moulded in relief with a grinning face, 7½in. high. (Christie's S. Ken.) $330 £200

PETIT

A Jacob Petit pot-pourri in the form of a fish, painted in iron-red and apricot and gilt scales, 19th century, 7½in. long. (Christie's S. Ken.) $330 £200

An attractive pair of early 19th century Jacob Petit porcelain taper holders, modelled as a Turkish sultan and his sultana, 16.5cm. high. (Henry Spencer) $2,295 £1,500

A Jacob Petit tapering oviform vase and domed cover with two blue rope-twist handles, blue JP monogram, mid 19th century, 20in. high. (Christie's S. Ken.) $908 £550

A Jacob Petit cornucopia vase, painted with flowers on a claret and gilt ground, 10in. high. (gilding worn) (Christie's S. Ken) $378 £242

A Jacob Petit porcelain figural vase, as a lady seated on a rocky mound encrusted with flowers, 27.5cm. high. (Henry Spencer) $459 £300

One of a pair of Jacob Petit cornucopia vases on rectangular bases, the bodies painted with flowers and moulded with leafy scrolls, blue JP monogram, 19th century, 9in. high. (Christie's S. Ken) Two $643 £418

PILKINGTON

A Pilkington Royal Lancastrian lustre vase decorated by W. S. Mycock, with short cylindrical neck, decorated with vertical bands of Tudor roses, dated 1927, 30cm. high high. (Christie's London)
$1,434 £880

A Pilkington Royal Lancastrian lustre charger decorated by William S. Mycock, decorated with a flamboyant armorial crest, dated 1924, 30.6cm. diam. (Christie's London) $574 £352

A massive Pilkington Royal Lancastrian lustre vase, decorated by Gordon Forsyth, decorated in gold with griffins passant on an iridescent greeny-blue ground, dated 1911, 63cm. high.
(Christie's) $6096 £3740

A Pilkington's Lancastrian lustre moonflask by Walter Crane and Richard Joyce, decorated with the coat of arms of the City of Manchester, 27cm. high.
(Spencer's) $2720 £1600

A Pilkington Royal Lancastrian lustre vase and cover decorated by William S. Mycock, decorated in gold with a double headed eagle, date code for 1913, 23.5cm. high. (Christie's London)
$717 £440

A Pilkington Royal Lancastrian lustre vase and cover decorated by Gordon Forsyth, with two central reserves each surrounded by laurel leaves and flanked by two lions, 29cm. high.
(Christie's) $5379 £3300

A Pilkington 'Royal Lancastrian' lustre vase by Richard Joyce, painted in golden lustre with two mounted Knights in armour, 26.5cm. high.
(Phillips) $1520 £950

A Pilkington lustre pottery charger, by W. S. Mycock, with concentrically ribbed interior, with foliate border, dated 1918, 33cm. diam. (Bonhams)
$249 £150

A Pilkington's lustre vase decorated by Gordon M. Forsyth, with gold lustre rampant lion with a cartouche, code for 1908, 28cm. high.
(Christie's) $645 £396

POOLE POTTERY

A pottery ovoid vase, shape no. 198, painted by Rene Hayes, with stylised flowers and foliage, impressed *Poole,* painted insignia and *W,* 6in. high. (Christie's S. Ken)
$381 £220

A Poole Pottery two handled oviform vase decorated with a design probably by Truda Carter, C.S.A. mark, painted decorator's mark and BT, 7in. high. (Christie's S. Ken) $655 £385

A Carter Stabler & Adams Ltd. vase, designed by James Radley Young, 25cm. high. (Lawrence Fine Arts) $317 £198

A Carter, Stabler & Adams Ltd. biscuit fired stoneware vase, with stepped and ribbed decoration, decorated in shades of brown with geometric, linear and floral designs, 33.7cm. high. (Christie's London) $924 £550

A pottery charger painted by Nellie Blackmore with a view of the ship the Harry Paye, by Arthur Bradbury, 15in. diam. (Christie's S. Ken)
$1,047 £605

A Poole Pottery two handled oviform vase, painted by Ruth Pavely with a pattern attributed to Truda Carter, C.S.A. mark, 9in. high. (Christie's S. Ken)
$1,272 £748

A terracotta twin handled oviform vase painted by Ruth Pavely with bluebirds and foliage between contrasting borders, impressed *CSA Ltd.* mark, 6½in. high. (Christie's S. Ken) $1,142 £660

A pottery table decoration modelled as a yacht in full sail, glazed white, on turquoise base moulded with waves, impressed *Poole,* 15½in. high. (Christie's S. Ken) $190 £110

A Poole Pottery baluster vase painted by Ruth Pavely with a design attributed to Truda Carter, impressed C.S.A. mark, painted rhebus, impressed 947, 11¾in. high. (Christie's S. Ken)
$1,346 £792

POOLE POTTERY

A Carter Stabler & Adams Ltd. vase, designed by James Radley Young, with vertical panels of dots within striped borders, 15.5cm. high. (Lawrence Fine Arts) $334 £209

A pottery oviform jug, shape no. 304, painted by Marjorie Batt with bluebirds and foliage in typical colours, impressed *CSA Ltd* mark, 5in. high. (Christie's S. Ken) $381 £220

A pottery biscuit barrel and cover with wicker handle painted by Sylvia Penney, with stylised flowers and foliage, impressed *Poole*, 5½in. high. (Christie's S. Ken) $228 £132

The Bull, a pottery group designed by Phoebe and Harold Stabler, modelled as two infants astride a bull in ceremonial trappings of swags and garlands, impressed *CSA* mark, 13in. high. (Christie's S. Ken) $3,996 £2,310

A Phoebe Stabler plaster bust of a young girl with pigtails, painted yellow, inscribed *Phoebe Stabler 1911*, 15in. high. (Christie's S. Ken) $419 £242

A pottery square honey pot and cover with beehive finial painted with floral sprigs, impressed *Poole*, 4¾in. high. (Christie's S. Ken) $362 £209

A Poole pottery vase of shouldered globular form, painted with the figures of two gazelle leaping, 20cm. high. (Phillips London) $489 £300

A terracotta plate painted by Anne Hatchard with a green spotted leaping gazelle amongst fruiting vines, impressed *CSA* mark, 12in. diam. (Christie's S. Ken) $1,484 £858

A Carter Stabler Adams Poole pottery vase, attributed to Truda Carter, painted in blue, green, mauve, black and yellow, 22.1cm. high. (Phillips London) $139 £85

PRATTWARE

A Prattware duck sauce boat, the cream body picked out in blue and ochre, the eyes circled in blue, 19.5cm. (Phillips London) $1,105 £650

Exceptional Prattware Postilion Toby Jug, England, 18th century, crisply modelled and decorated in underglaze blue, green, orange and ochre enamels, 7¼in. high. (Skinner Inc) $2200 £1447

A very rare 'C. Gresley' Pratt-ware teapot and cover, moulded in relief on both sides with three women at various domestic pursuits, 12cm. (Phillips London) $1,932 £1,200

A Pratt bottle vase, printed in colours with the exterior view of the Crystal Palace Exhibition, 6¾in. high. (Christie's S. Ken) $309 £198

A pair of Prattware oval plaques moulded in relief with classical profile heads of a man and a woman, 26.5cm. (Phillips London) $1,700 £1,000

A Prattware portrait bust of Admiral Earl St Vincent wearing a brown wig, ochre jacket with yellow frogging, 20cm. (Phillips London) $773 £480

An amusing Prattware model of a bear seated on its haunches, with head turned to face spectator, 13.5cm. (Phillips London) $3,230 £1,900

Prattware Cornucopia Wall Pocket, England, c. 1810, moulded in high relief with a figure of a child, (slight chips), 9in. long. (Skinner Inc) $600 £394

A Prattware Grey Goose jug moulded in relief with Old Mother Slipper-Slapper re-leasing the ochre coloured dog, 16cm. (Phillips London) $451 £280

ROCKINGHAM

A fine and impressive Rockingham porcelain basket, of shaped rectangular form with double entwined twig handle, griffin mark, 30cm. long.
(Spencer's) $1485 £900

Rockingham-Type Brown Glazed Figure of a Lion, England, mid 19th century, (chips under base rim), 11in. wide.
(Skinner Inc) $275 £180

A Rockingham flower encrusted circular basket with overgead handle, the exterior applied with flower heads, circa 1830, 11.2cm.
(Bearne's) $740 £460

ROOKWOOD

Rookwood pottery wax resist vase, Cincinnati, 1929, decorated with blue and green dogwood blossoms, 11¾in. high. (Skinner Inc.)
$300 £185

Rookwood pottery scenic plaque, 'The End of Winter', Cincinnati, Ohio, 1918, original frame, 12¼in. x 9¼in.
(Skinner Inc.) $2800 £1708

Rookwood pottery scenic vellum vase, Cincinnati, 1913, decorated with landscape scene in gray-blue on shaded yellow to peach background, 13⅝in. high.
(Skinner Inc) $2000 £1242

ROSENTHAL

A Rosenthal rectangular plaque, painted in colours with a 17th century Dutch scene, 13½in. x 15¾in.
(Christie's S. Ken) $2302 £1430

'Fright'. A Rosenthal porcelain bust of a faun by Ferdinand Liebermann, modelled as a young bare-chested faun holding a set of pan pipes, 39.4cm. high.
(Phillips) $1320 £800

An unusual Rosenthal white porcelain figure by Rosanowski modelled as a lean Jester with exaggerated limbs, 15.5cm. high.
(Phillips) $416 £260

ROYAL DUX

Royal Dux figure of harlequin and female companion, on oval base, 19in. high. (Phillips Manchester) $395 £250

A Royal Dux porcelain posy holder in the form of a rustic cart being drawn by a donkey, 27.5cm. long. (Bearne's) $248 £160

A Royal Dux porcelain lamp base modelled as an Egyptian slave girl wearing only a loin cloth, applied factory seal, 12½in. high. (Christie's S. Ken) $597 £385

A pair of Royal Dux figures in the form of a farmer carrying a sickle, his lady companion carrying a ewer, 33cm. high. (Bearne's) $496 £320

A pair of Royal Dux book ends in the form of clowns, cream, green and brown designs with gilt work. (G. A. Key) $493 £290

A Royal Dux porcelain group of a dancing couple in blue glazed and gilt Eastern costume, 12¼in. high. (Christie's S. Ken) $546 £352

A pair of Royal Dux porcelain figures in the form of a shepherd wearing a wolf skin, his companion with goats at her feet, 38cm. high. (Bearne's) $1127 £700

A Royal Dux centrepiece, the trefoil base with column modelled as three bare breasted girls kneeling and supporting lily-form bowl, 6½in. high. (Christie's S. Ken) $307 £198

A pair of Royal Dux figures of Eastern water carriers, 29cm. high. (Bearne's) $418 £270

RUSKIN

Ruskin circular footed dish, mottled blue fading to oatmeal, impress to base beneath feet, 6in. diam.
(Giles Haywood) $88   £55

Ruskin iridised circular footed bowl, being mottled yellow fading to pale-green, 1923, 7in. diam.
(Giles Haywood) $177   £110

Ruskin matte cylinder-shaped bulbous vase, pale-blue varying to cloud-effect orange and green, 1932, 9in. high.
(Giles Haywood) $88   £55

A Ruskin high fired stoneware vase, the grey ground covered in a speckled sang-de-boeuf and lustrous royal blue glaze, dated 1907, 32.2cm.m. high. (Christie's London) $1,386 £825

Ruskin matte circular footed vase with flared top, blue varying to orange/oatmeal, 8in. diam.
(Giles Haywood) $128   £80

A Ruskin high fired twin handled shouldered oviform vase, covered in a streaked lavender glaze flecked with green, 13¾in. high. (Christie's S. Ken) $656 £385

Ruskin matte cylinder-shaped bulbous vase, blue varying to orange/oatmeal, 3in. diam.
(Giles Haywood) $67   £42

A Ruskin high fired stoneware vase, the grey ground covered in mottled sang-de-boeuf, royal and sky blue and turquoise streaked glazes, dated 1908, 29.8cm. high. (Christie's London) $1,016 £605

A Ruskin crystalline glazed vase, with jade green, pale blue and cream glazes beneath two bands of sky and royal blue crystalline glazes, 21cm. high. (Christie's London) $222 £132

SATSUMA

A Satsuma oviform vase decorated with shaped panels of a pair of stylised ho-o birds meeting and displaying their plumage, signed *Kozan ga,* late 19th century, 20cm. high. (Christie's London)
$4,345 £2,750

A pair of Satsuma baluster vases boldly decorated with two panels of courtiers and attendants beside a veranda and samurai beneath blossoming trees, late 19th century, 62.5cm. high. (Christie's London)
$11,297 £7,150

A Satsuma oviform vase decorated with a continuous pattern of sages and divines amongst rocky pools, late 19th century, 23cm. high. (Christie's London)
$2,780 £1,760

A Satsuma koro and cover of quatrefoil shape decorated with four rectangular panels depicting warriors, ladies and pastoral scenes, signed *Hoen Seizo,* late 19th century, 8.5cm high. (Christie's London)
$1,564 £990

A Satsuma deep bowl decorated with a bamboo grove, the stalks issuing from a central mass of peony, chrysanthemum and other flowers, late 19th century, 14cm. diam. (Christie's London)
$6,952 £4,400

A Satsuma koro and cover decorated with a continuous pattern of two sprays of flowers and grasses, signed *Shozan,* late 19th century, 14cm. high. (Christie's London)
$4,692 £2,970

Satsuma pottery floor vase, late 19th century, one side decorated with samurai, the other with birds and an overall gilt moriage enamel ground, 59in. high. (Skinner Inc.)
$8,000 £5,000

A pair of tapering rectangular Satsuma vases decorated with four shaped panels surrounded by flowers and foliage, signed *Ryokuzan,* late 19th century, 24.5cm. high. (Christie's London)
$6,083 £3,850

A Satsuma moulded baluster vase decorated with various sages and scholars, oni and beasts under the boughs of a pine tree, signed *Satsuma yaki Tomonobu,* late 19th century, 45cm. high. (Christie's London)
$5,909 £3,740

SATSUMA

Satsuma Lohan Vase, Japan, late 19th century, of fine quality with excellent enamels, Shimazu crest and character marks, 6¼in. high.
(Skinner Inc) $350   £230

Important Pair of Satsuma Vases, Japan, 19th century, one depicting a Japanese Kuan Yin, the companion vase with similar Kuan Yin figure riding an elephant, 22in. high.
(Skinner Inc) $3750   £2467

Satsuma Koro and Cover, Japan, c. 1890, with two raised handles and standing on three raised feet with moulded lion head masks, 12¾in. high.
(Skinner Inc) $950   £625

Satsuma Globular Shaped Teapot, Japan, c. 1900, all over design of Lohans, attendants and a dragon, cover with Shimazu crests, 4in. high.
(Skinner Inc) $200   £131

A Satsuma octagonal shallow dish, the cavetto painted with three women and a child in a garden, 30cm. diam.
(Bearne's) $1333   £860

Satsuma Quatrefoil Lobed Tray, Japan, c. 1910, Lohans with attendants and dragon, Shimazu crest and character marks, 8½in. x 11in.
(Skinner Inc) $350   £230

Satsuma Square Shaped Bottle and Cover, late 19th century, each side with an elongated oval cartouche and with scenes of woman and children, 4¾in. high.
(Skinner Inc) $750   £493

Pair of Satsuma Panelled Vases, Japan, c. 1920, scenes of scholars and of courtesans, wide floral borders to top and bottom, 5in. high.
(Skinner Inc) $250   £164

A Satsuma Koro and cover, painted on either side with figures in a mountainous river landscape, 58cm.
(Bearne's) $744   £480

SEVRES

A Sevres fluted cup and saucer (tasse et soucoupe gaudrone), with radiating blue and white bands, date letter *K* for 1763, incised marks. (Christie's London) $409 £264

A Sevres oval seau, with wavy edge in blue and gold, painted with bouquets and sprays of flowers, 29.5cm., 1759. (Lawrence Fine Arts) $904 £572

A Sevres triangular tray (plateau triangle), the centre painted with sprays of colourful garden flowers, date letter *L* for 1764, painter's mark *X* for Xhrouet, 17cm. wide. (Christie's London) $5,115 £3,300

A pair of Sevres pattern gilt bronze mounted two handled pot pourri vases and covers, painted with youths and girls at various pursuits, circa 1880, 56cm. high. (Christie's London) $8,501 £5,280

A Sevres biscuit figure of L'Abbe Fenelon after the sculpture by Lecomte, wearing a hooded cloak over ecclesiastical robes bordered with lace, circa 1784, 47.5cm. high. (Christie's London) $6,820 £4,400

A pair of assembled Sevres pattern gilt bronze mounted oviform vases, the bodies decorated after Fragonard, the bodies signed *Jeanne,* late 19th century, 98cm. high overall. (Christie's London) $17,710 £11,000

A Sevres plate from the Egyptian service painted with the Dyvan Militaire by Swebach, the centre in brown heightened with white, red printed mark *M. Imp. le de Sevres 1811,* 24cm. diam. (Christie's London) $40,920 £26,400

A Sevres biscuit figure of *La Laitiere* by Fernex after Boucher, the charming young girl standing beside a plinth, 22.5cm., incised repairer's mark B. (Phillips London) $6,120 £3,600

A Sevres pattern turquoise ground circular tray, painted with a central portrait of Henri IV, surrounded by eight portraits of Court beauties, late 19th century, 48cm. diam. (Christie's London) $2,656 £1,650

SEVRES

A Sevres rose ground shaped oval tray, painted in colours with a watery landscape, a man fishing and another with a net, 29cm. wide. (Christie's London) $3,227 £1,980

A Sevres bleu de roi ground tasse litron and saucer, reserved with garlands of pink roses, 1766. (Christie's Geneva) $1,407 £858

A Sevres plate, painted with fishermen in two panels, with two others of fish and shellfish, 26.5cm. (Lawrence Fine Arts) $880 £550

A pair of Sevres pattern Napoleonic gilt metal mounted vases, decorated by Desprez, with continuous battle scenes including Napoleon Bonaparte on a white stallion, late 19th century, 100cm. high. (Christie's London) $21,252 £13,200

A Sevres vase hollandois and pierced stand painted en camaieu bleu with cottages and figures in rural landscapes, painter's mark script N to both pieces, 1757, 20cm. wide. (Christie's London) $9,861 £6,050

Pair of Sevres ormolu mounted vases, 19th century, decorated with continuous landscape containing a maiden and putto, signed *Labarre*, 28½in. high. (Robt. W. Skinner Inc.) $2,400 £1,463

A Sevres pattern turquoise ground circular tray, the centre reserved and painted by Paul Fortin, The village wedding by Greuze, interlaced L marks, late 19th century, 50cm. diam. (Christie's London) $2,656 £1,650

A Sevres caisse a fleurs, the sides painted in colours with sprays of wild flowers within camieu bleu rose and trellis borders, date letter *G* for 1759, 17.5cm. (Christie's London) $5,967 £3,850

A Sevres two handled seau a bouteille, painted in colours with large sprays of garden flowers, date letter *H* for 1760, painter's mark for Rosset, 19.5cm. high. (Christie's London) $5,456 £3,520

SEVRES

A Sèvres First Republic gold-ground two-handled ecuelle and cover painted in colours with baskets and vases of flowers, circa 1795, 18.5cm. wide.
(Christie's London) $1239   £770

A 'Sevres' green ground trembleuse cup, cover and stand, painted with Cupid handing Venus a basket of flowers, date code for 1756, 19th century decoration.
(Bearne's) $713   £460

A Sèvres Bleu Céleste tray, the centre painted in colours with a spray of garden flowers, date letter F for 1758, 17.5cm. wide.
(Christie's London) $1062   £660

A Sevres pattern royal blue ground two handled vase and cover, painted with a youth and a girl, imitation inter-laced L marks, circa 1870, 52cm. high. (Christie's London) $2,302 £1,430

A pair of Sèvres Charles X botanical tazzas, the centres painted in colours with Fleurs d'Amandier and Fleurs d'Oranger, within a bleu lapis border, 21.5cm. diam.
(Christie's London)
          $4604   £2860

A Sevres biscuit figure of a boy *Le Joueur de Musette* by Blondeau after Boucher, 22.5cm., incised repairer's mark F. (Phillips London)
          $4,250 £2,500

A Sèvres blue nouveau 'Jewelled' two-handled cup, cover and trembleuse saucer, the date letter CC for 1780 and L.G. for Le Guay.
(Christie's London) $1328   £825

A pair of Sevres-pattern cache-pots, the bleu celeste ground reserved with oval panels of Royal Children in attendance on mythical and other figures, 19th century, 7½in. high.
(Christie's S. Ken) $3751   £2420

A Sèvres biscuit bust of Napoleon Bonaparte wearing a jacket, on a Paris socle enriched with gilt palmettes and scrolls, circa 1810, 27cm. high.
(Christie's London) $974   £605

SPODE

A Spode blue and white rectangular octagonal meat dish printed with 'shooting a leopard in a tree' from the Indian Sporting Series, circa 1815, 20¼in. wide. (Christie's S. Ken) $508 £330

A pair of Spode beaded spill vases, each richly decorated with Japan pattern, of flowers in shaped cartouches, early 19th century, 11.5cm. high. (Bearne's) $611 £380

A Spode blue and white oval teapot and cover, bat-printed in blue with figures in landscapes, circa 1810, 10½in. wide. (Christie's S. Ken) $74 £44

One of a pair of Spode stone china oviform jugs with cylindrical necks and handles, printed and coloured in famille rose style, 12½in. high. (Christie's S. Ken.) $1,700 £1,100

A pair of spode gold-ground flared cylindrical vases painted with groups of luxuriant fruit and flowers on the rich gold ground, between white beaded rims, one vase with red mark and pattern no. 711, circa 1815, 16.5cm. high. (Christie's London) $3740 £2200

A Spode vase and pierced cover, finely painted with groups of flowers on a dark blue and gilt scale pattern ground, 24cm. (Lawrence Fine Arts) $1,443 £902

A Spode two handled vase, painted in Imari palette with panels of flowers on a blue and gilded ground, 16cm. (Phillips London) $884 £520

A pair of Spode two-handled vases, each painted with Chinese garden scenes in bright enamel colours and gold, 21cm. high. (Bearne's) $966 £600

A fine Copeland Spode vase and pierced cover, richly decorated with a jewelled and gilded green ground, 17.5cm. (Phillips London) $652 £400

STAFFORDSHIRE

A Staffordshire rectangular meat-dish printed with Oriental figures on a terrace before buildings in a river landscape, circa 1810, 20½in. wide. (Christie's S. Ken) $323   £209

A Staffordshire pottery pipe modelled in relief with Rugby and Association footballers, 21.5cm. long. (Lawrence Fine Arts) $104 £66

A large 19th century Staffordshire earthenware Masonic jug, circa 1831. (Phillips) $709   £430

A Staffordshire group depicting 'Lady Hester Stanhope' riding on the back of a camel, circa 1860, 10½in. high. (Christie's S. Ken) $545   £352

Combware pie plate, England, 19th century, with yellow slip decoration and coggled rim, 10½in. diam. (Skinner Inc.) $800 £473

A Staffordshire jug moulded as the head of 'Lord Rodney', the rim moulded with a flag and cannons, circa 1785, 6¼in. high. (Christie's S. Ken) $531   £330

A rare Staffordshire figure of Jenny Lind as Marie in a green hat, dark blue bodice and pink skirt, circa 1847, 8in. high. (Christie's S. Ken) $477   £308

A pair of Staffordshire lions facing to the left and right, painted in shades of brown, circa 1860, 6½in. high. (Christie's S. Ken) $1364   £880

A Staffordshire figure of a lady, carrying a basket of fruit on her head, wearing a floral sprigged dress, 15cm. (Phillips London) $476 £280

STAFFORDSHIRE

A rare moulded saltglaze sauce-boat with unusual fish handle, moulded on one side with a lion flanked by birds in trees, 21.5cm. (Phillips London) $2,254 £1,400

A pair of Staffordshire pottery figures of an old man and woman entitled 'Age', (restoration), 8¼in. high. (Christie's S. Ken) $255 £165

A Staffordshire porcelain part dessert-service, comprising two high comports, four low comports, and ten plates. (Christie's S. Ken.) $690 £418

A Staffordshire pottery oviform jug, printed in puce with a busy portrait of Admiral Lord Nelson flanked by a map of the Battle of Trafalgar, (cracked), 5½in. high. (Christie's S. Ken) $290 £187

Staffordshire figure, Garibaldi, polychrome decorated with name plaque, 15in. high. (G. A. Key) $270 £170

A Staffordshire group of two seated spaniels, one chained to a barrel with iron-red fur markings, 9½in. high. (Christie's) $399 £242

A Staffordshire figure of Dr Syntax in typical black costume seated between flowering branches reading a book, circa 1825, 5½in. high. (Christie's S. Ken) $596 £385

A pair of Staffordshire seated figures of Queen Victoria and Prince Albert, both brightly coloured, circa 1845, 6in. high. (Christie's S. Ken) $323 £209

A Staffordshire creamware equestrian group of Hudibras of Ralph Wood type, seated astride his bown-glazed horse, circa 1785, 30cm. high. (Christie's) $22176 £13200

STAFFORDSHIRE

A Staffordshire stirrup cup, modelled as a hound's head, the ears and part of the head coloured brown, one ear repaired, 12.5cm. (Lawrence Fine Arts) $563 £352

A Staffordshire silver resist lustre jug, decorated with birds standing in tubs among foliage branches, 14cm. diam. (Lawrence Fine Arts)$211 £132

A Staffordshire pearlware teapot and cover of lozenge section with leaf moulded handle, the body painted in colours with birds, 6¾in. high. (Christie's S. Ken) $334 £209

A Staffordshire group of two greyhounds before a tree stump spill vase, 10½in. high. (vase chipped) (Christie's S. Ken) $164 £105

A rare Staffordshire figure of James Braidwood, with black helmet and iron red uniform, circa 1861, 15in. high. (Christie's S. Ken) $847 £550

A Staffordshire gilt clock face, flanked by two seated spaniels and surmounted by a poodle, 9½in. high. (Christie's S. Ken) $269 £176

An interesting Staffordshire hybrid porcelain figure of a hurdy-gurdy player, on mound base, late 18th century, perhaps Enoch Wood, 8¼in. high. (Tennants) $468 £300

A pair of Walton type Staffordshire figures of a lady and gentleman playing a mandoline and a lute, 15.5cm. (Phillips London) $2,210 £1,300

A Staffordshire creamware group of Venus and Cupid of Ralph Wood type, the goddess scantily draped in a green robe, circa 1785, 27cm. high. (Christie's London) $637 £396

STAFFORDSHIRE

A Staffordshire tureen and cover modelled as a duck swimming in water, the base modelled with waves and painted in blue, 10¾in. long. (Christie's S. Ken) $757 £495

A Staffordshire figure of a Turk wearing a brown coat, black fez and yellow turban, 13.5cm. (Phillips London) $255 £150

A Staffordshire porcelain oval teapot and cover with feather moulded spout and painted in black with a windmill and cottage in a river landscape, perhaps Coalport, circa 1810, 10½in. wide. (Christie's S. Ken) $220 £143

A Staffordshire figure of a lady, wearing a brown sprigged dress and sitting on a green glazed tree trunk, 12cm. (Phillips London) $153 £90

A Staffordshire pearlware model of a roaring lion with brown mane and black muzzle, circa 1790, 33cm. long. (Christie's London) $2,656 £1,650

A Staffordshire pastille burner, modelled as a cottage on a grassy mound with floral encrusted decoration, 7in. high. (Christie s S. Ken) $144 £94

A Staffordshire jug, modelled in relief, with a stag, a faun and doe, 14.5cm. (Lawrence Fine Arts) $282 £176

A pair of late Staffordshire cats, seated on rectangular cushion bases painted in green and pink, 7in. high. (Christie's S. Ken) $337 £220

Staffordshire figure of Britannia on a rectangular base, polychrome decoration, 14in. high. (G. A. Key) $286 £180

Large Staffordshire pottery meat plate, blue and white Canova pattern, probably by Godwin and Hewitt. (G. A. Key) $213 £125

Staffordshire figure of Admiral C. Napier, named, 12in. high. (G. A. Key) $270 £170

Large Staffordshire china meat dish, mid-19th century, decorated with a cartouche to the centre depicting a pagoda and birds, in the style of Elkington & Knight. (G. A. Key) $90 £55

Staffordshire figure of Shakespeare, polychrome decorated, named, 14in. high. (G. A. Key) $262 £165

A pair of Staffordshire solid agate models of cats, seated upright, originally supporting candle nozzles, 12.5cm. (Phillips London) $3,220 £2,000

A Staffordshire saltglaze sugar sifter, moulded in relief with ozier and diaper panels, 14cm. (Phillips London) $1,369 £850

A rare enamelled saltglaze figure of a lady in Turkish dress, after a Meissen model, standing and wearing a long yellow lined blue cloak, 20.2cm. (Phillips London) $10,304 £6,400

A slipware circular dish, the brown ground trailed in dark and pale cream slip, probably Staffordshire, 18th century, 34.5cm. diam. (Christie's London) $1,417 £880

19th century Staffordshire vase, decorated in the Mason manner with Oriental flowers, birds etc., with a recumbent lion finial, 18in. high. (G. A. Key) $969 £570

STONEWARE

Incised and cobalt decorated stoneware crock, Thomas Warne and Joshua Letts, South Amboy, New Jersey, dated 1807, 9¼ in. high. (Skinner Inc.) $3,600 £2,209

Incised and cobalt decorated stoneware crock, impressed *W. Lundy and Co., Troy, New York*, circa 1825, 11¼ in., high. (Skinner Inc.) $4,750 £2,914

Cobalt decorated stoneware jug, William H. Farrar & Company, Geddes, New York, 1841-1858 (flake at base), 11in. high. (Skinner Inc.) $3,300 £2,025

A Boettger red stoneware cylindrical tankard, circa 1715, Danish silver mount, mark for Jens Isachsen Frus of Ringkobirg, Denmark, 1724-55, 24cm. high. (Christie's London) $12,787 £8,250

A stoneware oviform vase, by Katharine Pleydell-Bouverie, covered in lavender blue glaze, with olive green glaze at the rim and shoulder, impressed *KPB* seal, 22.1cm. high. (Christie's London)$1,663 £990

An Altenburg brown stoneware tankard applied in relief with dots forming the design of a hunter and his dog shooting a stag, first quarter of the 18th century, 20.5cm. high. (Christie's London) $2,152 £1,320

A stoneware bread plate designed by A. W. N. Pugin, moulded decoration of stylised foliage and wheat ears, the rim inscribed *Waste not, want not*, circa 1850, 33.8cm. diam. (Christie's London) $2,033 £1,210

Cobalt decorated stoneware jug, Boston, early 19th century, cobalt decorated at shoulder with three fish, 14½ in. high. (Skinner Inc.) $2,900 £1,779

A stoneware globular vase by Charles Vyse, covered in a lustrous mottled khaki and brown glaze with areas of crimson, incised *CV 1933*, 13cm. high. (Christie's London) $813 £484

TILES

A William De Morgan eight inch tile forming part of the Fan pattern, painted with two stylised flowers. (Phillips London) $815 £500

An early Dutch delft tile painted in blue with an elaborate sailing ship, 13.5cm. (Phillips London) $89 £55

A William De Morgan eight inch tile, hand painted with a large stylised rose in one corner. (Phillips London) $652 £400

A Minton's art pottery eight inch tile, hand painted with the head of a girl, 20.4cm. square. (Phillips London) $228 £140

A fine and important Rotterdam panel by Jan Pieter Aalmis, formed of thirty tiles, painted with an equestrian portrait of Frederick the Great, 78 x 65cm. (Phillips London) $5,053 £3,100

One of a pair of Dutch delft pictures both made up of four tiles, painted in blue with extensive Arctic whaling scenes, 25cm. square. (Phillips London) Two $554 £340

A large Craven & Dunhill tile panel comprising thirty-six six inch tiles, hand painted, with boats at full sail. (Phillips London) $424 £260

A Craven Dunhill & Co. metal mounted four tile jardiniere, each tile decorated with a design by William de Morgan, 21.2cm. high. (Christie's London) $1,111 £682

A William De Morgan eight inch Double Carnation tile, painted with two large stylised blooms and leaves. (Phillips London) $407 £250

264

TILES

A William De Morgan Gillow six inch tile painted with two yellow flowers on sinuous stems with green leaves. (Phillips London) $163 £100

An unusual Gibson Girl tile, printed from a design by the American illustrator Charles Dana Gibson, in underglaze blue, 15 x 14.8cm. (Phillips London) $57 £35

One of a set of three William De Morgan eight inch Chicago pattern tiles, painted in Persian colours. (Phillips London) Three $1,059 £650

A William De Morgan Marlborough Sands End eight inch tile, painted with a large stylised sunflower. (Phillips London) $359 £220

A large mounted panel of delft tiles, the centres alternately plain or painted in polychrome with birds in branches, each 14.5cm. (Phillips London) $293 £180

A Bernard Leach stoneware St Ives four inch tile painted with a weeping willow tree, 10.2cm. square. (Phillips London) $424 £260

Part of a set of twelve William De Morgan Peacock pattern six inch tiles, with stylised birds, flowers and leaves. (Phillips London) Twelve $4,564 £2,800

A rare part set of five Copeland Frog tiles, painted in shades of blue with amusing scenes of frogs variously engaged. (Phillips London) $1,043 £640

One of a pair of Dutch delft pictures made up of six tiles, painted in manganese with a milkmaid and cowhand both with a cow, 39 x 26cm. (Phillips London) Two $619 £380

TILES

Part of a set of twelve Minton Early English History six inch tiles, designed by John Moyr-Smith, painted underglaze in black. (Phillips London) Twelve $309 £190

Part of a set of twenty-two Dutch tin glazed tiles, each one hand painted in colours with an Oriental figure, 13.1cm. square. (Phillips London)   Twenty-two $522 £320

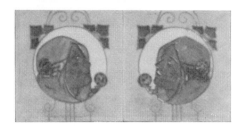

A pair of Art Nouveau tube lined six inch tiles, each one decorated with the head of a girl, 15.3cm. square, moulded England. (Phillips London) $456 £280

A pair of photographic six inch tiles forming a panel, showing the Clifton Suspension Bridge, Bristol, 15.2cm. high. (Phillips London) $261 £160

A Carters Poole Art Deco tile panel, comprising four tiles, block printed with a lady golfer teeing off, 30.2cm. square. (Phillips London) $1,239 £760

A set of four Pilkington six inch tiles from The Labours Series (circa 1902), designed by C. F. A. Voysey. (Phillips London) $717 £440

A Minton & Hollins horizontal tile panel, comprising six eight inch tiles, hand painted in red with putti, urns and scrolling foliage. (Phillips London) $244 £150

Part of a set of twelve Minton Idylls of the King six inch tiles designed by John Moyr-Smith, printed underglaze in two tones of brown. (Phillips London)
Twelve $359 £220

TILES

Part of a set of fourteen Minton Shakespeare series six inch tiles, designed by John Moyr-Smith, printed underglaze in brown against beige. (Phillips London)
Fourteen $359 £220

Part of a set of nine Sherwin & Cotton tiles, the design attributed to C. F. A. Voysey, each one moulded in relief. (Phillips London)
Nine $163 £100

A pair of six inch tiles, possibly made by Pilkington, each decorated in raised outline with a sailing galleon on the high seas. (Phillips London) $326 £200

A set of three Cinderella six inch tiles, depicting the two Ugly Sisters, Cinderella with the slipper and the Prince and Cinderella together. (Phillips London) $106 £65

A set of nine English delft Biblical tiles with barred oxhead corners, each 12.7cm. (Phillips London) $244 £150

A Carters Poole tile panel, comprising four six inch tiles, with a girl and boy, a cockerel, a pig and two sheep. (Phillips London) $685 £420

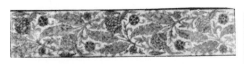

A run of five William De Morgan Merton Abbey eight inch tiles, painted with a stylised Persian pattern, 101.3 x 20.3cm. across. (Phillips London) $652 £400

Four Minton eight inch tiles, designed by John Moyr-Smith from subjects based on Sir Walter Scott's Waverley novels. (Phillips London) $179 £110

TILES

Grueby pottery two tile scenic frieze, Boston, circa 1902, depicting four cows in various states of grazing and repose. (Skinner Inc.)
$6,250 £3,858

A set of five Bird tiles, probably decorated by W. B. Simpson & Sons, each one painted with stylised birds in flight, 15.2cm. square. (Phillips London) $522 £320

A set of three small tiles by George Wooliscroft & Sons, printed marks on reverse, 4½ in. high.
(Phillips) $230   £143

Grueby pottery Polar Bear tile, Boston, rectangular-form with moulded decoration of polar bear, 5⅝ in. x 7in.
(Skinner Inc) $350   £217

One of a pair of W. B. Simpson & Sons decorated tile panels, each painted with medieval huntsmen. (Phillips London)
Two $1,206 £740

One of a set of three good Minton encaustic pictorial eight-inch tiles, moulded marks.
(Phillips) $283   £176

A painted tile, possibly by Arthur Wardle, hand painted, with the portrait of a cat, 28.8 x 14cm., image signed *A W* on face. (Phillips London)
$407 £250

A pair of Minton tile panels, each comprising five tiles and hand painted with a Classical maiden, 91.3 x 20.4cm.
(Phillips London) $734 £450

'Tuari Netana' a Sherwin & Cotton 'portrait' tile by George Cartlidge, modelled as the head and shoulders of the Maori Chief.
(Phillips) $389   £242

VIENNA

A Vienna plate painted in the Oriental style the centre with an exotic bird, incised *N,* circa 1735, 22.5cm. diam. (Christie's London)
$1,524 £935

A Vienna (Dupaquier) two handled double lipped baroque moulded sauce boat painted in the Imari style, circa 1740. (Christie's London)
$2,557 £1,650

A Vienna large circular dish, painted with Amor auf Reisen, signed *A. Becher,* 36cm. (Lawrence Fine Arts)
$1,390 £880

A Vienna figure of Neptune standing scantily clad with a puce cloak tied around his waist, circa 1760, 15.5cm. high. (Christie's London) $306 £198

A pair of Vienna baluster wine-coolers on stepped circular feet with high scroll handles, the broad waists painted in an Imari palette, circa 1770, 23.5cm. high. (Christie's London)
$3896 £2420

A Vienna group after a model by Anton Grassi, depicting a man and woman in 18th century costume, 29cm. high. (Bearne's) $1449 £900

A pair of Vienna putti dressed for the Commedia dell'Arte, in multi-coloured chequered harlequin dress and carrying their slapsticks, circa 1745, 10cm. high. (Christie's London)
$4,433 £2,860

A Vienna-style cylindrical cup, cover and stand, the apple-green ground reserved with an oval panel enclosing a cherub, circa 1880. (Christie's S. Ken) $523 £308

An impressive pair of Vienna style ewers, both colourfully painted with continuous Classical scenes, with high square plinth bases, 57cm. (Phillips London)
$4,186 £2,600

VIENNA

A Vienna figure allegorical of Winter, modelled as a Hungarian nobleman with a black tricorn hat, blue beehive mark, circa 1770, 21cm. high. (Christie's London) $1,614 £990

A 'Vienna' puce ground plate, the centre painted with a scantily draped nymph standing beside a flaming altar, imitation blue beehive mark, circa 1880, 25.5cm. diam. (Christie's London) $796 £495

A Vienna style vase, the claret lustrous ground reserved with a shaped panel of two maidens in a garden, signed *Legles,* 14¾in. high. (Christie's S. Ken) $624 £385

A Vienna documentary biscuit bust of the sculptor Canova modelled by Anton Grassi, beehive mark, impressed *6* and the date letter code *806,* 44cm. high. (Christie's Geneva) $5,628 £3,432

A pair of Vienna vases and covers, decorated with groups of classical figures in oval panels, signed *Cauffmann,* 32cm. (Lawrence Fine Arts) $634 £396

A Vienna figure of a pretzel seller standing beside a tree stump, a wicker basket slung over his left arm, holding a pretzel, circa 1760, 19.5cm. high. (Christie's London) $3,945 £2,420

A Vienna porcelain mug with an oval panel painted with two Classical figures in a landscape after Angelica Kauffman, 13.5cm. high. (Henry Spencer) $275 £180

A Vienna style rectangular porcelain plaque with 'Fruhling' painted by Bauer, with two maidens accompanied by children, with blue beehive mark and inscription, circa 1880, 11 x 8½in. (Christie's S. Ken) $1,016 £660

A 'Vienna' circular dish, painted by Falera with the head and shoulders of a young woman, inscribed *Coquetterie,* imitation blue beehive mark, circa 1900, 34cm. diam. (Christie's London) $850 £528

WEDGWOOD

A Wedgwood fairyland lustre bowk, the interior decorated with the Fairey in a Cage design, 22.3cm. diam.
(Bearne's) $1178 £760

A Wedgwood/Greatbach red-ware teapot and cover, the two main sides moulded in relief with chinoiserie children amidst scrolling foliage, 12cm.
(Phillips London) $2,898 £1,800

A Wedgwood earthenware fluted centre-dish with entwined double serpent handles, painted by Emile Lessore with Youthful Architects studying a Plan, circa 1865, 32cm. wide. (Christie's London)
$1062 £660

Two of four Wedgwood black basalt column candlesticks, carved in gilt with stiff leaves to the tops and spiralling bands of foliage, circa 1900, 11$\frac{1}{2}$in. high.
(Christie's S. Ken) $4944 £3190

A Wedgwood fairyland lustre slender baluster vase and cover, the iridescent black ground printed in gold and coloured with three faires, 1920s, 21.5cm. high. (Christie's London)
$4114 £2420

A pair of early 19th century Wedgwood three colour Jasper baluster vasese and covers with gilt metal pine-cone finials, female mask handles and bases, 11$\frac{1}{2}$in. high.
(Christie's S. Ken) $2618 £1540

A mid-18th century Wedgwood Wheildon type cauliflower moulded coffee pot and cover, 24.5cm. high.
(Spencer's) $2550 £1500

'Sun & Wind', a Wedgwood green and white Jasper plaque designed by Anna Katrina Zinkeisen, 12.5cm. diam. (Phillips) $478 £299

Wedgwood Glazed Caneware Honey Pot, England, early 19th century, moulded to form a beehive, impressed mark, 4in. high.
(Skinner Inc) $225 £148

WEDGWOOD

A Wedgwood/Whieldon lobed hexagonal teapot and cover with scrolling handle, in green with ochre streaks, 12cm. (Phillips London) $2,898 £1,800

A Wedgwood Daventry lustre octagonal bowl decorated in gold with chinoiserie panels of flowers and figures on a lilac ground, 18cm. (Phillips London) $1,449 £900

A Wedgwood bone china oval teapot, cover and stand, moulded with vine leaves and edged in gold, 15cm. (Phillips London) $850 £500

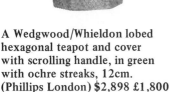

A rare Ralph Wedgwood & Co. creamware ovoid jug, printed in black with the full arms of the Cordwainers Company, 18cm. (Phillips London) $515 £320

A fine Wedgwood basalt figure group of Eros and Euphrosyne modelled by Thomas Woolner, the winged putto seated on her shoulder, 53cm. (Phillips London) $2,720 £1,600

A Wedgwood/Whieldon cauli-flower moulded coffee pot and domed cover, of pear shape, 25.5cm. (Phillips London) $2,415 £1,500

A good Wedgwood Fairyland lustre bowl, decorated with numerous figures on a water-side, printed mark in brown, circa 1920, 8¾in. diam. (Tennants) $1,872 £1,200

A Wedgwood pottery charger designed by Keith Murray, covered in a matt straw yellow glaze, printed facsimile signature *Keith Murray,* and *Wedgwood, Made in England,* 35.5cm. diam. (Christie's London) $850 £506

A Wedgwood creamware punch pot and cover, transfer printed in black with two oval panels of Aurora in chariots representing day and night, 25cm. (Phillips London) $1,700 £1,000

WEDGWOOD

A Wedgwood, Greatbatch red-ware teapot and cover moulded in relief with Chinese ladies and children, 12cm. (Phillips London) $3,740 £2,200

Zodiac Bull, a Wedgwood porcelain bull, designed by Arnold Machin, the cream glazed body with brown painted features, stars and signs of the Zodiac, circa 1945, 40.5cm. long. (Christie's London) $1,016 £605

A Wedgwood & Bentley black basalt teapot and cover of globular shape with a curved collar and reeded handle, 21.5cm. wide. (Phillips London) $2,040 £1,200

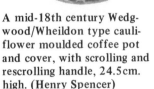

A mid-18th century Wedgwood/Wheildon type cauli-flower moulded coffee pot and cover, with scrolling and rescrolling handle, 24.5cm. high. (Henry Spencer) $2,295 £1,500

A Wedgwood Boat Race cup designed by Eric Ravilious, decorated with three oval coloured panels showing scenes associated with the Boat Race, 25.5cm. high. (Phillips London) $3,672 £2,400

A Wedgwood black basalt vase of bottle shape, the mask terminals in the form of Pan, impressed marks, 9¾in. high. (Christie's S. Ken) $457 £286

A Wedgwood & Bentley black basalt oval portrait medallion of Oldenbarneveld in high relief, circa 1780, 7cm. high. (Christie's London) $283 £176

19th century blue and white Jasperware Stilton cheese dish and cover, possibly Wedgwood. (G. A. Key) $175 £110

Duiker, a Wedgwood earthen-ware animal figure modelled by John Skeaping, covered in a matt crackled white glaze, 8½in. high. (Christie's S. Ken) $263 £153

WEMYSS

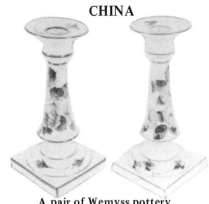

A Wemyss character jug modelled as the Fair Maid of Perth and painted with a floral sprigged yellow dress, 21.5cm. (Phillips London) $612 £380

A pair of Wemyss pottery candlesticks, painted with roses in colours and edged in green, 18cm. high. (Henry Spencer) $489 £320

A Wemyss sauce boat or flower holder modelled as a goose, with green neck, yellow beak, purple and blue breast. (Phillips London) $1,208 £750

WESTERWALD

A Westerwald tankard decorated in blue and aubergine, with a band of scrolling flowers and foliage, 17.5cm. (Phillips London) $322 £200

A Westerwald jug, coloured in aubergine and blue, relief decorated with a maskhead at the neck, 28cm. (Phillips London) $644 £400

A Westerwald tankard of cylindrical shape, the body with two bands of square panels incised and moulded in relief with floral motifs, 19.5cm. (Phillips London) $547 £340

A German Westerwald stoneware baluster jug with horizontally ribbed neck and pewter cover and mount, 17th century, 8in. high. (Christie's S. Ken) $647   £418

A Westerwald stoneware Sternkanne, the oviform body impressed with a starburst enclosing a heart within a circular cartouche with roundels, circa 1700, 30cm. high. (Christie's London) $1,449 £935

A Westerwald buff stoneware jug of large globular shape with cylindrical grooved neck and loop handle, circa 1700, 22cm. high. (Christie's London) $767 £495

WHIELDON

A Whieldon teapot and cover with crabstock handle and spout, 3½in. high (spout and cover restored). (Christie's S. Ken) $303 £187

A pair of creamware Arbour figures of Whieldon type, modelled as a musician playing the fiddle in streaked grey topcoat and yellow waistcoat, his companion in a green splashed crinoline and holding a pug dog on her lap, circa 1750, 15cm. high. (Christie's) $59136 £35200

A 7in. 18th century Whieldon pottery study of a ram on naturalistic base. (Riddetts) $1964 £1220

WOOD

A well modelled and brightly glazed Enoch Wood bust of Wesley, the head and hair in white, 32cm. (Phillips London) $1,870 £1,100

A pair of rare Ralph Wood models of a stag and a doe both at lodge, on green glazed bases, 16cm. and 17cm. (Phillips London)$5,440 £3,200

A documentary self portrait bust by Enoch Wood, in white smear glazed stoneware, cast in 1899 by Macintyre & Co., 56cm. high. (Phillips London) $293 £180

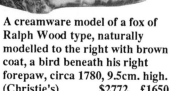

A Ralph Wood white pearlware group of Roman Charity, the veiled woman suckling a child at her breast, circa 1790, 20cm. high. (Christie's) $1008 £600

A creamware model of a fox of Ralph Wood type, naturally modelled to the right with brown coat, a bird beneath his right forepaw, circa 1780, 9.5cm. high. (Christie's) $2772 £1650

A pair of creamware figures of Ralph Wood type, each modelled as a youth in translucent blue, yellow and manganese clothes, circa 1780, 12.5cm. and 12cm. high. (Christie's) $702 £418

WORCESTER

Early 19th century porcelain comport by Grainger of Worcester, brightly painted with blue Japanese pattern, 10in. (G. A. Key) $246 £155

A Worcester (Flight) Royal armorial sauce tureen and cover from the service made to the order of the Duke of Clarence, circa 1789, 17.5cm. wide. (Christie's London) $1,239 £770

A Worcester vase, by Flight Barr & Barr, painted in ancient Greek style with figures of Cadmus and Actaeon in flesh colour. (Lawrence Fine Arts) $1,043 £660

A good Worcester transfer printed mug, crisply printed in black with the Whitton Anglers, circa 1765, 5¾in. high. (Tennants) $1,248 £800

A pair of Royal Worcester figures of lady musicians, the ivory porcelain painted in green peach and gilt, 1899, 32cm. (Osmond Tricks) $913 £560

A Royal Worcester green ground oviform vase, painted by Jas Stinton with a continuous frieze of pheasants in a woodland and a misty river landscape, date code for 1897, 33cm. high. (Christie's London) $3,010 £1,870

A late 19th century Royal Worcester porcelain figure of a Yankee resting against a post, date letter for 1881, 18cm. high. (Henry Spencer) $245 £160

A Chamberlain's Worcester yellow ground reticulated two handled cup and saucer pierced with gilt hexagons, script marks, circa 1830. (Christie's London) $1,063 £660

One of a pair of Grainger Worcester vases, painted by John Stinton, with views of Melrose Abbey and Stratford on Avon, 26.5cm. (Lawrence Fine Arts) Two $1,147 £726

WORCESTER

A rare Worcester teapot and cover, painted in a combination of famille rose and famille verte with a Chinese mother and child, 14cm. (Phillips London) $1,852 £1,150

A Worcester oblong tray, by Flight Barr & Barr, painted with a group of blackcurrants, cherries and gooseberries arranged on a cabbage leaf, 13cm. (Lawrence Fine Arts) $869 £550

A Grainger's Worcester reticulated porcelain ewer, the whole pierced with scrolling foliage, with pink and gilt jewelled enamelled borders, 30cm. high. (Henry Spencer) $857 £560

A Royal Worcester two handled slender oviform vase, the sides painted by Sedgley, date code for 1914, 36.5cm. high. (Christie's London) $1,062 £660

A Worcester flared cylindrical mug with strap handle, painted in a typical famille rose palette with The Beckoning Chinaman Pattern, circa 1758, 11.5cm. high. (Christie's London) $1,062 £660

A Royal Worcester slender oviform ewer, painted by C. Baldwyn with swans in flight among brown reeds and richly gilt foliage, date code for 1902, 35cm. high. (Christie's London) $6,729 £4,180

A Worcester porcelain two handled pot pourri vase and cover, painted with a horizontal band of landscape within moulded bands of beads, 5½in. high. (Christie's S. Ken) $160 £99

A Chamberlain's Worcester watch stand modelled as Apollo holding his lyre and draped in a gilt flowered robe, circa 1795, 23cm. high. (Christie's London) $744 £462

A Worcester yellow ground armorial baluster mug with grooved loop handle, circa 1770, 12cm. high. (Christie's London) $13,282 £8,250

WORCESTER

A Royal Worcester shallow vase with twin leaf moulded handles the spirally moulded body painted by Jarman, date code for circa 1911, 12in. across. (Christie's S. Ken)
$762 £495

A very fine Grainger Lee and Co wall plaque, painted with a view of Worcester from the North West, 27.5cm., marked *Grainger Lee and Co. Worcester.* (Phillips London)
$3,570 £2,100

A rare Worcester teapot and cover of early fluted silver shape, painted in blue with the Prunus Root pattern, 12.5cm. (Phillips London)
$5,610 £3,300

A Worcester hunting jug, painted in the manner of John Wood, with two dogs stalking a capercaillie, a horseman approaching, 18.7cm. (Phillips London) $1,304 £800

One of a pair of Royal Worcester tapering vases with tall slender tapering necks and gilt ring and scroll handles, date code for circa 1892, 11½in. high. (Christie's S. Ken)
Two $932 £605

A large Worcester porter mug, printed in blue with a rare print of The Temple Bells, circa 1780, 15cm. (Phillips London) $1,275 £750

A Royal Worcester pepper pot modelled as an owl perched on a barrel, 10cm., date code for 1908. (Phillips London)
$212 £130

A pair of Worcester Hogarth comports modelled as a girl and boy leaning on tree trunks, in the style of Kate Greenaway, 21cm., date codes for 1886. (Phillips London) $1,275 £750

A Worcester blue and white baluster flaring vase painted with two tall Chinese maidens, circa 1765, 8in. high. (Christie's S. Ken) $474 £308

WORCESTER

A Royal Worcester chamber candlestick modelled as a mouse nibbling at the sconce, 15cm., date code for 1912. (Phillips London) $424 £260

A Worcester vase, painted with two Highland cattle on a misty mountainside, signed *H. Stinton,* 16.5cm., date code for 1911. (Phillips London) $1,105 £650

A Worcester leaf shaped dish moulded in the form of two overlapping cabbage leaves with crossed stalk handle, circa 1765, 25.5cm. (Phillips London) $1,870 £1,100

A fine early Worcester coffee cup of quatrelobed shape, painted in stronger than usual colours with a Long Eliza figure, circa 1752-53, 7cm. (Phillips London) $5,950 £3,500

A First Period Worcester junket dish, painted with three classical vases adorned with flower branches, 23cm., cracked. (Lawrence Fine Arts) $405 £253

A Kerr & Binns vase in Limoges enamel style, by Thomas Bott Snr., signed and dated 1862, 24cm., shield mark and signature. (Phillips London) $424 £260

A pair of Royal Worcester figures of Joy and Sorrow modelled by James Hadley, modelled as maidens standing on waisted circular bases, date code for circa 1933, 9½in. high. (Christie's S. Ken) $711 £462

A small Worcester vase, painted with festoons of pink and yellow roses, signed *Chair,* below the fine arabesque piercing by George Owen, 10.8cm. (Phillips London) $3,400 £2,000

A pair of Kerr and Binns reticulated perfume bottles and stoppers with jewelled panels, 16cm., 1862. (Phillips London) $1,222 £750

279

BRACKET CLOCKS

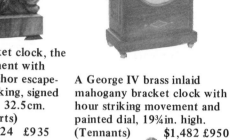

A George III mahogany bracket clock, the arched silvered dial signed Kemp, Yoxford and with strike/silent subsidiary in the arch, 1ft. 9¼in. high.
(Phillips) $3300   £2000

A rosewood bracket clock, the twin fusee movement with domed plates, anchor escapement and bell striking, signed *Wilson, Stamford,* 32.5cm.
(Lawrence Fine Arts)
          $1,524   £935

A George IV brass inlaid mahogany bracket clock with hour striking movement and painted dial, 19¾in. high.
(Tennants) $1,482 £950

Dutch Japanned Bracket Clock, c. 1750, red laquered case, enamelled dial and calender dial inscribed Ellicot London, 24in. high.
(Skinner Inc) $1800 £1168

A 19th century mahogany bracket clock, the twin fusee movement with anchor escapement, 43cm. (Phillips London)
          $1,010 £620

A substantial late 19th century walnut quarter chiming bracket clock, signed *John Carter,* the triple fusee movement chiming on eight bells, 75cm. high.
(Phillips London)$1,711 £1,050

A Georgian mahogany bracket clock, the bell top case surmounted by a carrying handle, signed Thomas Gardner London, the twin fusée movement with verge escapement, 1ft. 8½in. high.
(Phillips) $1650   £1000

An 18th century ebonised musical and repeating bracket clock, made for the Turkish market, the case of rectangular form with a bell top, signed *Edward Pister, London,* the three train movement with verge escapement, 22½in.
(Phillips Sevenoaks)
          $5,780 £3,400

An 18th century bracket clock, the rectangular mahogany case formerly ebonised with a bell top, signed *John Miller, London,* 21in. high. (Phillips Sevenoaks) $2,380 £1,400

BRACKET CLOCKS

A Georgian mahogany bracket clock, signed Baker London, the twin fusée movement with verge escapement, signed on the backplate, 1ft. 4½in. high. (Phillips) $5610   £3400

A George III mahogany musical bracket timepiece, the arched case surmounted by a spire and finial, signed M. Miller London, the twin fusee movement with verge escapement, 1ft. 7¾in. high. (Phillips) $3630 £2200

A 19th century mahogany and brass inlaid bracket clock, signed *Wand & Hills, Rochester,* the twin fusee movement with anchor escapement, 1ft. 11in. high. (Phillips London) $815 £500

A brass inlaid mahogany bracket clock, the two train fusee movement with shaped plates, signed Edward Newman, London, 17½in. (Lawrence Fine Art) $1525   £924

A George III scarlet japanned musical bracket clock for the Turkish market by Wm. Kipling London, the bekk-top case decorated overall with gilt chinoiseries, 25in. high (Christie's London) $44902   £28600

A Georgian ebonised and brass mounted quarter chiming musical bracket clock, signed De Lasall, the triple fusee movement converted to anchor escapement, 1ft. 7¾in. high. (Phillips) $3795   £2300

An 18th century ebonised quarter chiming bracket clock, signed *Chas Bosley,* chiming on six bells, 46cm. high. (Phillips London) $4,075 £2,500

An ebony veneered quarter repeating bracket clock, the five pillar chain fusee movement with verge escapement, signed *Sub:i Boverick, London,* 46.5cm. (Lawrence Fine Arts) $11,117 £6,820

A Regency mahogany and brass mounted bracket clock, the case with stepped canted top and cone finial, flanked by lion mask ring handles, 1ft. 7in. high. (Phillips) $1328   £805

CARRIAGE CLOCKS

A French brass carriage clock, the repeating movement with lever escapement, contained in a corniche case, 18cm. (Lawrence Fine Arts)
$466 £286

A French brass carriage timepiece, the movement with cylinder escapement and stamped *R & Co. (Richard)*, 16cm. (Lawrence Fine Arts)
$394 £242

A petite sonnerie and alarm carriage clock in gorge case by Drocourt, the white enamel dial with Roman numerals and Arabic five-minute divisions, 4³/₄ in. high.
(Christie's S. Ken.) $1496 £880

A French brass carriage clock, the enamel dial with a painted scene of a watermill and signed for Henry Atkinson & Wells Paris, 7¹/₂ in. high.
(Phillips) $1072 £650

A 19th century French gilt brass and champleve enamel carriage timepiece and barometer, centred by a thermometer, 15cm. high. (Phillips London) $1,222 £750

A 19th century French gilt brass carriage clock, the movement with replaced lever platform, 18.5cm. high. (Phillips London) $815 £500

A 19th century French gilt brass quarter striking carriage clock, the lever movement striking on gongs, with alarm and push repeat, signed Barraud and Lund, in a gorge case, 5¹/₂ in. high.
(Phillips) $1155 £700

A miniature French 19th century brass and enamel carriage timepiece, bearing the mark of Auguste Margaine, in an anglaise case, 10cm. high. (Phillips London) $1,369 £840

A 19th century brass and porcelain panelled carriage clock, signed for Marshall & Sons London, the case decorated with four porcelain panels, 6³/₄ in. high.
(Phillips) $2970 £1800

CARRIAGE CLOCKS

A French silver mounted miniature tortoiseshell carriage timepiece, inscribed *Edwards & Sons, 161 Regent St., W.,* hallmark for 1904. (Lawrence Fine Arts) $968 £594

A French miniature brass carriage timepiece, the movement with later lever escapement, 10.7cm. (Lawrence Fine Arts) $323 £198

An attractive French repeating carriage clock, the rectangular gilt dial richly engraved with acanthus leaves, 20.4cm. high. (Henry Spencer) $1,123 £720

A 19th century French gilt brass carriage clock, the lever movement striking on a gong with alarm and push repeat, 8in. high.
(Phillips) $891 £540

A 19th century bronze and gilt brass carriage timepiece, the circular movement with going barrel and lever platform escapement, 13.5cm. high. (Phillips London) $880 £540

A 19th century French gilt brass carriage clock, the lever movement striking on a bell and signed on the backplate Ch. Frodsham Paris, 6in. high.
(Phillips) $1237 £750

A 19th century French brass carriage clock, with replaced platform escapement striking on a gong and fitted with Le Roy's patent bottom wind, 13.5cm. high. (Phillips London) $782 £480

A gilt brass porcelain mounted striking giant carriage clock, the porcelain dial and sides painted with genre scenes of carousing cavaliers, signed H. Desprez, 8¹/₂in. high. (Christie's London) $7771 £4950

A 19th century French brass carriage clock, the lever movement striking on a gong with alarm and push repeat, 8in. high.
(Phillips) $891 £540

CLOCK SETS

A French porcelain clock garniture by Jacob Petit, the rococo moulded clock painted with panels of flowers on a gold decorated green ground, 32cm high.
(Bearne's) $1320   £820

A Sitzendorf clock case of circular form surmounted by a cherub and flanked by two nymphs kneeling to the rectangular pierced base, 16½in. high; and a pair of Sitzendorf candelabra, 19½in. high. (Christie's S. Ken) $1,683 £1,100

19th century brass and blue and white china clock set in the Renaissance manner, the side urns of baluster form with figure designs.
(G.A.Key) $731 £460

Victorian brass clock garniture, the clock of rococo form with applied and embossed C-scroll and foliate decoration, having a French striking movement. (G. A. Key) $336 £200

A large Art Deco marble, onyx and bronze clock garniture, the top of the clock's case mounted with a charioteer and horses, and mounted on a stepped base, 62.5cm. high, 44.1cm. across, and a pair of candelabra en suite. (Phillips London) $1,630 £1,000

A French porcelain mounted gilt spelter clock garniture, the movement with Brocot suspension, outside locking plate and bell striking. (Lawrence Fine Arts) $1,614 £990

CLOCK SETS

A pink marble and ormolu clock garniture, the clock with enamel dial inscribed *Made in France for Jas Crighton & Co., Edinburgh,* the clock 8¾in. high. (Christie's London)
$885 £550

A small French champleve enamel clock garniture, the movement with Brocot suspension and gong striking, the gilt dial with Arabic numerals, 28cm. (Lawrence Fine Arts)
$1,793 £1,100

A 19th century French enamel clock, surmounted by a foliate finial, 35cm. high, together with the matching pair of candlesticks, each sconce held aloft by a putto. (Phillips London) $2,282 £1,400

A French ormolu and bronze matched clock garniture comprising a pair of four light candelabra and a mantel clock in the form of a chariot driven by a putto, mid-19th century, the candelabra 24in. high. (Christie's London)
$8,855 £5,500

LANTERN CLOCKS

A brass lantern clock with anchor escapement, the dial surmounted by a dolphin fret and a chapter ring inscribed *Danl. Hoskins,* 15½in. (Phillips Sevenoaks) $884 £520

A miniature winged brass lantern clock with verge escapement and pendulum bob in the form of an anchor, 9½in. (Phillips Sevenoaks) $2,210 £1,300

A brass lantern clock of standard form with verge and balance escapement, outside countwheel, strike on bell above the cast dolphin frets, 14¼in. high. (Christie's London) $1123 £715

A small lantern/alarum timepiece, the movement with verge escapement and bob pendulum, signed *Kefford, Royston,* 25cm. (Lawrence Fine Arts) $3,586 £2,200

An early lantern clock, yagura-dokei, the brown-lacquered brass case etched with a hemp-leaf pattern, on four stump feet, unsigned, circa 1700, 45cm. high. (Christie's) $8266 £4950

An Eureka Clock Company electric timepiece, the circular brass chapter ring with black Roman numerals, 41cm. high. (Henry Spencer) $905 £580

A Charles II brass lantern clock of standard form, the florally engraved dial signed Henry Burges Fecit, 14½in. high. (Christie's London) $2673 £1650

A George III brass lantern alarm timepiece, signed Jno Silke Elmsted, the movement with anchor escapement, 8½in. high. (Phillips) $2062 £1250

A silver and giltmetal miniature lantern clock of standard form, the dial engraved with scrolling foliage bearing inscription Fromanteel, 6in. high. (Christie's London) $10692 £6600

LANTERN CLOCKS

A brass lantern clock, the dial with brass chapter and engraved centre signed Tho Muddle, Rotherfield, 1ft. 3¹/₂in. high. (Phillips) $1023 £620

A late Stuart brass striking winged lantern clock of standard form, with verge escapement and arrowhead pendulum, 15¹/₄in. high.(Christie's London) $2936 £1870

A Charles II brass striking lantern clock of standard form previously with anchor escapement now with verge and balance, signed Grigoris Itersprot ner Aldersgate, 16in. high.
(Christie's) $1947 £1100

Lantern clock, late 17th century, by Nicholas Coxeter at the Three Chaires in Lothbury, London, 15in. high.
(Brian Loomes) $4125 £2500

An early 18th century brass lantern clock of typical form, the engraved centrefield inscribed Humphrey Marsh, Highworth, fecti, number 105, with a single steel hand, 16in. high. (Christie's S. Ken.) $2244 £1320

A Rhennish chamber clock with iron posted frame to trains of brass wheels, vertical verge and balance escapement, countwheel strike/alarm on bell above, 17th-18th century, 15¹/₂in. high.
(Christie's) $7788 £4400

An unusual silver lantern timepiece, perhaps German, the movement with verge escapement and verge alarm, the dial plate engraved with tulips, 9in. high. (Phillips Sevenoaks)
$4,420 £2,600

Lantern clock, late 17th century, by James Delaunce of Frome, converted later to twin fusee eight-day key-wound movement, 15in. high
(Brian Loomes) $1980 £1200

A brass lantern clock of typical form, the rectangular case with turned pillars at the corners, 15¹/₂in. high.
(Christie's S. Ken.) $1089 £660

LONGCASE CLOCKS

A mahogany long case clock, the 12in. silvered dial with engraved centre, subsidiary seconds and date aperture, signed in the arch *John Croft, Plymouth Dock,* 7ft.1in. (Lawrence Fine Arts)
$1,972 £1,210

A fine and important Federal inlaid mahogany long case clock, signed by Simon Willard, Roxbury, Massachusetts, circa 1805, 105¾in. high. (Christie's New York)
$110,000 £69,182

A Georgian mahogany longcase clock, signed *Robt. Hynam London* the twin train movement with anchor escapement 2.40m. high. (Phillips London)
$4,238 £2,600

A late 18th century oak longcase clock, the hood with swan neck pediment, plaque to the centre inscribed *Vincent Menil, Amsterdam,* the eight day movement with anchor escapement, 7ft.8in. high. (Phillips Sevenoaks) $5,780 £3,400

A Chippendale carved mahogany long case clock, by John Wood, Philadelphia, circa 1770, the hood with moulded swan neck pediment, 96in. high, 17¼in. wide, 9½in. deep. (Christie's New York) $18,700 £11,761

An inlaid mahogany eight day quarter chiming longcase clock, the brass dial with a silvered Tempus Fugit boss, 18th century in part, 98in. high. (Tennants)
$5,148 £3,300

A late 18th century mahogany longcase clock, signed *Wyke & Green,* twin train movement with anchor escapement, 2.45m. high. (Phillips London)
$6,194 £3,800

A George III mahogany longcase regulator, signed *Richd Pendleton Pentonville,* the later flat steel pendulum with mercury bob, 1.81m. high. (Phillips London)
$14,996 £9,200

LONGCASE CLOCKS

A rare Federal inlaid cherrywood long case clock, dial signed *Caleb Davis,* Woodstock, Virginia, circa 1804, 97in. high. (Christie's New York)
$8,250 £5,188

A mahogany long case clock, the eight day movement rack striking, signed *Hewitt, Marlbro,* the arch with painted moon phase, 7ft.7in. (Lawrence Fine Arts)
$8,248 £5,060

A George III mahogany longcase clock, signed *J. Winterbourn,* the five pillared movement with anchor escapement, 2.40cm. (Phillips London)
$4,890 £3,000

An oak and mahogany long case clock, the eight day movement rack striking, signed on the chapter ring *W. G. Hyde,* 7ft.9in. (Lawrence Fine Arts)
$1,399 £858

A late Georgian mahogany longcase clock, signed *Saml. Whichcote London* and with strike silent in the arch, 2.56m. (Phillips London)
$2,608 £1,600

An Edwardian walnut and panel marquetry miniature longcase clock, signed *John Morgan London,* 1.59m. high. (Phillips London)
$4,238 £2,600

A late 17th century walnut and panel marquetry month going longcase clock, signed *Jno Pleydell,* with anchor escapement, 2.01m. high. (Phillips London)
$16,300 £10,000

Late Federal mahogany and mahogany veneer long case clock, William Brenneiser, Lancaster County, Pennsylvania, 1780-1830, 99½in. high. (Skinner Inc.)
$2,600 £1,677

LONGCASE CLOCKS

American mahogany long case chiming clock, 20th century, swan neck pediment above a break arch glazed door, 97in. high. (Robt. W. Skinner Inc.) $1,600 £976

John Warrone, Kirby Moorside, a good George III oak and mahogany longcase clock of slender proportions, 96in. high.
(Phillips) $2640 £1600

Fine putty painted long case clock, Silas Hoadley, Plymouth, Connecticut, circa 1830, the case painted in tones of red orange and mustard on ivory, 85in. high. (Skinner Inc.) $9,000 £5,325

Thos. Bembow, Newport, a late 18th century oak and mahogany longcase clock, the trunk with quarter reeded brass capped pillasters, 94in. high.
(Phillips) $1980 £1200

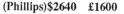

A mahogany long case clock, the eight day movement rack striking, signed Saml. Baines, Kensington. (Lawrence Fine Art) $15427 £9350

A mahogany and boxwood strung longcase clock with flat moulded pediment, signed J. Charlton, Durham, 83in. high. (Christie's S. Ken.) $1309 £770

An oak long case clock, the eight day movement with inside count wheel, signed on the chapter ring Josiah Stringer, 7ft. 4in. (Lawrence Fine Art) $4174 £2530

Gustav Stickley tall case clock, c. 1902, with copper numerals within tall slightly flared case, 70³/₄in. high (Skinner Inc) $7500 £4658

LONGCASE CLOCKS

A Georgian mahogany Irish longcase clock, signed *Jam. Lahee, Wexford*, 2.33m. high. (Phillips London) $1,630 £1,000

W.B. Cornforth Macclesfield, a good early 19th century mahogany longcase clock, 93in. high. (Phillips) $2145 £1300

A William and Mary walnut and marquetry longcase clock, the 12in. sq. dial signed Jn Gavell, London on the silvered chapter ring, 7ft. high. (Christie's London) $8635 £5500

Federal mahogany and bird's-eye maple long case clock, New Hampshire, circa 1800, 86in. high. (Skinner Inc.) $1,900 £1,226

An 18th century quarter chiming mahogany longcase clock, signed Richard Style London, the later four pillar movement chiming the quarters, 8ft. 3¼in. high. (Phillips) $3795 £2300

An unusual Art Deco ebonised and chromium plated cocktail cabinet, fashioned as a longcase clock, having a 'Temco' electric timepiece and a 'Rola Company' wireless at the top, 170cm. high. (Phillips) $2240 £1400

An Edwardian satinwood and painted miniature longcase clock, the pagoda topped hood flanked by turned columns, 5ft. high. (Phillips) $6072 £3680

An early 20th century burr walnut quarter-chiming grandmother clock, the arch moulded top above plain trunk, 69in. high. (Christie's S. Ken.) $1870 £1100

MANTEL CLOCKS

Louis XVI style marble and ormolu mantel clock, France, 19th century, lyre form frame on stepped oval base (key missing), 48cm. high. (Skinner Inc.) **$1,900 £1,226**

A Louis XVI ormolu and white marble clock, the glazed enamel dial signed *Guydamour a Paris*, with drum shaped case flanked by Venus and Cupid, 18½in. high. (Christie's London) **$5,214 £3,300**

A giltmetal mounted mantel clock with glazed enamel dial set within a Japanese porcelain case supported by an elephant, 19th century, 9¼in. high. (Christie's London) **$3,128 £1,980**

L. & J. G. Stickley mantel clock, Fayetteville, New York, circa 1910, designed by Peter Heinrich Hansen, signed with Handcraft decal, 22in. high. (Skinner Inc.) **$7,500 £4,630**

An Arts and Crafts silvered metal mantel clock, the embossed circular dial with Arabic chapters, with stud decoration, 14½in. high. (Christie's S. Ken) **$146 £94**

French mahogany hall clock with four columns on a rectangular base, the enamel face in a palmetto surround, circa 1830, 44cm. high. (Kunsthaus am Museum) **$1,242 £714**

Seth Thomas brass mantel clock, 20th century, with convex front and conforming glazed sides, mercury pendulum and key, 11in. high. (Skinner Inc.) **$275 £169**

French ormolu and gilt metal mantel clock, surmounted by an urn, the clock with attendant Cupid figures either side. (G. A. Key) **$504 £300**

A highly elaborate walnut fretwork architectural clock by Japy Freres & Cie, with visible Brocot escapement, 37½in. high. (Tennants) **$1,248 £800**

MANTEL CLOCKS

A good 18th century ormolu mounted ebony table clock, made for the Turkish market, the case of typical domed form, rococo scroll feet, engraved *Geo. Prior London,* 20in. high. (Phillips Sevenoaks)
$10,540 £6,200

Moineaux, a Lalique frosted glass clock of domed outline, the central dial enclosed by nestling sparrows. (Phillips London) $1,630 £1,000

Bronzed spelter mantel clock, the striking French movement by Badier, installed in a stump design with a Hercules type man attendant. (G. A. Key)
$636 £400

Cinq Hirondelles, a Lalique glass timepiece, moulded with five swallows in flight amid branches of blossom, 15cm. high. (Phillips London)
$2,608   £1,600

Edwardian mahogany cased mantel clock with Art Nouveau shell inlay and striking movement behind an enamel dial. (G. A. Key) $246 £155

A French Art Deco Van Cleef & Arpels small mantel time-piece, the lapis lazuli body with diamond chip surround and diamond set hands, 4in. high. (Tennants)
$31,200 £20,000

A Liberty & Co. Tudric pewter timepiece designed by Archibald Knox, embellished in relief with stylised plant forms, two buds set with blue enamel, 14cm. high. (Phillips London)
$4,238 £2,600

French bronze mantel clock, late 19th century, time and strike movement striking the half hour impressed *Raingo Freres, Paris,* (finish rubbed) 21in. high. (Skinner Inc.)
$1,000 £645

A fine decorated mahogany chain and fusee movement mantel clock, the dial in-scribed *L.N.E.R.,* 50cm. high. (Onslow's) $852 £510

MANTEL CLOCKS

An ormolu and dark blue ground porcelain mantel clock, the shaped dial centred with a maritime scene above a cartouche painted with a harbour scene, 17in. high. (Christie's London) $1,328 £825

A French blue-john and ormolu mantel clock, the case in the form of an urn flanked by rams' head masks, 55cm. high. (Phillips London) $22,950 £15,000

An ormolu and dark blue ground Sevres pattern porcelain mantel clock, the circular dial with a dark blue border enclosing putti and trophies, late 19th century, 21¼in. high. (Christie's London) $3,896 £2,420

A Liberty & Co. oak and enamel mantel clock designed by Archibald Knox, the circular dial with a red scrolling design on a mottled blue and green ground, 29.3cm. high. (Christie's London) $2,152 £1,320

A French gilt and patinated metal mantel clock in the form of the Eiffel Tower, backplate stamped R & C for Ricard & Co., 25in. high. (Christie's London) $3,365 £2,090

Classical Revival gilt gesso mantle timepiece, probably Atkins Clock Company, Connecticut, circa 1840, 18½in. high. (Skinner Inc.) $1,300 £798

A rare 19th century black marble mantel chronometer timepiece, signed *Arnold London,* the movement of small size, 41cm. high. (Phillips London) $4,890 £3,000

An Arts and Crafts copper and brass mantel clock, the pagoda style top with strapwork embellishment, 42cm. high. (Phillips London) $796 £520

A French rosewood and marquetry mantel clock in the Turkish market manner, inscribed *Meyer, 6 Rue de Grenelle, Ste. Honore,* 46.5cm. (Lawrence Fine Arts) $861 £528

MANTEL CLOCKS

A French ormolu mantel clock, the circular glazed enamel dial signed *Lerolle Freres a Paris,* flanked by scrolls with bacchic putti, 31in. high. (Christie's London) $3,542 £2,200

A small gilt brass mantel clock, the French carriage clock type movement with lever escapement and gong striking, 18cm. (Lawrence Fine Arts) $287 £176

An ormolu and dark blue ground Sevres pattern porcelain mantel clock, signed *Lister & Sons S F 20 Paris,* late 19th century, 20in. high. (Christie's London) $3,542 £2,200

An 18th century French ormolu and white marble mantel clock, the circular enamel dial signed *Le Masurier a Paris,* 35cm. high. (Phillips London) $733 £450

A French gilt and silvered bronze gothic cathedral clock, the movement with silk suspension, signed *Vieyres,* 52cm. (Lawrence Fine Arts) $1,434 £880

A brass electric mantel timepiece by Eureka, the movement with signed enamel dial and substantial compensated balance, 30cm. high. (Phillips London) $1,010 £620

A French ormolu mantel clock in the form of the front facade of Notre Dame Cathedral, 22in. high. (Christie's London) $5,313 £3,300

A miniature 19th century French ormolu mantel clock, with enamel dial signed *L. Leroy & Cie Paris,* 11.5cm. high. (Phillips London) $1,010 £620

A 19th century French red tortoiseshell and ormolu mounted mantel clock, signed *Balthazar a Paris,* 33cm. high. (Phillips London) $978 £600

MANTEL CLOCKS

A French black marble perpetual calendar mantel clock, the movement beel striking, the two piece white enamel dial with roman numerals, dated 1884, 22¹/₂in. high. (Lawrence Fine Art) $1779 £1078

A French Art Deco gilt bronze timepiece, the circular dial with gilded hands, 26.5cm. high, the case marked *G. Dunaime.* (Phillips London) $1,875 £1,150

Rare Sinclaire cut glass mantel clock, with vintage motif and stepped platform base with ribbing and diamonds, housing, 11¹/₂in. high. (Skinner Inc.) $3700 £2257

A French white marble and ormolu mounted mantel clock in drum-shaped case surmounted by a stylisd urn finial, 18¹/₂in. high. (Christie's S. Ken.) $1215 £715

A 19th century rosewood mantel timepiece, the square painted dial signed Webster & Son London, the fusée movement with anchor escapement and passing strike, 23cm. high. (Phillips) $1485 £900

Louis Philippe Ebonized Mantle Clock, mid 19th century, ormolu framed enamel dial, raised on spiral turned supports, striking the half-hour, case 26in. high. (Skinner Inc) $700 £454

A Lalique opalescent table clock, catalogued 'Inseparables', moulded 'R. Lalique', 11cm. high. (Bearne's) $1255 £780

A Ginori pottery clockcase, moulded as a two-handled pilgrim flask with mask-moulded neck, 16in. high. (Christie's S. Ken.) $200 £121

An Aesthetic movement Elkington & Co. black marble mantel clock, with porcelain panels painted with stylised daisies, inscribed *Elkington & Co.,* 31.8cm. high. (Christie's London) $1,848 £1,100

MANTEL CLOCKS

An Art Deco marble and enamel timepiece, the corners set with cloisonne enamel panels decorated in black, brown, yellow, beige and white, 26.2cm. high. (Phillips) $416 £260

A Louis Philippe ormolu and baccaret portico mantel clock, the enamel dial signed *Hry Marc a Paris,* with foliate bezel drum shaped case, 16¾in. high. (Christie's London)

$3,302 £2,090

A French 19th century white marble and ormolu mounted mantel clock of Louis XVI design, signed Crosnier à Paris, 20¼in. high. (Christie's S. Ken.) $1589 £935

A Liberty & Co. 'Cymric' silver and enamelled timepiece, embellished with a tree motif against a ground of coloured enamels, Birmingham marks for 1903, 11.5cm. high. (Phillips) $8320 £5200

An ormolu and bronze table clock of Louis XVI design, the terrestrial globe case supported by three putti on shaped base edged with scrolls, 30in. high. (Christie's London)

$5,562 £3,520

A 19th century French ormolu mantel clock, the case surmounted by a twin-handled urn with floral swags, flanked by two fluted Doric columns, 12½in. high. (Phillips) $1897 £1150

A Germanic early giltmetal timepiece, the case surmounted by a floral pierced and chased galleried dome surmounted by an urn finial, case and frame basically c. 1650, movement 18th century, 6¼in. high. (Christie's London)

$4277 £2640

A French 19th century ormolu and bronze mantel clock formed as a classical maiden, standing and leaning pensively on a classical urn, 22½in. high. (Christie's S. Ken.)$1776 £1045

Federal mahogany and gilt-wood banjo timepiece, probably Boston, circa 1820, with original painted eglomise tables, 32in. high. (Skinner Inc.)

$2,200 £1,302

MANTEL CLOCKS

A 19th century French red tortoiseshell and cut brass inlaid mantel clock, signed for Payne & Co., London, 1ft. 1in. high.
(Phillips) $1320 £800

A 19th Century bronze and ormolu mantel clock, the case surmounted by the figure of Venus with winged Cupid in a cage, 2ft. 12in. high.
(Phillips) $4620 £2800

A 19th century French ormolu and white marble mantel clock, the movement contained within a bronzed sphere, 1ft. 5in. high.
(Phillips) $1617 £980

An early 19th century Austrian quarter chiming Pendule d'Officer, the gilt dial with machined centre, 6½in. high.
(Phillips) $1485 £900

A 19th century French ormolu and white marble mantel clock, the circular case with a winged cherub to the side, 12in. high.
(Phillips) $2062 £1250

A 19th century Austrian silver and enamel mantel timepiece, the movement set within a Chinese pale celadon Bi disc, 6½in. high.
(Phillips) $1287 £780

A 19th century French ormolu and porcelain mounted mantel clock, the case surmounted by an urn on a shaped base, 16in. high.
(Phillips) $1567 £950

An Empire ormolu mantel clock, first quarter 19th century, signed LeRoy h'r, Palais Royal, 15¾in. high.
(Christie's) $4950 £3018

A French gilt bronze and bronze Elephant mantel clock, the movement with Brocot suspension, 22½in. high.
(Lawrence Fine Art)
 $2904 £1760

MANTEL CLOCKS

A French green tortoiseshell and boulle mantel clock in waisted case surmounted by a figure of a Cherub, 17in. high.
(Christie's S. Ken.) $935   £550

A 19th century French ormolu mantel clock, ther spherical blue painted case supported on the outstretched wings of an eagle, 1ft. 2in. high.
(Phillips) $1897   £1150

A French Ormolu mantel clock, the two train movement with silk suspension, outside locking plate and bell striking, 20³/₄ in. high.
(Lawrence Fine Art)
                          $1179   £715

A 19th century French green onyx, gilt brass and enamel mantel clock, 10in. high.
(Phillips) $594   £360

A 19th century ormolu and porcelain mantel timepiece, with a stylised emu mounted in front, the case made by Samson, 10¹/₄ in. high.
(Phillips) $2640   £1600

A Scottish Arts and Crafts ebony and silver timepiece with rectangular case in dark wood with flat metal top, signed 'J. H. McNair', 23.8cm. high.
(Phillips) $12800   £8000

A 19th century French ormolu mantel clock, the case with a figure of a dancing female to the side holding a harp, 12¹/₂ in. high.
(Phillips) $858   £520

A German 'Secessionist' plated timepiece, the circular dial with gilded hands mounted in a face with pointed and pierced top, 44.5cm. high.
(Phillips) $1122   £680

An Empire ormolu and patinated bronze figural large mantel clock, first quarter 19th century, signed LeRoy h'ger du Roi à Paris, the movement with anchor escapement, 30in. high.
(Christie's) $8250   £5030

SHELF CLOCKS

A Federal mahogany pillar-and-scroll shelf clock, by Eli Terry & Sons, Plymouth, Connecticut, 1815–1825, on bracket feet, 31in. high.
(Christie's) $1980   £1245

A Federal pillar and scroll shelf clock by Seth Thomas, Plymouth, Connecticut, circa 1805, the swan's-neck pediment centering three brass urn finials, 31in. high.
(Christie's) $3850   £2290

A Federal inlaid mahogany shelf clock by William Cummens, Roxburgh, Massachusetts, 1800–1810, with flame and urn finials above a pierced fretwork, 36¼in. high.
(Christie's) $17600   £10470

Round gothic mahogany veneer shelf clock, Brewster and Ingrahams, circa 1845, with eight day brass spring movement, 19¾in. high.
(Skinner Inc.) $500 £296

A Liberty & Co. Tudric pewter clock, the stepped rectangular form with overhanging top, moulded with panels of foliate decoration, 18.3cm. high. (Christie's London) $466 £286

Rosewood shelf timepiece, probably Atkins Clock Mfg. Co., Bristol, Connecticut, circa 1855, 30-day wagon spring movement, 17½in. high.
(Skinner Inc.) $1,100 £651

A Federal mahogany pillar-and-scroll shelf clock, by Eli Terry & Sons, Plymouth, Connecticut, 1815–1825, on bracket feet, 31in. high.
(Christie's) $1500   £943

A Federal mahogany eglomise shelf clock, by Eli Terry and Sons, Plymouth, Connecticut, circa 1820, with swan neck pediment, 30½in. high.
(Christie's New York)
          $3,300 £2,075

Massachusetts mahogany shelf timepiece, John Bailey, Lynn, Massachusetts, circa 1808, flaring French feet, 36in. high. (Skinner Inc.)
          $4,300 £2,638

SKELETON CLOCKS

An attractive Victorian brass skeleton timepiece, signed *J. Blackhurst, Crewe,* of scrolling balloon design, 20in. high overall. (Tennants) $1,404 £900

A 19th century French brass skeleton alarm timepiece, with engraved A plates, 10¹/₄ in. (Phillips) $693 £420

A 19th century brass striking skeleton clock, the pierced shaped and waisted plates with six turned screwed pillars, on oval ebonised base, with glass dome, 13in. high. (Christie's S. Ken.)$2245 £1430

A brass framed skeleton clock, the pierced chapter ring with black Roman numerals, contained in a glass dome (cracked), 51cm. high overall. (Henry Spencer) $1,123 £720

A French alarm skeleton timepiece with A-shaped plates, and five screwed pillar movement, with glass dome, 9in. high. (Christie's S. Ken.) $897 £528

A fine skeletonized mantel regulator with calendar, signed Edward François, H'Ger, 14 Boulevard ds Filles du Calvaire, circa 1900, 15¹/₂ in. high. (Christie's) $12650 £7713

A 19th century brass skeleton clock, the pierced plates of 'Brighton Pavilion' design, signed on an applied swag W & M. Dodge Manchester, 1ft. 9¹/₂ in. high. (Phillips) $5280 £3200

A 19th century brass skeleton timepiece, the substantial seven spoked great wheel with going barrel, Robt. Roskell, 1ft. 4¹/₂ in. high. (Phillips) $2970 £1800

A 19th century brass skeleton clock, the pierced screwed plates with six baluster pillar movement, 13³/₄ in. high. (Christie's S. Ken.) $1402 £825

WALL CLOCKS

A mahogany wall timepiece, the chain fusee movement with anchor escapement, the eight inch painted dial with roman numerals.
(Lawrence Fine Art)
$1089   £660

Baroque Revival patinated bronze wall clock, circa 1900, the works by E. Howard & Co., Boston, the whole decorated with pierced strapwork, 37in. square. (Skinner Inc.)
$3,750 £2,301

Austrian giltwood cartel clock, Anton Koppel, Vienna, early 19th century, circular dial with hands for calendar and days of week, 30in. high. (Skinner Inc.)
$1,600 £982

A 19th century Japanese hardwood stick wall timepiece, the movement with verge bob pendulum escapement, the trunk with adjustable register, 2ft. 3½in. high.
(Phillips) $1650   £1000

An ebonized and rosewood Vienna regulator by Lechner M., Pesten, mid 19th century, the case with moulded chamfered corners, 44½in. high.
(Christie's New York) $1210
£741

A 19th century mahogany cased regulator wall clock, the movement with maintaining power and dead beat escapement. (Henry Spencer)
$1,216 £780

A late 19th century black japanned act of parliament clock, the circular dial with gilt Roman numerals and Arabic minutes, 60in. high.
(Spencer's) $4950   £3000

A late 18th century French brass alarm travelling clock, the rectangular case with shaped and engraved dial plate and circular enamel dial, 6in. high.
(Phillips) $2640   £1600

Viennese regulator clock, attributed to Gustav Becker, early 20th century, with weight driven time and strike movement, 44½in. high. (Robt. W. Skinner Inc.) $400 £244

302

WALL CLOCKS

An oak gothic quarter chiming bracket clock, the three train chain fusee movement with anchor escapement, signed *Craighead Webb, Royal Exchange, London*, 82.5 cm. (Lawrence Fine Arts) $2,062 £1,265

Georgian inlaid mahogany wall clock, designer Moore, London. (H.P.S) $1114 £675

A XIX century walnut Vienna wall clock, the circular cream enamelled dial with black Roman numerals enclosing a subsidiary seconds dial, 59 in. high. (Spencer's) $990 £600

A 19th century oak Dutch 'Staartklok', the arched hood surmounted by three gilt wood figures, 4ft. 7in. high. (Phillips) $1122 £680

Federal gilt gesso and mahogany banjo timepiece, Aaron Willard Jr., Boston, circa 1820, the circular brass moulded bezel enclosing a painted iron dial, 40 in. high. (Skinner Inc.) $7,500 £4,601

A late 18th century oak striking wall clock, in the gothic taste, the engraved centre with subsidary rings for seconds and date signed Rollison, Sheffield, 72 in. high. (Christie's S. Ken.) $2418 £1540

A walnut veneered and ebonised Vienna regulator, the movement with dead beat escapement, maker's mark *H.E. & Co.,* 131 cm. (Lawrence Fine Arts) $1,219 £748

An 18th century alarm wall timepiece, signed Cartwright, London, with single steel hand and alarm set disc to the centre, 8 in. high. (Phillips) $1320 £800

A Federal gilt and eglomisé lyre-shaped wall clock, dial signed Aaron Willard, Boston, early 19th century, 40¹/₂ in. high. (Christie's) $2860 £1790

A rare late 18th century gilt metal lever watch, signed on backplate *Josiah Emery Charing Cross London 1094,* the later consular case with case maker's mark *TG,* 58mm. diam. (Phillips London)
$23,635 £14,500

An 18ct. gold slim half hunting cased keyless lever watch, the Swiss gilt movement with compressed balance, inscribed *Asprey, Bond St., London,* 1908. (Lawrence Fine Arts)
$1,793 £1,100

An 18ct. gold open faced key wind watch, signed *Swinden & Sons, Temple St., Birmingham,* hallmarked 1824, 47mm. (Lawrence Fine Arts)
$502 £308

A silver and tortoiseshell triple case Turkish market verge watch, the movement signed *Geo Charle London,* 63mm. diam. (Phillips London)
$554 £340

A 19th century French gold quarter repeating musical cylinder watch, inscribed *Breguet et Fils,* with enamel dial, 56mm. diam. (Phillips London) $3,260 £2,000

An 18th century silver pair cased watch, signed *P. Litherland & Co.,* the enamel dial with subsidiary seconds and gold hands, 62mm. diam. (Phillips London)
$2,608 £1,600

A late George V gentleman's 18 carat gold cased pocket watch with engine turned gilt metal dial, London 1933. (Henry Spencer) $391 £230

Art Deco gentleman's dress pocketwatch, silvered dial with Roman numerals, within a platinum case. (Skinner Inc.)
$2,700 £1,698

A French Empire silver verge watch, the movement with pierced bridge cock, the enamel dial with centre seconds, 53mm. diam. (Phillips London)
$1,271 £780

WATCHES

A Swiss gun metal keyless lever watch, the movement with tourbillion visible through the back, 53mm. diam. (Phillips London)$1,434 £880

An 18 carat gold half hunter case minute repeating keyless lever chronograph, signed *Cha's Frodsham 84 Strand London*, 54mm. diam. (Phillips London) $5,868 £3,600

An 18 carat gold and enamel keyless lever watch, the movement signed *Phillip & Phillip, London*, 1868, 36mm. diam. (Phillips London) $749 £460

A rare 19th century Continental gold watch, the gilt cuvette signed *S. F. Ravene Horloger du Roi a Berlin*, 55mm. diam. (Phillips London) $2,608 £1,600

A Continental silver hunter case Chinese duplex watch, signed *Euge Bournand & Cie A Ste Croix*, 56mm. diam. (Phillips London)$815 £500

A Swiss gold minute repeating keyless lever watch with perpetual calendar, signed *Ls Audemars, Brassus & Geneve*, 56mm. diam. (Phillips London) $15,485 £9,500

A good 19th century French gold quarter repeating Jacquemart watch, the dial with enamel chapter and skeletonised centre, 64mm. diam. (Phillips London) $11,736 £7,200

A Swiss nickel eight day keyless lever Goliath watch, the gilt and silvered dial containing moonphase aperture, 71mm. diam. (Phillips London) $587 £360

An 18 carat gold half hunter case keyless pocket chronometer with one minute tourbillion, signed *Joseph White & Son*, 55mm. diam., together with the original presentation case. (Phillips London) $22,005 £13,500

WRISTWATCHES

A Swiss gold Oyster perpetual date wristwatch by Rolex, the signed grey dial with date aperture, 35mm. diam. (Phillips London) $3,260 £2,000

A gent's 9ct. gold wristwatch, the Swiss movement stamped *Two Adjustments, 16 jewels,* and signed *Berino Watch Co., 1924,* 37 x 25mm. (Lawrence Fine Arts) $377 £231

An unusual circular
An unusual circular gilt metal gentleman's wristwatch, the case with triangular aperture, inscribed *Lord Elgin,* 31mm. diam. (Phillips London)
$358 £220

A rectangular gold gentleman's wristwatch, the movement stamped *Rolex,* with silvered dial, 40mm. long. (Phillips London) $815 £500

A Swiss gold circular gentleman's wristwatch, the movement signed *International Watch Co.,* 35mm. diam. (Phillips London) $489 £300

A silver gentleman's quartz wristwatch, the black dial inscribed *Gucci,* 43mm. long. (Phillips London)$293 £180

A Swiss gold circular wristwatch, by Jaeger le Coultre, 32mm. diam. (Phillips London)
$358 £220

A 9 carat gold octagonal Rolex Oyster wristwatch, circa 1935, the cream dial with applied gilt Arabic and baton numerals. (Spencer's) $1485   £900

A circular Swiss gilt metal gentleman's wristwatch, the movement signed *Ernest Borel,* 32mm. diam. (Phillips London)
$212 £130

WRISTWATCHES

A circular Swiss gold gentleman's wristwatch, inscribed *Mendys, La Chaux de Fonds,* 38mm. diam. (Phillips London) $309 £190

A Swiss gold square wristwatch, the circular movement signed *Mido,* 38mm. long. (Phillips London) $978 £600

A circular steel gentleman's chronograph, the black dial with subsidiaries for seconds, 39mm. diam. (Phillips London) $293 £180

A Swiss 18 carat two coloured gold wristwatch, the circular gilt movement signed *Peerless,* 24mm. wide. (Phillips London) $309 £190

A Swiss gold circular gentle man's wristwatch by Patek Philippe, the case with rounded splayed lugs, 35mm. diam. (Phillips London) $2,445 £1,500

A gilt metal rectangular gentleman's wristwatch, by Gruen, Arabic numerals, 45mm. long. (Phillips London) $489 £300

A Swiss silver circular wristwatch, by *Rolex,* the signed enamel dial with subsidiary seconds, London 1910, 34mm. diam. (Phillips London) $163 £100

A gold Rolex Oyster Elegante gentleman's wristwatch with centre sweep seconds. (Phillips Manchester) $727 £460

A Swiss gold circular gentleman's wristwatch by Patek Philippe, the signed silvered dial with subsidiary seconds, 34mm. diam. (Phillips London) $4,564 £2,800

CLOISONNE

A cloisonné enamel Censer, of globular form, raised on tripod feet, 4¹/₄in. diam., Qianlong. (Bonhams) $693   £420

Chinese cloisonne enamel covered ewer, 18th century, elephant handle and serpent spout, overall foliate enamel on a turquoise ground, 11in. high. (Skinner Inc.) $8,750 £5,469

A Russian cloisonne enamel cheroot case, each side decorated with a roundel enclosing a fabulous bird, Moscow, 1893, by Pavel Ovchinnikov, 88 zolotniki, 10.7cm. (Lawrence Fine Arts) $1,510 £968

Chinese cloisonne enamel on copper figural container, 18th century, in the form of a crouching sea turtle, 5in. high. (Skinner Inc.) $900 £563

A pair of 19th century Japanese cloisonne two handled vases, 21.5cm. high. (Auktionshaus Arnold) $414 £268

A 20th century Japanese cloisonne enamel vase, with birds perched amongst chrysanthemums, daisies and lilies, 46cm. high. (Henry Spencer) $652 £400

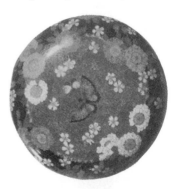

A Phoebe and Harold Stabler cloisonne pendant, with enamel decoration of ballerinas, painted signature, London 1922. (Christie's London) $536 £319

A pair of cloisonne vases by Ando Jubei, the elongated baluster bodies decorated in various coloured enamels, 19cm. high. (Christie's) $2245   £1430

A fine flattened globular cloisonne kogo and cover decorated in coloured enamels, signed Kyoto Namikawa, late 19th century, 6.2cm. diam. (Christie's) $1641   £1045

A cloisonne enamel casket of rectangular form, worked with stylised calligraphy and scattered blooms, 13½in. wide. (Lawrence Fine Arts) $69 £44

One of a pair of Chinese cloisonne enamel moon flasks, mid 19th century, dragon handles, polychrome floral and geometric decoration, 14½in. high. (Skinner Inc.) $1100 £671

Pair of Chinese cloisonne deer figures, 20th century, blue ground, animal handled lids on back, height to horns 8½in. (Skinner Inc.) $650 £414

One of a pair of ovoid cloisonne vases decorated in various coloured enamels and thicknesses of gold and silver wire, late 19th century, 24cm. high. (Christie's) $6563 £4180

A pair of 19th century Japanese cloisonne jars with covers, on wooden socles, 39cm. high. (Auktionshaus Arnold) $552 £358

A cloisonne snuff bottle decorated in coloured enamels with a bird and morning glories, and butterflies flying above autumn flowers, signed Kyoto Namikawa, late 19th century, 6cm. high. (Christie's) $6044 £3850

One of an atttractive pair of cloisonné enamel Cockerels, worked in colourful enamels, each standing on rockwork bases, 21½in. high. (Bonhams) $1732 £1050

A cloisonné enamel ox and cart, decorated in coloured enamels on a turquoise and blue ground, 19in. wide (Bonhams) $907 £550

Chinese cloisonne enamel figure of a rabbit, 19th century, sitting on its haunches, with copper base, 23.2cm. (Skinner Inc.) $700 £438

Moulded copper building ornament, America, late 19th century, figure of an American eagle with outspread wings, 35 in. high with base. (Skinner Inc.) $1,100 £710

An Eastern style brass casket, of cushioned form, extensively engraved with flowers, foliage and strapwork and inlaid with turquoise beads, 27 cm. wide. (Henry Spencer) $379 £240

A pair of late 18th century wrought iron and brass andirons, the ring turned uprights centred by spiral open twist knops, 25¾ in. high. (Christie's S. Ken) $986 £605

Pair of brass candlesticks, 17th century, near matching baluster form with drip pan below the socket, 28.3 cm. (Skinner Inc.) $425 £274

Metcalf Co. hammered copper vase with silver strapwork, circa 1910, silver tacked border on conical form, 12 in. high. (Robt. W. Skinner Inc.) $90 £55

A pair of mid 18th century brass candlesticks, with knopped stems and octagonal stepped and reeded bases, both signed Joseph Wood, 7½ in. high. (Christie's S. Ken) $1,294 £770

A Newlyn copper umbrella stand, the body with a relief pattern of fish and crabs swimming amid embossed banding, 58 cm. high. (Phillips London) $847 £520

An 18th century gilt brass curfew of typical form, repousse decorated with portraits, animal and figure subjects, 17 in. wide. (Christie's S. Ken) $1,165 £715

Roycroft copper American Beauty vase, East Aurora, New York, circa 1910, flared rim, original patina, signed with logo, 19¼ in. high. (Skinner Inc.) $2,000 £1,235

A rare copper tea kettle, marked *Hunneman*, Boston, circa 1810, with flat arched swing handle, 11in. wide. (Christie's New York)
$2,420 £1,522

Chinese brass brazier, 19th century, raised on a cylindrical support with globular base and three cabriole legs, 25in. high. (Skinner Inc) $800 £496

Jarvie brass candlestick, Chicago, Illinois, circa 1910, with angled handle, signed on base, 6in. high. (Skinner Inc.) $850 £525

A pair of brass candlesticks, English, late 18th century, each with scalloped bobeche above a trumpet turned stem, 17.5cm. (Christie's New York) $770 £484

A late 19th century beaker, the plated on copper outer sleeve cast in high relief with 18th century Continental figures in a continuous rural landscape , 13.5cm. high. (Henry Spencer) $150 £95

Pair of George III brass candlesticks, circa 1800, each with urn nozzle with bobeche over a baluster and urn shaped standard, 18¼in. high. (Robt. W. Skinner Inc.) $400 £244

A late 19th century English copper electrotype figure of Caractacus, after a model by J. H. Foley, stamped *Elkington & Co. Founders*, 82cm. high. (Christie's London) $974 £605

Pair of brass candlesticks, possibly Jarvie, Chicago, circa 1910, unsigned, 6in. high, 5in. diam. (Robt. W. Skinner Inc.) $400 £245

A Hagenauer brass bust of a highly stylised woman with slender neck, a beaded necklace and small pouting lips, 48cm. high. (Phillips London) $7,038 £4,600

Large and good quality heavy brass ink stand with two pots and decorative gallery. (G. A. Key) $269 £165

A George III brass bound mahogany tray of oval shape with scrolled carrying handles, 22in. wide. (Christie's London) $1,216 £770

A chased copper hibachi modelled as a fishing basket, decorated with a lobster, seaweed, coral and a variety of shells, unsigned, late 19th century, 31cm. diam. (Christie's London) $1,564 £990

19th century, Rhenish, brass pear shaped coffee urn, with two S-shaped knopped handles, on three cabriole legs with claw feet. (Kunsthaus am Museum) $1,188 £683

A Dutch brass jardiniere of cylindrical form with repousse scenes of drinking men, the sides with lion masks, 17in. wide. (Christie's London) $567 £352

An Art Nouveau brass and copper jug, embossed in relief with cartouches between linear and foliate borders, 15½in. high. (Christie's S. Ken) $129 £83

A large John Pearson beaten copper charger, the rim and central reserve with repousse foliate decoration, the reverse signed *J. Pearson, 1889,* 51.4cm. diam. (Christie's London) $1,072 £638

Unusual 19th century copper coal scuttle with swing handle and shovel. (G. A. Key) $264 £170

An Arts and Crafts hammered copper and iron log bin, with relief decoration of stylised foliage, with lacquered iron mounts and on bracket feet, 43.4cm. high. (Christie's London) $832 £495

A brass inkstand centred by a candle nozzle flanked by a sander and an inkwell, early 18th century, 12in. wide. (Christie's London) $1,029 £660

A copper bedwarmer with carrying handle, circa 1900. (Auction Team Koeln) $17 £11

An Art Union brass and copper pen tray, designed by Katie Harris, cast with a central seated female figure flanked by two male busts, stamped *Art Union of London 1902,* 33cm. wide. (Christie's London) $628 £374

A hexagonal brass hall lantern with pierced domed top, one plate engraved with a bird on a branch, 21½in. high. (Christie's London) $1,040 £638

Copper coal shute and shovel, late 19th century period. (G. A. Key) $186 £120

A French Provincial brass ewer with scrolling handle and coat-of-arms, early 18th century, formerly silver plated, 9in. high. (Christie's London) $1,738 £1,100

Silver wash hammered copper kettle on stand, Europe, circa 1905, riveted loop handle, 11½in. high. (Skinner Inc.) $600 £370

Pair of Continental brass candlesticks, Belgium or France, mid- 18th century, with knopped shaft and turned nozzles, 9in. high. (Skinner Inc.) $375 £230

Kayser patinated copper covered punch bowl, probably Austria or Germany, circa 1905, stamped with hallmark, 12in. diam. (Skinner Inc.) $425 £262

CORKSCREWS

A Thomason 1802 brass barrelled corkscrew with bone handle and hanging loop, the wire helix affixed to the double action hermaphrodite screw. (Christie's S. Ken) $269 £176

A good example of a James Heeley's bronzed double lever corkscrew by Weir, marked with a catalogue no. 428. (Christie's S. Ken) $673 £440

A brass barrelled example of a Thomason 1802 patent corkscrew with bone handle, hanging loop and wire helix. (Christie's S. Ken) $252 £165

A bone handled King's Screw corkscrew with brass barrel, metal winding handle and fine wire helix. (Christie's S. Ken) $286 £187

A Victorian engine-turned silver gilt travelling set comprising sandwich box and pair of roundlets with corkscrew and railway carriage key. London 1869. (Graves Son & Pilcher Fine Arts) $2025 £1250

A signed Lunds King's pattern with silvered patent tablet, lacking 2 of 3 bottle grips. (Graves Son & Pilcher Fine Arts) $295 £170

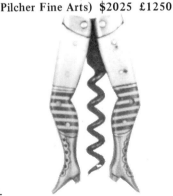

A Thomason 1802 patent corkscrew with brass barrel and wire helix, a brass Royal coat of arms affixed to the case. (Christie's S. Ken) $303 £198

A Gay Nineties folding corkscrew modelled as a pair of lady's stockinged legs. (Christie's S. Ken) $404 £264

A Hull's presto patent screw with solid brass thin barrel and rosewood handle with pusher. (Graves Son & Pilcher Fine Arts) $680 £420

A rare glove of knitted cotton, with fingerless tips to the index finger and thumb and worked with pots of flowers at the knuckles, early 18th century. (Christie's S. Ken)
$289 £176

Painted and decorated parade fire hat, probably Philadelphia, last half of 19th century, inscribed *Lafayette Hose Company*. (Skinner Inc.)
$7,000 £4,294

A dress of mauve silk taffeta woven with a purple pin stripe, trimmed with black lace, circa 1868.
(Christie's S. Ken.) $272   £165

A fine sleeved waistcoat of strawberry pink silk, with large flowering trees in silver thread and pink, brown, green and blue silk, circa 1740.
(Christie's S. Ken.)$3085   £1870

A pair of mittens of ivory silk with a long sinuous insertion at the inner wrists embroidered in pink silk, circa 1770.
(Christie's S. Ken.) $817   £495

A knitted waistcoat of burgandy coloured silk, knitted with gold lace patterns at the borders and seams, 17th century.
(Christie's S. Ken.)$1724   £1045

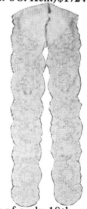

A single cotton glove printed in black with two Vestal Virgins and a chain around the wrist inscribed *l'Amitie Sincere,* circa 1800. (Christie's S. Ken)
$162 £99

A 19th century Taoist priest's robe of burnt prange silk, richly worked in couched metal threads and coloured silks.
(Phillips) $1980   £1200

A pair of early 18th century Brussels bobbin lace lappets designed with flowers, fruits and foliage, each 64cm. long.
(Phillips West Two)$782 £460

An open robe of cotton printed with exotic flowering branches in rose madder, brown and blue, circa 1770. (Christie's S. Ken) $8,118 £4,950

A young girl's dress of blue striped silk, with a tiered skirt and cuirasse bodice with blue braided buttons, circa 1870s. (Christie's S. Ken) $295 £176

A sleeveless evening dress of lime green velvet, labelled *Schiaparelli, 21 Place Vendome, Paris, Hiver 1936-7.* (Christie's S. Ken) $1,353 £825

A rare baby's closed robe of salmon pink silk satin woven with white flowers, early 18th century. (Christie's S. Ken) $5,051 £3,080

A fine dress of red chiffon, with a wrap over bodice of red chiffon, trimmed with gilt bugle beads at the neck and sleeves, circa 1910. (Christie's S. Ken) $261 £154

A young girl's dress of egg shell blue wool and silk, with a tiered skirt and short pleated cap sleeves, circa 1878. (Christie's S. Ken) $480 £308

A dress of blue cotton printed with brown leaves, the over-sleeves, neckline and trained hem printed a disposition with a patterned border, circa 1800. (Christie's S. Ken) $6,314 £3,850

A wedding dress of ivory gros-grain silk, lavishly trimmed with lace, fastening with simu-lated pearl buttons, circa 1874. (Christie's S. Ken) $758 £462

A child's matador fancy dress outfit, comprising black velvet breeches, a waistcoat and bolero, a hat, cummerbund and pair of ivory silk stockings, early 20th century. (Christie's S. Ken) $137 £88

A mid 19th century gown of chine silk, designed with grey flecks on a finely striped ivory and fawn ground. (Phillips West Two) $2,720 £1,600

An open robe and petticoat of ivory silk woven with a ribbed stripe and garlands of blue flowers, circa 1770. (Christie's S. Ken) $3,247 £1,980

A sleeveless dress of apple green muslin, embroidered overall with clear bugle beads, circa 1925. (Christie's S. Ken) $466 £286

An 18th century gentleman's coat of dark blue corded silk velvet, having silk covered buttons. (Phillips West Two) $4,080 £2,400

A dress of chine silk, the tiered skirt composed of bands of chine roses, 1850s and a day bodice, 1860s. (Christie's S. Ken) $1,353 £825

A robe of purple velvet, densely embroidered with beaten silver gilt wire arabesques, Turkish, 19th century. (Christie's S. Ken) $601 £385

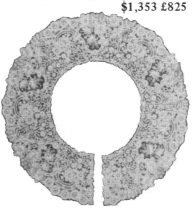

A pair of mid-19th century jointed lappets of Brussels bobbin and needlepoint applique designed with rushes, flowerheads and leaves, circa 1860s, 1.3m. (Phillips West Two) $240 £150

A late 19th century Brussels bobbin lace bertha collar with needlepoint insertions designed with flowers. (Phillips West Two) $576 £360

A mantua of blue silk damask woven with large sprays of exotic flowers and leaves, circa 1730-1740 (slight alterations).(Christie's S. Ken) $9,020 £5,500

A photograph of Grace walking away from the field, 7½ x 5½in., mounted with a 2pp a.l.s. from Grace to Lord Bessborough. (Christie's S. Ken) $612 £385

Wisden's Cricketers' Almanack, 1865, some corners creased, binder's green cloth. (Christie's S. Ken) $2,623 £1,650

Dickinson and Foster (Publishers): Lords — The Pavilion — Before the Match, photogravure, published 1 June 1895, 23½ x 39½in. (Christie's S. Ken) Two $787 £495

The Tour of the West Indian Cricketers, Demerara, 1887, photographic frontispiece, marginal browning. (Christie's S. Ken) $332 £209

A Coalport blue and white and gilt plate, manufactured for S. J. Kepple & Son, Bristol, commemorating W. G. Grace's century of centuries, the central reserve signed and dated 1895. (Christie's S. Ken) $7,345 £4,620

A photograph of Trumper at the crease, autographed in the negative by Trumper, and with original autographs around image, inscribed on verso *Trumper Testimonial Match N.S.W. v Rest of Australia, 8th Feb. 1913,* 6 x 4in. (Christie's S. Ken) $559 £352

Grace (W.G.), Robert Abel — A full length photograph of the two players signed by Grace, 4½ x 3½in. (Christie's S. Ken) $734 £462

An electroplated six division novelty toastrack, with cricket ball and wicket handle, 6in. long. (Christie's S. Ken) $542 £341

Wisden's Cricketers' Almanack, 1882, original paper covers. (Christie's S. Ken) $734 £462

Dickinson and Foster (Publishers): Lords on a Gentlemen v Players day, photogravure, published 1 June 1895, 19½ x 39½in. (Christie's S. Ken) $787 £495

The Third Australian Team in England, 1882 (Padwick 4975), wood engraved portraits, original wrappers, soiled. (Christie's S. Ken) $297 £187

After William Drummond and Charles J. Basebe: The cricket match between Sussex and Kent at Brighton, engraving, published by E. Gambart and Co, 01 May 1849 26 x 39in. (Christie's S. Ken) $349 £220

Surrey Cricket Team, 1896, mounted team photograph, 10½ x 12in. (Christie's S. Ken) $332 £209

A Staffordshire tobacco jar and cover sprigged in white with batsman and bowler on a peach ground, early to mid 19th century, 5in. high. (Christie's S. Ken) $454 £286

A commemorative cotton handkerchief with various team captains on the four corners, including A. Hunter, Aston Villa and W. Draper, Old Boys, Liverpool, 1890s, 26½ x 28½in. (Christie's S. Ken) $612 £385

Great Bowlers and Fielders, Beldam (G.W.) and C.B. Fry, 1906, coloured frontispiece. (Christie's S. Ken) $227 £143

English School: Boy with bat, early 19th century, oil on canvas, in oval frame, 7 x 6in. (Christie's S. Ken) $2,098 £1,320

Vanity Fair: 'Ranji' (K.S. Ranjitsinhji), chromolithograph by Spy, 15¼ x 10in. (Christie's S. Ken) $209 £132

The Australians, 1886, played at Sheffield Park, May 13th, 14th, 15th, a team photograph by E. Hawkins and Company, 9 x 11¼in. (Christie's S. Ken) **$699 £440**

A Staffordshire cylindrical tobacco jar, moulded in relief with batsman and bowler on a blue ground, later 19th century, 4in. (Christie's S. Ken) **$240 £154**

Gloucestershire XI, 1895, a team photograph mounted on card with inscription above and team list below, 9 x 11½in. (Christie's S. Ken) **$297 £187**

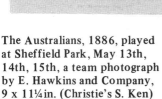

Wisden's Cricketers' Almanack, 1916, original paper covers, spine partly lacking. (Christie's S. Ken) **$559 £352**

The Australian Cricket Team, 1905, a commemorative cotton handkerchief naming the team with their fifteen portraits, 18 x 18½in. (Christie's S. Ken) **$446 £286**

Wisden's Cricketers' Almanack, 1867 original paper covers, some wear to spine. (Christie's S. Ken) **$1,574 £990**

A mid 19th century Valentine card on embossed paper with hand coloured wood engraving of a youth at the wicket. (Christie's S. Ken) **$77 £50**

A cricket ball with a white metal plaque inscribed *Surrey v Kent, Blackheath, 1923, "The Bogey Laid", P. G. H. Fender, Captain of Surrey.* (Christie's S. Ken) **$309 £198**

A tinted glass panel, the centre section painted with a scene of a cricket match, 1900s, 38¼ x 20½in. (Christie's S. Ken) **$734 £462**

A Staffordshire transfer printed jug, the ovoid body depicting a cricket match in progress, 4½in. high. (Christie's S. Ken)
$240 £154

Sussex, 1901 a mounted team photograph by E. Hawkins & Co., Brighton, with printed title and team list below, 9 x 11½in. (Christie's S. Ken)
$94 £61

A cricket ball stamped in gilt with the inscription *F. C. Cobden Esq. 3 wickets in 3 balls Lord's, June 28, 1870.* (Christie's S. Ken) $858 £550

The Empire's Cricketers, Chevallier Tayler (Albert), folio, 1905, 48 chromolithograph plates. (Christie's S. Ken)
$3,498 £2,200

A marble figure of a boy cricketer in forward defensive stance by William Day Keyworth the younger, dated 1895, 33in. high. (Christie's S. Ken)
$13,992 £8,800

Thomas Hayward, Born March 21st 1835 and Robert Carpenter Born Nov 18th 1831, a full length portrait photograph of the two players in 1863 before the tour to Australia, 9½ x 7½in. (Christie's S. Ken) $326 £209

To the Admirers of the Noble Game of Cricket, a commemorative cotton handkerchief, printed with the England XI of 1847, after the watercolour by Felix, 26½ x 32½in. (Christie's S. Ken) $489 £308

A Sandham, Strudwick & Bale Special bat signed on the face by the 1922-23 South African and England teams. (Christie's S. Ken) $1,201 £770

W. D. & H. O. Wills Cricketer Series, 1901, a set of 50 cigarette cards depicting notable cricketers of the day. (Christie's S. Ken)$686 £440

DOLLS

A painted felt child doll, with blue eyes, blonde wig and original green and white frilled organdie dress, marked on the soles *Lenci,* circa 1930, 14in. high. (Christie's S. Ken)
$869 £550

A wax over papier mache headed doll, the cloth body with pink kid arms with separated fingers, wearing original clothes, mainly 1780-1790, 17½in. high. (Christie's S. Ken) $1,303 £825

Percy, a bisque headed bebe with fixed brown eyes, closed mouth, pierced ears and short light brown wig, stamped on the body *Jumeau,* 18in. high. (Christie's S. Ken)$3,476 £2,200

An all bisque googlie eyed doll, with open/closed watermelon mouth, brown sleeping eyes glancing to the side, marked *222 28,* by Kestner, 11in. high, and a quantity of doll's clothes. (Christie's S. Ken)$2,607 £1,650

A wax over papier mache headed doll, with fixed bright blue eyes and hair wig, the stuffed body with waxed arms, 14in. high, circa 1840, in glazed case. (Christie's S. Ken)
$330 £209

William, a felt headed character doll, with side glancing eyes, fair mohair wig, the felt body dressed as a boy, Lenci 300 Series, circa 1930, 16in. high. (Christie's S. Ken)$2,086 £1,320

A bisque swivel headed Parisienne, with closed mouth, pale blue bulbous eyes and rigid kid body, by Gaultier, 11in. high. (Christie's S. Ken)
$695 £440

A bisque headed bebe, with fixed blue eyes, a wedding dress, petticoat, underclothes, shoes and socks, 12½in. high. (Christie's S. Ken)$1,564 £990

An all bisque child doll, with closed mouth, fixed brown eyes and moulded socks and grey tasselled boots, by J. D. Kestner, 6in. high. (Christie's S. Ken) $556 £352

An all bisque googlie eyed doll, with blue painted eyes glancing to the left, closed watermelon mouth and moulded blue socks and black shoes, by Kestner, 5½in. high. (Christie's S. Ken) **$521 £330**

A bisque headed child doll, with blue sleeping eyes, pierced ears and blonde wig, the composition jointed body wearing robe with lace insertions, marked *Simon & Halbig K,* 19in. high. (Christie's S. Ken) **$869 £550**

A pressed bisque headed bebe, with fixed pale blue eyes outlined in dark blue, shaded lids, closed mouth and pierced ears, by Emile Jumeau, 1880s, 16½in. high. (Christie's S. Ken) **$7,821 £4,950**

A celluloid headed teddy doll with plush covered body, beige felt hands and feet, moulded hair and painted features, circa 1908, 16in. high. (Christie's S. Ken) **$156 £99**

A wax headed doll, with bead eyes, painted short hair, cloth body and wax arms, circa 1840, 7½in. high. (Christie's S. Ken) **$782 £495**

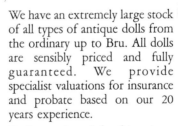

A bisque headed bebe, the pressed head with closed mouth, fixed brown eyes, pierced applied cars and blonde wool wig, impressed *7 EJ,* 1880s, 19in. high. (Christie's S. Ken) $6,952 £4,400

Eliza, a wax over composition doll, with wired eye mechanism, brown mohair ringlets, the stuffed body with wax over composition limbs, circa 1845, (wax cracked) 22in. high. (Christie's S. Ken) $782 £495

A bisque headed bebe, with fixed blue eyes, heavy brows, closed mouth, pierced ears and blonde hair wig, stamped in red *Depose Tete Jumeau 12,* 26in. high. (Christie's S. Ken) $2,780 £1,760

A carved and painted wooden doll, with rouged cheeks, dark enamel eyes, stitched brows and lashes, carved ears and adolescent figure, circa 1740 (arm missing, two fingers broken, legs detached), 18in. high. (Christie's S. Ken) $16,511 £10,450

A George III wooden doll, circa 1780, the carved ovoid head with high forehead, black and white enamelled eyes and pink mouth, 59cm. high. (Henry Spencer) $994 £650

A pressed bisque swivel headed lady doll, the fixed sky blue eyes with shaded lids and grey brows, the kid body wearing original novice's habit of the Augustinian order, Jumeau, circa 1875, 31in. high, with original stand. (Christie's S. Ken) $5,561 £3,520

Carved and painted dancing toy, probably America, 19th century, in the form of a black man wearing a black vest, 11½in. high. (Skinner Inc.) $1,400 £859

A George III wooden doll, circa 1800, the carved ovoid head with the remains of a styled ginger wig, jointed pine legs and primitively carved feet, 67cm. high. (Henry Spencer) $2,528 £1,600

A shoulder bisque marotte, with blond mohair curly wig, fixed blue glass eyes, painted features and open mouth, 35cm. high overall. (Henry Spencer) $244 £160

An Armand Marseille bisque socket head girl doll with painted features, closing blue glass eyes with hair eyelashes, open mouth with four upper teeth, 59cm. high. (Henry Spencer)　　$268 £170

A bisque swivel headed Parisienne, wearing original peacock green silk dress with matching sleeveless jerkin, marked on head and shoulder D, by Bru, circa 1862, 15in. high. (Christie's S. Ken) $2,607 £1,650

A rare bisque-headed character doll, modelled as a laughing baby, with open/closed mouth with upper and lower teeth, impressed Gebruder Heubach square mark, 11½in. high. (Christie's S. Ken.) $1361　£825

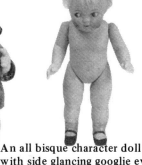

An Armand Marseille bisque socket head girl doll, with painted features, blue glass closing eyes and with a white cotton dress with floral white-work hem. (Henry Spencer)　　$411 £260

A pair of all bisque character dolls modelled as Max and Moritz, with painted black and ginger hair, by J. D. Kestner, 5in. high. (Christie's S. Ken) $2,085　£1,320

An all bisque character doll with side glancing googlie eyes, water melon mouth and blonde An all bisque character doll with side glancing googlie eyes, watermelon mouth and blonde mohair wig, marked *Kestner*, 5½in. high. (Christie's S. Ken) $312 £198

A bisque swivel headed doll, with closed mouth, blue sleeping eyes, pierced ears and gusseted cloth body with bisque arms, wearing provincial costume, marked *S 5 H 719DEP* 14½in. high. (Christie's S. Ken) $1,129 £715

Simon and Halbig bisque headed child doll made for Luno and Otto Dresall, right shoulder with red Dresall stamp of a winged helmet, circa 1910, 21in. (G. A. Key) $477　£300

Izannah Walker doll, Central Falls, Rhode Island, 1870-1880, moulded, painted stockinette figure of a girl with corkscrew curls, 18in. high. (Skinner Inc.)　　$2,500 £1,534

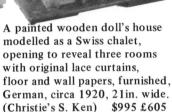

A painted wooden toy stable, with two stalls, coach house and furnished living quarters above and with blue cart and composition horses, 28½in. wide. (Christie's S. Ken) $521 £330

A wooden doll's house, opening at the front to reveal six rooms, hall and staircase, the kitchen with dresser and fire surround, with Christian Hacker stamp on the base, 33in. high. (Christie's S. Ken) $921 £583

A painted wooden doll's house modelled as a Swiss chalet, opening to reveal three rooms with original lace curtains, floor and wall papers, furnished, German, circa 1920, 21in. wide. (Christie's S. Ken) $995 £605

A painted wood and printed brick paper on wood doll's house, opening at the front to reveal four rooms with original kitchen paper, dresser and fire surrounds, 28in. high, (Christie's S. Ken) $347 £220

A painted wooden doll's house, of five bays and four storeys, opening to reveal ten rooms with hall, staircase and landings, interior doors, bathroom fittings, four side windows and contemporary wall and floor papers, 50in. wide. (Christie's S. Ken) $17,380 £11,000

A wooden doll's house, of three bays and two storeys, opening at the front to reveal four rooms with staircase and landing, interior doors and fire surrounds, by G. and J. Lines, circa 1910, 37in. high. (Christie's S. Ken) $2,085 £1,320

A late Georgian wooden carpenter made doll's house, painted to simulate brickwork, circa 1830, 4ft. long, 45in. high. (Christie's S. Ken) $3,476 £2,200

A painted wooden doll's house of late Georgian style, opening in three hinged sections to reveal seven rooms, the staircase rising from the front hall to the first floor with separate treads, early Victorian, 46in. wide. (Christie's S. Ken) $2,433 £1,540

A wooden doll's house, painted to simulate brickwork with grey roof with scalloped eaves, opening to reveal four fully furnished rooms, circa 1900, 50in. high. (Christie's S. Ken) $3,823 £2,420

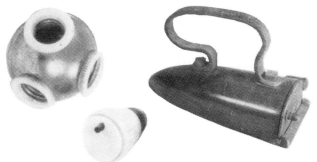

A porcelain screw-in lamp valve and porcelain insulator, circa 1922. (Auction Team Koeln)
$15 £9

An Ox tongue iron complete with core, and iron handle, circa 1860. (Auction Team Koeln)
$70 £44

Prancing horse tobacco cutter, America, late 19th century, cutting blade and wooden handle mounted on a swivel, 16½in. long. (Skinner Inc.)
$1,700 £1,043

An original Miele mangel with wooden rollers, restored, circa 1910. (Auction Team Koeln)
$14 £9

A Wella Masterpiece hairdrier, on movable base, circa 1935. (Auction Team Koeln) $126 £78

A fully automatic Morison's wooden washing machine, complete with tub, Belgian, circa 1900. (Auction Team Koeln)
$193 £122

A nickel plated Friho-Sol hand held hairdrier of contemporary angular form, circa 1920. (Auction Team Koeln) $44 £27

A large Danish three part coffee grinder by Schroder & Jorgensen Eff, Copenhagen, circa 1950. (Auction Team Koeln)
$27 £17

A CAL coffee grinder with ceramic holder and glass dispenser, circa 1925. (Auction Team Koeln)
$82 £52

A gallows mousetrap with two holes, 1920. (Auction Team Koeln) $23 £14

An Alexanderwerk bread cutting machine, circa 1910. (Auction Team Koeln) $70 £43

An old padlock with original key, circa 1875. (Auction Team Koeln) $11 £7

An OBM Mokkadomat coffee machine, circa 1920. (Auction Team Koeln) $296 £183

A wooden coffee grinder with coloured tinplate sides and harvest thanksgiving motif, circa 1900. (Auction Team Koeln) $240 £148

An early Kadus hairdrier, on cased movable stand, circa 1930. (Auction Team Koeln) $536 £331

A W. Feldmeyer spirit iron, with transverse tank and wooden handle, 1905. (Auction Team Koeln) $83 £51

A stamped Ovenex patty tin oven tray, circa 1925. (Auction Team Koeln) $6 £4

A brass flat iron with wooden handle and sleeve, circa 1850. (Auction Team Koeln) $41 £25

A moulded bakelite Siemens hand held hairdrier, circa 1930. (Auction Team Koeln) $26 £16

Flowerpress for dry pressing of flowers and herbs, circa 1900. (Auction Team Koeln) $35 £22

A bronze boot pull in the form of an erotic recumbent figure, circa 1900. (Auction Team Koeln) $57 £35

A World Patented Mechanical Darner beard cutter, with adjustable levels and bakelite housing, English, circa 1930. (Auction Team Koeln) $25 £16

A richly decorated cast metal Agrippina mangel, with the arms of Cologne and peacock feathers on both supports, stamped *HK & Co* circa 1880. (Auction Team Koeln) $442 £273

A peanut dispenser with original key, circa 1958. (Auction Team Koeln) $57 £35

A German Schott bakelite hairdrier, circa 1935. (Auction Team Koeln) $21 £13

The Boye Needle Co. 'Needles & Shuttles', 1910, a circular magazine with numerous wooden tubes for needles and bobbins. (Auction Team Koeln) $164 £101

A Rievel regulated iron, circa 1905. (Auction Team Koeln) $70 £44

DOMESTIC EQUIPMENT

A heavy duty iron with replaceable wooden handle, circa 1920. (Auction Team Koeln) $19 £12

An Ozonomat wall hanging air purifier, circa 1955. (Auction Team Koeln) $47 £30

A Dual dynamo pocket lamp, aluminium cased, circa 1940. (Auction Team Koeln) $19 £12

A very early AEG table fan, circa 1925. (Auction Team Koeln) $41 £25

A small fruit and wine must press, circa 1900. (Auction Team Koeln) $52 £33

A Mistral chromium plated electric coffee grinder, circa 1958. (Auction Team Koeln) $37 £23

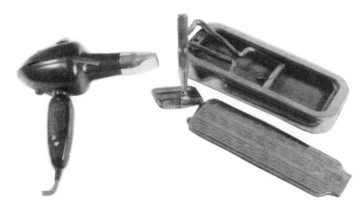

A German bakelite Forfex hand held hairdrier by Eisemann, circa 1935. (Auction Team Koeln) $70 £43

A Rolls Patent razor in plated case, circa 1910. (Auction Team Koeln) $23 £14

A Germania cast charcoal eye iron with six segment openings (eyes) for better draught, circa 1880. (Auction Team Koeln) $44 £28

A Greif-Roto double cylinder copier with box of unused stencils and five original printing ink tubes, circa 1935. (Auction Team Koeln) $93 £59

A German Ormig D10 Merkur spirit transfer printer, circa 1970. (Auction Team Koeln) $23 £15

An Edison Mimeograph No. 75 cylinder copier for wax stencils, circa 1905. (Auction Team Koeln) $32 £20

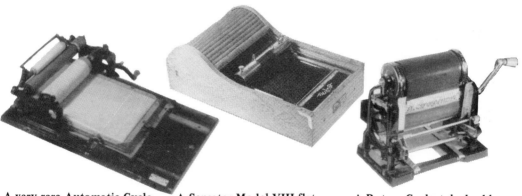

A very rare Automatic Cyclostyle mechanised frame copier, for wax stencils capable of 1200 copies per hour, 1897. (Aution Team Koeln) $160 £98

A Sensator Model VIII flat copier in attractive wooden roll top case, circa 1920. (Auction Team Koeln) $212 £130

A Rotary Cyclostyle double cylinder copier for wax stencils with metal hood, circa 1910. (Auction Team Koeln) $38 £24

A Roneo No 6 single cylinder copier for wax stencils, with metal hood, circa 1910. (Auction Team Koeln) $105 £67

A Gestetner Diaphragm Duplicator No. 70 portable copier, for wax stencils with colour board, coating platen and frame holder in mahogany case, circa 1890. (Auction Team Koeln) $41 £25

A Universal Duplicator double cylinder copier by Gestetner, complete with cardboard roll with original wax stencils and metal cassette with unused stencils, circa 1925. (Auction Team Koeln) $128 £81

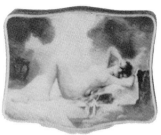

A set of four Edwardian disc menu holders finely enamelled with various game birds, in a fitted case, Chester. (Christie's S. Ken) $1,515 £990

A Viennese shaped oval dish, enamelled with various classical scenes, supported by a gilt-metal figure stem, 3.2in. high. (Christie's S. Ken.) $726 £440

An attractive enamelled rectangular box, the top depicting a naked woman, resting in an ethereal setting, being showered from above with golden coins, 9cm. wide, marked *935*. (Phillips London) $2,142 £1,400

A fine Limoges enamel plaque by Thomas John Bott, signed and dated *T. J. Bott, Worcester, 1883*, 24 x 14.5cm. (Phillips London) $4,238 £2,600

A gold and enamel heart-shape box, decorated with a group of three children at play, 6.5cm., French, early 19th century. (Lawrence) $4900 £2970

A Chinese pear shaped enamel scent bottle, one side painted with a shepherd and shepherdess in a landscape, Canton, early 19th century, 4½in. high. (Christie's London) $1,076 £660

A good quality enamelled vase, apparently unmarked, probably French, decorated in naturalistic colours with anemones and foliage, 28.3cm. high. (Phillips London) $6,031 £3,700

A pair of 18th century English enamel candlesticks, the white ground heightened in gilt and blue and painted with sprays of flowers, 9½in. high. (Christie's S. Ken.) $1996 £1210

A South Staffordshire enamel necessaire, painted with five reserves, with gilt metal mounts, circa 1765, 7.3cm. high. (Christie's London) $2,152 £1,320

A 19th century Viennese silver gilt and enamel quatrefoil dish, painted with figures in landscapes, 7in. wide. (Christie's S. Ken) $1,115 £715

A Birmingham circular enamel snuff box, the cover painted with a lady and a gentleman in a landscape, circa 1755, 6.7cm. diam. (Christie's London) $896 £550

A rare Birmingham rectangular enamel casket, the cover printed in puce with Paris awarding the apple to Hibernia with Britannia looking on, Birmingham, 1756-60, 10¼in. long. (Christie's London) $3,586 £2,200

A Viennese enamel cornucopia with silver and gilt metal mounts, raised with jewelled bosses, 16in. high. (Christie's S. Ken) $9,862 £6,050

An unusual Arts and Crafts enamelled stand made by J. P. Barraclough, R.C.A., each facet set with a coloured cloisonne enamelled panel, 11.5cm. high, 1913. (Phillips London) $587 £360

A Limoges enamel on copper baluster jar and domed cover by Camille Fauré, 13in. high. (Christie's S. Ken.) $1053 £638

A Limoges enamel on copper vase by Camille Faure, the foil backed enamel forming a raised abstract geometric design, 6¾in. high. (Christie's S. Ken) $1,125 £660

A 19th century Viennese silver gilt and enamel model of a sedan chair, with inset rock crystal windows, 5½in. high. (Christie's S. Ken) $1,287 £825

A Battersea enamel scent bottle, modelled in the form of a peach, gilt metal stopper and fitting, 6.5cm. (Lawrence) $1815 £1100

A Royalist fan, the silk leaf printed in
mezzotint or maniere noir with an oval
portrait of Louis XVI, 9in., 1793. (Christie's
S. Ken) $535 £330

A mid 19th century Chinese cabriolet fan
with painted silk insets of flowers, the leaves
decorated with figures of ivory and silk
applique, 22cm. long. (Phillips West Two)
                                    $680   £400

Souvenir des Montagnes Russes du Bould. des
Capucines, a chromolithographic fan of putti
riding on a Big Dipper, 14in., circa 1880.
(Christie's S. Ken) $446   £275

A mid-19th century Chinese fan with carved
and pierced ivory sticks, the guards carved in
high relief, the painted leaf decorated with a
central panel, 25cm. long, circa 1850s.
(Phillips West Two) $512 £320

An 18th century chinoiserie fan with carved,
pierced ivory sticks and silvered decoupe
vellum leaf, painted with cartouches of
figures playing games, 29cm. long, circa
1770s. (Phillips West Two) $480 £300

An Arts and Crafts fan, the dark blue leaf
painted with pairs of dragonflies in silvered
paint, 11in., circa 1890. (Christie's S. Ken)
                                    $1,693 £1,045

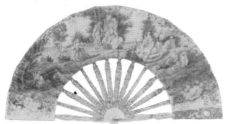

A fan, the leaf painted with Classical figures
in a park, the ivory sticks carved and pierced
with putti, 10¼in., the leaf mid-19th century,
the sticks circa 1770. (Christie's S. Ken)
                                    $535 £330

A fan, the leaf painted with an elegant shepherd and shepherdess, the ivory sticks pique
with silver, 11in., possibly English, circa
1690. (Christie's S. Ken) $3,564 £2,200

A mid 19th century Chinese black and gilt lacquer brise fan designed with a central cartouche of figures in a courtyard, 25cm. long. (Phillips West Two) $612 £360

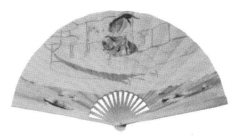

Parfum Pompeia, L.T. Piver, a chromolithographic fan of a lady in a flying machine, published by Maquet, 9in., circa 1918. (Christie's S. Ken) $570 £352

A fan with carved pierced blonde tortoiseshell sticks, decorated with mother-of-pearl and carved with foxgloves and convolvulus, 28cm. long, circa 1900s. (Phillips West Two) $1,360 £850

A late 18th century Chinese ivory brise fan, carved and pierced with trailing leaves and flowers and designed with a central roundel, 27cm. long, circa 1780s. (Phillips West Two) $1,040 £650

A late 18th century French fan with carved, pierced silvered and gilt ivory sticks, the silk leaf painted with a central cartouche of a pair of fashionably dressed lovers and cherubs, 28cm. long, circa 1770s. (Phillips West Two) $800 £500

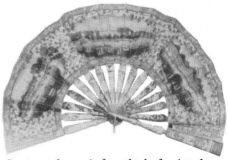

A Canton telescopic fan, the leaf painted with three views of the Hongs of Canton and Macao, circa 1860, in fitted lacquer box. (Christie's S. Ken) $2,317 £1,430

A fan, the leaf painted with the Family of Darius before Alexander, painted in mainly tones of green and terracotta, 11in., circa 1710. (Christie's S. Ken) $2,851 £1,760

An unmounted fan leaf on kid, painted with a trompe l'oeil a watercolour of Vesuvius erupting, Tarot cards, music sheets, lace and ribbons, 20in. wide, Italian, circa 1770. (Christie's S. Ken) $3,208 £1,980

A head and shoulders portrait photograph of Laurence Olivier signed and inscribed, with a portrait photograph of Vivien Leigh also signed and inscribed *For Ginger With My Best Wishes,* both 10 x 8in. (Christie's S. Ken) $695 £440

Laurel and Hardy — a half length publicity photograph signed twice by both individuals above and below each portrait *Stan Laurel* and *Oliver Hardy,* 5 x 7in. (Christie's S. Ken) $521 £330

Walt Disney Studios — Snow White and the Seven Dwarfs, 1937, gouache on celluloid, 10½ x 13¾in. (Christie's S. Ken) $1,738 £1,100

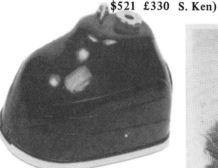

Gary Cooper — a half length portrait photographer signed and inscribed *Sincerely Gary Cooper,* 9 x 7in., circa 1937. (Christie's S. Ken) $261 £165

A 1920s Morrisharp Art Deco style electric pencil sharpener, accompanied with letter of authenticity from Peter Noble, stating that the composer Max Steiner used the pencil sharpener when writing the score for the film Gone With The Wind. (Christie's S. Ken) $313 £198

A half length publicity photo-graph of Nat King Cole signed and inscribed *To Lou Best of Luck, Nat King Cole,* 10 x 8in. (Christie's S. Ken) $226 £143

Louis Armstrong — One of two publicity photographs, signed and inscribed *My Best Wishes to E. H. Wilkinson From Louis Armstrong, 10/11/32,* (Christie's S. Ken) Two $487 £308

Marilyn Monroe — a Shannon Free Airport postcard signed *Marilyn Monroe* and *Arthur Miller,* with a previously un-published black and white snap shot. (Christie's S. Ken) $695 £440

A half length portrait photo-graph of Bela Lugosi, signed and inscribed *To My Friend Ginger in Rememberance, Bela Lugosi,* 10 x 8in. (Christie's S. Ken) $322 £198

A polychrome film poster The Fall Of The House Of Usher, featuring Vincent Price, 30 x 40in. (Christie's S. Ken) $52 £33

A gentleman's flat curb link identity bracelet with concealed clasp, the rectangular plate engraved on the obverse *Laurence Harvey Oct 1 1960.* (Christie's S. Ken) $695 £440

Marilyn Monroe — a polychrome film poster Gentlemen Prefer Blondes, printed by The Haycock Press, London, 30 x 40in. (Christie's S. Ken) $278 £176

A head and shoulders publicity photograph signed and inscribed *To Marjorie From Ronald Reagan "Good Luck" Always,* 10 x 8in. (Christie's S. Ken) $165 £105

A half length portrait photograph of Marilyn Monroe by Cecil Beaton, 9¼ x 9¼in., mounted on card, signed and inscribed, with original envelope frankmarked *Beverly Hills Calif. March 9th 1960.* (Christie's S. Ken)

$3,824 £2,420

Charlie Chaplin — August Leymarie *Everest Films presente Charlot,* lithograph in colours printed by L'Affiche d'Art, Paris, circa 1920, 62½ x 46½in. (Christie's S. Ken) $695 £440

Laurel and Hardy — a three-quarter length photograph of Stan Laurel playing the banjo whilst he unwittingly hits Oliver Hardy in the eye, signed and inscribed, 10 x 8in. (Christie's S. Ken) $869 £550

A Wadeheath pottery Walt Disney series novelty musical jug, the handle modelled as the Big Bad Wolf, printed factory mark and original paper label, 10in. high. (Christie's S. Ken) $785 £495

A three-quarter length photograph of Katharine Hepburn by Bob Willoughby on the set of the film The Lion In Winter, 1967, signed and inscribed, 12½ x 9¼in. (Christie's S. Ken) $348 £220

FILM MEMORABILIA

A brass key ring, one side inscribed with the MGM lion trade mark, the other inscribed *Dressing Room 24 Clark Gable,* 2¼in. diam. (Christie's S. Ken) $417 £264

Stan Laurel and Oliver Hardy — a pair of bowler hats, both with *Hal Roach Studios Wardrobe Department,* accompanied by a typescript letter, signed, dated *February 2nd 1938.* (Christie's S. Ken) $17,380 £11,000

Laurence Olivier — a head and shoulders portrait photograph of Laurence Olivier by photographer Gaston Longet, signed and inscribed, circa 1931, 9¾ x 7¾in. (Christie's S. Ken) $261 £165

A two piece evening outfit comprising a skin tight cocktail dress of aubergine coloured silk crepe, accompanied by a letter of authenticity from the executors of Marilyn Monroe's estate. (Christie's S. Ken) $7,172 £4,400

A surcoat of velvet in alternating burgundy and blue panels embroidered with raised gold thread, worn by Laurence Olivier in the title role of the 1944 Rank/Two Cities film Henry V. (Christie's S. Ken) $1,564 £990

Humphrey Bogart — a half length film still signed on the margin *Humphrey Bogart,* 10¼ x 8in. (Christie's S. Ken) $869 £550

Douglas Fairbanks Snr — a piece of paper signed and inscribed *Don Q. To Louella Parsons with great admiration and regard from Douglas Fairbanks 1925.* (Christie's S. Ken) $348 £220

Laurel and Hardy — a half length publicity photograph signed and inscribed *Hello Clive! Stan Laurel* and *Oliver Hardy,* 5 x 7in. (Christie's S. Ken) $452 £286

A collection of autographs from four of the leading characters in the 1939 MGM film The Wizard of Oz, in common mount with a reproduction still from the four characters standing, 23¼ x 15¼in. (Christie's S. Ken) $782 £495

Alfred Hitchcock — an illustrated souvenir programme for the Broadway production of Sleuth, 1970, signed by Alfred Hitchcock. (Christie's S. Ken) **$330 £209**

Laurel and Hardy — a head and shoulders publicity photograph signed and inscribed on the margin *Hello Gerald! Stan Laurel* and *Oliver Hardy,* 8 x 10in. (Christie's S. Ken) **$834 £528**

Marilyn Monroe — a typescript letter, signed, dated *April 17, 1958,* to Charles Henry Crowther, on Marilyn Monroe headed paper, thanking Crowther for sending a copy of the Golden Treasury. (Christie's S. Ken) **$1.130 £715**

A head and shoulders publicity portrait of Chet Baker, signed and inscribed *Hope to See You Soon Chet Baker,* 10 x 8in. (Christie's S. Ken) **$156 £99**

Errol Flynn — a rare collection of six autograph letters, signed, each written by South West London College schoolboy Errol Flynn to Mary White, the sister of a colleague, majority written by Flynn at the age of thirteen, various dates 8th–17th November 1922 and 24th January 1924.(Christie's S. Ken) **$4,519 £2,860**

A piece of Cunard White Star RMS Queen Elizabeth headed paper illustrated with a pencil drawing of Mickey Mouse, signed and inscribed *Best Wishes, Walt Disney,* 17.4 x 13.7cm. (Christie's S. Ken) **$4,866 £3,080**

Charlie Chaplin — a souvenir menu for the *Critics' Circle Film Section Luncheon,* in honour of *Charles Chaplin Esq. Empress Club, W1. 10-X-52,* signed, 9½ x 6in. (Christie's S. Ken) **$348 £220**

Richard Williams — The Pink Panther Standing In The Centre Of A Spotlight, signed, gouache on celluloid, 8 x 8in. (Christie's S. Ken) **$869 £550**

Marilyn Monroe — a re-issue promotional thermometer of bright orange and yellow enamel, for the United Artists film Some Like It Hot, made in the USA, 13 x 7¼in. (Christie's S. Ken) **$79 £50**

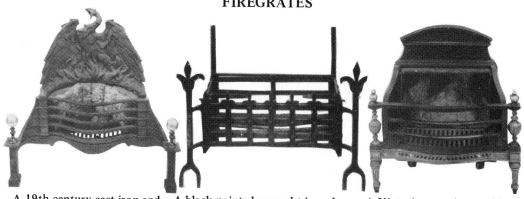

A 19th century cast iron and brass mounted fire grate, the concave backplate in the form of a phoenix rising from the flames, 36in. wide. (Christie's S. Ken) $986 £605

A black painted wrought iron dog grate, 33in. wide. (Christie's S. Ken) $341 £209

A Victorian cast iron and brass fire grate with serpentine railed front, the fret pierced with vitruvian scrolls flanked by baluster column standards, 24in. wide. (Christie's S. Ken) $807 £495

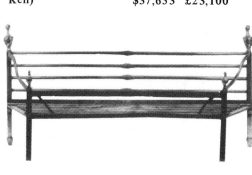

A brass and steel serpentine basket grate with pierced frame and scrolled supports, 21in. wide. (Christie's London) $434 £275

An Irish Georgian Carrara marble chimney-piece, with rectangular moulded shelf, the frieze inlaid with siena marble to simulate fluting with interspersed flowerheads within dotted roundels, 72 x 58in. high, the brass faced inset with raised classical figures within ovals flanking a bowed grate. (Christie's S. Ken) $37,653 £23,100

A Victorian iron and brass fire grate, the serpentine barred front above a pierced fret flanked by tapering standards, 27¾in. wide. (Christie's S. Ken.) $1,434 £880

A wrought iron fire grate, in the manner of Ernest Gimson, the shaped back cast with stylised and entwined foliage, 105.5cm. high. (Phillips London) $522 £320

An iron log grate, the rectangular barred front flanked by plain standards with applied navette shaped bosses, 44in. wide. (Christie's S. Ken.) $1,165 £715

A George III cast iron and brass serpentine fire grate with arched armorial back, 67cm. wide. (Phillips London) $2,745 $2,754 £1,800

FIREGRATES

A 19th century iron fire grate, the rectangular barred front above a pierced fret flanked by tapering column standards, 30½in. wide.(Christie's S. Ken) $3,227 £1,980

A cast iron fire grate, the inverted, barred front flanked by lion monopodiae standards with conical shaped finials, 35¼in. wide. (Christie's S. Ken) $897 £550

A brass and iron serpentine fronted fire grate, the waved fret pierced and incised with scrolling foliage and mythical beasts, part 18th century, 31½in. wide. (Christie's S. Ken) $717 £440

An engraved pierced brass and steel serpentine basket grate with urn finials and square tapering legs, 27in. wide. (Christie's London) $1,564 £990

One of a pair of brass cast iron fireplace insets, the frieze and uprights with applied figures of amorini emblamatic of the arts within panels of trophies and foliage, basically Victorian, 40 x 39¼in. (Christie's S. Ken) $4,662 £2,860

A Victorian iron and brass fire grate, the bowed front with pierced fret flanked by stylised lion monopodiae standards, 26in. wide. (Christie's S. Ken) $1,434 £880

An iron and brass grate, the barred rectangular front above a pierced fret incised with dragons and foliage, 28¼in. wide. (Christie's S. Ken) $1,793 £1,100

A Victorian cast iron and brass mounted fire grate, the bow railed front on paw feet with urn finials, 21½in. wide. (Christie's S. Ken) $1,076 £660

A Georgian iron and brass fire grate, the rectangular railed front flanked by applied oval bats' wing paterae above a pierced fret, 31in. wide. (Christie's S. Ken) $1,972 £1,210

A George III serpentine brass fender, the frieze pierced and incised with foliate ornament, 48in. long. (Christie's S. Ken) $1,793 £1,100

An Empire ormolu and bronzed adjustable fender with recumbent lions on scrolling plinth ends, 59½in. wide. (Christie's London) $4,345 £2,750

A late 19th century massive serpentine brass fender, the frieze pierced and incised with an urn of flowers, dragons and scrolling foliage, 90½in. wide. (Christie's S. Ken) $1,793 £1,100

A Georgian steel fender of bowed outline, with pierced and applied oval lozenges and foliage, 50in. wide.
(Christie's S. Ken.) $508 £308

A giltmetal adjustable fender of Empire style with winged seated griffins upon plinth ends applied with flaming winged lightning trophies, 44in. wide.
(Christie's) $1030 £660

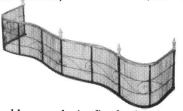

A Federal brass and wire fire fender, American, early 19th century, with moulded brass rim and urn form finials, 55in. long.
(Christie's New York) $9,350 £5,880

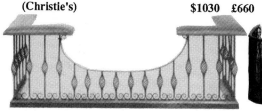

A black painted wrought iron club fender, the square section uprights with central open spiral twist knops, 75½in. long. (Christie's S. Ken) $1,255 £770

A brass and iron wire fire fender, early 19th century, D-shaped with three brass oval finials above a patterned woven screen decorated with scrolls, 56in. wide.
(Christie's) $2200 £1384

A 19th century brass 'D' shaped fender, the frieze pierced and engraved with foliage, 50in. wide.
(Christie's S. Ken.) $172 £104

An early 19th century steel fender with four urn finials, the frieze pierced with Vittuvian scrolls, 67¹/₂in. long .
(Christie's S. Ken.) $1361 £825

An early 19th century brass fender of bowed outline, the frieze pierced with lattice work and urns, 46in. wide.
(Christie's S. Ken.) $508 £308

A George III serpentine brass fender, the frieze pierced and engraved with linked lozenges and flowerheads, 44in. long.
(Christie's S. Ken) $1,076 £660

FIREPLACE FURNITURE

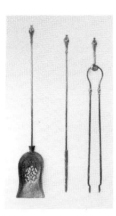

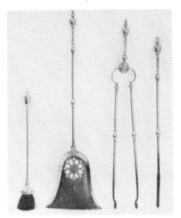

A set of three late George III steel fire irons, comprising a poker, tongs and pierced shovel, the shovel 30½in. long. (Christie's London) $274 £176

A set of three George III steel fire irons with pommel finials and pierced shovel about 31in. long, and associated brush. (Christie's London) $869 £550

A set of three Georgian steel fire irons, the baluster brass grips chased with foliage. (Christie's S. Ken) $502 £308

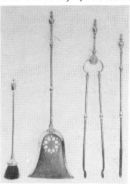

A set of three William IV ormolu mounted fire irons comprising a pierced shovel, tongs and a poker, 30in. long. (Christie's London) $1,029 £660

A pair of Federal steeple top faceted plinth brass andirons with matching shovel and tongs, New York, 1790-1810. (Christie's New York) $9,680 £6,088

A set of George III fire irons, comprising a pierced shovel, tongs and a poker and an associated brush. (Christie's London) $772 £495

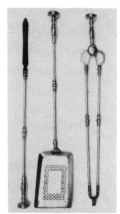

A set of three Georgian paktong fire irons, comprising shovel, poker and tongs. (Christie's S. Ken) $3,586 £2,200

A set of three Georgian brass fire irons with urn finials, the shovel 31in. long, and a fire-brush. (Christie's London) $1,217 £770

Four piece wrought iron fire-place set, attributed to Gustav Stickley, circa 1905, with strapwork log holder, unsigned, 33½in. high. (Skinner Inc.) $5,500 £3,395

A Victorian white marble chimneypiece, the serpentine moulded shelf above a plain frieze centred by a keystone tablet carved with floral spray, 72½ x 49½in. high. (Christie's S. Ken) $4,841 £2,970

A Scottish Georgian polychrome pine and gesso chimneypiece, the inverted breakfront shelf above a panelled frieze modelled with sea shells, seaweed and flowers, 83 x 60½in. high. (Christie's S. Ken) $2,152 £1,320

A Georgian pine and gesso chimneypiece, the breakfront shelf above a swagged, dentilled and pineapple moulded cornice, the centre panel of the frieze depicting a turreted tower within a wooded landscape, 68 x 58in. high. (Christie's S. Ken) $4,124 £2,530

A Victorian white painted pine and gesso chimneypiece in the Adam taste, the inverted breakfront shelf with stiff leaf moulding above an egg and dart cornice, 70½ x 57½in. high. (Christie's S. Ken) $1,434 £880

A French dove grey marble and ormolu mounted fire surround, circa 1820, with plain moulded rectangular shelf, the frieze applied with masks within wreaths and anthemion leaf motifs, 59½ x 47¼in. high. (Christie's S. Ken) $5,020 £3,080

A Regency carrara marble and bronze mounted chimneypiece, the rectangular moulded shelf above a plain frieze centred by an applied anthemion leaf motif flanked by wreaths 53¼ x 41½in. high. (Christie's S. Ken) $2,689 £1,650

BEDS

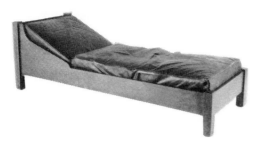

Limbert oak day bed, Michigan, circa 1910, shaped headrest and wide skirt accommodating spring cushions, square raised feet, 79in. long. (Robt. W. Skinner Inc.) $500 £307

An Ebene de Macassar single bed designed by Emile Jacques Ruhlmann, mounted on chrome plated plinth bases, 109cm. wide. (Christie's London) $4,482 £2,750

A Chinese black lacquered marriage bedstead, the pierced profusely carved gilded frieze and serpentined apron flanking interior picture panels, 96½in. high. (Christie's S. Ken.) $4,303 £2,640

An Italian parcel gilt, walnut and ebonised bed with distressed padded solid headboard, shaped foot rest and sides with turned finials, 70 x 85in.(Christie's London) $5,562 £3,520

Chinese opium bed, 19th century, open lattic work and carved canopy with gilded frieze, raised on a base fitted with drawers, 81in. wide. (Skinner Inc.) $2,000 £1,250

A late Federal carved mahogany high post bedstead, Massachusetts, 1810-1820, the footposts spiral turned with acanthus and waterleaf carved inverted balusters, 58in. wide. (Christie's New York)$2,860 £1,798

BEDS

L. & J. G. Stickley oak double bed, Fayetteville, New York, circa 1910, signed, 50in. high, 58in. wide. (Skinner Inc.) $5,250 £3,241

German gondola shaped cradle cross banded in black, slung between lyre shaped end pieces, on ogee feet, circa 1820. (Kunsthaus am Museum) $3,783 £2,174

An Empire ormolu mounted mahogany lit bateau, each of the panelled ends with a rounded toprail and with box spring and mattress. (Christie's London) $3,128 £1,980

An oak four poster bed of panelled construction, the head-board with arched architectural panel inlaid with birds and flowers, the footboard carved with lozenges, 76in. long. (Christie's London) $5,313 £3,300

A mahogany and parcel gilt four poster bed, the arched canopy with foliate moulded cornice hung with ribbon tied tasselled drapery swags, 18th century and later, 87in. long. (Christie's London) $9,862 £6,050

A George III green, buff, red and blue painted four post bed, the arched canopy decorated with panels of flowers and beading, extensively restored and redecorated, 79in. wide. (Christie's London) $37,653 £23,100

A George III mahogany four post bedstead, the two foot posts fluted and stop- fluted above acanthus carved baluster and square bases, 224cm. high. Lawrence Fine Arts) $5,020 £3,080

An oak cradle with shaped hood and sides, basically 17th century, 36½in. wide. (Christie's S. Ken) $1,109 £660

An oak four poster bed, the tester panels carved with lozenges, the frieze carved with lunettes and foliage, basically 17th century. (Christie's London) $9,740 £6,050

BOOKCASES

A William IV mahogany bookcase, with cavetto cornice above a pair of glazed doors and a pair of panelled doors, 54in. wide. (Christie's S. Ken) $2,125 £1,320

A scarlet japanned dwarf bookcase decorated in gilt with two shaped glazed doors, the panelled sides painted with Chinese landscapes, on bun feet, 37in. wide. (Christie's London) $2,059 £1,320

A Regency simulated rosewood japanned dwarf bookcase decorated in gilt with chinoiserie figures, birds, plants and buildings, on square tapering feet, 25in. wide. (Christie's London) $8,965 £5,500

A Victorian mahogany bookcase applied with scroll carved mouldings, the top section with a moulded cornice enclosed by a pair of arched glazed doors, 46in. wide. (Christie's S. Ken) $1,434 £880

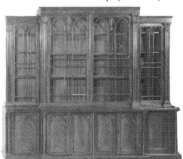

A William IV mahogany breakfront library bookcase, with four gothic arched glazed doors applied with honeysuckle and divided by reeded pilasters with acanthus capitals, 122in. wide. (Christie's London) $55,616 £35,200

A late Regency mahogany bookcase with two glazed doors enclosing adjustable shelves and divided by pilasters inlaid with scrolling ebony lines and anthemions, 59½in. wide. (Christie's London) $16,511 £10,450

A second Empire walnut bookcase, the finialled serpentined cornice with cartouche and foliate cresting, 43½in. wide. (Christie's S. Ken) $1,062 £660

An oak bookcase, with column supports and small shelf, the base column moulding supporting two shelves on trestle ends, 121.5cm. wide. (Christie's London) $2,772 £1,650

A late 19th century light oak bookcase, the base having twin drawers with brass pulls with twin doors panelled with slanting planks. (Phillips) $1,312 £820

BOOKCASES

L. & J. G. Stickley single door bookcase, circa 1907, no. 643, gallery top with exposed key tenons over single door, 36in. wide. (Robt. W. Skinner Inc.) $2,000 £1,227

A Georgian mahogany break-front library bookcase with a moulded cornice above four glazed doors with rectangular astragals, on plinth base, 280cm. wide. (Lawrence Fine Arts) $15,642 £9,900

Shop of the Crafters inlaid bookcase, Cincinnati, Ohio, 1906, with pierced detail over two glass doors, 28¼in. wide. (Robt. W. Skinner Inc.) $1,700 £1,043

A Classical rosewood desk and bookcase, probably Boston 1825-1835, on flaring hex-agonally faceted legs above a shaped medial shelf, 50½in wide. (Christie's New York) $14,300 £8,993

A pair of painted satinwood dwarf bookcases, each with open shelves, on tapered feet, 19¾in. wide. (Christie's S. Ken) Two $1,524 £935

A late George III mahogany library bookcase, with arched cornice above a pair of geo-metrically glazed doors with arched and lobed astragals, 1.48m. wide. (Phillips London) $6,120 £4,000

L. & J. G. Stickley two door bookcase, Fayetteville, New York, circa 1907, unsigned, (escutcheons replaced) 42in. wide. (Skinner Inc.) $3,100 £1,914

A Victorian mahogany standing bookcase with a cavetto cornice and enclosed by a glazed gothic astragal door, on ogee bracket feet, 44½in. wide. (Christie's S. Ken) $3,011 £1,870

Limbert open book rack, Michigan, circa 1910, flat sides centring three open shelves, 28in. high. (Robt. W. Skinner Inc.) $650 £399

BOOKCASES

A mahogany breakfront bookcase with moulded cornice above four glazed doors and four radial panelled cupboard doors, 64in. wide. (Christie's S. Ken) $2,218 £1,320

L. & J. G. Stickley three door bookcase, circa 1906, no. 647, gallery top and exposed key tenons over three doors, unsigned, 70in. wide. (Robt. W. Skinner Inc.) $4,000 £2,454

A Chinese hualiwood bookcase, carved with lion scaped panels depicting figures, on block feet, 48in. wide. (Christie's S. Ken) $1,201 £715

A Peter Waals rosewood bookcase, the lower part with two pairs of cupboard doors, on plinth base and bracket feet, 166cm. wide. (Christie's London) $1,793 £1,100

A William IV rosewood bookcase with moulded cornice and four glazed panelled doors between pilasters headed by foliate volutes, 72in. wide. (Christie's S. Ken) $7,392 £4,400

A Victorian mahogany library bookcase, the moulded cornice and four glazed doors above a pair of panelled doors, 100 x 96in. wide. (Christie's S. Ken) $3,048 £1,870

A Chippendale period mahogany bookcase, with a dentil moulded cornice and broken architectural pediment, 1.35m. wide. (Phillips London) $6,120 £4,000

A good early Victorian mahogany breakfront library bookcase, with five glazed doors, the upper section applied with rich flower head and acanthus carved glazing bars, 350cm. wide. (Henry Spencer) $8,965   £5,500

A George III mahogany, boxwood and ebony strung secretaire bookcase enclosed by a pair of arched astragal glazed doors applied with Prince of Wales feather cresting, 1.20m. wide. (Phillips London) $6,120 £4,000

BUREAU BOOKCASES

An early George III carved bureau cabinet, the upper part with a swan neck pediment terminating in rosettes and with a dentil cornice, on later bracket feet, 1.13m. wide. (Phillips London)$9,945 £6,500

A good George II red walnut bureau cabinet of narrow proportions, the architectural upper part with a moulded dentil cornice and fitted with adjustable shelves, 86cm. wide. (Phillips London)
$53,550 £35,000

Chippendale cherry desk and bookcase, probably Hartford County, Connecticut, 1780-1810, on shaped bracket feet, refinished (pediment and brasses replaced), 40in. wide. (Skinner Inc.)$14,000 £8,589

A walnut bureau bookcase, the arched top with two glazed doors above a feather banded slope, 36in. wide. (Christie's S. Ken) $3,198 £2,090

Baroque walnut and kingwood inlaid bureau cabinet, with faceted mirror, 200cm. high, 120cm. wide. (Auktionshaus Arnold) $12,143 £7,885

A North Italian walnut bureau cabinet with arched moulded cornice and a glazed cupboard door enclosing a partly fitted interior and well, 44in. wide. (Christie's London)
$83,424 £52,800

A George III mahogany bureau cabinet, the bureau with hinged slope and fitted interior above two short and three long drawers, on bracket feet, 43in. wide. (Christie's London)
$6,521 £4,180

German Brunswick mid-18th century walnut, burr walnut and marquetry cabinet, with writing compartment and three drawers under, on bun feet, 110cm. wide. (Kunsthaus am Museum) $10,807 £6,211

A George III oak bureau book-case, with two short and three graduated long drawers, on bracket feet, 50½in. (Christie's S. Ken) $1,703 £1,045

BUREAU BOOKCASES

A George III mahogany bureau bookcase, the interior with drawers and pigeon holes, the drawer inlaid with Prince of Wales feathers, 48in. wide. (Christie's London) $3,604 £2,310

A mahogany bureau bookcase, with fretwork broken pediment, the bureau with baize lined flap and fitted interior above four drawers, 44in. wide. (Christie's London) $5,379 £3,300

A Victorian mahogany bureau bookcase, the top section with a moulded cornice, on bracket feet, 42in. wide. (Christie's S. Ken.) $2,402 £1,430

A Dutch East Indies (Sri Lanka) kaliatur and calamander brass mounted bureau cabinet, the moulded arched cornice above two glazed doors, 18th century, 57in. wide. (Christie's London) $3,542 £2,200

A George III oak bureau cabinet with cream painted paterae above two panelled doors, on bracket feet, 50in. wide. (Christie's London) $4,662 £2,860

German mid-18th century walnut and burr walnut tabernacle bureau cabinet, the door and drawers with secret locks, on bun feet, 116cm. wide. (Kunsthaus am Museum) $24,317 £13,975

A George III oak bureau cabinet, now stripped to a golden colour, crossbanded in walnut and with stained inlay, 44¼in. wide. (Tennants) $1,896 £1,200

A George II walnut bureau cabinet, the bevelled rectangular plate with shaped upper corners, on later bracket feet, 33in. wide. (Christie's London) $14,872 £8,800

A mahogany bureau bookcase with arcaded cornice above a pair of geometrically glazed doors, George III. 51in. wide. (Christie's S. Ken.) $8,870 £5,280

BUREAUX

A Dutch walnut and marquetry bombe bureau, with flower filled vases and birds, the fitted interior including a well, 42in. wide. (Christie's S. Ken) $8,415 £5,500

Federal mahogany inlaid slant lid desk, New England, circa 1810, on shaped inlaid base with French feet, 38in. wide. (Skinner Inc.) $1,800 £1,161

A Dutch marquetry and mahogany bombe cylinder bureau, the cylinder inlaid with a lyre flanked by bowls of fruit enclosing a slide and well fitted interior, late 18th century, 49in. wide. (Christie's London) $9,559 £6,050

A George I olivewood bureau, the hinged slope enclosing drawers and pigeon holes flanking a door and two pilaster drawers, on bracket feet, restorations, 36in. wide. (Christie's London) $5,148 £3,300

A small burr elm bureau inlaid with chequered lines, the interior with arcaded drawers and pigeon holes flanking columns and a drawer, on bracket feet, 28in. wide. (Christie's London) $2,917 £1,870

A mahogany bureau, the hinged sloping flap enclosing a fitted interior above six drawers, on bracket feet, early 19th century, 47½in. wide. (Christie's S. Ken) $1,515 £990

An ormolu mounted kingwood and marquetry cylinder bureau with fitted interior and sliding writing surface, on clasp headed cabriole legs, 29½in. wide. (Christie's S. Ken) $1,496 £880

An early Georgian walnut bureau, cross and feather banded and in figured veneers throughout, on later elm base, the top 36in. wide. (Tennants) $2,844 £1,800

A rosewood and foliate marquetry bureau de dame, the serpentine slope enclosing a fitted interior including a lined writing surface, late 19th century, 27in. wide. (Christie's S. Ken) $1,408 £880

FURNITURE

BUREAUX

An ormolu mounted king-
wood and marquetry bureau
a cylindre of Louis XV style,
flanked by bacchic putti and
scrolling foliage, on cabriole
legs, modern. (Christie's London) $10,626 £6,600

Chippendale mahogany
veneered slant lid desk,
probably Massachusetts, circa
1800, on moulded bracket
base, replaced pulls, 39¾in.
high. (Skinner Inc.)
          $3,500 £2,258

Biedermeier walnut bureau,
restorations to veneer, 128cm.
wide. (Auktionshaus Arnold)
          $1,379 £896

Louis XV Provincial walnut
bureau en pente, mid 18th century, shaped slant front
opening to black leather
writing surface, 45in. wide.
(Skinner Inc.) $4,750 £3,025

A late Victorian rosewood
bureau inlaid with ivory and
marquetry panels depicting
gryphons, cornucopiae, scrolling
arabesques and a falconry hunt,
31in. wide. (Christie's S. Ken)
          $1,859 £1,155

A Louis XV tulipwood and
kingwood parquetry bureau,
the shaped hinged slope lined
in green leather enclosing a
stepped interior with drawers
and shelves around a well, 44½in.
wide. (Christie's London)
          $10,428 £6,600

An oyster veneered walnut
bureau, the sloping flap enclosing a fitted interior
including a well above a pair of
short and two graduated long
drawers, on bun feet, 32in.
wide. (Christie's London)
          $6,506 £3,850

William and Mary oak slant
front desk, the fitted interior
with drawers, doors and cubbyholes, 30in. wide. (Skinner Inc,)
          $3,900 £2,484

A George II walnut bureau,
the hinged flap enclosing a
fitted interior with a door
flanked by columns, pigeon
holes and stepped drawers, on
bracket feet, 36½in. wide.
(Christie's London)
          $2,788 £1,650

BUREAUX

A late 18th/early 19th century Dutch mahogany and floral bombe fronted bureau in two sections, the upper part with hinged sloping ogee fall inlaid with a basket of flowers, 1.35m. wide. (Phillips London) $16,065 £10,500

A Louis XV style rosewood and marquetry inlaid bureau de dame, the serpentined rectangular panelled top with a pierced three quarter gallery, on cabriole legs, 30½in. wide. (Christie's S. Ken) $1,682 £1,045

A Chippendale carved cherrywood reverse serpentine desk, Massachusetts, 1780-1800, with thumb moulded slant lid enclosing a compartmented interior, 44¼in. wide. (Christie's New York) $10,450 £6,572

A Chippendale figured maple slant front desk, New England, 1760-1780, with thumb moulded slant lid opening to a fitted interior with six valanced pigeonholes, 93.7cm. (Christie's New York) $12,100 £7,610

A Chippendale carved mahogany slant front desk, signed *Joseph Davis,* Newburyport, Massachusetts, circa 1775, on ball and claw feet, 40in. wide. (Christie's New York) $7,700 £4,842

A George III mahogany bureau with hinged slope and fitted interior, the three graduated long drawers on bracket feet, 44in. wide. (Christie's S. Ken) $1,848 £1,100

Gustav Stickley dropfront desk, circa 1912, no. 732, gallery top with tenon sides, 32in. wide. (Robt. W. Skinner Inc.) $850 £521

An unusual George III sycamore, tulipwood crossbanded and marquetry bombe bureau de dame, in the manner of Christopher Furlogh and George Haupt, on cabriole legs, 78cm. wide. (Phillips London) $6,885 £4,500

A George III mahogany bureau, the hinged sloping front enclosing an inlaid fitted interior above four graduated long drawers, on bracket feet, 36½in. wide. (Christie's S. Ken) $2,302 £1,430

BUREAUX

A George III mahogany bureau, the hinged rectangular slope enclosing an elaborately fitted arcaded interior, on ogee bracket feet, 48in. wide. (Christie's S. Ken) **$3,142 £1,870**

A South German walnut and ebonised bureau cabinet inlaid with stars and geometric bands, on turned tapering bun feet, basically 19th century, 51in. (Christie's S. Ken) **$4,114 £2,420**

A late George III oak bureau, the slope and fitted interior above four graduated long drawers on bracket feet, 33in. wide. (Christie's S. Ken) **$2,032 £1,210**

Maple grained desk, Southern New England, circa 1800, the interior with valanced compartments and recessed panel prospect door, old refinish, 38½in. wide. (Skinner Inc.) **$5,000 £3,067**

A Neo Classical style satinwood and rosewood banded cylinder bureau, painted and decorated with cherubs and riband flowersprays, 32½in. wide. (Christie's S. Ken) **$5,544 £3,300**

Fine Queen Anne tiger maple slant lid desk, New Hampshire, circa 1750, the slant lid opens to a double tier stepped interior, old finish, 37½in. wide. (Skinner Inc.) **$55,000 £33,742**

Chippendale carved maple desk, New Hampshire, attributed to the Dunlaps, 1780-1800, on an ogee bracket moulded base, 35in. wide. (Skinner Inc.) **$51,000 £31,288**

A late 18th century Dutch walnut bureau, of bombe form, raised upon lion paw and ball front supports and bracket back supports, 93.5cm. wide. (Henry Spencer) **$5,216 £3,200**

Country Queen Anne maple desk on frame, New England, circa 1740, the slant lid opens to reveal interior with compartments and drawers, 34in. wide. (Skinner Inc.) **$4,250 £2,607**

CABINETS

Mahogany cabinet with cockle shell doors, 20th century, cut out crest on arched gallery top, 34½in. wide. (Robt. W. Skinner Inc.) $325 £199

A Dutch Colonial ebony and rosewood cabinet on stand, the two fielded doors enclosing a hinged architectural interior with sixteen false drawers, 19th century and later, 39in. (Christie's S. Ken) $1,515 £990

An unusual Edwardian mahogany drinks cabinet, the fall front opening to reveal a suspended shelf retaining three cut glass decanters, 31in. wide. (Tennants) $1,326 £850

Gustav Stickley smoker's cabinet, circa 1907, over-hanging top above single drawer and cabinet door, 20in. wide. (Robt. W. Skinner Inc.) $1,500 £920

A late 17th century japanned cabinet on contemporary carved giltwood stand, the upper part enclosed by a pair of panel doors decorated with chinoiserie landscapes, 1m. wide. (Phillips London) $4,896 £3,200

A Federal walnut cabinet on chest, Pennsylvania, 1800-1820, in two sections, the upper cabinet with moulded cornice above two recessed panel covered doors, on French feet, 41¼in. wide. (Christie's New York) $9,900 £6,226

A Victorian ormolu mounted walnut and marquetry display side cabinet with shaped glazed door and clasp headed uprights, 33in. wide. (Christie's S. Ken) $1,309 £770

A French Provincial aumbrey with arched top inlaid in a foliate pattern, mainly 17th century, 99 x 130cm. high. (Lawrence Fine Arts) $9,324 £5,720

An ormolu mounted ebony and black lacquer side cabinet, the door decorated with a Chinese landscape, on paw feet, 28in. wide. (Christie's London) $3,010 £1,870

CABINETS

A Dutch ebonised fruitwood and walnut cabinet on stand, with chequer stringing, on four square supports, late 17th century, 56cm. wide. (Lawrence Fine Arts) $3,997 £2,530

A good Victorian porcelain mounted walnut side cabinet of broken shallow D-form, with small floral porcelain ovals, 60in. wide, 39½in. high. (Tennants) $4,368 £2,800

A black lacquer cabinet on a stand decorated in red and gilt with landscapes and birds, distressed, 18th century, 37in. wide. (Christie's S. Ken)
$2,059 £1,320

An early 18th century walnut cabinet on chest, the upper part with a moulded cornice and cushion frieze drawer, on bracket feet, 1.03m. wide. (Phillips London)
$5,355 £3,500

A pair of ebonised and boulle side cabinets with gilt metal mounts incorporating female caryatid figures, 19th century, 82cm. wide. (Lawrence Fine Arts) $1,793 £1,100

A good 19th century French ebonised and amboyna salon cabinet, the high stepped superstructure with arched cresting to the canopied top, 183cm. long. (Henry Spencer)
$3,749 £2,300

A walnut cabinet crossbanded and inlaid with feather bands, the moulded cornice above a pair of mirror glazed doors, 41in. wide. (Christie's S. Ken)
$3,696 £2,200

Painted pine wall cabinet, America, early 18th century, the rectangular case with applied double arched moulding, 18in. wide. (Skinner Inc.) $3,700 £2,270

A Gothic Revival oak cabinet, the upper part with a moulded cornice and two panelled doors, 54in. wide. (Phillips Sevenoaks)
$2,040 £1,200

CABINETS

A Dutch mahogany side cabinet, with broken pediment applied with rushes and wheatears above a pair of radial glazed doors, basically late 18th century, 68in. wide. (Christie's S. Ken)$7,172 £4,400

A William IV mahogany library cabinet with leather lined articulated rounded rectangular top, the sides with foliate bronze handles, on plinth base, 54in. wide. (Christie's London) $27,808 £17,600

Oak liquor cabinet with copper slide, probably Michigan, circa 1910, with fitted compartments, unsigned, 40¾in. high. (Skinner Inc.) $550 £340

A Louis XVI mahogany semanier, with seven panelled drawers inlaid with brass lines and turned oak feet, 38½in. wide. (Christie's London) $1,390 £880

19th century oak hall cupboard, with panelled doors and drawers at the base, 177cm. wide, 227cm. high. (Auktionshaus Arnold) $607 £394

A 19th century mahogany table cabinet, the hinged, panelled doors to the front enclosing a compartmented interior, 12½in. wide. (Christie's S. Ken)$224 £132

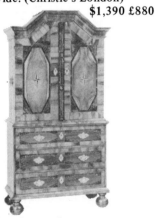

A walnut and marquetry cabinet on chest in the baroque style, restorations, 109cm. wide. (Auktionshaus Arnold) $4,968 £3,226

An oak dwarf cabinet with two doors each carved with a grotesque mask, a basket of fruit, a bowl of flowers, a bunch of grapes, a scroll and a sheaf of foliage, 16th century, probably Spanish, 34in. wide. (Christie's London) $7,436 £4,400

A mahogany and satinwood banded side cabinet and associated bookcase, top with two glazed doors above a fall-front, early 19th century, 55in. wide. (Christie's S. Ken) $1,287 £825

CABINETS

An early Georgian walnut cabinet on chest with moulded cornice above a pair of cupboard doors enclosing twelve drawers, on later bracket feet, 43in. wide. (Christie's London) $8,923 £5,280

A French gilt metal mounted mahogany breakfront side cabinet with eared Carrara marble top and frieze applied with riband tied swags of flowers, 75in. wide. (Christie's S. Ken) $3,198 £2,090

An Edwardian mahogany smoker's table cabinet, the lower part with a compartment and drawer enclosed by a glazed panel door, 12½in. high. (Christie's S. Ken) $202 £132

A George IV rosewood side cabinet with a pair of recessed panel doors flanked by richly figured brass mounted pillars, 44in. wide. (Tennants) $2,028 £1,300

A Victorian walnut serpentine side cabinet, the eared Carrara rectangular marble top below a mirrored back, 60in. wide. (Christie's S. Ken) $1,010 £660

A fine Goanese ivory, ebony and hardwood cabinet on stand inlaid overall with geometric marquetry with rectangular top and ten various size drawers, 40in. wide. (Christie's London) $33,022 £20,900

A Dutch tulipwood side cabinet with D-shaped top and one frieze drawer above a pair of tambour cupboards, 27in. wide. (Christie's London) $2,086 £1,320

A Regency mahogany and satinwood side cabinet with two frieze drawers above a pair of panelled cupboards inlaid with ovals, 36½in. wide. (Christie's London) $1,544 £990

A Dutch mahogany and marquetry inlaid serpentined side cabinet, the frieze drawer above a panel door between Corinthian column pilasters, 19th century, 30in. wide. (Christie's S. Ken) $2,869 £1,760

CABINETS

A late George III amboyna collector's cabinet, eleven cedar-lined satinwood drawers, on later brass bound base, 32in. wide. (Christie's London) $3,089 £1,980

A mid-19th century ebonised and boullework credenza, with gilt brass bacchus mask corbels, and with boullework panels to the frieze, 12cm. long. (Henry Spencer) $3,726 £2,300

An Iberian ebonised and bone inlaid table cabinet, the top inset with tortoiseshell and mother-of-pearl panels depicting birds and foliage, 17th century, 18½in. wide. (Christie's S. Ken) $2,288 £1,430

A walnut cabinet on stand, the stepped top with moulded cornice and arcaded frieze above two partly glazed panelled doors, on ribbed and fluted naturalistic cluster columns carved with acanthus, 42in. wide. (Christie's London) $8,606 £5,280

A walnut cabinet on stand, the crossbanded rectangular top with moulded frieze above a pair of featherbanded doors, 42½in. wide. (Christie's S. Ken) $2,510 £1,540

A Flemish oak cabinet on stand carved with acanthus scrolls and cherub mask, the moulded cornice and deep frieze above a fielded panelled door, basically early 17th century, 29½in. wide. (Christie's London) $4,250 £2,640

A mahogany and brass mounted side cabinet with a pair of panel doors enclosing a recess flanked by cedar lined drawers, on cabriole legs, 25½in. wide. (Christie's S. Ken) $1,255 £770

Empire Style Mahogany and Ormolu Mounted Cabinet, last-quarter 19th century, moulded cornice above a pair of cabinet doors, 37in. wide. (Skinner Inc) $1600 £1038

Henry II style walnut cabinet, late 19th century, the upper section with carved, pierced cornice above a pair of carved cabinet doors, raised on bun feet, 55in. wide. (Robt. W. Skinner Inc.) $750 £457

CANTERBURYS

A rosewood two tier canterbury with rectangular top on column supports above a divided shelf, on turned feet, 30in. wide (Christie's London)
$2,331 £1,430

A late Regency rosewood canterbury with three division top and single drawer, on turned tapered legs, 20in. wide. (Christie's S. Ken)$2,479 £1,540

An early Victorian rosewood Canterbury, the foliate laurel slatted three division rectangular top, 18$^1/_2$in. wide. (Christie's S. Ken.)$1996 £1210

A Regency mahogany Canterbury, the concave partitions above a drawer, on ring turned tapered legs, 20in. wide.
(Bonhams) $1815 £1100

A mid-Victorian walnut Canterbury whatnot with C-scrolling three-quarter galleried rectangular top on open fretwork vase-shaped supports, 24in. wide. (Christie's S. Ken.)$2722 £1650

Regency Rosewood Caterbury, 18th/19th century, with turned supports on a single frieze drawer, raised on turned legs ending in brass casters, 18in. high.
(Skinner Inc) $1900 £1233

A Regency mahogany Canterbury with dished rectangular top and turned baluster spindles to the sides, with giltmetal paw feet, 21in. wide.
(Christie's) $20592 £13200

A Victorian mahogany Canterbury Whatnot, the rectangular top with a pierced fretwork gallery, 20$^1/_2$in. wide. (Bonhams) $891 £540

A William IV rosewood canterbury, the divided top enclosed by baluster posts above a drawer on turned feet, 24¼in. wide. (Christie's S. Ken)
$2,510 £1,540

DINING CHAIRS

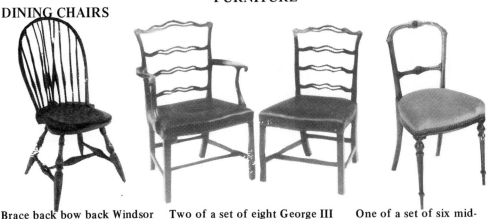

Brace back bow back Windsor side chair, probably Rhode Island, circa 1780, painted green, 35½in. high. (Skinner Inc.) $850 £548

Two of a set of eight George III mahogany dining chairs, the pierced shaped ladder backs above padded seats. (Christie's S. Ken) Eight $7,531 £4,620

One of a set of six mid-Victorian walnut side chairs, each with a carved flower-head to the arched crest rail. (Tennants)
Six $1,060 £680

A Queen Anne maple side chair, Massachusetts, 1730-1750, with carved yoke crest above a solid vase shaped splat, 42in. high. (Christie's New York) $3,520 £2,214

A pair of late George III mahogany dining chairs, each with a pierced lattice back and padded seat on turned tapered reeded legs. (Christie's S. Ken) $1,571 £935

One of a set of six Victorian walnut dining chairs, the cresting rails carved and pierced with flowers and foliage. (Henry Spencer)
Six $2,037 £1,250

A William and Mary painted maple side chair, Essex County, Massachusetts, 1740-1760, on cylinder and ring turned front legs, 42½in. high. (Christie's New York) $1,100 £691

Pair of Dutch walnut and marquetry side chairs, second quarter 19th century, shaped, rounded back above a solid baluster form splat. (Robt. W. Skinner Inc.) $700 £427

Gustav Stickley leather upholstered side chair, circa 1904, signed with small red decal, 33¼in. high. (Skinner Inc.) $1,500 £926

DINING CHAIRS

Italian marquetry and ivory inlaid hall chair, the panel back depicting a courtier, X stretcher base. (G. A. Key) $952 £560

Two of a set of eight late George III mahogany dining chairs, including two carvers, on ring turned tapered legs. (Christie's S. Ken)
Eight $8,069 £4,950

One of a pair of Valabrega sidechairs, each back of carved curvilinear pierced form. (Christie's London)
Two $5,199 £3,190

Rosewood laminated side chair, circa 1860, pierced and carved oval back, raised on cabriole legs, 34¾in. high. (Skinner Inc.) $400 £258

Two of a set of three Regency mahogany dining chairs, each with a curved scroll top rail, and three similar, partly early 19th century. (Christie's S. Ken)
Six $3,511 £2,090

A composite set of eight George III faded mahogany dining chairs, on square legs with stretchers. (Tennants)
$4,740 £3,000

Queen Anne walnut side chair, Massachusetts, circa 1780, the serpentine crest rail with scrolled ears, 37¾in. high. (Skinner Inc.) $2,200 £1,419

Two of a set of eight mahogany dining chairs, the acanthus carved backs with padded seats and gadrooned aprons. (Christie's S. Ken)
Eight $6,059 £3,960

One of a set of six George IV mahogany dining chairs, with curved cresting rails, fluted and turned front legs. (G. A. Key)
Six $1,210 £720

DINING CHAIRS

Two of a Harlequin set of ten North Country ash and elm ladder back chairs including two carvers, late 18th century and later. (Christie's S. Ken)
Ten $7,069 £4,620

A Chippendale mahogany side chair, Philadelphia, 1780-1800, the back with four horizontal moulded and pierced slats, 38in. high. (Christie's New York) $1,100 £691

A pair of Regency yew rustic chairs, constructed from branches, on squared legs with shaped brackets. (Christie's London) $6,506 £3,850

Two of a set of eight black and polychrome painted side chairs, with ribbon tied Prince of Wales' feathers, on square tapering legs with spade feet. (Christie's S. Ken)
Eight $7,172 £4,400

An Italian walnut chair upholstered in worn velvet on spirally twisted legs and stretchers, 17th century. (Christie's London)
          $2,231 £1,320

A pair of oak side chairs designed by C. A. Voysey, each back splat pierced with heart-shaped motif, on square section legs joined by plain stretchers. (Christie's London)
          $12,012 £7,150

Two of a set of eight Irish George III mahogany harlequin dining chairs, the pierced splat backs above close nailed up-holstered seats. (Christie's S. Ken) Eight $2,956 £1,760

Michigan Chair Co. spindle back side chair, Grand Rapids, Michigan, circa 1910, partial label, 39in. high. (Skinner Inc.)
          $800 £494

A pair of German, mid-18th century, beechwood chairs, with waved and pierced splat and curved seatrail, on cabriole legs. (Kunsthaus am Museum)
          $919 £528

DINING CHAIRS

Two of a set of eight mahogany dining chairs, the shield and pierced splat backs with draped urns and wheatsheaves, part George III. (Christie's S. Ken) $4,114 £2,420 Eight

One of a set of six early 20th century French walnut salon chairs, the spoon backs with rococo scroll carved arched cresting, dated 1906. (Henry Spencer)   Six $1,059 £650

Two of a set of eight George III style mahogany dining chairs, each with a shield shaped back centred by a pierced splat, on square tapered legs. (Christie's S. Ken)   Eight $3,366 £2,200

Two late Federal carved mahogany chairs, New York, 1810-1815, each with tablet crest rail above a carved lyre, 32½in. high. (Christie's New York) $24,200 £15,220

A Napoleon III parcel gilt and polychrome chaise with circular padded back and seat with moulded frame and turned uprights. (Christie's London) $1,043 £660

Two of a set of eleven Victorian mahogany dining chairs, the C-scrolling balloon moulded backs above upholstered seats. (Christie's S. Ken)   Eleven $5,632 £3,520

Two of a set of four German cherrywood chairs with curved bar backs on carved baluster legs. (Kunsthaus am Museum)   Four $865 £497

North German carved mahogany chair with fruit basket motif, on carved baluster front supports, mid-19th century. (Kunsthaus am Museum) $243 £140

Two of a set of four North Italian fruitwood chaises en gondole, each with a scrolled curved toprail, on square tapering legs with paw feet. (Christie's S. Ken)   Four $7,531 £4,620

DINING CHAIRS

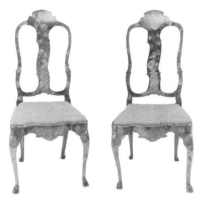

One of a set of six Victorian
small walnut chairs, the open
oval backs carved with leafage.
(Lawrence Fine Arts)
Six $2,690 £1,650

Pair of Dutch rococo walnut
and marquetry side chairs,
circa 1760, arched crest rail
above a solid serpentine splat.
(Robt. W. Skinner Inc.)
$1,300 £793

A Chippendale carved walnut
slipper chair, Philadelphia
1740-1760, on short cabriole
legs with trifid feet, 37¾in.
high.(Christie's New York)
$4,400 £2,767

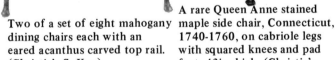

One of a set of six mahogany
dining chairs in George II style,
with cabriole front supports
with pad feet. (Lawrence Fine
Arts) Six $956 £605

Two of a set of eight mahogany
dining chairs each with an
eared acanthus carved top rail.
(Christie's S. Ken)
Eight $4,620 £2,750

A rare Queen Anne stained
maple side chair, Connecticut,
1740-1760, on cabriole legs
with squared knees and pad
feet, 43in. high. (Christie's
New York) $44,000 £27,672

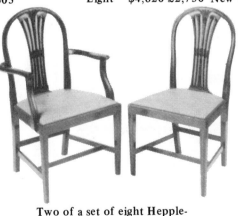

One of a set of seven
George III mahogany dining
chairs, including two with arms,
repairs and restorations.
(Lawrence Fine Arts)
Seven $5,200 £3,190

Two of a set of eight Hepplewhite style mahogany dining
chairs including two armchairs,
on square tapering legs joined
by cross stretchers. (Christie's
S. Ken) Eight $2,956 £1,760

An early Georgian red walnut
single chair, on front cabriole
supports with pad feet. (Lawrence Fine Arts) $610 £374

DINING CHAIRS

One of a set of six George III style mahogany dining chairs, the pierced undulating ladder backs above upholstered leather. (Christie's S. Ken)
    Six $1,478 £880

Two of a set of six mahogany occasional chairs, the beaded sunburst crested spindled rail backs above cane filled seats, second quarter of 19th century. (Christie's S. Ken)
    Six $1,755 £1,045

One of a set of six Victorian rosewood dining chairs, the scrolling railed semi balloon backs above upholstered seats, on cabriole legs. (Christie's S. Ken) Six $4,066 £2,420

A George II walnut dining chair with shaped uprights flanking a solid vase shape splat carved with birds' heads. (Lawrence Fine Arts)
    $2,600 £1,595

Two of a set of eight mahogany boardroom chairs, each with a waisted back and seat close-nailed upholstered in brown leather. (Christie's S. Ken)   Eight $3,586 £2,200

One of a composite set of eight ash ladder back chairs, including two with arms, early 19th century. (Lawrence Fine Arts)   Eight   £3,048 £1,870

One of a set of four oak up-right chairs, with upholstered green leather seats, on shaped front supports and square back united by stretchers. (Phillips London) Four $428 £280

Two of a set of six George III style mahogany shield back dining chairs, 20th century. (Robt. W. Skinner Inc.)
    Six $2,100 £1,280

One of a set of six single mahogany chairs, with gold coloured silk lift-out seats. (Lawrence Fine Art)
    Six $1,614 £990

DINING CHAIRS

One of five 19th century Liverpool spindle back dining chairs with fan carved top rails. (Phillips Manchester)

Five $2,444 £1,300

A pair of Biedermeier fruitwood open armchairs, each with a shaped toprail hung with a quiver of arrows. (Christie's S. Ken) $2,690 £1,650

Late 18th century German carved oak chair, the carved top rail with heart shape between acanthus leaves, on turned legs with stretchers. (Kunsthaus am Museum)

$324 £186

One of a set of six ebonised brass mounted Regency style side chairs, on sabre legs. (Tennants) Six $936 £600

Two of a set of eight George III mahogany dining chairs, the bowed bar and rail backs above padded seats. (Christie's S. Ken)

Eight $4,039 £2,640

A George III mahogany child's chair with serpentine toprail and pierced splat, on square legs, 26in. high. (Christie's London) $1,883 £1,155

One of a set of four gothic Revival oak chairs, supported on X-frame with chamfered edges. (Phillips London)

Four $261 £160

Two of a set of six early Victorian grey and cream painted side chairs, on bobbin turned legs with stretchers. (Christie's London)

Six $2,241 £1,375

Painted Queen Anne side chair, New England, 18th century, the carved yoked crest above moulded back posts, 41¾in. high. (Skinner Inc.) $1,600 £982

DINING CHAIRS

One of a set of six late **Regency** mahogany dining chairs, **with** bar backs, on tapering reeded supports, 86cm. (Osmond Tricks) Six $3,016 £1,850

Two of a set of four George I style walnut dining chairs, the acanthus scrolled vase backs above padded seats and out-curving arms with eagle head terminals. (Christie's S. Ken)
Four $1,935 £1,265

Painted fan back brace back Windsor side chair, New England, circa 1780, old black paint, 36¾in. high. (Skinner Inc.) $1,900 £1,226

An Empire giltwood chaise, the arched cresting with displayed eagle within a wreath above a frieze centred by an oval patera flanked by laurels. (Christie's London) $8,342 £5,280

Two of a composite set of eight early 19th century spindle back dining chairs of Lancashire type. (Tennants)
Eight $5,616 £3,600

Rhenish, 18th century, carved oak chair, the curved back with pierced struts, on turned, fluted legs. (Kunsthaus am Museum) $216 £124

One of a set of six George III mahogany ladder back dining chairs, the undulating toprails with scrolled ends. (Phillips London)
Six $6,426 £4,200

A pair of Victorian papier mache bedroom chairs, profusely inlaid with foliate cut mother-of-pearl and heightened in gilt. (Christie's S. Ken)
$711 £418

Mid-19th century German cherrywood straightbacked chair with marquetry inlay, on tapering legs. (Kunsthaus am Museum) $244 £140

EASY CHAIRS

A William IV simulated rose-wood tub chair, with scrolled moulded arms on lappeted turned legs headed by paterae. (Christie's London)
$3,048 £1,870

A beechwood bergere in the shape of a shell, covered in faded pink corduroy, on turned legs. (Christie's London)
$1,594 £990

A Regency mahogany bergere, the reeded seat rail and arms carved with paterae and lotus leaves, on reeded tapering legs. (Christie's London)
$6,864 £4,400

A William IV walnut bergere with upholstered back, down-swept arms and serpentine seat, on turned ribbed legs. (Christie's S. Ken) $1,972 £1,210

An Italian blue painted and parcel gilt sedan chair with domed top and panelled sides decorated with cartouches of flowers and vignettes of courting couples, mid-18th century, 65in. high. (Christie's London) $2,955 £1,870

A George II mahogany wing armchair with arched rect-angular padded back, on cabriole legs with shell headings and pad feet. (Christie's London)
$5,917 £3,630

A mahogany wing armchair with curved back, scrolling arms and serpentine seat up-holstered in red damask on square tapering legs. (Christie's London) $1,345 £825

A Rod Arad Rolling Volume sheet steel armchair, with rounded back and sides polished and acid painted to give black patina. (Christie's London)
$9,240 £5,500

A Victorian mahogany armchair the scrolling arms and seat up-holstered in figured brocatelle, on cabriole legs with knob feet. (Christie's S. Ken) $1,144 £715

EASY CHAIRS

A George IV mahogany bergere, the moulded frame with turned arm supports and reeded legs, with brass socket for a book rest. (Christie's London)
$2,917 £1,870

A Regency maplewood bergere chair with overscrolled toprail and lotus scroll carved arm terminals and supports. (Phillips London) $5,814 £3,800

An Empire mahogany bergere de bureau, the moulded frame with Egyptian caryatid arm supports reaching to claw feet. (Christie's London)
$10,080 £6,380

A Victorian walnut armchair, the foliate carved cresting and frame with a buttoned brocade balloon back and seat. (Christie's S. Ken)
$1,672 £1,045

A George III mahogany invalid's chair attributed to John Joseph Merlin, the winged buttoned back, arms and padded seat upholstered in close nailed burgundy hide. (Christie's London)
$3,128 £1,980

Renaissance Revival rosewood armchair, third quarter 19th century, floral and ribbon turned crest, continuing to griffin carved arm terminals, 48in. high. (Skinner Inc.)
$1,200 £736

A beechwood fauteuil, the moulded frame carved with a flowerhead and foliate cresting and centre to the seat rail, mid-18th century, possibly German. (Christie's London) $1,130 £715

A Victorian walnut armchair, the buttoned cartouche and foliate carved crested back, serpentined seat and arm pads upholstered in green velvet. (Christie's S. Ken) $669 £418

Victorian walnut framed and upholstered armchair with spoon shaped panel back, turned front supports, upholstered in red dralon. (G. A. Key) $716 £450

EASY CHAIRS

A mahogany wing armchair with arched back, down swept arms and bowed seat upholstered in tapestry, basically 18th century. (Christie's S. Ken) $1,478 £880

An early Victorian mahogany reclining chair with buttoned panel back and adjustable seat, on curved legs. (Christie's S. Ken) $1,165 £715

A Chippendale mahogany easy chair, Salem, Massachusetts, 1770-1790, on square corner moulded legs joined by a moulded H-stretcher, 33in. wide. (Christie's New York) $8,250 £5,188

A Victorian walnut open armchair with waisted buttoned back, the moulded frame carved with scrolls, on cabriole legs. (Christie's S. Ken) $2,421 £1,485

A pair of Louis XIV style giltwood fauteuils each with a serpentine back and seat upholstered in blue silk damask. (Christie's S. Ken) $1,870 £1,100

A Federal mahogany barrel back easy chair, Philadelphia, 1800-1815, with curving wings above scrolled arms, 47½in. high. (Christie's New York) $5,500 £3,459

Gustav Stickley fixed back armchair, circa 1907, no. 324, flat arm over six vertical slats, 39in. high. (Robt. W. Skinner Inc.) $800 £491

Chinese export bamboo reclining armchair, early 19th century, with extending caned foot rest, on wheels, 62in. long extended. (Skinner Inc.) $1,800 £1,125

A William IV mahogany Dawes patent reclining chair with high curved back, adjustable by finger grips beneath the arms. (Lawrence Fine Arts) $1,972 £1,210

EASY CHAIRS

A Federal mahogany easy chair, American, 1790-1810, with arched crest flanked by shaped wings, 45¾in. high. (Christie's New York)
$1,650 £1,037

Renaissance Revival walnut side chair, circa 1875, raised on trestle form legs ending in stylised paw feet, 32in. high. (Robt. W. Skinner Inc.)
$700   £427

One of a pair of mahogany and caned panel bergeres, the arms terminating in turned uprights, on turned legs. (Christie's S. Ken)
Two $1,614 £990

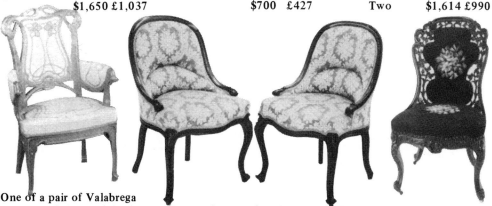

One of a pair of Valabrega open armchairs, each back with central shaped, upholstered and braided panel within a curved curvilinear, pierced framework. (Christie's London) Two $7,889 £4,840

Two mahogany drawing room chairs, almost identical, with upholstered curved backs and moulded cabriole supports, 19th century. (Lawrence Fine Arts) $4,518   £2,860

Rococo Revival rosewood laminated side chair, attributed to J. H. Belter, circa 1860, on carved seat rail and cabriole legs, 33¾in. high. (Skinner Inc.) $425 £274

A William IV mahogany library armchair, the upholstered panelled back, arm pads and seat in a moulded frame carved with acanthus. (Christie's S. Ken)
$1,663 £990

A walnut wing armchair, with padded back, on cabriole legs and pad feet, early Georgian and later. (Christie's S. Ken)
$5,984 £3,520

An early Victorian mahogany library armchair, the arms carved with acanthus and paterae, on turned tapered fluted legs. (Christie's S. Ken)
$1,201 £770

EASY CHAIRS

An oak open arm chair designed by Denham MacLaren, with shaped trestle ends, supporting deep upholstered black hide and zebra skin seat backrest. (Christie's London)
$4,805 £2,860

A Flemish walnut open arm-chair, upholstered in gros-point needlework, the back woven with two musicians, a lady and a dog, 17th century. (Christie's London) $10,224 £6,050

Bentwood rocking chair, by Thonet, arched twined top rail and cut velvet fabric fitted back, 53in. long.
(Skinner Inc) $700 £434

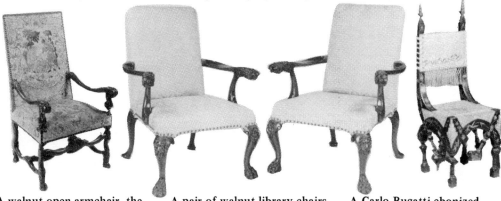

A walnut open armchair, the front stretcher carved with a flowerhead and foliage on scrolling legs with later paw feet and waved stretchers, part late 17th century. (Christie's London) $5,313 £3,300

A pair of walnut library chairs of George II style, on cabriole legs and hairy paw feet headed by lion masks and rings with bellflowers and scrolled brackets. (Christie's London) $16,137 £9,900

A Carlo Bugatti ebonized, inlaid and painted vellum side chair, the uprights with turned finials, above a rope tied rectangular vellum panel. (Christie's London)
$4,303 £2,640

L. & J.G. Stickley adjustable back armchair, Fayetteville, New York, c. 1909, no. 470, flat arm with arched cupport, 27½in. wide. (Skinner Inc) $800 £496

Rare Gustav Stickley oak Eastwood chair, circa 1902-1904, signed with a red decal in a box, 36in. wide. (Skinner Inc.) $19,000 £11,728

A George I walnut wing arm-chair, (upholstery lacking) on cabriole legs and claw and ball feet carved with shells. (Christie's London)
$8,855 £5,500

EASY CHAIRS

Plail Co. barrel back armchair, Wayland, New York, circa 1910, spring cushion seat over wide front seat rail, 40in. high. (Skinner Inc.) $900 £556

A Victorian mahogany sociable of trefoil outline with three deep bowed padded seats and shaped arched backs, on turned legs, 32in. high. (Christie's London) $5,562 £3,520

An Arts and Crafts oak armchair showing the influences of the designs of C. F. A. Voysey, the woven fabric 'slung' combined back and seat held by large brass hemispheres. (Phillips) $544 £340

A Venetian parcel gilt, silvered and painted grotto chair with scalloped shell back and seat with addorsed dolphin arms. (Christie's London) $6,604 £4,180

A Victorian walnut gentleman's armchair, the acanthus carved scrolling frame with buttoned back, and the lady's chair en suite. (Christie's S. Ken) $1,964 £1,155

An unusual ebonised and upholstered Arts and Crafts armchair, with upholstered drop-in seat, on curved back supports and turned front supports. (Phillips) $480 £300

A walnut wing armchair of William and Mary style with rectangular back, padded arms and loose cushion in green cotton. (Christie's London) $1,487 £880

Pair of 19th century French boulle armchairs, having shield backs with upholstered panels and ormolu mountings. (Auktionshaus Arnold) $2,760 £1,792

Empire Mahogany Bergere, first-quarter 19th century, moulded crest rail above an upholstered back, dolphin carved arms. (Skinner Inc) $1600 £1038

ELBOW CHAIRS

A Regency mahogany bergere, the reeded frame caned throughout, on turned front legs. (Tennants) $1,326 £850

Rare leather sling seat arm chair, Toby Furniture Co., Chicago, circa 1900, design attributed to Gustav Stickley, unsigned, 33in. wide. (Skinner Inc.) $2,900 £1,790

An Empire mahogany and parcel gilt open armchair applied with giltmetal mounts, and with dolphin's head arm terminals. (Christie's S. Ken) $1,458 £935

A George II oak open armchair, the shaped toprail with scrolled ends above a solid vase splat and outscrolled arms. (Christie's London) $1,165 £715

A William IV mahogany library chair, the tub caned back with scroll corner infills, on reeded tapering supports with brass cup castors, 81cm. (Osmond Tricks) $9,454 £5,800

Chinese hardwood inlaid armchair, last third 19th century, with pierced and carved splats above octagonal seat (minor repairs), 35in. high. (Skinner Inc.) $400 £250

An early George III mahogany open armchair, the shaped toprail with tasselled pagoda centre flanked by acanthus. (Christie's London)$1,201 £770

A late Victorian brass mounted oak seat, the back with balustrade, the sides with circle, centred by bosses, on moulded downswept legs, 22in. wide. (Christie's London) $1,115 £715

An oak open armchair, the geometrically panelled back inset with fielded larch panels, the shaped toprail carved with scrolls and foliage. (Christie's London) $5,205 £3,080

ELBOW CHAIRS

A William IV mahogany bergere with caned back, fitted to the right with brass swivel attachment for a reading arm. (Christie's London) $1,458 £935

A 'Makers of Simple Furniture' laminated birchwood open arm chair, designed by Gerald Summers, cut and shaped to form a curved top rail. (Christie's London) $10,164 £6,050

An oak caqueteuse chair, the panelled rectangular back with linked roundels carved with flowerheads, the top rail geometrically carved with lunette cresting, Salisbury, early 17th century. (Christie's London) $5,205 £3,080

One of a pair of green painted open armchairs, each with an oval wheel back painted with a rosette, on square tapering legs. (Christie's S. Ken)
Two $2,152 £1,320

An oak chair table with hinged oblong top, the back and arms on spindle supports with solid seat on turned legs joined by stretchers, 41½in. wide. (Christie's London) $1,022 £605

George III mahogany corner chair, third quarter 18th century, with outscrolled arms above two pierced vase shaped splats, 32¾in. high. (Skinner Inc.) $950 £583

A very rare Charles II walnut open armchair carved with stylised leaves and flowers, 39½in. high. (Tennants)
$869 £550

A satinwood and lacquer open armchair with trellis work back, arms and padded seat on square legs. (Christie's S. Ken)
$1,614 £990

Chinese hardwood swivel armchair, 19th century, with mother-of-pearl circular seat, raised on stylised cabriole legs, 36½in. high. (Skinner Inc.)
$350 £219

ELBOW CHAIRS

One of a set of eight Regency mahogany dining chairs with moulded frames, the panelled bar toprails with paper scroll crestings. (Phillips London)
Eight $12,240 £8,000

Slat back maple child's high chair, Philadelphia or the Delaware River Valley, 1720-1760, old colour, old twisted hemp seat, 39in. high. (Skinner Inc.) $6,000 £3,681

One of a pair of George III mahogany elbow chairs, the oval backs of curved form with splat in the form of stylised fleur de lys slats. (Phillips London)   Two $2,754 £1,800

A Federal mahogany arm chair, Salem, Massachusetts, 1790-1810, the rectangular back with reeded crest, stiles and three vertical bars, 32¼in. high. (Christie's New York)
$2,200 £1,383

Queen Anne walnut armchair, Rhode Island, mid 18th century, the yoked crest above a vasiform splat, 39½in. high. (Skinner Inc.)
$46,000 £28,221

An Arts and Crafts oak tub chair, the curved toprail and rail below embellished with carved leaf motifs. (Phillips London) $474 £310

A comb back Windsor armchair, Pennsylvania, late 18th century, on flaring baluster turned and cylindrical legs with ball feet, 42in. high. (Christie's New York)
$4,400 £2,767

Anglo-Indian carved rosewood armchair, circa 1830, raised on circular fluted legs ending in stylised claw feet, 36½in. high. (Robt. W. Skinner Inc.)
$1,100 £671

A Regency mahogany elbow chair with a solid curved cresting rail, on sabre supports, 84cm. high. (Lawrence Fine Arts) $628 £385

ELBOW CHAIRS

An 18th century oak Lambing chair, the arched toprail carved, with panelled seat fitted with a side drawer. (Phillips Manchester) $2,528 £1,600

Painted writing arm Windsor chair, Connecticut, 1780-1800, with baluster and ring turned splayed legs. (Skinner Inc.) $7,000 £4,294

An English mahogany high backed open armchair, with marquetry decoration, on tapering square section legs. (Christie's London) $717 £440

An Arts and Crafts mahogany armchair, having a cushion and seat upholstered in Liberty & Co. fabric. (Phillips London) $490 £320

Painted ash and maple child's ladderback highchair, New England, 18th century, original black paint (missing foot rest), 38½in. high. (Skinner Inc.) $3,250 £1,994

Painted maple slat back armchair, New Jersey or Hudson River Valley, 1725-1775, 40in. high. (Skinner Inc.) $1,300 £798

Painted turned slat back armchair, New England, last quarter 17th century, rush seat, 42in. high overall. (Skinner Inc.) $12,000 £7,362

A rare Queen Anne maple armchair, probably Rhode Island, 1740-1760, on lambrequin scrolled cabriole legs with pad feet, 39½in. high. (Christie's New York) $12,100 £7,610

A late George II mahogany elbow chair with solid carved splat, outswept arms and scrolled terminals. (Phillips London) $1,071 £700

ELBOW CHAIRS

A George III satinwood and decorated elbow chair in the manner of Seddon, the shield-shaped back with interlaced pierced splat.
(Phillips) $2970 £1800

Late 18th century German carved oak lug armchair, the seatrail carved with stylised leaves and lions' heads, on cabriole legs. (Kunsthaus am Museum) $973 £559

A George III mahogany open armchair, the pierced splat with a roundel of trefoils, on square chamfered legs, restorations. (Christie's London) $1,373 £880

A Charles II oak child's chair, the toprail with scrolled ends, the back panel carved with an interlaced design and flower-heads, on squared and turned legs. (Christie's London) $11,511 £7,150

A George III carved mahogany ladderback elbow chair, with pierced foliate undulating splats, on square chamfered legs united by stretcher.
(Phillips) $1402 £850

An Edwardian satinwood open armchair of George III style, the shield shaped back with ribbon tied splat.
(Christie's London) $1,151 £715

An early Victorian oak Glastonbury chair, with solid seat on X-legs, inscribed below the seat *Thomas Shepp...d(?) maker February 21 1846.* (Christie's London) $619 £385

One of a pair of Regency beech open armchairs, each with trellis back below a turned crest rail. (Tennants)
Two $936 £600

A yew and elm child's Windsor rocking chair, with solid seat on turned legs, mid-19th century. (Christie's London) $1,264 £748

ELBOW CHAIRS

A George III carved mahogany ladderback dining chair with turned carved splayed uprights, on simulated bamboo front legs. (Phillips) $1402 £850

One of a pair of early Victorian mahogany armchairs each with curved shaped back and shepherd's crook arms. (Christie's London)
Two $8,342 £5,280

A George III mahogany open arm elbow chair in the Sheraton taste, the rectangular back with turned uprights. (Phillips) $2310   £1400

Painted and decorated Salem rocking chair, by J. D. Pratt, Lunenburg, Massachusetts (minor paint loss), 43½in. high. (Skinner Inc.)
$1,400 £859

A late Regency mahogany library chair with a movable hinged writing slope supported on a folding brass quadrant and with two small ink drawers, 30in. high.
(Lawrence Fine Arts) $3630   £2200

Shaker child's maple rocking chair, Mt. Lebanon, New York, circa 1870, the horizontal shawl bar over three arched slats, 27½in. high. (Skinner Inc.)$1,800 £1,104

A rare early 19th century Dutch mahogany and floral marquetry metamorphic library step chair after a patent by Morgan and Saunders. (Phillips) $4620   £2800

German cherrywood armchair with solid cresting rail and down scrolled arms, early 19th century. (Kunsthaus am Museum) $2,431 £1,397

A George III carved mahogany elbow chair, in the Hepplewhite taste, on square tapered legs united by stretchers. (Phillips) $1402   £850

CHESTS OF DRAWERS

One of a matched pair of Empire walnut chests each with a blind frieze drawer above three other drawers, 48in. wide and 50in. wide. (Christie's S. Ken) Two $4,250 £2,640

A fine Federal inlaid mahogany bowfront chest of drawers, Massachusetts, 1790-1810, the bowfront top edged with lozenge pattern inlay, 41¾in. wide. (Christie's New York) $7,700 £4,842

A fine Chippendale cherrywood reverse serpentine chest of drawers, Connecticut, 1760-1780, the rectangular top with serpentine moulded edge, 38¾in. wide. (Christie's New York) $71,500 £44,968

A Queen Anne walnut, crossbanded and featherstrung bachelor's chest, with a quarter veneered hinged top, on bracket feet, 77cm. (Phillips London) $15,300 £10,000

A Federal inlaid figured maple tall chest of drawers, New England, 1790-1810 with cove moulded cornice, on French feet, 44½in. wide. (Christie's New York) $8,800 £5,534

A Federal mahogany and bird's eye maple chest of drawers, Salem, Massachusetts, 1800-1815, the rectangular top with reeded edge and outset rounded corners, 42in. wide. (Christie's New York) $3,520 £2,213

An oak chest with rectangular moulded top above three geometrically panelled long drawers, on bun feet, late 17th century. (Christie's S. Ken) $2,331 £1,430

19th century brass bound military chest in two sections, with brass inset handles, on turned feet, 35½in. long. (Phillips Manchester) $1,422 £900

A George III mahogany chest of drawers, the top with a moulded edge fitted with a brushing slide, on bracket feet, 88cm. (Phillips London) $1,453 £950

CHESTS OF DRAWERS

A Chippendale cherrywood reverse serpentine chest of drawers, signed by George Belden, Hartford, Connecticut, circa 1790, the moulded rectangular top with an oxbow front edge, 34¾in. wide. (Christie's New York)
$20,900 £13,144

Small Chippendale mahogany chest of drawers, Massachusetts, late 18th century, the four graduated drawers with cockbeaded surrounds, 36in. wide overall. (Skinner Inc.)
$18,000 £11,043

A late 18th century Dutch walnut and marquetry chest, the undulating moulded top inlaid with a vase of flowers, on later paw feet, 89cm. wide. (Phillips London) $5 202 £3,400

A Victorian teak military chest in two sections, with inset brass handles and corners, on turned bun feet, 41in. (Christie's S. Ken)$1,870 £1,100

A Japanese black lacquer, gold-painted and brass-mounted chest decorated with stylised roundels. (Christie's S. Ken.)$4537 £2750

A George III mahogany chest of four long graduated drawers fitted with a brushing slide, on bracket feet, 33in. wide. (Christie's S. Ken) $1,478 £880

A Federal inlaid cherrywood bow front chest of drawers, New England, 1790-1810, the bowed top with inlaid crossbanding, on French feet, 40¾in. wide. (Christie's New York) $3,520 £2,213

Federal grain painted chest of drawers, New England, circa 1820s, the scrolled back board above the two tiered bureau, 39in. wide. (Skinner Inc.) $3,500 £2,147

Federal mahogany inlaid bowfront bureau, probably New York, circa 1800, the rectangular inlaid top with bowed front, 41¾in. wide. (Skinner Inc.) $1,600 £982

CHESTS OF DRAWERS

Gustav Stickley chest of drawers, circa 1907, two half drawers over three long drawers, 37in. wide. (Robt. W. Skinner Inc.)
$1,900 £1,166

Chippendale cherry oxbow chest of drawers, Connecticut, circa 1780, with three reverse serpentine graduated drawers, 44in. wide. (Skinner Inc.)
$1,500 £968

An oyster veneered walnut chest, the rectangular top above three graduated long drawers on bracket feet, 31½in. wide. (Christie's S. Ken)
$1,887 £1,210

A walnut chest of drawers by E. P. Gardiner, the plain top having a raised band at the back, on square supports, 84cm. wide. (Phillips London)
$1,607 £1,050

A Victorian brass mounted walnut secretaire military chest with five graduated drawers flanking a central fitted drawer, 39in. wide. (Christie's S. Ken)
$1,346 £880

Queen Anne painted pine blanket chest, New England, circa 1750, the moulded lift lid above case of two false and two working thumb moulded drawers, 40in. wide. (Skinner Inc.) $6,000 £3,681

A George III mahogany chest of four long graduated drawers flanked by plain canted angles, on bracket feet, 104cm. (Lawrence Fine Arts)
$1,255 £770

A Victorian mahogany Wellington chest with coffered rectangular top and five drawers, on plinth labelled *Lady Melville, London,* 23in. wide. (Christie's S. Ken) $1,940 £1,155

A Federal carved mahogany chest of drawers, Salem, Massachusetts, 1810-1820, with four cockbead moulded long drawers flanked by spiral turned columns, 44in. wide. (Christie's New York)
$3,520 £2,213

CHESTS OF DRAWERS

Chippendale mahogany chest of drawers, on moulded bracket base, brasses are old replacements, old refinish, 38½in. wide. (Skinner Inc.)
$17,000 £10,429

George III mahogany bow-front chest of drawers, early 19th century, on a scrolled drawers skirt, raised on splayed feet, 41in. wide. (Skinner Inc.) $700 £452

William and Mary inlaid walnut chest of drawers, with string inlay and replaced brass drop pulls, raised on bun feet, 36in. wide. (Skinner Inc.)
$1,200 £764

William and Mary oak chest of drawers, circa 1690, pair of short drawers above three long drawers, 37½in. wide. (Robt. W. Skinner Inc.) $700 £427

A Victorian mahogany bow-front chest, with two short and four graduated long drawers on bracket feet, 45in. wide. (Christie's S. Ken) $935 £550
2987

Federal cherry inlaid chest of drawers, possibly Pennsylvania, circa 1800, the projecting moulded top above row of inlaid diamonds, 43¾in. high. (Skinner Inc.) $1,100 £710

A mahogany dwarf chest with four graduated long drawers, on bracket feet, basically 18th century, 37½in. wide. (Christie's S. Ken) $1,165 £715

A French ormolu mounted kingwood semainier cross-banded in rosewood, the canted angles with foliate plaques, 21½in. wide. (Christie's London)
$4,959 £3.080

An early George III mahogany serpentine fronted chest of four long drawers, on shaped bombe bracket feet, 39¾in. wide. (Tennants)
$7,900 £5,000

CHESTS OF DRAWERS

A George I style burr walnut and banded bachelor's chest, the rectangular foldover top above four graduated long drawers, 29½in. wide. (Christie's S. Ken) $1,239 £770

A Regency mahogany bachelor's chest with four long drawers, on turned tapering feet, the sides with carrying handles, 33in. wide. (Christie's London) $2,259 £1,430

A George III mahogany serpentine chest with eared moulded top above four graduated drawers, 45½in. wide. (Christie's London) $5,491 £3,520

A mid-Georgian walnut chest crossbanded and inlaid with feather bands, the moulded rectangular top above four drawers on bracket feet, 33½in. wide. (Christie's London) $6,276 £3,850

A Gordon Russell satin birch dwarf chest of drawers, two short and two long drawers, with moulded ebonised handles and stringing, on stepped trestle ends, 83.5cm. wide. (Christie's London) $3,511 £2,090

A walnut and oak rectangular chest fitted with four graduated long drawers, on turned bun feet, basically late 17th century, 38½in. wide. (Christie's S. Ken) $3,344 £2,090

A mid-Georgian mahogany chest with brushing slide above four graduated drawers between quarter-column angles, on later bracket feet, 33in. wide. (Christie's London) $3,603 £2,310

A walnut feather banded dwarf chest with four graduated drawers on bracket feet, 18th century, 21in. (Christie's S. Ken) $13,801 £9,020

A Dutch mahogany chest inlaid with cornucopiae and foliate marquetry trails, the rectangular top with low ledge back, on turned tapering bun feet, 40in. wide, 19th century. (Christie's S. Ken) $4,124 £2,530

CHESTS OF DRAWERS

A George III mahogany serpentine chest, with four graduated long drawers, the top one formally fitted, on later front feet, 46½in. wide. (Christie's S. Ken) $3,188 £1,980

An oak ebonised low chest designed by Denham MacLaren, the rectangular top above two long drawers with rectangular slit hand grips, 106.7cm. wide. (Christie's London)
          $1,756 £1,045

A walnut and marquetry chest, with two short and three long similarly inlaid drawers, on bracket feet, early 18th century, the marquetry later, 28in. wide. (Christie's London)
          $6,198 £3,850

A George I burr elm chest crossbanded and inlaid with feather banding, the rectangular moulded top above a slide, 35in. wide. (Christie's London)
          $7,064 £4,180

A Victorian mahogany secretaire Wellington chest, the eared rectangular top above a deep writing drawer and four long drawers, 28¼in. wide. (Christie's S. Ken)
          $3,168 £1,980

A George II mahogany rounded rectangular top above a slide and four graduated drawers, on bracket feet, 30¼in. wide. (Christie's London)
          $5,491   £3,520

A burr walnut chest with moulded quarter veneered top above a brushing slide and four graduated drawers on bracket feet, 28in. wide. (Christie's London) $3,765 £2,310

Painted chest on frame, New Hampshire, circa 1830, with six graduated thumb moulded drawers, on cabriole legs with arris pad feet, 36in. wide. (Skinner Inc.)
          $151,000 £92,638

A William and Mary blue, black and red painted chest with rectangular top naively painted with a black speckled panel on a cream ground, 41in. wide. (Christie's London)
          $40,898 £24,200

CHESTS ON CHESTS

A George II walnut chest on chest with ogee moulded cornice, on later bracket feet, restored, 68½in. high.
(Lawrence Fine Arts)
$5082   £3080

A George III mahogany tall-boy, the top section with a dentilled cornice, the lower section with a brushing slide, 44½in. wide. (Christie's S. Ken)
$2,690 £1,650

A George III mahogany chest on chest, the lower part with a slide above three long drawers, on bracket feet, 115cm. wide. (Lawrence Fine Arts)
$4,519 £2,860

A walnut and oak tallboy, the moulded cornice above three short and six graduated long drawers, 41½in. wide. (Christie's S. Ken) $7,392 £4,400

A walnut cabinet on chest, the top section with two doors enclosing ten drawers surrounding a door with architectural parquetry interior, the top late 17th century, the associated base 18th century, 67½in. high. (Christie's London)
$13,282 £8,250

A Victorian mahogany secretaire tallboy inlaid with satinwood fanned spandrels, on bracket feet, 43in. wide. (Christie's S. Ken)
$5,984 £3,520

A George III mahogany chest on chest, the lower part with three long drawers, all oak lined with brass loop handles, and on bracket feet, 45in. wide. (Lawrence Fine Arts)
$4174   £2530

A George I walnut chest on chest, the drawer front inlaid with narrow bands, the sides varnished pine and on later replaced bracket feet, 90cm. wide. (Lawrence Fine Arts)
$1,738 £1,100

A George II walnut chest on chest with a cavetto cornice above three short and three long drawers, with oak sides and bracket feet, restored, 101cm. wide. (Lawrence Fine Arts) $5,562 £3,520

CHESTS ON CHESTS

A walnut tallboy, the cavetto moulded cornice above five small and five long drawers, on bracket feet, early 18th century, 43in. (Christie's S. Ken) $4,675 £2,750

Chippendale cherry reverse serpentine buit-in chest on chest, attributed to George Belden, Elisha Strong house, Windsor, Conecticut, early 1790s. (Skinner Inc.) $20000 £12200

An early Georgian walnut tallboy, the top section with moulded cornice and convex frieze drawer above three short and three long feather banded drawers, 67in. high. (Christie's London) $9,438 £6,050

Chippendale birch chest on chest, New Hampshire, circa 1780, old refinish, brasses and escutcheons replacements, 38in. wide. (Skinner Inc.) $8,000 £4,734

A George III mahogany tallboy with moulded cornice above two short and six graduated long drawers on bracket feet, 43½in. wide. (Christie's S. Ken) $1,478 £880

An early 19th century mahogany chest on chest, the upper section with stepped moulded cornice over an arcaded blind fret frieze, 107cm. long. (Henry Spencer) $2,247 £1,450

A George I walnut chest on chest, the lower part with three graduated long drawers, on later ogee bracket feet, 3ft. 6in. wide. (Phillips) $7260 £4400

George III Mahogany Chest on Chest, last-quarter 18th century, Greek key cornice above two short and three long graduated drawers, 71in. high. (Skinner Inc) $3500 £2272

An early George III mahogany chest on chest with blind-fret carved frieze above four short and six long drawers, 44½in. wide. (Christie's S. Ken) $3,326 £1,980

CHESTS ON STANDS

An oak chest on stand, the chest with four geometrically panelled drawers, the stand with a drawer and arcaded apron, late 17th century, the stand later, 40in. wide. (Christie's London)
$2,974 £1,760

Chippendale mahogany carved high chest, Massachusetts, circa 1770-1790, with fan carving and cabriole legs ending in ball and claw feet, 38in. wide. (Skinner Inc.)
$19,000 £11,656

A walnut chest with moulded cornice, the stand fitted with three short drawers, on cabriole legs and pad feet, 40in. wide. (Christie's S. Ken)
$2,510 £1,540

A Queen Anne walnut high chest of drawers, Massachusetts, 1740-1760, on cabriole legs with pad feet, the rear legs of maple, 41½in. wide. (Christie's New York)
$9,900 £6,226

Maple tall chest on frame, New Hampshire, circa 1780, on cabriole legs ending in pad feet, brasses replaced, 36in. wide. (Skinner Inc.)
$9,000 £5,521

A walnut and feather banded chest on stand fitted with three short and three graduated long drawers, basically early 18th century. (Christie's S. Ken)
$4,065 £2,420

An oak chest on stand, on inverted cupped baluster legs and cross stretchers, basically 18th century, 40in. wide. (Christie's S. Ken) $1,683 £1,100

A Queen Anne maple high chest of drawers, New England, 1740-1760, the upper case with moulded swan neck pediment centring three ball and spire finials, 38¾in. wide. (Christie's New York)
$26,400 £16,603

Queen Anne maple high chest of drawers, Salem, Massachusetts, 1740-1760, on cut out skirt joining four cabriole legs, 37¾in. wide. (Skinner Inc.) $16,000 £9,816

CHIFFONIERS

A Regency rosewood, satinwood crossbanded and brass inlaid Secrétaire, having a shelved superstructure with pierced gallery and turned uprights, 3ft. 4in. wide.
(Phillips) $6930   £4200

A simulated rosewood and marbilized chiffonier with shelved superstructure on scroll supports above two simulated grill doors, early 19th century, 38in. wide.
(Christie's S. Ken.)$3993   £2420

A fine Victorian mahogany Chiffonier, the arched superstructure with a single shelf on scroll supports, 44in. wide.
(Bonhams) $1402   £850

Roycroft oak chiffonier, East Aurora, New York, circa 1907, signed with *Roycroft* across front, 42in. wide.
(Skinner Inc.) $6,000 £3,704

Regency rosewood chiffoniere, early 19th century, the top with a three quarter pierced brass gallery, on a rectangular base, 29¾in. long. (Skinner Inc.)
$6,000 £3,681

A Dutch mahogany side buffet, the hinged rectangular lid enclosing folding shelves, on square tapering legs, 19th century, 42in. wide. (Christie's S. Ken) $1,386 £825

A George IV brass inlaid rosewood chiffonier, the super-structure with galleried shelf above three drawers inlaid with foliage, 36½in. wide. (Christie's London) $7,722 £4,950

A Regency mahogany chiffonier with reeded uprights and graduated shelves, slight restoration, 31in. wide. (Christie's S. Ken.)$2541   £1540

A William IV mahogany chiffonier, the bolection moulded frieze drawer above two cupboard doors between uprights headed by foliate volutes, 42½in. wide. (Christie's S. Ken) $2,464 £1,540

COMMODE CHESTS

An early Louis XV kingwood, crossbanded and ormolu mounted bombe commode, surmounted by a moulded rance marble top with rounded re-entrant corners, 1.32m. wide, stamped *G. Schwingkens.* (Phillips London)$11,016 £7,200

A Louis XV/XVI Transitional kingwood and inlaid commode containing three short and two long drawers veneered a quatre faces with purple heart borders, stamped *J.G.T. SAR,* 1.30m. wide. (Phillips London) $5,202 £3,400

A Louis XVI mahogany, brass mounted and ebony strung rectangular commode, with projecting rounded angles, surmounted by a breccia marble top, 1.25m. wide. (Phillips London)$4,590 £3,000

A Dutch oak bombe commode carved with leafy acanthus scrolls, on block feet, 19th century, 33in. (Christie's S. Ken) $1,776 £1,045

Swedish rococo elmwood and ormolu mounted commode, mid-18th century, with three drawers, raised on cabriole legs, 27in. long. (Skinner Inc.) $5,000 £3,067

An ormolu mounted marquetry mahogany and harewood commode after Leleu with rounded rectangular mottled top, the panelled frieze applied with scrolling foliage, 34in. wide. (Christie's London) $2,955 £1,870

Italian four drawer commode, part 17th century, on bun feet, 131cm. wide. (Auktionshaus Arnold) $1,270 £824

A Dutch burr walnut bombe commode with eared serpentine quarter veneered top, with keeled angles and scroll feet, mid-18th century, 38in. wide. (Christie's London) $6,083 £3,850

A French Provincial fruitwood commode of arc en arbalette outline, the top with moulded edge, on scrolled feet, mid-18th century, 51¾in. wide. (Christie's London) $7,436 £4,400

COMMODE CHESTS

18th century Louis XVI oak commode, repairs to feet, 123cm. wide. (Auktionshaus Arnold) $828 £538

A giltmetal mounted mahogany commode of Louis XVI style, with eared mottled liver marble top with false frieze drawer, 52in. wide. (Christie's S. Ken) $1,663 £990

A North Italian fruitwood and banded serpentine commode with two long drawers and a shaped apron on bracket feet, late 18th century, 48in. wide. (Christie's S. Ken) $2,772 £1,650

A George III mahogany commode, the D-shaped top above two drawers and two doors with shaped apron, on bracket feet, 26½in. wide. (Christie's London) $2,317 £1,485

A North Italian walnut bombe commode, the sides with cupboards, on cabriole legs carved with flowerheads and trefoil feet, 41in. wide. (Christie's London) $6,604 £4,180

Louis XV style kingwood marquetry commode, early 20th century, with ormolu banding and bombe front above three drawers, 31in. wide. (Skinner Inc.) $1,300 £828

One of a pair of ormolu mounted mahogany bombe commodes, each with a serpentine marble top above two drawers inlaid sans traverse, 50½in. wide. (Christie's S. Ken)
Two $10,758 £6,600

A Dutch burr walnut commode with waved moulded top and five shaped long drawers with waved chamfered angles, 43½in. wide. (Christie's London) $2,781 £1,760

Early 18th century walnut and kingwood commode in the baroque style, 121cm. wide. (Auktionshaus Arnold) $4,692 £3,046

COMMODE CHESTS

Rococo style bombe chest, 20th century mahogany and burled wood, black/white marble top over two drawers, 51in. wide. (Skinner Inc.) $3,100 £1,975

Dutch mahogany and floral marquetry commode of bombe outline, on claw feet, 91cm. wide. (Kunsthaus am Museum) $3,242 £1,863

Louis XV style parquetry commode, late 19th century, moulded serpentine mottled violet top, 45in. long. (Skinner Inc.) $850 £548

George II Walnut Commode Table, mid 18th century, raised on cabriole legs ending in pad feet, 25³⁄₄in. high. (Skinner Inc.) $2100 £1363

Mid-19th century North German boxwood inlaid mahogany commode with rounded corners and three drawers of varying sizes, 90cm. wide. (Kunsthaus am Museum) $973 £559

A North Italian walnut and bone inlaid secretaire commode decorated with putti amid scrolling flowerheads with shaped inset top, basically 17th century, 27in. wide. (Christie's London) $7,821 £4,950

Italian rococo walnut partial gilt commode, serpentine crossbanded top over three drawers on cabriole legs (restoration), 36½in. long. (Skinner Inc.) $6,000 £3,822

An Italian commode, veneered, crossbanded and inlaid with geometric bands, raised on square tapering supports, late 18th/19th century, 117cm. wide. (Lawrence Fine Arts) $1,217 £770

German Aachen late 18th century carved oak commode with fluted rounded corners, the three drawers carved with flower baskets and birds, 128cm. wide. (Kunsthaus am Museum) $3,513 £2,019

COMMODES & POT CUPBOARDS

A George IV mahogany commode armchair, the solid hinged seat with brass recessed handle to the right above two panelled doors, with buttoned green leather cushion, 25in. wide. (Christie's London) $1,030 £660

George III mahogany commode table, late 18th century, three quarter gallery above two drawers and a pair of cupboard doors, 20in. long. (Skinner Inc.) $475 £291

An antique French Provincial carved walnut bidet in the Louis XV taste, with raised padded end with hinged compartment. (Phillips) $1567 £950

An early George III mahogany bedside cupboard with pierced galleried top, and chamfered square legs. 16in. Wide. (Christie's London) $1,564 £990

A pair of George III mahogany inlaid tray top bow front pot cupboards, each enclosed by a panel door. (Phillips) $12375 £7500

A Victorian Marriott portable water closet, painted in black with floral spandrels and borders, 55cm. wide. (Henry Spencer) $558 £360

A George III mahogany bedside commode with a sliding drawer enclosing a glazed ware bowl, 23in. wide. (Christie's S. Ken.)$2359 £1430

An early 19th century mahogany commode chest, the hinged cover enclosing fitted interior with water reservoir. (Allen & Harris) $644 £400

A Regency mahogany step commode with three leather lined treads, the pull out middle with porcelain bowl on six turned legs, 22in. wide. (Christie's London) $1,287 £825

CORNER CUPBOARDS

An early Georgian burr walnut corner cabinet with later moulded cornice above two fielded panelled doors, on later bracket feet, 45in. wide. (Christie's London)
$9,295 £5,500

A George III mahogany standing corner cupboard with a bolection moulded cornice above a pair of fielded arched doors, 48in. wide. (Christie's S. Ken) $3,703 £2,420

A fine Chippendale carved walnut corner cupboard, probably Lancaster County, Pennsylvania, 1760-1780, the upper part with moulded swan neck pediment, 91½in. high. (Christie's New York)
$8,800 £5,535

A Louis Philippe ormolu mounted kingwood and tulipwood corner cabinet of serpentine outline with two quarter veneered doors, 37½in. high. (Christie's London) $869 £550

A Liberty & Co. oak corner cabinet, carved below the cornice with stylised leaves and foliage, with leaded glass doors enclosing shelves, 218cm. high. (Phillips London) $1,312 £805

A mahogany, ebonised and parquetry corner cabinet, having a door with parquetry panels of maize motifs and painted with a butterfly and flowers, 78.3cm. high. (Phillips London) $490 £320

A late George III mahogany straight front floor standing corner cupboard, raised upon slightly ogee bracket feet, 118cm. long. (Henry Spencer) $3,240   £2,000

A standing mahogany corner cupboard, inlaid with narrow kingwood bands in geometric patterns, the door with a central oval floral motif, 239cm. high. (Lawrence Fine Arts) $3,128 £1,980

A Regency mahogany corner cupboard with blind fret carved frieze above four panelled doors, on plinth, 45½in. (Christie's S. Ken)$1,683 £990

CORNER CUPBOARDS

A George III mahogany standing corner cabinet the moulded cornice above a glazed lancet door, on bracket feet, 37in. wide. (Christie's S. Ken)
$1,703 £1,045

Country Chippendale walnut corner cabinet, Pennsylvania, circa 1780, the shaped backboard joining three-quarter round shelves, 24in. wide. (Skinner Inc.) $7,000 £4,294

A green lacquer standing bow front corner cupboard, enclosing a later red painted interior, restored top portion 18th century, 181cm. high. (Lawrence Fine Arts)
$1,182 £748

Walnut corner cabinet, in the rococo style, with swan neck pediment, some older parts, 140cm. wide. (Auktionshaus Arnold) $4,416 £2,867

Renaissance style walnut corner cabinet, late 19th century, carved throughout with scrolling acanthus leaves and masks, 59½in. wide. (Robt. W. Skinner Inc.) $1,100 £671

One of a pair of pine corner cabinets with broken scrolling pediment, the open shelves carved with scallops above panelled cupboard doors, 38in. wide. (Christie's S. Ken)
Two $3,945 £2,420

A mahogany corner cabinet with carved dentilled moulded cornice above two arched panelled doors and two rectangular panelled doors, 87½in. high. (Christie's London) $3,142 £1,870

A Louis XV ormolu mounted Chinese black lacquer encoignure with waved moulded breche d'Alep top above a bowed cupboard door, reconstructed, 29in. wide. (Christie's London)
$2,607 £1,650

A Federal carved mahogany corner cupboard, mid-Atlantic States, 1800-1810, with overhanging broken moulded cornice above two panelled cupboard doors, 80½in. high. (Christie's New York)
$3,300 £2,075

CUPBOARDS

A painted rosewood aesthetic movement hanging wall cupboard, with galleried shelf above twin doors enclosing shelves, 90cm. wide. (Phillips London) $1,148 £750

A Spanish oak buffet, the front with seven doors, the moulded corner posts with scrolled tops, 17th century, 79in. wide. (Christie's London) $2,125 £1,320

Country Federal cherry two-part cupboard, possibly Pennsylvania, circa 1820, on shaped bracket feet (refinished, replaced pulls, restoration), 46in. wide. (Skinner Inc.) $1,500 £968

19th century Chinese apothecaries cupboard, with numerous drawers, 81cm. wide. (Auktionshaus Arnold) $1,766 £1,146

Walnut glazed cupboard, Pennsylvania, circa 1810, the flaring cornice moulding above two glazed cupboard doors, 85in. high. (Skinner Inc.) $3,250 £2,097

Pine slant back cupboard, New England, 18th century, four thumb moulded shelves, old stain and varnish, 75in. high. (Skinner Inc.) $5,500 £3,374

A rare Federal grain painted step-back cupboard, Vermont, early 19th century, the entire surface painted olive with brown sponge painted grain decoration, 63½in. wide. (Christie's New York) $44,000 £27,672

A good late 17th century north of England oak press cupboard, the frieze carved with a band of stylised flower-heads, 75in. wide. (Tennants) $7,900 £5,000

An oak court cupboard with strapwork panels, the canopy top with two doors above three fielded cupboard doors, 55½in. dated 1668 & 69. Christie's S. Ken) $1,683 £1,100

CUPBOARDS

Grain painted and bird's-eye maple decorated pine apothecary cupboard, New Ipswich, New Hampshire, early 19th century, 51in. wide. (Skinner Inc.) $13,500 £8,282

Carved oak milk cupboard, with bevelled corners and three doors moulded in high relief, Westphalian, mid-18th century, 212cm. wide. (Kunsthaus am Museum)
$2,433 £1,398

Carved pine buffet, Canadian Provinces, 18th century, the rectangular top above two moulded single drawers and two carved diamond point cupboard doors, 58¾in. wide. (Skinner Inc.) $3,900 £2,393

An oak press cupboard of small size, carved overall with guilloche, conjoined scrolls, fluting and flowerhead designs, basically 17th century, 144cm. high. (Lawrence Fine Arts)
$2,085 £1,320

A pair of Georgian mahogany dining pedestal cupboards, one opening to reveal two drawers, the other with zinc lining, 49.5cm. wide. (Lawrence Fine Arts) $7,172 £4,400

An oak cupboard, three doors each carved with a saintly figure, on square uprights joined by an undertier, 17th century, 45in. wide. (Christie's S. Ken) $4,662 £2,860

Pine stepback cupboard, Canadian Provinces, 18th century, the moulded cornice above two raised panel cupboard doors, 58in. wide. (Skinner Inc.) $3,250 £1,994

Mid-17th century oak press cupboard, the separate base with two quartered doors, 64½in. wide. (Tennants)
$1,106 £700

German Brunswick mid-18th century, richly inlaid walnut cupboard chest with two drawers, 148cm. wide. (Kunsthaus am Museum)
$14,051 £8,075

DAVENPORTS

A late Victorian bamboo and black-laquer Davenport decorated with birds amongst foliage, on splayed feet, 23¹/₂ in. wide.
(Christie's S. Ken.) $1089 £660

A Victorian ebonised and amboyna Davenport inlaid with geometric boxwood lines, the leather-lined hinged sloping flap below a brass galleried lid, 22in. wide.
(Christie's S. Ken.) $1543 £935

An Edwardian mahogany Davenport with hinged three-quarter gallery compartment fitted with a pen trough above a lined-slope, 20in. wide.
(Christie's S. Ken.) $817 £495

A padouk and ivory inlaid davenport, the sliding boxed top with a hinged leather lined sloping flap, on turned tapering block feet, basically 19th century, 22in. wide. (Christie's S. Ken) $3,696 £2,200

A mid-Victorian walnut piano top Davenport, the rising superstructure with a concealed mechanism, drawers and pigeon-holes, 21in. wide.
(Christie's S. Ken.)$3448 £2090

A William IV rosewood Davenport, the sliding slpe above ink tray slide and three drawers, 20in. wide.
(Bonhams) $3300 £2000

A Victorian walnut davenport with hinged stationery compartment, pen trays and a lined slope enclosing a bird's-eye maple interior, 21in. wide.
(Christie's S. Ken) $1,663 £990

An Anglo-Indian Vizigatapam ivory, sandalwood and tortoiseshell Davenport engraved overall with scrolling foliage, Indian figures, deities and beasts, 18in. wide.
(Christie's) $21450 £13750

A Victorian rosewood Davenport with raised pen, ink and envelope compartments, the sloping top enclosing fitted interior.
(Lawrence Fine Arts) $2359 £1430

DAVENPORTS

An early Victorian rosewood Davenport, the slope revealing a bird's-eye maple interior of drawers, 22^1/$_2$ in. wide.
(Bonhams) $2805 £1700

A Victorian walnut piano top davenport, the interior fitted with a lined sliding writing surface and pen trough, on bar feet and castors, 22in. wide. (Christie's S. Ken)
$3,775 £2,420

A Victorian walnut Davenport, surmounted by turned finials flanking a pierced gallery, 24in. wide.
(Bonhams) $2475 £1500

An attractive George IV rosewood Davenport, with a pierced brass gallery, the writing slope inset with leather, circa 1825, 21in. wide.
(Bonhams) $3960 £2400

A Victorian figured walnut piano top davenport with a hinged lid to the stationery compartment, the top 22½in. wide. (Tennants)
$3,120 £2,000

A Victorian walnut davenport, the back with galleried hinged stationery compartment, on turned feet, 22in. wide.
(Christie's S. Ken) $1,201 £770

A George IV satinwood Davenport, the three-quarter galleried top with sloping inset leather flap above two slides, 1ft. 8in. wide.
(Phillips) $4785 £2900

A Victorian inlaid burr walnut davenport with a brass galleried superstructure, the top with a pull out writing slope, 22in. wide. (Tennants)
$2,652 £1,700

A George IV pollard oak davenport in the manner of Richard Bridgens, the rectangular top with undulating three quarter gallery, on concave fronted plinth base, 26in. wide.
(Christie's London)
$2,574 £1,650

DISPLAY CABINETS

One of a pair of Victorian cut brass and ebony veneered display cabinets, with lacquered brass mounts and bracket feet, 33in. wide. (Tennants)
Two $1,014 £650

A Victorian giltmetal walnut and ebonised credenza with glazed door flanked by bowed doors divided by pilasters, 66in. wide. (Christie's S. Ken) $2,057 £1,210

A black and gold lacquer cabinet on stand, the shaped moulded cornice with cartouche cresting above a pair of glazed cupboard doors, 51½in. wide. (Christie's London)
          $2,433 £1,540

Louis XVI style giltwood vitrine, 20th century, demilune top above conforming case with glazed door and sides, 54in. high. (Robt. W. Skinner Inc.) $1,300 £793

19th century baroque walnut and kingwood banded bombe fronted glazed display cabinet, 215cm. wide. (Auktionshaus Arnold) $2,318 £1,505

A Dutch mahogany display cabinet inlaid with marquetry foliate bands enclosed by two glazed doors and side panels, 19th century, 40in. wide. (Christie's S. Ken) $3,227 £1,980

A George III satinwood display case of arched form and glazed panel construction with single door, 18in. wide.   (Christie's S. Ken) $1,010 £660

An Art Nouveau mahogany inlaid display cabinet, with glazed doors enclosing shelves, inlaid and coloured with stylised roses and leaves, 181cm. high. (Phillips London)
          $2,119 £1,300

A giltmetal mounted kingwood bombe vitrine with a glazed door and side panels on cabriole legs with sabots, 29in. wide. (Christie's S. Ken)
          $1,403 £825

DISPLAY CABINETS

An Edwardian mahogany display cabinet, the raised mirrored back with shell carved pediment, on short turned supports, 31in. wide. (Phillips Manchester) $1,504 £800

German carved oak display cabinet with carved cornice, the upper doors glazed, the lower with lozenge carvings, 161cm. wide. (Kunsthaus am Museum) $5,944 £3,416

A late Victorian mahogany and satinwood banded pedestal display cabinet, on square tapering legs with spade feet, 42½in. high. (Christie's S. Ken) $531 £330

Louis XV style ebonized vitrine, 20th century, moulded D-shaped top above conforming case, 55½in. high. (Skinner Inc.) $475 £306

An Art Nouveau inlaid mahogany display cabinet, having a central bevelled mirror with an arched apron above with twin cupboards below, 1.45m. wide. (Phillips London) $2,907 £1,900

Chinese hardwood vitrine, 20th century, raised on cabriole legs, inlaid throughout with mother-of-pearl, 70in. high, 36in. wide. (Skinner Inc.) $800 £500

A seaweed marquetry glazed cabinet of William and Mary style with moulded cornice above two shaped, glazed doors, the base with two panelled doors, 42½in. wide. (Christie's London) $8,923 £5,280

A Dutch East Indies (Sri Lanka) brass mounted jackwood and kaliatur display cabinet on stand, on moulded cabriole legs, 18th century, 38in. wide. (Christie's London) $2,479 £1,540

An attractive Edwardian mahogany salon cabinet, of reverse break bow front form, with shallow arched pediment, 122.5cm. long. (Henry Spencer) $1,472 £950

DRESSERS

A Georgian oak dresser base fitted with three mahogany crossbanded drawers above pierced spandrel brackets, 184 x 89cm. wide. (Lawrence Fine Arts) $7,531 £4,620

An oak dresser with waved frieze, the front with six drawers on square chamfered legs joined by an undertier, 59½in. wide. (Christie's London) $6,506 £3,850

An oak low dresser fitted with three frieze drawers applied with geometric mouldings, parts 17th century, 77in. wide. (Christie's S. Ken) $9,324 £5,720

An oak dresser with rectangular moulded top and later plate rack with dentilled cornice and two open shelves above six small drawers, the base late 17th century, 74in. wide. (Christie's London)
$4,647 £2,750

A Georgian oak dresser with open rack, the concave cornice above a pierced frieze, 72in. high.
(Lawrence Fine Art)
$3630   £2200

A Georgian oak dresser, the plate rack with moulded cornice and arcaded frieze above two shelves fitted with iron hooks, 57in. wide. (Christie's London)
$5,313 £3,300

An oak dresser, the top section with a cavetto moulded cornice and open shelves, on baluster columns, 71½in. wide. (Christie's S. Ken)
$7,480 £4,400

A George III oak low dresser, the planked rectangular top above three frieze drawers and twin panel cupboard doors, 63in. wide. (Christie's S. Ken)
$2,869 £1,760

A small oak dresser in the Georgian style with a dentil cornice above a pierced frieze, on front cabriole supports, 201cm. high. (Lawrence Fine Arts) $2,241 £1,375

DRESSERS

A late George III oak dresser, the whole inlaid with chequered banding, lozenge and circular motifs and fan shaped patera, on bracket feet, 174cm. long. (Henry Spencer)
$4,890 £3,000

An oak dresser inlaid with ivory and chequer bands, the dentilled top with open shelves, on turned bun feet, 55½in. wide. (Christie's S. Ken)
$2,331 £1,430

An Arts and Crafts oak dresser, having a central mirror flanked by carved flowers, the base with twin drawers and cupboards, 1.55m. wide. (Phillips London) $918 £600

An oak dresser, the plate rack with moulded cornice and shaped frieze above three shelves, 18th century, restorations, 72in. wide. (Christie's London)
$8,365 £4,950

George III oak Welsh cupboard, late 18th century, with mahogany banding, plate racks and cubbyholes above, 72in. long.(Skinner Inc.)
$5,000 £3,185

An oak dresser, with three shelves and moulded cornice, the base with five drawers, on turned legs with undertier, early 19th century, 62in. wide. (Christie's London)
$5,313 £3,300

An 18th century oak pot board dresser, the delft rack with swept moulded cornice over three open shelves, 158cm. long. (Henry Spencer)
$3,667 £2,250

Victorian oak carved dresser, carved with foliate and scrolls, the base with two door cupboard and bracket formed feet, 59in. wide. (G. A. Key)
$782 £480

A George III oak dresser with open shelves above six frieze drawers and a planked undertier, adaptions, 59in. wide. (Christie's S. Ken)
$3,366 £2,200

KNEEHOLE DESKS

A mahogany kneehole desk, the arched kneehole flanked by four drawers, on short cabriole legs and paw feet carved with acanthus scrolls, 51½in. wide. (Christie's London) $7,172 £4,400

A Regency Revival black lacquer and simulated bamboo pedestal desk, the rectangular leather lined top above four central drawers flanked by two false drawers, 53½in. wide. (Christie's S. Ken) $25,998 £15,950

A Flemish walnut and marquetry desk, the rectangular top depicting an episode from Classical mythology with an orator addressing a crowd, 67½in. wide. (Christie's London) $6,729 £4,180

A walnut and feather kneehole desk, the banded cross rectangular top above eight drawers, on bracket feet, modern, 36in. wide. (Christie's S. Ken) $1,599 £1,045

A Victorian walnut cylinder bureau with satinwood fitted interior and sliding writing surface, 48in. wide. (Christie's S. Ken) $2,861 £1,870

A George I kneehole desk with crossbanded quarter veneered fold out top above a frieze drawer, on bracket feet, adapted, 30in. wide. (Christie's London) $8,069 £4,950

An elm and mahogany banded desk with a long frieze drawer and six small drawers flanking a central kneehole, part 18th century, 40½in. wide. (Christie's S. Ken)$1,165 £715

A walnut kneehole desk with crossbanded rectangular top and central recessed cupboard door flanked by eight drawers, Queen Anne and later, 30½in. wide. (Christie's London) $7,808 £4,620

George III mahogany kneehole desk with fielded panel cupboard flanked by six small drawers on shaped bracket feet, 35in. wide. (Phillips Manchester) $4,108 £2,600

KNEEHOLE DESKS

A Victorian larch and satin-wood kneehole desk, the lined rectangular top above nine drawers on undulating plinth base, 54in. wide. (Christie's S. Ken) $1,683 £1,100

An Italian walnut pedestal desk, the rectangular top with moulded edge, the frieze with brushing slide and three drawers, on bracket feet, 18th century, 54½in. wide. (Christie's London)
$7,436 £4,400

American walnut pedestal desk, circa 1860, with moulded edge, over two banks of three drawers, 49in. long. (Skinner Inc.) $925 £567

George III mahogany kneehole desk, third quarter 18th century, with a central cupboard flanked by three short drawers, raised on bracket feet, 27¼in. long. (Skinner Inc.) $800 £491

A mid Georgian mahogany kneehole desk, with recessed cupboard below between six small drawers, on shaped bracket feet, 87cm. wide. (Phillips London)$2 601 £1 700

LINEN PRESSES

A George III mahogany clothes cupboard with a fluted frieze above two fielded panel doors, 52in. wide. (Lawrence Fine Arts) $1906 £1155

Chinese Export campaign camphorwood clothes press, second quarter 19th century, with one long fitted drawer above a pair of cupboard doors enclosing drawers, 38¼in. long. (Skinner Inc.) $3,000 £1,840

A George III mahogany clothes press, the pediment with Gothic arches above a pair of panelled doors crossbanded with rosewood, on splayed feet, 48in. wide. (Christie's S. Ken) $3,188 £1,980

A Regency mahogany linen press with broken pediment applied with metal gilt paterae, on splayed bracket feet, 52in. wide. (Christie's S. Ken) $2,861 £1,870

Chippendale cherry linen press, Eastern America, circa 1780, the moulded cornice above two panelled doors, 42in. wide. (Skinner Inc.) $3,700 £2,387

Early 19th century mahogany linen press, the unusual raised cornice above a pair of ebony banded panel doors, 43in. wide. (Phillips) $3201   £1940

A George III mahogany clothes press with dentilled moulded cornice above two panelled doors, on splayed bracket feet, 41in. wide. (Christie's London) $2,059 £1,320

A fine George III mahogany linen press by Gillows, Lancaster, the upper section with moulded and dentil cornice, 50½in. wide. (Bonhams) $3630   £2200

A Regency mahogany clothes press inlaid with ebony lines with shaped pediment flanked by akrotiri inlaid with anthemions above a moulded cornice, on splayed bracket feet, 48in. wide. (Christie's London) $3,586 £2,200

LOWBOYS

A mid-Georgian mahogany low-boy with moulded rectangular top above three drawers, on square chamfered legs, 32½in. wide. (Christie's London)
$1,458 £935

A good lacquered Lowboy, the bevelled rectangular top decorated with figures and pavilions in a watery landscape, 47in. wide.
(Bonhams) $1815 £1100

An early 18th century green japanned and chinoiserie decorated Lowboy, the top with a moulded edge painted with pagoda landscapes, 2ft. 5in. wide.
(Phillips) $7260 £4400

A George II oak Lowboy, the bevelled rectangular top above three short drawers and a shaped apron, 32¼in. wide.
(Bonhams) $4620 £2800

A George III oak lowboy, the rounded rectangular top over a small frieze drawer flanked by two deeper drawers. (Henry Spencer) $1,173 £720

A walnut lowboy with quarter veneered moulded rectangular top and three drawers on cabriole legs with pad feet, 30in. wide. (Christie's London)
$1,793 £1,100

A walnut lowboy, the canted rectangular top above four frieze drawers, part 18th century, 31in. wide. (Christie's S. Ken) $2,188 £1,430

George II Elm Lowboy, rectangular moulded top over three small drawers, on cabriole legs and pad feet, 32in. long.
(Skinner Inc) $1700 £1103

George III oak low boy with moulded plank top above three small drawers, 30½in. wide. (Phillips Manchester)
$758 £480

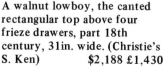

SCREENS

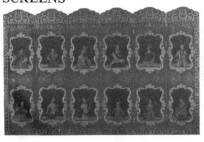

A Chinese export scarlet, black and gilt-japanned six-leaf screen painted with twelve three-quarter length portraits of European men and women in late 17th century costume, each leaf 21¼in. x 80in.
(Christie's) $120120   £77000

A French giltwood Cheval firescreen inset with a cartouche-shaped Aubusson tapestry panel of a girl with a dog in a farmyard, the frame 19th century, 29in. wide.
(Christie's) $2231   £1430

A Japanese four-fold screen, enriched with mother o' pearl and ivory mounts depicting birds flying and perched in flowering branchwork, each fold 26in. x 65in.
(Lawrence Fine Arts)
$2178   £1320

One of a pair of Regency black and gilt-japanned and parcel-gilt tole two-leaf screens, painted in colours with figures before pagodas and other buildings in chinoiserie landscapes, each leaf 27in. x 61in.
(Christie's) $51480   £33000

A pair of early Victorian black lacquered papier mache pole screens, with decoratively pierced borders and finely painted with differing designs of exotic birds, flowers and scrolls.
(Geering & Colyer)
$1732   £1050

A six-leaf screen, each leaf painted with chinoiserie figures in a landscape after Boucher, the figures taking tea, fishing and playing musical instruments, each leaf 24in. x 74in.
(Christie's) $4805   £3080

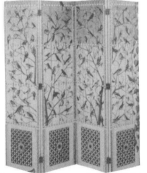

An Art Nouveau carved three leaf screen, the rectangular panels with bud finials, fluted borders and tapering legs, 135cm. wide. (Christie's London) $753 £462

A four-fold screen, designed by Piero Fornasetti, one side depicting brightly coloured birds, the other showing guitars, each panel 200cm. high x 50cm. wide.
(Christie's) $6376   £3960

Chinese four panel screen, 19th century, with scenes in relief carved in small pieces of multi-coloured soapstone, agate and quartz, 69in. high. (Skinner Inc.) $2,800 £1,783

SCREENS

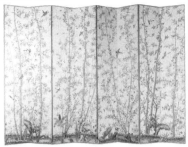

An eight leaf screen decorated with Chinese wallpaper with songbirds amid flowering shrubs and bamboo shoots on a grey blue ground, each leaf 105 x 20in. (Christie's London) $8,690 £5,500

Charles X Three Panel Paper Screen, c. 1830, grisaille decorated with arched crests painted with a laurel leaf frame surrounding an Italian landscape scene, 67in. high. (Skinner Inc) $2100 £1363

Early 19th century European four-fold screen, with painted paper panels depicting figures in an architectural setting, 5ft. 9in. x 2ft. ½in. (Phillips) $1815 £1100

A dated Coromandel lacquer twelve-leaf screen, one side decorated with flowers, birds and rocks, the reverse with a Chinese inscription between circular panels of Chinese figures, Kangxi 20th year, each leaf 258cm. x 51cm. (Christie'sLondon) $34320 £22000

A mahogany cheval fire-screen with arched needlework panel depicting a parrot and peacock, the needlework 18th century. (Christie's) $496 £308

A four-fold screen, designed by Piero Fornasetti, one side depicting a collector's bookshelves, the other showing guitars, each panel 130cm. high x 35cm. wide. (Christie's) $5313 £3300

A Dutch embossed leather four leaf screen, decorated in gilt with strapwork scrolls, on a green, red and grey ground, the leather 17th century, each leaf 85 x 23½in. (Christie's London) $2,125 £1,320

A Victorian giltwood fire-screen, the arched tufted beadwork panel depicting the Royal pets, after Landseer, 57½in. high. (Christie's London) $1,151 £715

A decorative chinoiserie four-fold screen, painted with oriental landscape, figures amongst pavilions, 75½in. x 24½in. (Bonhams) $1237 £750

411

SECRETAIRE BOOKCASES

A Georgian mahogany secretaire bookcase with a dentil frieze above two thirteen pane glazed doors, on bracket feet, 112cm. wide. (Lawrence Fine Arts) $5,562 £3,520

A Federal ladies' secretaire, Salem, Massachusetts, 1790-1810, with tambour doors enclosing a compartmented interior, 30½in. wide. (Christie's New York)
$2,640 £1,660

A mahogany secretaire bookcase with a fitted secretaire drawer and two cupboard doors enclosing sliding tray shelves, 122 x 224cm. high. (Lawrence Fine Arts)
$1,883 £1,155

A late Victorian walnut secretaire bookcase etched and carved with acanthus scrolls, the top section with a moulded cornice enclosed by two glazed astragal doors, 47½in. (Christie's S. Ken) $1,165 £715

A William IV mahogany breakfront secretaire bookcase, the later moulded cornice applied with foliate motif above open shelves, 112in. wide. (Christie's S. Ken) $7,531 £4,620

A mahogany secretaire bookcase the top with a pair of geometrically glazed doors above a rosewood banded writing drawer, on splayed bracket feet, early 19th century, 44½in. (Christie's S. Ken) $2,861 £1,870

A Victorian mahogany secretaire bookcase, with a deep secretaire drawer and three graduated long drawers, on bracket feet, 44in. wide. (Christie's S. Ken) $4,488 £2,640

A George III mahogany breakfront secretaire bookcase, the central fitted writing drawer above a pair of panelled doors flanked by two other doors, 68in. wide. (Christie's S. Ken)
$9,438 £6,050

A late Victorian oak secretaire bookcase carved with roundels and acanthus arabesques, the base with two drawers and two doors, on bracket feet, 52in. wide. (Christie's S. Ken) $1,408 £880

SECRETAIRE BOOKCASES

Renaissance Revival walnut bureau bookcase, circa 1870, drop-front desk enclosing a fitted interior, 51in. wide. (Robt. W. Skinner Inc.) $1,500 £915

A mahogany secretaire bookcase inlaid with boxwood and ebonised lines, the top section with a broken scroll pediment and inlaid frieze above two glazed doors, 42in. wide. (Christie's S. Ken) $3,696 £2,200

Late George III Satinwood Bureau Bookcase, first quarter 19th century, uper case with a pair of glazed doors, on bracket feet, (restorations), 66in. high. (Skinner Inc) $4500 £2922

A fine and rare Classical secretaire bookcase, New York, 1822-1838, the double glazed cupboard doors with gothic pattern mahogany and giltwood muntins, 58in. wide. (Christie's New York) $41,800 £26,289

Late George III Mahogany Secretary, early 19th century, triangular pediment above a pair of glazed mullioned doors, 42in. long. (Skinner Inc) $3000 £1948

A George III mahogany secretaire bookcase, with a deep fitted drawer and a pair of panelled cupboard doors, on plinth base, 48in. (Christie's S. Ken) $4,862 £2,860

English mahogany bureau bookcase with glazed doors, circa 1840, one pane restored, 117cm. wide. (Auktionshaus Arnold) $1,932 £1,254

A George III mahogany secretaire bookcase, the fascia hinged and falling to reveal pigeon holes, French bracket feet, 138cm. wide. (Henry Spencer) $6,031 £3,700

A Regency mahogany secretaire bookcase, the lower section with a satinwood fitted secretaire drawer above three graduated long drawers, 45½in. wide. (Christie's S. Ken) $3,945 £2,420

SECRETAIRES

A 17th century Portuguese walnut and ivory inlaid vargueno on contemporary stand, 1.07m. wide. (Phillips London) $9,945 £6,500

A Regency secretaire cupboard of breakfront form with a bowed central section, on later turned feet, 186cm. wide. (Lawrence Fine Arts) $5,379 £3,300

A 19th ventury faded teak secretaire military chest, the top drawer fitted inside with tooled leather to the fall front, 3ft. wide. (Wooley & Wallis) $3040 £1900

A Franco Flemish mahogany secretaire a abattant, the frieze drawer above a fall front with a fitted interior, on reeded block feet, early 19th century, 38½in. (Christie's S. Ken) $2,693 £1,760

A Marsh & Jones satinwood and marquetry bureau cabinet, the design attributed to Charles Bevan, the superstructure with galleried shelves above elaborated brackets, 174cm. wide. (Christie's London) $22,176 £13,200

A gilt metal mounted walnut and parquetry secretaire abattant after Riesener, with chamfered and moulded rectangular Louis XVI breccia marble top, 32in. wide. (Christie's London) $7,084 £4,400

A French mahogany secretaire a abattant with a fall front enclosing oak lined interior with pigeon holes, drawers and central cupboard, early 19th century, 102cm. wide. (Lawrence Fine Arts) $1,303 £825

A George III mahogany and satinwood pedestal secretaire, the fitted drawer veneered with an apsidal panel within contrasting banding, 48¾in. wide. (Tennants) $2,370 £1,500

A Dutch kingwood and marquetry inlaid pedestal secretaire chest, the pierced three quarter galleried top above a writing drawer, 20in. wide. (Christie's S. Ken) $2,214 £1,375

SECRETAIRES

A Louis XVI tulipwood, purple heart and inlaid secretaire a abattant of small size with canted angles surmounted by a rance marble top, 78cm. wide. (Phillips London) $5,355 £3,500

A gilt tooled leather secretaire cabinet on stand, the fall front engraved with a crest of a boar's jaws held apart by two hands within strapwork borders, stamped *H. Samuel*, 32in. wide. (Christie's London) $6,276 £3,850

A fine and rare Classical mahogany and bird's eye maple secretaire a abattant, Philadelphia, 1820-1830, on acanthus carved lion's paw feet, 36½in. wide. (Christie's New York) $46,200 £29,056

A Louis XVI tulipwood and inlaid secretaire a abattant, bordered with purple heart lines and stringing, on turned tapered feet, stamped *J. M. Schiler*, 91cm. wide. (Phillips London) $3,366 £2,200

Empire Mahogany and Ormolu Secretaire à Abbatant, first-quarter 19th century, mottled grey rectangular marble top, (with later mounts, damaged), 54½in. high. (Skinner Inc) $1500 £974

A Regency mahogany secretaire a abattant attributed to Gillows, with frieze flap enclosing pigeon holes, the base with two doors, 43¾in. wide. (Christie's London) $3,476 £2,200

An Arts and Crafts oak secrétaire of tapering form, having twin-glazed doors, with drop-fronted bureau below. (Phillips) $960 £600

Louis XVI mahogany and ormolu mounted secretaire a abattant, stamped *L. Craisson, JME,* fourth quarter 18th century, 37½in. long. (Skinner Inc.) $2,900 £1,779

George III style mahogany secretaire, circa 1900, scrolled crest above a pair of glazed doors, raised on square tapering legs, 78in. high. (Skinner Inc.) $1,700 £1,097

SETTEES & COUCHES

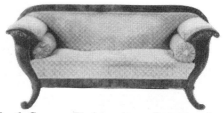

A French Provincial fruitwood daybed with outscrolled ends and moulded rail, 19th century, 78in. wide. (Christie's S. Ken) $1,178 £770

North German Biedermeier mahogany sofa, on scroll feet, 217cm. wide. (Auktionshaus Arnold) $1,214 £788 1626

An Art Deco two seater sofa, upholstered in coloured velvet fabric depicting tigers walking through foliage, 166cm. long. (Phillips London) $456 £280

A Victorian mahogany three seater sofa, the upholstered buttoned bowed back and seat on cabriole legs, 82in. wide. (Christie's S. Ken) $1,431 £935

A Biedermeier satin birch sofa, the scrolled toprail centred by an oval patera, the scrolled ribbed arms with turned roundels, the seat rail with leafy paterae on sabre legs, 89in. wide. (Christie's London) $5,214 £3,300

An attractive walnut chair back settee in the 18th century style, the back pierced with triple interlaced loops, raised upon three cabriole front supports. (Henry Spencer) $2,557 £1,650

An Edwardian mahogany daybed, the arched back, scrolled arms, long seat and pleated skirt upholstered in green and white shamrock pattern chintz, 71in. long. (Christie's London) $956 £605

A mid-Victorian walnut settee with one reclined outscrolled end, downswept back, bowed end and serpentine seat, on cabriole legs, 77in. wide. (Christie's S. Ken) $1,584 £990

SETTEES & COUCHES

A mahogany sofa with shaped arched back, padded arms and triple serpentine seat upholstered in yellow silk, on cabriole legs with acanthus, 78in. wide. (Christie's London)
$3,432   £2,200

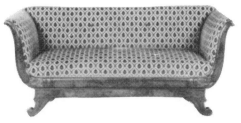

Walnut upholstered Empire sofa, on scroll feet, 197cm. wide. (Auktionshaus Arnold)
$1,546 £1,004

Regency style mahogany quadruple chairback settee, 19th century, raised on turned legs (fretwork sections showing breaks), 80in. long. (Skinner Inc.) $3,100 £1,975

A Victorian walnut chaise longue carved with flowerheads, foliage and C-scrolls, on cabriole legs with knob feet, 64in. wide. (Christie's S. Ken) $1,232 £770

American Empire mahogany settee, second quarter 19th century, with carved griffin heads, acanthus carved scrolled arms, 60½in. long. (Skinner Inc.) $1,300 £798

A massive sofa with deep seat, low back, scrolled arms and bolster cushions upholstered in tartan with tasselled seat rail, 132in. wide. (Christie's London) $1,912 £1,210

Louis XV beechwood canape, mid-18th century, floral and leaf carved scrolling crest above a caned back and seat, 73in. long. (Skinner Inc.) $900 £552

Rococo Revival walnut cassapanca, late 19th century, scrolling crest rail of C-scroll and acanthus leaves with a central cartouche, 56in. wide. (Robt. W. Skinner Inc.) $1,500 £915

SETTEES & COUCHES

A Classical carved mahogany small recamier, attributed to Quervelle, Philadelphia, circa 1820, on anthemion carved paw feet, 72 in. long. (Christie's New York) $8,800 £5,535

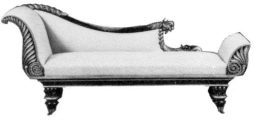

A Classical carved and giltwood meridienne, New York, 1825-1835, the scrolling half back carved with a lion's head terminal, 85 in. wide. (Christie s New York) $5,500 £3,459

An Aesthetic Movement ebonized and painted daybed, the upright back with baluster ends and reeded ornament, 168 cm. long. (Christie's London) $5,737 £3,520

Federal mahogany inlaid sofa, New Hampshire, circa 1815, attributed to John Gould, Jr., the swelled reeded legs on casters, 79 in. wide. (Skinner Inc.) $2,750 £1,687

A George I walnut twin chair back settee, the moulded balloon shaped back with solid vase splats with scroll ornament. (Phillips London) $22,950 £15,000

A Victorian walnut chaise longue, the graduated cresting rail carved with acanthus scrolls above an upholstered bowed back, 68 in. wide. (Christie's S. Ken) $1,771 £1,100

One of a pair of French giltwood canapes upholstered in green watered silk, the arms carved with guilloche, on turned legs carved with foliage, 86¼ in. wide. (Christie's London)
Two $8,855 £5,500

A late Victorian mahogany bergere three seater sofa, the acanthus carved crestings above double caned side panels and back, with claw and ball feet, 77 in. wide. (Christie's S. Ken) $4,662 £2,860

SETTEES & COUCHES

A Gothic mahogany chaise longue, the curved seat with arched back, raised on solid panelled and arched supports, 1.675m. long. (Phillips London) $995 £650

A Classical carved mahogany sofa, Boston, 1820-1830, on carved sabre legs with leafy feet, 35in. high, 85in. wide (Christie's New York) $7,700 £4,842

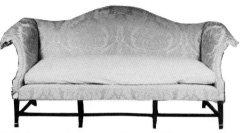

A Federal mahogany sofa, New York or Philadelphia, 1785-1810, on square, tapering legs with spade feet, 91in. long. (Christie's New York) $17,600 £11,069

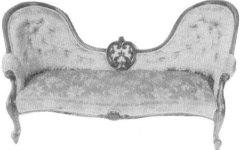

An attractive Victorian mahogany cameo back settee, scroll arm terminals extending down to cabriole front supports. (Henry Spencer) $1,630 £1,000

A Dutch walnut and marquetry inlaid sofa, the twin splat chair back above an undulating drop-in tapestry rectangular seat, 50in. wide. (Christie's S. Ken) $2,152 £1,320

A giltwood day bed, the arched back, down-swept arms and bowed seat upholstered in blue silk damask, on cabriole legs and scroll feet, 19th century, 80in. long. (Christie's S. Ken) $2,479 £1,485

A green painted and giltwood sociable of Louis XVI style, the padded back, arms and seats upholstered in floral cotton, on fluted turned tapering legs, 90½in. wide. (Christie's London) $5,313 £3,300

Gustav Stickley knock-down settee, New York, circa 1907, 12in. wide horizontal back slat, 84in. long. (Skinner Inc.) $7,750 £4,784

SIDEBOARDS

A late George III mahogany sideboard, fitted with a central drawer flanked by deep drawers, on six square tapering supports, 168cm. wide. (Lawrence Fine Arts) $3,824 £2,420

A French Provincial fruitwood buffet with moulded rounded rectangular top above two shaped fielded panelled doors, on scrolled feet, mid-18th century, 58in. wide. (Christie's London) $4,462 £2,640

A late George III mahogany bowfront sideboard, the central frieze drawer flanked by two deep drawers divided by reeded panels, on canted tapering legs, 60¼in. wide. (Christie's London) $8,236 £5,280

A late George III mahogany bow fronted sideboard, the lacquered brass back rail with urn finials and two candle branches, on square tapering legs with spade feet, 66in. wide. (Christie's London) $21,450 £13,750

Renaissance Revival walnut sideboard, circa 1870, upper case with carved crest above a pair of glazed doors, 46½in. wide. (Skinner Inc.) $500 £323

A mid-Victorian oak, sycamore and alder sideboard, by Charles Bevan, inlaid with dots, chevrons and stylised flowers, the mirrored back with crenellated cornice and gothic columns, 84½in. wide. (Christie's London)$2,917 £1,870

L & J. G. Stickley sideboard, circa 1912 panelled plate rail with corbels, (refinished, some stains and scratches) 54in. wide. (Skinner Inc.) $1,300 £798

Renaissance style oak sideboard, circa 1860, with three frieze drawers and three cabinet doors carved throughout, 84½in. wide. (Robt. W. Skinner Inc.) $700 £427

A Regency mahogany sideboard in the manner of Gillows, with double brass rail back, with later feet, 184cm. wide. (Lawrence Fine Arts) $5,379 £3,300

SIDEBOARDS

A George III mahogany sideboard with D-shaped breakfront top, on square tapering legs and spade feet, 67in. wide. (Christie's London)
$2,317 £1,485

A French Provincial oak buffet, the two drawers flanked by two panelled doors carved with scrolls and foliage, on incurved feet, 18th century, 66½in. wide. (Christie's London) $7,064 £4,180

A mahogany and marquetry bowfront sideboard with short drawer and two panelled doors, on square tapered legs, 72in. wide. (Christie's S. Ken)
$1,777 £1,045

Walnut sideboard, circa 1870, backsplash with carved crest above shelves and mirror on a moulded white marble top, 82in. high. (Skinner Inc.)
$1,700 £1,097

A satinwood sideboard crossbanded in tulipwood and inlaid with fanned spandrels with rectangular slightly bow front top, on square tapering legs, 51in. wide. (Christie's London)
$1,793 £1,100

A large oak sideboard by Romney Green, the top with four open shelves flanked by two stepped compartments, on four bracket feet, 298cm. wide, (Christie's London)
$13,860 £8,250

Part of an Art Deco dining room suite, comprising: a dining room table, a sideboard and four chairs with beige simulated leather upholstered seats. (Phillips London)
$459 £300

A Regency mahogany sideboard, the bowfronted top with three quarter gallery above a drawer and kneehole drawer flanked by deep drawers on ring turned legs, 48in. wide. (Christie's London)
$5,020 £3,080

A good Victorian ebonised credenza, of D-shape, with a central oval panel applied with a bird perched amidst branches of foliage, 180cm. long. (Henry Spencer) $3,749 £2,300

STANDS

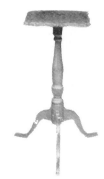

A rare George II walnut reading stand, with a drawer at one side and fitted with two small slides, adjustable in height, 56cm. wide. (Lawrence Fine Arts) $11,297 £7,150

George III style mahogany plate stand, 19th century, shaped top above a conforming body with paterae headed, square tapering legs, 25½in. high, 32in. wide. (Robt. W. Skinner Inc.) $1,200 £732

A late Federal grain painted maple candlestand, New England, early 19th century, the square top elaborately scalloped, 25in. high. (Christie's New York) $7,150 £4,497

Gustav Stickley Toby magazine stand, circa 1904, square top with corbel supports, unsigned (top reglued), 43in. high. (Skinner Inc.)$600 £368

A pair of fruitwood and ebonised fluted columns with square capitals and plinths, 40¼in. high. (Christie's S. Ken) $1,478 £880

Limbert octagonal plant stand with cut-outs, Michigan, circa 1910, on box base with double trapezoidal cut-outs, 28½in. high. (Skinner Inc.) $1,500 £926

L. & J. G. Stickley dinner gong, Fayetteville, New York, 1912, arched frame supporting circular bronze gong. (Robt. W. Skinner Inc.) $7,000 £4,294

Painted cherry stand, Connecticut River Valley, early 19th century, the scrolled two board top above a base with single beaded drawer, 26in. high. (Skinner Inc.) $3,750 £2,301

Federal painted and decorated candlestand, probably New England, on a tripod base with an arris leg, mid 19th century, 28in. high. (Skinner Inc.) $850 £521

Double sided walnut music stand, last third 19th century, each ratcheted side of pierced scrolling foliage, 67½in. high. (Skinner Inc.) $900 £581

A George III mahogany two division cutlery stand with pierced carrying handle, on ring turned splayed legs, 66cm. wide. (Phillips London) $2,295 £1,500

Hammered copper plant stand, design attributed to Joseph Maria Olbrich, Germany, late 19th century, unsigned, 29in. high. (Robt. W. Skinner Inc.) $1,600 £982

Weller Art Nouveau pattern umbrella stand, Zanesville, Ohio, early 20th century, moulded floral design in green matte glaze, 24in. high. (Skinner Inc.) $375 £231

An unusual mid-Victorian oak tabernacle of architectural form, the fluted super-structure with pepperpot finials, 39in. wide. (Christie's S. Ken) $2,869 £1,760

Roycroft oak umbrella stand, East Aurora, New York, circa 1910, signed with logo, (finish partially removed) 29¾in. high. (Robt. W. Skinner Inc.) $500 £307

A Federal mahogany tilt top stand, Salem, Massachusetts, 1790-1810, on tripod cabriole legs with pad feet, 69cm. high. (Christie's New York) $1,210 £761

A George III mahogany butler's tray, the rectangular galleried top pierced with carrying handles on a turned beech folding stand, 26in. wide. (Christie's S. Ken) $1,848 £1,100

Hammered copper umbrella stand, attributed to Benedict Studios, East Syracuse, New York, circa 1910, unsigned, 25in. high. (Skinner Inc.) $600 £370

STANDS

A Regency mahogany double sided bookstand with spindle filled ends and divided top, inlaid with satinwood stripes, 14½in. wide. (Christie's London) $1,008 £638

A mahogany book trough on moulded square legs and cross stretchers, 31in. wide. (Christie's London) $869 £550

A late George III mahogany booktray with carrying handle and galleried sides, 17in. wide. (Christie's London) $608 £385

Japanese lacquered dumbwaiter, 19th century, three circular tiers decorated with takamakie with abalone, mother-of-pearl and gilt accents, 43½in. high. (Skinner Inc) $300 £186

A George III mahogany oval wine bin, brass banded with two brass handles, lead lined, 25½in. high. (Wooley & Wallis) $5280 £3300

A late George III mahogany pedestal dumb waiter, on a turned bulbous tapering shaft with splayed legs, 54in. high. (Christie's S. Ken) $1,408 £880

L. & J. G. Stickley square drink stand, Fayetteville, New York, circa 1910, signed with Handcraft decal, 27in. high. (Skinner Inc.) $600 £370

A Regency specimen wood parquetry pedestal teapoy, the octagonal top with a hinged lid enclosing two caddies and bowl apertures. (Christie's S. Ken) $3,029 £1,980

An ormolu mounted kingwood and marquetry three tier etagere with galleried top, turned supports and two shelves, 14in. wide. (Christie's London) $1,738 £1,100

FURNITURE

A William IV rosewood
pedestal plant stand, the
drum top with metal liner,
31in. high. (Tennants)
$967 £620

A Regency rosewood teapoy
with chamfered corners and
inlaid with stringing, on four
square curved supports joined
by X turned stretchers, 48cm.
wide. (Lawrence Fine Arts)
$3,302 £2,090

Regency mahogany two tiered
dumb waiter, first quarter 19th
century, two octagonal drop
leaf shelves, raised on splayed
legs, 44in. high. (Skinner Inc.)
$1,500 £920

A Biedermeier style mahogany
stand, on double S-scroll supports with finial on serpentine
platform base with gilt feet,
38in. high. (Christie's S. Ken)
$896 £550

A George III mahogany jardiniere, the oval brass bound
body with carrying handles on
square chamfered legs with
C-scroll brackets, 27in. wide.
(Christie's London)
$11,117 £6,820

Paint decorated Federal
candlestand, New Hampshire,
attributed to the Dunlap
family of cabinetmakers,
1780-1810, 26½in. high.
(Skinner Inc.) $8,000 £4,908

A green stained oak magazine
rack made by H. Lamberton of
Glasgow, with graduated slots,
inlaid at the bottom with an
Art Nouveau plant motif,
92.5cm. high. (Phillips London)
$571 £350

An Arthur Simpson of Kendal
oak tea trolley, the swivel
hinged rectangular top above
carved frieze of stylised flowerheads, on square section legs,
75cm. high. (Christie's London)
$1,294 £770

A mahogany plant stand, possibly by Ellwood, having four
uprights with hemispherical
finials, 93.2cm. high. (Phillips
London) $245 £150

STOOLS

A Regency mahogany window seat, the scrolling X-frame applied with paterae and joined by spirally reeded arms and stretchers, 64½in. wide. (Christie's London) $13,728 £8,800

A Classical carved mahogany footstool, English, 1820-1830, on reeded baluster feet, 6¾in. high. (Christie's New York) $550 £345

Louis XIII cherrywood bench, late 17th century, with 18th century needlepoint seat of gros and petit point, 31in. long. (Skinner Inc.) $2,800 £1,718

An ormolu mounted satinwood stool, the padded rectangular seat upholstered in green velvet and decorated with laurel wreaths, 22½in. wide. (Christie's London) $1,304 £825

A Classical mahogany piano stool, New York, 1800-1815, the upholstered circular seat turning above a threaded support, 14in. diam. (Christie's New York) $700 £484

A Classical mahogany stool, Boston, 1820-1830, on a scrolled curule base joined by a turned stretcher, 20in. wide. (Christie's New York) $1,870 £1,176

A James II walnut stool, the cabriole legs headed by cabochons with scroll feet joined by moulded waved stretchers, 20in. square. (Christie's London) $4,250 £2,640

Limbert oak window bench, Grand Rapids, Michigan, 1907, with original leather cushion, branded mark (minor nicks), 24in. wide. (Skinner Inc.) $11,000 £6,790

A George III mahogany stool with concave sided drop in seat on square legs and cross stretchers, 17in. wide. (Christie's London) $1,303 £825

FURNITURE

A Gordon Russell oak stool, the rectangular top woven with hide straps, on square section notched legs, 72cm. wide. (Christie's London) $702 £418

An early Victorian mahogany footstool, upholstered in strapwork and floral patterned needlework, on turned feet, 17½in. wide. (Christie's London) $782 £495

Louis XVI giltwood footstool, signed *P. Forget*, late 18th century, rectangular needlepoint upholstered seat, 13in. long. (Skinner Inc.)$325 £199

A walnut stool, with turned baluster legs and stretchers, late 17th century, with restorations, 19in. wide. (Christie's London) $1,771 £1,100

One of a pair of Windsor stools, New England, 1800-1820, the oval tops on bamboo turned splayed tapering legs, 13in. high. (Skinner Inc.)
$13,000 £7,975

A mahogany stool of Empire design, on winged lion's head supports with cabriole legs and gilt metal paw feet, 22in. wide. (Christie's S. Ken)
$3,407 £2,090

An early Georgian walnut stool, the rectangular seat upholstered in needlework depicting a bird among flowering branches, 18in. wide. (Christie's London)
$3,765 £2,310

A George III mahogany stool with drop in seat on chamfered square legs and stretchers, 21in. wide. (Christie's London)
$695 £440

A 17th century oak joint stool with moulded rectangular seat and shaped seat rail on turned legs, 19in. wide. (Christie's London) $1,859 £1,100

STOOLS

A George III mahogany meta-morphic stool, on square chamfered legs joined by slanting stretchers incorporating three treads. (Christie's London)
$1,972 £1,210

Roycroft oak upholstered footstool, New York, circa 1910, no. 048, needlepoint cover, 10in. high. (Skinner Inc.) $375 £230

A mahogany stool, upholstered in close nailed dark brown leather, on six fluted and reeded legs, 35in. wide. (Christie's London) $1,459 £935

A beech and ash milking stool with dished circular seat on three splayed legs, 19th century, 11½in. high. (Christie's London) $148 £88

A pair of Regency mahogany footstools, each with square floral needlework seat, the tapering sides fitted with ring handles on paw feet, 12in. sq. (Christie's London) $1,614 £990

An oak joint stool, the seat rail with chiselled edge on turned and squared legs with stretchers, 17th century, one foot restored, 18½in. wide. (Christie's London) $1,948 £1,210

A George IV white painted and parcel gilt stool, on channelled cabriole legs headed by flowers, the seat rail inscribed *Bartholomew*, 25in. wide. (Christie's London) $897 £550

A pair of Regency rosewood dressing stools, raised upon inverted X-frame supports tied by a baluster turned stretcher. (Henry Spencer) $2,325 £1,500

An early Georgian style walnut stool, on shell and husk carved cabriole legs headed by 'C'-scrolls, 25½in. wide. (Bonhams) $1072 £650

FURNITURE

A Victorian giltwood stool, on cabriole legs with scroll feet and cabochon headings, 25in. wide. (Christie's S. Ken.) $508 £308

A Regency rosewood foot stool, after a design by George Smith, the S-scroll padded top upholstered in striped repp, on ribbed bun feet, 15½in. wide. (Christie's London)
$1,887 £1,210

An Irish mahogany stool, the seat rail carved with leaves and scrolls on a pounced ground, on cabriole legs and paw feet, 18th century, 28½in. wide. (Christie's London)
$2,231 £1,430

A French giltwood stool after a design by A. C. M. Fournier, the four legs and X-shaped stretcher carved in the form of knotted rope, 19in. diam. (Christie's) $4462 £2860

A pair of Victorian walnut stools each with a distressed rectangular upholstered top on hipped, cabriole legs, 17½in. wide. (Christie's S. Ken) $3,227 £1,980

A Louis XIV giltwood tabouret with padded rectangular seat on scrolling legs carved with acanthus joined by an X-shaped stretcher, 22in. wide. (Christie's London) $1,217 £770

Queen Anne Walnut Footstool, 18th century, rectangular upholstered seat raised on cabriole legs, 20in. long. (Skinner Inc) $4250 £2759

Pair of Italian Neoclassical Cream Painted Parcel Gilt Footstools, early 19th century, (one foot repaired), 19¾in. long. (Skinner Inc) $2000 £1298

A walnut stool of George II design, on cabriole legs with pad feet and shell and bellflower carved headings, 21½in. wide. (Christie's S. Ken.) $581 £352

Four piece suite of Heywood-Wakefield wicker seat furniture, a settee, armchair and two
side chairs, raised on circular legs. (Skinner Inc.) $650 £419

Early 20th century German suite of furniture consisting of: a round table, four chairs
and a cupboard, in cherrywood with teak inlay, the cupboard with three glazed doors,
190cm. wide, the table on four sided base with corner columns. (Kunsthaus am Museum)
$1,891 £1,087

An Empire mahogany and ormolu mounted salon suite, comprising: a canape and four
fauteuils, the upholstered and slightly arched carved backs with neo-Classical decorated
toprails. (Phillips London) $9,180 £6,000

A pair of early Victorian rosewood open armchairs, each with a shaped, curved back, the shepherd's crook arms with eagle's head supports, with claw and ball feet and a sofa en suite, 100in. wide. (Christie's London) $27,560 £17,380

Seven piece suite of Directoire style walnut seat furniture, circa 1900, comprising a settee, two armchairs and four side chairs, raised on stop fluted, circular tapering legs. (Skinner Inc.) $1,800 £1,161

Louis XV style beechwood suite of seat furniture, 19th century, a settee and two side chairs, moulded crest rail with C-scroll and acanthus carving, carved apron raised on cabriole legs. (Robt. W. Skinner Inc.) $800   £488

A seven-piece late Victorian mahogany salon suite upholstered in coral fabric, comprising a settee, two armchairs and four chairs. (Bonhams) $1237 £750

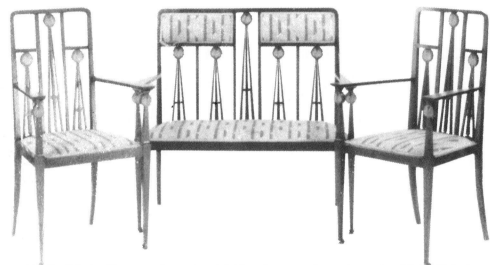

An English Art Nouveau three piece inlaid mahogany salon suite, each with inlaid fruit-wood roundels of buds, the tapering arms and padded seats on tapering legs, 104cm. width of sofa. (Christie's London) $5,174 £3,080

A Louis XVI style giltwood suite with foliate beaded frame comprising a canape with a tapestry upholstered back and seat on fluted turned tapering legs, 57in. wide, two arm-chairs and two side chairs. (Christie's S. Ken) $4,114 £2,420

SUITES

A Victorian carved giltwood salon suite in the Louis XV style, having leafage scroll decoration, floral tapestry upholstered back panels and seats, on slender cabriole front supports. (Russell Baldwin & Bright) $5115   £3300

A pair of Louis XV style carved giltwood fauteuils, the tapestry upholstered channelled frames below a foliate shell carved cresting. (Christie's S. Ken) $1,663   £990

A suite of grey-painted seat furniture of Louis XVI style with shaped padded backs and bowed seats upholstered in gold and grey floral silk, the channelled toprails carved with ribbon-tied urns. (Christie's) $2449   £1540

CARD & TEA TABLES

Federal cherry veneered card table, Southern Massachusetts, circa 1810, on four ring turned reeded tapering legs ending in turned feet, 35¼in. wide. (Skinner Inc.) $2,600 £1,595

A good Regency mahogany tea table in the manner of Gillows, on slender fluted legs, 33½in. wide. (Phillips Manchester) $1,975 £1,250

Federal mahogany veneered card table, probably Connecticut, circa 1820, the serpentine top with ovolo corners, 36in. wide. (Skinner Inc.) $1,300 £798

An Italian burr yew card table, the banded rectangular top centred by an inlaid geometric motif on square tapered legs, 33in. wide. (Christie's S. Ken) $2,033 £1,210

A William IV mahogany pedestal card table the crossbanded rectangular fold-over top with a scroll and tablet banded frieze, 36in. wide. (Christie's S. Ken) $1,755 £1 045

A Chippendale carved mahogany card table, Rhode Island or Massachusetts, 1770-1790, with hinged serpentine top, 32in. wide. (Christie's New York) $2,750 £1,729

A Georgian D-shape card table veneered in amboyna and kingwood crossbandings, raised on four square tapering supports, 92cm. wide. (Lawrence Fine Arts) $3,407 £2,090

A Classical gilt stencilled mahogany card table, New York, 1825-1835, on four acanthus carved legs with lion's paw feet 36in. wide. (Christie's New York) $2,090 £1,314

A mahogany card table, the elliptical fold-over top above frieze drawers, on club legs, part 18th century, 30in. wide. (Christie's S. Ken) $1,570 £935

CARD & TEA TABLES

Classical Revival carved mahogany card table, Salem, Massachusetts, circa 1820, the rectangular top with reeded edge, 35½in. wide. (Skinner Inc.) $2,500 £1,534

A George III card table with rounded fold-over top, raised on four square tapering supports, the frieze and legs with flowers and swags, repairs, 91cm. wide. (Lawrence Fine Arts) $1,564 £990

A fine Federal inlaid mahogany card table, Massachusetts, 1790-1810, on square tapering line-inlaid legs with inlaid cuffs, 91cm. wide. (Christie's New York) $2,420 £1,522

A late Regency mahogany and inlaid bowfront tea table, the eared shaped rectangular fold-over top above a tablet applied frieze, 39in. wide. (Christie's S. Ken) $1,570 £935

A Dutch walnut card table, inlaid with urns, flowerheads and foliate marquetry, on cabriole legs with pad feet, part late 17th century, 30½in. (Christie's S. Ken) $2,712 £1,595

Federal mahogany inlaid card table, Newport, Rhode Island, circa 1800, on four square tapering front legs; two back legs swing to support the top. (Skinner Inc.) $20,000 £12,270

A late Regency rosewood card table, with rectangular base and four short sabre shape supports, 91cm. wide. (Lawrence Fine Arts) $956 £605

A George II concertina action mahogany card table, on cabriole legs carved with C-scrolls at the knee, on hoof feet, 91cm. wide. (Phillips London) $3,366 £2,200

A Regency rosewood, brass inlaid card table decorated with flowerheads, foliate and stellar cut brass ornament, 91cm. wide. (Phillips London) $4,284 £2,800

CARD & TEA TABLES

A Regency ormolu mounted card table, the frieze applied with anthemions and geometrically inlaid on turned splayed tapering legs, 36in. wide. (Christie's London)
$1,614 £990

A Victorian walnut and marquetry inlaid serpentine card table, on a reeded tapering shaft and foliate lappeted quadruple splayed legs, 35in. wide. (Christie's S. Ken)
$1,076 £660

An ormolu mounted ebonised and scarlet boulle serpentine card table, the shaped frieze centred by a mask clasp, 19th century, 35in. wide. (Christie's S. Ken)
$1,683 £990

A George II red walnut and mahogany serpentine tea table, on chamfered square moulded legs with acanthus carved wings, adapted, 33in. wide. (Christie's S. Ken)
$2,510 £1,540

A walnut and seaweed marquetry card table of William and Mary style, the demi-elliptical folding top with concave centre lined in needlework, 32in. wide. (Christie's London)
$17,660 £10,450

A George III mahogany card table, the fluted frieze applied with paterae on square tapering fluted legs, 36in. wide. (Christie's London)
$3,407 £2,090

A Regency rosewood tea table, inlaid with brass, the D-shaped top on beaded moulded shaft and concave platform, 35in. wide. (Christie's S. Ken)
$2,152 £1,320

A William IV rosewood card table, with square tapering outward splayed quadruped supports terminating in brass lion paw feet, 91cm. long. (Henry Spencer)
$1,141 £700

George III satinwood games table, breakfront with single frieze drawer, on tapered square legs, 36in. wide. (Skinner Inc.)
$1,300 £828

CARD & TEA TABLES

Regency Rosewood and Brass Mounted Card Table, c. 1810, with rounded corners and anthemion inlay, 35½in. wide. (Skinner Inc) $2400 £1558

Dutch Mahogany and Marquetry Card Table, third-quarter 18th century, rectangular folding top above a shaped skirt, 32¾in. long. (Skinner Inc) $1800 £1168

A Victorian walnut card table, the serpentine rectangular top on cabochon tapering shaft and scrolling quadruple supports, 36in. wide. (Christie's S. Ken) $1,683 £1,100

A walnut card table, the eared top and single frieze drawer on shell headed club legs, 32½in. wide, early Georgian and later. (Christie's S. Ken) $1,682 £1,045

Rare small mahogany serpentine Chippendale card table, probably Rhode Island, circa 1760 (minor imperfections), 24in. wide. (Skinner Inc.) $7,500 £4,438

Dutch rococo walnut marquetry tea table, 18th century, raised on cabriole legs, pull out with candleslides, 29in. wide. (Skinner Inc.) $5,250 £3,344

A George IV rosewood pedestal card table, on a turned ribbed pedestal, the concave sided platform base on down scroll feet, 36in. wide. (Christie's S. Ken) $1,793 £1,100

Classical carved veneered brass inlaid table, probably New York, circa 1820s, the green marble top with triple banded edge, 33in. wide. (Skinner Inc.) $6,500 £3,846

Regency Satinwood Card Table, first quarter 19th century, D-shaped top opening to a baize-lined playing surface, 36in. long. (Skinner Inc) $3000 £1948

CENTRE TABLES

Renaissance Revival walnut centre table, third quarter 19th century, stamped *W. Gertz,* with carved laurel leaf frieze, 28¾in. long. (Skinner Inc.) $3,250 £1,994

An ebonised and parcel gilt centre table with circular black, grey and beige veined marble top on a fluted shaft and concave sided base with paw feet, 51in. diam. (Christie's London) $1,972 £1,210

A giltmetal mounted walnut, amboyna and foliate marquetry centre table, decorated with a vase of flowers amidst scrolling foliage and strapwork, 54in. wide. (Christie's S. Ken) $5,379 £3,300

An early Victorian rosewood centre table by Gillows, on three cabriole legs and paw feet carved with scrolls and acanthus, 48in. wide. (Christie's London) $4,662 £2,860

A pine centre table with circular black marble top and spirally turned shaft carved with an eagle, 24in. diam. (Christie's S. Ken) $1,255 £770

A mahogany centre table, the waved circular tip up top with acanthus carved border on splayed legs with dolphin head pad feet, part 18th century, 34in. diam. (Christie's S. Ken) $2,587 £1,540

Rosewood centre table, late 19th century, raised on single baluster form pedestal supported by three griffon headed C-scroll legs, 26in. high. (Robt. W. Skinner Inc.) $450 £274

A Regency pollard oak centre table, the quarter veneered circular tip up top banded in calamander on a concave sided triangular shaft with turned angles, 52½in. diam. (Christie's London) $8,236 £5,280

An early Victorian mahogany centre table with circular Italian specimen marble top on three scrolled supports headed by carved dragons, 23in. diam. (Christie's London) $9,862 £6,050

CENTRE TABLES

A George IV rosewood and parcel gilt centre table, on a spreading hexagonal shaft and triangular base with acanthus and scroll feet, 53¾in. diam. (Christie's London)
$25,102 £15,400

Painted Queen Anne tavern table, Rhode Island, 18th century, scrubbed top on original red washed base, 38in. wide. (Skinner Inc.)
$12,000 £7,101

A William IV rosewood, marquetry and ebony centre table, the spreading triangular shaft and concave sided platform inlaid with panels of foliate marquetry, 52in. diam. (Christie's London)
$4,483 £2,750

An ormolu mounted bois de citron and harewood centre table by A. Beurdeley fils, the circular top with a verre eglomise panel decorated with a naked woman playing the flute, 32in. diam. (Christie's London)
$26,565 £16,500

A Gordon Russell oak drop leaf centre table, the twelve sided moulded drop leaf top above four octagonal legs joined by chamfered stretcher, with swivel gate leg, 1930, 55.9cm. wide. (Christie's London)
$1,571 £935

Carved Lotus centre table, executed by John Bradstreet, Minneapolis, circa 1905, original black finish, unsigned, 30in. diam. (Skinner Inc.)
$25,000 £15,432

A walnut centre table, the rectangular marble top on foliate carved cabriole legs with pad feet, 46½in. wide. (Christie's S. Ken) $896 £550

A George IV brass inlaid rosewood centre table with circular tip up top, concave sided tripartite platform and foliate scrolling claw feet, 42½in. wide. (Christie's London)
$8,923 £5,720

An Irish mahogany centre table with moulded rectangular grey and coral vine marble top, on cabriole legs with hairy paw feet, 34in. wide. (Christie's S. Ken) $3,407 £2,090

CONSOLE TABLES

A French giltwood console table in Louis XV style with semi-circular marble top, on shell headed scrolling legs with finialled stretcher, 47½in. wide. (Christie's S. Ken) $1,703 £1,045

Louis XVI mahogany console desserte, 20th century, with antico verde breakfront marble top, 72in. wide. (Robt. W. Skinner Inc.) $1,600 £976

A George IV giltwood console table, the serpentine brocatella marble top above a frieze with foliate C-scrolls and shells, 58in. wide. (Christie's S. Ken) $7,172 £4,400

A mahogany and brass-inlaid console side table, the eared and crossbanded rectangular top above a tablet applied banded frieze, early 19th century, 35in. wide. (Christie's S. Ken.) $2359 £1430

A George II giltwood console table with a later rectangular white marble top, the frieze carved with drapery flanked by egg-and-dart and gadrooning, 39½in. wide. (Christie's) $68640 £44000

Regency Mahogany Console Table, c. 1810, D-shaped top raised on circular carved tapering legs, 31¼in. long. (Skinner Inc) $2900 £1883

A Classical carved and gilt stencilled mahogany marble top pier table, Philadelphia, 1825-1835, on scroll supports with acanthus knees, 42in. wide. (Christie's New York) $4,620 £2,905

One of a pair of George III style demilune console tables, antico verde marble tops with ogee edge, 51in. wide. (Skinner Inc.) Two $6,250 £3,981

A Classical rosewood marble top pier table, Philadelphia, 1820-1830, with ormolu medallion and leafage above gilt scrolled supports, 42in. wide. (Christie's New York) $7,700 £4,842

CONSOLE TABLES

One of two early Victorian giltwood console tables, each with shaped serpentine white marble top, the pierced frieze carved with flowerheads and foliage, 33½in. high. (Christie's London) Two $14,168 £8,800

A 19th century painted and marble console table in the manner of John Vardy, supported upon a pair of carved griffins with heads inclined inwards, 1.14m. wide. (Phillips London) $48,960 £32,000

A Regence giltwood console table with serpentine front on scroll supports carved in relief with shell medallions , scrolls, masks and foliage, 46in. wide. (Christie's) $4462   £2860

One of a pair of brass inlaid rosewood console tables, each with a verde antico marble top on displayed eagle support, 43½in. wide. (Christie's S. Ken)   Two $12,551 £7,700

A mid 19th century cast-iron console table with variegated serpentine marble top, the back legs stamped James Yates, Totherham, registered March 1842, 59in. wide. (Christie's) $10890   £6600

Classical pier table, New York, circa 1820, with mirror above carved gilded leafage and paw feet, 36in. wide. (Skinner Inc.) $3,250 £1,994

An Anglo-Indian rosewood console-table with rectangular scagliola top, S-scroll end-supports carved with acanthus leaves and paterae, 19th century, 48in. wide. (Christie's) $2834   £1760

One of a pair of giltwood console tables, each with a rectangular bréche d'alep marble top, 54¼in. wide. (Christie's) $17160   £11000

A French bowed giltwood console table, the eared Griotte Uni marble top above a pierced acanthus frieze applied with swags and paterae, 19th century, 50in. wide. (Christie's S. Ken) $7,531 £4,620

DINING TABLES

A mahogany D-end extending dining table with ripple moulded frieze on turned tapered reeded legs, extending to 190in. (Christie's S. Ken)
$3,945 £2,420

A Victorian burr walnut pedestal breakfast table, on a fluted central baluster shaft flanked by quadruple columns, stamped *Gillow,* 48in. wide. (Christie's S. Ken)$2,241 £1,375

A late George III mahogany D-ending dining table on square tapered fluted legs each headed by a fanned oval, 84½in. wide, including an extra leaf. (Christie's S. Ken)$2,525 £1,650

A George III mahogany breakfast table, the rounded rectangular top on a quadripartite support with reeded legs, 52in. (Christie's S. Ken)
$1,683 £990

A William IV mahogany extending pedestal dining table, the later D-end top on a flared chamfered support, extending to 90in. including three extra leaves. (Christie's S. Ken)
$4,250 £2,530

A calamander breakfast table with circular cross banded top on chamfered stepped triangular shaft, 48in. diam. (Christie's S. Ken) $3,740 £2,200

A mid-Victorian burr walnut breakfast table, the oval tip up top inlaid with Tonbridge ware diamonds within boxwood line borders, 56in. wide. (Christie's S. Ken) $2,402 £1,540

A mahogany breakfast table, the rectangular tilt-top on a ring turned shaft, basically early 19th century, 41 x 60in. (Christie's S. Ken) $924 £550

A Victorian figured walnut breakfast table, the oval snap top quarter veneered, with thumb moulded edge, 150cm. long. (Henry Spencer)
$1,627 £1,050

DINING TABLES

A mahogany breakfast table, with reeded splayed legs and lion's paw caps, Regency and later, 53in. wide. (Christie's S. Ken) $1,703 £1,045

A mahogany dining table, the rounded rectangular top on turned tapered legs, extending to 95in. including three extra leaves. (Christie's S. Ken) $1,851 £1,210

A William IV mahogany break-fast table, the D-end tilt top on a pedestal carved with lotus leaves, 61in. (Christie's S. Ken) $3,366 £1,980

A late Victorian walnut break-fast table, the oval moulded tip up top on a turned quadri-partite support with foliate carved splayed legs, 54in. wide. (Christie's S. Ken)$1,072 £638

A rosewood pedestal breakfast table, the circular tip up top with Grecian key pattern satin-wood banded border, basically early 19th century, 54in. diam. (Christie's S. Ken) $7,084 £4,400

Roycroft pedestal base dining table, East Aurora, New York, circa 1910, signed with logo, no leaves, 48in. diam. (Robt. W. Skinner Inc.) $2,100 £1,288

A late Regency mahogany breakfast table, on a turned pillar with four sabre shape supports with brass claw feet. (Lawrence Fine Arts) $1,390 £880

A Victorian burr walnut pede-stal dining table, on a carved tapering bulbous column and quadripartite base with scrol-led feet, 53in. diam. (Christie's S. Ken) $1,870 £1,100

A rosewood breakfast table, the octagonal top banded in burr maple on an octagonal shaft and four downswept legs, 42½in. wide. (Christie's London) $2,331 £1,430

DRESSING TABLES

An ormolu mounted tulip-wood marquetry and parquetry toilette a transformations of transitional style, on cabriole legs, 22¾ in. wide. (Christie's London)
$6,729 £4,180

A George IV mahogany dressing table, the rectangular top above five frieze drawers and a simulated panelled door, on ring turned tapering legs, 45½ in. wide. (Christie's S. Ken)
$1,515 £990

A rosewood bow front dressing chest fitted with a rectangular rising mirror and splayed supports, 19th century, 140cm. (Lawrence Fine Arts)
$1,004 £616

A fine Queen Anne carved mahogany dressing table, Salem, Massachusetts, 1740-1760, on cabriole legs with pad feet, 34in. wide. (Christie's New York)
$66,000 £41,509

Louis XV style mahogany dressing table, 19th century, lifting lid to reveal mirror, fitted interior with sliding tray and hidden jewellery drawer. (Skinner Inc.) $1,200 £764

Rare William and Mary japanned maple and pine dressing table, Boston area, 1710-1715 (one leg and foot, an old replacement), 34in. wide. (Skinner Inc.)
$45,000 £27,607

An Art Deco oak and painted dressing table, the red painted table surface with curved up ends, 1.66m. high, with stool en suite. (Phillips London)
$612 £400

A rare Queen Anne figured maple dressing table, Delaware River Valley, 1750-1770, on square tapering cabriole legs with Spanish feet, 39in. wide. (Christie's New York)
$41,800 £26,289

Roycroft mirrored dressing table, East Aurora, New York, circa 1910, with swing handles, tapering MacMurdo feet, signed with orb, 39in. wide. (Skinner Inc.) $900 £556

DRESSING TABLES

An Arthur Simpson of Kendal dressing table, with three quarter galleried top, on square section tapering legs, stool en suite, 114cm. wide. (Christie's London) $1,201 £715

George I burr walnut kneehole dressing table, rectangular moulded top on one long drawer above a central cupboard flanked by three short drawers, 35½in. long. (Skinner Inc.) $1,000 £613

A Biedermeier mahogany pedestal dressing table mounted with brass and inlaid with bands of scrolling foliage heightened with mother-of-pearl, with conforming stepped base, 18¾in. wide. (Christie's London) $3,824 £2,420

A French kingwood and tulipwood dressing table, the serpentine top enclosing a fitted interior, 15in. wide. (Christie's S. Ken) $3,048 £1,870

A parquetry and marquetry dressing table, the folding rectangular top part lined in maroon leather and enclosing three compartments, 35in. wide. (Christie's London) $2,607 £1,650

Eastlake lockend walnut chest of drawers, late 19th century, superstructure of mirrored cabinet and raised galleried shelves, 35¼in. wide. (Skinner Inc.) $1,200 £774

Prairie School style oak bureau with swivel mirror, Illinois, circa 1912, central portion with square posts and moulded cornice over vertical mirror, 87in. high. (Robt. W. Skinner Inc.) $1,600 £982

Queen Anne mahogany and mahogany veneered dressing table, probably Rhode Island, circa 1770, the moulded overhanging top above cockbeaded case, 30½in. wide. (Skinner Inc.) $10,000 £6,135

Federal mahogany veneered Beau Brummel, probably Eastern United States, circa 1820, on turned tapering legs, 40in. high. (Skinner Inc.) $6,000 £3,871

DROP LEAF TABLES

A Queen Anne mahogany drop leaf table, Massachusetts, 1730-1750, on cabriole legs and pad and disc feet, 29in. high. (Christie's New York) $2,200 £1,383

A Regency mahogany dining table, the folding rectangular top on ring turned tapering legs, 46 x 55in. (Christie's S. Ken) $1,178 £770

A mid Georgian mahogany drop leaf dining table, the oval twin flap top on club legs and pad feet, 55in. wide. (Christie's S. Ken) $1,571 £935

Large Georgian mahogany oval drop leaf table of good colour on four tapering legs, measuring 48 x 45in. when erected. (G. A. Key) $874 £520

Queen Anne mahogany drop leaf table, Massachusetts, 1750-1780, with hinged square leaves over a shaped skirt, 27in. high. (Skinner Inc.) $5,500 £3,374

Queen Anne tiger maple drop leaf table, New England, on cabriole legs ending in pad feet, 48in. wide. (Skinner Inc.) $6,600 £4,258

Gustav Stickley cut-corner drop leaf table, circa 1906, no. 638, signed with red decal (some restoration to base), 30in. high. (Robt. W. Skinner Inc.) $1,700 £1,043

A Queen Anne cherrywood drop leaf table, Massachusetts, 1740-1760, on cabriole legs with pad feet, 26½in. high. (Christie s New York) $5,500 £3,459

Country Queen Anne maple dining table, New England, mid 18th century, the rectangular drop leaf top above a shaped skirt, 26¾in. high. (Skinner Inc.) $3,000 £1,840

DROP LEAF TABLES

A Queen Anne cherrywood drop leaf table, Massachusetts, 1740-1760, on turned legs with pad feet, 28in. high. (Christie's New York) $3,080 £1,937

A Regency mahogany drop leaf dining table of Cumberland action, on quadruple columns and splayed legs terminating in brass paw cappings, 1.50 x 1.21m. (Phillips London) $6,426 £4,200

A Georgian mahogany drop-leaf dining table of rectangular shape, raised on eight square tapering supports, 123 x 177cm., extended. (Lawrence Fine Arts) $1,076 £660

A Classical carved mahogany breakfast table, New York, 1815-1825, the clover shaped top with two drop leaves, 29½in. high. (Christie's New York) $5,500 £3,459

Victorian walnut Sutherland table, on dual turned end stretchers, all supported on brass castors, the top measuring 39 x 36in. when erected. (G. A. Key) $437 £260

Diminutive Queen Anne maple drop leaf table, New England, circa 1750, on four cabriole legs terminating in pad feet, 25¼in. high. (Skinner Inc.) $3,500 £2,258

Queen Anne maple drop leaf table, Rhode Island, circa 1760, the rectangular top with rounded leaves, 26in. high. (Skinner Inc.) $1,700 £1,043

A Federal mahogany pedestal base drop leaf table, Boston or Salem, Massachusetts, 1800-1815, on four moulded sabre legs fitted with casters, 28¼in. high. (Christie's New York) $2,860 £1,798

A Queen Anne cherrywood drop leaf table, probably Connecticut, 1740-1760, on cabriole legs with pad feet, 28in. high. (Christie's New York) $1,870 £1,176

GATELEG TABLES

William and Mary walnut gate-leg table, Massachusetts, 1715-1740, the rectangular top with half round hinged leaves, 28½in. high. (Skinner Inc.)
$20,000 £12,270

An oak gateleg table, fitted with a drawer either side and on reel turned supports, 18th century, 152cm., extended. (Lawrence Fine Arts)
$2,607 £1,650

A Charles II oak gateleg dining table with spirally twisted supports and turned feet joined by square stretchers, 68 x 53in. (Christie's London)
$16,731 £9,900

An oak gateleg table, the oval top with single flap on baluster legs joined by squared stretchers, 34in. wide. (Christie's London) $2,138 £1,265

A chestnut and polychrome painted gateleg table, on turned legs with turned and squared stretchers, 17th century, restorations. (Christie's London) $3,896 £2,420

An 18th century oak gateleg table, the oval top with two drop flaps, 122cm. long extended. (Henry Spencer) $899 £580

A reconstructed early 18th century oval oak gateleg table with baluster turned columnar supports, 47in. x 55in. (Michael Newman) $660   £400

A George III mahogany circular dining-table in two semi-circular sections on square chamfered legs, one with gateleg action, 70in. diam. (Christie's) $15988   £9380

A large late 17th century oak gateleg table, the oval twin flap top above an end frieze drawer, on turned feet, 4ft.8in. x 5ft. 9.5in. (Woolley & Wallis)
$14850   £9000

GATELEG TABLES

A Charles II oak gateleg table with oval top above a single drawer, the top 49½in. by 62¼in. open. (Tennants) $3,160 £2,000

A William and Mary yew gateleg table with oval twin flap top on turned and square legs joined by moulded stretchers, 45in. wide. (Christie's London) $13,013 £7,700

An oak gateleg table with oval twin-flap top above a bobbin frieze and spiral-twist legs joined by stretchers, basically late 17th century, adapted, 61½in. wide. (Christie's S. Ken.)$2904 £1760

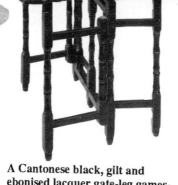

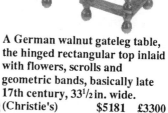

Maple gateleg table, Massachusetts, circa 1740, old scrubbed top on early base, 42½in. wide. (Skinner Inc.) $3,250 £1,923

A Cantonese black, gilt and ebonised lacquer gate-leg gamestable, the eared rectangular flap opening to reveal a card-table, circa 1830, 31½in. wide. (Christie's) $4959 £3080

A German walnut gateleg table, the hinged rectangular top inlaid with flowers, scrolls and geometric bands, basically late 17th century, 33½in. wide. (Christie's) $5181 £3300

A William and Mary oak gateleg dining table, the oval twin flap top on turned legs joined by square stretchers, 60in. wide. (Christie's London) $4,647 £2,750

A rare pine gateleg table, probably Southern, 18th century, the rectangular top with two drop leaves, on turned feet, 29⅓in. high. (Christie's New York) $2200 £1330

A George III mahogany gateleg table, the oval twin-flap top on chamfered legs, 67in. wide. (Christie's) $5643 £3300

LARGE TABLES

A William IV mahogany six leaf dining table with rounded ends in four sections, one with twin flap, on turned legs, 154¾in. long. (Christie's London) $14,071 £9,020

A mahogany and inlaid three part D-end dining table, the centre section with drop-leaf sides on fourteen square tapering legs, basically early 19th century. (Christie's S. Ken) $4,435 £2,640

A large Victorian wind-out mahogany dining table, with rounded corners and moulded edge, 4ft.6in. wide, 11ft.9½in. extended length. (Tennants) $3,900 £2,500

A mid Victorian mahogany D-end extending dining table, the moulded top on turned ribbed legs, extending to 96in. including three extra leaves. (Christie's S. Ken) $2,992 £1,870

A Victorian mahogany dining table, the cavetto banded rectangular top with rounded ends, on turned tapering bulbous legs, extending to 142 x 62in. (Christie's S. Ken) $4,435   £2,640

A Regency mahogany D-end dining table with concertina action, the frieze applied with roundels and centred by a quatrefoil tablet, on ring turned tapered legs, 132in. wide, including four modern leaves. (Christie's S. Ken) $6,732 £3,960

A William IV mahogany extending dining table, the rounded rectangular moulded top on turned tapered legs, each with a lotus leaf carved collar, extending to 135in. (Christie's S. Ken) $4,862 £2,860

A fine Classical mahogany two part dining table, Boston, 1820-1830, on moulded sabre legs with cylindrical feet, 29¼in. high. (Christie's New York) $28,600 £17,987

A mahogany three pedestal dining table with rounded ends, twin turned spreading shaft and splayed bases with brass claw caps, 40 x 130in. (Christie's S. Ken) $3,696 £2,200

A Regency mahogany extending dining table in two sections, in the manner of Gillows, the reeded D-end top on ring turned and reeded legs, 2.85m. long. (Phillips London) $8,415 £5,500

LARGE TABLES

A mahogany D-ended dining table, the central section with gate leg action, early 19th century, 4ft.3in. wide, 11ft.6in. assembled length. (Tennants) $5,530 £3,500

A late Regency mahogany extending dining table with a fluted edge to the rounded top, on two D-shape ends, 292cm., extended. (Lawrence Fine Arts) $5,214   £3,300

Country Federal mahogany two part dining table, New England, circa 1820, the D-end tops with moulded edge and hinged drop leaves, extended 91in. (Skinner Inc.) $4,250 £2,607

A late Regency mahogany extending dining table with two rounded ends, raised on four reeded tapering supports, 274cm., extended. (Lawrence Fine Arts) $7,995 £5,060

A George III style mahogany D-end dining table on triple turned tapering shafts and fluted quadruple splayed legs, extending to 124in. x 46½in. including two extra leaves. (Christie's S. Ken) $3,719 £2,310

A Regency mahogany three pedestal dining table, each pedestal with turned shaft and three moulded downswept legs with reeded caps, 118 x 45½in. (Christie's London)
$19,118 £12,100

A late George III mahogany dining table in three sections, the D-ended top with drop leaf centre section on square tapering legs, 118in. long. (Christie's London)
$6,952 £4,400

A George IV mahogany two pillar dining table, the frieze with tablets at each end, each pedestal with turned shaft and four downswept legs carved with acanthus, 75in. long, including one leaf. (Christie's London)
$6,006 £3,850

George III mahogany banquet table, late 18th century, demilune shaped ends joined by a rectangular drop leaf centre, raised on square tapering legs, 102in. extended. (Skinner Inc.) $2,750 £1,687

A George IV mahogany three part dining table, the rectangular top with rounded ends and folding central section on ring turned tapering legs, 42 x 81½in. (Christie's S. Ken)
$3,366 £1,980

OCCASIONAL TABLES

A Victorian giltmetal mounted walnut and marquetry jardiniere the rectangular glazed top on cabriole legs, 31in. wide. (Christie's S. Ken)$1,948 £1,210

A Chinese Export black lacquer and mother-of-pearl tripod table, the octagonal top with a scene of quail feeding by a stream, 30in. wide. (Christie's London) $986 £605

A George III mahogany and satinwood oval tray, inlaid with a fanned oval and leafy bands, on a later stand, 27in. wide. (Christie's London) $2,607 £1,650

An early George III mahogany architect's table, the frieze with pull out drawer, on chamfered legs with turned inner legs, 36in. wide. (Christie's London) $1,372 £880

A Dutch painted and ebonised tripod table, the tip up top painted with figures in front of the Town Hall, Amsterdam, on cabriole legs with pad feet, 18th century, 43in. wide. (Christie's London) $4,427 £2,750

A mid-Georgian mahogany reading table, the shaped hinged top crossbanded and fitted with a reading stand with two candle slides to the sides, 27in. wide. (Christie's London) $3,407 £2,090

A George III sycamore and marquetry occasional table in the manner of John Cobb in the French Transitional style crossbanded in rosewood and tulipwood, 46cm. (Phillips London) $16,065 £10,500

George III mahogany snap top occasional table with Chippendale border, terminating in claw and ball feet, the top 27in. diam. (G. A. Key) $1,034 £650

A Louis XV laburnum wood small table with quartered shaped rectangular top and leather lined writing slide, stamped *Migeon,* 16½in. wide. (Christie's London) $6,083 £3,850

OCCASIONAL TABLES

A Spanish walnut brazier, the circular copper dish with brass handles, the octagonal top inlaid with tortoiseshell, bone and ebony panels depicting hunting scenes, 19th century, 36½in. wide. (Christie's London)
$2,433 £1,540

A Finmar tea trolley, designed by Alvar Aalto, raised on bentwood supports with two large circular disc shaped wheels, 90cm. long. (Phillips London)
$1,593 £977

An early Victorian mahogany coaching table with folding rectangular top and an undulating underframe, extending to 34in. (Christie's S. Ken) $496 £308

A satinwood tea table, inlaid with musical instruments and foliate marquetry arabesques, 35in. wide. (Christie's S. Ken)
$1,515 £990

Victorian mahogany circular loo table with drop frieze, octagonal tapering column, 35in. diam. (G. A. Key)
$456 £280

An early George III mahogany architect's table with cross-banded hinged and ratcheted rectangular top above a frieze drawer, on square chamfered legs, 34in. wide. (Christie's London) $8,580 £5,500

A triangular oak table, the canted triangular top with an applied rim on three chamfered legs, 18th century, 26in. wide. (Christie's London) $743 £440

Country maple and pine tea table, New England, 18th century, on tapering turned legs, 25½in. high. (Skinner Inc.) $1,200 £774

A good late Victorian inlaid rosewood tripod table, the top with a band of winged horses and warriors, 26in. diam. (Tennants)
$2,184 £1,400

OCCASIONAL TABLES

An oak draw leaf refectory table with cup and cover trestle supports, 68in. wide. (Christie's S. Ken) $1,165 £715

Dutch walnut and marquetry table, late 19th century, on carved baluster legs joined by carved stretchers, 29½in. high. (Skinner Inc.) $800 £516

Gustav Stickley two drawer library table, circa 1907, signed with red decal (minor stains and nicks), 48in. wide. (Skinner Inc.) $1,400 £864

A mahogany tripod reading table with circular adjustable tip-up top on splayed legs and pad feet, 36in. wide. (Christie's S. Ken) $1,614 £990

A mahogany pedestal drum table, the inset leather lined circular top above a simulated frieze fitted with four drawers, part 19th century, 39in. diam. (Christie's S. Ken) $1,771 £1,100

One of a pair of cast iron pub tables, circa 1900, circular mahogany top raised on three legs, headed by caryatids, 29in. high. (Skinner Inc.) Two $600 £387

A Dutch walnut and foliate marquetry silver table, the dished rectangular top decorated with spandrels and birds amongst foliage, 19th century, 36in. wide. (Christie's S. Ken) $3,775 £2,420

A Georgian carved mahogany tea table, on knopped column, birdcage action and tripod supports, 86cm. (Phillips London) $2,754 £1,800

A Louis XV style ormolu mounted tulipwood vitrine table, the glazed serpentined box top enclosed by a hinged lid, 32in. wide. (Christie's S. Ken) $2,587 £1,540

OCCASIONAL TABLES

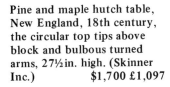

Pine and maple hutch table, New England, 18th century, the circular top tips above block and bulbous turned arms, 27½in. high. (Skinner Inc.) $1,700 £1,097

An Irish mahogany serving table with rope carved borders, on rope carved tapering legs with paw feet, 72in. wide. (Christie's S. Ken) $5,379 £3,300

A mid-19th century rosewood pedestal table with squat baluster stem and four leaf carved scroll legs, the top 47in. x 58¼in. (Tennants) $2,028 £1,300

A mahogany silver table with fret blind outlines, on chamfered square moulded legs with Marlborough block feet, 32½in. wide. (Christie's S. Ken) $842 £550

An interesting and impressive 18th century Venetian carved wood figure of a crouching blackamoor as an occasional table, 82cm. high. (Henry Spencer) $3,097 £1,900

Gustav Stickley table with twelve Grueby tiles, 1902-1904, four flat rails framing 4in. green tiles, 24in. wide. (Skinner Inc.) $20,000 £12,346

Roycroft pedestal base lamp table, East Aurora, New York, circa 1910, with four curving legs joining in the middle, 29½in. high. (Skinner Inc.) $1,700 £1,049

Fine 19th century satinwood two tier occasional table, with painted detail in the style of Vernis Martin, the bottom tier measuring 34in. x 21in. (G. A. Key) $2,295 £1,350

A Regency style yew wood drum table, on a fluted tapering shaft and scrolling triform base, 24in. diam. (Christie's S. Ken) $807 £495

OCCASIONAL TABLES

Limbert double oval table with cut out base, Grand Rapids, Michigan, circa 1907 (bangs and stains on surface). (Robt. W. Skinner Inc.) $4,250 £2,607

Late Regency mahogany serving table, circa 1840, with two leaves, supported by a turned pedestal raised on four scrolled legs, 43in. long. (Robt. W. Skinner Inc.) $800 £488

A Victorian walnut and ebony circular top table, the frieze carved with a band of guilloche pattern, 103cm. diam. (Lawrence Fine Arts) $3,048 £1,870

Louis XVI mahogany table de nuit, late 18th century, raised on square tapering legs joined by kidney shaped shelf, (damaged) 28in. high. (Robt. W. Skinner Inc.) $1,300 £793

A Chippendale cherrywood dish top tea table, Pennsylvania, 1770-1800, with circular dish top revolving and tilting above a birdcage support, 28½in. high. (Christie's New York) $7,700 £4,842

A Napoleon III walnut etagere, the curvilinear crossbanded rectangular top with a three-quarter gallery, on cabriole legs with sabots, 19½in. (Christie's S. Ken) $1,524 £935

Chippendale cherry tilt top tea table, Norwich, Connecticut, 1760-1790, on cabriole leg tripod base, 26½in. high. (Skinner Inc.) $1,300 £798

A late Federal carved mahogany serving table, New York, 1815-1825, the reeded rectangular top with outset rounded corners, 36in. wide. (Christie's New York) $3,300 £2,075

A Victorian papier mache screen table, the shaped oval top tilting and rising on a rod, 43cm. wide. (Lawrence Fine Arts) $1,345 £825

OCCASIONAL TABLES

Fine painted country maple
tea table, New England,
circa 1800, rectangular top
with shaped corner overhangs,
27in. high. (Skinner Inc.)
$10,000 £6,135

Chippendale carved walnut
tilt top tea table, Connecticut,
1760-1780, on a cabriole leg
tripod base, 34in. diam.
(Skinner Inc.) $3,250 £1,994

A mahogany tripod table, the
circular tip up top with a
waved border carved with
shells and husks, 31in. diam.
(Christie's S. Ken) $887 £528

A Louis XV style kingwood
and marquetry inlaid table en
chiffoniere of oval form, the
inset rouge royale top with a
pierced three quarter gallery
above, 19½in. wide. (Christie's
S. Ken) $1,558 £968

Round table with caned
pedestal base, probably
Michigan, circa 1915, un-
signed, (refinished), 36½in.
diam. (Robt. W. Skinner Inc.)
$350 £215

A Carlo Bugatti ebonized,
inlaid and painted vellum
table, the octagonal top with
central vellum panel, painted
with Arabic script, 74cm. high.
(Christie's London)
$12,192 £7,480

A set of three rosewood rectangular quartetto tables on
twin turned tapering column
end standards, 23in. wide.
(Christie's S. Ken) $1,848 £1,100

Painted pine hutch table,
Massachusetts, 18th century,
the round two board top
above a two board seat, 49in.
diam. (Skinner Inc.)
$4,750 £2,914

George III mahogany tilt-top
table, raised on three cabriole
legs ending in pad feet
(repaired), 18in. diam. (Robt.
W. Skinner Inc.) $700 £427

OCCASIONAL TABLES

A George IV burr elm pedestal table, the circular top inlaid with specimen wood segments centred by a boxwood star, with scroll feet, 20in. diam. (Christie's London)
$2,059 £1,320

A Gallé walnut and inlaid card table, the sides with halved panels depicting oriental figures representing the card suits, 66.6cm. high. (Phillips) $2160   £1350

A Victorian papier mache occasional table, painted with a view of Newstead Abbey, with a pleasure boat in the foreground, 51cm. diam. (Henry Spencer) $652 £400

An oak tripod table, the oval top with birdcage on baluster shaft and flat cabriole legs, restorations, early 18th century, 24½in. wide. (Christie's London) $2,125 £1,320

A Regency simulated calamander drum table, the frieze with four drawers and four false drawers on turned shaft and downswept legs, 48in. diam. (Christie's London)
$7,722 £4,950

A mid-Georgian burr yew tripod table with circular top, turned shaft and anthro-pomorphic cabriole legs with shoe feet, 27½in. deep. (Christie's London)
$8,855 £5,500

A rare Chippendale mahogany tilt top tea table, attributed to John Goddard, Newport, Rhode Island, 1760-1790, on three arched legs, 69.5cm. high. (Christie's New York)
$28,600 £17,987

A Federal figured maple work table, on ball and ring turned reeded tapering legs with ball turned feet, 27½in. high. (Christie's New York)
$2,420 £1,522

A Chippendale carved mahogany scallop top tea table, Pennsylvania, 1765-1785, on tripod cabriole legs with ball and claw feet, 28in. high. (Christie's New York)
$13,200 £8,302

OCCASIONAL TABLES

A Louis XV style kingwood and marquetry inlaid gueridon, the curvilinear top with brass mounted borders, 19in. wide. (Christie's S. Ken) $986 £605

A Regency mahogany library table with unusual leather lined double hinged rectangular top, on four reeded downswept legs, 54in. wide. (Christie's London) $2,574 £1,650

A George III mahogany tripod table with circular galleried top, some spindles replaced, 60cm. high. (Lawrence Fine Arts) $6,604 £4,180

A mid-Victorian ormolu and porcelain mounted kingwood jewel box with rounded rectangular hinged lid, 12½in. wide. (Christie's London) $2,302 £1,430

An oak table with semi-circular twin flap top enclosing a well on turned legs with curved stretcher, 17th century, 27in. wide. (Christie's London) $2,479 £1,540

A German fruitwood and marquetry table en chiffonniere with oval mottled grey marble top above four engraved panels depicting ladies in a garden, 18th century, reconstructed, 60½in. wide. (Christie's London) $2,433 £1,540

Chippendale mahogany tilt top tea table, New England, circa 1780, the circular top above a birdcage support, 34in. diam. (Skinner Inc.) $2,000 £1,227

A Marsh & Jones burr-walnut, ebonised and inlaid octagonal table, having an inlaid floret and ebonised border, 71cm. high. (Phillips) $3520 £2200

Chippendale tiger maple bird cage tilt top tea table, on tripod cabriole leg base, 19½in. diam. (Skinner Inc.) $3,200 £2,065

PEMBROKE TABLES

A George III mahogany serpentine Pembroke table on four canted moulded supports joined by a shaped X platform stretcher. (Lawrence Fine Arts) $4,124 £2,530

A plum pudding mahogany and painted pembroke table painted with a band of peacock feathers and poppies on a cream ground crossbanded with rosewood, 40in. wide, open. (Christie's London) $5,148 £3,300

A George III mahogany Pembroke supper table, the frieze with a drawer above a shelf enclosed by brass grilles with two concave doors, 42in. open. (Christie's London) $6,634 £4,070

George III mahogany Pembroke table, late 18th century, oval drop leaf top above one drawer. (Skinner Inc.) $2,100 £1,338

A George III mahogany butterfly Pembroke table, on square moulded legs and spade feet, 38½in. wide. (Christie's S. Ken) $2,302 £1,430

George III mahogany Pembroke table, late 18th century, with serpentine leaves, above a single frieze drawer, raised on square tapering legs, 28in. long. (Skinner Inc.) $1,900 £1,166

Chippendale walnut Pembroke or breakfast table, probably Philadelphia, circa 1800, pierced fret cross stretchers, 28¾in. high. (Skinner Inc.) $6,000 £3,681

A mahogany supper table, the serpentine top with a frieze drawer and wire mesh undertier on square tapering legs, 32½in. wide. (Christie's S. Ken) $2,869 £1,760

A George III mahogany and satinwood Pembroke table, on square tapering legs with brass caps, 32in. wide. (Christie's S. Ken) $1,255 £770

PEMBROKE TABLES

A late Federal figured maple and cherrywood Pembroke table, signed by A. J. Baycock, Brookfield, Madison County, New York, 1810-1830, on spirally reeded tapering cylindrical legs, 28¼in. high. (Christie's New York)
$3,850 £2,421

A George III mahogany Pembroke table with crossbanded serpentine shaped top, the frieze with a drawer, on faceted tapering legs, 38in. wide, open. (Christie's London)$2,231 £1,430

A Federal figured maple Pembroke table, New York or Bermuda, 1800-1820, the rounded rectangular top with two drop leaves, 28in. high. (Christie's New York)
$3,080 £1,937

Federal mahogany inlaid Pembroke table, Rhode Island, circa 1790-1810, on four square tapering inlaid legs terminating in spade feet, measures 32 x 40½in. (Skinner Inc.) $4,250 £2,742

George III mahogany Pembroke table, late 18th century, raised on square tapering legs ending in spade feet and casters, 37in. long extended. (Skinner Inc.)
$3,100 £1,902

George III Satinwood Pembroke Table, last-quarter 18th century, oval inlaid top with rosewood crossbanding above a single frieze drawer, 29¾in. long. (Skinner Inc.) $3,750 £2,435

A George III mahogany serpentine Pembroke table with narrow rosewood crossbanding, on four square section cabriole legs. (Lawrence Fine Arts)
$6,257 £3,960

An Edwardian mahogany Pembroke table, the rounded rectangular top painted with amorini amid scrolling foliage and flowerheads, 63½in. wide. (Christie's S. Ken)
$3,227 £1,980

An early George III mahogany serpentine Pembroke table, on four square tapering supports with block feet and leather castors. (Lawrence Fine Arts)
$5,735 £3,630

SIDE TABLES

An early Victorian rosewood sidetable with a moulded rectangular Carrara marble top, on cabroile legs with scroll feet, 66in. wide.
(Christie's S. Ken.)$2359 £1430

An early 19th century carved giltwood side table in the manner of William Kent, with a rectangular green verde antico top, 5ft. 3in. wide.
(Phillips) $14025 £8500

A George III style mahogany side table, the crossbanded rectangular top with a foliate moulded rim, on carved cabriole legs, 19th century, 54½in. wide.
(Bonhams) $1237 £750

A Regency mahogany side table in the manner of George Smith, with grey marble top containing an end drawer to the frieze, 3ft. 6in. wide.
(Phillips) $2640 £1600

A Galle marquetry sidetable, the rectangular tray top with two handles, inlaid in fruit-woods with a butterfly in a wooded landscape, 61.3cm. wide. (Christie's London)
$1,793 £1,100

A Victorian pollard oak serving side table, the serpentined top with an oak leaf carved border above a shaped frieze, 93in. wide.
(Christie's S. Ken) $2,587 £1,540

A Dutch ebony and marquetry side table, inlaid in fruitwoods, stained and natural ivory with songbirds and an urn of flower-ing foliage, moulded X-stretchers and bun feet, 27in. wide. (Christie's London)
$2,974 £1,760

A mahogany, sycamore and marquetry side table, the elliptical top on square tape-ing legs, basically late 18th century, 48in. wide. (Christie's S. Ken) $1,309 £770

A mid-Georgian oak side table with rectangular top and shaped frieze on cabriole legs and pointed pad feet, 32in. wide. (Christie's London)
$1,951 £1,155

SIDE TABLES

A walnut side table, the cross-banded rectangular top above two short and one long frieze drawers on later cabriole legs, 38in. wide. (Christie's S. Ken)
$567 £352

An Irish late Regency mahogany bowfront serving side table with reduced ledge back with quartefoil cresting, on cabriole legs and lion's paw feet, 90in. wide.
(Christie's S. Ken.)$3630 £2200

An unusual Arts and Crafts side table, supported at the front on supports with three plant form branches, 1.11m. long. (Phillips London)
$612 £400

A giltwood side table with later terracotta and white veined marble top, on cabriole legs with leafy scroll feet, early 18th century, re-gilded, 37in. wide. (Christie's London)
$8,580 £5,500

A William IV carved satinwood and paraquetry side table, the crossbanded rectangular top inlaid with a variety of exotic woods, 2ft. 9½in. wide. (Phillips)
$4950 £3000

A Flemish oak side table with planked rectangular top, on turned and squared legs joined by a rectangular under tier, 17th century, 35½in. wide. (Christie's London)
$7,064 £4,180

A good George II mahogany side table, the later green marble slab above a frieze with a drawer to the one end.
(Bonhams) $3630 £2200

An oak credence table, with folding semi-circular top, the frieze applied with lozenges and fitted with a drawer, 48½in. wide. (Christie's London) $4,276 £2,530

A walnut and marquetry side table, the moulded rectangular top inlaid with a songbird amid floral sprays with one frieze drawer, on spirally turned legs, 17th century and later, 31½in. wide. (Christie's London)
$5,391 £3,190

SOFA TABLES

A rosewood sofa table inlaid with brass, on quadruple baluster shaft with paw feet, early 19th century. (Christie's S. Ken) $7,574 £4,950

A William IV mahogany sofa table with fluted edge to the top, the frieze fitted with a drawer either side. (Lawrence Fine Arts) $2,694 £1,705

An Anglo-Indian ebony sofa table, on spirally reeded end standards and scrolled gadrooned base with reeded stretcher, early 19th century, 50½in. wide. (Christie's London) $11,154 £7,150

A good regency rosewood sofa table with a wide burr-wood band edged and inlaid with stringing, 36½in. x 26in. (Lawrence Fine Art) $14520 £8800

A Regency rosewood sofa table with two drawers and raised on twin turned end supports jointed by a pole stretcher, some warping to flaps. (Lawrence Fine Arts) $7,821 £4,950

A red lacquer and gilt chinoiserie sofa table with rounded rectangular twin-flap top, on down-curved legs, 46in. wide. (Christie's S. Ken.)$2904 £1760

A late Regency mahogany sofa table with moulded twin flap top and two frieze drawers on twin ring turned end standards, 59in. wide. (Christie's S. Ken) $3,326 £1,980

A Regency fiddleback mahogany sofa table, the frieze with two cedar lined drawers on tapering end standards and downswept legs, 48½in. wide. (Christie's London) $8,237 £5,280

A Regency mahogany sofa table, the rounded rectangular twin flap top above a frieze fitted with two drawers, on square tapering sabre legs, 60in. wide, open. (Christie's London) $4,804 £3,080

SOFA TABLES

A Regency maplewood and ebonised sofa table, on twin ring turned end standards applied with rams' masks and anthemions and reeded down-swept legs, 55½in. wide. (Christie's London)
$5,379 £3,300

A Regency maple sofa table with kingwood crossbanding, inlaid with stringing and anthemion motifs, 91.5 x 66 x 150cm. extended. (Lawrence Fine Arts)
$12,730 £7,810

A mahogany sofa table, inlaid with ebony lines, on square end-standards and splayed legs with brass caps, 63in. wide. (Christie's S. Ken) $1,972 £1,210

A late George III mahogany sofa table, on trestle supports and reeded outswept legs, tied by a turned stretcher, 62in. wide (open). (Bonhams) $3630   £2200

Regency rosewood sofa table, circa 1810, having four flared feet with ormolu pawed caps, on casters. (Skinner Inc.)
$3,500 £2,229

An early 19th century satin-wood inlaid and decorated sofa table, the hinged top cross-banded in purple heart and having rounded corners, 1.76m. x 56cm. (Phillips London) $11,475 £7,500

A rosewood and satinwood banded sofa table with a rounded rectangular twin-flap top above two frieze drawers, 55in. wide. (Christie's S. Ken.)$4719   £2860

A Regency brass inlaid sofa table, with two drawers divided by trellis inlaid panels on a U-shaped support with downswept legs and paw feet, 59½in. wide. (Christie's London)
$5,663 £3,630

A mahogany sofa table, on twin turned end-standards with acanthus dog's leg supports and gilt paw feet, 45½in. open. (Christie's S. Ken)
$2,510 £1,540

WORKBOXES & GAMES TABLES

A Victorian mahogany work table with hinged cover revealing fitted interior, on an octagonal tapering pillar, 43cm. wide. (Lawrence Fine Arts) $1,008 £638

Unusual Roycroft sewing table, East Aurora, New York, circa 1910, incised with logo, (some stains, one knob broken) 30in. wide. (Robt. W. Skinner Inc.) $1,600 £982

A Victorian burr walnut work table, the rectangular hinged top with marquetry inlaid and fret carved interior, on scrolling end standards, 22in. wide. (Christie's S. Ken) $1,720 £1,012

A Classical stencilled rosewood work table, New York, 1815-1825, on four gilt acanthus leaf carved lion's paw feet, the top and corners with gilt stencilling, 29¼in. high. (Christie's New York) $6,600 £4,150

An 18th century Dutch walnut and marquetry games table in the baroque taste, the top with twin panels concealing compartments inlaid for backgammon and inlaid for chess, 1.15m. x 69cm. (Phillips London) $7,344 £4,800

Regency mahogany work table, Philadelphia, circa 1830s, with recessed facade of two convex drawers, 21in. wide. (Skinner Inc.) $1,600 £982

A Regency satin birch work table, on U-shaped support, the faceted shaft with concave platform and scroll feet, 18in. wide. (Christie's S. Ken) $2,059 £1,320

A Classical gilt stencilled mahogany work table, New York, 1820-1830, on acanthus carved lion's paw feet with casters, 23in. wide. (Christie's New York) $3,520 £2,213

An early Victorian rosewood sewing table, on pierced scrolling end standards joined by conforming stretcher, 27in. wide. (Christie's S. Ken) $1,848 £1,100

WORKBOXES & GAMES TABLES

Stickley Brothers flip-sided sewing table, Grand Rapids, Michigan, circa 1912, rectangular box with applied handle, 18in. wide. (Skinner Inc.) $350 £216

A Victorian rosewood butterfly hinged triple fold games table, the shaped top unfolding to reveal a chequer board, 85cm. long. (Henry Spencer) $1,264 £780

A Victorian rosewood sewing table, the octagonal hinged top with thumb moulded edge, 52cm. wide. (Henry Spencer) $652 £400

A Classical grain painted and stencilled work table, New York, 1825-1835, the rectangular top with drop leaves, 28¾in. high. (Christie's New York) $2,640 £1,660

A William IV period Colonial satinwood parquetry and crossbanded games table, the rectangular top with a slide inlaid on the reverse for chess, concealing a tray inlaid for backgammon, 83cm. wide. (Phillips London) $7,344 £4,800

A Victorian walnut games/work table, opening to reveal a green baize playing surface, a drawer to the frieze over a draw out sewing well, 77cm. long. (Henry Spencer) $1,701 £1,050

Federal bird's-eye maple veneered sewing table, Massachusetts, 1790-1810, with two maple veneered cockbeaded drawers, 27½in. high. (Skinner Inc.) $1,400 £859

A Regency mahogany work table with two-flap top above two drawers and a further drawer incorporating the silk pleated covered work bag, 93cm., extended. (Lawrence Fine Arts) $1,564 £990

Federal mahogany veneered work table, Boston or North Shore, circa 1800, the mahogany veneered top with four carved ovolo corners, 18½in. wide. (Skinner Inc.) $3,000 £1,840

WORKBOXES & GAMES TABLES

A George IV rosewood and calamander work and writing table, on trestle ends and gilt paw feet with turned stretcher, 22in. wide. (Christie's London) $1,255 £770

William IV mahogany sewing table, second quarter 19th century, with two drop leaves, above a single fitted frieze drawer and work drawer with bag, 35½in. long. (Skinner Inc.) $475 £291

A George III oak and mahogany work table, the hinged cross-banded rectangular top inlaid with a cross, 18in. wide. (Christie's London) $520 £308

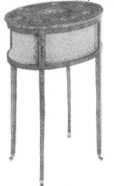

A late Victorian painted satin-wood work table, the hinged oval top with panel of children at play, on square tapering legs, 22¼in. wide. (Christie's London) $1,564 £990

A George III mahogany games table, the turned shaft on an arched cabriole tripod base with pad feet, 44½in. diam. (Christie's London) $4.483 £2,750

A Regency tortoiseshell boulle and rosewood workbox on stand, inlaid with berainesque designs within ebony borders, on lotus carved bun feet, 31in. high. (Christie's London) $1,614 £990

A Victorian walnut work table, in coloured woods supported upon turned legs and cross stretchers ending in knurled foliate carved feet, 60cm. wide. (Henry Spencer) $652 £480

A George III mahogany work table with crossbanded rounded rectangular top, the frieze with an end drawer above a tapered well, on square tapering legs, 22½in. wide. (Christie's London) $2,510 £1,540

Continental Neoclassical Fruitwood Work Table, c. 1830, raised on square tapering S-scroll legs, joined by a shelf-stretcher, 21¼in. wide. (Skinner Inc) $1500 £974

WORKBOXES & GAMES TABLES

A mahogany work table, the chevrette top fitted with two drawers above a frieze drawer on square tapering legs with platform and spade feet, 18in. wide. (Christie's S. Ken)
$1,434 £880

A George IV penwork and ebonised games table, the square tip up top decorated with flowers and Classical vignettes within a border of scrolling foliage, 21in. square. (Christie's London)
$5,491 £3,520

A George III mahogany work table, the rectangular double hinged top with a leather lined interior, on ring turned tapering legs with brass caps, 23½in. wide, open. (Christie's S. Ken)
$2,331 £1,430

Paint decorated and grained work table, probably New England, circa 1825, yellow ground, green and black striping, 17¾in. wide. (Skinner Inc.)
$1,600 £947

A fruitwood work table, the rounded rectangular grained burr top on U-shaped square support and splayed legs, 26¾in. wide. (Christie's S. Ken)
$2,152 £1,320

An unusual George IV mahogany pedestal work table, the octagonal top with rising lid, 19½in. across. (Tennants)
$624 £400

Dutch rococo walnut and marquetry games table, mid-18th century, hinged top opening to inlaid interior. (Skinner Inc.)
$950 £583

An Edwardian satinwood pedestal work table, the folding rectangular top with rosewood banded borders enclosing a buttoned silk lined interior, 14½in. wide. (Christie's S. Ken)
$1,434 £880

Dutch mahogany games table, mid-18th century, with a central front and a side drawer, raised on cabriole legs ending in pad feet, 28in. long. (Skinner Inc.)
$850 £521

WRITING TABLES & DESKS

An Edward Barnsley mahogany desk with writing tablet, having a plain rectangular top with two drawers, inlaid with satinwood banding, 96.5cm. wide. (Phillips London) $765 £500

Italian rococo style walnut desk, 20th century, with one long drawer flanked by four short drawers, raised on cabriole legs, 49in. wide. (Robt. W. Skinner Inc.)
$400 £244

A late Regency mahogany library table with inset tooled leather top, fitted with two drawers opposite two dummy drawers, 140 x 79cm. (Lawrence Fine Arts) $6,096 £3,740

Rococo style rosewood and marquetry lady's writing desk, late 19th century, with shaped apron, and cabriole legs with ormolu mounts, 28in. wide. (Skinner Inc.) $1,300 £828

An early Victorian mahogany writing table by Holland & Sons, the rectangular top inset with simulated blue leather, 48in. wide. (Christie's S. Ken)
$1,848 £1,100

A fine Regency rosewood, gilt brass and ormolu mounted cylinder desk by John McLean, the shelved superstructure with pierced brass gallery and trellis sides, 93cm. wide. (Phillips London)
$35,190 £23,000

Charles Rohlfs dropfront oak desk, Buffalo, New York, circa 1907, shaped gallery top above slant front, 25½in. wide. (Robt. W. Skinner Inc.)
$2,400 £1,472

Gateleg dropfront desk, circa 1912, arched gallery top and flat sides, branded *The Work of L. & J. G. Stickley*, 31½in. wide. (Robt. W. Skinner Inc.)
$850 £521

An ebonised gilt metal and porcelain mounted desk in the Louis XV style, on four square section cabriole legs, late 19th century, 110cm. (Lawrence Fine Arts) $1,564 £990

WRITING TABLES & DESKS

Louis XV style kingwood and walnut marquetry bureau plat, on cabriole legs with ormolu mounts, 69in. long. (Skinner Inc.) $4,750 £3,025

A Regency mahogany library table, the rounded rectangular top with wide crossbanding, on trestle end supports applied with large paw feet, 153cm. wide. (Lawrence Fine Arts) $8,690 £5,500

Edwardian mahogany desk, circa 1900, signed *Edwards & Roberts,* rectangular top with four short drawers raised above the surface, 48in. wide. (Robt. W. Skinner Inc.) $1,600 £976

Rococo Revival rosewood lady's writing desk, circa 1860, with four short drawers resting on a serpentine, sliding, leather lined desk top, on cabriole legs. (Robt. W. Skinner Inc.) $850 £518

George III mahogany cylinder desk, rectangular top above a roll top opening to a fitted interior, 44½in. wide. (Robt. W. Skinner Inc.) $900 £549

A walnut and giltmetal mounted writing table, on clasp headed cabriole legs with sabots, restorations, late 19th century, 24½in. wide. (Christie's S. Ken) $1,373 £880

A Liberty & Co. mahogany desk, the rectangular top having a drawer below flanked with three drawers on each side, 85.5cm. high. (Phillips London) $949 £620

Rare Charles Rohlfs carved drop front desk with swivel base, Buffalo, New York, 1900, Gothic style, signed with logo, 25½in. wide. (Skinner Inc.) $12,000 £7,407

An attractive late George III mahogany small writing table, the rectangular top with a 19th century superstructure, 93cm. long. (Henry Spencer) $1,116 £720

WRITING TABLES & DESKS

An early Victorian ormolu mounted kingwood bureau plat inlaid with mother-of-pearl and polychrome marquetry, on cabriole legs, 45½in. wide. (Christie's London)
$8,237 £5,280

A William IV mahogany writing table, on partly fluted spreading turned trestle ends carved with bands of egg and dart, 63¾in. wide. (Christie's London) $6,952 £4,400

A Louis XV style kingwood and marquetry inlaid bureau plat applied with gilt metal mounts and borders, on cabriole legs and sabots, 19th century, 45½in. wide. (Christie's S. Ken)
$4,881 £3,190

A George III satinwood cylinder bureau, the rectangular top with three-quarter gallery, the interior with three drawers below pigeonholes, on square tapering legs, 28in. wide. (Christie's London)
$17,034 £10,450

19th century mahogany Louis Philippe roll top desk, some damage to veneer, 132cm. wide. (Auktionshaus Arnold)
$1,380 £896

A George III mahogany roll top desk, the tambour shutter composed of alternating strips of satinwood and rosewood, 34in. wide. (Christie's London)
$8,690 £5,500

A late Victorian rosewood writing table inlaid with marquetry arabesques, the inset leather lined top below an elevated cabinet back, 26¾in. wide. (Christie's S. Ken)
$2,152 £1,320

Late 18th century Rhenish carved oak writing desk, the writing compartment behind a slanting board with drawers and pigeonholes, the serpentine commode base with three drawers, 127cm. wide. (Kunsthaus am Museum)
$2,702 £1,553

A William and Mary oak bureau, with ledge and pen drawer to the right, on turned supports and bar feet joined by stretchers, 30in. wide. (Christie's London) $2,045 £1,210

WRITING TABLES & DESKS

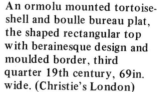

French Louis XV style rosewood and mahogany writing table with three drawers and leather lined top and additional surmount to one side containing two extra drawers, 185cm. wide. (Kunsthaus am Museum) $2,433 £1,398

An Edwardian mahogany and satinwood bowfront writing table, a leather lined plateau and five frieze drawers, 36½in. wide. (Christie's S. Ken) $1,063 £660

An ormolu mounted tortoiseshell and boulle bureau plat, the shaped rectangular top with berainesque design and moulded border, third quarter 19th century, 69in. wide. (Christie's London) $8,500 £5,280

A late Victorian amboyna and calamander writing table, the tambour roll top enclosing a fitted interior, with square tapering legs and concave platform, 19½in. wide. (Christie's S. Ken) $1,076 £660

Biedermeier walnut secretaire, second quarter 19th century, rectangular top of one long frieze drawer above roll top revealing fitted parquetry interior, 42in. long. (Skinner Inc.) $2,500 £1,534

A Regency rosewood and satinwood strung bonheur du jour, the superstructure with a three-quarter gallery and two graduated shelves on shaped uprights, 76cm. wide. (Phillips London) $7,344 £4,800

An Art Deco oval oak writing table, the oval top inset with green leather supports, the two pedestals enclosing drawers and a shelf, 69.6cm. high. (Phillips London) $522 £320

German, late 19th century, rosewood roll top desk with neo-gothic style top and two doors on either side of kneehole with three drawers over, 135cm. wide. (Kunsthaus am Museum) $3,783 £2,174

A mahogany writing table, on shaped end standards and downswept legs with curved stretcher, 39in. wide. (Christie's London) $2,145 £1,375

TRUNKS & COFFERS

Charles II oak coffer with moulded hinged top enclosing candlebox, 1670, 52in. long. (Phillips Manchester) $711 £450

A Louis Vuitton travelling trunk, 44in. wide. (Christie's S. Ken) $539 £352

Paint decorated dower chest, Pennsylvania, late 18th century, the overhanging top with moulded edge (feet added; repainted), 54in. wide overall. (Skinner Inc.) $800 £516

Grain painted pine blanket chest, probably New England, 18th century, the overhanging top with thumb moulded edge, 42in. wide. (Skinner Inc.) $2,500 £1,534

A George III black lacquer chest decorated in the Chinese taste, enclosed by a hinged panelled lid on later turned baluster legs, 54in. wide. (Christie's S. Ken) $1,860 £1,155

A boarded oak coffer, the front carved with a double row of nulling above a band of leafage lunettes, 100cm. (Lawrence Fine Arts) $1,614 £990

A leather and brass bound travelling trunk by Louis Vuitton, the hinged rectangular top enclosing a fitted interior, 36in. wide. (Christie's S. Ken) $2,816 £1,760

Japanese hardwood miniature spice chest, 19th century, with five drawers and a cabinet door enclosing two drawers (missing lock), 15in. wide. (Skinner Inc.) $350 £219

Arts & Crafts veneered cedar chest with strap hinges, 1919, with burled walnut veneer and geometric bronze strapwork, unsigned, 46¼in. wide. (Skinner Inc.) $500 £309

TRUNKS & COFFERS

An oak joined coffer with quadruple panel cover and the front with triple panels carved with arches, 17th century, with repairs. (Lawrence Fine Arts)
$1,112 £704

Charles II oak blanket chest, late 17th century, rectangular moulded lift top, 71in. long. (Skinner Inc.) $700 £452

Painted and decorated poplar six board chest, Soap Hollow, Somerset County, Pennsylvania, 1875, probably by John Sala, Sr., (1810-1882) 46in. wide. (Skinner Inc.)
$3,200 £1,963

Chinese export dome top trunk on stand, early 19th century, painted throughout with bird and floral decoration, 20¼in. wide. (Skinner Inc.) $500 £313

A decorative coaching trunk, circa 1870. (Auction Team Koeln) $117 £72

Grain painted pine blanket chest, New England, 18th century, the moulded top overhangs a dovetailed case with a well, 43¼in. wide. (Skinner Inc.)
$27,000 £16,564

Japanese bronze mounted lacquered storage chest, 18th century, decorated in hira-makie with the aoi crest of the Tokugawa family, 47½in. wide. (Skinner Inc.) $14,000 £8,750

Italian Renaissance walnut cassone, 19th century, the top with figures in bas-relief, carved with caryatids and full form figures at corners, 54½in. wide. (Robt. W. Skinner Inc.)
$750 £457

A massive 17th century Westphalian oak chest, the two plank top with hammered iron strap hinges, 70½in. wide. (Tennants) $4,108 £2,600

Carved oak box chest, the front decorated with three carved panels separated by pilasters, on bun feet, Westphalian, 18th century, 170cm. wide. (Kunsthaus am Museum) $1,350 £776

An oak chest with hinged rectangular top and boarded front and sides, the front decorated with horizontal grooves, 17th century, 48in. wide. (Christie's London) $929 £550

German 18th century, carved oak chest, the base with pierced fretwork border and floral inlay, on bun feet, 145cm. wide. (Kunsthaus am Museum) $2,702 £1,553

An early George III mahogany mule chest, the frieze with gothic blind fretwork with two drawers below on shaped bracket feet, 56½in. wide. (Christie's London) $2,045 £1,210

A Flemish giltmetal mounted and kingwood strongbox on stand, the rectangular top with pierced hinges and foliate border enclosing a fitted interior, 17th century, 28in. wide. (Christie's London) $5,214 £3,300

A Dutch East Indies camphor coffer, the hinged rectangular top with brass studs, the sides with carrying handles, 18th century, 45in. wide. (Christie's London) $619 £385

A mid-Georgian oak mule chest, the front with three fielded panels above two drawers crossbanded with mahogany, on bracket feet, 49¾in. wide. (Christie's London) $1,022 £605

Grain painted six-board chest, New England, early 19th century, the yellow ochre and burnt umber fanciful graining in imitation of mahogany, 38½in. wide. (Skinner Inc.) $850 £518

A walnut coffer with slightly domed top and panelled sides inlaid overall with mother-of-pearl flowerheads and foliage, 18th century, near Eastern, 52in. wide. (Christie's London) $2,045 £1,210

TRUNKS & COFFERS

A Heal's oak blanket chest, the rectangular overhanging panelled top above plain panelled sides, on turned legs joined by plain stretchers, 93cm. wide. (Christie's London)
$1,016 £605

An oak chest, the front and sides with carved fielded panels on block feet, 17th century, 69in. wide. (Christie's London)
$3,532 £2,090

A fine German oak and iron bound coffer, dated 1736, with domed top, the whole applied with iron bindings in the form of scrolls, strapwork and grotesque masks, 46in. wide.
(Bonhams) $1980 £1200

A German steel armada chest, the lock engraved with mermaids and foliate scrolls and locking at fourteen points around the rim, early 17th century, 49in. wide. (Christie's London) $1,208 £715

An oak domed coffer on stand, the domed hinged top and sides covered in cut floral plush, the base late 17th century, 27in. wide. (Christie's London)
$708 £440

A large mid-Georgian brass mounted mahogany campaign chest with brass corner mounts and side handles, 49½in. wide. (Tennants)
$1,422 £900

Painted dower chest, probably Pennsylvania, early 19th century, original worn green paint, old replaced brasses and hinges, 45¼in. wide.
(Skinner Inc.) $1400 £854

Northwest German 15th century carved oak chest, iron clasps and bands with fleur-de-lys finials, 189cm. wide.
(Kunsthaus am Museum)
$3,242 £1,863

Polished oak and marquetry chest, decorated in reserves with birds, with metal fittings, on bun feet, German, 18th century, 117cm. wide.
(Kunsthaus am Museum)
$1,891 £1,087

An 18th century Dutch burr walnut and feather banded armoire, the upper part of ogee arched form with mould--ed cornice, 1.75m. wide. (Phillips London) $6,120 £4,000

A Tyrolean painted and marbled armoire, the frieze dated 1810 above two panelled doors painted with roses, early 19th century, 61½in. wide. (Christie's London) $9,559 £6,050

An Italian walnut armadio with two panelled doors carved with cabochons in guilloche borders framed by strapwork scrolls, foliage and masks. 59½in. wide. (Christie's London) $18,590 £11,000

An ebonised lacca povera wardrobe with moulded cornice above a pair of double panelled doors applied with prints of flowers and birds, on bun feet, 19th century, 41in. wide. (Christie's London) $3,586 £2,200

A Victorian mahogany wardrobe, the stepped top with gothic arched centre carved with foliate crockets, on plinth base, 71in. wide. (Christie's London) $2,690 £1,650

A Heal & Sons Arts & Crafts oak wardrobe, with central mirrored door enclosing hanging space with single drawer below, 128.3cm. across. (Phillips London) $862 £529

A Louis XVI boulle cabinet en armoire, the upper part with convex frieze above two cupboard doors, inlaid with engraved pewter scrolling foliage, 42½in. wide. (Christie's London) $13,904 £8,800

A 19th century French Provincial cherrywood armoire, with round headed brass studs over a pair of triple panelled doors with shaped thumb moulded edges, 148cm. wide. (Henry Spencer) $1,782 £1,100

Painted pine stepback cupboard, New England, early 19th century, old wooden pulls and catches, old red paint with later varnish, 73¼in. high. (Skinner Inc.) $3,750 £2,301

WARDROBES & ARMOIRES

A George II oak press with moulded cornice above two shaped arched fielded panelled doors divided by a reeded pilaster, 55in. wide. (Christie's London) $2,125 £1,320

A painted wardrobe, coloured in navy blue, red and green with linear decoration, combed wavy banding and roundels, 76cm. across. (Phillips London) $391 £240

A Polish polychrome pine armoire with a pair of cupboard doors painted with flowers, Saint Dorata and Saint Maria Boskowska, 18th century, 51in. wide. (Christie's London) $12,514 £7,920

A Dutch burr walnut armoire banded in ash with arched moulded cornice above two arched panelled doors, on shaped bracket feet, mid-18th century, 65in. wide. (Christie's London) $13,035 £8,250

Pine wardrobe or Kas, Hudson River Valley or Delaware, circa 1750, on large turnip feet painted black, 59½in. wide. (Skinner Inc.) $6,500 £3,988

A French Provincial oak armoire, the frieze carved with a basket of flowers above two doors with shaped fielded panels carved with flowers and foliage, 18th century, 62in. wide. (Christie's London) $5,667 £3,520

An oak wardrobe by E. P. Gardiner, having a plain cornice above twin panelled doors, raised on square legs, 1.275m. across. (Phillips London) $428 £280

A Dutch Colonial oak and rosewood kas applied with ebony fret mouldings, on turned onion feet, 18th century and later. (Christie's S. Ken) $5,020 £3,080

A French Provincial oak armoire, the arched moulded cornice carved with a cabochon within scrolls and foliage, mid-18th century. (Christie's London) $2,603 £1,540

WASHSTANDS

A Liberty & Co. tiled oak washstand, the tapering back and base similarly covered with narrow green tiles, 1.23m. high. (Phillips London)
$995 £650

A Regency mahogany dressing-commode washstand, the hinged rectangular top with reeded edge, on square tapering legs, 45in. wide.
(Christie's)　　$4267　£2750

Country Federal tiger maple corner washstand, New England, circa 1810, the shaped backboards above cut out shelf, 40½in. high.
(Skinner Inc.)　$2,500 £1,534

A Dutch mahogany toilet cabinet inlaid with urns and foliate marquetry with folding rectangular top enclosing a telescopic mirror plate, early 19th century, 29in. wide.
(Christie's S. Ken.)$4900　£2970

A George III mahogany bowfront washstand, the top fitted with three bowl apertures and a three-quarter galleried superstructure, 24in. wide.
(Christie's S. Ken.)$1996　£1210

Victorian mahogany tray top wash stand with centre dummy drawer and two side drawers, 2ft. 6in. wide.
(Hobbs & Chambers)
$330　£200

Mahogany bow-fronted corner wash stand with tray top, the cupboard enclosed by pair panel doors, 1ft. 10½in. wide.
(Hobbs & Chambers)
$346　£210

A late Regency mahogany washstand with raised back and sides, on turned supports joined by undershelf, 121cm. wide. (Lawrence Fine Arts)
$1,598　£1,012

Georgian mahogany corner washstand having boxwood string inlay with satinwood crossbanding.
(Michael G. Matthews)
$577　£350

WHATNOTS

A Victorian rosewood serpentine front whatnot of three tiers with pierced gallery and turned supports, 102cm. high. (Lawrence Fine Arts)
$1,219 £748

A Victorian walnut bowfront corner whatnot, the fret gallery above triple graduated tiers, on turned tapering legs, 26in. wide. (Christie's S. Ken) $1,151 £715

An early Victorian mahogany whatnot of three rectangular tiers, joined by turned supports, 86cm. high. (Lawrence Fine Arts) $1,345 £825

An Irish mid-Victorian walnut three tier buffet, on double fluted column supports with turned bun feet, 43½in. (Christie's S. Ken) $1,115 £715

A late Regency mahogany four tier whatnot, each tier with concave sides on ring turned finialled uprights, 53in. high. (Christie's S. Ken)
$2,587 £1,540

An elegant Regency mahogany Whatnot, the upper tier with fretwork gallery, the lowest with a drawer, on lion's paw feet, 35in. wide. (Bonhams) $1650 £1000

A mahogany six tier whatnot with a drawer in the lower tier and each with slender turned supports, 19th century, 67½in. high. (Lawrence Fine Art)
$1724 £1045

Mid Victorian rosewood three tier what-not, with fretwork gallery over turned barley twist supports, 40in. high. (Phillips) $825 £500

A George III mahogany whatnot of three tiers by slender turned supports, 47in. high. (Lawrence Fine Art)
$3085 £1870

WINE COOLERS

A George III mahogany wine cooler on stand, of rectangular shape with tapering sides, on four fluted tapering supports. (Lawrence Fine Arts)
$9,733 £6,160

A William IV ash wine cooler with hinged coffered rectangular top, panelled tapering body and plinth base, 43½in. wide. (Christie's London)
$1,115 £715

A brass bound mahogany hexagonal wine cooler, with hinged top enclosing a zinc lined interior, late 18th century and later. (Christie's S. Ken)
$2,805 £1,650

An early 19th century mahogany cellaret, the rectangular top with ovolo moulded edge, raised upon gadroon carved ogee bracket feet, 42cm. wide. (Henry Spencer)
$3,875 £2,500

A brass bound mahogany urn wine cooler on pedestal cupboard, the cover with pineapple finial. (Lawrence Fine Arts)
$5,020 £3,080

A Regency mahogany wine cooler, the tapering front with reeded pilasters, the sides with carrying handles, on paw feet, 22½in. wide. (Christie's London)
$2,421 £1,485

An early Victorian mahogany wine cooler, the hinged coffered top enclosing a fitted interior, on stiff leaf scroll feet, 35in. wide. (Christie's S. Ken)
$5,174 £3,080

A George III style mahogany brass bound wine cooler with oval fanned top centred by a turned handle, 28in. wide. (Christie's S. Ken) $1,386 £825

A George IV mahogany wine cooler of tapered form with beaded coffered rectangular top, with later interior, 26½in. wide. (Christie's S. Ken) $2,037 £1,265

WINE COOLERS

An attractive early 19th century mahogany casket of sarcophagus cellaret form, the ovolo moulded hinged top with reeded edge, 78cm. long. (Henry Spencer) $1,956 £1,200

A mahogany wine cooler of sarcophagus shape, with convex curved sides, 19th century, 72cm. (Lawrence Fine Arts) $1,470 £902

A George IV mahogany wine cooler, the frieze carved with scrolling acanthus, the tapering sides with carrying handles on paw feet, 29in. wide. (Christie's London) $3,227 £1,980

A fine and rare figured mahogany veneer cellarette, attributed to Duncan Phyfe, New York, 1815-1825, of sarcophagus form, with gilt leaf carved lion's paw feet, 25¼in. high. (Christie's New York) $13,200 £8,301

George III mahogany cellaret, 18th century, oval form, hinged lid, brass florette and ring handles, on square tapered legs. (Skinner Inc.) $2,200 £1,401

A George III carved mahogany cellaret with a hinged cavetto top and fluted canted angles, 43cm. wide. (Phillips London) $3,825 £2,500

A George III brass bound mahogany wine cooler, the hinged octagonal lid enclosing a lead lined interior, on moulded tapering legs, 19½in. wide. (Christie's London) $6,006 £3,850

A Regency brass inlaid wine cooler carved overall with gadrooned bands, the stepped rectangular top with re-entrant corners enclosing a later lead lined interior, 28½in. wide. (Christie's London) $3,407 £2,090

A George III brass bound mahogany wine cooler with octagonal lid and carrying handles, the stand with square tapering legs, 19½in. wide. (Christie's London) $4,866 £3,080

A lead caricature figure of an obese drunkard, standing on circular base, 15in. high. (Christie's)　$316 £198

A Coadestone type figure of a recumbent lion, the well modelled mane with head slightly turned to dexter, 22¼in. wide. (Christie's)　$968 £605

One of a pair of lead troughs in the 18th century style, the sides applied with lion masks, 16in. high. (Christie's)
Two　$968 £605

One of a set of four 19th century white marble garden urns of campana form with fluted bodies and gadrooned lower halves, 40in. high. (Christie's)
Four　$21,120 £13,200

A 19th century white marble figure of Athena standing on oval base, 48in. high. (Christie's)　$2,464 £1,540

One of a pair of late 19th century lead Medici urns, cast in relief with a running frieze of Classical figures with loop and mask handles, 30½in. high. (Christie's)
Two　$3,520 £2,200

A 19th century Coadestone over life size figure of a Classical maiden depicting Plenty, stamped *Coade, Lambeth*, 71in. high. (Christie's)　$66,880 £41,800

A lead corner trough, the facetted front cast with vintage scenes, 41in. high. (Christie's)　$3,520 £2,200

A white marble figure of a Classical nymph seated on oval base, bearing inscription, 27in. high. (Christie's)　$2,640 £1,650

A reconstituted marble fountain mask depicting a river god with curled coiffure, 30in. high. (Christie's)$2,992 £1,870

One of a pair of white marble figures of seated lions on rectangular shaped bases, 19in. high. (Christie's)
Two $4,576 £2,860

One of a pair of lead jardinieres of cylindrical form, the sides cast with lion masks, 10½in. high. (Christie's) $492 £308

One of a pair of 19th century white painted cast iron garden urns, the flared rims with fluted lower halves, 24¾in. high. (Christie's)
Two $282 £176

A 19th century white marble group of Venus and Cupid, on oval shaped base, 40in. high. (Christie's) $2,816 £1,760

One of a pair of 19th century white painted cast iron garden urns of campana form, the beaded rims with gadrooned lower halves, 31½in. high. (Christie's)
Two $1,936 £1,210

A mid 19th century Italian white marble figure of Rebecca at the well, signed *G. Masini, Roma 1882*, 57in. high. (Christie's)
          $5,632 £3,520

A late 18th/early 19th century white marble plinth of octagonal form, the front panel with Latin inscription, 38 x 29in. (Christie's)
          $14,080 £8,800

An 18th century white marble half length figure of Venus Marina holding a conch shell, 39in. high. (Christie's)
          $1,144,000 £715,000

An 18th century lead small fountain as a putto, standing on one leg, holding a dolphin, 64cm. high. (Henry Spencer) $1,271 £780

An early 19th century brass horizontal sundial, signed *Chars Harrison, Limerick,* the gnomon with scroll support, 13¾in. diam. (Christie's S. Ken) $777 £495

A stone figure of a Tudor worthy, standing with cloak held behind his back, on rectangular base, 88½in. high. (Christie's S. Ken) $7,172 £4,400

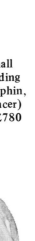

A 19th century white marble bust of a gentleman with mutton chop whiskers and Classical drapery, 28in. high. (Christie's S. Ken) $1,524 £935

A 19th century white marble figure of Flora, classically draped holding flowers, standing on octagonal base, 65in. high. (Christie's S. Ken) $11,654 £7,150

One of a pair of Doulton terracotta figures of eagles with outstretched wings, on square bases stamped *Doulton, London,* 37in. high. (Christie's S. Ken) Two $4,662 £2,860

A white marbled figure of Apollo, after the antique, both arms damaged, the figure leaning against a tree stump on base, 42in. high. (Christie's S. Ken) $1,524 £935

One of a pair of massive gate pier limestone urns with scrolled angular handles and waisted bodies, 57½in. high. (Christie's) $3448 £2090

An 18th century white marble bust of a gentleman with Classical robes in the style of Peter Scheemakers, 20in. high. (Christie's S. Ken) $896 £550

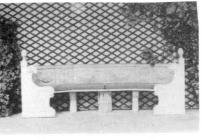

One of a pair of 19th century lead urns, the wide scrolled rims above squat bulbus bodies, cast with roseheads, 15in. high. (Christie's) $3267 £1980

A white marble garden seat of D-shaped form, the scrolled end supports carved with paw feet and ram and lion mask terminals, 113in. wide. (Christie's S. Ken) $21,516 £13,200

A late 18th century Coade stone keystone, modelled with a mask of an elderly bearded man with cap, stamped Coade, London 1790, 16in. high. (Christie's) $3993 £2420

A white marble bust of a young Moroccan woman with coins in her ears and headdress, signed on the back *Guasti, Firenze, 1877,* 27½in. high. (Christie's S. Ken) $1,345 £825

A white marble bust of a young girl with headdress signed *Angelo Bertozzi Carra,* 16in. high. (Christie's S. Ken) $1,703 £1,045

A white marble bust of a young signorina on circular socle, the back signed *C. Lapini, Firenze, 1891,* 29in. high. (Christie's S. Ken) $1,793 £1,100

A 19th century white marble bust of a Classical lady, with curled coiffure interlaced with fruiting grapevines, on circular socle, 26in. high. (Christie's S. Ken) $4,303 £2,640

One of a pair of 19th century white-painted cast-iron garden urns, the dish-shaped gadrooned bodies with trailing grapevine rims, 45in. (Christie's) $1996 £1210

A stone figure, possibly of Sir George Canning, cloaked and standing on rectangular shaped base, 87in. high. (Christie's S. Ken) $7,172 £4,400

A massive mid 19th century lead urn, with flambeau finial, the sides applied with lion masks and cartouches with cherubs, 68½in. high. (Christie's) $16,720 £10,450

A white marble trough, of rectangular form, carved with cherubs riding chariots, raised on winged sphinx supports, 45½in. wide. (Christie's) $14,080 £8,800

A 19th century white marble column, carved with swags of flowers and foliage, on octagonal base, 39½in. high. (Christie's) $2,288 £1,430

A white painted composition figure of Venus, standing beside a tree stump, holding an apple in her right hand, 64in. high. (Christie's) $616 £385

A pair of cast iron Coalbrookdale fern leaf pattern armchairs, the pierced cast backs above slatted seats. (Christie's) $1,144 £715

A French limestone figure of Venus, after Canova, the naked goddess shown holding drapery to her breast, 74in. high.(Christie's) $8,800 £5,500

A cast iron urn, the ovoid fluted body with stiff leaf cast lower halves, 30½in. high. (Christie's) $968 £605

A massive 18th century lead garden urn, the dish shaped bowl with egg and dart rim, 49in. high. (Christie's) $14,960 £9,350

One of a set of four white painted cast iron garden urns, with egg and dart rims and gadrooned bodies above fluted socles and square bases, 35in. high. (Christie's) Four $1,408 £880

One of a pair of 19th century bronze figures of athletes, after Pompeiian originals, on rectangular bases, 45in. high. (Christie's)
Two $15,840 £9,900

A Coalbrookdale cast iron garden seat of unusual small size of gothic design, 37in. wide. (Christie's)
$1,936 £1,210

A 19th century white marble figure of Arianna, signed *Calvi, Milano*, 37in. high, on cylindrical granite plinth. (Christie's) $3,168 £1,980

A mid 19th century Doulton Lambeth terracotta plinth, the circular top with gadrooned rim, 44in. high. (Christie's) $492 £308

Part of a collection of ten stone garden gnomes, some playing bowls, the others as attendants, 25in. high. (Christie's)
Ten $2,640 £1,650

A lead and stone sun dial formed as a figure of Atlas supporting a sphere incorporating a sun dial, 39in. high. (Christie's) $457 £286

A Victorian white painted cast iron garden seat, with stiff leaf back and grape vine feet. (Christie's) $352 £220

A pair of Suffolk stone gargoyles, possibly 14th century, the grotesque figures with open, oversized mouths, 5 3½in. high. (Christie's)
$2,112 £1,320

A white painted cast iron Medici urn, the campana shaped body cast with Classical frieze, with mask and loop handles, 27in. high. (Christie's) $616 £385

Old Hickory outdoor porch glider, Indiana, 20th century, basket woven settee suspended from T-shaped floor frame, 62in. wide. (Skinner Inc.)
$900 £552

Cast zinc fountain, J. W. Fiske, Ironworks, New York, late 19th century, young boy and girl beneath an open umbrella, 27in. high. (Skinner Inc.)
$3,250 £1,994

A white marble group depicting a fox catching a hen on naturalistic rocky base, 34in. wide. (Christie's)
$2,552 £1,595

An Italian 19th century white marble figure of Ariadne dressing her hair, leaning against a tree stump, 69in. high. (Christie's) $10,560 £6,600

A 19th century Italian white marble figure of Eve seated on a rocky outcrop with entwined serpent, 64in. high. (Christie's) $8,800 £5,500

A 19th century white marble figure of Hebe holding a tazza and a ewer, left arm loose, 62in. high. (Christie's)
$4,928 £3,080

A 19th century white marble figure of Diana the Huntress with hound, on square base, 52in. high. (Christie's)
$6,160 £3,850

One of a set of four French folding iron garden chairs, the slightly arched backs with down curved scroll arm rests. (Christie's)
Four $2,816 £1,760

An 18th century lead figure of a Classical priestess, with flowing robes, standing beside a Classical urn, 70in. high. (Christie's)
$15,840 £9,900

A Coalbrookdale cast iron garden seat of Louis XV design, the arched pierced back cast with a central flower motif, 75in. wide. (Christie's) $3,168 £1,980

A white marble figure of Modesty, the draped female figure holding flowers, inscribed *Modestia,* 62in. high. (Christie's) $5,280 £3,300

A cast iron Coalbrookdale nasturtium pattern seat, the pierced cast back and ends with wood slatted seat, 71in. wide. (Christie's) $3,520 £2,200

A white marble figure depicting an allegory of Wealth, clasping a wreath of berries with bird at her feet, 43in. high.(Christie's) $7,392 £4,620

One of a pair of 18th century lead gate pier finials, the urn shaped bodies with grotesque mask scroll handles, 33in. high. (Christie's) Two $4,224 £2,640

A 19th century white marble group of Venus running with Cupid on her shoulders, on circular base, 42in. high. (Christie's) $2,640 £1,650

An early 20th century bronze figure of Venus disrobing, standing on circular base, signed *Ferd. Lepke Fec,* 72in. high. (Christie's) $19,360 £12,100

A set of Coalbrookdale cast iron bench ends, designed by Dr Christopher Dresser, with elaborate pierced scrolling decorations. (Christie's) $968 £605

An Italian 19th century white marble figure of a pensive Classical lady, standing on square base, 49in. high. (Christie's) $1,232 £770

BASKETS

Steuben art glass basket, flared rim on reticulated glass woven basket of pomona green crystal, 8in. diam. (Robt. W. Skinner Inc.) $175 £109

Three Art glass baskets, one of pink rose, in the Stevens & Williams manner, 7–8in. high. (Skinner Inc.) $400 £244

A German moulded oval swing-handled cake basket on vine feet, fitted with a blue glass liner, 10in. (Christie's) $842 £550

Steven & Williams Victorian glass basket, applied crimped amber glass rim and handles on transparent blue folded pedestalled bowl, 6in. high. (Skinner Inc.) $225 £137

Rare Val St. Lambert cameo glass basket, overlaid in emerald green, cameo cut and wheel cut in Vintage pattern, 11in. high. (Skinner Inc.) $2000 £1220

Mount Washington cameo glass bride's basket, shaped rim on flared half-round bowl of opal glass layered in pink, 9½in. high. (Robt. W. Skinner Inc.) $175 £109

BEAKERS & TUMBLERS

A dated Zwischengoldglas beaker of faceted cylindrical shape decorated in gold and colours with a continuous boar hunting scene, 1751, 8.8cm. (Phillips London) $816 £480

A Bohemian 'Zwischengoldglas' flared beaker and cover, the double-walled fluted sides gilt with Eastern scenes of figures, circa 1735, 18.5cm. high. (Christie's) $3179 £1870

A gilt-decorated opaque opaline flared tumbler from the atelier of James Giles, circa 1770, 10cm. high. (Christie's) $5236 £3080

BEAKERS & TUMBLERS

An amusing beaker of slightly flared cylindrical shape, engraved with a showman and a dancing bear, 9.5cm., German or Bohemian. (Phillips London) $544 £320

A North Bohemian 'Lithyalin' hexagonal beaker attributed to Friedrich Egermann, the exterior of pale marbled mauve, blue and ochre colours, Blottendorf, circa 1830–40, 10.5cm. high. (Christie's) $8925 £5250

Blown three mould flip glass, colourless with gray tint, pontil scar, 5¾in., New England, 1825-1840. (Robt. W. Skinner Inc.) $175 £109

A Biedermeier Heiligenbild clear glass tumbler of oviform shape supported on six claw feet, engraved, possibly by Anton Simm, 12.8cm. (Phillips London) $2,040 £1,200

A Bohemian engraved tumbler, the flared sides with a lady presenting a heart to a gentleman, first quarter of the 18th century, 13cm. high. (Christie's) $711 £418

A German amber-tinted ringbeaker (Ringelbecher), the slender conical body with a gadrooned collar to the lower part, 17th century, 16.5cm. high. (Christie's) $14960 £8800

A Biedermeier beaker, engraved with a spray of roses, carnation and other flowers, 12cm. (Phillips London) $646 £380

Early enamelled shot glass, in white along with multi-coloured florals and bird, Bohemia, mid 18th century, 2½in. high. (Skinner Inc.) $120 £73

A North Bohemian 'Lithyalin' flared beaker attributed to Freidrich Egermann, Blottendorf, circa 1830–40, 11.5cm. high. (Christie's) $3553 £2090

493

BOTTLES

E. G. Booz's Old Cabin Whiskey bottle, honey amber, 7¾in., Whitney Glassworks Glasshouse, New Jersey, 1860-1870. (Robt. W. Skinner Inc.) $900 £559

David Andrews vegetable/ jaundice/bitters bottle, with sloping shoulders, 8¼in., America, 1850-1865. (Robt. W. Skinner Inc.) $460 £286

Lancaster Glass Works NY soda bottle, very rare, medium sapphire blue, 1855-1865. (Robt. W. Skinner Inc.) $150 £93

Pineapple Bitters bottle, W & Co., NY, amber, double collared lip, 8½in., probably New Jersey Glasshouse, 1850-1860. (Robt. W. Skinner Inc.) $200 £124

Stiegel type flask, 16oz., deep amethyst, sheared lip, pontil scar, 5½in., possibly Stiegel's American Flint Glass Manufactory, Manheim, Pennsylvania, 1770-1774. (Robt. W. Skinner Inc.) $3,700 £2,298

T.C. Pearsall on seal spirits bottle, some of the original wax on lip, olive green, 10½in. high, perhaps America, 1780-1795. (Robt. W. Skinner Inc.) $425 £264

Flora Temple pictorial flask, crudely applied lip, smooth base, pint, Whitney Glassworks, Glassboro, New Jersey, 1859-1865. (Robt. W. Skinner Inc.) $200 £124

I Alsop 1763 seal spirits bottle, deep olive green, 12in. high, probably England, circa 1763. (Robt. W. Skinner Inc.) $700 £435

Pressed bar bottle, amethyst, oversized doughnut lip, polished pontil, 11in., probably Bakewell Pears and Co., Pittsburgh, 1860-1880. (Robt. W. Skinner Inc.) $650 £404

BOTTLES

Washington Taylor portrait flask, smoky mauve sheared lip pontil scar, quart, Dyottville Glassworks, Pennsylvania, 1840-1860. (Robt. W. Skinner Inc.) $1,200 £745

Beiser and Fisher pig figural whiskey bottle, amber, double collared lip smooth base, 9½in. America, 1865-1875. (Robt. W. Skinner Inc.) $200 £124

Bininger's Regulator whiskey bottle, clock shape, honey amber, 6in., America, 1861-1864. (Robt. W. Skinner Inc.) $200 £124

Pineapple Bitters bottle, citron, double collared lip, pontil scar, 8½in., probably New Jersey, 1850-1865. (Robt. W. Skinner Inc.) $2,700 £1,677

Harrisons Columbian Ink master ink bottle, 11¼in. high, probably Whitney Bros. or Isabella Glassworks, New Jersey, 1855-1865. (Robt. W. Skinner Inc.) $24,000 £14,907

Large chestnut bottle, olive amber, sloping collar, pontil scar, 10¼in. high, New England, 1790-1830. (Robt. W. Skinner Inc.) $150 £93

Large barrel bottle, wide opening, emerald green, tooled lip, smooth base, 9¾in., America, 1870-1885. (Robt. W. Skinner Inc.) $75 £47

Rohrer's Expectoral Wild Cherry Tonic bottle with label, pyramid shape, 10½in. high, America, 1860-1865. (Robt. W. Skinner Inc.) $375 £233

Sunburst flask, olive amber, pint, Keene Marlboro St. Glassworks, Keene, New Hampshire, 1822-1830. (Robt. W. Skinner Inc.) $300 £186

GLASS

Greeley's Bourbon Bitters bottle, barrel, puce amber, smooth base, 9¼in. high, America, 1860-1880. (Robt. W. Skinner Inc.) $125 £78

A large Leith green glass bottle, the globular body incised 'Andrew and Maria Glass, London, 1846', 27cm. high. (Bearne's) $563   £350

A sealed and dated octagonal wine-bottle of dark-olive tint and shouldered form, applied with a seal inscribed R S 1739, 25cm. high.
(Christie's) $5610   £3300

Ribbed pinch bottle, deep sapphire blue, tooled lip pontil scar, 8½in., Germany/Austria, mid 18th century. (Robt. W. Skinner Inc.) $500 £311

Pair of Mary Gregory type barber bottles, cobalt blue with boy and girl tennis scene, 8¼in., probably England, late 19th century. (Robt. W. Skinner Inc.) $350 £217

Pillar moulded bar bottle, conical with eight heavy pillars, gray, pontil scar, 12in., Pittsburgh area, 1850-1870. (Robt. W. Skinner Inc.) $1,900 £1,180

Morse's Celebrated Syrup, Providence, R.I., medicine bottle, whittled, flattened sides, 9½in., America, 1855-1865. (Robt. W. Skinner Inc.) $500 £311

An early Armorial 'Onion' wine-bottle, the depressed body applied with a seal bearing a coat-of-arms, circa 1680, 17cm. high.
(Christie's) $1402   £825

J & A Dearborn, N. Y., Albany Glassworks, New York, soda bottle, extremely rare, cobalt blue, 7¼in., 1848-1856. (Robt. W. Skinner Inc.) $450 £279

BOTTLES

A rare sealed and dated octagonal wine-bottle of green tint and rectangular section, the tapering neck with a string-ring, 1736, 26.5cm. high. (Christie's) $5610   £3300

Pottery book figural bottle, Bennington type, white body with brown mottling, 5½ in., America, 1850-1875. (Robt. W. Skinner Inc.) $225 £140

Martha Washington Hair Restorer bottle with full label and contents, colourless, 7 in., America, 1870-1880. (Robt. W. Skinner Inc.) $160 £99

An early 'Shaft and Globe' wine-bottle of green tint, and with kick-in base, circa 1660, 17.5cm. high. (Christie's) $3366   £1980

'E.G. Booz's', figural Whiskey bottle, cabin shape, bevelled roof edge variety, Whitney Glassworks, Glassboro, New Jersey, 1870–80, 7³/₄ in. high. (Skinner Inc.) $950   £579

An early sealed 'Shaft and Globe' wine-bottle of green tint, the depressed and tapering oviform body applied with a seal, circa 1670, 20cm. high. (Christie's) $11220   £6600

The Fish Bitters bottle, amber, applied lip, smooth base, 11½in. high, America, 1870-1880. (Robt. W. Skinner Inc.) $125 £78

An 'Onion' serving-bottle of dark olive-green tint with shallow kick-in base, circa 1725, 17cm. high. (Christie's) $1589   £935

Skull figural poison bottle, crossed bones on base, cobalt blue, tooled lip-smooth base, 4¹/₈ in. high. (Skinner Inc.) $1300   £793

BOWLS

Pairpoint cobalt blue centre bowl, with raised pedestal foot, brilliant crystal clarity, 14¼in. diam. (Robt. W. Skinner Inc.) $275 £171

Pairpoint mounted centrebowl of white and clear glass hand-painted within with floral designs and ladybugs, 9in. high. (Robt. W. Skinner Inc.) $250 £155

An amber tinted circular glass bowl, painted in enamels and raised gilt with sprigs of flowers, on a scrolling five footed base. (Christie's S. Ken) $404 £264

A Daum carved and acid textured coupe, overlaid with leafy branches and lapis blue umbel seed heads, 21.8cm. high. (Christie's London) $4,303 £2,640

An Orrefors enamel painted bowl designed by Gunnar Cyren, with painted decoration of women and sailors dancing among flowers, 15.2cm. high. (Christie's London) $1,883 £1,155

A Schneider tazza, the bowl with facetted flange rim, on a knopped violet glass stem, 14.6cm. high. (Christie's London) $681 £418

Kosta Swedish crystal bowl, bright transparent pink internally decorated with crossed white spirals in diamond pattern, 3½in. high. (Robt. W. Skinner Inc.) $125 £78

Freeblown bowl, early form, nearly straight sided walls, 4½in. high, America, probably Pennsylvania/New Jersey area, 1800-1830. (Robt. W. Skinner Inc.) $300 £186

Freeblown swagged cuspidor, wide flaring lip, bowl with swag decoration, possibly Ellenville Glassworks, New York. (Robt. W. Skinner Inc.) $1,800 £1,118

BOWLS

A good Galle cameo glass bowl and cover, overlaid with orange, the bowl carved with trailing strands of seaweed, 11cm. high. (Bonhams) $3,652 £2,200

Perruches, a Lalique opalescent glass bowl, moulded on the exterior with a broad frieze of budgerigars, 24.5cm. diam. (Phillips London) $1,989 £1,300

South Jersey type footed bowl, freeblown thickly made,15.5cm. wide, probably South Jersey, or Pittsburgh area glasshouse, 1820-1850. (Robt. W. Skinner Inc.) $300 £186

Large sweetmeat glass bowl, 16 ribs, ogee bowl connected to heavy wafer, short stem and large foot, 19.38cm., probably England, late 18th century. (Robt. W. Skinner Inc.) $200 £124

Ondine Ouverte, a Lalique opalescent glass bowl, the exterior moulded in relief with undulating water nymphs, 8¼in. diam. (Christie's S. Ken) $1,125 £660

A Decorchemont pate de verre bowl, with moulded decoration of stylized flowers, 8.5cm. high. (Christie's London) $3,765 £2,310

A Loetz iridescent squat oviform bowl with everted undulating rim, the green glass splashed with turquoise iridescence, 3½in. high. (Christie's S. Ken) $750 £440

A Gabriel Argy-Rousseau pate de verre bowl, overlaid in shades of green and red with berried branches, 7cm. high. (Christie's London) $3,945 £2,420

Steuben blue aurene centre bowl, with fine silver blue iridescence and areas of mirror brilliance, 11½in. diam. (Robt. W. Skinner Inc.) $600 £373

BOWLS

A Daum oval glass bowl, acid-etched with fuchsias in relief, heightened with gilding and contained within a silver-coloured metal mount, 35cm. wide.　(Phillips) $2480　£1550

Tiffany bowl and undertray, decorated with pulled swirled knobs, matching knobby tray, each with strong gold iridescence, 6in. diam. (Robt. W. Skinner Inc.) $375　£233

Victorian satin glass centrebowl, crimped and folded camphor rim, enamel decoration with blossoms and butterflies, 5½in. high. (Skinner Inc.)　$550　£335

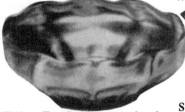

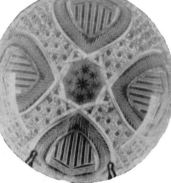

Tiffany Favrile blue centrebowl, the moulded shaped cobalt blue bowl with strong lustre, 8in. diam. (Skinner Inc.)　$1400　£854

Steuben Cluthra centrebowl, massive heavy-walled conical form of shaded black-grey to colourless, 15in. diam. (Skinner Inc.)　$800　£488

A Daum cameo glass bowl, with cameo cut and enamel painted wintry landscape on acid treated matt pale amber ground, 13cm. diam. (Henry Spencer)　$1,232 £780

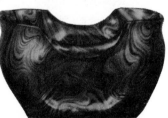

An Arsall acid etched and carved double overlay cameo glass oviform bowl, the pale grey glass overlaid in pink and green with flowering branches, 5½in. diam. (Christie's S. Ken) $682 £440

Rare American brilliant cut glass shield bowl, possibly commemorating President McKinley, 10in. diam. (Skinner Inc.)　$650　£396

Brilliant cut glass two-part punch bowl, raised on matching flared pedestal base, 9½in. high. (Skinner Inc.)　$150　£91

A Delatte cameo glass powder bowl, overlaid in deep purple and etched with convolvulus on a lighter ground, 14cm. wide. (Henry Spencer)　$397 £260

A lalique opalescent glass bowl of inverted conical form with children dancing below, catalogued 'Farandole', 26cm. diam. (Bearne's)　$5270　£3400

Oval glass bowl by Wilhelm Kralik Sohn, the long sides dimpled beneath a raised rim, in clear glass with combed and trailed violet and yellow pattern, circa 1900, 12.5cm. high. (Kunsthaus am Museum)　$432 £248

BOWLS

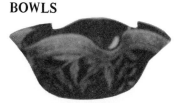

Webb Gem Cameo bowl, unusual emerald green ruffle-edge bowl carved with apple blossoms, 5¹/₂ in. diam.
(Skinner Inc.) $1800   £1098

A Gallé enamelled glass bowl of smoky-brown tone and painted in coloured enamels with thistles and cross of Lorraine, 23cm. wide.
(Phillips) $1472   £920

'Calypso', a Cristal Lalique opalescent glass bowl, moulded on the underside with five mermaids swimming amid angular waves, 35.5cm. diam.
(Phillips) $6400   £4000

Tiffany gold Favrile centre bowl, crimped and scalloped ten rib moulded bowl with overall iridescence, 10¹/₂ in. diam.
(Skinner Inc.) $950   £579

A Façon-de-Venise low tazza, the shallow tray moulded with husk ornament, on a conical foot, perhaps Germany, 17th/18th century, 22.5cm. wide.
(Christie's) $1683   £990

Four Steuben gold Aurene salad bowls, shallow flared form with extraordinary brilliance, 8¹/₂ in. diam.
(Skinner Inc.) $800   £488

A giltmetal stand with associated cut glass bowl and two bands of pierced scrolling foliage, on scrolling feet, 11¼ in. high. (Christie's London)
$1,182 £748

A 'Lynn' green finger-bowl, of dark tint and ogee form, second half of the 18th century, 11.5cm. diam.   (Christie's) $748   £440

An Evald Nielsen circular bowl with incurving rim and twin loop handles, mark for 1935, 24cm. diam.
(Phillips) $416   £260

An American cut glass caviar bowl with outer ice bowl and white metal mounts, early 20th century, 13in. diam.
(Tennants) $2,652 £1,700

A Daum Art Deco glass bowl overlaid with olive-green transparent glass acid-etched with a geometric design of birds on foliate branches, 22.5cm. high.
(Phillips) $3040   £1900

A Gallé twin-handled cameo glass bowl, the translucent body overlaid with orange glass acid-etched with sunflowers and foliage, 8.5cm. high.
(Phillips) $6720   £4200

BOXES

A Galle carved and acid etched cameo bonbonniere and cover, of compressed cylindrical form with swollen sides, 16.5cm. diam. (Christie's London)　$1,434 £880

Tiffany Studios double inkwell, designed as a treasure chest in Venetian pattern with two ink bottle receptacles, 5in. x 3in. (Skinner Inc.)　$425　£259

An engraved oval turquoise casket with gilt mounts and feet, 8$\frac{1}{2}$in. diam. (Christie's)　$508　£308

A Bohemian milk white overlay and painted casket, painted with flower sprays within blue and gilt scrolling borders, 13cm. (Phillips London)　$1,288 £800

Two Wavecrest covered dresser boxes, one swirled with colourful lily decoration, the other of bulbed moulded form, 7in. diam. (Skinner Inc.)　$750　£457

A Mary Gregory style black glass perfumery casket, painted in white with a youth on a swing between trees, 10cm. wide. (Henry Spencer)　$535 £350

A French opaline gilt metal-mounted rectangular casket, the mounts with lion mask terminals, 4$\frac{3}{4}$in. wide. (Christie's S. Ken.)　$1234　£748

A Bohemian ruby glass casket of tapering rectangular and fluted form, with metal mounts, 9.5cm. (Phillips London)　$515 £320

A Bohemian overlay and painted casket of deep rectangular shape, in milk white glass overlaid with pale lilac ribbing, 21.5cm. (Phillips London)　$3,570 £2,100

CANDLESTICKS

A pair of 19th century French ormolu and glass candlesticks, with flower chased nozzles and drip pans, 10½in. high. (Christie's S. Ken) $598 £352

Tiffany Studios bronze and favrile glass candleholder, candlecup with seven green iridescent jewelled glass inserts, 8in. high. (Robt. W. Skinner Inc.) $1,500 £932

Pair of dolphin candlesticks, double step base, colourless, 10in. high, Boston & Sandwich Glassworks, Massachusetts, 1845-1870. (Robt. W. Skinner Inc.) $150 £93

Pair of dolphin candlesticks, single step base, 10¼in., Boston & Sandwich Glass Co., Sandwich, Massachusetts, 1845-1870. (Robt. W. Skinner Inc.) $3,800 £2,360

A light-Baluster candlestick, the cylindrical nozzle with everted rim, supported on a multi-knopped stem, circa 1750, 23.5cm. high. (Christie's) $1683 £990

Pair of gold Aurene candlesticks, baluster and ring-turned shaft on cupped pedestal foot, 8¼in. high. (Skinner Inc.) $700 £427

Pair of early candlesticks, columnar with petal socket, colourless, 9¼in., probably Boston & Sandwich Glassworks, Sandwich, Massachusetts, 1850-1865. (Robt. W. Skinner Inc.) $110 £68

A Baluster candlestick, the cylindrical nozzle with folded rim supported on a cushion knop above an acorn knop, circa 1725, 17.5cm. high. (Christie's) $1683 £990

Pair of candlesticks, sand finish, two colour, clambroth petal socket and stem, 9¼in., Boston & Sandwich Glassworks, Massachusetts, 1850-1865. (Robt. W. Skinner Inc.) $150 £93

503

DECANTERS

A Venini Vetro Pesante Inciso decanter and stopper, designed by Paolo Venini, of topaz glass cased in clear, 22cm. high. (Christie's London) $430 £264

Blown three mould decanter, type two stopper, colourless, pontil, quart, New England, 1825-1835. (Robt. W. Skinner Inc.) $100 £62

A Victorian green flash decanter and stopper, 29cm. (Osmond Tricks) $187 £115

A Brierley glass decanter, designed by Keith Murray, with flared stepped neck and conical fluted stopper, 28.3cm. high. (Christie's London) $665 £396

An oak and plated metal mounted tantalus, fitted with three cut glass decanters and stoppers, 13in. wide. (Christie's S. Ken) $401 £242

Blown three mould decanter, with original stopper, type 2, colourless, flaring lip, pontil scar, quart, New England, 1830-1845. (Robt. W. Skinner Inc.) $175 £109

Early pressed decanter, plume and arch pattern, deep cobalt amethyst, tooled lip, pontil scar, 11½in. high, probably France, mid 19th century. (Robt. W. Skinner Inc.) $200 £124

A Victorian electro plated trefoil decanter stand, fitted with three bottle shaped glass decanters enamelled and gilt with trailing vines, overall height of decanter stand 17in. (Christie's S. Ken) $1,262 £825

An unusual glass decanter and stopper, probably Dutch, the 'ring' body engraved with fish, foliage and a jardiniere of flowers, 35cm. high. (Bearne's) $434 £270

DECANTERS

A Continental dark green faceted decanter with clear stopper and pierced silver foot mount, 1930, 29.5cm. (Osmond Tricks) $139 £85

Broken chain decorated decanter, colourless lead glass, 8in., probably Thomas Cains Phoenix Glassworks, Boston, 1820-1830. (Robt. W. Skinner Inc.) $125 £78

A James Powell vaseline glass decanter and stopper, the blown form with applied prunts and border decoration, 24.7cm. high. (Christie's London) $627 £385

Blown three mould decanter, colourless, pontil scar, quart, probably New England, 1825-1840. (Robt. W. Skinner Inc.) $100 £62

An attractive pair of early 19th century barrel shaped Bristol green decanters and stoppers, inscribed 'Hollands' and 'Brandy', 19cm. high. (Spencer's) $644 £400

An Edwardian clear glass dimpled decanter of wrythen fluted square form, Birmingham 1902, 21.5cm. high. (Henry Spencer) $384 £240

A blue decanter and stopper for RUM, named in gilt within a pendant fruiting-vine cartouche, early 19th century, 26cm. high. (Christie's) $524 £308

A brass bound mahogany decanter box of rectangular shape, and a set of four decanters and stoppers, mid 19th century, 8¼in. wide. (Christie's S. Ken) $1,215 £715

An Italian post war polychrome glass decanter modelled as a clown, with the stopper forming the head, 15¼in. high. (Christie's S. Ken) $131 £77

DISHES

Rare Libbey silhouette compote, designed by Douglas Nash, supported by fiery opalescent Jumbo elephant figural stem, 7¹/₂ in. high.
(Skinner Inc.) $550   £335

A Venetian enamelled dish, the depressed well rising to a central point with gadrooned underside and applied footrim, circa 1500, 25cm. diam.
(Christie's) $24310   £14300

Unusual Mt. Washington Amberina compote, with tooled scalloped rim, applied pedestal and foot, extremely deep fuchsia and dark amber colour, 5in. high.
(Skinner Inc.) $600   £366

An Almeric Walter Pâte-de-Verre dish of tri-lobed shape modelled in high relief and naturalistically coloured with a lizard clambering among ivy leaves, 17.5cm. wide.
(Phillips) $5940   £3600

A clear glass dish by Ann Wolff and Wilke Adolfsson, with transparent grey-blue overlay, with etched central motif on round foot, 33cm. diam., signed and dated 1979, Swedish. (Kunsthaus am Museum) $2,672 £1,572

Early lacy oblong tray, Hairpin pattern, rare size, colourless, 9¾ x 7½in., Boston & Sand-wich, Sandwich, Massachusetts, 1830-1845. (Robt. W. Skinner Inc.) $375 £233

Brilliant cut glass covered cheese dish, with fan pattern plate and domed cover with faceted knob, 7¹/₂ in. high.
(Skinner Inc.) $225   £137

Austrian Art glass dish, Loetz-type mottled pink, blue and yellow iridescent shell mounted within gilt bronze metal footed holder, 11in. long.
(Skinner Inc.) $1000   £610

Cigales, a Lalique opalescent bonbonniere, the slightly domed lid decorated with a moulded pattern of insects, 25.5cm. diam. (Christie's London) $1,255 £770

DRINKING SETS

A Lalique frosted glass Lemonade Set, comprising, a flared jug, six glasses.
(Phillips) $2400 £1500

Art Deco cameo cut beverage set, twelve tumblers and an ice bucket of frosted glass with red bamboo and stylised leaf decoration.
(Skinner Inc.) $175 £107

Rene Lalique orangeade service, golden amber moulded crystal set comprising pitcher, six tumblers and the serving tray. (Robt. W. Skinner Inc.)
$1,800 £1,118

An Austrian glass eight-piece liqueur service, enamel painted in black and green with a foliate pattern, 25.5cm. high.
(Christie's) $753 £462

A Bohemian ruby carafe and beaker, with applied opaque panels painted in colours, 8½ in. high.
(Christie's S. Ken) $204 £132

An oviform cut jug painted in colours with two girls fighting over a young boy, and a pair of goblets en suite.
(Christie's) $944 £572

An Art Deco glass decanter set, comprising: a decanter and stopper with faceted sides, 25cm. high, and six glasses.
(Phillips London) $424 £260

New England Amberina Pitcher and two tumblers, with strongest 'chocolate blue' colour at rim and spout, 7in. high.
(Skinner Inc.) $600 £366

A Daum Art Deco glass decanter set, comprising: a bullet-shaped decanter, and six flared glasses en suite, each of pale orange-amber tone.
(Phillips) $1088 £680

507

FIGURES

Source de la Fontaine, a Lalique frosted glass ashtray centred with a slender female figure, 11.50cm. high.(Phillips London)　　$490 £320

Chrysis, a Lalique presse papiers, moulded as a nude maiden with flowing hair, with acid stamped signature, 13.3cm. high. (Christie's London)　　$2,510 £1,540

Naiade, an opalescent, blue stained statuette, moulded as a mermaid, balanced on her coiled tail, moulded R. Lalique, 13cm. high. (Bonhams)　　$2,822 £1,700

An Almeric Walter pate de verre religious rectangular plaque depicting in moulded relief and pale colours a female saint, 30.5 x 16.5cm. (Phillips London)　　$918 £600

Rene Lalique amber Suzanne statuette, frosted fiery amber moulded figure of a woman with arms outstretched holding a gossamer drapery behind her nude body, 8½in. high. (Robt. W. Skinner Inc.) $17,000 £10,559

An Italian clear glass sculpture of a pugilist standing with fists raised, 12in. high. (Christie's S. Ken) $597 £385

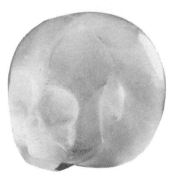

Source de la Fontaine, a Lalique frosted glass luminaire in the form of a young woman with flowered headdress, 19½in. high. (Christie's S. Ken)　　$10,878 £6,380

The Skull, by Raoul Goldoni, in layered iridescent clear and turquoise glass, signed and dated 1972, 16cm. high. (Kunsthaus am Museum)　　$7,485 £4,403

Sirene, a Lalique opalescent glass figurine modelled as a mermaid with her legs drawn up, 10.3cm. high. (Phillips London)　　$1,454 £950

A Bohemian cameo glass goblet in clear glass overlaid in dark blue, carved in the manner of and probably by Franz Zach, 27.3cm. (Phillips London) $2,720 £1,600

Tiffany blue goblet, of dark cobalt blue glass with overall iridescence and mirror finish below, 7in. high. (Robt. W. Skinner Inc.) $425 £264

A large baluster goblet, supported on an inverted baluster stem with basal knop above a folded conical foot, circa 1700.
(Bearne's) $998   £620

A Bohemian amber flashed large goblet and cover, engraved with two running horses, on an amber flashed octagonal knop, 38.5cm. (Phillips London) $1,288 £800

A pair of Bohemian amber-flashed goblets and covers, the octagonal faceted bowls with large amber-flashed panels, one engraved with a landua with two passengers, a coachman and postillion, the other with two spirited horses, on amber flashed octagonal faceted stems and actafoil feet, 28cm.
(Phillips) $1529   £950

Bohemian style engraved and covered goblet, colourless with ruby flash, engraved with stag and forest scene, 12½in. high, probably Bohemia, 1860-1880.
(Robt. W. Skinner Inc.)$50 £31

A pair of St Louis white overlay goblets on red and blue colour twist stems, 7in. high. (Christie's S. Ken) $925 £605

Early 19th century Bohemian goblet, green glass with coloured enamelling, 16cm. high. (Auktionshaus Arnold) $414 £269

A goblet with large ovoid bowl, set on a stem containing a double series opaque twist, circa 1765, 18.7cm. high.
(Bearne's) $434   £270

GOBLETS

A cylinder-knopped Baluster goblet, the flared funnel bowl with a solid lower part enclosing a tear, circa 1715, 17cm. high. (Christie's) $7106 £4180

Engraved covered goblet, colourless with bright green overlay, engraved with stag and forest scene, 10¼in., 1860-1880. (Robt. W. Skinner Inc.) $150 £93

A dated electioneering goblet, the ogee bowl inscribed Succefs to Sir Francis Knollys 1761, 1761, 17cm. high. (Christie's) $1309 £770

A Bohemian large goblet, with medallions of flowers and portraits of courtly men and women, the ground with gilt arabesques, 19th century, 12½in. high. (Lawrence Fine Arts) $852 £550

An interesting engraved goblet on short plain stem and circular foot, the bowl finely engraved with a running stag and a town in the distance, flanked by two crowned Irish harps and a crest of a helmet in a circular panel, between borders of fruiting vine and key fret, 15cm. (Phillips) $740 £460

A South Bohemian 'Lithyalin' goblet of marbled pale-green/grey opalescent glass, the faceted bowl with a raised band, circa 1835–45, 12.5cm. high. (Christie's) $4114 £2420

A 'Newcastle' engraved light-Baluster goblet, the funnel bowl decorated with a border of floral swags, circa 1750, 18cm. high. (Christie's) $1776 £1045

Pair of Tiffany Company Commemorative goblets, designed as thistles, impressed 'Engineers Club December 9th 1907', 7½in. high. (Skinner Inc.) $550 £335

A large Venetian or Facon de Venise latticinio goblet, on a stem composed of two fluted knops between collars and with opaque white serpent handles, 32cm. (Phillips London) $3,703 £2,300

JARS

Handel ware humidor, flat sided opal glass jar with knobbed cover attached with hinged rim, 7½in. high. (Robt. W. Skinner Inc.) $500 £311

Muller Fres scenic cameo glass jar, with conforming cover, layered in dark amethyst, cameo cut with birds in flight, trees and an ivy covered chapel, 5½in. diam. (Robt. W. Skinner Inc.) $1,100 £683

Potter and Bodine's Air Tight Fruit Jar, barrel shaped, wax seal groove, pint, Bridgeton Glassworks, Bridgeton, New Jersey, 1858-1863. (Robt. W. Skinner Inc.) $700 £435

Potter & Bodine's Air Tight Fruit Jar, barrel shape, wax seal groove, 1½ quart size, Bridgeton Glassworks, New Jersey, 1858-1863. (Robt. W. Skinner Inc.) $325 £202

Crown Milano glass and silver-plated cracker jar, late 19th century, globular body with scrolled reserves depicting flowers, 5¼in. high. (Skinner Inc.) $450 £290

Early rum jar, tall square container with tapering sides, deep olive green, 11in. high, probably America, late 18th century. (Robt. W. Skinner Inc.) $850 £528

Mt. Washington jewelled crown Milano biscuit jar, square form with applied glass beads in fan and circle designs, 8in. high. (Skinner Inc.) $950   £579

Mason's Patent, Nov. 30th, 1858, fruit jar, honey amber, ground lip, smooth base, half gallon, America, 1870-1880. (Robt. W. Skinner Inc.) $130 £81

Lithyalin covered jar, attributed to Frederick Egermann, overlaid with darker shades, cut, faceted and polished in geometric agate design, 6in. high. (Skinner Inc.) $600   £366

Early freeblown pitcher, thinly blown, applied handle with multiple crimping at bottom, Pittsburgh area glasshouse, 1820–50.
(Skinner Inc.) $60   £37

Tiffany gold cocktail pitcher, applied handle on waisted cylindrical amber vessel with pouring lip, 6½in. high. (Robt. W. Skinner Inc.) $500 £311

Lily pad decorated pitcher, solid, uncrimped foot, aqua, 6½in. high. (Robt. W. Skinner Inc.) $375 £233

A cut oviform white overlay jug, decorated with shaped panels with crossed diamonds and prisms, 13½in. high.
(Christie's S. Ken.) $726   £440

Rare pillar moulded pitcher, cranberry body with clear cased cranberry blown handle, 9½in., possibly Pittsburgh area, 1850-1870. (Robt. W. Skinner Inc.) $8,800 £5,466

A finely engraved Nurnberg wine ewer, the flattened pear shaped body engraved on one side with a putto, 33.5cm., overall, maker's mark HH conjoined. (Phillips London)
          $34,000 £20,000

Daum cameo glass pitcher with silver mounts, the frosted clear glass body layered in bright emerald green, cameo cut with lilies, buds and con- voluted leaves, 12½in. high. (Robt. W. Skinner Inc.)
          $4,500 £2,795

A Clutha glass jug, the tinted lime green glass striated with pink and with silver foil inclusions, 18.2cm. high. (Christie's London)
          $6,468 £3,850

Crimped foot handled jug, globular body, with thick crude handle, 6½in., probably South Jersey glasshouse, 1820-1840. (Robt. W. Skinner Inc.) $550 £342

Exceptional freeblown pitcher, round handle, applied crimped foot, deep blue, 6½in. high, probably South Jersey, possibly Whitney Glassworks, 1835-1850. (Robt. W. Skinner Inc.) $1,100 £683

Freeblown creamer, high arched lip, ear handle with crimping, 3¾in., possibly South Jersey/Pittsburgh area, 1830-1850. (Robt. W. Skinner Inc.) $500 £311

Very rare lily pad decorated pitcher, a beautiful early piece, 7in. high, probably South Jersey glasshouse, early 19th century. (Robt. W. Skinner Inc.) $2,400 £1,491

Overshot champagne pitcher, gooseneck form, 10½in., probably Boston & Sandwich Glass, Sandwich, Massachusetts, 1870-1887. (Robt. W. Skinner Inc.) $75 £47

Extremely rare Hawkes presentation pitcher, carved with the likeness of 'Thomas G. Hawkes', signed by the artist 'W.H. Morse', 15in. high. (Skinner Inc.) $4000 £2440

Moser enamel decorated pitcher, bright transparent blue with applied salamander handle, 11¾in. high. (Skinner Inc.) $2300 £1403

An attractive Wrockwardine jug with spherical body and lipped cylindrical neck, the loop handle with turned-up terminal, the green glass flecked in white, red, blue and yellow, 21.8cm. (Phillips) $676 £420

A Baluster jug, the everted rim with pouring lip and with a shallow kick-in base, 18th century, 14cm. high. (Christie's) $654 £385

Carder Steuben gold Aurene pitcher, broad bulbous vessel with applied conforming handle, 9¾in. high. (Skinner Inc.) $950 £575

MILK BOTTLES

Square tin-top milk bottle, with embossed line and liquid measurement on side, 'Climax patd 1898', pint.
(Skinner Inc.) $80   £49

Thatcher's milk bottle, 'Absolutely Pure Milk' with man milking cow and 'The Milk Protector Thatcher Mfg. Co.'
(Skinner Inc.) $275   £168

'Pure Milk' milk jar, very rare tin screw top with handle, Adlam patent on base, colourless.
(Skinner Inc.) $850   £518

A.G. Smalley handled milk bottle, no side embossing, colourless, quart size.
(Skinner Inc) $124 £75

Tin-type dairy bottle, with embossed Indian's head, no cap seat, 'Indian Head Farm/ Framingham, Massachusetts'
(Skinner Inc.) $100   £61

Rare cream separator milk bottle, colourless with red pyroglazed 'Deluxe Cream Separator'.
(Skinner Inc.) $350   £213

Square tin-top milk bottle, 'NL Martin, Boston' 'Climax 107' on base, (light haze, some acid lettering on side), quart.
(Skinner Inc.) $375   £229

'Langs Creamery', Buffalo, New York, milk bottle, UD51-12, green, quart.
(Skinner Inc.) $300   £183

'Alta Crest Farms' milk bottle, green, (light wear), quart.
(Skinner Inc.) $700   £427

MILK BOTTLES

A.G. Smalley handled milk bottle, rare half-pint size, side embossing reads 'this bottle to be washed and returned', colourless.
(Skinner Inc.) $400   £244

'Big Elm/Dairy/Company' milk bottle, green, quart.
(Skinner Inc.) $250   £152

A.G. Smalley handled milk bottle, with embossing on side, colourless, quart size.
(Skinner Inc.) $140   £85

Alta Crest milk bottle, crown top with blue pyroglazed, 'Patent 1929' on base, colourless, quart.
(Skinner Inc.) $70   £43

'Alta Crest Farms' milk bottle, UD51-1, green, with paper seat cap, and Alta Crest top cover.
(Skinner Inc.) $700   £427

'Brighton/Place Dairy' milk bottle, UD51-3, green, quart.
(Skinner Inc.) $325   £198

'Weckerle' milk bottle, green, quart.
(Skinner Inc.) $150   £91

Rare milk pail, 'pat. glass pail, Boston, Massachusetts, June 24, 84' on base, tin band around lip with handle.
(Skinner Inc.) $275   £168

Rare cream separator, square pyroglaze deluxe, colurless, quart.
(Skinner Inc.) $400   £244

MISCELLANEOUS

Tiffany Studios bookends, Venetian pattern with border of ermine, in gold dore finish, 6¼in. high. (Robt. W. Skinner Inc.) $375 £233

A very large tazza, on an eight sided pedestal stem and domed foot, with a folded rim, 30cm. diam. (Phillips London) $580 £360

Six Figurines, a set of six Lalique liqueur glasses, moulded with rectangular panels enclosing classical maidens, stained pink, in original fitted box, 3¾in. high. (Christie's S. Ken) $6,002 £3,520

Bottle Baby flask by Asa Brandt, in clear blown glass with a baby face in relief on the front and profiles of a couple in a red lustre circle on reverse, 24.5cm. high, signed *A sa*, 1982, Swedish. (Kunsthaus am Museum) $588 £346

Orrefors Swedish crystal ice bucket, of brilliant dark sapphire blue with pulled and applied handle openings, 7¾in. high. (Robt. W. Skinner Inc.) $120 £75

A good early 19th century two handled loving cup, the bell shaped bowl with two strap handles, 25cm. high. (Henry Spencer) $367 £240

A pair of Masonic bucket bowl drinking glasses, engraved with two circular cartouche and Masonic symbols, 19th century, 4in. high. (Christie's S. Ken) $305 £187

A late 19th century opaque glass wine cooler, painted in colours with a group of men in a rural setting with a river beyond, 33cm. high. (Henry Spencer) $382 £250

Large handled tankard with cover, thick strap handle, colourless non lead glass, 10¾in. high, probably Bohemia, early 19th century. (Robt. W. Skinner Inc.) $125 £78

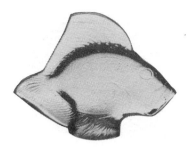

Extremely rare Mount Washington Burmese whimsey bellows, with applied rigaree, 11½in. high. (Robt. W. Skinner Inc.) $1,800 £1,118

Rare spill holder, Sandwich star pattern, 13.02cm.,. probably Boston & Sandwich Glassworks, Massachusetts, 1840-1860. (Robt. W. Skinner Inc.) $900 £559

Gros Poisson, a large Lalique glass model of a carp, its body forming an arc and moulded with scale and fin details, 31.3cm. high. (Phillips London) $5,216 £3,200

One of a pair of ormolu and glass tazze, emerging from a column flanked by three putti on concave sided triangular plinth 16in. high. (Christie's London)
Two $5,313 £3,300

A pair of George III Irish tapering octagonal glass sugar casters on star cut shaped circular bases, Dublin, circa 1780, 8½in. (Christie's S. Ken) $853 £550

A Masonic round bowled rummer, engraved with various Masonic symbols and a circular cartouche initialled G within a six pointed star, 6in. high. (Christie's S. Ken) $215 £132

A cut glass spirit barrel, with plated bands, tap and stand, with four angled square supports, length 23cm. (Osmond Tricks) $717 £440

A clear glass bell shaped flask by Hanns Model, the outside in opaque matt glass with a leaf motif running from top to bottom, signed and dated, 27cm. high, German, 1979. (Kunsthaus am Museum)
$214 £126

A Galle cameo glass moon flask, with cup shaped rim and two small applied loop handles, cameo mark Galle with a star, 21cm. (Bonhams)$3,320 £2,000

MISCELLANEOUS

Rare signed Sinclaire cut glass tray, with cut and engraved motif, centrally signed with S-in-wreath trademark, 11½ in. wide. (Skinner Inc.) $4200 £2562

A pair of Clichy concentric millefiori door-handles, the central pale-pink and green cluster surrounded white-centred blue star canes, mid-19th century, 5.3cm. diam. (Christie's) $1215 £715

A 'Nailsea' sealed Armorial spirit-flask of rectangular section with canted angles and olive-green tint, 19th century, 16cm. high. (Christie's) $2805 £1650

A honeycomb moulded pedestal stem champagne glass, on domed folded foot, circa 1725, 7in. high. (Christie's S. Ken) $466 £286

A pair of Almeric Walter 'Pâte-de-Verre' bookends designed by André Houillon as two dolphins with angular scaly bodies, 17cm. high. (Phillips) $2000 £1250

Glass sculpture by Erwin Eisch with elongated body narrowing sharply at the neck and spun green and brown threads combed in peacock style, signed and dated *1976*, German, 37cm. high. (Kunsthaus am Museum) $267 £157

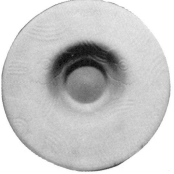

A two-handled posset-pot, the bell bowl applied with two scroll handles flanking a curved spout, mid-18th century, 18.5cm. high. (Christie's) $1870 £1100

A Charder acid etched Art Deco charger, the shaded pink glass decorated with geo-metric stylised flowers, 41.8cm. diam. (Christie's London) $1,219 £748

A Cameo biscuit-barrel with plated mounts, the pale-blue matt ground overlaid in white and carved with sprays of foliage, circa 1890, 14cm. high. (Christie's) $1496 £880

A sweetmeat glass, the shallow bowl cut with shallow diamonds below a scalloped and dentate rim, 13.5cm. (Phillips London) $354 £220

A Central European dated 'Glass-blower's' flask, enamelled in colours with the gaffer standing blowing a glass before a flaming furnace, perhaps South Germany, 1767, 16.5cm. high. (Christie's) $20570 £12100

Glossy Webb peachblow roundel, the crimped edge plate with gold enamelled butterfly, 8¾in. diam. (Robt. W. Skinner Inc.) $400 £248

A Tiffany 'Favrile' iridescent glass Seal moulded with the bodies of three scarab beetles, 4.5cm. high. (Phillips) $576 £360

A pair of Bohemian white overlay, green glass lustre vases, painted with panels of flowers in enamel colours and gold, 30.3cm. high. (Bearne's) $1271 £820

An important 'Whitefriars' glass, silver and enamelled centrepiece designed for James Powell and Sons by Harry Powell, 36cm. high. (Phillips) $15680 £9800

Anti Fleur, a Daum/Salvador Dali pate de verre piece in clear glass and yellowish green, free flower form, glazed signature *Dali 70*, 38cm. high. (Kunsthaus am Museum) $2,139 £1,258

A pair of engraved moon-flasks, painted in colours with flowering prunus trees, on Buddhistic lion feet, 9¾in. high. (Christie's S. Ken) $968 £605

A sweetmeat glass, with diamond and geometric cutting, on a faceted centre knopped stem and domed foot, 16.3cm. (Phillips London) $354 £220

PAPERWEIGHTS

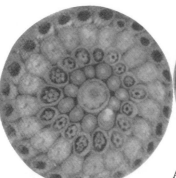

A small clear glass paper weight, enclosing a single pink clematis flower flanked by two buds and five leaves, probably Baccarat, 4.5cm. diam.
(Spencer's) $693   £420

A Bacchus close concentric millefiori weight, the five circles of canes including iron-red-lined and pale-green-lined hollow crimped tubes, mid-19th century, 8.5cm. diam.
(Christie's) $524   £308

A Baccarat pink gentian weight, the curved green stalk with three white-lined pink bell-shaped flowers, mid-19th century, 7.5cm. diam.
(Christie's) $14960   £8800

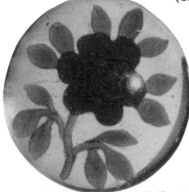

A Baccarat 'Thousand petalled' rose weight, the multi-petalled dark-red flower with seven green leaves showing behind, mid-19th century, 6.5cm. diam.
(Christie's) $5984   £3520

A Baccarat miniature primrose weight, the flower with six white heart-shaped petals edged in inscribed on the base 18 4/72 mid 19th century.
(Christie's) $1,400   £825

A St. Louis fruit weight including a ripe pear, an unripe pear, an apple and three cherries, mid-19th century, 8cm. diam.
(Christie's) $1309   £770

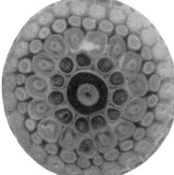

A Bacchus close concentric millefiori weight, the five circles of canes in shades of iron-red, pale-blue, green, yellow and white, mid-19th century, 8.7cm. diam. (Christie's) $1309 £770

A Paul Ysart double-snake pedestal weight, the two coiled reptiles with raised heads and red tongues, 20th century, 7.5cm. diam.
(Christie's) $1215   £715

A St. Louis faceted amber-flash posy weight, the posy with five florettes in shades of pink, yellow, white and blue resting on six green leaves, mid-19th century, 6.5cm. diam.
(Christie's) $1683   £990

PAPERWEIGHTS

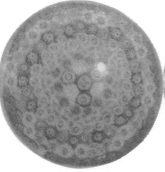

A St. Louis close concentric mushroom weight, the tuft with seven concentric circles of canes, on a star-cut base, mid-19th century, 7.8cm. diam. (Christie's) $1776 £1045

A Clichy close concentric millefiori weight, the eight circles of canes in pale shades of pink, green, yellow, white and torquoise, mid 19th century, 7cm. diam. (Christie's) $710 £418

A St. Louis fruit weight, the large ripe pear and three cherries resting among numerous green leaves, mid 19th century, 7.5cm. diam. (Christie's) $1,309 £770

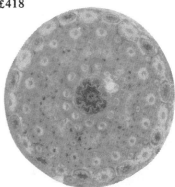

Charles Kaziun silhouette paperweight, rare cameo portrait in black and white millifiore, 2in. diam. (Skinner Inc.) $750 £457

A Paul Ysart bouquet weight, the loose bouquet tied with a blue cord comprising five flowers and a bud, 20th century, 7.2cm. diam. (Christie's) $898 £528

A Bacchus close concentric millefiori weight, the five circles of canes in pale shades of pink, mauve, blue, green, white, and yellow, mid 19th century, 8.5cm. diam. (Christie's) $655 £385

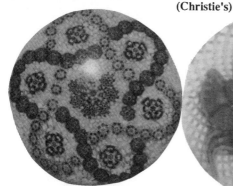

A Baccarat carpet-ground patterned millefiori weight, the central circular cluster of canes enclosed by two interlocking trefoil garlands, mid-19th century, 7.8cm. diam. (Christie's) $9350 £5500

A St. Louis double-clematis weight, the dark-blue flower with fifteen ribbed petals about a salmon-pink cogwheel centre, mid-19th century, 5.8cm. diam. (Christie's) $1309 £770

A St. Louis dated mushroom paperweight, the concentric millefiori cluster with rows of red, blue, white and green canes, dated 1848, 7cm. (Phillips) $2093 £1300

GLASS

SCENT BOTTLES

Fancy pressed cologne, drape and dot lacy pattern, 5½in., possibly Baccarat, France, mid 19th century. (Robt. W. Skinner Inc.) $200 £124

A Galle enamelled glass perfume flask decorated in the Persian manner with an acid etched ground of trellis and stylised flowers, 18cm. long. (Phillips London) $1,683 £1,100

Gardenia, a scent bottle for Worth, moulded with an all-over design of flowerheads, moulded *R. Lalique*, 8.5cm. high. (Bonhams) $149 £90

Mille Fleurs, a frosted blue stained Brule Parfums, the bullet shaped cover moulded with flowers, cover moulded *R. Lalique*, 16cm. high. (Bonhams) $2,324 £1,400

Ambre Antique, a Lalique frosted and sepia stained glass scent bottle, moulded with a frieze of classical maidens and with quartered foliate stopper, moulded *R. Lalique*, 5.4cm. (Bonhams) $1,328 £800

Dans la Nuit, a large display scent bottle for Worth, the spherical body moulded with stars, faint moulded mark *R. Lalique*, 25.5cm. high. (Bonhams) $1,328 £800

Imprudence, a clear glass bottle for Worth, moulded as five graduating discs, each rimmed with silver, stencilled *R. Lalique*, 9cm. high. (Bonhams) $631 £380

D'Argental cameo glass perfume burner, of fiery opal frosted glass layered in orange amber and brown, 6¼in. high.(Robt. W. Skinner Inc.) $300 £186

Blue overlay cologne bottle, overlaid in dark cobalt blue deeply cut in Gothic arches, 9in. high. (Robt. W. Skinner Inc.) $200 £124

SCENT BOTTLES

A Venini vetro a file scent bottle and stopper, of chocolate brown colour decorated with internal red glass fragmented threads, 15cm. high. (Phillips London) $275 £180

A clear glass scent bottle with tiara stopper, for Roger et Gallet, stopper moulded *Lalique* (minute chips to stopper), 8.2cm. (Bonhams) $3,320 £2,000

Le Jade, a green scent bottle for Roger et Gallet, moulded with a bird of paradise perched amidst entwined branches, base moulded *RL France,* 8.3cm. (Bonhams) $1,162 £700

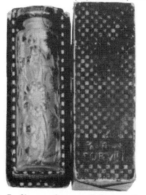

Cut blue overlay cologne, overlaid in cobalt blue cut to accent ribbed design, conforming stopper, 7¼in. high. (Robt. W. Skinner Inc.) $300 £186

A Lalique clear and frosted glass scent bottle and stopper, in original box, moulded *R. Lalique*, base and stopper engraved *332*, 4in. high. (Christie's S. Ken) $1,275   £748

Le Provencal, a sienna stained frosted perfume atomiser, designed for Molinard, the cylindrical base moulded with six nude female figures, moulded *R. Lalique,* 15.5cm. (Bonhams) $498 £300

Je Reviens, a large perfume display bottle for Worth, the dark blue bottle of ribbed cylindrical form, stencilled *R. Lalique Worth Made in France,* 29cm. high. (Bonhams) $913 £550

Palmes, a Lalique clear and frosted glass Brule Parfums, moulded with a design of overlapping palm leaves, moulded *R. Lalique, Made in France,* 18cm. (Bonhams) $465 £280

Palerme, a clear scent bottle, moulded with graduated beaded swags and with pierced bead stopper, moulded *R. Lalique,* 12cm. (Bonhams) $365 £220

SCENT BOTTLES

A white satin glass tear-drop
fluted scent bottle, Sampson
Mordan, London 1884, 3½in.
(Christie's S. Ken) $341 £220

A rare Lithyalin square
perfume bottle in green glass
overlaid in deep mulberry and
gilt with butterflies and
flowers, 10cm. (Phillips
London) $580 £360

A cameo glass scent bottle, in
blue glass overlaid in white,
with American silver mount,
by Gorham of Massachusetts,
16cm. (Phillips London)
                $748 £440

A Victorian green glazed champagne bottle scent spray, the
plated mount impressed with
the diamond registration mark,
4¾in. (Christie's S. Ken)
                $887 £528

Two Daum enamelled glass scent
bottles and stoppers, acid-etched
and naturalistically painted with
violets, 10.5cm. high.
(Phillips) $4480   £2800

A Galle carved and acid
etched cameo perfume
atomiser, the yellow tinted
glass overlaid in red, 23.5cm.
high. (Christie's London)
                $1,255 £770

A Lalique frosted glass Perfume
Bottle and Stopper of cylindrical
shape moulded with satyr masks
and swags of roses, 12.5cm. high.
(Phillips) $1440   £900

A pair of English opaque glass
scent bottles in a shagreen case,
each decorated in the manner of
James Giles, 18th century, slight
damage, 4.5cm. high.
(Bearne's) $3255   £2100

A Continental pedestal scent
flask, the hinged lid and body
profusely enamelled with
garden scenes and butterflies,
4in. high. (Christie's S. Ken)
                $1,010 £660

SCENT BOTTLES

A Lalique frosted glass Perfume
Burner of cylindrical shape
moulded with mermaids, 17.3cm.
high.
(Phillips) $1760 £1100

A Victorian novelty scent bottle
in the form of a swan's head,
C. S. & F. S., Birmingham,
1884, 6in. (Christie's S. Ken)
$1,016 £605

A Victorian novelty silver top -
ped scent bottle in the
form of a mottled brown
bird's egg, Sampson Mordan,
London, 1885, 2¼in.
(Christie's S. Ken) $256 £165

A Gallé carved and acid-etched
cameo perfume atomiser, the
milky-white and pink glass
overlaid in purple with
labernum, 22.5cm. high.
(Christie's) $1614 £990

Fleurs Concaves, a pair of
Lalique glass scent bottles,
impress moulded with florets
graduating in size, heightened
with grey staining, 13cm. high.
(Phillips London) $3,749 £2,300

A French blue opaque glass
scent bottle decorated in gilt
with berried foliage, 3in.
(Phillips Sevenoaks) $94 £55

A French rectangular glass and
gold mounted perfume flask,
the shoulders engraved rococo
scrolls and flowers, 4½in.
(Phillips Sevenoaks) $561 £330

An unusual Rolex scent bottle,
with openwork front
incorporating the Rolex crown
symbol and fluted sides, 5.7cm
high. (Phillips London)
$179 £110

A fine and attractive late
Victorian silver sheathed cran-
berry glass dressing table
bottle, by Sampson Morden
& Co., 13cm. high, 1892.
(Henry Spencer) $720 £450

SHADES

Madagascar, a Lalique opalescent plafonnier, moulded in high relief with a band of monkey masks, 30cm. diam. (Christie's London)
$3,048 £1,870

Leaded glass hanging clematis shade, John Mathot, Holliston, Massachusetts, fine contemporary conical hanger, 29in. diam. (Skinner Inc.)
$1,000 £645

A Daum Cameo glass hanging lampshade, finely decorated with leaves in autumnal colours, 45cm. diam.
(Bearne's) $4185   £2700

Boule de Gui, a Lalique green stained hanging shade, the clear and satin finished glass moulded with mistletoe, 44cm. high. (Christie's London) $28,688 £17,600

A pair of Lalique wall light panels, moulded in high relief with a putto between floral friezes, 47cm. high. (Christie's London) $7,172, £4,400

Deux Sirenes, a Lalique frosted glass plafonnier, moulded with two swimming water nymphs, their hair forming streams of bubbles, 39.5cm. (Bonhams)
$2,822 £1,700

A Daum cameo glass lampshade, the body streaked with yellow and orange, overlaid with brown glass acid etched with Chinese lanterns and foliage, 19.5cm. diam. (Phillips London) $4,401 £2,700

A Venini wall light designed by Fulvio Bianconi, with diagonal stripes of clear, red, green and blue glass, mounted on a brass wall bracket, 29cm. high. (Christie's London) $1,076 £660

Leaded glass dragonfly hanging shade, with six dragonfly motifs at edge in blue with leaded mesh covered wings, 24in. diam. (Skinner Inc.)
$350 £226

STAINED GLASS

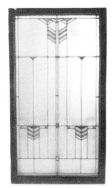

A tinted glass panel, the centre section painted with a golfing scene, 1900s, 38¼ x 20½in. (Christie's S. Ken) $3,498 £2,200

French scenic window plaque, signed by artist *R. Boutillie*, of clear and opal glass etched and painted in shades of blue, yellow and pink, 15½ x 12½in. (sight) (Robt. W. Skinner Inc.) $500 £311

One of a pair of leaded glass windows, Midwest, circa 1910, two repeating arrow medallions in orange centring vertical strip, 48½in. high. (Skinner Inc.)
Two $500 £309

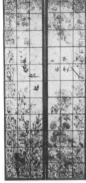

Two pairs of French stained and painted glass doors, circa 20th century, each depicting finches among various flowers, 89in. x 21in.
(Skinner Inc.) $2300 £1403

'Four Corners to my Bed', a circular stained and leaded glass panel by William Glasby, in brass frame, 87.3cm. diam. (Christie's London)
$3,696 £2,200

One of a pair of Arts and Craft leaded and stained glass panels, with swallows before clouds in a border of stylised flowerheads in oak frames, 180 x 111cm. each panel. (Christie's London)
Two $2,772 £1,650

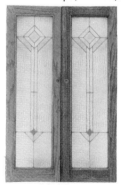

A late 19th century arched stained glass window painted in the Romanesque style, 121in. high. (Christie's)
$2,288 £1,430

An Art Nouveau stained glass window by Muller Freres, fashioned from segments of stained glass supported with lead, signed, 111cm. high x 117cm. across.
(Phillips) $1485 £900

Four tall and two short Prairie School style leaded glass windows, circa 1910, 40in. and 32in. high. (Skinner Inc.)
$425 £261

VASES

Satin glass gold enamelled vase, attributed to Thomas Webb & Sons, decorated in the Jules Barbe manner, 7½in. high. (Robt. W. Skinner Inc.)
$550 £342

Legras art glass vase, decorated with yellow green, white and brown striations between layers of clear glass, 10in. high. (Robt. W. Skinner Inc.)
$650 £404

Piriac, a frosted, blue stained vase, moulded in high relief with a band of fish above a waved base, wheel cut *R. Lalique France,* 18.5cm. high. (Bonhams) $1,029 £620

A glass vase attributed to Monart, of flaring shouldered cylindrical form, cased in crystal glass, 11½in. high. (Christie's S. Ken) $179 £105

Lithyalin vase, attributed to Frederick Egermann, of agate glass in variegated earth tones of browns, beige, yellow amber and green, 10½in. high. (Robt. W. Skinner Inc.)
$1,200 £745

Moser art glass vase, of heavy walled cobalt blue glass faceted in ten panels and banded with a frieze of classically dressed women, 8¼in. high. (Robt. W. Skinner Inc.) $425 £264

Pattern moulded vase, herringbone pattern, bubbly glass, deep amethyst folded under lip, pontil scar, 8¾in. (Robt. W. Skinner Inc.) $125 £78

European art glass vase, decorated with alternating stripes of frosted and amber textured panels, mounted in gilt metal fittings, signed *Lovakia* on base, 12in. high. (Robt. W. Skinner Inc.) $500 £311

Orrefors cut and etched crystal vase, The Shark Killer, by Vicke Linstrand, with dramatic underwater scene, 14in. high. (Robt. W. Skinner Inc.)
$11,000 £6,832

VASES

Dom Remy, a Lalique opalescent glass vase of broad oviform, moulded in relief with globular thistles, 21.4cm. high. (Phillips London) $704 £460

Formose, a fine cased jade green vase, moulded with swimming shubunkin fish, etched script mark *R. Lalique France,* 17cm. high. (Bonhams) $6,972 £4,200

Blown vase, deep cobalt blue, rolled over lip, pontil scar, 8in., probably New England, probably mid 19th century. (Robt. W. Skinner Inc.) $550 £342

A Loetz iridescent vase, of tapering cylindrical form with applied handles of pale amber splashed with turquoise, 6¼in. high. (Christie's S. Ken) $1,032 £605

Tiffany morning glory paperweight exhibition vase, of colourless glass with internal paperweight frieze of blue and purple red morning glory blossoms, 6¼in. high. (Robt. W. Skinner Inc.)$14,000 £8,696

A Loetz iridescent vase, the dimpled quatrefoil body tapering to waisted base, 6½in. high. (Christie's S. Ken) $563 £330

Grimpereaux, a clear and frosted vase, moulded with horizontal and vertical panels decorated with birds, wheel cut *R. Lalique France,* 21.2cm. high. (Bonhams) $996 £600

Serpent, a fine amber glass vase, a serpent coiled around the body, the head with gaping jaws, intaglio moulded *R. Lalique,* 25cm. (Bonhams) $13,280 £8,000

A James Couper & Sons clutha glass vase, designed by Christopher Dresser, of waisted form with a short neck, 8.5cm. high. (Phillips London) $1,143 £747

VASES

An ormolu mounted opaline vase, the lid pierced with scrolls, the sides with winged caryatids, 12½in. high. (Christie's London)
$1,239 £770

A stylish Muller Freres Art Deco glass vase, the lower part decorated with pale lemon geometric motifs acid etched in relief, 19.5cm. high. (Phillips London) $2,282 £1,400

A good Galle artichoke vase, the pale mutton fat coloured body having pale brown vertical strips, 20.5cm. high. (Phillips London)
$97,800 £60,000

A Humppila vase by T. Wirkkala in clear glass lightly tinted with brown, the body slightly waisted, broadening in a fountain shape at the top with irregular fluting, 42cm., signed. (Kunsthaus am Museum)
$294 £173

La Giroflee de Muraille, a fine quality Galle marquetrie-sur-verre and wheel carved glass vase, applied with coloured stems and blooms, 20.5cm. high. (Phillips London) $122,250 £75,000

A clear glass sculpture by Mieke Groot, on rectangular base, with raised inflated rim, painted in yellow and black, spray painted yellow and red band on long sides, 32.5cm. high, 1985. (Kunsthaus am Museum) $481 £283

A finely carved Stourbridge cameo glass vase of small size, overlaid in white and carved with a Persian style design, 11.5cm. (Phillips London)
$1,449 £900

A Brierley glass vase, designed by Keith Murray, of broad bucket shape and engraved with stylised foliate sprays, 20cm. high. (Phillips London)
$2,282 £1,400

An attractive Galle enamelled glass vase, the body of pale amber tint, acid etched with pendant and circular blooms picked out in vivid red, 21.5cm. high. (Phillips London)
$4,890 £3,000

VASES

Jugendstil glass vase, possibly Loetz, 24cm. high. (Auktionshaus Arnold) $386 £251

A Loetz iridescent glass vase, the olive green glass decorated with iridescent silvery blue ribbons, 5½ in. high. (Christie's S. Ken) $1,330 £858

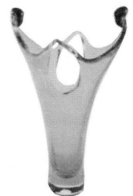

A vase by J-G. Kizinska, the rim moulded to four points, two with knops and the others with handle type openings, 38.5cm. high, signed, Polish. (Kunsthaus am Museum) $145 £85

A Loetz green Phenomenon glass vase of bulbous tapering cylindrical form, encased in pewter twin handled mount, 7¾ in. high. (Christie's S. Ken) $682 £440

Fulper pottery glass vase, Flemington, New Jersey, circa 1910, black drip glaze over copper dust ground, 12¼ in. high. (Skinner Inc.) $1,400 £864

An Arts and Crafts twin handled overlay glass vase of campana form, intaglio and cameo cut with a frieze of tulips, 9½ in. high. (Christie's S. Ken) $546 £352

A Lalique opalescent glass vase, moulded in relief with scaly fish swimming amid horizontal waved ribs, 13.8cm. high. (Phillips London) $1,956 £1,200

A cylindrical white glass sculpture by Albin Schaedel, designed with four spirals on round base and triangular rim, 16cm. high, signed S, East German. (Kunsthaus am Museum) $882 £519

Danaides, a Lalique opalescent glass vase, moulded in relief with a frieze of six naked female water carriers with jars on their shoulders, 18cm. high. (Phillips London) $3,423 £2,100

VASES

An unusual Loetz iridescent glass vase, decorated with random splashes exhibiting shades of mauve blue lustre and applied with vertical glass bands, 23.5 cm. high. (Phillips London) $673 £440

English cameo glass vase, attributed to Thomas Webb & Sons, cameo cut and intricately carved with broad poppy blossoms, buds, pods and leaves, 8½ in. high. (Robt. W. Skinner Inc.) $2,250 £1,398

A Daum overlay vase, the clear glass overlaid with a green, blue, yellow and white pattern, 26.2 cm. high. (Christie's London) $1,345 £825

One of a pair of large oviform Bohemian vases with flaring necks, broadly cut with flutes and lozenge shaped lenses, 14 in. high. (Christie's S. Ken) Two $1,313 £858

An Italian two handled glass vase, the design attributed to Dino Martens, decorated with diagonal lines, 29 cm. high. (Christie's London) $896 £550

A Galle carved and acid etched, double overlay vase, overlaid in scarlet and red with flowering phlox, 32.8 cm. high. (Christie's London) $5,379 £3,300

A Loetz vase, the clear glass decorated with an iridescent trailed silver green, purple and blue pattern, 35.5 cm. high. (Christie's London) $645 £396

Satin glass portrait vase, attributed to American decorator company, probably Gillinder, marked in white on base 'Cameo', 8 in. high. (Skinner Inc.) $550 £335

Wheeling Peachblow Morgan vase on holder, flared rim and extended shaped neck on classic oval body, 10 in. high. (Robt. W. Skinner Inc.) $750 £466

VASES

A Daum carved and acid etched cameo vase, the mottled yellow, red and green body overlaid in darkest amber with fruiting vines, 34.5cm. high. (Christie's London) $5,379 £3,300

Austrian art glass vase, attributed to Pallme-Konig, of orange amber, opal and deep pink layers with blue black threading, 7¾in. high. (Robt. W. Skinner Inc.) $100 £62

De Vez scenic cameo glass vase, of mottled yellow overlaid in orange and blue, cameo cut and carved with an intricate woodland scene, 11in. high. (Robt. W. Skinner Inc.) $1,800 £1,118

A Loetz vase, the clear glass decorated with an iridescent trailed silver purple, green and yellow pattern, 26cm. high. (Christie's London) $627 £385

A Daum carved and acid etched vase, the mottled yellow and orange glass overlaid with hazelnut leaves and nuts, 25cm. high. (Christie's London) $2,689 £1,650

Webb cameo vase, cameo cut and carved with a bouquet of wild geranium blossoms, buds and leaves, 9in. high. (Robt. W. Skinner Inc.) $2,500 £1,553

A Gabriel Argy-Rousseau pate de verre vase, with moulded decoration in green and red with stylised thistles, 15.5cm. high. (Christie's London) $7,172 £4,400

A Galle acid etched and carved cameo glass vase, the flattened oviform body with slender neck and flaring trefoil rim, cameo signature *Galle*, 10in. high. (Christie's S. Ken) $2,813 £1,650

A Legras enamel painted vase, the milky white glass with grey, amber and orange painted decoration, 30.2cm. high. (Christie's London) $861 £528

VASES

A Loetz vase, of swollen form on short flared base with everted rim, with three applied stylised flowerheads, 5½in. high. (Christie's S. Ken) $338 £198

Victor Durand art glass vase, slightly raised and flared rim on ovoid iridescent blue body with white random leaf and vine decoration, 6¼in. high. (Robt. W. Skinner Inc.) $750 £466

Loetz type vase in bronze mount, of green with blue threading fitted within three-footed elaborate bronzed Art Nouveau floral and scrolled cage, 9¾in. high. (Robt. W. Skinner Inc.) $300 £186

A Galle fire polished cameo glass vase, the aquamarine glass overlaid in violet and carved with trailing, flowering tendrils of convolvulus, 25cm. high. (Bonhams) $2,822 £1,700

Pair of Bohemian type engraved vases, engraved with grapes, florals and leaves, 10½in. high, possibly Boston & Sandwich Glassworks, Massachusetts, 1880s. (Robt. W. Skinner Inc.) $200 £124

Rare panelled vase, so-called Stiegel type, twelve panels, 8½in., probably New England, 1840-1860. (Robt. W. Skinner Inc.) $1,700 £1,056

A large and finely carved cameo vase, decorated in white relief with a large spray of Christmas roses, 22cm. (Phillips London) $2,040 £1,200

Rare Rene Lalique amethyst vase, Courges pattern, with moulded overall design of gourd shaped vegetables, 7½in. high. (Robt. W. Skinner Inc.) $22,000 £13,665

A Galle wheel carved cameo glass vase, the clear glass body overlaid with deep ruby red glass wheel carved with clematis flowers, 20.5cm. high. (Phillips London) $5,661 £3,700

VASES

Renoncules, a Lalique opalescent glass vase of globular shape, moulded in high relief with stylised flowers and foliage, 15 cm. high. (Phillips London)
$1,040 £680

Victor Durand opal crackle glass vase, of amber with opal, blue and gold expanded, crackled and textured surface decoration overall, 9½ in. high. (Robt. W. Skinner Inc.) $400 £248

Rampillon, a Lalique opalescent glass vase moulded on the exterior with lozenge shaped protrusions against a floral ground, 12.7 cm. high. (Phillips London) $643 £420

Rare Mount Washington jewelled Royal Flemish vase, decorated with enamelled and gilt bordered blossoms, buds, autumn leaves and thorny stems, 9 in. high. (Robt. W. Skinner Inc.) $1,400 £870

Wiener Werkstatte vase, attributed to Otto Prutscher, completely faceted and outlined in black with square design, 8¾ in. high. (Robt. W. Skinner Inc.) $1,200 £745

Sauterelles, a Lalique emerald green oviform vase, moulded in relief with numerous grasshoppers, 27.5 cm. high. (Phillips London)
$11,016 £7,200

Muller Fres art glass vase, of brilliant royal blue with gold metallic inclusions and streaks of yellow and brown, 11 in. high. (Robt. W. Skinner Inc.)
$600 £373

Yvelines, a Lalique clear glass vase, the cylindrical body flanked by two disc handles, wheelcut *R Lalique France,* etched *No. 975,* 20.02 cm. high. (Christie's S. Ken)
$3,751 £2,200

Galle blow moulded cameo vase, of three colours blown into a mould with golden amber gourds, amber and brown leaves and brown tendrils and vines, 7½ in. high. (Robt. W. Skinner Inc.) $2,800 £1,739

VASES

Stueben green jade vase, flared rim on oval spirally ribbed body of pastel green jade, 6¾in. high. (Robt. W. Skinner Inc.) $200 £124

Formose, a Lalique amber glass vase, moulded in relief with scaly fish with fanned tail feathers, 16cm. high. (Phillips London) $2,934 £1,800

A Lalique opalescent glass vase of cylindrical shape moulded in high relief with vines and berries, 16cm. high. (Phillips London) $842 £550

Quezal floriform lily vase, of gold iridescent lined opal glass decorated with five extra-ordinary green and gold pulled feather repeats, 9½in. high. (Robt. W. Skinner Inc.) $1,200 £745

Rare pair of Mount Washington lava vases, each with irregular glass inclusions in shades of blue, green, white, pink, aqua and some red, 8in. high. (Robt. W. Skinner Inc.) $3,500 £2,174

Tiffany favrile peacock vase, of opal glass lined with orange gold iridescence and decorated in amber gold with green symmetrically pulled feather devices, 10¼in. high. (Robt. W. Skinner Inc.) $6,000 £3,727

Formose, a fine red vase, moulded with swimming shubunkin fish, intaglio moulded *R. Lalique*, 17cm. high. (Bonhams) $7,470 £4,500

Charles Lotton art glass vase, of opaque white glass with five iridescent blue green pulled leaf designs ending in red orange four petalled blossoms, 8¾in. high. (Robt. W. Skinner Inc.) $325 £202

Montargis, a frosted and grey stained vase, moulded on the shoulders with curved fern leaves on a stained ground, intaglio moulded *R. Lalique France*, 21cm. high. (Bonhams) $5,810 £3,500

VASES

Austrian art glass vase, atrributed to Loetz, of threaded bright green raised on low pedestal disc foot, iridescence overall, 8in. high. (Robt. W. Skinner Inc.)
$200 £124

Prunes, a clear and opalescent glass vase, the bulbous base moulded in high relief with clusters of plums amidst foliage, engraved *R. Lalique France,* 17.8cm. (Bonhams)
$3,652 £2,200

A clear, frosted and grey stained vase, moulded with slender vertical leaves, alternately folded at the tips, stencilled *R. Lalique France,* 14.5cm. high. (Bonhams)
$797 £480

An unusual and fine quality wheel carved cameo glass vase, the clear body overlaid with amber and green glass wheel carved with four Classical female dancers, 30.5cm. high. (Phillips London) $6,426 £4,200

A good Argy-Rousseau pate de verre oviform vase, moulded in relief with a frieze of four black wolves padding along a shelf of icy snow, 24.5cm. high. (Phillips London)
$24,480 £16,000

A Galle cameo glass vase, the greyish body amber tinted and overlaid with pale blue and amethyst glass acid etched with tropical foliage, 21cm. high. (Phillips London)
$6,732 £4,400

Durand art glass vase, of cobalt glass with blue iridescence and trailing heart shaped leaf and vine decoration, 9½in. high. (Robt. W. Skinner Inc.)
$750 £466

A frosted glass vase, moulded at the base with a panel of recumbent ibex beneath myriad stars, stencilled *Lalique France,* 20.3cm. high. (Bonhams) $747 £450

A large Daum cameo glass, the body tinted rose pink, orange and yellow overlaid with orange and dark green acid etched, 44.5cm. high. (Phillips London)
$3,978 £2,600

VASES

Quezal vase with silver overlay, raised rim and elongated neck on bulbous amber body with iridescence overall, 8½ in. high. (Robt. W. Skinner Inc.)
$2,200 £1,366

A Tiffany vase, with two applied shell shaped handles, with engraved signature, 11cm. high. (Christie's London) $1,165 £715

Rare swagged vase with ball cover, aqua, 7in., pontil scar. (Robt. W. Skinner Inc.)
$700 £435

A Samuel Hermann vase, of compressed section rising to a narrow neck, the clear glass decorated with a grey and yellow hailed pattern, 17.5cm. high. (Christie's London)
$287 £176

A Vallerysthal vase, with an applied glass tendril and enamel painted decoration of a butterfly and buds, 23cm. high. (Christie's London)
$6,096 £3,740

Sauges, a Lalique coloured glass vase, the emerald green glass moulded in high relief with four bands of overlapping leaves, 24cm. high. (Christie's London)
$8,965 £5,500

A Daum and Louis Majorelle blown glass and wrought iron vase, the mottled pink glass protruding through an elaborately decorated wrought iron framework, 22.5cm. high. (Christie's London) $1,972 £1,210

A Galle carved and acid etched vase, overlaid with blue and violet flowering clematis, 31.4cm. high. (Christie's London)
$11,116 £6,820

Tulipes, a Lalique blue stained vaseline glass vase, moulded with tulips, 21cm. high. (Christie's London)
$4,303 £2,640

VASES

Steuben dark blue aurene vase of green body with dark purple green blue iridescence overall, 8¾in. high. (Robt. W. Skinner Inc.) $300 £186

Formose, a Lalique satin finished vase, the globular body moulded with fantailed goldfish, 17.2cm. high. (Christie's London) $753 £462

Daum cameo glass vase, of mottled cobalt blue and frosted clear overlaid in blue and opaque pastel green, 12in. high. (Robt. W. Skinner Inc.) $8,500 £5,280

A Mueller Croismaire vase, overlaid with acid etched and carved brown tiger lilies, 27cm. high. (Christie's London) $6,454 £3,960

A Lalique vaseline glass vase, moulded with stylised flowering thistles, with moulded signature *R. Lalique,* 21.5cm. high. (Christie's London) $1,255 £770

A d'Argental carved and acid etched landscape vase, the white glass overlaid in amber with the view of a castle in a mountainous landscape, 20cm. high. (Christie's London) $861 £528

A Loetz white metal mounted vase, decorated with an iridescent blue and green oil splashed pattern, 20cm. high. (Christie's London) $1,076 £660

A James Powell glass vase, the opalescent green glass decorated with milky striations forming stylised flowers, 25.5cm. high. (Christie's London) $1,524 £935

A Galle carved and acid etched cameo vase, of flask form with short everted neck and two applied handles, 30.8cm. high. (Christie's London) $5,738 £3,520

WINE GLASSES

A gilt decorated wine glass, the ogee bowl gilt in the manner of James Giles, on an opaque twist stem, 15cm. (Phillips London) $1,054 £620

An interesting cordial glass, the small ogee bowl engraved with a spray of blackcurrants, 14cm. (Phillips London) $442 £260

A Beilby enamelled wine glass, the rounded funnel bowl enamelled in white with fruiting vine leaves, 14.8cm. (Phillips London) $2,210 £1,300

A Newcastle engraved wine glass, the bell bowl with a wide rim border of scrolls, leaf scrolls and foliage, 17cm. (Phillips London) $741 £460

One of a pair of Beilby enamelled wine glasses, the bell bowls enamelled in white with bunches of grapes, 17.8cm. (Phillips London)
                Two $3,400 £2,000

A rare enamelled Royal Armorial wine glass by William Beilby, enamelled, with the arms of William V, Prince of Orange and his wife, Frederica Wilhelmina, 18.5cm.(Phillips London) $7,480   £4,400

A wine glass, the rounded funnel bowl engraved with a carnation spray and an insect, possibly of Jacobite significance, 14.8cm. (Phillips London) $646 £380

A rare yellow twist wine glass with ogee bowl, the stem composed of a central six strand spiral, 15cm. (Phillips London)
            $9,860 £5,800

A colour twist wine glass, the stem composed of a thin central blue thread within a pair of opaque corkscrews, 17cm. (Phillips London)
            $2,550 £1,500

WINE GLASSES

A Lynn wine glass, the rounded funnel bowl on an opaque twist stem of a four-ply column, 13cm. (Phillips London) $493 £290

A colour twist wine glass, the stem composed of a central red ribbon within a pair of six-ply corkscrews, 15cm. (Phillips London)
          $2,380 £1,400

A wine glass, with honeycomb moulding round the lower part on a shoulder knopped multiply air twist stem, 16cm. (Phillips London) $419 £260

A bell bowled wine glass, on composite multiple air twist stem, 6½in. high (some chips to foot). (Christie's S. Ken)
          $249 £154

A Beilby enamelled wine glass, the rounded funnel bowl painted in white enamel with a ruined classic column, 15.5cm. (Phillips London) $1,156 £680

A round funnel bowled wine glass with basal flutes, on a double series opaque twist stem, 6½in. high. (Christie's S. Ken)
          $230 £143

A Lynn wine glass, the opaque twist stem composed of a lace corkscrew enclosed by a six-ply spiral band, 14.2cm. (Phillips London) $816 £480

A baluster wine glass, supported on a wide angular knop over a basal knop and enclosing an elongated tear, 15cm. (Phillips London) $515 £320

A Jacobite airtwist drinking glass on airtwist stem and conical foot, 5¼in. high. (Christie's S. Ken) $808 £528

WINE GLASSES

A wine flute, on an opaque twist stem composed of a gauze corkscrew encircled by three opaque spiral strands, 19.2cm. (Phillips London)
$451 £280

An unusual cordial glass with waisted bell bowl, on an opaque twist stem, 16cm. (Phillips London) $255 £150

An engaved opaque-twist cordial-glass of Jacobite significance, the funnel bowl with two flower-sprays, circa 1770, 16.5cm. high. (Christie's) $1028 £605

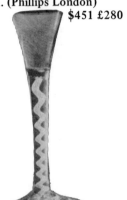

A wine glass with wrythen-moulded trumpet bowl on single series enamel gauze twist stem, 6in. (Russell Baldwin & Bright) $742 £450

A gilt-decorated wine glass with rounded funnel bowl, gilt in the manner of the Giles Workshop with sprays and sprigs of flowers and an insect, on an opaque twist stem composed of a central glaze cable encircled by a multiply spiral, 14.4cm. (Phillips) $644 £400

A cordial glass with pineapple-moulded funnel bowl on double series air-twist stem, 7in. (Russell Baldwin & Bright) $907 £550

A baluster wine glass, the rounded funnel bowl with solid base containing a small tear, on a baluster stem also containing a tear and with basal knop, above a domed and folded foot, 15cm. (Phillips) $805 £500

A wine glass, the bell bowl set on a multi-series airtwist stem with vermicular collar, circa 1750. (Bearne's) $515 £320

A two-colour opaque-twist wine-glass, the cobalt-blue ogee bowl supported on a clear stem with swelling waist knop filled with spiral threads, circa 1765, 16.5cm. high. (Christie's) $24310 £14300

WINE GLASSES

A Mercury cordial-glass, the stem with a spiral air core within a seven-ply spiral, circa 1750, 16.5cm. high.
(Christie's) $748   £440

A Balustroid wine-glass of 'Kit-Kat' type and drawn-trumpet shape, set on an inverted baluster knop, circa 1720, 16.5cm. high.
(Christie's) $748   £440

A Beilby opaque-twist wine-glass, the funnel bowl enamelled in white with a border of fruiting-vine, circa 1770, 15cm. high.
(Christie's) $1683   £990

A pan topped drinking glass on multi spiral opaque twist stem, 6$^{1}/_{2}$ in. high.
(Christie's S. Ken.) $436   £264

An attractive Newcastle light baluster wine glass, the funnel bowl engraved with the arms of Utrecht, the reverse with a shining star, on a cusped and a small ball knop above a baluster section with two rows of air bubbles and a basal knop, wide conical foot, 19cm.
(Phillips) $1577   £980

A rare ratafia glass on 3-piece knopped stem with double series enamel twist section, 7$^{1}/_{4}$ in.
(Russell Baldwin & Bright)
                    $5775   £3500

An engraved wine glass, the bell bowl with an encircling band of vines on a shoulder knopped multi-series airtwist stem, circa 1750.
(Bearne's) $434   £270

A cordial glass with drawn trumpet bowl, on a mercurial air twist stem, 18cm. (Phillips London) $451   £280

A Jacobite drawn-trumpet wine-glass, the bowl engraved with a six-petalled rose, mid-18th century, 16cm. high.
(Christie's) $1028   £605

A Continental rectangular enamelled gold snuff box, engraved with a bear hunt, 19th century, 3¼ in. long. (Christie's London)
$3,227 £1,980

A 9 carat gold cigarette case by Boucheron, hand finished to simulate leather, London 1962, 8.5 x 9cm. (Henry Spencer) $608 £380

An antique gold rectangular vinaigrette, decorated with flowers, shells and scrollwork, the grill pierced and engraved with flowers and thistles, 1¼ in. (Christie's S. Ken) $591 £352

A Louis XVI vari-coloured gold paste-set scent-bottle, formed from a sword grip, Paris, 1775-81, with the décharge of Jean-Baptiste Fouache, 4¹/₂ in. high. (Christie's) $4250   £2640

A pair of gold fundame kobako modelled as male and female Mandarin ducks (oshidori), their plumage decorated in gold, silver and black hiramakie, late 19th century, both about 18.4cm. long. (Christie's London) $7,299 £4,620

A English gold snuff-box formed as a pug seated on a plinth, the hinged base set with a bloodstone matrix, circa 1750, 3¹/₄ in. high. (Christie's) $7969   £4950

A stylish French gold vesta case, with rounded top and base set with bands of calibre set rubies, flanking a row of five small diamonds. (Phillips London) $522 £320

A gold equestrian statue of Henri IV of France, set on a rectangular lapis lazuli base, 19th century, 394gr., 4¼ in. long. (Christie's London)
$8,965 £5,500

A circular enamelled gold pill-box, the cover with a zodiacal sign of Taurus, probably American, late 19th century, 2¹/₈ in. diam. (Christie's) $1417   £880

A horn flask engraved with crown, *GR* cypher, Hanoverian motto figure of a Grenadier and a map marked *Road to Lexington.* (Christie's S. Ken) $336 £220

An Anglo-Indian horn tea caddy of sarcophagus shape, the ivory and ebony interior fitted with two hinged zinc lined caddies, 15in. long. (Christie's London) $686 £440

Hammered copper presentation cup with three horn handles, Thomas G. Brown & Sons, New York, circa 1903, 6¼in. high. (Robt. W. Skinner Inc.) $200 £123

An engraved powder horn, the body decorated with a map of Fort Sant Mark, showing various buildings. (Phillips) $2310 £1400

A Rhinoceros horn libation cup carved with two male figures seated under a willow-type tree beside a stream watching two horses at play, 17cm. wide. (Christie's London) $7722 £4950

An engraved Masonic horn cup, American, early 19th century, three circular reserves with Masonic iconography, coloured red and black, 3¾in. high. (Christie's New York) $330 £207

A Chinese rhinoceros horn libation cup carved in relief with officials and sages wearing tabbed hats, the handle formed as pine boughs, 16/17th century, 3½in. high. (Christie's S. Ken) $5,738 £3,520

Engraved Siege of Boston Rhyme powderhorn, Charles Town Camp, (Massachusetts) dated 1775, curving cow horn engraved on one side, 14in. long. (Skinner Inc.) $5,500 £3,374

A Chinese rhinoceros horn libation cup carved in relief with a figure teaching children, the handle formed as pine boughs coming over the rim of the cup, 17/18th century, 5in. high. (Christie's S. Ken) $9,861 £6,050

A 19th century Russian icon in
two registers, the upper part
with the Godhead, 17½in. x
12½in., in a gilt surround.
(Christie's S. Ken.) $1180 £715

18th century Russian icon
Eliseus, 27 x 24.5cm.
(Auktionshaus Arnold)
$883 £573

South Russian icon of the
Praise of the Mother God,
early 19th century (losses,
flaking), 9¼in. wide. (Robt. W.
Skinner Inc.) $300 £183

A circa 1800 Russian icon of
Christ Pantocrator, full length,
flanked by Saints, Patriarchs
and Forefathers, 17½ x 13¾in.
(Christie's S. Ken)$1,589 £935

Russian icon of The Virgin of
the Sign, Moscow, circa 1905,
Virgin and Child below the
Lord Savaoth, 8¼in. wide.
(Robt. W. Skinner Inc.)
$1,200 £732

Russian icon of The Virgin and
Child, 18th century, with an
embossed silver riza, Moscow
1787, 6¾in. wide. (Robt. W.
Skinner Inc.) $650 £396

An 18th century unusually large
Russian icon on canvas of The
Transfiguration, 62in. x 47½in.
(Christie's S. Ken.)
$8712 £5280

A 19th century Russian icon of
the Mother of God of Kazan,
overlaid with a silver oklad,
9in. x 7in.
(Christie's S. Ken.) $998 £605

19th century Russian icon of
The Three Saints of Marriage,
31.5 x 25.5cm. (Auktionshaus
Arnold) $442 £287

Russian icon, The Virgin of Vladimir, with ormolu oklad, 32.5 x 26.5cm. (Auktionshaus Arnold) $1,104 £717

A 19th century Greek icon of the Resurrection, 15¾ x 12in. (Christie's S. Ken) $785 £462

Multiple icon, Russian, 19th century, 35 x 30.5cm. (Auktionshaus Arnold)
$773 £502

Russian Icon of St. Nicholas, late 19th century, riza by Ovchinnikov, Moscow, 1884, silver-gilt with foliate cloisonne enamel border, 10½ in. high. (Skinner Inc) $1700 £1103

A 19th century Russian icon of the Deisis, The Enthroned Christ with intercessionary figures, 12in. x 10in. (Christie's S. Ken.) $817   £495

A 19th century Russian icon of the Smolenskaya Mother of God, 8³/₄ in. x 7in. (Christie's S. Ken.) $871   £528

19th century Russian icon, Moscow stamp, maker's mark GX, St Nicholas, gilded silver oklad, 31 x 26cm. (Auktionshaus Arnold) $1,877 £1,219

A 19th century Russian icon of the Archangel Michael with sword, 18¹/₂ in. x 10¹/₂ in. (Christie's S. Ken.) $907   £550

A 19th century Russian icon of the Nativity, the Christ Child and Mother of God with angels and saints, 9in. x 7in. (Christie's S. Ken.) $327   £198

A four case inro decorated with kiku flowers and stylised kotobuki characters in hiramakie on a fundame ground, 19th century, 8.5cm., with an attached ojime. (Christie's London) $3,476 £2,200

A large wood tonkotsu decorated with a fruiting persimmon branch tied to a bamboo trellis, unsigned, early 19th century, with gold fundame ojime, 13cm. high. (Christie's London)
$4,866 £3,080

A four case inro decorated with two Bugaku dancers, fundame interiors, signed *Jokasai*, 18th century, with an umimatsu ojime formed as a magatama, 8cm. high. (Christie's London)
$7,821 £4,950

A four case inro decorated in hiramakie and silver and shakudo inlay with a man seated watching a Noh actor in the role of Shojo, signed *Kogyokusai*, 19th century, 8.7cm. high. (Christie's London) $5,214 £3,300

A three case inro decorated in hiramakie on a makibokashi ground with a recumbent ox near a rocky outcrop, unsigned, 19th century, 5.5cm. high. (Christie's London)
$3,128 £1,980

A four case inro decorated in hiramakie, yasuriko and aogai with a group of poem papers in a variety of designs, unsigned, circa 1700, 8.4cm. high. (Christie's London)
$5,214 £3,300

A rare four-case Inro decorated in takamakie, hiramakie and nashiji with groups of seashells and seaweed at low tide, unsigned, 17th century, 6.5cm. high.
(Christie's) $4317   £2750

A four case inro decorated in hiramakie on a fundame ground with a hawk on a pine tree branch, signed *Kajikawa saku*, 19th century, 8.3cm. high. (Christie's London)
$3,128 £1,980

A four-case Rioronuri Inro decorated in red and gold togidashi with dancers performing beneath a blossoming cherry tree, signed Shunsho Masayuki saku, circa 1800, 9cm. high.
(Christie's) $12434   £7920

A Husbands fine walnut bodied table stereoscope with focusing eyepieces and hinged top section. (Christie's S. Ken) $986 £605

A fine 18th century silver Butterfield type dial, signed *N. Bion A Paris,* calibrated for latitudes 40°, 45°, 50° and 55°, 3in. long. (Christie's S. Ken) $1,727 £1,100

A Negretti and Zambra walnut 'Magic Stereoscope' with two pairs of eyepiece lenses, rack and pinion focusing front section and hinged lid. (Christie's S. Ken) $1,255 £770

A Philips 19in. terrestrial globe with brass support and turned oak stand, 28½in. high overall. (Christie's London) $382 £242

A transmitting valve for Brown Boveri T 1000-1, circa 1955, on wooden base. (Auction Team Koeln) $17 £11

A Philips small library globe with brass calibrated scale mount, on ring turned stand, 17in. high. (Christie's S. Ken) $1,434 £880

A Regency mahogany waywiser, the steel dial calibrated for yards, poles, miles and furlongs and signed *Dollond, London,* 52in. high. (Christie's London) $2,152 £1,320

An American Stereoscopic Co. Brewster pattern hand held stereoscope with gilt tooled leather covered body. (Christie's S. Ken) $305 £187

A late 19th century time globe, unsigned, but with monogram, the mechanism within an enamelled casing, 8in. high. (Christie's S. Ken) $1,174 £748

INSTRUMENTS

A late 19th century veterinary medical chest by Day & Sons, Crewe, Ltd., the lid with colourful trade label, 13½in. wide. (Christie's S. Ken) $449 £286

A pair of 19th century aluminium and mother-of-pearl opera glasses, unsigned, probably French. (Christie's S. Ken) $242 £154

A rare 19th century oxidised and lacquered brass drum double sextant, signed, *J. Hicks, London,* 10¼in. wide. (Christie's S. Ken) $1,209 £770

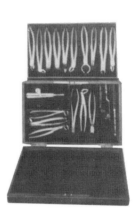

A late 19th century Kaiser-Marine brass sextant of small size stamped *W. Bening Wilhelmshaven,* with ivory scale and vernier. (Christie's S. Ken) $1,209 £770

French inlaid walnut burl and bronze humidor, mid 19th century, mother-of-pearl and brass scroll design, 11½in. diam. (Skinner Inc.) $1,400 £903

A collection of dental forceps by J. Wood, York, in plush lined mahogany case, 14in. wide. (Christie's S. Ken) $414 £264

A surgical instrument case by Aitken, York, containing fifteen various knives, a hook, saw and other instruments, in fitted mahogany case, 23.2cm. wide. (Christie's S. Ken) $553 £352

An early 19th century ebony octant with brass fittings and ivory scale, the makers plate stamped *Spencer, Browning & Co.,* 9¾in. radius. (Christie's S. Ken) $691 £440

A 19th century brass drawing protractor signed *T. B. Winter,* with well divided scale, in fitted case. (Christie's S. Ken) $311 £198

INSTRUMENTS

An 18th century medical saw, the blade secured by rivet and wing nut, and with tapering walnut handle, 9¾in. long. (Christie's S. Ken) $240 £143

A surgical instrument case, containing three saws, three Liston knives, forceps, tourniquet and other items in a fitted mahogany case, 17in. wide. (Christie's S. Ken) $656 £418

A late 18th century brass Culpeper type compound monocular microscope, signed on the circular stage *Dollond London*, 44.2cm. high. (Christie's S. Ken) $1,209 £770

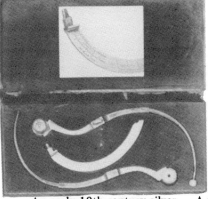

A late 19th century oxidised brass transit theodolite, the dial signed *A. Buccellati, Cairo*, 11½in. high. (Christie's S. Ken) $691 £440

An early 19th century silver cranium measure, signed and engraved in the quadrant arm *To W. A. F. Brown Esqr. Surgeon*, Edinburgh, 1833, 26.4cm. wide. (Christie's S. Ken) $2,418 £1,540

A fine late 19th century composition anatomical figure of the human male, arranged to reveal the internal organs for instructional purposes, 23½in. high. (Christie's S. Ken) $1,036 £660

A rare Crookes' multi-sphere tube, the seven pale green spheres interconnected with five bulbs, 12¼in. high. (Christie's S. Ken) $294 £187

An early 19th century 12in. celestial globe with label and ebonised stand (globe and horizon ring repaired). (Christie's S. Ken) $2,072 £1,320

A fine oxidised and lacquered brass compound monocular microscope, signed *C. Baker*, with rack and pinion course focusing, 13in. high. (Christie's S. Ken) $484 £308

INSTRUMENTS

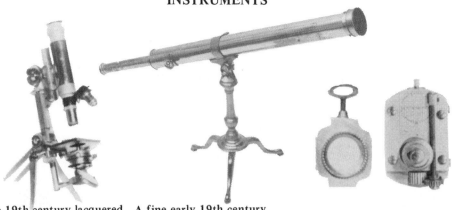

A late 19th century lacquered brass folding microscope by J. Swift & Son, with rack and pinion focusing double nosepiece. (Christie's S. Ken)
$347 £220

A fine early 19th century lacquered brass 2in. refracting telescope, signed on the end plate *Grubb London*, 31in. long. (Christie's S. Ken)
$1,382 £880

A brass epicycloidal chuck signed Bonsall, Marshall & Guy, with operating ring. (Christie's S. Ken)
$314 £187

A black enamelled and satin chrome binocular microscope by E. Leitz, Wetzlar, with rack and pinion coarse and micrometer fine focusing, 16in. high. (Christie's S. Ken) $382 £242

A black enamelled microtome by Bausch & Lomb Optical Co., with three cased blades, 13½in. long. (Christie's S. Ken)
$208 £132

An early 19th century lacquered brass Culpeper type microscope, with draw tube focusing, 13in. high. (Christie's S. Ken)
$887 £528

A late 19th century lacquered and oxidised brass microscope by W. Watson and Sons, with rack-and-pinion focusing, 13in. high. (Christie's S. Ken)
$314 £187

A terrestrial globe, by Gilman Joslin, Boston, Massachusetts, early 19th century, the stand on ring and baluster turned legs joined by an X-stretcher, 14in. high. (Christie's New York) $1,650 £1,037

A wooden stereo graphoscope and photograph viewer with white metal decoration and five stereocards. (Christie's S. Ken) $202 £121

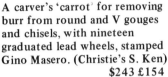

A carver's 'carrot' for removing burr from round and V gouges and chisels, with nineteen graduated lead wheels, stamped Gino Masero. (Christie's S. Ken) $243 £154

A fine brass and black lacquered single draw Brewster Kaleidoscope with signed eyepiece *P. Carpenter. Sole maker.* (Christie's S. Ken) $1,470 £880

A rare Crookes' watering can tube, on turned wood stand, 17½in. high. (Christie's S. Ken) $864 £550

A brass 19th century simple theodolite bubble level, on mahogany circular base, 9½in. high. (Christie's S. Ken) $185 £110

A rare Irish cannon scribe, signed *Lynch, Dublin,* the instrument made of brass with steel feet, contained in the original mahogany case. (Lawrence Fine Arts) $753 £462

An early 20th century black painted twin cylinder vertical hot air engine by J. Falk, Germany, 27.5cm. high. (Henry Spencer) $379 £240

An oxidised brass theodolite, by Elliott Bros., the telescope with rack and pinion focusing, 29.8cm. (Lawrence Fine Arts) $932 £572

Gaumont, Paris, a 45 x 107mm. mahogany bodied table stereoscope with internal mechanism and slide holders. (Christie's S. Ken) $598 £352

A vacuum pump, the double action mechanism mounted between tapering brass pillars, on a rectangular base with bracket feet, 42cm. high. (Henry Spencer) $702 £450

INSTRUMENTS

A dovetailed steel panel plane by Mathieson with rosewood infill and handles, gunmetal lever and Mathieson cutter, 15½in. long. (Christie's S. Ken) $156 £99

A fine mahogany-bodied Kaleidoscope with lacquered brass eyepiece stamped W. Harris & Co., 50 Holborn, London. (Christie's S. Ken.) $5445 £3300

A Norris A14 annealed iron tapered heel smoother with iron knobbed 1913 twin thread patent adjustment. (Christie's S. Ken) $139 £88

A painted brass bodied kaleidoscope with rotating glass holder and mounted on a three legged stand. (Christie's S. Ken) $1,683 £990

A fine quality wax model of the human head, in glazed ebonised case, 9¾in. high. (Christie's S. Ken) $414 £264

A late 19th century 3in. terrestrial globe by Malby, 37 Parker Street, London, dated 1877, 4½in. high. (Christie's S. Ken) $1,900 £1,210

A mahogany and brass inlaid barograph, the lacquered brass instrument in a glazed case with drawer below, 1ft. 5in. wide. (Phillips) $1237 £750

A mammoth walnut combined graphoscope and stereoscope with ornate carved wood decoration, front panel with plaque *E. Ziegler, Bd. des Capucines 35, Paris.* (Christie's S. Ken) $524 £308

A burr walnut Brewster pattern stereoscope with rack and pinion focusing, shaped lens hood mounted on hinged lens section. (Christie's S. Ken) $337 £198

A Stanley 72 adjustable cham-fer plane with standard nose section and rosewood handles. (Christie's S. Ken) $156 £99

A rare Norris A11 adjustable mitre plane, the dovetailed steel stock with rosewood rear infill, the sole 10¼in. cutter, width 2¼in. (Christie's S. Ken) $4,345 £2,750

A fine Votra stereo transparency viewer. (Christie's S. Ken) $654 £385

A mahogany pedestal dual viewer stereoscope with split hinged lid and hinged wood mounted glass cover. (Christie's S. Ken) $524 £308

A 19th century brass binocular telescope by Broadhurst Clarkson & Co London, in fitted mahogany carrying case. (Andrew Hartley Fine Arts) $1237 £750

A Brewster-pattern hand-held stereoscope with Japanese lacquer-work decoration depicting flying storks and trees. (Christie's S. Ken.) $726 £440

 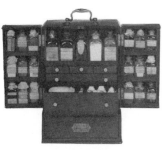 

Early 20th century oak cased barograph by J H Steward, 406 & 457 The Strand, London, in oak case with drawer to base. (G.A. Key) $660 £400

An early 19th century mahogany domestic medicine chest, the double doors, each containing nine bottles, 1ft. 7¹/₄in. high. (Phillips) $3960 £2400

A walnut bodied stereo-graphoscope with front hinged eyepiece section and rear hinged ground glass screen. (Christie's S. Ken) $287 £176

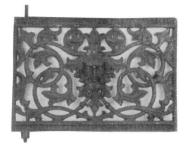

A wrought iron triangular clamping device with rack and pinion and button release pawl, 10in. radius, 18th century. (Christie's S. Ken) $52 £33

Oriental cast iron gate, Baltimore area, 19th century, 20in. high, 28in. long. (Skinner Inc.) $700 £427

A very early hand cast iron with welded on handle, possibly French, circa 1700, 15cm. long. (Auction Team Koeln) $152 £94

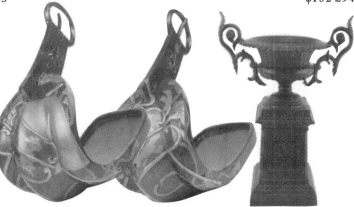

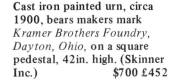

A polychrome cast iron panel of the Royal Arms as used in Scotland, the lion rampant quartered twice, 40in. wide. (Christie's S. Ken.)$1906 £1155

A pair of iron stirrups decorated in takamakie, hiramakie and heidatsu with sahari, hossu and gunsen, the last decorated with dragons in clouds, unsigned, 19th century, each 29cm. long. (Christie's London) $5,214 £3,300

Cast iron painted urn, circa 1900, bears makers mark *Kramer Brothers Foundry, Dayton, Ohio,* on a square pedestal, 42in. high. (Skinner Inc.) $700 £452

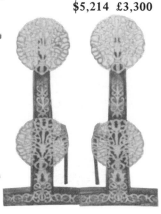

A pair of iron gates, each panel centred by scrolling iron work applied with repoussé foliate rosettes, 68in. high x 32$\frac{1}{2}$in. wide. (Christie's) $581 £352

A pair of iron and brass Fire-Dogs, possibly a design by Ernest Gimson, each tapering upright with raised sides, 68.6cm. high. (Phillips) $1280 £800

A brass and iron footman, 19th century, the shaped and pierced top above a conforming apron, 9$\frac{1}{2}$in. high. (Christie's) $440 £275

Elihu Vedder wrought iron fireback, New York, 1882, The Sun God, cast with the face of a man surrounded by flowing hair, 27¾in. wide. (Skinner Inc.) $3,100 £1,914

A cold painted iron Vesta case in the form of a German soldier, standing wearing a spiked helmet, trench coat and rucksack, 3in. high. (Spencer's) $140 £85

A pair of cast iron andirons, with scrolled capitals above a shield shaped crest cast with fleur de lys on a trefoil arch, 21in. high. (Christie's London) $967 £572

Pair of painted cast iron garden figures, Whitman Foundry, Whitman, Massachusetts, late 19th/early 20th century, 64in. high. (Skinner Inc.) $8500 £5185

A wrought iron brazier, the circular bowl on scrolling column shaft and tripod base, late 17th/early 18th century, 22½in. high. (Christie's London) $2,479 £1,540

A pair of painted cast iron hitching post finials, American, second half 19th century, each modelled as a horse head, 12¾in. high. (Christie's) $1430 £895

A wrought iron fire screen, in the manner of Edgar Brandt, with openwork form of stylised foliage, 91.5cm. high. (Phillips London) $489 £300

A painted cast iron trade sign, American, 19th century, modelled in the form of a top hat, 7in. high. (Christie's New York) $2,200 £1,383

Cast iron stove plate, Pennsylvania, c. 1750, 'Dance of Death', pattern, the inscription translated 'Here fights with me the bitter death/And brings me in death's stress' 22in. x 24in. (Skinner Inc.) $500 £305

An early 19th century German carved ivory Corpus Christi, his head lowered to his right, the perizonium tied with cord to his left, 16in. high.
(Christie's S. Ken.)
$1815   £1100

A 19th century Dieppe ivory bust of Queen Henrietta Maria opening to reveal a triptych depicting the execution of her husband Charles I, 12cm. high. (Christie's London)
$567 £352

'Futuristic Dancer', a gilt-bronze and ivory figure cast and carved from a model by Gerdago.
(Christie's) $9740   £6050

A very fine German carved ivory powder flask, carved in low relief with a small circular central frame within four larger oval ones, the screws and spring retaining their original blueing, late 17th century, 5½in. high. (Christie's S. Ken)
$17,380 £11,000

A pair of early 19th century Dieppe ivory figures of Rousseau and Voltaire, attributed to Antoine or Jacques Rosset, 6in. high.
(Christie's S. Ken.)
$2359   £1430

A Japanese ivory carving of an elderly fish seller, standing wearing a shirt and short jerkin, 12½in. high.
(Hamptons Fine Art)
$5610   £3300

An F Preiss ivory figure of a naked boy, seated on a tree stump, removing a splinter from his foot, 11cm. high.
(Henry Spencer) $692 £400

An early 19th century Vizigapatnam ivory veneered two compartmented workbox, the twin rising flap covers centred by a swing carrying handle, 12½in. wide.
(Christie's S. Ken.) $1180   £715

A 19th century ivory presentation spill vase on raised and moulded base, bearing inscription 'Patty and Emma, Inglis & Harris', 11½in. high.
(Andrew Hartley Fine Arts)
$1186   £760

A substantial turned ivory cup and cover, the body with two graduated drum sections of octagonal form with serpentine panels and mouldings, 40cm. high. (Phillips London) $9,180 £6,000

Polychromed scrimshaw Civil War watch fob, Massachusetts, second half 19th century, heightened in red, blue and green, 2in. high. (Skinner Inc.) $350 £213

A 19th century French ivory tankard, with figures of two Bacchantes on the lid (one hand missing), 43.5cm. (Christie's London) $6,375 £3,960

A 19th century French ivory statuette of Joan of Arc, opening to reveal a triptych with Joan of Arc pleading before the King, 14.5cm. high. (Christie's London) $1,151 £715

A pair of 19th century French ivory triptych figures of Henry VIII and Anne Boleyn, the hinged fronts revealing court scenes, 8¼in. high. (Christie's S. Ken) $2,059 £1,320

A Japanese sectional marine ivory figure of a travelling entertainer holding a balalaika over one shoulder, 32cm. high. (Henry Spencer) $684 £420

A 19th century French ivory statuette of a lady in 18th century costume, wearing a plumed hat, 37.5cm. high. (Christie's London) $3,896 £2,420

An early 19th century Vizigapatnam ivory veneered tea caddy, the moulded cavetto lid and sides with engraved architectural landscapes, 10½in. wide. (Christie's S. Ken.) $2269 £1375

A 19th century French ivory group of classically dressed musicians and a maiden supporting a basket of fruit on her head, 8in. high. (Christie's S. Ken.) $6897 £4180

A Victorian gold hinged bangle, the front with a row of half pearls flanked by bar piercing, the reverse plain. (Lawrence Fine Arts) $1,235 £792

A pair of circular cut diamond bow shaped diamond clips, the centres set with diamond quatrefoils. (Bonhams) $2,198 £1,400

A Theodor Fahrner Art Deco brooch with central faceted plaque of rose quartz flanked by two batons set with marcasites, 4.2cm. wide. (Phillips London) $1,193 £780

An amusing 1950s chrysoprase, ruby diamond and gold Daffy Duck brooch. (Bonhams) $440 £280

A fine pair of ruby and diamond flower cluster earrings, oval shaped two stone ruby centres with a border of brilliant and marquise shaped diamonds. (Bonhams) $11,050 £6,500

An Arts and Crafts peacock brooch, designed in the manner of Ashbee for the Guild of Handicraft, 6cm. long. (Phillips London) $796 £520

A Victorian garnet pendant brooch of shaped open scroll form engraved with foliage. (Lawrence Fine Arts) $1,201 £770

Brooch, the spray of cabochon sapphire buds held by pave set circular cut diamond leaves. (Bonhams) $942 £600

An Art Nouveau pendant formed as a winged maiden, her outspread wings embellished with shaded pink and green translucent enamels, 4.5cm. wide. (Phillips London) $765 £500

An emerald and diamond crescent brooch, centred by a square cut emerald flanked by graduating circular emeralds. (Lawrence Fine Arts) $326 £209

A large citrine brooch, the rectangular cut citrine with canted angles, and each side with an engraved gold block. (Lawrence Fine Arts) $343 £220

A Georg Jensen white metal brooch designed by Arno Malinowski, the pierced oval decorated with a kneeling hind. (Christie's London) $107 £66

A Guild of Handicrafts Ltd., cloak clasp, the design attributed to Charles Robert Ashbee, its body picked out with opal cabochons, 13cm. wide. (Phillips London) $1,377 £900

An attractive diamond roundel brooch, the centre brilliant cut stone within a surround of thirteen smaller stones. (Lawrence Fine Arts) $3,432 £2,200

A French gold, garnet and pearl bracelet, the head centred by a cabochon oval garnet on a slide. (Lawrence Fine Arts) $1,853 £1,188

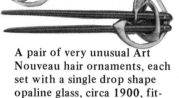

A very attractive Edwardian baroque pearl and rose-cut diamond turtle pendant. (Bonhams) $884 £520

A pair of very unusual Art Nouveau hair ornaments, each set with a single drop shape opaline glass, circa 1900, fitted Liberty case. (Bonhams) $6,460 £3,800

A large Arts and Crafts pendant with a large piece of turquoise matrix suspended from an openwork foliate mount, 8cm. long. (Phillips London) $306 £200

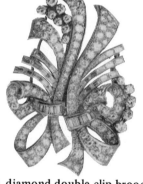

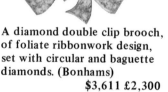

A Georg Jensen white metal brooch, the pierced circle composed of four leaves, with central cabochon, usual marks. (Christie's London) $681 £418

A diamond double clip brooch, of foliate ribbonwork design, set with circular and baguette diamonds. (Bonhams) $3,611 £2,300

A good cameo brooch, carved with the bust of a young woman, in a gold frame. (Lawrence Fine Arts) $2,093 £1,342

An antique gold cannetille, ruby and turquoise brooch, in the original fitted case. (Lawrence Fine Arts) $686 £440

A Victorian diamond and garnet brooch, hung with two carved ivory fuchsia and gem set pendants. (Bonhams) $707 £450

A fine and attractive Edwardian diamond brooch, central brilliant cut diamond with diamond and rose diamond set quatrefoil surround. (Bonhams) $2,295 £1,350

Platinum and diamond ring, an emerald cut diamond weighing 4.09ct., surrounded by 18 marquise diamonds. (Skinner Inc.) $43,000 £27,044

Pearl and onyx ring, containing one pear shaped green onyx surmounted by clusters of small multi-coloured pearls, bead set with 24 round diamonds. (Skinner Inc.) $1,500 £943

Sapphire and diamond ring, a centre oval sapphire weighing approx. 3.45ct., surrounded by two rows of round diamond beads set into the platinum mounting. (Skinner Inc.) $4,200 £2,642

Victorian gold locket, heart shaped with applied gold detail highlighted by pearls, turquoise and diamonds. (Skinner Inc.) $1,700 £1,069

An unusual gold coloured metal locket in the form of a portmanteau, unfolding to reveal six oval photograph frames, 1850. (Henry Spencer) $840 £500

Victorian locket, 14ct. gold with platinum screws, centred by a carved onyx cameo of a man. (Skinner Inc.) $900 £566

An attractive mid-Victorian lapel pin, the circular porcelain panel painted in colours by W. Essex, dated 1862. (Henry Spencer) $272 £170

Pink tourmaline and gold pendant, attributed to Margaret Vant, Boston, circa 1925, shield shaped open gold filigree form, 2in. wide. (Skinner Inc.) $850 £525

Victorian citrine brooch, containing one large oval faceted citrine set into a triple frame with engraved decoration, stamped 18ct. (Skinner Inc.) $800 £503

Art Deco star sapphire and diamond ring, centred by one oval cabochon star sapphire, approx. 25.00ct., surrounded by 20 baguette and 22 square cut diamonds. (Skinner Inc.) $5,500 £3,459

Victorian 15ct. gold brooch, of ribbon design. (Skinner Inc.) $425 £267

Art Nouveau pin, 14ct. gold, depicting the face of a woman with flowing hair. (Skinner Inc.) $375 £236

Victorian 18ct. gold locket, centred by a carved black onyx cameo, edged by two natural pearls. (Skinner Inc.) $1,100 £692

An Arts and Crafts enamelled pendant, with enamelled panel depicting in naturalistic colours the profile head and shoulders of a girl, 3.5cm. (Phillips London) $424 £260

Antique painted miniature pendant, gouache on paper, signed *E. Pescador,* set in a 14ct. gold bezel, European hallmarks. (Skinner Inc.) $350 £220

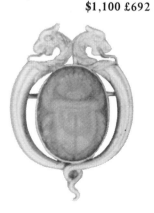

Egyptian Revival pin, 14ct. gold, centred by a carved chrysophrase scarab, framed by a pair of gold griffins. (Skinner Inc.) $750 £472

Victorian diamond brooch, 14ct. gold base, set with table cut diamonds with three pear shaped drops. (Skinner Inc.) $2,100 £1,321

Centaur pin, David Webb, 40 round brilliant cut diamonds, set in platinum, total weight approx. 2.50ct. (Skinner Inc.) $2,500 £1,572

Diamond and synthetic ruby retro style ring, containing one round old European cut diamond weighing approx. 1.35ct. (Skinner Inc.)
$1,600 £1,006

18ct. yellow gold and diamond pin, executed by Edward Oakes, Boston, early 20th century, approximate weight 5ct. (Skinner Inc.)
$6,250 £3,858

Art Deco sapphire and diamond ring, with seven round diamonds, total weight approx. .60ct. (Skinner Inc.) $950 £597

Platinum, diamond and sapphire ring, containing one sapphire approx. weight 1.80ct. and one diamond approx. weight 2.05ct. (Skinner Inc.)
$9,000 £5,660

18ct. gold and diamond ear-clips, Van Cleef & Arpels, France, gold spirals centred by a cluster of 19 round brilliant cut diamonds. (Skinner Inc.)
$5,100 £3,208

Emerald and diamond ring, a cabochon emerald surrounded by 16 round diamonds, total weight approx. .60ct. (Skinner Inc.) $900 £566

A Norwegian Arts and Crafts brooch of elliptical shape embossed with a bird flanked by three green stained chalce-dony cabochons, 9.5cm. long. (Phillips London) $367 £240

Victorian suite of carved onyx cameo jewellery, 14ct. gold plaquard shape with applied gold bead work. (Skinner Inc.)
$1,300 £818

An attractive Edwardian pearl and peridot open work brooch, with a faceted tear-drop peri-dot. (Henry Spencer)
$748 £440

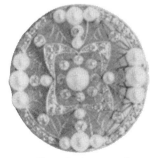

Art Nouveau pin of a peacock against a sunset background, 14ct. gold. (Skinner Inc.)
$350 £220

Edwardian platinum and diamond circle pin, set with numerous diamonds and en-hanced by 15 pearls. (Skinner Inc.) $2,300 £1,447

An attractive gold and enamel portrait brooch of canted rect-angular form, set with numerous small rose cut diamonds. (Henry Spencer)
$347 £220

Frank Gardner Hale gold and silver brooch with opals, Boston, circa 1917, a gold scroll filigree setting, 1½in. long. (Skinner Inc.) $2,300 £1,420

Bi-colour 14ct. gold bow brooch, circa 1940, set with six diamonds in platinum, 10 dwt., hallmarked. (Skinner Inc.) $750 £472

A seven stone diamond ring, the central brilliant cut stone of 1.08 carats, flanked by three smaller stones, gold shank. (Henry Spencer) $1,920 £1,200

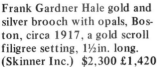

An emerald and diamond ring, the square cut emerald claw set and flanked by two brilliant cut diamonds. (Henry Spencer) $2,480 £1,550

Gold brooch, Verdura, France, in the form of a snail, set with an emerald bead. (Skinner Inc.) $5,500 £3,459

Antique diamond bow brooch, circa 1800, containing 76 rose, table and mine cut diamonds. (Skinner Inc.) $1,600 £1,006

Antique diamond and pearl brooch, set with approx. 135 old mine cut diamonds and centred by one 9½mm. pearl. (Skinner Inc.) $4,600 £2,893

Large 9ct. gold framed cameo brooch depicting a young lady with eagle feeding from a bowl. (G. A. Key) $561 £330

Demantoid, fire opal and diamond pin/pendant, circa 1900, centred by one buff top, navette shaped Mexican fire opal. (Skinner Inc.) $1,700 £1,069

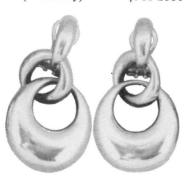

18ct. gold and enamel brooch, Cartier, an enamelled scarecrow highlighted by two diamonds. (Skinner Inc.) $1,600 £1,006

18ct. gold double hoop earpendants, Italy, Cartier, 21.5dwt. (Skinner Inc.) $1,200 £755

A very attractive sapphire and diamond fob watch, suspended from a sapphire and diamond bow brooch, case by Mappin & Webb. (Bonhams) $3,297 £2,100

Micro mosaic pendant, oval shaped, of a dog, with blue glass frame mounted in 14ct. gold. (Skinner Inc.) $600 £377

An unusual and rare Loetz glass pendant of lobed oviform, exhibiting random splashes of violet and peacock blue iridescence, 5.3cm. long. (Phillips London) $765 £500

An historical silver-gilt and citrine watch fob pendant, early 19th century, according to the affidavit this fob descended directly from Paul Revere. (Christie's) $3850 £2421

Art Deco platinum and diamond brooch, set with 62 old European cut diamonds and three single cut diamonds, approx. 4.00ct. (Skinner Inc.) $3,400 £2,138

A Victorian cameo brooch, the oval shell carved with the head of Jupiter in profile, maker's mark C&F. (Lawrence) $1270 £770

Buccellati pin, 24ct. gold branch design with platinum leaves set with rose cut diamonds and four round cabochon sapphires, marked *Buccellati Italy 1000.* (Skinner Inc.) $1,800 £1,132

A Liberty & Co. gold and enamelled pendant, designed by Archibald Knox, suspended from a Liberty gold and enamelled brooch, 8.5cm. long. (Phillips London) $2,754 £1,800

An Arts and Craft style moonstone set pendant, set with three cabochon polished moonstones and hung with three tear shaped moonstones. (Spencer's) $280 £170

A carved amber pendant by Sybil Dunlop, the foliate drop suspended from a scroll and foliate mount, set with cabochon amber detail. (Christie's London) $2,772 £1,650

LAQUER

A Ming red lacquer rectangular box and cover carved with a scholar and three attendants in the foreground of a river landscape, 16th/17th century, 13.6cm. wide.
(Christie's London)

$8580   £5500

An elaborately carved and lacquered model of three figures in a bird prowed boat, signed on a red lacquer tablet *Shoun,* Meiji period, 45cm. long.
(Christie's London)

$9,559 £6,050

Japanese lacquer and copper tabako-bon, 19th century, lacquered surfaces decorated with finely detailed cranes, pines and boats, 9in. wide.
(Skinner Inc.) $2,000 £1,250

Pair of Japanese lacquer vases, late 19th century, baluster form, decorated with a gold hiramakie and takamakie dragon, $10^{3}/_{8}$ in. high.
(Skinner Inc) $13000   £8074

A pair of lacquer bowls in roiro-nuri and tame-nuri richly decorated in hiramakie, hirame and nashiji with massed butterflies, unsigned, 19th century, each 15.5cm. diam. (Christie's London) $5,040 £3,190

A miniature tansu in the form of a silver temple lantern decorated with cloisonné enamels with a variety of subjects in Shibayama inlay, unsigned, late 19th century, 21.5cm. high.
(Christie's) $10707   £6820

A red lacquer pentafoil floral box and cover carved to the centre of the cover with Shoulao flying on a crane above three other Daoist Immortals, 17th/18th century, 25cm. wide.
(Christie's London)

$3775   £2420

A handsome lacquered wood saddle frame decorated in takamakie, hiramakie and yasuriko-nashiji with red capped cranes on a bekko patterned ground, signed with a kakihan, 19th century, 37cm. long. (Christie's London)

$6,083 £3,850

A large Shibuichi-Ji Natsume decorated in coloured takamakie and gold nashiji, unsigned, probably school of Shibata Zeshin, 19th century, 10.7cm. high.
(Christie's) $2590   £1650

LAMPS

Pairpoint seascape table lamp, colourfully reverse painted Directoire shade with expansive full round ocean scene, 16in. diam. (Robt. W. Skinner Inc.) $3,600 £2,236

Wrought iron lamp with mica shades, possibly England, early 20th century, cast leaf detail, unsigned, 17½in. high. (Robt. W. Skinner Inc.) $1,600 £982

Pairpoint seascape boudoir lamp, reverse painted dome shade with whimsical Viking ships, 14½in. high. (Robt. W. Skinner Inc.) $1,600 £994

Tiffany bronze lamp with crocus shade, with three prong shade holder and six footed bulbous platform base, 22½in. high, shade diam. 16in. (Robt. W. Skinner Inc.) $16,000 £9,938

A Daum satin finished table lamp, the knopped mushroom cap shade with quatrefoil border, 46.5cm. high. (Christie's London) $10,399 £6,380

Handel parrot lamp, domical Teroma glass shade signed *Handel 7128,* and by artist *Bedigie,* handpainted interior with three colourful parrots, 18in. diam. (Robt. W. Skinner Inc.) $23,000 £14,286

A Legras glass table lamp having a domed shade, painted in coloured enamels with a pair of budgerigars and foliage, 36.5cm. high. (Phillips London) $1,271 £780

Tiffany bronze ten-light lily lamp, slender decumbent stem shade holders above lily pad stepped platform base with broad leaves, buds and vines, 16½in. high. (Robt. W. Skinner Inc.) $13,000 £8,075

A Sabino frosted glass table lamp, the shade formed as a triple cascade of water supported on three metal arms, 19.5cm. high. (Phillips London) $367 £240

568

Handel reverse painted lamp, hand painted on the interior with wide multicoloured border band of predominantly lavender and fuchsia red scrolls, shade diam. 18in. (Robt. W. Skinner Inc.) $4,000 £2,484

A Lalique blue stained table lamp, the shade moulded with six dancing maidens wearing classical dresses, 23.5cm. width of shade. (Christie's London)
$12,909 £7,920

Leaded glass table lamp, with four repeating clusters of lavender iris blossoms and green spiked leaves, shade diam. 18in. (Robt. W. Skinner Inc.) $450 £280

A Handel leaded glass table lamp, the domed circular shade having rows of honey coloured marbled glass segments on the upper section, 59cm. high. (Phillips London)$4,896 £3,200

A Victorian gilt metal shaving/ reading lamp, fitted inside with a gimbal candle holder, 20cm. high from base to top, circa 1860. (Phillips London)
$349 £220

Leaded glass table lamp, attributed to Handel, of mottled green brickwork banded with border of bright pink apple blossoms, 23in. high. (Robt. W. Skinner Inc.)
$1,000 £621

French cameo glass lamp, cut with Roman gladiators and Art Deco borders, supported on three arm metal fixture 19in. high. (Robt. W. Skinner Inc.) $1,700 £1,056

A gilt bronze table lamp cast in the form of a frog with its arms outstretched, the floral motifs and frog's eyes studded with ruby glass cabachoms, 14½in. high. (Christie's S. Ken)
$3,376 £1,980

A Le Verre Francais acid etched cameo table lamp, the milky white acid textured glass overlaid with amber fruiting vines, 46cm. high. (Christie's London)
$7,172 £4,400

English cameo glass miniature lamp, attributed to Thomas Webb & Sons, cameo cut and carved. 9in. high. (Robt. W. Skinner Inc.) $7,000 £4,348

Art Deco Daum style table lamp, on rectangular silvered base, the club shaped frosted glass shades sitting on out-stretched arms, circa 1925, 29cm. high. (Kunsthaus am Museum) $973 £559

Copper and mica piano lamp, attributed to Benedict Studios, East Syracuse, New York, circa 1910, unsigned, 21½in. high. (Skinner Inc.) $1,800 £1,111

A fine Galle carved, table lamp, overlaid with bats in the evening sky, 59cm. high. (Christie's London) $48,411 £29,700

A W.M.F. figural pewter lamp, fashioned as an Art Nouveau maiden with children at her feet, 48cm. high. (Phillips London) $815 £500

An oil lamp, the white overlay ruby glass stem cut with symmetrical designs, surmounted by a clear glass reservoir, 76.5cm. high. (Bearne's) $2092 £1350

Pairpoint blown-out puffy lilac and trellis lamp, reverse painted with four panels of pink and lavender blossoms against latticework back-ground, 18in. diam. (Robt. W. Skinner Inc.) $5,500 £3,416

A Galle triple overlay cameo glass table lamp, the greyish body overlaid with lemon, pink and brownish olive glass acid etched with horse chest-nut leaves and blossom, 54cm. high. (Phillips London) $16,830 £11,000

An acid-etched and cut glass cameo table lamp, the mushroom form shade supported by three-branch chromed metal mount, 20½in. high. (Christie's S. Ken) $2479 £1540

Grueby pottery lamp base, Boston, c. 1905, having an elongated neck flaring towards bulbous base, artist signed 'A.L.' for Annie Lingley, 24¼in. high. (Skinner Inc) $3250   £2018

A Guerbe patinated bronze figure, in the form of a table lamp cast as an Art Deco maiden, 51cm. high, base signed. (Lawrence Fine Arts) $834 £528

A Quezal iridescent glass and bronze table lamp, decorated externally with green and silver-blue iridescent feathering, 64cm. high. (Phillips) $2400   £1500

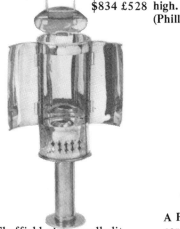

A Galle cameo glass lamp base, overlaid in deep red and etched with bell like flowers and foliage, 10in. high. (Christie's S. Ken) $597 £385

A Sheffield plate candle lit folding carriage lamp, with suspension hooks, vents, double door and candle holder, 5¾in. high. (Christie's S. Ken) $143 £88

A French Art Nouveau ceramic lamp stand modelled as a maiden in strapless dress holding a shawl billowing behind her head, 26in. high. (Christie's S. Ken) $716 £462

Bradley-Hubbard panelled table lamp, of eight curved ribbed glass panels reverse painted with a border of tulip blossoms and stylised leaf designs, 24in. high. (Robt. W. Skinner Inc.) $900 £559

Cut overlay lamp, with reeded brass standard and marble base, ovals, brass collar, 11in., probably Boston & Sandwich Glass, Sandwich, Massachusetts, 1855-1870. (Robt. W. Skinner Inc.) $400 £248

A Lalique glass and metal table lamp, the frosted pyramidal shade moulded on the inside with stepped bands of beads, 51cm. high. (Phillips) $2160   £1350

Arabesque, a Charlotte Rhead spherical pottery lamp base decorated in a Chinese style pattern of peonies in foliate roundels, 6in. high. (Christie's S. Ken) $163 £105

Rare Limbert copper and mica Prairie School table lamp, Michigan, circa 1913, branded on foot, 19in. high, 24in. wide. (Skinner Inc.) $50,000 £30,864

Quezal art glass shade on gilt lamp base, with four green and gold double hooked and pulled feather repeats, 8in. high. (Robt. W. Skinner Inc.) $650 £404

Rare Steuben plum jade acid cut back lamp with gold aurene shades, mounted in gilt metal fittings, 13in. high. (Robt. W. Skinner Inc.) $1,300 £807

Handel reverse painted scenic table lamp, Meriden, Connecticut, early 20th century, with brilliant sunset coloured tropical island scene, 21in. high. (Skinner Inc.) $2,400 £1,548

A 19th century cast brass oil lamp, the boat shaped reservoir applied with masks in the Renaissance style, 57cm. high. (Henry Spencer) $749 £490

Handel leaded glass table lamp, Meriden, Connecticut, late 19th century (some leading damage, base polished to high copper gloss), 24in. high. (Skinner Inc.) $1,200 £774

An Art Deco spelter and pink alabaster table lamp, with a spelter model of an Egyptian slave girl perching with a torch form shade upon her knees, 20½in. high. (Christie's S. Ken) $525 £308

Arts & Crafts oak and slag glass table lamp, circa 1910, pyramidal shade lined with green slag glass, 26in. high. (Skinner Inc.) $650 £401

A gilt metal mounted cast iron lamp with inscription *Prussian Souvenir of The Passage of General Read across the River Seine, Thursday, January 5th, 1871,* 18in. high. (Christie's London) $619 £385

Handel moonlight desk lamp, with reverse painted pine forest landscape scene centring a full moon, shade 8¼in. long. (Robt. W. Skinner Inc.) $1,600 £994

Handel moonlight boudoir lamp, with reverse painted landscape scene with mountains and rolling meadows, 14in. high. (Robt. W. Skinner Inc.) $1,800 £1,118

Copper and mica table lamp, Upstate New York, circa 1910, mushroom topped flaring shade with four mica panels, 29in. high. (Skinner Inc.) $3,000 £1,852

An ormolu and porcelain lamp with amorous children in a trellis arbour entwined with flowers, 10½in. high. (Christie's London) $1,239 £770

Tiffany favrile experimental mosque light, octagonal wooden lamp base mounted with gilt bronze conforming rim centring a light socket with octagonally panelled shade, total height 8½in. (Robt. W. Skinner Inc.) $3,000 £1,863

Handel banded poppy table lamp, reverse painted with wide border band of orange poppy blossoms, buds, pods and leaves, shade diam. 18in. (Robt. W. Skinner Inc.) $4,750 £2,950

Handel type pond lily desk lamp, early 20th century, green slag and white leaded glass full blossom shade, 13¾in. high. (Skinner Inc.) $450 £290

Copper and mica table lamp, circa 1910, flaring shade with four mica panels divided by copper straps, 26in. high. (Skinner Inc.) $1,600 £988

Jodocus Hondius — Virginiae Item et Floridae, hand coloured engraved map, 340 x 480mm., (1607 or later) (Christie's S. Ken) $574 £352

Willem Blaeu — Nova Virginiae Tabula, engraved map, 370 x 480mm. (1630 or later) (Christie's S. Ken) $537 £330

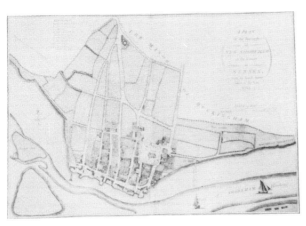

James Edwards — A Companion from London to Brighthelmston in Sussex, 4to, 1801. (Christie's S. Ken) $861 £495

Johnson & Ward (Publishers): New Illustrated Family Atlas, folio, New York, 1864, 61 hand coloured maps and plates. (Christie's S. Ken.) $669 £418

Charles Felix Marie Texier Manuscript plans of Port au Prince, 170 x 170mm. (Christie's S. Ken.) $497 £286

Christopher Saxton — Lancastriae Comitatus palatin vera et absoluta descripio, engraved map, hand coloured in outline, 400 x 480mm., 1577. (Christie's S. Ken.) $1,722 £990

Edward Wells: A New Map of the Terra-
queous Globe (1 and 2), 2 hand coloured
engraved maps, each 360 x 500mm., 1700
or later. (Christie's S. Ken.) $968 £605

William Camden — Britannia, Newly Translated into English, folio, by Edmund Gibson,
1695, 49 doublepage maps. (Christie's S.
Ken) $986 £605

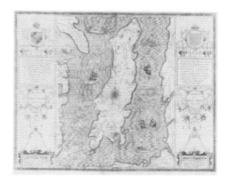

John Speed — Oxfordshire Described . . . ,
hand coloured engraved map, 380 x 530mm.,
Bassett and Chiswell. (1676 or later)
(Christie's S. Ken) $502 £308

John Speed — The Isle of Man, hand
coloured engraved map, 380 x 500mm.
(1627 or later) (Christie's S. Ken) $215 £132

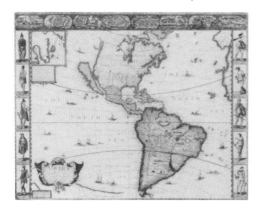

John Speed — American, hand coloured
engraved map, 390 x 510mm., 1626
(1676 or later), laid down on paper.
(Christie's S. Ken.) $1,722 £990

R. Montgomery Martin — Tallis's Illustrated
Atlas, folio, London and New York, 80
maps only (of 81). (Christie's S. Ken)
$1,972 £1,210

A late 19th century Florentine marble statue of Night, by F. Andreini, shown as a voluptuous, lightly draped girl, (fingers and crescent broken and left arm repaired at two points) 127cm. high. (Christie's London) $6,198 £3,850

A white marble bust of Charles Morgan Bart., by John Evan Thomas, dated 1841, on circular socle, 27½in. high. (Christie's S. Ken) $3,227 £1,980

A 19th century English marble statuette of a Hindu girl placing her lamp upon the Ganges, by Joseph Gott, 57cm. high. (Christie's London) $8,855 £5,500

A pair of late Victorian black and red marble obelisks, each decorated with hieroglyphics on a stepped and rusticated base, 20¼in. high. (Christie's London) $3,586 £2,200

An 18th century variegated rouge marble twin handled urn, 16in. high. (Christie's S. Ken) $4,712 £3,080

A pair of Italian grey and cream marble columns with circular foliate capitals and spirally turned shafts, 41in. high. (Christie's London) $1,564 £990

A 19th century Italian marble bust of (?) Minerva, by G. Pecoraro, the Grecian head shown crowned, 60cm. high. (Christie's London) $2,479 £1,540

A French rouge marble and ormolu mounted hexagonal pedestal, the plateau supported on three tapering foliate chased legs, 30½in. high. (Christie's S. Ken) $2,957 £1,760

A 19th century sculpted white marble bust of a young girl, on a conforming waisted socle, 16in. high. (Christie's S. Ken) $1,544 £990

A 19th century English marble bust of Queen Victoria, signed *L A Malempre 1887,* on turned marble socle, 50cm. high. (Christie's London) $885 £550

Ancient Roman marble bust of a male, 1st century B.C., carved after the classical Greek with idealistic features, 19$\frac{1}{2}$in. high. (Skinner Inc) $3200 £1987

A late 19th century Danish white marble bust of King Christian IX, in military uniform, attributed to Ludvig Brandstrup, 58.5cm. high. (Christie's London) $797 £495

A fine grey veined marble pedestal urn mounted in ormolu, the cover cast with fruiting vines, 63cm. high. (Henry Spencer) $918 £600

A German statuary marble coat-of-arms carved in relief with a displayed eagle and quarterings of crenellated towers, 17/18th century, 25in. wide. (Christie's London) $4,519 £2,860

A monumental mid-19th century English marble statue of the Eagle Slayer, by John Bell, signed on the back, 245cm. high. (Christie's London) $88,550 £55,000

A 19th century sculpted white marble bust of the Duke of Wellington, his shoulders draped to the truncation, 13in. high. (Christie's S. Ken) $411 £242

Pair of Italian white marble torcheres, with fluted half columns, each approx. 44in. high. (G. A. Key) $734 £450

A 19th century Scottish marble bust of William Small, by Sir John Steell, Small shown looking forward, on turned marble socle, 74cm. overall. (Christie's London) $4,605 £2,860

Meccano Aeroplane Constructor Outfit No. 2 (2nd series), silver and red, assembled as a single seater fighter, with pilot, circa 1932, 18½in. wingspan. (Christie's S. Ken) $634 £396

Meccano No. 2 Motor Car Constructor Outfit, green and cream, assembled as a Grand Prix Special, circa 1937, 11¾in. long. (Christie's S. Ken) $704 £440

Meccano No. 2 Special Aeroplane Outfit, red and cream, assembled as a three engine airliner, with No. 2 Aero motor, circa 1937, 20½in. wingspan. (Christie's S. Ken) $792 £495

Meccano Dealers Parts Display, blue and gold, on original card, circa 1936. (Christie's S. Ken) $704 £440

Dealer's Meccano Display Model, yellow and blue Double Ferris Wheel fairground ride, electric motor, on wood base with Meccano signs, late 1970s, 19½in. wide. (Christie's S. Ken) $440 £275

Rare Meccano Dealers Display Cabinet, red and green, six drawers, original velvet card, circa 1928. (Christie's S. Ken) $2,816 £1,760

Assembled blue and gold Showman's Engine, electric motor, steerable front wheels, circa 1934, 29½ x 20in. (Christie's S. Ken) $1,126 £704

Meccano Radio Crystal Receiving Set No. 1, on wood board, with phones, circa 1921. (Christie's S. Ken) $634 £396

Assembled early nickel plated 'B' type Omnibus, with clockwork motor, 1916 parts, 21¾in long. (Christie's S. Ken) $493 £308

Meccano Kemex Chemical Experiments No. 3L, with assorted glass bottles, in original box, circa 1933. (Christie's) $563 £352

Meccano, No. 2 Constructor Car with spare parts, good condition, key. (Phillips West Two) $643 £420

Meccano Aeroplane Constructor Outfit No. 1 (2nd series), blue and cream, assembled as a Monoplane Racer, with pilot, circa 1936, 18½in. wingspan. (Christie's S. Ken) $739 £462

Meccano Aeroplane Constructor Outfit No. 1, silver, disassembled, in original box with instructions, circa 1931. (Christie's S. Ken)$1,672 £1,045

Dealer's Meccano Display Model, red and green opening and closing No. 2 Outfit, electric motor, on wood base, circa 1960, 15in. wide. (Christie's S. Ken) $528 £330

Rare Meccano Mechanised Army Outfit No. MA, in original box, with instructions, circa 1939. (Christie's S. Ken) $1,496 £935

Meccano Elektron Electrical Experiments Outfits, comprising Sets No. 1 and 2, including electric motors, circa 1936. (Christie's S. Ken)
$616 £385

Meccano Steam Engine, a live steam spirit fired vertical steam engine, with japanned boiler, original fittings, circa 1929, 7½in. high. (Christie's)
$1,144 £715

Rare Italian Meccano Outfit No. 3, red and green, with removable tray, in original box, circa 1928. (Christie's S. Ken)
$229 £143

An early Georgian gilt looking glass, the later plate below a shaped leaf carved cresting, 37¾in. high. (Tennants) $790 £500

A George I gilt gesso mirror, the moulded frame carved with flowerheads and leaves on a punched ground, 25 x 20in. (Christie's London) $4,662 £2,860

A Regency giltwood overmantel, the channelled frame with acorn and oak leaf border applied with rosettes, 54 x 53½in. (Christie's S. Ken) $4,089 £2,420

A Charles II stumpwork and walnut mirror, the cushion frame worked with flowers, butterflies, insects and birds with a king and queen to either side, 35½ x 29in. (Christie's London) $17,661 £10,450

A Masonic giltwood mirror with verre eglomise frame painted with flowerheads, the shaped cresting with balustraded vista and Masonic eye, part 18th century, 51 x 23in. (Christie's S. Ken) $3,048 £1,870

A late Victorian oblong dressing table mirror with easel support and bevelled glass, Goldsmith & Silversmith Co. Ltd., 1900, 17½in. (Christie's S. Ken) $1,023 £660

A Venetian engraved and moulded glass mirror with arched bevelled plate, the mirrored border engraved with flowers with spiral twist mouldings, mid-19th century, 72 x 37in. (Christie's London) $2,479 £1,540

A large copper wall mirror by John Pearson, embossed in high relief with stylised mythical creatures reserved against a textured ground, 63cm. diam. (Phillips London) $2,437 £1,495

A giltwood overmantel, the rectangular plate flanked by fruiting foliate uprights, the frieze with riband tied flowerswags, 83 x 43in. (Christie's S. Ken) $1,309 £770

A Regency giltwood convex mirror, the ebonised slip within a surround of bronze lattice work motifs, surmounted by an heraldic eagle, with dolphin supports, 37in. high. (Christie's S. Ken) $1,683 £990

Giltwood mirror, probably Philadelphia, circa 1830, half round colonnettes ornamented with raised floral baskets, 32½ x 22in. (Skinner Inc.) $650 £399

A Continental porcelain mirror frame of shaped rectangular outline, painted with scattered fruit and flowers, late 19th century, 56cm. high. (Christie's London) $797 £495

A 19th century Dieppe ivory domed wall mirror, decorated with putti, hippocampi, flowers and a coat-of-arms, 34in. high. (Christie's S. Ken) $2,152 £1,320

An important early George III giltwood chimney glass, in the manner of John Linnell, 56½in. high, 65in. wide. (Tennants) $37,920 £24,000

An interesting and elaborate composite giltwood cheval mirror, the rectangular bevelled plate within a carved frame, 42in. wide, basically circa 1840. (Tennants) $1,738 £1,100

One of a pair of giltwood pier glasses, each with an arched bevelled plate in a gilt vert eglomise frame, 31 x 51in. (Christie's S. Ken)
Two $3,586 £2,200

Louis XVI style giltwood mirror, oval ribbon moulded frame with floral crest, 50in. high. (Skinner Inc.) $425 £274

A giltwood mirror, the canted rectangular plate in a rope carved and riband barbola cushioned frame, late 19th century, 43 x 31in. (Christie's S. Ken) $1,255 £770

A Regency parcel ebonised mahogany cheval mirror, the finialled ring turned frame with brass tightening handles cast with rosettes, 64in. high. (Christie's London) $1,477 £935

A French hand mirror, the porcelain frame encrusted with flower and fruit branches, 28cm. (Lawrence Fine Arts) $261 £165

An early George III carved giltwood pier glass, in the manner of Francis and John Booker of Dublin, with cartouche and swan neck pediment, 1.67m x 77cm. (Phillips London) $30,600 £20,000

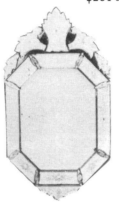

A William and Mary oyster veneered walnut mirror with bevelled rectangular plate in a moulded cushion frame, 39 x 32in. (Christie's London) $2,417 £1,430

A Venetian glass octagonal wall mirror, the surround etched with flowers, below a foliate surmount, 37in. high. (Christie's S. Ken) $655 £385

One of a pair of Italian giltwood mirrors with rectangular plates, the moulded channelled frames with trelliswork and recesses carved with foliage and ribbon tied husks, 96 x 84in. (Christie's London)
Two $27,808 £17,600

German polished mahogany and marquetry mirror with corniced pediment and two black half columns, mid-19th century, 160 x 72cm. (Kunsthaus am Museum) $595 £342

A Regency mahogany toilet mirror inlaid with ebonised lines on ring turned supports, the serpentine base with two drawers, 22in. wide. (Christie's London) $1,029 £660

George II style burl walnut and giltwood mirror, broken arch pediment with bird atop, 58in. high. (Skinner Inc.) $3,400 £2,166

A Japanese lacquer dressing glass, the shield shaped mirror plate suspended between shaped uprights, 77.5cm. high. (Henry Spencer) $1,956 £1,200

A Regency giltwood and ebonised convex mirror, the foliate cresting with displayed eagle, the apron with bronzed lion mask, 38½ x 27½in. (Christie's London)
$4,805 £3,080

A Chinese Export green lacquer toilet mirror decorated in gilt with a trellis and flowers, the oval base with two fitted drawers on bracket feet, early 19th century, 21in. wide. (Christie's London) $897 £550

A late Victorian arched oblong dressing table mirror mounted on green plush and with an easel support, H. M., Birmingham, 1900, 16½in. (Christie's S. Ken) $713 £440

A mahogany cheval glass with rectangular bevelled plate and bobbin turned uprights on splayed feet, 33½in. high. (Christie's S. Ken) $1,524 £935

A Keswick School of Industrial Art brass mirror, with repousse decoration of fruit laden foliage and a Tudor rose at each corner, 66.8 x 51.1cm. (Christie's London) $813 £484

A giltwood mirror with bevelled rectangular plate, the frame with flowerhead and ribbon entwined border within pierced acanthus scrolls, part 18th century, 44 x 34½in. (Christie's London)$2,231 £1,430

'Cope's Tobaccos Cigars Cigarettes', mirror, 203 x 21cm. framed. (Onslow's) $359 £220

A Dutch carved giltwood mirror, in a pierced frame carved with putti amongst scrolling foliage, late 17th century, 27 x 20in. (Christie's London) $1,580 £935

A late George I gilt and gesso wall mirror with projecting foliate scroll cresting and swan neck pediment, 1.03m. x 53cm. (Phillips London)$8,415 £5,500

A gilt frame convex wall mirror with reeded ebonised inner border and displayed eagle surmount, 102cm. high. (Lawrence Fine Arts) $1,738 £1,100

A George II style pine wall mirror, the frieze applied with shells and acanthus beneath a broken pediment, 72 x 37in. (Christie's S. Ken)$3,366 £1,980

A Chippendale giltwood and mahogany veneer mirror, probably English, late 18th century, with moulded scrolled pediment centring a spread wing eagle, 61in high. (Christie s New York)
$6,600 £4,150

A William IV giltwood overmantel, the eared moulded cornice and frieze applied with trailing foliage, 72 x 65in. (Christie's S. Ken) $897 £550

A Chippendale mahogany and giltwood mirror, labelled by James Musgrove, Philadelphia, circa 1780, the pierced and scrolled pediment centring a carved phoenix, 30in. high. (Christie's New York)
$3,300 £2,075

Courting mirror, Europe, 18th century, shaped eglomise inset moulded crest, 17¾in. high. (Skinner Inc.)
$2,200 £1,350

A circular gilt frame wall mirror, surmounted by gilt leafage and black painted display eagle, 19th century, 99cm. high. (Lawrence Fine Arts) $1,040 £638

Painted Chippendale mirror, New England, mid 18th century, the shaped crest over moulded and incised frame, 19¾in. high. (Skinner Inc.)
$6,000 £3,681

Chippendale mahogany veneered looking glass, America or England, 18th century (restoration), 37½in. long. (Skinner Inc.)
$1,300 £798

A Hagenauer chromium plated table mirror cast as a stylised leaping deer, stamped monogram, 30.5cm. (Bonhams)
$1,328 £800

A WMF large electroplated dressing table mirror, the semi-circular base incorporating a recessed stand, 66cm. high. (Bonhams) $1,992 £1,200

A giltwood and composition pier glass, the shaped cresting with a mask, flanked by grotesque birds' heads, 78 x 148cm. high. (Lawrence Fine Arts) $3,048 £1,870

A Liberty & Co. hammered copper mirror, the design attributed to John Pearson, decorated with two stylised cranes, 71cm. high. (Christie's London) $1,972 £1,210

A gilt pier mirror, probably American, 1815-1825, the broken rectangular cornice hung with acorn pendants, 58in. high. (Christie's New York) $2,200 £1,383

A 19th century Venetian rectangular wall mirror, the mirrored cushion frame etched with foliate motifs, 45¼in. high. (Christie's S. Ken) $1,028 £605

A giltwood and gesso circular convex wall mirror, the moulded frame with applied orbs and fitted with twin brass candle sconces, 40½in. high. (Christie's S. Ken) $3,696 £2,200

A WMF Art Nouveau electro-plated mirror, a female figure cast in semi relief at one side gazing at her reflection in the glass, 37cm. high. (Bonhams)
$1,162 £700

Stuffed tench, 4½lb., *Caught in the 16th foot by Fred Rowe, 1925.* (G. A. Key) $370 £220

A buffalo foot doorstop with brass carrying handle, 18in. high. (Christie's S. Ken) $108 £66

A rare French Revolutionary period standard of the Sans Culottes de Sainte Anne, in the form of a cotton swallow tailed pennant, 196 x 40cm., circa 1790-92. (Phillips London) $5,024 £3,200

A deck of fifty two playing cards manufactured by Goodall & Son, London, circa 1882. (Christie's S. Ken) $515 £330

A 14oz. 'Demon' tennis racket by Slazenger with convex wedge and fish tail handle, and a box of six Slazenger 'Demon' tennis balls. (Christie's S. Ken)$139 £88

Regency thuya wood miniature Wellington chest, circa 1810, with a lock end on a plinth base, 23½in. high. (Skinner Inc.) $900 £552

A walnut and yew dwarf chest with feather banded inlay, the rectangular top above a brushing slide, on bracket feet, basically 18th century, 28½in. (Christie's S. Ken) $4,488 £2,640

A Jacobean plaster overmantel, the central oval decorated with the Annunciation amid strapwork clusters of fruit and masks, 58 x 74in. (Christie's London) $4,781 £2,970

An agate and white metal tazza, the circular bowl supported by a male figure, 6in. high. (Christie's S. Ken) $652 £418

Painted sunburst fixed slat louvred blind, New England, early 19th century, bearing the inscription *Mrs Mary Stone dec'd AEt. 26,* 23½in. wide. (Skinner Inc.) $2,100 £1,243

A stuffed model of a turtle, 27in. long. (Christie's S. Ken) $251 £154

A set of six pottery carpet bowls, with a red, green or blue cross-hatched design, some glaze chipping. (Bearne's) $325 £210

A leather wallet, the front and back decorated with a bead-work panel, worked in brown and grisaille beads, 3 x 5in., 19th century. (Christie's S. Ken) $168 £99

Sand jar, America, late 19th century, colourful sand arranged in geometric patterns centring an eagle with American flag, 9in. high. (Skinner Inc.) $2,100 £1,243

Miniature country Chippendale bureau, America, late 18th century, raised on a moulded bracket base (refinished, minor repairs), 14in. high. (Skinner Inc.) $400 £258

A pair of Jefferies Racquets rackets, 30¾in. long, in a mahogany glazed case, the interior applied with a silver shield shaped plaque inscribed *'J. P. Rodger, Winner of the Single Racquets, Eton 1869'.* (Christie's S. Ken) $2,448 £1,540

Green jade figure of a laughing man, 19th century, reclining in flowing robes, 6in. high. (Skinner Inc.) $300 £188

A millweight, attributed to Elgin Wind Power and Pump Company, second half of 19th century, modelled in the form of a full bodied rooster with ribbed rainbow tail, 46 x 41 x 8cm. (Christie's New York) $3,850 £2,421

A finely engineered and detailed live steam, spirit fired model of the Passenger Tramp Steamer Belle Morss of London, 22^1/$_2$in. x 51^1/$_2$in. (Christie's) $2722 £1650

A finely detailed electric powered radio controlled model of the paddle steamer Albion, 16in. x 52in. (Christie's) $2722 £1650

A well detailed and presented fibreglass wood and metal electric powered, radio controlled model of the Lowestoft Herring Drifter Gull, Licence No. H241, built by W.A. Williams, London. 68in. x 35in. (Christie's) $3630 £2200

Sutcliffe live steam spirit fired battleship, with burner, in original paintwork, circa 1928, 16½ in. long, in original box. (Christie's S. Ken.) $299 £187

Cased, carved and painted ship model, America, late 19th/early 20th century, polychrome model of the steam ship City New York, 35½in. wide. (Skinner Inc.) $1,400 £903

An ^{1}/$_8$th scale wooden display model of the German cruiser S.M.S. Viktoria Louise, the hull carved from the solid, masts and rigging and deck details including anchors, deck rails, bridge, stayed funnels, guns in turrets and other details, 29in. x 67^1/$_2$in. (Christie's) $762 £462

Kron Prinzessin Cecilie, a rare hand painted tinplate display model of the Norddeutscher Line Trans-Atlantic liner, by Fleischmann, Germany, circa 1907, 154cm. long. (Christie's S. Ken) $12,166 £7,700

A finely planked and pinned unrigged model of the ship rigged sloop Myridon of circa 1881, built by P. Danks, Leighton Buzzard, from plans supplied by the National Maritime Museum, 8in. x 32in. (Christie's) $2359 £1430

A well presented fully planked and framed model of a 30ft. Royal Navy armed pinnace of circa 1877, built by P. Smith, Ealing, 15in. x 23.5in.
(Christie's) $799   £484

Shadow box with model of the 'Cumberland', America, late 19th century, of polychrome wood, paper and thread, 15¹/₂in. x 26in.
(Skinner Inc.) $800   £488

An extremely fine and detailed exhibition standard fibreglass wood and metal, electric powered radio controlled model of H.M.S. Warspite built by G. Edwards, Cheddington, 17¹/₂in. x 61in. (Christie's) $6897   £4180

A finely detailed and well researched fully planked and framed electric powered radio controlled model of a Thornycroft 55ft. coastal motor torpedo boat, built by R.R. Bullivant, Leighton Buzzard, 14¹/₂in. x 38in.
(Christie's) $1633   £990

A well detailed and presented 1:150 scale static display model of the Spanish paddle/sail corvette San Isldefonso of circa 1840, built by W.M. Wilson, Carlisle, 10¹/₂in. x 19in.
(Christie's) $399   £242

A well presented radio controlled, electric powered model of the Mississippi Stern Wheel Steamer Creole Queen, built by R. Burgess, Mayfield, 15¹/₂in. x 48in.
(Christie's) $544   £330

A fine and detailed exhibition standard ¹/₇₅th scale model of the French 64-gun ship of-the-line Le Protecteur, built to drawings supplied by Le Musee de la Marine, Paris, 32¹/₂in. x 39in.
(Christie's) $3630   £2200

An extremely fine and detailed builder's model of the steel schooner rigged single screw steam yacht Wakiva, built by Ramage & Ferguson Ltd. of Leith for W.E. Cox, Boston, Massachusetts, 19in. x 52in.
(Christie's) $54450   £33000

Model steam locomotive, 'Lion' 0-4-2, 3¹/₂in. gauge. (H.P.S) $1815 £1100

Model steam locomotive, Union Pacific Railroad, 4-4-0, 7¹/₄in. gauge. (H.P.S) $6600 £4000

Model steam locomotive, London Brighton & South Coast, 'Atlantic' class, 4-4-2, 3¹/₂in. gauge. (H.P.S) $4125 £2500

Model steam locomotive, Great Western Railway 'Castle' class, 4-6-0, 7¹/₄in. gauge. (H.P.S) $11962 £7250

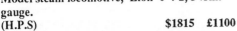

A No. 2-E Engine Shed (lacks light fittings). (Christie's S. Ken) $493 £308

Hornby book of trains 1927-1939 (three incomplete. (Christie's S. Ken.) $1,320 £825

A well engineered and presented 3½in. gauge model of the Japanese Climax 0-4-0 plus 0-4-0 geared logging locomotive No. 3, built by P. Higgins, Renhold, 10½ x 28in. (Christie's S. Ken) $3,407 £2,090

An exhibition standard 5in. gauge model of the LMS (ex L & Y) 2-4-2 side tank loco-motive No. 10637, built to the designs of Don Young by Major F. R. Pearce, West Byfleet, 14 x 39¼in. (Christie's S. Ken) $5,738 £3,520

Model steam locomotive, London Midland & Scottish, shunting tank engine, 0-6-0, 5in. gauge. (H.P.S) $3465 £2100

A rare clockwork model of the SAR 0-4-0 No. 1 tank locomotive No. 7206, in original box, circa 1926. (Christie's S. Ken) $493 £308

Rare Hornby-Dublo pre-war (3-rail) EDL7 S.R. 0-6-2 tank locomotive No. 2594, in original box, circa 1938. (Christie's S. Ken) $968 £605

A (3-rail) electric model of the LNER 4-4-0 No. E220 special locomotive and tender No. 201 'Bramham Moor'. (Christie's S. Ken) $1,496 £935

Model steam locomotive, London Brighton & South Coast, Brighton terrier class, 0-6-0, 5in. gauge. (H.P.S) $3300 £2000

A rare (3-rail) electric model of the 0-4-0 No. LE220 locomotive No. 10655, finished in green livery with grey roof, circa 1934. (Christie's S. Ken) $2,288 £1,430

Painted and stencilled tin train, Stevens and Brown, Cromwell, Connecticut, 1868-1872, black, green and red engine inscribed *Thunderer,* engine 6in. long. (Skinner Inc.) $4,000 £2,454

A well engineered and presented 3½in. gauge model of the Heisler 0-4-0 plus 0-4-0 geared logging locomotive No. 5, built by P. Higgins, Renhold, 10 x 28½in. (Christie's S. Ken) $3,048 £1,870

A well engineered and presented 3½in. gauge model of the Shay 0-4-0 plus 0-4-0 geared logging locomotive No. 2 built by P. Higgins, Renhold, 11 x 27½in. (Christie's S. Ken) $3,765 £2,310

A finely detailed exhibition standard 7¼in. gauge model of the GWR Class 1101 0-4-0 Dock tank Sisyphus, originally built by the Avonside Engine Company, Bristol, 19 x 38½in. (Christie's S. Ken) $9,861 £6,050

A (3-rail) electric model of the LMS 4-6-2 locomotive and tender No. 6201 'Princess Elizabeth', in the original maroon paintwork, circa 1937. (Christie's S. Ken) $2,816 £1,760

591

Carette hand painted portable steam engine, with burner, single cylinder and flywheel in original paintwork, circa 1912, 8½in. (Christie's S. Ken)
$704 £440

A finely engineered model of an early 19th century four column single cylinder beam pumping engine originally designed by D. E. Alban, 9½ x 9in. (Christie's S. Ken)
$1,016 £605

A 2in. scale model of a single cylinder single speed three shaft general purpose traction engine, cylinder approx. 1¼in. bore x 2in. stroke, 19½ x 28in. (Christie's S. Ken) $1,911 £1,210

A Marklin live steam spirit fired horizontal stationary steam engine, in original paintwork, circa 1921, 52in. high. (Christie's S. Ken)$1,216 £770

Marklin for Gamages, a spirit-fired portable horizontal over-type steam engine, with single cylinder driving governer, circa 1910 (worn), 27cm. long. (Christie's S. Ken) $1,034 £638

A Marklin for Gamages live steam spirit fired horizontal stationary steam engine, with brass boiler, chimney, original fittings, German, circa 1920, 12½in. wide. (Christie's S. Ken)
$608 £385

A fine exhibition standard 2in. scale model of the Burrell 5 m.p.h. double crank compound three shaft, two speed, agricultural tractor, built by D. Burns, Pennington, Australia, 19¾ x 29in. (Christie's S. Ken)
$9,861 £6,050

A finely engineered unique steam-powered Crawler Tractor built on a Ransome's MG 6 chassis by A. Pickering, 1985. Overall length 90 x 43in. (Christie's S. Ken)
$16,137 £9,900

An early 19th century wrought iron and brass, single cylinder, four pillar overcrank model engine with cylinder approx. 2in. bore x 2in. stroke, 19 x 11¼in. (Christie's S. Ken)
$382 £242

'I always did 'spise a mule"
savings bank by J & E
20cm. high.
(Auktionsverket, Stockholm)
$279 £169

An amusing savings bank in the
form of a typewriter. (Auction
Team Koeln) $24 £15

Plated clockwork Bulldog
Savings Bank by Ives Blakes -
lee & Co. 18cm. high.
(Auktionsverket, Stockholm)
$1,012 £613

A German lithographed tinplate
money box, with lever action
eyes and extending tongue,
1920's, 7½in. high.
(Christie's S. Ken.) $544 £330

Black and gold Jep tin money
bank, in the form of an old
safe with combination lock,
French, circa 1920. (Auction
Team Koeln) $70 £43

Stump Speaker, a cast iron
mechanical moneybox, with
movable right arm and unusual
counterbalanced talking mouth,
pat. June 8 1886, 25cm. high.
(Christie's S. Ken) $1,426 £880

Jolly Nigger bank, with
movable right arm, in original
paintwork, by Shepard Hard-
ware Co., Buffalo, N.Y., circa
1883, 7in. high. (Christie's
S. Ken) $295 £187

Pussycat chromium cast money
bank, with key, circa 1935.
(Auction Team Koeln) $34 £21

Wooden Jug savings bank, with
key, circa 1920. (Auction
Team Koeln) $19 £12

1922 Rolls Royce Silver Ghost tourer, Reg. No. NN3740, the engine comprising six cylinders set in-line in blocks of three cylinders, with water cooling and side valves with rather attractive skiff type body fitted some 35 years ago. (Christie's London) $83,655 £49,500

1949-50 2.5litre Alfa Romeo 6C-2500 Super Sport Cabriolet, coachwork by Pininfarina, in excellent condition and an impressive example of one of the most handsome of all post-war Alfa Romeos. (Christie's London) $167,310 £99,000

1957 BMW 507 sports, in the original black colour, with red leather upholstery. (Christie's London) $250,965 £148,500

1960 Bentley S2 Continental 2-door saloon, coachwork by H. J. Mulliner, Reg. No. 8889RW, extensively restored in 1984-85. (Christie's London) $223,080 £132,000

1979 Aston Martin V8 Volante convertible. Reg. No. GAG730T, V8 engine, twin overhead camshaft, 5,340cc, gearbox: five speed synchromesh, finished in Midnight Blue with light blue interior, the car is in excellent condition. (Christie's London) $204,490 £121,000

1964 AC Cobra 289 MKII sports two seater, Reg. No. KHX345B, Ford V8 engine, overhead valve, 289cu. in. (4,727cc), 280bhp, resprayed in pearl black, with black leather interior, the original engine replaced in 1973 and the current engine having covered some 54,000 miles. (Christie's London) $316,030 £187,000

1930 Packard Deluxe 8 Sedanca de Ville, Chassis No. 150481, in generally good order, with the brakes and engine having recently been overhauled. (Christie's London) $52,052 £30,800

1973 BMW 3.0 CSL coupe, Reg. No. UMP12M, with 206bhp, 3,158cc engine, aluminium wheels, Recaro seats, and electric sun roof. (Christie's London) $29,744 £17,600

1950 Bristol 401 2litre two door sports saloon, Reg. No. BRC4, six cylinder engine, overhead valve, monobloc, bore 66mm, stroke 96mm, capacity 1,971cc, finished in blue with cream interior. (Christie's London) $40,898 £24,200

1979 Ferrari 308 GTS, Reg. No. KNL555, V8 engine, double overhead camshaft per bank, 2,962cc, 250bhp, finished in black with a red interior. (Christie's London) $89,232 £52,800

1952 Buick Riviera, model 45R, odometer reading 69,060, eight cylinder, very good condition. (Robt. W. Skinner Inc.) $3,500 £2,134

1987 replica Bugatti Type 41 Royale, Chevrolet V8 engine, 7.7litres developing 260bhp at 6,500rpm, 6.3m in length and currently with 7.00 x 24in. tyres. (Christie's London) $148,720 £88,000

1974 BMW 3.0 CSi two door coupe, coachwork by Karmann, Reg. No. DNP237N, fuel injected six cylinder engine, overhead camshaft, 2,985cc, 200 bhp, finished in blue with matching interior. (Christie's London) $6,507 £3,850

1965 Mercedes Benz 230SL convertible sports two seater, Reg. No. KPJ668C, six cylinder engine, overhead camshaft, 2,306cc, 150bhp, originally silver, but now finished in red with black interior. (Christie's London) $17,661 £10,450

1974 Rolls Royce Silver Shadow I, four door sedan, right hand drive, odometer reading 96,300, green exterior. (Robt. W. Skinner Inc.) $10,000 £6,098

1964 Austin Healey 3000 MkIII sports two seater, Reg. No. JHX363B, the six cylinder in-line BMC engine of 2,012cc producing 148bhp, right hand drive, finished in black over red with red leather upholstery. (Christie's London) $44,616 £26,400

1953 MG TF Sports two seater, engine: four cylinder, overhead valve, 1,250cc, 57bhp; gearbox: four speed synchromesh; brakes: four wheel hydraulic. (Christie's London)
$27,791 £17,050

1959 Aston Martin DB MkIII Drophead Coupe, engine: six cylinder, twin overhead camshaft, 2922cc, 162bhp; gearbox: four speed synchromesh; brakes: disc front, drum rear. (Christie's London) $268,950 £165,000

1965 Aston Martin DB5 Vantage Grand Touring four seater, engine: six cylinder, twin overhead camshaft, 3,955cc, 314bhp; gearbox: five speed synchromesh; brakes: four wheel servo disc; wheels: wire spoked centre lock; right hand drive. (Christie's London) $98,615 £60,500

1962 Mercedes Benz 300SE two door Cabriolet, engine: six cylinder, overhead camshaft, 2,996cc, fuel injection, 160bhp; gearbox: four speed automatic with hydraulic clutch; brakes: four wheel servo disc; right hand drive. (Christie's London)
$48,411 £29,700

1980 Ferrari 400i convertible, V12 engine, double overhead camshaft, 4,823cc, 340bhp, fitted with the traditional Ferrari five speed manual gearbox, finished in Ferrari red with biscuit interior. (Christie's London)
$120,835 £71,500

1913 Fiat T52B 12-seater Shooting Brake, engine: four cylinder, side valve, 2.6 litre, 15/20hp; gearbox four speed sliding mesh; brakes: rear wheel mechanical; suspension: semi-elliptic; right hand drive. (Christie's London) $17,930 £11,000

1931 Morris Minor Model 60 McEvoy Special Prototype Tourer, engine: four cylinder, side valve, 847cc, 8hp; gearbox: three speed sliding mesh; brakes: four wheel hydraulic. (Christie's London)
$7,530 £4,620

1908 Standard 20hp 4litre Single Phaeton with Dickey, engine: six cylinder, side valve, 4 litre, 29.5 RAC hp; gearbox: gate change three speed sliding mesh; brakes: on transmission and rear wheels; right hand drive. (Christie's London) $71,720 £44,000

1957 Ford Thunderbird Convertible, engine:
V8, overhead valve, 5,800cc, 300bhp, power
steering; gearbox: automatic; brakes: four
wheel hydraulic; left hand drive. (Christie's
London) $27,791 £17,050

1958 Mercedes Benz 300SL roadster, Reg.
No. TSU915, six cylinder engine, overhead
camshaft, 2,996cc, 215bhp, in metallic light
green with beige interior. (Christie's London)
                                 $250,965 £148,500

1934 Rolls Royce 20/25 four door Sports
Saloon, coachwork by Thrupp & Maberly,
engine: six cylinder, overhead valve, 3.7 litre,
20/25hp; gearbox: four speed with synchromesh on third and top; brakes: four wheel
servo mechanical. (Christie's London)
                                 $60,962 £37,400

1935 Rolls Royce Phantom II Continental
saloon, long chassis coachwork by Park
Ward, Reg. No. FUR323B, the body in
Oxford blue with black wings, trimmed with
light blue Connolly hide and Wilton carpets.
(Christie's London) $111,540 £66,000

Circa 1900 Benz Duc Victoria, engine: single
cylinder, side valve, 5hp; transmission: three
forward, one reverse by belt with chain final
drive; wheels: wooden spoked with solid
rubber tyres. (Christie's London)
                                 $116,545 £71,500

1925 Hispano-Suiza H6B four door Sports
Saloon, coachwork by Kellner et Cie, engine:
six cylinder, overhead camshaft, 6,597cc,
135bhp; gearbox: three speed sliding mesh;
brakes: four wheel servo mechanical.
(Christie's London) $134,475 £82,500

1966 Jaguar E-type 4.2 litre 2x2 fixed head
Coupe, engine: six cylinder, twin overhead
camshaft, 4,235cc, 265bhp; gearbox: three
speed automatic; brakes: four wheel servo
disc; suspension: fully independent.
(Christie's London) $29,584 £18,150

1965 MGB 2x2 Berlinette, coachwork by
Jacques Coune, Brussels, engine: four
cylinder, overhead valve, 1,798cc, 95bhp;
gearbox: four speed synchromesh; brakes:
disc front, drum rear. (Christie's London)
                                 $16,137 £9,900

1935 Aston Martin Ulster MkII, 2/4 seater sports, 1,500cc, Reg. No. CMF764, in fine original condition. (Christie's London) $241,670 £143,000

1955 Mercedes Benz 300 SL Gullwing Coupe, engine: six cylinder, overhead camshaft, 2,996cc, 215bhp; gearbox: four speed synchromesh; brakes. four wheel servo drum suspension; fully independent; left hand drive. (Christie's London) $286,880 £176,000

1934 Rolls Royce Phantom II Continental four door Sports Saloon, coachwork by Park Ward, engine: six cylinder, overhead valve, 7,668 cc, 40/50 horsepower; gearbox: four speed sliding mesh, brakes: four wheel servo-mechanical; right hand drive. (Christie's London) $161,370 £99,000

1931 Ford Model AA Service Car, engine: four cylinder, side valve, 200.5cu. ins., 40bhp; gearbox: four speed sliding mesh; brakes: four wheel mechanical; suspension: leaf springs; right hand drive. (Christie's London) $34,067 £20,900

1929 Mercedes Benz Nurburg four door convertible, Reg. No. USJ1538, the bodywork and upholstery in the currently fashionable green. (Christie's London) $130,130 £77,000

1922 Maxwell Model 25 four door Tourer, engine: four cylinder, side valve, 3 litre, 18/22hp; gearbox: three speed sliding mesh; brakes: rear wheel mechanical. (Christie's London) $10,758 £6,600

1970 Jaguar D-type replica, fitted with a 4.2litre engine, with triple Weber carburettors, very well finished in silver with a red interior. (Christie's London) $78,078 £46,200

1903 Peugeot twin cylinder Forecar, engine: air cooled, V-twin, atmospheric inlet, overhead exhaust valve, 344cc, transmission: single speed, belt drive; wheels: wire spoked. (Christie's London) $12,551 £7,700

1948 Jaguar 1½ litre four door Sports Saloon engine: four cylinder, overhead valve, 1,775cc, 65bhp; gearbox: four speed synchromesh; brakes: four wheel mechanical. (Christie's London) $14,344 £8,800

1932 Aston Martin New International 2/4 seat Tourer, coachwork by Bertelli, engine: four cylinder, overhead camshaft, 1,495cc, 60bhp; gearbox: four speed sliding mesh; brakes: four wheel mechanical; wheels: wire spoked centre lock. (Christie's London)
$107,580 £66,000

1964 Ferrari 250 GT/Lusso, Reg. No. 542EMW, V12 engine, single overhead camshaft, 2,953cc, 250bhp, finished in silver, with black leather upholstery. (Christie's London) $743,600 £440,000

1963/64 Morris Mini Cooper S, Reg. No. 24PK, four cylinder engine, water cooled unit, 1,293cc, set across the chassis in the Issigonis style, a semi works-prepared survivor of the apogee period of Mini Coopers in competition. (Christie's London)
$35,321 £20,900

1967 Mercedes Benz 250 SL Sports two seater, engine: six cylinder, overhead camshaft, 2496cc, 150bhp; gearbox: automatic; brakes: four wheel disc; suspension: fully independent; right hand drive. (Christie's London) $30,481 £18,700

1951 MG TD sports two seater, Reg. No. MLT842, four cylinder engine, twin carburettors, overhead valve, 1,250cc, finished in red with beige leather upholstery. (Christie's London) $31,603 £18,700

1932 Bugatti Type 49 coupe, coachwork by Gangloff, Reg. No. USV854, the engine eight cylinders in line bi-block, single overhead camshaft, three valves per cylinder with 72mm bore x 100mm stroke giving a capacity of 3,257cc, finished in green and black with tan leather interior. (Christie's London)
$334,620 £198,000

1953 Mercedes Benz 300 Adenauer four door Cabriolet, engine: six cylinder, overhead camshaft, 2,996cc, 115bhp; gearbox: four speed synchromesh; brakes: four wheel hydraulic drum. (Christie's London)
$44,825 £27,500

1962 Chevrolet Corvette convertible roadster, Reg. No. SSU778, V8 engine, overhead valve, 327cu. in. (5,360cc), 250bhp, recently totally restored, the body removed, the chassis overhauled and the car repainted in white. (Christie's London) $40,898 £24,200

1950 Riley RMC 2½litre roadster, Reg. No. LRO426, four cylinder engine, single overhead camshaft, 2,443cc, 85bhp, paint-work, upholstery and carpets are all in as-new condition and the car holds a current MOT test certificate. (Christie's London) $42,757 £25,300

1965 Aston Martin DB5 Vantage Grand Touring, Reg. No. FPR117D, six cylinder engine, twin overhead camshaft 3,995cc, 314bhp, finished in Florida blue metallic with fawn leather upholstery and in excellent condition. (Christie's London) $148,720 £88,000

1973 Porsche 911 Carrera RS2.7 2 plus 2 sports coupe, flat six cylinder engine rear mounted, overhead camshaft, 2,687cc, 210bhp, repainted in its original Grand Prix white with blue lettering on the flanks. (Christie's London) $74,360 £44,000

1950 AEC/Merryweather fire engine (100ft. steel turntable ladder), Reg. No. LYB388, Chassis No. 9766 EXA82355, in complete working order with a current V5 certificate. (Christie's London) $7,436 £4,400

1977 Porsche 935, with 2.8litre air cooled engine with single turbocharger, developing in excess of 600bhp, finished in Grand Prix white with a black bucket seat. (Christie's London) $817,960 £484,000

1949 Bentley MkVI convertible, Reg. No. LMB222, six cylinder engine, overhead valve, 4,257cc, 135bhp, finished in black, with a red/grey interior. (Christie's London) $59,488 £35,200

1982 Ferrari 400i, Reg. No. AHH55Y, V12 engine, double overhead camshafts, 4,823cc 340bhp, painted blue with a beige interior, serviced regularly by Maranello Concession-aires. (Christie's London) $74,360 £44,000

1914 Rolls Royce Silver Ghost tourer, coachwork by Van den Plas, the engine, of just over 7 litres has its six side valved cylinders set in two blocks of three, fitted with a blue Van den Plas tourer body. (Christie's London) $278,850 £165,000

1935 SS1 four seat sports tourer, Reg. No. WS5777, six cylinder engine, overhead valves, 2.5litre, 20hp, finished in Old English white with red leather interior, in concours condition following total body-off restoration. (Christie's London)
                         $85,514 £50,600

1952 Bentley R type two door lightweight convertible, coachwork by H. J. Mulliner, Reg. No. RAU3, six cylinder engine, overhead inlet, side exhaust valve, twin SU carburettors, 4,566cc, finished in bottle green with fawn interior and hood. (Christie's London) $130,130 £77,000

1972 AC 428 convertible, coachwork by Frua, Reg. No. SPD268L, V8 engine, 7,106cc, overhead valve, hydraulic tappets, 345bhp at 5,250rpm, torque 460ft. lbs at 2,600rpm. painted bright red with a black interior. (Christie's London) $139,425 £82,500

1955/6 Rolls Royce Wraith touring limousine, coachwork by Park Ward, Reg. No. HLD1, one owner, chauffeur driven, finished in Arden green, with tan hide upholstery. (Christie's London) $115,258 £68,200

1930 Rolls Royce Phantom II 4-door tourer, coachwork by Gaston Grummer of Paris, the engine a 7.7litre six cylinder unit, with the in-line cylinders set in two groups of three. (Christie's London) $185,900 £110,000

1958 Mercedes Benz 190SL roadster, four cylinder engine, overhead camshaft, 1897cc, 105bhp, finished in white with a pleasantly original red leather interior. (Christie's London) $26,026 £15,400

1932 Chevrolet sports roadster, two door convertible, Reg. No. YF2993, chassis No. M101710, right hand drive. (Christie's London) $22,308 £13,200

601

A rare Libellion musical box with twin combs and spring motor in walnut case with simulated inlaid panels to sides. (Christie's S. Ken)
$4,114 £2,420

A Monopol 7½in. disc musical box formed as a child's pull along car with original red paintwork, 20in. long, with six discs. (Christie's S. Ken)
$785 £462

A Sublime Harmony interchangeable cylinder musical box by Paillard, with one eight-air cylinder, tune selector and indicator, the cylinder 13¼in. (Christie's S. Ken) $1,403 £825

A 50cm. upright coin slot polyphon with zither attachment, in typical walnut case with pediment and coin-drawer, 49in. high, with twelve discs. (Christie's S. Ken)
$10,285 £6,050

Swiss cylinder music box with bells, late 19th century, 13in. cylinder with six bells playing twelve airs, 25in. long. (Skinner Inc.) $1,500 £968

A Euphonion coin operated metal disc player with 13 discs (50cm.). (Auction Team Koeln)
$2,921 £1,849

A Polyphone with glockenspiel and six tin discs, circa 1900. (Auction Team Koeln)
$1,643 £1,014

A French musical bronze encrier, the inkwell concealed by a standing figure of a lady, with (defective) HMG movement in wood base, 9½in. high. (Christie's S. Ken) $935 £550

A musical box playing twelve airs, with nickel plated movement, zither attachment, double-spring motor and ebonised case with stringing, 28½in. wide. (Christie's S. Ken)
$2,618 £1,540

A late 19th century Swiss lever wound Drum Bells Castanets musical box, with 9¼in. cylinder, 23½in. long. (Tennants) $1,872 £1,200

A Gramophone Company Senior Monarch gramophone in oak case with triple spring motor, gooseneck tone arm and G & T brass horn, 22in. long. (Christie's S. Ken) $1,346 £792

A Charles Ullmann musical box playing eight airs, with painted automaton striker with two dancing dolls, 17in. wide. (Christie's S. Ken) $2,244 £1,320

A 'Symphonion' coin operated gramophone with 52cm. tin disc and wall attachment. (Auction Team Koeln) $4,547 £2,807

An Othello Orchestrion by Popper & Co., Leipzig, the cabinet with Art Nouveau decoration and equipped with mechanical piano, mandoline, xylophone, drums, triangle and cymbals, in working order, 1912. (Auction Team Koeln) $8,764 £5,547

A Commodaphone gramophone built into the seat of a wooden armchair, circa 1920. (Auction Team Koeln) $632 £390

An HMV Model 2a horn gramophone with double spring motor, gooseneck tone arm and mahogany horn, dated on base *10 Jul 1917*. (Christie's S. Ken) $1,402 £825

A D. Le Coultre key wound cylinder musical box, the 10¾in. cylinder playing six airs. (Lawrence Fine Arts) $1,076 £660

An EMG Mark XV oversize gramophone with oak case, spring motor, EMG four-spring soundbox and papier mache horn, 33¼in. (Christie's S. Ken) $3,179 £1,870

A rare Edison Fireside phonograph, Model B, with four-
minute gearing, Diamond B
reproducer and No. 10 Cygnet
horn. (Christie's S. Ken)
$1,122 £660

Ideal sublime harmonie cylinder
music box, late 19th century,
Swiss movement with four 11-
inch cylinders, 30in. wide.
(Skinner Inc.) $4000   £2440

A Bassanophone table grand
gramophone with double out-
let sound box, automatic stop
acting on governor, circa 1910.
(Christie's S. Ken) $448 £264

Victorian inlaid musical box
playing eight airs, No. 8240,
striking on five bells.
(Michael G. Matthews)
$1485   £900

An orchestral musical box
playing ten airs accompanied
by 21-key organ, drum,
castanet and nine engine
turned bells, 27½in. wide.
(Christie's S. Ken)
$6,545 £3,850

Swiss cylinder music box with
bells, circa 1900, playing eight
airs and a 6in. cylinder with
single comb and three bells.
(Skinner Inc.) $550 £337

A Baillard's Echophone
phonograph with model C
reproducer shaped brass horn
and transfer printed beech case,
13½in. wide.
(Andrew Hartley Fine Arts)
$495   £300

An unusual 19th century Swiss
musical box, in the form of an
organ of vertical rectangular
form, the top, sides and fascia
inset with ten enamel plaques
painted in colours, 23cm. high.
(Spencer's) $2145   £1300

Wind-up Expert phonograph in
an oak case, with brass trumpet.
(Southgate Antique Auction
Rooms) $478   £290

A rare and interesting viola da gamba, attributed to Barak Norman, circa 1710, 780mm. (Phillips London) $7,820 £4,600

An E-flat Helichon, by Boosey and Co., and engraved Solborn class A, and numbered 9908. (Christie's S. Ken.) $254   £154

Painted and decorated parade drum, J. & G. Dennison, Freeport, Maine, late 19th century, the green ground decorated in polychrome, 16½in. diam. (Skinner Inc.) $850 £503

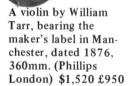

A violin by William Tarr, bearing the maker's label in Manchester, dated 1876, 360mm. (Phillips London) $1,520 £950

A rare mandolin by Vincentius Vinaccio, bearing the maker's label, 1760. (Phillips London)
     $2,160 £1,350

An interesting patent design violin by T. Howell, bearing the maker's label, overall length 24in. (Phillips London) $992 £620

Large painted and decorated parade bass drum, inscribed *William Bridget Maker & Painter, Belfast,* late 19th century, 37in. diam. (Skinner Inc.) $4,250 £2,515

A fine mandolin bearing the signed label of Umberto Ceccherini, Naples, circa 1900. (Phillips London) $576 £360

Painted and decorated tambourine, America, early 20th century, painted in polychrome, pressed brass bells, 9½in. diam. (Skinner Inc.) $1,400 £828

A violoncello by
Pierre Le Lievre, bear-
ing the maker's label,
dated 1755, 27¾in.
(Phillips London)
$6,460 £3,800

A violin by John Simp-
son, bearing the
maker's label, London,
circa 1790, 357mm.
(Phillips London)
$2,880 £1,800

A good viola by
Honore Derazey Pere,
bearing the maker's
label, circa 1860,
399mm. (Phillips
London)
$9,860 £5,800

A good violin by
Alexander Smillie,
bearing the maker's
label, *Fecit Crosshill,
Glasgow*, dated 1898,
357mm. (Phillips
London)
$2,480 £1,550

A rare and early violin
by Benjamin Banks,
inscribed on lower
inner back, 1751,
359mm. (Phillips
London)
$1,876 £1,100

A fine violin by
Arthur Richardson,
bearing the maker's
label in Crediton and
dated 1936, 14in.
(Phillips London)
$6,720 £4,200

A fine violin by Henry
Werro, bearing the
label *J. Werro fecit a
Berne*, dated 1922,
357mm. (Phillips
London)
$4,000 £2,500

A viola by Giovanni
Schwarz, bearing the
maker's label and
signed *S. Sefano
fecit anno 1913*,
16in. (Phillips London)
$8,840 £5,200

A good violin by W. E. Hill & Sons, bearing the label dated 1913, 359mm., with two bows in case. (Phillips London)

$4,784 £2,990

A handsome baroque pattern violin of the Vuillaume School, circa 1850, bearing a manuscript label *Nicolo Paganini, 1828,* 365mm. (Phillips London)

$2,000 £1,250

A violin labelled *Carolus Baderello fecit in Taurini anno Domini 1929,* 357mm. (Phillips London)

$4,160 £2,600

A violin by Ch. J. B. Collin-Mezin, bearing the maker's label in Paris, dated 1911, 360mm. (Phillips London)

$1,600 £1,000

A violin by Honore Derazey, bearing the maker's label in Mirecourt, circa 1870, 359mm. (Phillips London)

$6,800 £4,000

A fine violin by Honore Derazey Pere, bearing the maker's label *a Mirecourt,* circa 1850, 14in., with a bow in a rosewood case with cover. (Phillips London)

$9,860 £5,800

A viola bearing the maker's label *Joseph Guadagnini Cremonensis fecit Mediolani anno 1796,* 390mm. (Phillips London)

$8,840 £5,200

A violin of the John Betts School, London, circa 1810, 14in., with a silver mounted violin bow by Roderich Paesold. (Phillips London)

$2,640 £1,650

An ivory netsuke of two karako pulling each other's hair as they fight over a drum, unsigned, mid 19th century, 4.4cm.
(Christie's) $1053 £638

A finely patinated ivory netsuke of a fukura suzume bearing on its back the tiny figure of the man, signed Hidemasa, late 18th century, 3.7cm. long.
(Christie's) $2072 £1320

A finely patinated ivory netsuke of a karashishi sitting and turned to its right, its eye pupils inlaid in black horn, late 18th/early 19th century, 4cm. wide. (Christie's London) $3,128 £1,980

A finely lacquered netsuke formed as a boy-doll standing holding a pearl in a small dish and a Chinese fan, unsigned, 19th century, 5.4cm.
(Christie's) $3630 £2200

A fine boxwood netsuke of a human skull entwined by a snake, signed *Hogen Rantei*, 19th century, 4cm. high.
(Christie's London) $5,214 £3,300

A red-lacquered wood netsuke depicting two wrestlers in the Kawazu throw, their fundoshi lacquered brown, unsigned, early 19th century, 7.6cm.
(Christie's) $2904 £1760

An ivory netsuke of an ape sitting holding a persimmon, a fruiting branch on its back, signed *Masatami*, late 19th century, 4.5cm. long. (Christie's London) $1,738 £1,100

An unusual ivory netsuke depicting a tiger curled up inside a bisected bamboo node, signed *Okakoto*, circa 1800, 4.1cm. high. (Christie's London) $2,259 £1,430

A kagamibuta netsuke with ivory bowl and iron disc decorated with takaramono in cloisonné enamels, unsigned, the disc early 19th century, 4.4cm.
(Christie's) $817 £495

A brown stained ivory netsuke of a recumbent karashishi, signed *Gyokuyosai,* mid-19th century, 4.3cm. long. (Christie's London) $1,077 £682

An ivory netsuke of a tiger sitting snarling, its fur engraved and stained brown with black stripes, unsigned, style of Otoman, circa 1850, 3.5cm. (Christie's) $12705 £7700

A well detailed ivory netsuke depicting three karako, two playing instruments, signed *Ryomin* (Ono school), 19th century, 4cm. wide. (Christie's London) $1,129 £715

A finely patinated stag antler netsuke of a horse standing with its head and neck turned sharply, signed *Tsunemasa* (of Shima Province), 18th century, 5.3cm. high. (Christie's London) $1,738 £1,100

An ivory netsuke of Oguri Hangan leaping his horse on to a go table, signed *Ryosho,* late 19th century, 6.2cm. high. (Christie's London) $1,390 £880

An ivory netsuke of Hotei standing holding a Chinese fan and his sack suspended from a staff on his shoulder, signed Hidekazu, late 19th century, 3.8cm. high. (Christie's) $725 £462

A walrus ivory ryusa manju netsuke carved with a Bugaku stage with a gilt metal figure on Ran Ryo-o inset, signed *Koku,* 19th century, 4.3cm. diam. (Christie's London) $3,128 £1,980

A finely patinated ivory netsuke of a rat emerging from a hole in a pumpkin, unsigned, early 19th century, 3.7cm. wide. (Christie's London) $2,607 £1,650

A patinated bronze netsuke of a snail emerging from and turning back upon its shell, signed *Shugetsu,* 19th century, 4.5cm. wide. (Christie's London) $660 £418

Early German Courant letter opener, circa 1910.
(Auction Team Koeln) $119   £71

A two tier gold-bronze painted stamp holder, circa 1900.
(Auction Team Koeln)
$16 £10

Early German DRGM 114.189 stapler, with unusual reverse stapling facility, 1900.
(Auction Team Koeln) $132   £79

An Olympic pencil sharpener.
(Auction Team Koeln) $93 £59

A Brical calculator, with five scales and windows for L.S.D., in plush lined case, 7in. wide.
(Christie's S. Ken) $216 £132

An Ergo Extra pencil sharpener,
(Auction Team Koeln) $128 £81

A Pilot desk punch, metal on wooden base, circa 1910.
(Auction Team Koeln)
$29 £19

The Jeffers Calculator, calculating aid with interchangeable cardboard strips, in folding wooden case, 1907. (Auction Team Koeln) $1,027 £630

An Art Nouveau nickel plated cast iron stapler, circa 1890.
(Aution Team Koeln)
$58   £37

Parlograph dictating machine with taping and erasing modules and 11 new wax rolls, by Carl Lindstrom AG Berlin, circa 1920.
(Auction Team Koeln)
$777 £465

A decorative block stamp having floral decoration to the sides complete with plug and mat. (Auction Team Koeln)
$93 £59

A Jupiter pencil sharpener by Guhe & Harbeck, Hamburg, with case, circa 1920. (Auction Team Koeln) $113 £68

A very rare J. N. Williams US cheque writer for Automatic Bank Punch Co., New York City, 1885. (Auction Team Koeln) $289 £177

A calculating ape: Consul the Educated Monkey, a very rare tin calculating toy, in original cover, 1918. (Auction Team Koeln) $706 £433

A Boston Pencil Pointer pencil sharpener. (Auction Team Koeln) $41 £26

A brass pen brush for quill pens, circa 1900. (Auction Team Koeln) $39 £24

The Rapid adhesive label dampener of decorative Art Nouveau style, German, circa 1900.
(Auction Team Koeln)
$184 £110

A cast iron Adressograph Model 500 hand address-ing machine for metal plates, 1930's. (Auction Team Koeln) $51 £32

Bank of England Note. 10 shilling note 1948 specimen, serial R00 000000 with metal thread. (Phillips London) $1,422 £900

Great Britain, Exchequer Bill for £100 signed by Walpole and dated 1745. (Phillips London)
$1,137 £720

South Africa, 1860, London & Natal Bank Ltd. £10 unissued. (Phillips London)
$412 £260

Treasury Notes, N.K. Warren Fisher, 10 shilling note 1922-27 prefix M/700001. (Phillips London) $411 £260

Belgian Congo, 1944, 1,000 francs colour trial in blue for Waterlow & Sons Ltd. (Phillips London) $442 £280

Scarborough Old Bank, £5 note 1895, cut cancelled. (Phillips London) $174 £110

Canada, 1906 Eastern Townships Bank $100. (Phillips London) $1,106 £700

Bank of England Note. K. O. Peppiatt, £5, 2 February 1935 issued at Newcastle. (Phillips London) $664 £420

Bermuda, 1927 Government £1. (Phillips London) $189 £120

Brazil, 1940, Giori-Garrasi uniface trial in orange of 1,000 cruzeiros note. (Phillips London) $142 £90

Beverley Bank, £10 1864. (Phillips London) $316 £200

Norwich & Norfolk Bank, £5 note 1893. (Phillips London) $189 £120

Bank of England Note. Henry Hase, Perkins, Baron £1 uniface proof on thin paper 1820. (Phillips London) $506 £320

Great Britain, Perkins, Fairman & Heath Sideographic specimen note 1820. (Phillips London) $269 £1·70

Canada, 1883 La Banque Nationale $5 front and back proofs in black on white thin paper, light repair top edge and small piece of print missing by right panel of value on front. (Phillips London) $284 £180

New Zealand, 1928 Bank of Australasia £1. (Phillips London) $332 £210

Barbados, 1922 Canadian Bank of Commerce $5. (Phillips London) $338 £210

Canada, 1912 Molsons Bank $10 specimen colour trial in brown/black and light green with red back, two punch holes. (Phillips London) $322 £200

Canada, 1821 Hudsons Bay Company £1, with counterfoil (P. S1098), 10mm split at top of centre crease. (Phillips London) $193 £120

Bank of England Note. C. P. Mahon £5, 3 August 1927 issued at Hull. (Phillips London) $332 £210

Town & County Bank Ltd., £1, 1890. (Phillips London) $419 £260

Scotland, Sir William Forbes, James Hunter & Company, £1, 181-, unissued. (Phillips London) $316 £200

Huddersfield Bank, £5, 18--, proof on card. (Phillips London) $225 £140

Greece, 1870 National Bank 100 drachmai. (Phillips London) $580 £360

Bank of England Note, J. S. Fforde, 10/-, 1966-68 error with large piece of extra paper at right. (Phillips London) $338 £210

Canada, 184- La Banque du Peuple uniface proof of $10 printed by Toppan, Carpenter & Co. (as P. S907). Four small punch holes at bottom. (Phillips London) $515 £320

Bank of England Note, Abraham Newland, £1, 2 March 1797, note number 4 (Dugg. B200), first date of issue for the first £1 notes ever produced by the Bank of England, (Phillips London) $27,370 £17,000

States of Guernsey, £5 essay on thin paper produced in 1836 with a covering letter to Perkins, Bacon & Petch approving the general design and requesting delivery of 2,000 notes. (Phillips London) $6,636 £4,200

Timor, 1924 5 patacas. (Phillips London)
$177 £110

Cyprus, 1949 George VI £5. (Phillips London) $258 £160

Seychelles, 1919 Government 50 cents, emergency issue. (Phillips London) $934 £580

Japan, 1885 1 yen. (Phillips London)
$419 £260

U.S.A., 1934 $500 Federal Reserve note.
(Phillips) $528   £320

Ludlow Bank: £20 unissued 18.
(Phillips) $124   £75

Bank of England note £1 Applegarth and
Cowper essay in red and blue on black 1821.
(Phillips) $363   £220

Bermuda, 1927 Government £1. (Phillips
London) $209 £130

Bank of England note £20 1985–89 with large
piece of extra paper at bottom, including
colour bars.
(Phillips) $825   £500

Bank of England note £1 17 December 1825,
piece missing upper left but not infringing on
design.
(Phillips) $462   £280

Paraguay: 1870 Lezica y Lanus (Argentine
occupation) 5 pesos.
(Phillips) $165   £100

Sri Lanka, 1900c Diyatalawa P.O.W. camp 5
rupees. (Phillips London) $129 £80

Singapore: 1860 Chartered Bank $50 Post Bill,
used as currency at the time.
(Phillips) $264   £160

Canada: 1897 Dominion of Canada $1.
(Phillips) $264   £160

British Guiana 1928 Barclays Bank $5.
(Phillips London) $306 £190

Sri Lanka, 1865 Asiatic Banking Corporation
£1, Colombo. (Phillips London) $419 £260

Great Britain: Five francs 1914–18 P.O.W.
note at 'Depot des Prisonniers de Guerre
Anglais'.
(Phillips) $132   £80

Town and County of Southampton Bank: £1,
1810.
(Phillips) $313   £190

Sweden, 1921, 1,000 kronor. (Phillips
London) $209 £130

Sudan: 2,500 piastres Siege of Khartoum.
(Phillips) $214   £130

U.S.A., 1970 Military Payment Certificate $10
Series 692.
(Phillips) $264   £160

Nicaragua, 1908 100 pesos, specimen.
(Phillips London) $322 £200

Great Britain treasury note, August 1914.
(Phillips) $660   £400

National Commercial Bank: £100 1959.
(Phillips) $231   £140

Bank of England Note, Abraham Newland,
£1, 12 June 1804 (Dugg. B200), few small
holes in body otherwise very well preserved
for this issue. (Phillips London)
                              $2,576 £1,600

Bank of England note £1 1940–48 error with
extra paper.
(Phillips) $231   £140

Egypt: 1916 £10 National Bank.
(Phillips) $363   £220

British Guiana, 1940 Barclays Bank $20.
(Phillips London) $290 £180

Canada, 1897 Dominion of Canada $1.
(Phillips London) $644 £400

U.S.A., Military Payment Certificate $20
Series 692.
(Phillips) $264   £160

Bank of England Note. K. O. Peppiatt, £100,
29 September 1936 issued at Liverpool.
(Phillips London) $822 £520

St Helena, 1722 2/6d issued by The Governor
and council of the Island; the first paper
currency of St Helena was produced in 1717
for a total issue of £400. This note is believed
to be the only surviving paper money of that
period. (Phillips London) $8,855 £5,500

Wellingborough & Higham Ferrers, Northamp-
tonshire Bank, £10, 179-, unissued. (Phillips
London) $209 £130

British Guiana, 1918 Government $2.
(Phillips London) $708 £440

Paisley Commercial Banking Company, £20,
1843. (Phillips London) $1,320 £820

French Equatorial Africa, 1941, 1,000 francs,
Phoenix note. (Phillips London) $592 £368

A Regency red ground rectangular papier mache tray, the sandwich edge border painted and heightened in gilt with flowers and birds, 30in. wide. (Christie's S. Ken) $3,142 £1,870

A Victorian papier mache and mother-of-pearl inlaid teapoy painted in gilt with foliage, on bulbous fluted shaft and scroll feet, 17½in. wide. (Christie's S. Ken) $1,165 £715

A large 19th century papier mache tray, of cartouche form, richly decorated with Chinese style insects amongst sprays of flowers, 31cm. wide. (Henry Spencer) $826 £540

Papier mache tray by B. Walton & Co., painted with a Tudor hall interior scene, gilt raised border, approx. 18 x 15in. (G. A. Key) $884 £570

An attractive late 19th century Russian papier mache tea caddy, painted in sombre colours with a family riding in a troika drawn by three harnessed horses, 21cm. wide. (Henry Spencer) $537 £340

A 19th century oval papier mache tray, painted with a scene of English and French men o' war in battle on the high seas, 29½in. wide. (Christie's S. Ken) $858 £550

An early 19th century Stobwasser circular papier mache snuff box lid, painted with a couple in a bedroom scene, the reverse inscribed *Le cocu galant* 3¾in. diam. (Christie's S. Ken) $1,201 £770

A Victorian papier mache chair painted in gilt and inlaid with mother-of-pearl, on cabriole legs. (Christie's S. Ken) $359 £220

Fine papier mache tray, interior hand painted with a scene from Southern Hall interior, stamped to the rear *B. Walton & Co.*, 26 x 19in. (G. A. Key) $1,145 £720

PARASOL HANDLES

A jewelled rock crystal parasol handle, cut around the neck with geese and set with a trellis of rubies in gold collets, late 19th century, 2in. high. (Christie's London) $1,255 £770

A gold-mounted walking cane, the handle of tao form, one end engraved with a crest, the other tapering to a sea-monster's head, circa 1760, 34in. long. (Christie's) $4427 £2750

A French translucent blue guilloche enamel parasol handle, the body mounted with a band of foliage and flowers, by Cartier, Paris, 2¼in. long. (Christie's London) $2,689 £1,650

 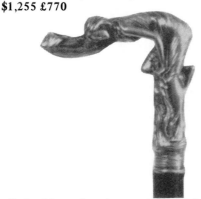 

An Edward VII jewelled gold mounted tortoiseshell parasol handle, with a collar of matted gold set with diamonds and demantoid garnets, by Charles Cooke, 1906, 10¾in. long. (Christie's London)$1,165 £715

A malacca walking stick, the white metal handle modelled with a figure of a young woman kneeling amidst reeds. (Christie's S. Ken.) $871 £528

An Edward VII jewelled gold mounted tortoiseshell parasol handle, 1906, by Charles Cooke, in original fitted case, 6½in. long. (Christie's London) $1,076 £660

A gold mounted silver and rock crystal parasol handle, by Tiffany & Co., late 19th century, 4¼in. in fitted case. (Christie's London) $2,510 £1,540

A walking stick with silver collar, the ivory handle carved with the heads of two reined horses. (Christie's S. Ken.) $327 £198

A George III tortoiseshell veneered dandy's cane, the baluster shaped knop with embossed wrythen decoration and additional flowers. (Phillips London)$1,683 £1,100

A Liberty & Co. pewter and enamel clock, with scrolling decoration and four turquoise enamelled hearts, the circular face with Arabic chapters, 10.3cm. high. (Christie's London) $370 £220

A W.M.F. pewter letter tray of curvilinear form, modelled with a maiden reading a letter, stamped marks, 12½in. long. (Christie's S. Ken) $938 £550

A Liberty & Co. pewter rose bowl designed by Rex Silver, embellished in relief with heavy plant form motifs, set with glass studs, 15.6cm. high. (Phillips London) $587 £360

Late 18th century Walzenkrug with ball thumbpiece, engraved with the arms of Saxony, monogram *1784* on lid. (Kunsthaus am Museum) $270 £155

Pair of Chinese pewter deer, 17th/18th century, stylized standing animals with glass eyes and articulated tails, 11½in. high. (Skinner Inc) $1500 £930

A WMF electroplated pewter centrepiece, the trumpet form body with pierced panels of floral decoration and two buttress supports, 51cm. high. (Christie's London) $466 £286

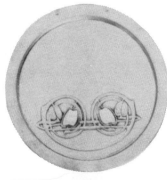

A Liberty & Co. Art Nouveau pewter circular tray designed by Archibald Knox, embellished in relief with entwined tendrils terminating with stylised honesty leaves, 25.2cm. diam. (Phillips London) $978 £600

A German scarlet japanned pewter coffee pot with domed lid and baluster body, with tap and scrolled legs on turned feet, 18th century, 17½in. high. (Christie's London) $929 £550

A Liberty & Co. English pewter bowl, with clutha glass liner, the mount pierced and embellished with plant forms, 16.5cm. high. (Phillips London) $1,454 £950

A W M.F. pewter letter tray, of curvilinear form, cast in shallow relief with a naked maiden, 10in. long. (Christie's S. Ken) $338 £198

A Liberty & Co. enamelled pewter tray, decorated with organic patterns and central turquoise enamel reserve, stamped *English Pewter,* 31cm. long. (Christie's London) $591 £352

A W. M. F. pewter letter tray, with pierced and raised scrolling floral decoration and modelled with a maiden stretching her hand towards a lily, 10¼in. long. (Christie's S. Ken) $597 £385

Cylindrical pewter coffee pot with knop finial and wrapped handle, marked *Zwickau 1855,* 22.5cm. high. (Kunsthaus am Museum) $541 £311

Pair of Persian pewter covered vases, 19th century, turned brass finial on a domed cover with wide undulating rim (minor dents), 18in. high. (Skinner Inc.) $800 £500

A W.M.F. polished pewter frame mirror, on easel support, cast in full relief with an Art Nouveau maiden gazing at her reflection, 14½in. high. (Christie's S. Ken) $1,782 £1,045

Heavily chased Seder pewter plate, German, probably Ulm, dated 1739, 33cm. diam. (Kunsthaus am Museum) $1,622 £932

Chased Walzenkrug with domed lid and ball thumb-piece, engraved on lid, 1810, Meissen, 24cm. high. (Kunsthaus am Museum) $485 £279

A pewter basin, by William Danforth, Middletown, Connecticut, 1792-1820, with a single reed brim, 20cm. diam. (Christie's New York) $935 £588

A metal enamelled sign in the form of a film spool advertising *'Illingworth's Films stocked here. Films developed & Printed'*, 20 x 7¼in. (Christie's S. Ken) $246 £154

A mahogany bodied, sliding box reflex camera obscura with a 5 x 4in. ground glass focusing screen. (Christie's S. Ken) $3,945 £2,420

A large brass bound portrait lens with brass mounting flange and Waterhouse stop, lens barrel engraved *Voigtlander & Sohn in Wien und Braunschweig.* (Christie's S. Ken) $753 £462

Houghtons Ltd., London, box of six boxed Ticka films in original packaging, outer box stamped Batch 01256. (Christie's S. Ken.) $581 £352

A brass 'Canary songster' photographer's birdie in maker's original box by the Risden Mfg. Co., Naugatuck, U.S.A. (Christie's S. Ken) $861 £528

A painted Brownie figure holding a brown coloured box camera with maker's marks '6360 JMK Czechoslovak', 23in. high (approx.) (Christie's S. Ken) $187 £110

W. Bruns Chem. Fabrik, Halberstadt, Germany, photographic colouring outfit comprising original colours in maker's bottles, all contained in a fitted wooden box. (Christie's S. Ken) $394 £242

A cut away display Leica IIIc camera no. 476784 mounted in a glass case. (Christie's S. Ken) $1,122 £660

A black rexine covered portable developing tent with folding down sides, built-in red glass safelight. (Christie's S. Ken) $359 £220

Noel Coward — a three-quarter length portrait photograph by Dorothy Wilding, signed and inscribed *For Ginette with love always Noel 1903*, 9½ x 7in. (Christie's S. Ken) $257 £165

Walter L Brock photograph in Bleriot cockpit, signed and dated September 18th 1913 by the subject. (Onslow's) $280 £170

HM Queen Victoria — a full length platinum print photograph by A. Bassano with photographer's credit, 21 x 15.5cm., signed and inscribed *Victoria R.I. 1886*. (Christie's S. Ken) $1,030 £660

Julia Margaret Cameron, Joachim, 1868, albumen print, 10¾ x 8½in., remounted on modern card. (Christie's S. Ken) $449 £264

H.R.H.Edward Prince of Wales A half-length profile portrait photograph in his regalia as Prince of Wales, by Campbell Gray, signed and inscribed *'Edward 1911'*. 11½ x 9¾in. (Christie's S. Ken) $686 £440

Tommy Sopwith, full length portrait standing beside aerodrome railings. (Onslow's) $264 £160

A full length photograph of HRH Princess Mary with her two eldest sons in Highland dress, signed and inscribed in Princess Mary's hand, *Victoria Mary 1906, Albert, Edward*, 7¾ x 6in. (Christie's S. Ken) $309 £198

Marcus D Manton photograph seated in Farman biplane, signed and inscribed Hendon and dated 13-9-13. (Onslow's) $165 £100

A full length seated portrait photograph by Alice Hughes of Princess Mary with her three eldest children, signed and inscribed in Princess Mary's hand *Victoria Mary, Albert, Victoria, Edward 1897*, 6 x 4in. (Christie's S. Ken) $275 £176

David Bailey — John Lennon and Paul McCartney, 1965, gelatin silver print, image size 9 x 9in., signed, dated and inscribed in pencil. (Christie's S. Ken) $1,165 £715

Mother and child, mid-late 1850s, albumen print, oval 6½ x 8¼in., possibly Oscar Gustave Rejlander. (Christie's S. Ken) $8,965 £5,500

David Bailey — Michael Caine, 1965, gelatin silver print, image size 18 x 18in., signed, dated and inscribed in pencil. (Christie's S. Ken) $1,255 £770

Dorothy Wilding — The Duchess of Windsor, autographed portrait, 1942, gelatin silver print, 23.8 x 18.7cm., mounted on tissue then card. (Christie's S. Ken) $538 £330

David Octavius Hill and Robert Adamson — James Linton, 1844-45, Calotype, 7½ x 5½in. (Christie's S. Ken) $6,813 £4,180

Oscar Gustave Rejlander — Mary Rejlander, semi-nude study in classical costume, 1850-60s, albumen print, oval, 5¼ x 3¼in. (Christie's S. Ken) $681 £418

David Bailey — Joseph Beuys, 1987, gelatin silver print, image size 9 x 9in., monogrammed and dated in ink and pencil on reverse. (Christie's S. Ken) $807 £495

Edward Curtis (1868-1952) — Zuni Governor, 1903, brown toned silver print, 45.1 x 25.7cm. (Christie's S. Ken) $1,076 £660

Cecil Beaton — Katherine Hepburn, 1950s, gelatin silver print, 9¼ x 9½in., with pencil annotations on the reverse. (Christie's S. Ken) $323 £198

PHOTOGRAPHS

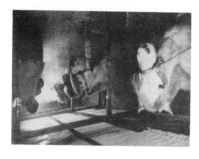

Herbert Ponting — In the stable, 1910-1912, mammoth gelatin silver print, 16½ x 23½in., (the figure is that of Capt. Oates). (Christie's S. Ken) $1,614 £990

An 8 x 4½in. paper 'The Menai Bridge', hold to light view, paper with watermark *J. Green, 1818.* (Christie's S. Ken) $305 £187

Gustave Le Gray — Portrail milieu d' Aubeterre, 1851-52, salt print from a waxed paper negative, 23.2 x 28.3cm. (Christie's S. Ken)
$11,655 £7,150

Claude Harris — Auguste Rodin in his studio, early 1900s, gelatin silver print, 7¾ x 4¾in. (Christie's S. Ken) $269 £165

Clarence Sinclair Bull — Female nude, circa 1927, gelatin silver print, image size 13 x 10in., photographer's blindstamp on image and M.G.M. ink credit stamp on the reverse. (Christie's S. Ken)
$1,165 £715

Algerine Woman, early 1850s, Calotype, 22.6 x 18.1cm., titled in ink on mount, possibly Charles Marville. (Christie's S. Ken)
$25,102 £15,400

Cecil Beaton — Pablo Picasso in his studio at Mougins in the South of France, 1965, gelatin silver print, 14 x 14in. (Christie's S. Ken) $1,434 £880

Portrait of a lady, 1840s, sixth-plate daguerreotype, octagonal paper surround, green morocco case. (Christie's S. Ken) $143 £88

Henry Peach Robinson (1830-1901) — 'She never told her love', 1857, albumen print, 7¼ x 9½in. (Christie's S. Ken) $39,446 £24,200

Robert Capa — General de Gaulle, Chartres, 1944, gelatin silver print, image size 9 x 13½in., ink copyright stamps and typescript title label on reverse. (Christie's S. Ken) $502 £308

A carpenter in his workshop, 1850s, a fine stereoscopic daguerreotype, hand tinted, oval surrounds, passe-partout. (Christie's S. Ken) $3,945 £2,420

William Henry Fox Talbot — Melrose Abbey, 1844, Calotype, 7¼ x 9in. (Christie's S. Ken) $807 £495

Clarence Sinclair Bull — Greta Garbo, 1936, gelatin silver print, 10 x 8in., photographer's blindstamp on image and ink credit stamp on the reverse. (Christie's S. Ken) $1,040 £638

Potteau — No Zanva Ikonta, 1862, albumen print, 7 x 5½in., trimmed at corners, pencil manuscript captions on the reverse. (Christie's S. Ken) $2,510 £1,540

Julia Margaret Cameron — Mrs Herbert Duckworth, 1867, albumen print, 13½ x 9¾in., mounted on grey card in original oak frame. (Christie's S. Ken) $23,309 £14,300

Lucia Moholy (born 1894) — Bella Kangil, 1920s, gelatin silver contact print, 4¾ x 3½in., signed in pencil on reverse, matted. (Christie's S. Ken) $717 £440

Roger Fenton (1819-69) — The Croat Chiefs, 1855-6, salt print, 18.1 x 15.2cm. (Christie's S. Ken) $1,076 £660

Claude Harris — George Bernard Shaw, 1910-20, gelatin silver print, 8 x 5¾in. (Christie's S. Ken) $574 £352

Harry Diamond — Francis Bacon and Lucien Freud, 'Dean St. Soho', 1974, gelatin silver print, image size 10½ x 15½ in. (Christie's S. Ken) $1,076 £660

T. R. Williams — Two young men with a woman plucking game, 1850s, stereoscopic daguerreotype, hand tinted, printed paper label on reverse. (Christie's S. Ken) $7,172 £4,400

George Bernard Shaw, early 1940s, gelatin silver print, image size 2½ x 3½ in., inscribed in pen (later) *Charlotte snaps GBS 'posing'* on the reverse. (Christie's S. Ken) $359 £220

Julia Margaret Cameron (1815-1879) — Henry Taylor, 1864, albumen print, 25.1 x 20cm., mounted on card, titled in ink on mount. (Christie's S. Ken) $717 £440

Herbert Ponting — The Terra Nova Icebound in the Pack, 1910-12, green toned carbon print, 75.9 x 55.3cm., photographer's blindstamp signature on image. (Christie's S. Ken) $1,434 £880

Herbert Lambert — 'Young England', 1917, gelatin silver print, 17 x 13¾ in., photographer's pencil monogram, border and title on image. (Christie's S. Ken) $807 £495

David Octavius Hill and Robert Adamson — Miss Matilda Rigby, mid 1840s, Calotype, 8¼ x 5¾ in. (Christie's S. Ken) $1,614 £990

John Thomson (1837-1921)— Covent Garden Flower Women, circa 1876-77, woodburytype, 10.8 x 8.6cm., mounted on card. (Christie's S. Ken) $215 £132

Dorothy Wilding — HM Queen Elizabeth, 1952, gelatin silver print, 11½ x 8¾ in., with photographer's facsimile printed signature. (Christie's S. Ken) $430 £264

William Henry Fox Talbot — The Fruit Sellers, 1842, Calotype, 18.4 x 22.6cm. (Christie's S. Ken) $1,165 £715

Attributed to Baron Adolphe de Meyer — Edward VII, circa 1903, brown toned platinum print, 9½ x 11½in., with clipped signature *Edward R.* (Christie's S. Ken) $1,345 £825

Group at Niagara Falls, circa 1855, half-plate daguerreotype, gilt surround, attributed to Platt D. Babbit. (Christie's S. Ken) $3,586 £2,200

Man Ray — Marie-Laure Comtesse de Noaille, 1936, gelatin silver print, 8.3 x 6cm., signed and dated in ink on image. (Christie's S. Ken) $7,172 £4,400

Cecil Beaton — Yul Brynner, 1946, gelatin silver contact print, 25.1 x 20.3cm., photographer's ink copyright stamp (facsimile signature) on reverse, matted. (Christie's S. Ken) $1,076 £660

Cecil Beaton — Bomb victim in a London hospital, 1940, gelatin silver print, 11¾ x 10in., typescript title and copyright label on reverse, matted. (Christie's S. Ken) $1,255 £770

Cecil Beaton (1904-1980) — The Marquis and Marchioness of Cholmondeley, circa 1939, gelatin silver print 9½ x 7¾in., signed and dated. (Christie's S. Ken) $986 £605

Portrait of a man with sliding box camera, globe and fez, 1850s, quarter-plate ambrotype. (Christie's S. Ken) $1,703 £1,045

Henry Peach Robinson — 'The Valentine', 1885, albumen print, 21½ x 16¼in., mounted on card, framed. (Christie's S. Ken) $8,606 £5,280

PHOTOGRAPHS

Cecil Beaton — Marlene Dietrich, 1937, gelatin silver print, 12¾ x 16¼in., printed later. (Christie's S. Ken) $807 £495

William Henry Fox Talbot — Botanic Garden, Oxford, 1842, Calotype, 16.2 x 19.7cm., (Christie's S. Ken) $717 £440

Horst P. Horst — Luchino Visconti, 1953, gelatin silver print, image size 19.4 x 24.5cm., signed in pencil in margin, printed 1980s. (Christie's S. Ken) $897 £550

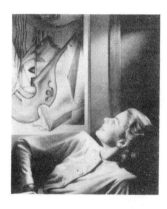

Ernest Bachrach — Ingrid Bergman, 1945, mammoth gelatin silver print, 24 x 20in., printed later. (Christie's S. Ken) $430 £264

Man Ray — Lee Miller in a bathing costume, circa 1932, gelatin silver print, 6½ x 4¼in., signed in pencil on image. (Christie's S. Ken) $23,309 £14,300

Yousuf Karsh — HRH the Duke of Windsor, 1971, gelatin silver print, 11¾ x 9½in. typescript copyright title label on reverse. (Christie's S. Ken) $305 £187

Charles Marville — La Porte Rouge, before 1853, Blanquart-Evrard process print from waxed paper negative, 8¼ x 6in. (Christie's S. Ken) $4,662 £2,860

Horatio Ross — Self-portrait preparing a collodion plate, 1850s, albumen print, 8 x 6¼in., mounted on card. (Christie's S. Ken) $5,738 £3,520

Yousuf Karsh (born 1908) — Robert Frost, 1940s, glossy gelatin silver print, image size 12¼ x 10in., photographer's ink copyright stamp on reverse. (Christie's S. Ken) $538 £330

631

A fine Classical stencilled and carved mahogany piano, By E. N. Scherr, Philadelphia, 1825-1835, the pedal support formed of two carved dolphins in a lyre, 68in. wide. (Christie's New York)

$3,300 £2,075

A Regency mahogany square pianoforte by Robert Wilson, Musical Instrument Maker, Whitby, the rectangular case with boxwood stringing, 5¾ octaves. (Christie's S. Ken.)

$1089 £660

A street barrel piano by Keith Prowse & Co. Ltd., with ten-air barrel pinned by Tomasso with popular tunes of circa 1900, the case with typical incised Keith Prowse name and decoration, overall length 83in. (Christie's S. Ken.)

$4719 £2860

Baby grand piano by Steinbach, in a mahogany case. (Michael G. Matthews)

$825 £500

Piano forte in Victorian rosewood case. (J.R. Parkinson Son)

$742 £450

An early Victorian small mahogany harmonium, the folding top lifting to reveal a keyboard, 98cm. wide. (Lawrence Fine Arts)

$521 £330

A piano Melodico, modelled as a miniature grand piano in an ebonised case, the playing mechanism operating from punched concertina cards. (Henry Spencer)
$2,445   £1,500

18th century George III mahogany Clavichord by Broderip, London with Lemonwood interior, 150cm. wide. (Duran, Madrid)
$913   £546

A Chappell & Co. Ltd., rosewood overstrung upright piano, the panelled front inlaid with scrolling foliage and flowers, 52½in. x 59in. (Bearne's)
$1122   £680

An Ibach mahogany cased baby grand piano, overstrung, serial number 90576. (Abbotts)
$1,092   £670

An ormolu mounted harewood, bois clair and mahogany marquetry overstrung grand piano by Steinway and Sons, New York, the square tapering legs on hairy paw feet, circa 1882, 83in. wide.
(Christie's, London) $115,115 £71,500

A Kessels 61-note automatic piano in upright ebonised case with roll mechanism in cupboard below keyboard driven by hand crank or electric motor, 59in. wide, with thirty-one rolls.
(Christie's S. Ken.) $690   £418

An Italian 17th century carved, gilded and painted plate frame, the central panel with gilded scrolling foliage and flowers, 99.7 x 81.6cm. (Christie's S. Ken) $2,917 £1,870

An English 18th century carved and gilded frame, the corners with pierced opposed C-scrolls, trailing foliage running to pierced cartouche centres, a foliate sight edge, 41 x 50in. (Christie's S. Ken) $1,716 £1,100

A Dutch tortoiseshell frame, with ripple inner and outer edges, 12½ x 10¼in. (Christie's S. Ken) $858 £550

A Bolognese 18th century carved and gilded leaf frame, with acanthus leaf centres and corners, 32¾ x 31in. (Christie's S. Ken) $1,888 £1,210

An Italian 17th century carved, gilded and painted frame, with a gadrooned outer edge, 47.4 x 39.7cm. (Christie's S. Ken) $343 £220

An English 18th century carved and gilded swept frame, the corners with pierced foliate cartouche spandrils, 22½ x 18¼in. (Christie's S. Ken) $601 £385

A Louis XIV carved and gilded frame, the corners with anthemia flanked by opposed C-scrolls on a cross hatched ground, 60.6 x 72.1cm. (Christie's S. Ken) $1,373 £880

A French Provincial 18th century, carved and gilded frame, with anthemia corners, carved with flowers, 17 x 10in. (Christie's S. Ken) $446 £286

A Spanish 17th century carved and gilded frame, with scrolling leaves running from the centres to the corners, 24¼ x 28¼in. (Christie's S. Ken) $1,716 £1,100

An English 18th century carved and gilded swept frame, 27¼ x 31½in. (Christie's S. Ken) $515 £330

A Louis XIV carved and gilded frame, the anthemia corners and centres flanked by opposed C-scrolls, 15¼ x 17¼in. (Christie's S. Ken) $1,201 £770

A Louis XIII carved and gilded frame, with a holly leaf pattern running from the flowerhead centres, 25¼ x 31¼in. (Christie's S. Ken) $3,089 £1,980

A Louis XV style carved and gilded frame, the corners centred by shell flanked by opposed C-scrolls, 24 x 27in. (Christie's S. Ken) $1,115 £715

An English 18th century carved and gilded frame, the corners and centres with rosettes flanked by pierced opposed C-scrolls, 37 x 31½in. (Christie's S. Ken) $1,201 £770

An Italian 17th century carved and gilded frame, with overlapping leaves running from centres to corners and scrolling foliage, 15¾ x 14¼in. (Christie's S. Ken) $1,716 £1,100

A Dutch 17th century carved and ebonized frame, with various ripple and wave mouldings, 26½ x 23¼in. (Christie's S. Ken) $2,917 £1,870

An Italian late 16th century carved and painted tabernacle frame, a broken pediment with inlays supported on a pair of marble doric columns, 15½ x 10in. (Christie's S. Ken) $5,491 £3,520

A French Provincial 18th century carved and gilded frame, the corners with scrolling foliage and flowers, 18½ x 21½in. (Christie's S. Ken) $1,459 £935

Frederick Buck (1771-circa 1839-40) – Captain Hugh Irvine, in the scarlet uniform of the 16th Regiment of Foot, gold frame with bright cut border, oval, 3¼in. high. (Christie's London) $704 £440

Maximilien Villiers (b. circa 1760) – A lady, patterned shawl and gold chain necklace, striped scarf in her curly hair, signed on obverse and dated *1790*, oval, 2½in. high. (Christie's London) $3,520 £2,200

Frederick Buck (1771-circa 1839/40) – Ephraim Norton, in scarlet uniform with green facings and gold epaulettes, white cross sash and plate, gold frame with plaited hair reverse, oval, 2½in. high. (Christie's London) $704 £440

JW, circa 1730 – Charlotte Branfill, nearly full face, in blue dress with lace underslip and cuffs, signed with monogram, 1¾in. high. (Christie's London) $824 £528

William Grimaldi (1751-1830) after Sir Joshua Reynolds, P.R.A. (1723-1792) – King George IV, as Prince Regent, wearing the regalia of the Order of the Garter, signed on the reverse, 1789, gilt metal frame, oval, 4in. high. (Christie's London) $5,280 £3,300

A miniature of Lady Flint (nee Anna Maria Seton), by George Engleheart, signed with cursive E, circa 1805, oval 79mm., in papier mache frame. (Phillips London) $2,038 £1,250

Frederick Buck (1771-circa 1839/40) – One of two brothers, one in blue naval uniform, the other in blue coat and waistcoat, gilt metal frames, oval, 3in. high. (Christie's London)
Two $1,144 £715

Charles Shirreff (b. circa 1750) – A lady, in gold trimmed white dress and shawl, matching turban headgear, drop pearl earrings, unframed, oval, 3¼in. high. (Christie's London) $528 £330

Thomas Hazlehurst (circa 1740-1821) – A gentleman, believed to be John Beck, in blue coat, white waistcoat and tied cravat, signed with initials on obverse, oval, 74mm. high. (Christie's London) $1,144 £715

George Chinnery (1774-1852) — A gentleman, possibly Sir Charles D'Oyly, in dark blue coat, white waistcoat and stock, gilt metal mount, oval, 3½in. high. (Christie's London) $1,496 £935

Attributed to Matthew Snelling (1621-1678) — A gentleman, bust length, in red cloak edged with gold fringe, and lace cravat, on vellum, silver gilt frame with pierced spiral cresting oval, 2½in. high. (Christie's London) $12,320 £7,700

Andrew Plimer (1763-1837) — The Hon. Charlotte Shore, as a child, with frilled collar and blue ribbon waistband, gold frame, the reverse with lock of hair, oval, 66mm. high. (Christie's London) $3,168 £1,980

Archibald Skirving (1749-1819) — A lady, holding an embroidery tool, in white dress trimmed with blue ribbon, the reverse with gold monogram *CR* within plaited hair, oval, 3in. high. (Christie's London) $968 £605

Bernard Lens (1682-1740) — A young boy, in blue coat, white waistcoat and embroidered border, holding a black tricorn hat under his left arm, oval, 48mm. high. (Christie's London) $669 £418

Sir William John Newton (1785-1869) — A lady, possibly Mrs Rennell, in mauve coloured dress with frilled white fichu, rectangular gilt metal mount, oval, 79mm. high. (Christie's London) $1,144 £715

Peter Paul Lens (circa 1714-circa 1750) — A gentleman, in gold bordered rust coloured coat with blue lapel, plaited hair mount, gold frame with bright cut border, oval, 1¾in. high. (Christie's London) $4,928 £3,080

Samuel Shelley (1750/56-1808) probably after Angelica Kauffman, R.A. (1741-1807) — Lady Emma Hamilton, as Ariadne, in white robe with red waistband, oval, 113mm. high. (Christie's London) $3,344 £2,090

Attributed to Andrew Robertson (1777-1845) — A lady, in white dress with pearl brooch at her corsage, green bordered red shawl draped over her shoulders, oval, 2¾in. high. (Christie's London) $704 £440

John Bogle (1746-1803) — A gentleman, in gold bordered blue waistcoat and tied cravat, powdered hair en queue, signed with initials and dated *1778,* oval, 1½in. high. (Christie's London) $1,056 £660

John Hoskins (d. 1664/5) — Queen Henrietta Maria, in decollete black dress with lace collar, vellum on card, gold frame set between rose diamond foliage sprays, oval, 2in. high. (Christie's London) $2,640 £1,650

Ignazio Pio Vittoriano Campana (1744-1786) — A lady, in decollete white dress with pale blue ribbon sash, gilt metal mount, circular, 60mm. diam. (Christie's London)$1,144 £715

Karl Von Saar (1797-1853) — An officer, holding a black plumed helmet, in red and gilt edged breast plate, signed on obverse and dated *1836,* 4in. high. (Christie's London) $6,688 £4,180

Francois Dumont (1751-1831) — A child, facing right, in white bonnet trimmed with black lace, signed on obverse and dated *1772,* gilt metal frame, oval, 1½in. high. (Christie's London) $1,584 £990

Ozias Humphry, R.A. (1742-1810) — Miss Elizabeth Bagot, in decollete orange and white dress, rope of pearls at her corsage, gilt metal frame, rectangular, 4in. high. (Christie's London) $1,936 £1,210

Henry Edridge, A.R.A. (1769-1821) — A lady, seated with arms folded, in gold edged white dress and white turban in powdered hair, oval, 2½in. high. (Christie's London) $704 £440

Attributed to Alexander Gallaway (fl. circa 1794-1812) — Lt Col. Richard Jones Sankey, in red uniform with blue facings, silver lace and silver epaulettes, gold frame with split pearl border, circular, 1¾in. diam. (Christie's London) $669 £418

Thomas Hazlehurst (circa 1740-1821) — A lady, in decollete white dress with blue ribbon sash and bandeau in powdered hair, signed with initials on obverse, oval, 2¾in. high. (Christie's London) $1,320 £825

PORTRAIT MINIATURES

A miniature of a lady, by John Smart, signed with initials and *I* for India and dated *1785,* oval 53mm. (Phillips London) $10,106 £6,200

William Prewitt (fl. 1735-1750) — A young boy, in blue coat with silver frogging, signed on reverse, gold frame with diamond border, oval, 47mm. high. (Christie's London) $6,160 £3,850

Roger, circa 1800 — A child, standing half length holding a cat, wearing a blue dress trimmed with white, signed on obverse, oval, 3½in. high. (Christie's London) $493 £308

Heinrich Friedrich Fueger (1751-1818) — Field Marshal Gideon Ernst Von Loudon (1716-90), in armour and white ruff collar, powdered hair, inscribed on reverse, rectangular, 3¼in. high. (Christie's London) $5,280 £3,300

John Smart (1742-1811) — A lady, in decollete blue dress with lace border and pink rose at her corsage, signed with initials on obverse and dated 1767, oval, 35mm. high. (Christie's London) $1,936 £1,210

Sn. Duchosal, 19th century, after Jean Etienne Liotard (1702-1789) — Mme. Louise Florence d'Epinay (1726-1783), in blue dress, enamel, signed on obverse, gilt wood frame, rectangular, 4¼in. high. (Christie's London) $3,520 £2,200

Heinrich Friedrich Fueger (1751-1818) — A fine portrait of Emperor Joseph II of Austria, wearing the Breast Star of the Order of Maria Teresa, gilt metal frame, oval, 3¾in. high. (Christie's London) $31,680 £19,800

Mme. Adelaide Labille-Guiard (later Mme. Vincent) (1749-1803) — A lady, holding a pink rose and resting her arms on a plinth, ormolu frame with beaded border, circular, 2¾in. diam. (Christie's London) $1,232 £770

William Singleton (d. 1793) — A lady, in gold figured white dress with lace underslip, the reverse with a memorial miniature of a lady with turban headgear, oval, 1½in. high. (Christie's London) $1,408 £880

639

PORTRAIT MINIATURES

Thomas Hargreaves (1774-circa 1846/47) — A young girl, bust length, facing right, in white dress with pink ribbon sash, gilt mounted rectangular black wood frame, oval, 2¾in. high. (Christie's London) $528 £330

Samuel Rickards (circa 1735 d. after 1823) — Mrs William Russell, seated reading to her daughter Mary, lock of hair on reverse, oval, 2in. high. (Christie's London) $968 £605

Cornelius Linsell (fl. 1800-1832) — P. Wayt of Burton, in black coat and waistcoat, tied white cravat, signed with initials on obverse and dated *1813*, oval, 79mm. high. (Christie's London) $528 £330

A miniature of Sir Charles Flint by George Engleheart, signed with cursive E, circa 1805, oval 79mm., in papier mache frame. (Phillips London) $1,989 £1,150

Frederick Buck (1771-circa 1839/40) — Mrs Robinson, in white dress trimmed with blue ribbon, gold frame, the reverse with plaited hair, oval, 2½in. high. (Christie's London) $528 £330

John Wood Dodge (1807-1893) — Mr William R. Blackwell, in black coat, red waistcoat and tied black stock, signed and dated *New York April 26, 1837*, oval, 61mm. high. (Christie's London) $968 £605

Albert Theer (1815-1902) — A Lieutenant of infantry, in white uniform with red collar and matching braid, signed on obverse and dated *Vienna 1856*, oval, 3½in. high. (Christie's London) $1,760 £1,100

John Thomas Barber Beaumont (1774-1841) — Captain Peter Lely, in the scarlet uniform of the Royal Marines, signed on reverse with trade card, ormolu mounted rectangular black wood frame by John Miers, oval, 60mm. high. (Christie's London) $2,816 £1,760

James Scouler (circa 1740-1812) — A gentleman, in blue coat, white waistcoat and tied cravat, signed on obverse and dated 1794, gold frame, hair border, oval, 52mm. high. (Christie's London) $1,320 £825

Joseph Friedrich August Schall (1785-1867) — An officer, in blue uniform with silver buttons, wearing a decorative Order and gold fob, signed and dated *1808,* oval, 48mm. high. (Christie's London) $493 £308

John Smart (1742-1811) — A charming portrait of a young girl, in decollete white dress with thin yellow waistband, signed with initials and dated *1804,* oval, 80mm. high. (Christie's London) $13,200 £8,250

Nathaniel Plimer (1757-1822) — A lady, in lilac coloured dress with white fichu and frilled white bonnet, in the base of a gilt metal locket, 2¾in. high. (Christie's London) $1,408 £880

William Grimaldi (1751-1830) after Sir Joshua Reynolds, P.R.A. (1723-1792) — HRH Frederick Duke of York, wearing the regalia of the Order of the Garter, signed on reverse, oval, 4¾in. high. (Christie's London) $24,640 £15,400

Austrian School, circa 1840 — A lady, in black dress with red roses at her corsage, her triple pearl necklace set with blue jewel, gilt metal frame, oval, 2½in. high. (Christie's London) $387 £242

Moritz Michael Daffinter (1790-1849) — An officer, half length, in blue uniform, possibly of the Italian Light Dragoons, signed on obverse, gilt metal frame with monogram on reverse, oval, 61mm. high. (Christie's London) $2,992 £1,870

De Brea, circa 1790 — A lady, in decollete white dress and salmon bolero, in the lid of a circular gold mounted lava composition box, circular, 2¼in. diam. (Christie's London) $1,760 £1,100

Jean Theodore Perrache (1744-1789) — Mrs Maria Julia Shrine, aged 40, seated with her son Julian, enamel, signed on the reverse and dated *1785,* gilt metal mount, oval, 2¾in. high. (Christie's London) $704 £440

Andrew Plimer (1763-1837) — A lady, in white dress with blue bows, large straw hat tied with blue ribbons, gold frame, oval, 60mm. high. (Christie's London) $1,496 £935

Crystal Palace Road Circuit poster Saturday 21st May Grand Composite Meeting Cars, pub by London Midland & Scottish Railway, 102cm. x 64cm. (Onslow's) $907 £550

1920s Coca Cola advertising poster in wooden frame, Dutch, 93 x 50.5cm. (Auction Team Koeln) $60 £36

Nick, Terrot Cycles Motorcycles, pub by Pertuy, Paris, on linen, 158cm. x 119cm. (Onslow's) $462 £280

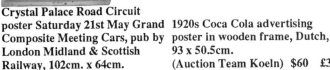

Paul Berthon Folies Bergere, a chromolithographic poster, printed by Le Mercier Paris, 163 x 64.5cm. (Phillips London) $704 £460

Gerald Spencer Pryse, Niger Steamers Loading Groundnuts, AB5. (Onslow's) $1,320 £800

'Flirt. Lefevre-Utile' 1900, signed *Mucha*, titled in gold across top and *Biscuits/Lefevre-Utile/Grand Prix 1900*, colour lithograph, 59.4 x 25.4cm. (Skinner Inc.) $2,100 £1,288

An 11½ x 17½in. lithographic poster advertising 'Lamb's Royal Diorama of Scotland', and with manuscript ink caption *These lithographs were issued on Friday April 18, 1873'.* (Christie's S. Ken) $486 £286

Bovril 17 types of standard cattle, advert on board, 43 x 68cm. framed. (Onslow's) $528 £320

An exhibition poster *Warhol*, The Tate Gallery, 17 February — 28 March 1971, signed *Andy Warhol* in black felt pen, 30 x 20in. (Christie's S. Ken) $1,075 £660

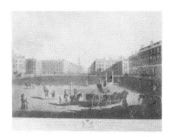

Thomas McLean, publisher — Windsor, Staines and South Western Railway Bridge over the river Thames at Richmond, by W. J. Gales, coloured lithograph, published, London, 1848, 12 x 19¾in. (Christie's S. Ken) $717 £440

After Edward Dayes — View of Hanover Square, by R. Pollard & F. Jukes, coloured aquatint, London 1787, 14¾ x 20¾in. (Christie's S. Ken) $1,219 £748

George Scharf — Zoological Gardens, Regent's Park, coloured lithograph, printed by C. Hullmandel, published by G. Scharf, London, 1835, 8 x 12¼in. (Christie's S. Ken) $717 £440

'Spanish Nights', by Louis Icart, etching and drypoint printed in colours, numbered 67, Copyright 1926, 53.5cm. x 34.5cm. (Christie's) $4605 £2860

'Attic Room', by Louis Icart, etching and drypoint printed in colours, numbered 261, Copyright 1940, 38cm. x 43.5cm. (Christie's) $7084 £4400

William Henry Payne, The half penny showman, aquatint, London, Jan 1, 1805, with contemporary printed description on reverse. (Christie's S. Ken) $827 £495

After James Pollard — Scenes on the Road, or A Trip to Epsom and Back: Hyde Park Corner, by J. Harris, coloured aquatint, published by Ackermann & Co, London, 1838, 13 x 20in. (Christie's S. Ken) $1,075 £660

After Francis Calcraft Turner — View on the Thames, showing Goding's new Lion Ale Brewery, the Wharfs, Shot Factories and the Lambeth end of Waterloo Bridge, by G. Hunt, coloured aquatint, published by J. Moore, London, 1836, 15½ x 24½in. (Christie's S. Ken) $3,048 £1,870

Franklin Square Lithographic Company, publishers, Bird's-eye View of the Great Suspension Bridge connecting the cities of New York and Brooklyn, lithograph printed in colours, published New York, 1883, 17½ x 35½in. (Christie's S. Ken) $574 £352

Glazed chintz quilt, America, early 19th century, light brown background with stylised floral bouquets, 120 x 104in. (Skinner Inc.) $600 £368

Applique quilt, probably Pennsylvania, late 19th century, the red and green cotton patches arranged in patriotic motif with eagle, 74 x 72in. (Skinner Inc.) $3,000 £1,840

An appliqued cotton and quilted coverlet, American, circa 1850, worked in a modified Princess Feather pattern, the green and red feathers stitched in four pinwheels, centring a quilted pineapple, 88 x 88in. (Christie's New York) $4,620 £2,905

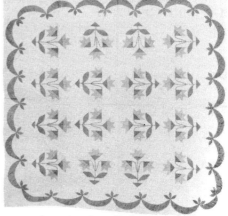

An appliqued and stuffed cotton quilt, Pennsylvania, 1840-1850, worked in sixteen blocks of appliqued flowers alternating with nine blocks of trapunto tulips, 79½ x 78in. (Christie's New York) $3,850 £2,421

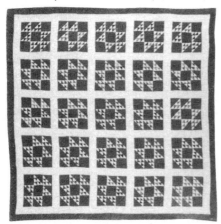

A pieced cotton quilted coverlet, Lincolnton County, Massachusetts, circa 1870, worked in 25 blocks of flying geese pattern with print fabrics on green ground framed in white sashing with green border, 82 x 82in. (Christie's New York) $990 £622

An Amish pieced cotton and wool quilted coverlet, initialled J.F.K., Lancaster County, Pennsylvania, circa 1920, the diamond-in-the-square pattern with slate centre diamond stitched in star and wreath framed in dusty pink with wide purple border, 82 x 82in. (Christie's New York) $2,860 £1,798

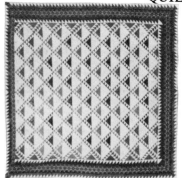

Pieced album quilt, probably New Jersey, circa 1843, various calico and muslin patches arranged in the little sawtooth pattern, 96 x 96in. (Skinner Inc.) $1,500 £920

An appliqued and quilted cotton coverlet, Hawaii, mid 19th century, worked with four enlarged floral and vine urns in blue fabric with white dots on a white ground, 78 x 80in. (Christie's New York) $5,500 £3,459

An appliqued and pieced album quilt, Maryland, mid 19th century, centring a square reserve with a lemon tree, the inner border with 38 pictorial squares including tulips, roses, oak leaves, flower baskets, wreaths, birds and flags, 85 x 95in. (Christie's New York) $6,050 £3,805

A pieced and appliqued cotton quilted coverlet, Hawaii, second half 19th century, centring a square reserve depicting the crest of the Hawaiian monarchy and inscribed *Kuu Hae,* above and *Aloha* below, 74 x 74in. (Christie's New York) $8,800 £5,534

A Mennonite pieced cotton quilted coverlet, Lancaster County, Pennsylvania, circa 1880, worked in the Joseph's Coat of Many Colours pattern in a spectrum of bright fabrics with rope twist stitching, 82 x 86in. (Christie's New York) $6,050 £3,805

A Mennonite pieced and appliqued cotton quilted coverlet, Lancaster County, circa 1880, worked in four blocks of Princess Star Feather in mustard and green fabric on red ground with floral baskets along the centre, 72 x 80in. (Christie's New York) $2,860 £1,798

A very early Braun Radio Model K transistor radio with glass transistors, original batteries and dials, circa 1959. (Auction Team Koeln) $164 £101

A single tube battery radio receiver with earphones, possibly home-made. (Auction Team Koeln) $93 £59

A French Excelsior 5 radio by SNR, with snakeskin decoration, circa 1953. (Auction Team Koeln) $164 £104

A wooden cased Berliner Wien radio with built in dual straight receiver and free swivel loud-speaker. (Auction Team Koeln) $35 £22

A German radiogram, the case designed in 1928 by Prof. Bruno Paul, made by Telephonefabrik Berliner, 1930. (Auction Team Koeln) $316 £195

An early Marconiphone battery powered pocket radio, circa 1955. (Auction Team Koeln) $76 £47

A French SNR Excelsior 5 radio, dark brown. (Auction Team Koeln) $158 £100

A Fada yellow plastic valve radio with green marbled louvred speaker, original label, 8¼in. wide. (Christie's S. Ken.) $998 £605

A Tefifon six band radio, circa 1958.(Auction Team Koeln) $126 £78

Great Western Railway cast brass nameplate, *Rhuddlan Castle,* removed from the Castle Class 4-6-0 locomotive No. 5039, 68½in. long. (Christie's S. Ken)
$10,758 £6,600

David Shepherd, 'Service by Night', published by BR, quad royal. (Onslow's) $391 £240

London and North Eastern Railway cast brass nameplate, *The Pytchley,* being the left hand side plate removed from the D.49 Hunt Class 4-4-0 locomotive, 33in. long. (Christie's S. Ken) $10,399 £6,380

London Brighton & South Coast Railway (SER) hand-lamp, with BR(SR) wick. (Onslow's) $101 £60

A pair of brass LNWR hand held acetylene lamps by Lucas, one with bull's-eye, the other with plain glass. (Christie's S. Ken) $179 £110

Lancashire & Yorkshire Railway lower quadrant signal lamp, lacking burner, 47cm. high. (Onslow's) $51 £30

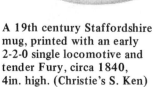

A 19th century Staffordshire mug, printed with an early 2-2-0 single locomotive and tender Fury, circa 1840, 4in. high. (Christie's S. Ken) $170 £105

An enamel sign, *G.W. and L.M.S. Railway Tickets Issued Here,* red on white ground, 24in. wide. (Christie's S. Ken) $681 £418

A 19th century blue and white printed earthenware jug depicting John Blenkinsop's locomotive and five coal wagons on a viaduct, possibly Dillwyn, 1830s, 5¾in. high. (Christie's S. Ken) $1,076 £660

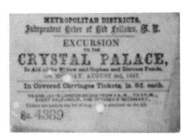

'Caution Do Not Look Over or Pass Along the Side of this Cab . . . ' cast iron Great Western locomotive sign, dated *Jan. 1909,* 19 x 30cm. (Onslow's) $110 £65

Great Eastern Railway brown earthenware ink pot. (Onslow's) $100 £60

Metropolitan Districts, Independent Order of Odd Fellows Excursion to the Crystal Palace Monday August 3rd 1857 covered carriage ticket 1/6d. (Onslow's) $84 £50

Great Northern North Eastern and North British Railway, Glasgow International Exhibition 1901, on linen. (Onslow's) $507 £300

Great Western Railway Hotels large milk jug, cream jug, small sugar basin and coffee cup. (Onslow's) $217 £130

W & SC Joint Line, punch ticket No. 7033. (Onslow's) $54 £32

Great Eastern Railway etched bevelled mirror, 45 x 40cm. (Onslow's) $287 £170

Great Central Railway silver plated toast rack, stamped with letter K. (Onslow's) $251 £150

London Brighton & South Coast Railway handlamp with metal plate stamped *Holmwood* with burner. (Onslow's) $118 £70

A Maclure, Great Central Railway, Grimsby Royal Docks 1879, colour lithograph, by Maclure and McDonald, 53 x 95 cm. (Onslow's) $334 £200

London & Greenwich Railway Company, bronze ticket with Company coat of arms on each side. (Onslow's) $135 £80

Great Western Railway 'No Unauthorised Person Allowed in this Box', cast iron sign, 21 x 28cm. (Onslow's) $101 £60

Great Eastern Railway Cavendish Station, black painted platform oil lamp, lacking burner, 51cm. high. (Onslow's) $118 £70

Great Northern & London & North West Railway Joint, cast iron gate warning sign, dated 1st November 1883, 47 x 46cm. (Onslow's) $980 £580

London Midland & Scottish Hotels, plated ice bucket. (Onslow's) $59 £35

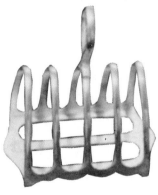

A mantel clock with mahogany case stamped *LMS Hotels*, 26cm. high. (Onslow's) $84 £50

Royal Victoria Hotel silver plated toast rack. (Onslow's) $100 £60

North Staffordshire Railway Company, silver free pass with blue enamel inscription *T. Thomas No. 101.* (Onslow's) $439 £260

Kenilworth 3325, cast brass Great Western Railway cab-side name/number plate, stamped with engine and boiler class numbers and letters. (Onslow's)
$6,591 £3,900

Great Eastern Railway, clothes brush with letters on bristles. (Onslow's) $93 £55

Midland Railway Hotels gilded water jug and washing bowl. (Onslow's) $456 £270

Kerr, 'If You Must Travel Travel Light I Can't You Can', double crown. (Onslow's)
$65 £40

Metropolitan Electric Tramways, enamel map of the system, 74cm. square. (Onslow's) $101 £60

'You May Have A Friend Here He's In Your Usual Train', published by Railway Executive Committee, double royal. (Onslow's) $57 £35

A Tyer's tablet machine, with brass label *Dersingham,* on original signal box cupboard, mounted with back board and block bell. (Onslow's)
$250 £150

Bert Thomas, 'Smaller Parcels Quicker Service', published by The Railway Executive Committee, 64 x 51cm. (Onslow's) $52 £32

London Brighton & South Coast Railway glass decanter. (Onslow's) $134 £80

Midland Grand Hotel, oval salmon dish with pierced tray and cover, lacking handle, with coat of arms. (Onslow's) $372 £220

The Talisman, London & North East Railway cast aluminium headboard, the reverse stamped with the names *Fenman, Comet, Manxman, Irishman, Irish Mail and Talisman.* (Onslow's) $2,535 £1,500

Cast iron smokebox plate 52108, together with receipt for 4/- dated *March 1962.* (Onslow's) $355 £210

L. A. Webb, 'Shabby? Yes this station does need smartening up', published by SR, double royal, 1945. (Onslow's) $122 £75

Furness Railway, blue and white enamel warning sign, 46cm. square, ex Grange-over-Sands. (Onslow's) $93 £55

Irish Tourist Ticket, issued Euston Station London, 26th July 1853 First Class valid for one month price £6.10.0. (Onslow's) $169 £100

'LNER Factory Sites'. (Onslow's) $98 £60

South Eastern & Chatham Railway poster, 'Fashionable Folkestone Kent', on South Eastern & Chatham Railway poster, 'Fashionable Folkestone Kent', on linen. (Onslow's) $1,723 £1,020

'Use Road-Rail Containers'. (Onslow's) $57 £35

An official Beatles fan club postcard, circa 1964, the Dezo Hoffmann group photograph signed by each member of the group. (Christie's S. Ken) $771 £473

A flight bag of blue vinyl trimmed with white, printed on both sides with white lettering *Star Club Hamburg*, 10½ x 14in. (Christie's S. Ken) $340 £209

A jacket of white lurex' decorated with strips of black and white brocade, with a photograph of David Bowie wearing the jacket in 1973 and a letter of authenticity. (Christie's S. Ken) $1,613 £990

A piece of paper signed and inscribed *To Lenny, Ritchie Valens*, 1½ x 3½in., with a head and shoulders colour machine print photograph, 10¾ x 9½in. (Christie's S. Ken) $394 £242

A presentation Multi-Platinum disc *Faith*, the album mounted with seven reductions of the cover *1 Million Sales* to *7 Million Sales*, a platinum cassette and a plaque inscribed *To commemorate the sale of more than 7,000,000 copies of the Columbia Records album and cassette Faith*, the disc, signed on the label *George Michael*, 21 x 17in., framed. (Christie's S. Ken) $896 £550

Printed sheet music for the song *Gimme Some Truth*, from the *Imagine* album, 1971, signed *love John Lennon*, 11½ x 8½in. (Christie's S. Ken) $1,613 £990

Two autographed albums *Led Zeppelin III* 1970, and *House of the Holy*, 1973, signed by all four original members of the band, Jimmy Page, Robert Plant, John Paul Jones, and John Bonham. (Christie's S. Ken) $537 £330

John Lennon, *Portrait Of A Lady*, biro drawing on the reverse of *Imperial Hotel, Torquay* headed paper, with pencil annotations in separate hand, 1964. (Christie's S. Ken) $3,944 £2,420

An album cover *Who's Next*, MCA Records, 1971, signed by Keith Moon, Pete Townshend, Roger Daltrey and John Entwistle. (Christie's S. Ken) $627 £385

A group photograph of The
Beatles, circa 1969, inscribed
With Best Wishes to Bevans,
signed by John Lennon, Ringo
Starr, George Harrison and
Paul McCartney, 8 x 10in.
(Christie's S. Ken) $986 £605

A promotional copy of a
Jurgen Vollmer photograph
used on the cover of the album
Rock 'n' Roll, signed by John
Lennon in blue felt pen,
9 x 7in. (Christie's S. Ken)
$753 £462

A three-quarter length colour
machine print photograph,
circa 1975, signed *Best Wishes
Elvis Presley*, 9½ x 7½in.
(Christie's S. Ken) $538 £330

Two albums *Thriller* and *Bad*,
both Epic Records, 1987 and
1988, each signed by Michael
Jackson in felt pen. (Christie's
S. Ken) $537 £330

An early autograph letter to a
fan, signed (n.d. but circa
April 20th 1962), from Paul
McCartney, thanking Anne?
for her letter —*Yours was the
first one I got. The Club where
we're playing is good but not
as good as Liverpool.. I think
we'll be making some records
soon, and we'll get them released in Liverpool as soon as
possible* . . . (Christie's S. Ken)
$5,379 £3,300

A rare printed colour proof
for the banned version of the
David Bowie album cover
Diamond Dogs, RCA Records,
1974, 13½ x 25½in.(Christie's
S. Ken) $1,255 £770

A self portrait caricature with
Yoko Ono, on a brown hard-
backed envelope, inscribed
Power To The People and
signed *Love John Lennon '71*,
8¼ x 12½in. (Christie's S. Ken)
$4,303 £2,640

A souvenir Rolling Stones
concert programme, circa
1965, signed on the cover by
Brian Jones, Keith Richards,
Bill Wyman, Charlie Watts and
Mick Jagger. (Christie's S. Ken)
$322 £198

A piece of paper signed *Sam
Cooke*, 2½ x 3½in., in com-
mon mount with a half length
machine print photograph of
Sam Cooke, 10½ x 8in.
(Christie's S. Ken) $358 £220

A machine print publicity photograph of The Doors, signed by Ray Manzarek, Robby Krieger, John Densmore, and inscribed *Cheers J. Morrison,* 6¾ x 7½in. (Christie's S. Ken) $896 £550

A Fender Stratocaster guitar, signed and inscribed *Eric Clapton '89,* 38½in. long, in fitted case; accompanied by a letter of authenticity. (Christie's S. Ken) $3,586 £2,200

A rare autographed souvenir concert programme, circa 1958, signed on the reverse by Buddy Holly. (Christie's S. Ken) $1,524 £935

A copy of the withdrawn album cover for The Rolling Stones *Some Girls* EMI Records, 1978. (The first version of the *Some Girls* album cover had to be withdrawn as permission had not been granted by the film stars included.) (Christie's S. Ken) $717 £440

A BOAC-Cunard menu, circa 1964, signed on the cover by John Lennon, Paul McCartney, Ringo Starr and George Harrison and inscribed *The Beatles* in the latter's hand. (Christie's S. Ken) $1,434 £880

An album cover *Revolver,* Capitol Records, 1966, signed by each member of the group in blue ink. (Christie's S. Ken) $2,510 £1,540

An album cover *Prince – Love Sexy* 1988, signed and inscribed *Love God, P. '88,* additionally signed by seven members of the band. (Christie's S. Ken) $573 £352

A machine print of a Dezo Hoffmann publicity photograph, 1964, signed by each member of the group in black ink, 5½ x 6in. (Christie's S. Ken) $1,219 £748

A rare souvenir concert programme for *BBC Top Beat,* April 27th, 1964, Royal Albert Hall, London, signed inside by various artists including The Rolling Stones. (Christie's S. Ken) $717 £440

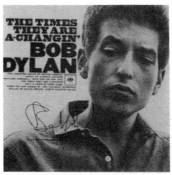

Four previously unpublished photographs of Jimi Hendrix by photographer Graham Howe, taken at The Round House, Chalk Farm, London, in February 1967. (Christie's S. Ken) $986 £605

An album cover *The Times They Are A-Changin'* Columbia Records, 1964, signed by Bob Dylan in blue felt pen, 12 x 12in. (Christie's S. Ken) $681 £418

R. Hughes, 1980 photographic silk screen print numbered 409 from an edition limited to 750, inscribed by subject *Elvis Costello best wishes,* 31¼ x 23¼in. (Christie's S. Ken) $860 £528

A rare colour machine print photograph from *Life* magazine, 1967, signed by each member of the group in blue ink, 13¾ x 10¼in. (Christie's S. Ken) $1,793 £1,100

A printed proof for an unissued version of The Beatles album cover *Let It Be,* Apple Records, 1970, 14 x 14in. (Christie's S. Ken) $179 £110

A page from an autograph book signed and inscribed *To Jerry, Best Wishes Elvis Presley,* 2¼ x 3¼in. (Christie's S. Ken) $538 £330

A rare colour machine print from The Beatles *Magical Mystery Tour* TV film, 1967, signed by each member of the group. (Christie's S. Ken) $1,793 £1,100

A souvenir concert programme for The Beatles/Roy Orbison tour 1963, signed by The Beatles and Roy Orbison. (Christie's S. Ken) $1,434 £880

An album cover *Never Mind The Bollocks Here's The Sex Pistols,* Virgin Records, 1977, signed by Sid Vicious, Paul Cook, Steve Jones and inscribed *John Rotten was here.* (Christie's S. Ken) $1,255 £770

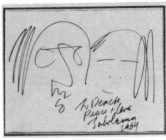

A self portrait caricature with Yoko Ono, in black felt pen, signed and inscribed *To Derek, Peace and Love, John Lennon, 1969,* 8 x 10½in. (Christie's S. Ken) $4,661 £2,860

A pair of high platform lace-up shoes of black and silver leather, the left shoe signed *Elton John* on the toe in blue biro. (Christie's S. Ken) $986 £605

A colour machine print photograph of the *Sgt. Peppers Lonely Hearts Club Band* album cover, signed by each member of the group. (Christie's S. Ken) $1,434 £880

A Michael Jackson presentation Platinum disc *Bad* mounted above a plaque bearing the R.I.A.A. Certified Sales Award and inscribed *Presented to Epic Records to commemorate the sale of more than 1,000,000 copies.* (Christie's S. Ken) $1,793 £1,100

A rare album *The Rolling Stones,* for American Radio, 1969, signed on the back cover by Mick Jagger, Bill Wyman, Charlie Watts, Keith Richards, and Mick Taylor. (Christie's S. Ken) $358 £220

An American Wurlitzer Model 1015 1948 style juke box, with visible electric record selector for twenty-four 78rpm records. (Christie's S. Ken) $12,192 £7,480

An exotic stage jacket of gold and black tiger skin patterned lurex, reputedly worn by Bryan Ferry on the inside cover of the first Roxy Music album *Roxy Music.* (Christie's S. Ken) $1,703 £1,045

An official Beatles fan club card, 1963, signed by each member of the group, with a souvenir programme for the Royal Command Performance, Monday November 4th, 1963. (Christie's S. Ken) $1,075 £660

A page from an autograph book signed and inscribed *Stay Groovy Jimi Hendrix,* 3½ x 4¾in., in common mount with a half length publicity photograph, circa 1968. (Christie's S. Ken) $537 £330

An autographed Christmas card, circa 1965, decorated with a printed reproduction of John Lennon's drawing *The Fat Budgie,* signed and inscribed inside. (Christie's S. Ken) $717 £440

A circular brass belt buckle, embossed with the Sun Record Company logo, inscribed *Good Rockin' Tonight (Ray Brown),* *Elvis Presley, Scotty and Bill,* 3in. diam. (Christie's S. Ken) $251 £154

A rare autographed souvenir concert programme, 1958, signed on the reverse by Buddy Holly, Jerry Allison and Joe Mauldin. (Christie's S. Ken) $1,972 £1,210

A presentation Gold disc *The Everly Bros. Greatest Hits,* above a plaque inscribed *Presented to Barnaby Records to commemorate the sale of more than 500,000 copies.* (Christie's S. Ken) $1,075 £660

A rare Beatles dress, signed by Brian Epstein, John Lennon, Paul McCartney, George Harrison, Ringo Starr and Cynthia Lennon, worn by one of the usherettes at the world premiere of The Beatles film *A Hard Day's Night,* July 6th, 1964. (Christie's S. Ken) $4,662 £2,860

A bomber jacket of black satin printed with a design of shooting stars and planets. Accompanying letter states that the jacket was given to actress Suzanna Leigh by Marc Bolan in the 1970s. (Christie's S. Ken) $1,524 £935

An Elvis Presley autograph letter, signed to a fan, *Dear Marlene,* with original envelope frankmarked Memphis, Tenn. January 24th 1961. (Christie's S. Ken) $897 £550

Rare handwritten and typescript lyrics by Bob Dylan, circa 1966, comprising four verses from *Obviously Five Believers,* 1966, three verses handwritten in black biro with alterations and deletions, one verse typescript, on a piece of paper 8.58 x 14.94cm. (Christie's S. Ken) $2,689 £1,650

A restaurant menu *Diner Au Choix . . . 22/6d* dated October 2nd, 1965, signed by Paul McCartney and John Lennon, 20½ x 4¼ in. (Christie's S. Ken) $573 £352

Yomud Ensi, West Turkestan, early 20th century, red ashik gul inner border, multi-coloured pole tree elems. (Skinner Inc.) $800 £516

Gustav Stickley drugget rug, circa 1910, honeycomb pattern and Greek key border, 7ft.11in. x 5ft.1in. (Skinner Inc.) $1,200 £741

A Kazak carpet, the red field with three red, ivory and blue medallions, 12 x 8ft. (Christie's S. Ken) $1,309 £770

Large hooked rug, America, early 20th century, patterned in the manner of an Oriental rug, 103 x 90in. (Skinner Inc.) $8,500 £5,215

Karabagh rug, South Caucasus, late 19th century, the centre field covered with four large latch hook medallions, 9ft. x 4ft.5in. (Skinner Inc.) $2,700 £1,656

An Iranian Sarouk rug, the shaded brick red field with a blue medallion and ivory spandrels, 4ft.8in. x 3ft.3in. (Christie's S. Ken) $561 £330

Armenian kazak, Southwest Caucasus, the dark blue linked medallions flanked by large stylised birds, 6ft.8in. x 4ft.7in. (Skinner Inc.) $550 £355

Malayer rug, Northwest Persia, late 19th/early 20th century, with scalloped midnight blue medallion on the ivory field, 6ft.3in. x 4ft.2in. (Robt. W. Skinner Inc.) $700 £427

Malayer rug, Northwest Persia, late 19th/early 20th century, the overall zili sultan design of rose-filled vases, 6ft.6in. x 4ft.3in. (Robt. W. Skinner Inc.) $1,700 £1,037

A Quasqhai tribal rug, the blue field with an overall Herati type design, 7ft.6in. x 4ft.9in. (Christie's S. Ken) $1,683 £990

Pictorial hooked rug, America, early 20th century, bearing the inscription *Old Shep,* 27 x 34in. (Skinner Inc.) $900 £552

A silk Hereke prayer rug, the ivory mehrab with brightly coloured flowering trees beneath a pink floral arch, 3ft.8in. x 2ft.8in. (Christie's S. Ken) $1,309 £770

Bidjar long rug, Northwest Persia, late 19th century, the scalloped midnight blue diamond medallion with large pendants, 9ft.6in. x 4ft.7in. (Skinner Inc.) $950 £613

Bordjalou Kazak prayer rug, Southwest Caucasus, second half 19th century (6in. tear, wear creases), 4ft x 3ft.8in. (Skinner Inc.) $1,400 £903

A Kazak-Gendje rug, the indigo field with columns of diagonal multi coloured boteh, 8ft.10in. x 4ft.2in. (Christie's S. Ken) $1,309 £770

An Ispahan rug, the pale blue field with a beige floral pole medallion surrounded by brightly coloured flowering vines, 5ft.3in. x 3ft.9in. (Christie's S. Ken) $1,109 £660

Hamadan rug, Northwest Persia, late 19th century, the medallion and anchor design in shades of medium and dark blue, 6ft.2in. x 4ft. (Skinner Inc.) $600 £387

A Kuba Seichur rug, the dark blue field with brightly coloured medallions, guls and flowerheads, 6ft.6in. x 4ft.8in. (Christie's S. Ken) $1,146 £715

Hamadan rug, Northwest Persia, early 20th century, the centre ivory keyhole covered with an angular rust medallion, 6ft x 3ft.4in. (Skinner Inc.) $500 £323

A 1930s Modernist woollen carpet, woven in brown, beige, salmon pink and russet red, with linear and geometric design, 319 x 265.6cm. (Christie's London) $1,201 £715

Joshogan rug, central Persia, early 20th century, the dark blue field with central stepped medallion (good condition), 6ft.10in. x 4ft.2in. (Skinner Inc.) $1,200 £736

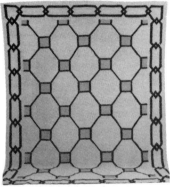

India drugget area carpet, circa 1910, broad honeycomb pattern joined by orange squares, approximately 9ft. x 12ft. (Skinner Inc.)$700 £432

An antique Khotan Rug, the flame-red field covered with two symmetrical vase and pomegranate designs within a boldly patterned geometric border, 18th century, 6ft. 9in. x 3ft. 7in. (Phillips) $9900 £6000

Gustav Stickley India hemp carpet, 1910, honeycomb pattern, brown on neutral ground, 11ft.8in. x 9ft.2in. (Skinner Inc.) $2,900 £1,790

An antique Kashgai Rug, South Persia, the large 'Botehs' covering the ivory field depicted alternately in indigo and red, 5ft. 5in. x 2ft. 11in. (Phillips) $18150 £11000

Drugget flatweave area rug, 20th century, orange and black zig-zag pattern, 5ft.9in. x 3ft.2in. (Skinner Inc.) $325 £201

An antique Melaz Rug, Western Anatolia, early 19th century, the striped brown field decorated with stylised carnations within a golden-yellow inner surround, 5ft. 4in. x 3ft. 11in. (Phillips) $1815 £1100

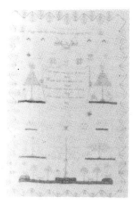

A sampler by Sarah Thornback, 1826, embroidered in coloured silks with a verse *Jesus permit,* framed and glazed, 16 x 13in. (Christie's S. Ken) $913 £550

Needlework sampler, worked by *Elisabeth Lyon, aged 14 years 1791 New Haven,* Connecticut, 17¾ x 20¾in. (Skinner Inc.) $4,250 £2,515

A sampler by Peggy Veale, 1819, worked in coloured silks with a verse *God spake,* 18 x 13in., framed and glazed. (Christie's S. Ken) $1,004 £605

A sampler, by Elizabeth Rennie, 1811, worked in coloured silks with a verse *Stretched on the cross,* 17 x 13in., framed and glazed. (Christie's S. Ken) $772 £495

A late 18th century needlework sampler by *Mary Bradfield, aged nine years, 1798,* the wool ground embroidered in coloured silks with carnations, morning glory and trailing summer flowers, 34 x 34cm. (Phillips West Two) $1,120 £700

A Perpetual Almanack sampler, by Ellen Stackhouse, 1781, Walton School, with a naturalistic pot of flowers and scrolling motifs worked beneath in coloured silks, 16 x 11in. (Christie's S. Ken) $515 £330

A sampler by Matilda Andrews, 1837, worked in coloured silks with a verse *Lord search, oh search,* 15 x 12in. (Christie's S. Ken) $1,309 £770

Needlework sampler, *Eliza Emory,* Rindge, New Hampshire, dated *183-,* 16¾ x 17¼in. (Skinner Inc.) $1,700 £1,006

An early 19th century needlework sampler by *Louisa Gawby 1811,* in brightly coloured silks, designed with a verse titled *Advice,* 43 x 30cm. (Phillips West Two) $512 £320

Needlework memorial sampler, Sarah Jane Campbell, America, 19th century, the upper panel depicting a woman mourning beside a tomb, 21½ x 17¼in. (Skinner Inc.) $1,100 £675

Needlework family record, *Wrought by Sarah E. Foster Aged 11 years Roxbury, Dec. 24th 1830,* Massachusetts (good condition), 19½ x 16¼in. (Skinner Inc.) $1,400 £859

A sampler by Mary Swiney 1815, worked in coloured silks with a windmill flanked by weeping willows, 15 x 13in. (Christie's S. Ken)$394 £242

Needlework sampler, *Mary Leavitt her Sampler made (in the four)teenth year of her age A.D. 17(18),* Salem, Massachusetts, 16½ x 7¾in. (Skinner Inc.) $1,000 £614

A fine and rare needlework sampler, by Alice Mather, Norwich, Connecticut, 1774, 13¾ x 11½in. (Christie's New York) $49,500 £31,132

A 17th century whitework sampler, bearing the inscription *The fear of God is an Excellent Gift,* 44 x 20cm. (Phillips West Two) $1,105 £650

Needlework sampler, Boston area, second half 18th century, rows of alphabet and numbers over scenic panel with Adam and Eve, 11½in. high. (Skinner Inc.) $8,500 £5,215

A 17th century whitework sampler, designed with bands of reticella of floral design, 45 x 23cm. (Phillips West Two) $1,360 £800

Needlework sampler, *Orpha Starkwather 1804,* possibly Virginia or South Carolina, framed, 15½ x 18in. (sight), (minor discoloration). (Skinner Inc.) $1,600 £1,032

An early 19th century needlework sampler by *C. May, aged 8 years, 1828,* the wool ground worked in mainly green, brown and ochre silk threads, 33 x 43cm. (Phillips West Two) $680 £400

A fine and rare needlework sampler, by Sarah Doubt, Massachusetts, 1765, worked in red, green, blue, purple, yellow and white silk threads, 50.5 x 30cm. (Christie's New York) $6,050 £3,805

Needlework sampler, *Wrought by Mary Attwill-Aged 10 Years, Lynn, September 3, 1812,* Massachusetts, worked with silk threads on a linen ground. (Skinner Inc.) $5,000 £3,067

An early Victorian child's needlework sampler, worked in full cross stitch in coloured wools, by Maria Rotherham aged 8 years, 1859, 61cm. square. (Henry Spencer) $221 £140

A mid 17th century needlework sampler dated 1669, in coloured silk threads with rows of stylised flowers, 78 x 18cm. (Phillips West Two) $3,230 £1,900

Needlework sampler, *Wrought by Eunice Goodridge Aet 16 yrs. Fitchburg 1825,* Massachusetts (fading, staining), 20½ x 16½in. (Skinner Inc.) $600 £387

A sampler by Emma Greaves, 1846, worked in coloured wools, with a verse *Jesus permit,* also with a large mansion flanked by formalised trees, 26 x 27in. (Christie's S. Ken) $369 £220

Needlework sampler *Betsey Sergent's Sampler,* Stockbridge, Massachusetts, dated *September 28, 1788,* (faded) 12 x 7¾in. (Skinner Inc.) $1,300 £839

A late 18th century needlework sampler, designed with tulips, bluebells and animals around two verses of a poem, 34 x 32cm. (Phillips West Two) $544 £320

A W. F. Thomas & Co. narrow-arm lockstitch machine for hand or treadle drive, on later baseboard (lacks shuttle). (Christie's S. Ken) $739 £440

A Taylor's Patent Friction Gear hand sewing machine with figure-of-eight base on scroll feet. (Christie's S. Ken) $782   £495

A Grover & Baker sewing machine of typical form with partial transfers, patents to 1863, original receipt dated February 9th 1876. (Christie's S. Ken) $2,402 £1,430

A German Opel Model S richly inlaid and gold mounted machine with swing shuttle, circa 1905. (Auction Team Koeln) $409 £259

A cabinet Grover & Baker sewing machine, with plated arm and lever arm, mother-of-pearl and transfer decoration, patents to 1861, 35in. high. (Christie's S. Ken) $1,353 £825

A rare Kimball & Morton Lion treadle sewing machine, the machine head formed as a standing lion, 26½in. wide, with Registration mark of 1868. (Christie's S. Ken) $7,762 £4,620

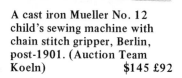

A lockstitch sewing machine with serpentine arm, gilt and coloured transfers and marble base (lacks shuttle cover). (Christie's S. Ken) $407 £242

A cast iron Mueller No. 12 child's sewing machine with chain stitch gripper, Berlin, post-1901. (Auction Team Koeln) $145 £92

A lockstitch machine with crescent shape semi-rotating shuttle, gilt transfers and iron base. (Christie's S. Ken) $702 £418

A Raymond Household lock-stitch sewing machine with partial transfers and Beaver trademark. (Christie's S. Ken) $333 £198

A German sewing machine by Clemens Mueller of Dresden, with original wooden case, circa 1870. (Auction Team Koeln) $455 £288

A Judkins chainstitch sewing machine, signed Judkins Patentee 4 Ludgate Hill London, with part gilt and red transfers. (Christie's S. Ken) $660 £418

A rare Nuremburg Clown sewing machine, No. 4024, the seated cast iron figure with nodding head and working arms operated by a porcelain handled crank, on iron base with lions paw feet, 8¾ in. high. (repainted) (Christie's S. Ken) $4,519 £2,860

A treadle machine by Howe Machine Co., with gilt decoration and brass Elias Howe medallion. (Christie's S. Ken) £739 £440

A Newton, Wilson & Co. Princess of Wales lockstitch machine with partial transfers and flat base with cusped outline (lacks shuttle). (Christie's S. Ken) $702 £418

A Jones English swing shuttle hand sewing machine, with copy instructions, post-1879. (Auction Team Koeln) $204 £129

A Smith & Egge Automatic sewing machine in rare nickel casing, 1901. (Auction Team Koeln) $303 £192

A J. Starley Swiftsure lock-stitch sewing machine, No. 22448, with 1869 patent date. (Christie's S. Ken) $739 £440

Palestine, The Jewish Colonial Trust (Juedische Colonialbank) Ltd. 1900, 1st year of issue, Cert No. 340 for 1 x £1 ordinary share. (Phillips London) $322 £200

American Express Company 1865, 1 x $500 share, signed by Wells as president, Fargo as secretary and Holland as treasurer. (Phillips London) $537 £340

Australian Agricultural Company, incorporated by Royal Charter in 1824, Certificate for ten subscribers shares of £100 each dated 1829, trimmed possibly in the 19th century due to change of directors. (Phillips London) $2,737 £1,700

State of Mississippi 1833, bond No. F1247 for $1,000 with coupons, printed at The Natchez Courier Office, signed by the Governor, A. M. Scott, dated 1831. (Phillips London) $395 £250

The Stockton & Darlington Railway Co., 1858, one £25 Class A Preferential share. (Phillips London) $1,975 £1,250

The Great North of England Railway Company 1836, £100 share. (Phillips London) $338 £210

Potosi, La Paz & Peruvian Mining Association 1827, vignette of city with large mountain in background, on vellum, slight staining. (Phillips London) $411 £260

Canadian, South Winnipeg Ltd. 1913, 10 x $5 shares, an attractive certificate, ideal for framing. (Phillips London) $322 £200

Chinese Central Government Loan of £300,000 sterling, March 1913 (Arnhold Karberg Loan III) £1,000 bond No. 167, possibly the rarest Chinese bond. (Phillips London) $3,213 £2,100

The Leeds & Thirsk Railway Co. 1848, a certificate of payment of subscriptions in advance of calls on 120 shares. (Phillips London) $612 £380

Canterbury Navigation & Sandwich Harbour, 1826, one £25 share. (Phillips London)
$300 £190

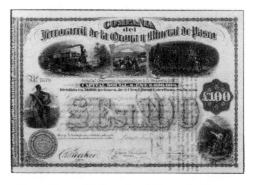

Peru, Oroya Railroad and Cerro de Pasco Mining Co. 1878, £100 shares (50 examples). (Phillips London) $676 £420

The Metropolitan Saloon Omnibus Co. Ltd., 1857, £1 share. (Phillips London) $205 £130

Bridlington Quay Public Rooms Association 1847, Cert. No. 197 for one share. (Phillips) $182 £110

The Norton Ventilator Co. Ltd. 1880, £10 shares, most attractive vignette of sail-assisted steamship, printed by Waterlow & Sons. (Phillips) $99 £60

China, Gold Loan 1898, £500, Deutsch-Asiatische Bank, small tears in centre, badly tape repaired. (Phillips London) $2,979 £1,850

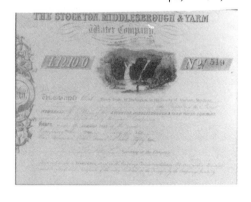

An early Italian bank, Monte di Pieta della citta di Firenze, a registered bond for six debentures (Loughi) of 100 scudi each, paying 4% per annum, dated 1682. (Phillips London) $2,254 £1,400

The Stockton, Middlesbrough & Yarn Water Co. 1885, issued to Henry Pease, vignette of High Force, Teesdale. (Phillips) $346 £210

Missouri, Kansas & Texas Railway Co., 1880, 100 x $100 shares, signed by Jay Gould as president. (Phillips London) $268 £170

Leeds Banking Co. 18609, Certificate No. 2 for five shares, attractive vignette, on Vellum. (Phillips) $198   £120

Hukuang Railways 1911, £20 bond, issued by American banks. Although 141 bonds outstanding out of 150 x £20 bonds issued, very few seen in reasonable condition, one of the rarest Chinese/American bonds. (Phillips London) $1,580   £1,000

China: Gold Loan 1908 (Anglo-French) £20, a rare bond, seldom seen in this cindition (Phillips) $957   £580   6156

Venezuela, The Orinoco Steam Navigation Co. of New York 1851-7, $1,000 share. Chartered by the State of New York. The company had exclusive right to navigate the Orinoco and Apure Rivers by steam for 18 years (9 examples). (Phillips London) $258 £160

Australian Agricultural Company, incorporated by Royal Charter in 1824, certificate for 5 x £100 shares dated 14th June, 1825. Elegant and decorative piece with a vignette of Sydney Harbour from the Observatory area. (Phillips London) $7,110 £4,500

A Hishigata gold fundame tsuba richly decorated in Shibayama style with Gama the toad, unsigned, late 19th century, 11.5cm. (Christie's) $3454   £2200

A lady's leather card case with ivory spine and covers richly decorated in Shibayama style, unsigned, Meiji period (1868–1912), 10.5cm. x 8cm. (Christie's) $3454   £2200

An ostrich egg finely decorated in hiramakie, shell and ivory inlay, with a Chinese sage holding a fan, unsigned, Meiji period, 15cm. long. (Christie's London) $6,604 £4,180

An ivory elephant inlaid in Shibayama style with an elegant caparison, decorated with a profusion of flowers and foliage, unsigned, Meiji period, 14cm. long. (Christie's London) $7,821 £4,950

A Japanese gold lacquer and Shibayama five case inro, the ground as frothing waves overlaid with fish, lobster and octopus, 3½in. long. (Hamptons Fine Art)

$3485   £2050

Japanese silver and Shibayama koro, late 19th century, with dragon handles, bird finial and pedestal base, (damage) 8in. high. (Skinner Inc.)$1,700 £1,063

A good silver mounted Shibayama vase, the body of rectangular section decorated with four Kinji lacquer panels in mother-o'-pearl, ivory, coconut shell and enamel, 30cm. high. (Phillips) $18,480 £11,000

Pair of Shibayama ivory tusks, Japan, late 19th century, each inlaid with birds among trees in tortoiseshell, mother-of-pearl and other materials, 13¾in. high. (Skinner Inc.)$2,800 £1,750

A large silver vase, the ovoid body supporting six ivory plaques inlaid in Shibayama style with various pictorial designs, Meiji period, 37cm. high. (Christie's London) $6,604 £4,180

A pair of ladies' shoes of pale blue kid printed with mauve stripes, with low heels, circa 1790 (worn). (Christie's S. Ken) $2,706 £1,650

A pair of red leather doll's shoes trimmed with red silk and with high pointed fronts and cross over straps, last quarter of the 18th century, 3in. long. (Christie's S. Ken) $330 £209

A pair of mauve brocade shoes trimmed with white silk ribbons and bows, with a low stepped heel, 1860's. (Christie's S. Ken.) $168 £100

A pair of cherry red leather lace up shoes, with circular heels labelled Ferrina, Created by Ferragamo, Made in England, and Harvey Nichols and Eros. (Christie's S. Ken.) $58 £35

A pair of ladies' shoes of pink kid, the uppers with a sandal decoration with a underlay of white kid, with low white kid wedge heels, circa 1795. (Christie's) $1,512 £900

A pair of mid 18th century shoes with fitted clogs of yellow damask silk, bound in yellow silk. (Phillips West Two) $6,120 £3,600

A pair of pink satin high heeled shoes trimmed with silver lace, circa 1730. (Christie's S. Ken) $3,247 £1,980

An interesting pair of late 19th century black leather clown's shoes with square cut toes and wooden soles, 45.75cm. long. (Henry Spencer) $229 £150

A pair of ladies' shoes, the uppers of linen embroidered in green and white beads with flowerheads, circa 1790, the embroidery Indian. (Christie's S. Ken) $1,984 £1,210

A silhouette of a gentleman, painted on plaster, by John Miers, oval 80mm., in ebonised wood frame. (Phillips London) $212 £130

A silhouette, depicting Mr & Mrs Small of Devon House, Newbold Terrace, Leamington Spa, being male and female full length portraits on a plain white ground, 12in. x 9in. (Black Horse Agencies) $264 £160

A bronzed silhouette of a gentleman, painted on plaster, by John Field, oval 83mm., in papier mache frame. (Phillips London) $326 £200

A bronzed silhouette on plaster of Reverend J. Babington, by J. Miers, oval 80mm., in papier mache frame. (Phillips London) $391 £240

August Edouart (1788-1861) — Silhouette of Three Children with Toys, Cat and Dog, cut paper applied to a watercolour, 17.8 x 34.6cm. (Skinner Inc.) $2,100 £1,243

Mrs Isabella Beetham (circa 1753-1825) — A gentleman, in profile, silhouette painted on convex glass, turned wood frame, oval, 80mm. high. (Christie's London) $528 £330

A. Charles (fl. circa 1780-1807), Mr. Fitzgerald, in profile to the right, in coat, waistcoat stock and hat, his hair tied in a pigtail, silhouette, painted on glass, 3in. high. (Christie's) $2449 £1540

Edouart, a paper cut silhouette, mounted on a coloured wash drawing room interior in Gothic style, depicting male and female in costume, signed and dated 1837, 12in. x 9in. (Black Horse Agencies) $511 £310

Mrs. Isabella Beetham (circa 1753-1825), Mrs. Sharland, seated half length in profile to the left, in lace trimmed dress and hat decorated with rosette, silhouette, painted on convex glass, 3$^7/8$in. high. (Christie's) $3498 £2200

BASKETS

A George III reeded oval swing handled cake basket on a rising foot, maker's initials M.H., London, 1799, 14in., 24oz. (Christie's S. Ken) $1,094 £715

A 19th century Chinese Export swing handled oval cake or fruit basket, by Cutshing, Canton, circa 1850, 28.4cm. long, 30.5oz. (Phillips London) $1,113 £700

A George II shaped oval bread basket, with shell and scroll border and swing handle, by John Swift, 1746, 12¾in. long, 45oz. (Christie's London) $21,516 £13,200

A George III swing handled sugar basket of shaped and pleated oblong form, 8cm. high, by William Abdy II, 1792, 5oz. (Phillips London) $477 £300

A George III pierced swing handled sugar basket, by Edward Aldridge, 1771, 11cm. high to top of handle, 1.75oz. (Phillips London) $795 £500

George III Silver Sugar Basket, Peter, Anne & William Bateman, London, 1800–1801, approximately 8 troy oz. (Skinner Inc) $400 £259

A George IV floral and foliate chased shaped circular swing-handled cake basket, William Bateman, London, 1823, 11in., 25¼oz. (Christie's S. Ken) $938 £605

A George III shaped oval cake basket, pierced and engraved with foliage, by Robert Breading, Dublin, 1794, 39.7cm. long, 38oz. (Christie's London) $4,124 £2,530

An early Victorian shaped circular cake basket, the plain centre within a band of well chased swirl leafage, 1838, by Joseph and John Angell, 36.5cm., 42.2oz. (Lawrence Fine Arts) $1,544 £990

BASKETS

A George III shaped oval cake basket, the centre engraved with a crest, 1802 by Robert and Samuel Hennell, 39.2cm., 31.5oz. (Lawrence) $2087 £1265

A leaf-form basket by Shiebler, New York, circa 1885, with a leaf-form handle surmounted by a cast bunch of grapes and a copper fly, 3³/₄in. high, 17 oz. 10 dwt.
(Christie's) $6050 £3805

A cake basket, American, circa 1895, with a pierced bail handle and four scroll feet, marked *Sterling* and *Tiffany & Co*, 9in. high, 33oz. (Christie's New York) $2,200 £1,383

A George III sugar basket, 1792 maker's mark of George Smith II and Thomas Hayter overstriking another, 14cm. overall height. (Lawrence) $871 £528

A late Victorian slat and roundel-pierced moulded circular cake basket, J.J., Sheffield 1900, 12¹/₄in., 27.75oz. (Christie's S. Ken.) $907 £550

An attractive George III sugar basket, with scrolling foliage within wrigglework scroll borders, London 1778, 202gr., 20cm. high. (Henry Spencer) $474 £300

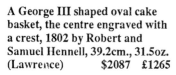

A Victorian sweet basket in the style of the 1760s, the shaped oval basket pierced with crosses above raised lozenges, 1866 by Robert Harper, 16.6cm., 5oz. (Lawrence) $617 £374

A plated cake basket by Rogers & Bro., Waterbury, last quarter 19th century, the everted brim with a die-rolled border in a geometric aesthetic pattern, 9¹/₂in. high, overall. (Christie's) $220 £138

George III style silver cake basket, 19th century, bearing marks of London, 1766–7, 14¹/₂in. long., approximately 29 troy oz. (Skinner Inc.) $1200 £732

BEAKERS

A Swedish, parcel gilt, mid 18th century, plain tapering beaker, the body engraved with elaborate flowers and scrolling foliage, Petter Gadd, Kristianstad, circa 1760, 3½in. (Christie's S. Ken) $673 £440

A French inverted bell shaped beaker, the bowl with a moulded rim and engraved with bright cut swags of fruit and flowers, 4¼in. (Christie's S. Ken) $673 £440

A Swedish mid 18th century parcel gilt tapering beaker, the bowl decorated with two narrow friezes of wriggle work, Henrik Norin, Norrkoping, circa 1755, 3¾in. (Christie's S. Ken) $673   £440

A beaker by Shepherd & Boyd, Albany, early 19th century, on a moulded circular foot, engraved *C. Van Rensselaer,* in script, marked, 8.5cm. high, 4oz. (Christie's New York) $462   £290

A tall beaker by John Burt Lyng, New York, 1760-1780, with a flaring rim, engraved with a ruffle border, 4½in. high, 5oz. (Christie's New York) $7,150 £4,496

A beaker, by William A. Williams, Alexandria, Virginia or Washington, D.C., early 19th century, with reeded rim and footrim, marked, 8cm. high, 4oz. (Christie's New York) $1,650 £1,037

A Dutch tapering beaker, on moulded rim foot, by Wibe Pibes, Harlingen, mid-18th century, 4½in. high, 148gr. (Christie's London) $5,379 £3,300

An 18th century christening beaker, plain, of good gauge, 9cm. high, maker's mark IL, possibly for Jacques Limbour, Jersey (of French origin), circa 1775. (Phillips London) $795 £500

A Charles II beaker, of thistle form, the upper part chased with stylised frieze of seeded flowers and leaves, 9cm. high, punched with the letters TD for Thomas Dare, circa 1660, 3oz. (Phillips London) $3,975 £2,500

BOWLS

A good hand wrought punch bowl, with a slightly everted rim, 1936, by Richard Comyns, 27.8cm. diam., 55.4oz. (Lawrence Fine Arts) $2,402 £1,540

An 18th century two handled marriage bowl, with cast double scroll handles either side, maker's mark PA, for Pierre Amiraux (II), Jersey, circa 1770, 4oz. (Phillips London) $1,351 £850

A Victorian silver gilt two handled campana shaped circular bowl, by C. F. Hancock, 1866, 10in. high, 81oz. (Christie's London) $4,662 £2,860

A Sibyl Dunlop Celtic silver stemmed bowl, applied on the exterior with Celtic entrelacs and beast masks in relief, 9.5cm. high, 1923. (Phillips London) $949 £620

Chinese export silver covered entree dish and serving bowl, 19th century, with beaded rim and domed cover, 8in. diam., 54 troy oz. (Skinner Inc.) $2,700 £1,688

An important Keswick School of Industrial Arts silver presentation rose bowl and cover, made to commemorate James William Lowther being elected as Speaker to the House of Commons in 1905. (Phillips London) $5,202 £3,400

An Edwardian large rose bowl chased with flowers and foliage, H. W., Sheffield, 1902, 12½in., 55oz. (Christie's S. Ken) $2,728 £1,760

A Georg Jensen footed bowl, designed by Johan Rohde, the lightly hammered bowl with everted rim, 5½in. high. (Christie's S. Ken) $938 £550

A late Victorian pedestal rose bowl, repousse with rococo scrolls and two vacant cartouche panels, London 1897, 1207gr., 29cm. diam. (Henry Spencer) $1,445 £860

BOWLS

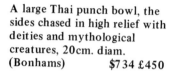

A large Thai punch bowl, the sides chased in high relief with deities and mythological creatures, 20cm. diam. (Bonhams) $734 £450

Kalo sterling silver bowl with attached underliner, Chicago, circa 1915, squat bulbous form, approximately 15 troy oz. (Skinner Inc.) $400 £247

A punch bowl by Herbert A. Taylor for Stone Associates, Gardner, Massachusetts, 1908-1937, the sides partly fluted, marked, 39cm. diam., 106oz. (Christie's New York)
$9,350 £5,880

A rosebowl, with leafy scroll and female mask border, Chester 1906, by Walker and Hall, 25cm., 33oz. (Bonhams)
$1,141 £700

An Art Nouveau spot hammered centre bowl on a domed circular foot, Albert Edward Bonner, London, 1909, 7½in., 23.25oz. (Christie's S. Ken) $702 £418

A late Victorian part oxidised fluted moulded circular rose bowl, Henry Wilkinson & Co. Ltd., London, 1900, 10¼in. 37.75oz. (Christie's S. Ken)
$1,144 £748

A George I two handled circular Monteith, with two winged grotesque mask and drop ring handles, by John East, 1718, 10¼in. diam., 52oz. (Christie's London)
$26,895 £16,500

A George III hemispherical punch bowl, by Paul Storr, on fluted circular foot, 1867, 30.5cm. diam., 91oz. (Phillips London) $9,858 £6,200

A Victorian punch bowl, chased with foliate swags pendent from ribbon ties, 1890, by Walter and John Barnard, 30.4cm. diam., 44oz. (Lawrence Fine Arts)
$2,745 £1,760

BOWLS

A foliate rimmed silver bowl chased and modelled in relief with a foliate band of irises on a stippled ground, stamped *jungin,* Meiji period, 20cm. diam. (Christie's London) $3,128 £1,980

A Ganetti silver modernist powder bowl and cover, the lift off cover with copper loop handle and mirrored interior, 7in. diameter.
(Henry Spencer) $165 £100

A rose bowl of compressed circular ogee form, 1936, maker's mark R&Co. Ltd., possibly for Robinson and Co., 26cm., 29.5 oz. excluding grille.
(Lawrence) $998 £605

Stieff Sterling Repousse Punchbowl, Baltimore, heavily chased with roses and assorted flowers, 12in. diam, approximately 75 troy oz.
(Skinner Inc) $8500 £5519

Silver bowl with red glass liner, on four cartouche feet, with fluted edge and with open pierced mouldings, flower baskets, garlands and Chinese scenes, German, 24.5cm. high.
(Kunsthaus am Museum) $649 £373

Georg Jensen Sterling Punchbowl, circular moulded edge resting on leaves and berries, circular base, 9$^{1}/_{2}$in. diam, approximately 42 troy oz.
(Skinner Inc) $3700 £2402

A late Victorian rose bowl, the hemispherical body chased with a band of scroll foliage, 1890 by George Maudsley Jackson, 21cm. diameter, 21.5oz.
(Lawrence) $1270 £770

A Scottish Art Nouveau spot hammered rose bowl, applied with three bracket handles, J.F., Glasgow, 1904, 12½in., 49oz. (Christie's S. Ken)
$1,158 £715

A late Victorian bunch bowl, of semi fluted circular form, London 1886, 1604 grammes, 35cm. wide over handles.
(Spencer's) $3465 £2100

BOWLS

A Victorian sugar bowl, chased with panels of scroll foliage on a matted ground, 1875 by Daniel and Charles Houle, 13cm., 8.3oz. (Lawrence) $635 £385

A centrepiece bowl marked 'Milton A. Fuller, Inc. New York/Palm Beach', circa 1900, on four lion's-paw feet, 14in diam, 68 oz. (Christie's) $4180 £2629

A fine silver and glass punch bowl by Gorham, Providence, 1893, with a flaring scalloped brim repoussé and chased with grapes and mixed fruit, 16¼in. diam, 352 oz. (Christie's) $24200 £15220

A Repouse Compote by Tiffany & Company, New York, 1883–1891, the sides formed of a finely repoussé and chased band of mythological figures, 33 oz. 10 dwt. (Christie's) $5500 £3459

A Georg Jensen circular bowl and cover of bulbous form and hammered finish, 6.5in. high, London 1921, 414gms., 13.3oz. (Bearne's) $990 £600

A Victorian parcel gilt sugar bowl, each lobe chased with a bird amid scroll foliage, 1891 by James Wakely and Frank Clarke Wheeler, 9,3cm., 7oz. (Lawrence) $726 £440

A mid-18th century Irish 7⅝in. circular silver punch bowl engraved a crest in the form of a double headed eagle, maker John Moore, 19³/₄oz. (Phillips) $4455 £2700

A footed fruit bowl by Whiting Manufacturing Company, North Attleboro or Newark, circa 1885, on a spreading cylindrical foot with a serpentine border, 4³/₄in. high, 21 oz. 10 dwt. (Christie's) $7150 £4497

Coin silver sugar bowl. Christof Christian Küchler for Hyde & Goodrich, (1816-1866), New Orleans, c. 1850, 6¼in. high. (Skinner Inc.) $3300 £2013

BOXES

A Russian rectangular gilt lined tobacco box, with a nielloed band picking out the word *Souvenir*, Moscow 1878, 4in. (Christie's S. Ken) $512 £330

A late Victorian jewellery casket, of rectangular form with canted corners, 524gr., 20cm. long. (Henry Spencer) $605 £360

An Italian silver gilt trinket box, the lid enamelled with a semi naked woman reclining on rockwork, 3½in. (Christie's S. Ken) $477 £308

A William Hutton & Sons silver casket, the hinged cover inset with high relief panel in mother-of-pearl, pewter, enamel and copper of a lakeside scene, 1902, 31.5cm. long. (Christie's London) $7,762 £4,620

An Eastern gilt box and cover modelled as a parrot with crocidolite eyes, a red enamelled beak and green, yellow, white and brown enamelled crest, 6¼in. (Christie's S. Ken) $785 £462

A silver and enamel circular box and cover, painted in white, pink and green enamels with the head and shoulders of a long haired maiden, 11.2cm. diam. (Phillips London) $1,141 £700

A rectangular silver rimmed Ryoshibako and inner tray, decorated in hiramakie, hirame and other techniques with bush clover and pampas grass against the full moon, 19th century, 22.5cm. wide. (Christie's London) $10,428 £6,600

A silver rimmed box, the top with a panel richly decorated in carved shell with chrysanthemums, peonies and other flowers, signed *Shinryosai Masayuki saku*, 19th century, 15.8 x 12cm. (Christie's London) $5,561 £3,520

A German oval bombe sugar box and cover, on four shell and scroll feet, with an oval plaque, enamelled in colours with figures of David and Jonathan, probably mid-18th century, 5in. long, gross 280gr. (Christie's London) $3,227 £1,980

BRANDY SAUCEPANS

An early 19th century Indian Colonial covered brandy saucepan, with baluster wood handle, by John Hunt, Calcutta, circa 1810, 10oz. (Phillips London) $715 £450

A George IV brandy warmer and cover, with a turned wood handle at right angles to the lip, Sheffield, 1821, by Samuel Roberts Jn and George Cadman and Co., 16.3cm. overall height, 13.3oz. all in. (Lawrence Fine Arts) $927 £594

An Old Sheffield plate plain tapering brandy saucepan and cover with ebonised turned wood side handle, 11in. overall. (Christie's S. Ken) $299 £176

BUCKLES

A rare early Mokume cloak clasp by Tiffany & Co., New York, 1876, in the Japanese taste, 6½in. wide, extended, 3 oz. 10 dwt. (Christie's) $2640 £1571

A leaf-form belt buckle by Frank M. Whiting, North Attleboro, circa 1885, applied with a spider, a fly, a bee, and a butterfly, 3⅛in. long, 1 oz. (Christie's) $462 £291

A William Comyns silver buckle in two pieces, of sinuous outline, formed by interwoven foliage, 11.5cm. wide, 1902. (Phillips London) $261 £160

A medallion silver and gold belt buckle by Schiebler, New York, circa 1885, comprised of one oval and one rounded rectangular medallion, 3in. long, 2⅛in. high, 1 oz. 10 dwt. (Christie's) $1760 £1107

Sterling silver Arts & Crafts belt buckle, England, circa 1900-1904, two turquoise stones in symmetrical openwork organic design, 3¼in. wide. (Skinner Inc.) $175 £108

French silver Joan of Arc belt buckle, possibly by Piel Freres, Paris, circa 1900, 5.4cm. diam. (Skinner Inc.) $550 £340

CANDELABRA

A pair of George III two-light candelabra, by John Romer, the branches by Thomas Heming, the candlesticks with detachable nozzles, 14¼ in. high, 114oz.
(Christie's) $13282   £8250

A German six-light candelabrum on a rising shaped circular base moulded with flowerheads, laurel leaves and berries, 24in. high.
(Christie's S. Ken.)
                      $2632   £1595

A good pair of three-light plated candelabra of circular baluster form with gadrooned edges, 20in. high.
(Phillips) $660   £400

A pair of French seven-light candelabra, each on a shaped-oblong base, by Jean-Baptiste Harleux, Paris, late 19th century, 22¾ in. high, 7,070grs.
(Christie's) $9209   £5720

A large and impressive four branch five light candelabrum, the bell shaped sockets with detachable sconces, 77cm. high.
(Spencer's) $1122   £680

A fine quality pair of five-light plated candelabra each in corinthian column form, 21¼ in. high.
(Phillips) $1320   £800

A four branch five light candelabrum with shaped square sconces, the whole with foliate stamped angles, 53cm. high.
(Spencer's) $198   £120

An impressive pair of Austro-Hungarian three branch candelabra, 17⅛ in. long, the branches supported by winged beasts, circa 1830.
(Bonhams) $4455   £2700

Sterling silver and copper candelabra, possibly Metcalf & Co., Upstate New York, circa 1905, 13in. high.
(Skinner Inc.) $300 £185

CANDLESTICKS

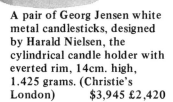

A George III pair of candlesticks, in the Neo Classical manner, 32cm. high, by Matthew Fenton, Richard Creswick & William Watson, Sheffield, 1799 (loaded). (Phillips London)
$2,862 £1,800

A pair of Georg Jensen white metal candlesticks, designed by Harald Nielsen, the cylindrical candle holder with everted rim, 14cm. high, 1.425 grams. (Christie's London) $3,945 £2,420

A George II rare pair of cast candlesticks, 28.5cm. high, by Nicholas Sprimont, 1742, 80oz. (Phillips London)
$310,000 £195,000

A pair of late Victorian table candlesticks, spirally fluted Corinthian columns on stepped square bases, London, 1892, 11½in. high.
(Bonhams) $1980 £1200

A pair of W.M.F. figural twin-branch candlesticks, each in the form of an Art Nouveau maiden, 27.5cm. high.
(Phillips) $2320 £1450

A pair of George III table candlesticks, the cast sticks with fluted knopped stems and shaped square bases, London 1777, by Jonathon Alleine, 21.5cm. high, 34½oz.
(Bonhams) $3,060 £2,000

A pair of Edwardian table candlesticks in the Neo Classical revival style, 1903, by William Hutton and Sons Ltd., 30.7cm., loaded. (Lawrence Fine Arts) $1,716 £1,100

A pair of Old Sheffield Plate telescopic candlesticks, on fluted circular spreading bases.
(Bonhams) $214 £140

A pair of Victorian Neo Classical style beaded candlesticks on rising square bases, with beaded circular detachable nozzles, J. B., London, 1887, 12¼in. (Christie's S. Ken) $1,963 £1,155

A large 18th century Norwegian sugar dredger of vase shape with waisted neck, by Andreas Lude, also bearing mark of Assay Master Dithmar Kahrs, Bergen, 1787, 23.5cm. high, 11.5oz. (Phillips London)
$2,862 £1,800

A caster by Elias Pelletreau, Southampton, 1760–1776, the pierced domed cover with a baluster finial, 3¼in. high, 2 oz. 10 dwt.
(Christie's) $3850   £2290

A William Hutton & Sons silver sugar caster, the cover with openwork decoration set with a cabochon amethyst, London hallmarks for 1902, 19.3cm. high, 320gr. (Christie's London)
$2,957 £1,760

A Charles II caster, of cylindrical form with knopped finial, bayonet lock, 280 grammes, 17.5cm. high. (Henry Spencer)
$7,426 £4,700

A pair of Dutch 19th century spiral fluted pear shaped sugar casters on rising shaped circular bases, 7¾in., 19.75oz. (Christie's S. Ken) $1,010 £660

A Dutch late 18th or early 19th century beaded and bright cut vase shaped sugar caster, with a spiral twist finial, 7½in., 8.25oz. (Christie's S. Ken)
$1,084 £682

George III lighthouse caster, London, 1768–9, domed bright-cut and pierced cover with button finial, 9½in. high, approximately 25 troy oz. (Skinner Inc) $800   £519

A caster, marked *HM*, probably New York, circa 1700, the domed and pierced cover with bayonet mounts and a turned finial, 3½in. high, 3oz. (Christie's New York)
$4,400 £2,767

A late Victorian spiral fluted lighthouse sugar caster in the early 18th century taste, Nathan and Hayes, Chester, 1898, 7¾in., 9oz. (Christie's S. Ken) $375 £242

CENTREPIECES

Gorham sterling and crystal centrepiece, circa 1900, on a spreading circular base chased with roses, 14in. diam., approx. 27 troy oz. (Skinner Inc.)
$2,100 £1,288

A Chinese centrepiece, the panelled sides chased with ceremonial dragons and prunus blossom, maker's mark *W.S.*, 30cm. high. (Bonhams)
$1,060 £650

An unusual Indian table centrepiece, the large bombé-shaped bowl chased with elephants and scrolling foliage. (Bonhams) $627   £380

An early Victorian six-light candelabrum centrepiece, by Joseph and John Angell, 1836 and 1837, the basket apparently unmarked, 17³/₄ in. high, 178oz. (Christie's) $8501   £5280

A George III epergné, 19in. overall length, on four leaf-chased scroll supports with pierced scroll feet, London, 1766, by John King, 86oz. (Bonhams) $10230   £6200

A fine Victorian centrepiece by Edward and John Barnard, the triform base cast on three massive leaf mounted feet, London, 1864, 16¹/₄ in. high, 108 oz.(Bonhams) $8250   £5000

A large and impressive table centrepiece, the stepped circular clear glass shallow bowl with leaf moulded decoration, 50cm. high. (Spencer's) $495   £300

A large and impressive table centrepiece as a gondola, raised upon waves and a shaped rectangular base, 22in. wide overall. (Spencer's) $462   £280

A table centrepiece with a large central vase, applied with rococo scrolling foliate rims, William Hutton & Sons Ltd., Sheffield, 1919, 12½in.. 27½oz. (Christie's S. Ken)
$546 £352

CHAMBERSTICKS

A pair of George III chamber candlesticks, 1811 by Thomas Hayter, the extinguishers York 1826, 13.2cm. diameter, 15.2oz. (Lawrence) $1996   £1210

A Victorian fluted and foliate-stamped taperstick on a rising shaped circular base, Henry Wilkinson and Co., Sheffield 1850, 5³/₄in.
(Christie's S. Ken.) $1089   £660

A pair of Victorian chamber candlesticks, the circular pans engraved with two crests, 1858 by Daniel and Charles Houle, 13.9cm., 16.2oz.
(Lawrence) $2359   £1430

George III Sheffield silver-plated chamber candlestick, Matthew Boulton, late 18th century, with slotted cylindrical sconce, 5¾in. (Skinner Inc.)
$225 £138

A pair of rare George III circular chamber candlesticks, each with scroll handle, by William Burwash, 1812, 5½in. diam., 24oz. (Christie's London)
$3,944 £2,420

A Victorian chamber candlestick in the Renaissance style, the cylindrical socket heavily cast with masks, London 1877, probably by George Fox, 392gr. (Henry Spencer)$672 £400

CHOCOLATE POTS

A Queen Anne plain tapering cylindrical chocolate pot, with curved spout and detachable domed cover, by Joseph Ward, 1706, 9¾in. high, gross 27oz. (Christie's London)
$9,861   £6,050

A Louis XV plain pear-shaped chocolate pot, on three spreading feet, with hinged flap to the curved lip, by Jean Gouel, Paris, 1734, 9¹/₂in. high 840grs.
(Christie's) $5909   £3740

An early 19th century French silver chocolate pot of bulbous form, marked on body, cover and supports, height 9.25in., makers initials P.L., gross 20.5oz.
(Graves Son & Pilcher)
$1567   £950

CIGARETTE CASES

An enamelled cigarette case decorated with a naked girl sitting on a wall catching water from a well in a bowl, 9cm. long, stamped *935*. (Phillips London) $643 £420

A Russian rectangular gilt lined cigarette case, one side nielloed with a domed building, Moscow, circa 1890, 3¾in. (Christie's S. Ken) $654 £385

A German enamelled cigarette case depicting a young woman wearing an off-the-shoulder dress and enjoying the amorous advances of her suitor in a boudoir setting, 8.7cm. long. (Phillips London) $1,301 £850

A Russian rectangular gilt lined cigarette case, the exterior cloisonne enamelled with flowers and scroll work, 4in. (Christie's S. Ken) $757 £495

A stylish French Art Deco lacquered cigarette case, decorated with egg shell roundels, red roundel and curved bands, 12cm. wide. (Phillips London) $1,011 £620

A German Jugendstil cigarette case decorated in niello with sinuous linear banding, 9cm. long. (Phillips London) $261 £160

A German enamelled cigarette case depicting a young girl wearing a lacy nightdress, falling from one shoulder, 9cm. long, stamped *935*. (Phillips London) $1,193 £780

An attractive German enamelled cigarette case, depicting a Titian haired beauty wrapped in a partly diaphanous shawl and seductively revealing a breast, 9.5cm. wide, 1906. (Phillips London) $1,875 £1,150

A Continental gilt lined cigarette case, the lid enamelled with a naked woman rising from the sea, 3½in. (Christie's S. Ken) $597 £385

CLARET JUGS

A Victorian silver mounted vase shaped clear glass claret jug with star cut base and applied scroll handle, Henry Wilkinson & Co. Ltd., London, 1898, 10¾in. (Christie's S. Ken) $1,496 £880

A Victorian silver mounted claret jug, the spherical glass body with cylindrical neck and cut overall with small stars, Sheffield 1862, by William and George Sissons, 24.8cm.,(Lawrence Fine Arts) $2,574 £1,650

An Edwardian silver mounted plain flaring clear glass claret jug with star cut base, Birmingham, 1905, 11½in. (Christie's S. Ken) $286 £187

A French claret jug, the ovoid glass body with leaf-chased scroll handle, circa 1880, 10in. high. (Bonhams) $495 £300

Fine glass claret jug, diamond cut with hallmarked silver pourer, lid and handle, Sheffield 1895. (G. A. Key) $505 £310

A Victorian silver mounted vase shaped clear glass claret jug with star cut base and applied scroll handle, John Foligno, London, 1867, 10in. (Christie's S. Ken) $748 £440

A Victorian part fluted vase shaped claret or hot water jug on a rising circular foot, Edward Hutton, London, 1886, 12½in., 20oz. (Christie's S. Ken) $818 £528

A cut glass and silver-gilt claret jug, marked by Theodore B. Starr, New York, circa 1900, the glass ovoid with melon-reeding, 11⁵⁄₈in. high. (Christie's) $1760 £1107

German Silver and Cut-Glass Claret Jug, late 19th century, silver lid and handle cast with Renaissance-style foliate scrolls, handle marked 800, 11¹⁄₂in. high. (Skinner Inc) $650 £422

CLARET JUGS

A claret jug, pear shaped with cross hatched bands to glass body, by Martin Hall and Company, 30cm. high.
(Bonhams) $275 £180

A Victorian silver mounted flaring clear glass claret jug engraved with ferns, the mount decorated with satyrs masks and trailing vines, Frederick Elkington, Birmingham, 1870, 11¼in. (Christie's S. Ken) $1,515 £990

A claret jug, with swollen amber glass body, Bacchus mask mounted spout and domed hinged cover, 33cm. high. (Bonhams) $321 £210

A cut glass and silver-gilt claret jug by William B. Durgin Company, Concord, New Hampshire, circa 1900, 12½in. high.
(Christie's) $7150 £4497

A late Victorian glass claret jug in the form of a duck, Sheffield 1894, by Henry Wilkinson, 20cm. high. (Henry Spencer) $2,400 £1,500

A tapering part fluted clear glass claret jug with star cut base, the body engraved with palm trees, bullrushes and herons, 11¼in. (Christie's S. Ken) $303 £198

A Victorian silvei gilt claret jug, the collar chased with Bacchanalian masks and vine leaves, London 1853, 26.7cm. high. (Bonhams) $689 £450

An attractive late Victorian claret jug, of ovoid form, with waisted cylindrical neck, Birmingham 1874, maker's mark H.P. and Co. 746 grammes gross. (Henry Spencer) $1,020 £600

A Victorian silver mounted claret jug, the cylindrical hob-nail cut body on a swelling base, 1886, by Charles Boyton, 27cm. (Lawrence Fine Arts) $1,682 £1,078

COASTERS

A pair of Old Sheffield plate wine coasters, with escallop shell, acanthus leaf and reeded stamped and filled borders, 16cm. diam. (Henry Spencer) $374 £220

A pair of Old Sheffield plate wine coasters, 5½in. diam., circular fluted sides with everted gadrooned borders, circa 1850. (Bonhams) $165 £100

A pair of Regency part-fluted moulded circular gadrooned wine coasters, William Elliot, London 1813, 6¼in. (Christie's S. Ken.)
$3085 £1870

A pair of George III 5in. circular silver wine coasters pierced and bright-cut engraved pointed arches, London 1810, makers mark rubbed.
(Phillips) $990 £600

A pair of George IV silver gilt wine coasters, applied with a band of shells and anthemion ornament, by John Bridge, 1827. (Christie's London)
$6,813 £4,180

A pair of George III 6in. circular silver wine coasters, makers Rebecca Emes and Edward Barnard.
(Phillips) $1336 £810

A pair of George III circular wine coasters, engraved with a crest within a garter cartouche with motto, 1817 by John Houle, 15cm.
(Lawrence) $2904 £1760

A pair of George IV wine coasters, each with similar border, the print engraved with a crest, by John Bridge, 1825.
(Christie's) $11511 £7150

A pair of William IV circular wine coasters, with ovolo borders and open wirework sides applied with vines, by John Edward Terrey, 1830.
(Christie's) $4990 £3080

COFFEE POTS

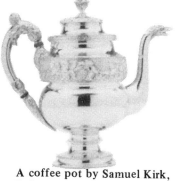

A George III plain baluster coffee pot, with a foliate chased rising curved spout, William and James Priest, London, 1766, 10½in., 19oz. gross. (Christie's S. Ken) $2,032 £1,210

A coffee pot by Samuel Kirk, Baltimore, with assay mark of 1824-1843, with a wide band of repousse and chased grapes and leaves at the shoulder, marked on base, 11½in. high, gross weight 38oz. (Christie's New York) $3,960 £2,490

A Maltese fluted pear shaped coffee pot, with moulded spout, scroll thumbpiece and flower finial, circa 1770, 8¼in. high, gross 611gr. (Christie's London) $4,303 £2,640

A French 19th century vase shaped coffee pot on leaf and flower capped lion's paw feet, 11¼in., 21oz. gross. (Christie's S. Ken) $1,934 £1,210

A George IV fluted pear shaped coffee pot on a rising shaped cicular foot, Richard Sibley, London, 1824, overall height 10¾in., 46¾oz. (Christie's S. Ken) $2,046 £1,320

A George II coffee pot, the body engraved with an heraldic device, raised upon a stepped circular foot, London 1741, 7772 grammes gross, 22.5cm. high. (Henry Spencer) $1,955 £1,150

A George I coffee pot, on moulded foot with wooden scroll handle and faceted spout, London, circa 1715, by William Penstone, 24.3cm. high, 25oz. (Bonhams) $3,912 £2,400

A George II fluted pear shaped coffee pot, on three lion's mask and claw feet, by David Willaume, 1736, 8in. high, gross 28oz. (Christie's London) $12,551 £7,700

A fine George I plain tapering octagonal coffee pot, with curved spout with duck's head terminal, by John Bache, 1724, 10¾in. high, gross 34oz. (Christie's London) $53,790 £33,000

COFFEE-POTS

A good Victorian coffee pot, the spirally fluted baluster form body supported on similarly decorated circular base, London, 1885, 10¼in. high.
(Bonhams) $1815   £1100

A Sheffield plated coffee pot, the plain baluster body divided into wide lobes and with a leaf capped scroll handle, 26cm.
(Lawrence) $436   £264

An electroplated coffee pot in the style of the 1760s, the plain baluster body on a gadrooned pedestal base, by F.B. Thomas and Co., 25.5cm.
(Lawrence) $290   £176

A coffee pot by Samuel Kirk & Son Co., Baltimore, 1903–1907, with a domed cover, cuirving spout and handle with insulators, 9¼in. high, 23 oz.
(Christie's) $1650   £982

A parcel-gilt coffee pot and sugar bowl by Tiffany & Company, New York, 1892–1902, coffee pot 8¾in. high; bowl 4in. diam.
(Christie's) $3520   £2214

A Victorian tapering octagonal coffee pot in the mid 18th century taste, with a leaf capped panelled rising curved spout, W. H., London, 1888, Britannia Standard, 8¾in., 18.25oz. gross.
(Christie's S. Ken) $1,159 £682

A black coffee pot by Gorham, Providence, 1888, with a narrow curving spout and handle with insulators, 9½in. high, 14 oz. 10 dwt.
(Christie's) $715   £425

A George IV coffee jug, the ovoid body chased with scroll foliage, 1821 by Joseph Angell, 21.5cm., 23.9oz.
(Lawrence) $1234   £748

A coffee pot by Dominick & Haff, New York, 1881, with a domed cover, a pointed finial scrolling handle and a narrow spout, 10¾in. high, 23 oz. 10 dwt.
(Christie's) $2420   £1440

CREAM JUGS

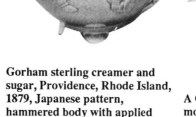

A good Victorian cow creamer by George Fox in the style of John Schuppe in the mid 18th century, 6¼in., London 1865, 6¼oz.
(Phillips) $7425   £4500

Gorham sterling creamer and sugar, Providence, Rhode Island, 1879, Japanese pattern, hammered body with applied butterflies and lily pads, approximately 15 troy oz.
(Skinner Inc.) $1800   £1098

A Continental novelty cream jug modelled as the head of Napoleon, his hat forming two spouts, London 1903, 3¾in.
(Christie's S. Ken.) $817   £495

A George II cream jug, with a sparrowbeak lip, 1735, maker's mark possibly for George Hindmarsh, 8.8cm. (Lawrence Fine Arts) $1,132 £726

A late Victorian Japanesque style barrel shaped cream jug, the planished body engraved with carp swimming amongst weeds, London 1887, by Martin Hall & Co. Ltd., 77 grammes, 7cm. high. (Henry Spencer) $578 £340

A George III bright cut fluted helmet cream jug on a reeded rising shaped oblong foot, London 1796, 6in. (Christie's S. Ken) $477 £308

Fine George III silver cream jug, helmet shaped with bright cut decoration, London 1797, by Peter and Anne Bateman.
(G. A. Key) $391 £240

A George III pedestal cream jug, the ogee body chased with an agricultural landscape, 1772 by Thomas Shepherd, 11.8cm.
(Lawrence) $690   £418

George III vase shaped milk jug with reeded loop handle, makers mark rubbed, London 1794 (loaded) (Phillips Manchester) $174 £110

SILVER

A George III, silver cruet, the stand with gadroon and reeded decoration raised on scrolled lions paw feet, maker Charles Fox, London 1815, 16oz. (Diamond, Mills & Co)
$978   £600

A very rare Scottish provincial four-bottle cruet frame of plain oblong form with rounded corners, maker's mark WF, circa 1825, 17.75oz. (Phillips) $14850   £9000

A George III beaded, pierced and bright cut oval cruet on claw and ball feet, William Abdy, London 1786, 10in. (Christie's S. Ken) $1,159 £682

A Hukin & Heath electroplated six piece cruet and stand designed by Dr Christopher Dresser, fitted with three faceted cut glass bottles and stoppers, two similar shakers and mustard pot with hinged cover, 1878, 23.1cm. high. (Christie's London) $7,392 £4,400

A good George III oil and vinegar bottle stand, with a cast beaded scroll handle, 1770, by Jabez Daniell and James Mince, the bottle mounts with standard and maker's marks only, circa 1770, by Robert Peaston, 25cm. high, 25.3oz. of weighable silver. (Lawrence Fine Arts) $3,947 £2,530

A George III gadrooned oval cruet on part-fluted curved feet, the mustard pot with a reeded scroll handle, London 1805, 8³/₄ in. (Christie's S. Ken.) $871   £528

A Victorian breakfast cruet stand of trefoil form, 1870 by Joseph and Edward Bradbury, the red pepper ladle and mustard spoon Sheffield 1871. (Lawrence) $436   £264

An early Victorian seven bottle cruet, Sheffield, 1838, by Henry Wilkinson & Co., stand 910gr. (Henry Spencer)
$1,142 £680

A George IV circular egg frame, on three foliage and paw feet, by James Fray, Dublin, 1825, with six fiddle pattern egg-spoons, 1816, 1822, 44oz. (Christie's) $2656   £1650

A Channel Islands christening cup, with two beaded scroll handles, Guernsey, circa 1720, maker's mark IS, 6.5cm. high. (Lawrence Fine Arts)
$1,064 £682

A rare spout cup by William S. Nichols, Newport, Rhode Island, circa 18921, with a tubular side spout, a moulded strap handle, and a reeded circular footrim, 2³/₈in. high, 3 oz. (Christie's) $1650 £982

A George II plain tapering cup on a skirted foot, Richard Bayley, London, 1747, 4½in. 8oz. (Christie's S. Ken)
$597 £385

A George III two handle cup and cover, the vase shape body engraved with a view of Magdalen Hospital, 1800 by Solomon Hougham, 33.5cm., 37.4oz.(Lawrence Fine Arts)
$3,432 £2,200

A trophy loving cup by Tiffany & Co., New York, circa 1889, with a serpentine brim and three curving handles formed as anchors, 9in. high, 57 oz. 10 dwt. (Christie's) $2530 £1505

A loving cup, by Gorham, Providence, circa 1905, with an applied grapevine border and three sinuous handles, 19¼in. high, 107oz. (Christie's New York) $7,700 £4,842

A Commonwealth small wine cup, the tapering cylindrical bowl punched with beading and chased with stylised flower-heads, 1656, maker's mark H.N 2¾in. high, 1oz. (Christie's London) $7,530 £4,620

An 18th century two handled christening cup, 6.5cm. high, maker's mark IH, crown above, (Jean Hardie, probably) Guernsey, circa 1770, 3oz. (Phillips London)
$1,113 £700

A Continental gilt lined rowing trophy cup modelled as a Classical dolphin supporting a nautilus shell, 13½in. high. (Christie's S. Ken) $429 £275

DISH RINGS

A dish ring in the Irish style, the spool shape body chased and pierced, 1911, by Robert Frederick Fox, of C.T. & G. Fox, 20.7cm., 17.2oz. (Lawrence Fine Arts) $652 £418

A waisted dish ring in the Irish 18th century taste, pierced and chased with various animals, birds, fruit, flowers and scrolling foliage, 7½in., 10oz. (Christie's S. Ken) $640 £418

A George III Irish potato ring, pierced and chased with pheasants, S and C scrolls and fruiting vines, by William Homer, Dublin, circa 1765, 20.2cm. diam., 16oz. (Phillips London) $4,134 £2,600

DISHES

A silver gilt basketweave dish, by Tiffany & Co., New York, circa 1890, in the form of an Indian basket, 5¾in. diam., 5oz. (Christie's New York) $1,320 £830

A George III gilt lined oval swing handled pedestal sugar basin, Duncan Urquhart and Napthali Hart, London 1796, 6¾in., 8¾oz. (Christie's S. Ken) $818 £528

A plated dish by James W. Tufts, Boston, last quarter 19th century, with a flaring lobed brim, the entire surface chased with stylised foliate and geometric borders, 11³/₈in. diam. (Christie's) $275 £173

A late Victorian revolving breakfast dish and liner, the cover stamped with wrythen fluting, 35cm. wide over handles. (Henry Spencer) $347 £220

A covered entree dish with a figural finial, by Samuel Kirk & Son, Baltimore, 1880-1890, the domed cover surmounted by a figure of a grazing deer, marked, 6¾in. high, 52oz. (Christie's New York) $5,280 £3,320

A Guild of Handicraft Ltd muffin dish and cover, probably designed by C. R. Ashbee, circa 1900, 25cm. diam. (Henry Spencer) $790 £500

DISHES

A covered entree dish, by Samuel Kirk & Son Co., Baltimore, 1896-1925, the cover and bowl repousse and chased with flowers and scrolls, 23cm. diam., 35oz. (Christie's New York) $3,520 £2,214

A rare Indian style silver mounted glass canoe form butter dish, by Shreve & Co., San Francisco, circa 1890, marked, 11cm. high, 24.78cm. long. (Christie's New York) $2,420 £1,522

An Old Sheffield Plate Tree and Well carving dish, on four bun feet, circa 1840, 68.6cm. wide. (Bonhams) $918 £600

An unusual Georg Jensen silver sweetmeat dish of shell shape, supported on an open-work foliate and beaded stem, 10.5cm. high. (Phillips London) $1,255 £820

A Victorian copy of the Temperantia dish of Francois Briot, chased with panels of Classical figures, by Robert Garrard, 1862, 17in. diam., 66oz. (Christie's London) $3,586 £2,200

Georg Jensen sterling tazza, Denmark, 1925-30, with pendant bunches of grapes on a spiral chased stem with spreading foot, 7¼in. high, approx. 18 troy oz. (Skinner Inc.) $1,600 £982

A good William IV butter dish, stand and cover, with a flowerhead finial, 1836, by Joseph and John Angell, 19cm. diam of base, 26.9oz. (Lawrence Fine Arts) $1,287 £825

A Dutch 19th century pierced moulded oval bonbon dish in the 18th century taste, 5in., 8oz. (Christie's S. Ken) $559 £352

A medallion butter dish by Gorham, Providence, circa 1865, repoussé and chased with a band of cartouches, scrolls, and foliage, 5in. high, 16 oz. (Christie's) $990 £623

FLATWARE

A. D. W. Hislop set of four silver spoons and forks designed by Charles Rennie Mackintosh, stamped with maker's marks and Glasgow hallmarks for 1902. (Christie's London)

$36,960   £22,000

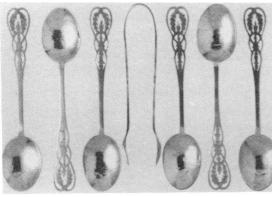

A set of six silver teaspoons with sugar spoons, designed by Sybil Dunlop, the terminals of each decorated with openwork floral decoration, hallmarks for 1923, 90gr. (Christie's London)

$407   £242

A George III composite Old English pattern table service, the majority by Peter, Ann & William Bateman, 1803, 1805, etc., comprising 66 pieces, 94oz. (Christie's London)

$6,275 £3,850

A pair of engraved fish servers by Albert Coles, New York, circa 1850-1855, the slice with a scrolled blade elaborately engraved with scrolls and foliage, 12in. long, 8oz.
(Christie's) $550   £346

A Charles I seal top, of good gauge, with the initials RW for Robert Wade, Senior, circa 1640. (Phillips London) $954 £600

A rare punch ladle, attributed to John Hastier, New York, 1725-1750, the circular bowl with a heart shaped join and an everted rim, marked (minor repair at handle join), 13½in. long. 3oz.
(Christie's New York) $1,870   £1,176

A George II Hanoverian pattern basting spoon, the terminal engraved with presentation initials. 1742 by James Wilks, 5.8oz. (Lawrence) $998   £605

A Charles II lace back trefid, punched in the bowl and punched twice on the stem with the letters TD and the T & Tun mark for Taunton, by T. Dare, Junior, circa 1680. (Phillips London) $1,749 £1,100

A rare early 17th century Barnstaple silver gilt seal top spoon, circa 1623, by Robert Mathew, 17.2cm.
(Lawrence Fine Arts) $7,893 £5,060

An unusual Victorian fish slice and fork, modelled as a garden spade and fork, with ivory handles. (Christie's S. Ken) $525 £330

FLATWARE

A Victorian pair of cast fish carvers, the heavy handles modelled as a stylised full length fish, assay marks for 1872, 1855, and the maker's mark HH for Hyam Hyams, 23oz. (Phillips London) $1,272 £800

A pair of sugar tongs, by John D. Germon, Philadelphia, 1785-1825, the arms pierced in the form of stylised leafage, 5½in. long, 1oz. (Christie's New York) $1,210 £761

A Commonwealth puritan, plain, of good gauge, punched in the bowl, possibly by Thomas Thornborough, Salisbury, circa 1650. (Phillips London) $1,352 £850

A Liberty & Co., Cymric silver spoon, designed by Archibald Knox on the occasion of Edward VII's Coronation in 1902, 16cm. long. (Phillips London) $490   £320

A Queen Anne Dog Nose pattern gravy spoon, the terminal engraved with a monogram, Britannia Standard bottom marks indistinct, probably 1707 maker's mark WD, 4.8oz. (Lawrence) $1097   £665

A George III Old English pattern gravy spoon, 1790 by Hester Bateman, 3.5oz. (Lawrence) $399   £242

A parcel gilt fish slice and fork, American, circa 1885, each engraved with two intertwined carp, 11½in. long, 8oz. (Christie's New York) $605   £380

A silver gilt composite dessert service, comprising twelve spoons, twelve four pronged forks, twelve knives, a pair of grape scissors, a pair of sugar nippers, a caddy spoon and a French fiddle pattern sugar sifter, 1798/1809, weight without knives 65oz. (Christie's London) $4,482 £2,750

A Georg Jensen 48 piece table service, stamped maker's marks, after 1945, 2,700grs. gross weight. (Christie's London) $4,482 £2,750

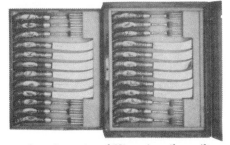

A set of twelve pairs of Victorian silver gilt dessert knives and forks, the Continental porcelain handles painted with various exotic birds, George Adams, London, 1868. (Christie's S. Ken) $1,848   £1,100

FRAMES

A late Victorian shaped rectangular photograph frame, the body pierced with acorns and oak leaves and inlaid with tortoiseshell, H. A., London, 1894, 3¼in. (Christie's S. Ken) $1,478 £880

An Edwardian easel backed bevelled mirror, of vertical rectangular form, 15in. x 10in., overall.
(Henry Spencer) $594   £360

A Victorian silver mounted dressing glass, on a ebonised base with easel supports, 1885 by William Comyns, 32.3cm.
(Lawrence) $1089   £660

A William Hutton & Sons Art Nouveau silver and enamel photograph frame, decorated with stylised honesty and green and blue enamelling, 1904, 22.3cm. high. (Christie's London) $4,066 £2,420

A silver repoussé picture frame of shaped rectangular form, decorated in relief with a stylised foliate pattern, Chester hallmarks, 32.7cm. high. (Christie's) $1594   £990

A silver repousse picture frame, shaped rectangular form, decorated in relief with flowers and insects, Birmingham hallmarks for 1907, 29.5cm. high. (Christie's London) $1,165 £715

A William Hutton & Sons silver and enamelled picture frame, the top having interwoven tendrils picked out in green and violet enamels, 20.5cm. high. (Phillips London) $4,131 £2,700

A William Hutton & Sons silver and enamel picture frame, the shaped square frame with repousse decoration, London hallmarks for 1903, 19.3cm. high. (Christie's London) $3,048 £1,870

A silver and enanmel repoussé photograph frame, decorated in relief with stylised and green enamel flowers, Birmingham hallmarks for 1904, 21.5cm. high.
(Christie's) $1505   £935

GOBLETS

A George IV gilt lined part fluted campana shaped goblet, the bowl applied with a frieze of vines and engraved with a crest, Rebecca Emes and Edward Barnard, London, 1824, 6¾in., 14.25oz.
(Christie's S. Ken) $707 £462

Peter and Ann Bateman, a goblet, 6¼in. high, vase-form engraved with rosettes, husk swags and waved bands, London, 1796, 5.5oz.
(Bonhams) $660   £400

A 19th century Chinese Export goblet, the sides chased in relief with arched panels, by Wang Hing & Co., Hong Kong, circa 1890, 21.4cm. high, 9.5oz.
(Phillips London) $477 £300

A gilt-lined goblet on a beaded rim foot, the bowl engraved with an armorial and crest, possibly American circa 1860, 6in., 10.75oz.
(Christie's S. Ken.) $254   £154

A matched pair of Regency gilt-lined goblets on reeded rising hexagonal bases, I.B., London 1816 and T.R., London 1812, 6¼in., 18oz.
(Christie's S. Ken.) $998   £605

A George IV gilt-lined part-fluted campana-shaped goblet on a rising circular foot, Langlands & Robertson, Newcastle, circa 1823, 7¼in., 12.75oz.
(Christie's S. Ken.) $817   £495

A George III goblet, the ovoid body on a gadrooned trumpet shape pedestal foot, 1774 by Emick Romer, 15cm., 8.6oz.
(Lawrence) $544   £330

An attractive Victorian silver gilt goblet, 6½in. high, chased with panels of cavorting putti, vines and masks, London, 1861, by George W. Adams, 7oz.
(Bonhams) $1072   £650

A George III wine goblet, gilt interior, on a gadroon knopped and banded circular stem foot, 5in. maker Peter Gillois, London 1769, 5.5oz.
(Wooley & Wallis) $412   £250

INKSTANDS

A late Victorian rectangular inkstand with three quarter gallery pierced with scroll foliage, 1893 maker's mark of William Gibson and John Langman, 18.4oz. (Lawrence Fine Arts) $1,802 £1,155

A martele inkstand, by Gorham, Providence, circa 1905, the stand repousse and chased with serpentine ribs and flowers, marked *Martele. 9584,* 10¼in. wide, 9oz. (Christie's New York) $2,200 £1,383

Regency ebonised double ink stand, early 19th century, with ormolu beading, florettes, and centre ring handle, 13in. long. (Skinner Inc.) $800 £510

A George II inkstand, the shaped oblong sunk base with a moulded rim, decorated in the Baroque manner, by Paul de Lamerie, length overall 22cm., bell, 14cm. high, 1730, 25.5oz. (Phillips London) $41,340 £26,000

A plated elephant's-head inkwell by Meriden Britannia Company, last quarter 19th century, the hinged cover with a cast figure of a monkey, 6½in. long. (Christie's) $1540 £968

An inkstand, with shell and florally chased border, on four scroll chased supports, the inkwell Birmingham 1895, 25.5 x 17.8cm., 21oz. (Bonhams) $897 £550

An Edwardian shaped oblong inkstand on openwork scrolling foliate feet, Heath & Middleton, London 1905, 10in., 17.25oz. free. (Christie's S. Ken) $1,122 £660

A commemorative inkstand by Tuttle Silversmiths, Boston, 1945-1949, marked with pine tree shilling mark and *HT1,* for President Truman's first term, 8in. high, 35oz. (Christie's New York) $1,430 £899

A Victorian rectangular ink-stand with two receivers, London, 1884, the central taperstick London 1881, 8½in. long. (Tennants) $2,028 £1,300

JUGS

A Cellini style plated wine ewer, 31cm. high. (Bonhams) $153 £100

A George III Irish hot water or coffee jug of squat circular form, profusely chased with flowers and scrolls, maker's mark overstruck by that of James Le Bass, Dublin, 1819, 24cm. high, 33.5oz. (Phillips London) $1,081 £680

A tall ewer, by William Forbes for Ball, Tompkins & Black, New York, 1839-1851, with a flaring cylindrical neck, 18¼in. high, 49oz. (Christie's New York) $2,860 £1,798

A Liberty & Co. silver jug, the lightly hammered tapering cylindrical body with domed hinged cover, with Birmingham hallmarks for 1915, 22cm. high, 536 gr. gross. (Christie's London) $739 £440

A Hukin & Heath electro-plated jug, decorated with three vertical copper bands, 20.3cm. high. (Christie's London) $161 £99

A George III beer jug, of plain baluster form, on a pedestal foot, 25cm. high overall, by Thomas & Richard Payne, 1777, 24oz. (Phillips London) $3,816 £2,400

Fine late Victorian hot water jug of baluster design, treen handle, Edinburgh 1895, by Hamilton and Inches, 22oz. all in. (G. A. Key) $646 £380

A George III plain pear shaped hot water jug, with partly wicker covered foliate scroll handle, with gadrooned borders, 1770, maker's mark I. B. 9½in. high, gross 23oz. (Christie's London) $2,331 £1,430

A George III gadrooned plain pear shaped hot water jug on a gadrooned rising circular foot, James Young & Orlando Jackson, London, 1774, 10¾in., 21.50oz. gross. (Christie's S. Ken) $1,262 £825

MISCELLANEOUS

A William IV silver mounted note case with three ivory leaves, Joseph Wilmore, Birmingham, 1836, 3¼in. (Christie's S. Ken) $517 £308

A Continental rectangular double sovereign and half sovereign case, the front stamped with two perched owls, 2¾in. overall. (Christie's S. Ken) $295 £176

An Edwardian foliate pierced shaped circular pedestal cake stand, G.H., London, 1910, 11¼in., 24.25oz. (Christie's S. Ken) $598 £352

A Danish white metal cock-tail shaker, the cylindrical form on a flared circular foot, Copenhagen marks for 1941, 23cm. high, 440 grams. (Christie's London) $538 £330

A Victorian novelty plated spoon warmer modelled as a stylised duck on periwinkle feet, 6in. (Christie's S. Ken) $455 £286

A Continental toby jug with caryatid scroll handle, the bewigged figure wearing a frock coat and tricorn hat, import marks, 9in. (Christie's S. Ken) $1,346 £880

A George III barrel shaped tobacco jar and cover, engraved to simulate staves and with applied hoops, by John Emes, 1803, 4¾in. high, 13oz. (Christie's London)
          $6,096 £3,740

A Sabattini electroplate picnic cocktail set comprising a cylindrical stacking system of six cups and decanter, 15¾in. high. (Christie's S. Ken)
          $222 £143

A Royal Irish Rifles officer's silver (J. & Co. Birmingham, 1893) whistle with holder, chains and chain boss. (Christie's S. Ken) $218 £143

A pap boat, by William Thompson, New York, 1809-1845, oval, with an everted rim, a curving spout and a scroll handle, 16cm. long, 3oz. (Christie's New York)
$440 £276

One of a pair of Sheffield plated meat plates and covers in sizes, the domed covers engraved with arms. (Lawrence Fine Arts) Two $995 £638

A French 18th century wine taster, engraved with the owner's name, with scrolling oval thumbpiece, 11.5cm. long, 79gr. (Henry Spencer)
$2,370 £1,500

An Edwardian child's silver rattle, stamped in the form of Mr Punch, Birmingham 1908, maker's mark *G & N,* 14cm. high. (Henry Spencer)
$192 £120

An Edwardian rectangular vesta case, the front enamelled with an oval vignette of a dog, R.B.S Chester, 1906, 2in.(Christie's S. Ken) $184 £110

An unusual pair of sugar nips formed as a Dutch doll, the head enamelled with a face and hair, London 1911, 3½in. (Christie's S. Ken) $841 £495

An early 19th century French silver metal needlework clamp, with netting hook and pin cushions. (Phillips West Two)
$170 £100

A George III argyle, of urn shape, on a pedestal foot, wood handle, 20cm. high overall, by Henry Green, 1791, 14oz. (Phillips London)
$4,134 £2,600

A rare George IV tapering cylindrical ear trumpet, engraved with a coat of arms, by Mary Ann and Charles Reily, 1828, 13in. long, 5oz. (Christie's London)
$5,020 £3,080

MISCELLANEOUS

A Victorian posy holder, the waisted and flared bowl stamped with flowers and foliage, 5½in. (Christie's S. Ken) $370 £220

An amusing flask, by Tiffany & Co., New York, 1891-1902, decorated with etched scenes of brownies frolicking and quarrelling and avoiding mosquitoes, marked, 7¾in. high, 15oz. (Christie's New York) $8,250 £5,188

Mauser Co. Sterling Bottle Carrier, New York, c. 1900, in the form of a wine bottle with repousse vine decoration, 11½in. high, approximately 27.5 troy oz.
(Skinner Inc) $1400   £909

A Victorian castle top card case, the cover chased in relief with a view of Balmoral, probably by Nathaniel Mills, Birmingham, 1855. (Phillips London) $445 £280

Liberty & Co. four piece dressing table set, comprising pin tray, hair brush, clothes brush and hand mirror, Birmingham 1924 and 1925, 25.2cm.
(Lawrence) $762   £462

A Victorian shaped rectangular card case, the front chased in high relief with a view of Westminster Abbey, Yapp & Woodward, Birmingham 1854, 3.9in.
(Christie's S. Ken.) $1089   £660

Russian Silver-Gilt and Shaded Enamel Easter Egg, Khlebnikov & Co., Moscow, 1908–1917, 4¾in. high.
(Skinner Inc) $2750 £1785

A Williams IV lady's rosewood dressing case, 1835 by Archibald Douglas, the small inkpot a replacement of 1836, 32.6cm.
(Lawrence) $799 £484

A figural cigar stand, Tiffany & Company, New York, 1865–1870, supported by three cast fully-modelled putti, on a shaped plinth base, 8⅜in. high, 29 oz. 10 dwt.
(Christie's) $1980 £1245

MISCELLANEOUS

A pair of George III candle snuffers with steel cutter and box, indistinct maker's mark only, c.1800, 18.2cm.
(Lawrence) $254   £154

A textured and beaded plated oval watering can with scroll handle and hinged cover, 7¹/₂ in.
(Christie's S. Ken.) $172   £104

A cigar lighter by Gorham, Providence, 1881, in the neo-Grecque taste, the top dished, in a petal pattern, 4³/₈ in. long, 4 oz.
(Christie's) $440   £277

A George V rattle/whistle, the collar stamped 'darling' on a mother of pearl teething stick, Birmingham 1920.
(Spencer's) $66   £40

A Victorian silver gilt christening set, comprising a mug, a spoon, fork and knife, the mug 1869 by Robert Garrard, 7.8cm.
(Lawrence) $653   £396

An unusual late Victorian silver mounted miniature mahogany long case clock, William Comyns, London, 1900, 14¼in.
(Christie's S. Ken) $1,069 £660

A Victorian shaped rectangular card case, stamped in high relief with a view of Osborne House, A.T., Birmingham, 1854, 4in. (Christie's S. Ken)
$787 £495

An Edwardian novelty pin cushion as a chick in an egg, by Samsons Morden and Co., Chester 1908, 2in. high.
(Spencer's) $190   £115

A Victorian silver visiting card case, with a gold monogram surmounted by a Viscount's coronet, 1875, 11.2cm. long.
(Henry Spencer) $622 £370

MUGS

A medallion mug by Gorham, Providence, circa 1865, with a squared handle and beaded borders, applied with two medallions, 3in. high, 4 oz. (Christie's) $440 £277

An unusual late Victorian shaving mug, the hinged cover engraved with a monogram, London 1899, by Alex Clark, 251 grammes gross. (Henry Spencer) $478 £290

A Chinese christening mug of tapering cylindrical form, embossed with chrysanthemums, stamped on the base with Chinese characters only, circa 1900, 7.9cm. high, 6oz. (Phillips London) $349 £220

A mug by Hands & Co 1846 of baluster form decorated with floral engraving, 10oz. (Michael Newman) $660 £400

A cann, by Joseph Richardson, Sr., Philadelphia, 1744-1784, with a moulded rim and a moulded circular foot, 5¼in. high, 11oz. (Christie's New York) $2,200 £1,383

A George III mug, with a leaf capped scroll handle, all on a domed foot rim, 1764 by Louis Black, 11.9cm., 10.4oz. (Lawrence) $944 £572

A George V christening mug of waisted octagonal form, with foliate cast handle and foot rim, London 1910, 148 grammes. (Henry Spencer) $134 £85

A mug by William B. Durgin Co., Concord, New Hampshire, circa 1880, with a curved handle, the spot-hammered surface repoussé and finely-chased, 3⅝in. high, 7 oz. (Christie's) $1100 £654

A George III christening mug, dated 1911, with plain curved handle and gilded interior, by Robert and David Hennell, 146 grammes, 7.5cm. high. (Henry Spencer) $205 £130

MUSTARD POTS

A mustard pot, 2³/₄ in. high, cylindrical bar pierced sides engraved with leaves and scrolls, London 1936, by A. & F. Parsons, 3oz.
(Bonhams) $297   £180

Crichton Brothers, a pair of mustard pots, 4in. diam., with moulded borders, scroll handles and detachable blue glass liners, London, 1913, 10.5oz.
(Bonhams) $594   £360

A mixed-metal mustard pot and spoon by Dominick & Haff, New York, 1880, with a circular low-domed hinged cover with a ball finial, 2¹/₂ in. high, gross weight 4 oz. 10 dwt.
(Christie's) $2200   £1383

A Victorian mustard pot, 3in. high, with leaf-capped scroll handle and domed fluted hinged cover, Sheffield 1875, by Henry Wilkinson, 4oz.
(Bonhams) $313   £190

Attractive Victorian silver drum mustard, London 1836 by Charles T Fox and George Fox.
(G.A. Key) $247   £150

A Victorian unusual mustard pot, the cauldron-shaped body finely embossed and matted with a desert oasis scene, 10cm. high, by A. Sibley, 1857, 7oz.
(Phillips) $742   £450

A Victorian mustard pot, 2³/₄ in. high, in 18th century style, the sides chased with floral swags, 2.5oz.
(Bonhams) $198   £120

A Victorian mustard pot, gourd-shaped, engraved in panels with scrollwork, Birmingham 1847, by Yapp and Woodward.
(Bonhams) $577   £350

A Victorian mustard pot, 3in. high, octagonal with leaf engraved sides, London 1858, by Reilly and Barnard, 5oz.
(Bonhams) $396   £240

PITCHERS

A pitcher, by Edwin Stebbins, New York, 1828-1835, the foliate scroll handle with a cast helmet thumbpiece, marked, 13¾in. high, 45oz. (Christie's New York) $1,045 £657

Georg Jensen sterling water pitcher, Denmark, 1925-30, with beaded base and ebony handle, 9½in. high, approx. 27 troy oz. (Skinner Inc.) $2,000 £1,227

A pitcher, by William Gale for Tiffany & Company, New York, 1856-1859, the neck and foot with repousse acanthus leaf borders, marked, 11½in. high, 29oz. (Christie's New York) $2,090 £1,314

A presentation pitcher, by Newell Harding & Co., Boston, circa 1854, with a cast rustic handle and a cast grapevine spout, marked, 13in. high, 39oz. (Christie's New York) $1,650 £1,037

A pitcher, by Haddock, Lincoln & Foss, Boston, circa 1855, with a rustic handle and a leaf form spout, marked (bruises), 9¾in. high, 33oz. (Christie's New York) $935 £588

A plated pitcher, by Meriden Britannia Co., circa 1885, the entire surface spot hammered, the sides repousse and chased with a dragonfly, waterlilies and flowers, marked, 26cm. high. (Christie's New York) $1,100 £691

A pitcher, by Tiffany & Co., New York, 1869-1891, the cast handle in the form of stylised leafage above classical mask handle join, marked, 22cm. high, 36oz. (Christie's New York) $3,520 £2,213

Georg Jensen sterling pitcher, Denmark, with openwork grapevine decoration, 9in. high, approx. 30 troy oz. (Skinner Inc.) $3,000 £1,840

A pitcher, by A. E. Warner, Balitmore, circa 1810, the neck and base with reeded banding, the front engraved with armorials, 8¼in. high, 32oz. (Christie's New York) $8,800 £5,534

PORRINGERS

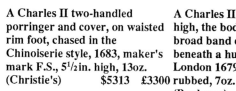

A Charles II two-handled porringer and cover, on waisted rim foot, chased in the Chinoiserie style, 1683, maker's mark F.S., 5¹/₂in. high, 13oz.
(Christie's) $5313   £3300

A Charles II porringer, 3¹/₄in. high, the body chased with a broad band of acanthus leaves beneath a husk chased band, London 1679, maker's mark rubbed, 7oz.
(Bonhams) $1650   £1000

A Charles II two-handled plain circular porringer and cover, with scroll handles, the base engraved with initials E.S., 1677, maker's mark T.K., the cover with maker's mark only, 4¹/₄in. high, 12oz.
(Christie's) $4427   £2750

A large porringer and cover, 7¹/₂in. high, in late 17th century style, with two cast scroll side handles, London, 1908, by the Crichtons, 33oz.
(Bonhams) $1105   £670

Silver porringer, Samuel Casey maker, South Kingston, Rhode Island, mid-18th century, 5in. diam., approx. 8 troy oz.
(Skinner Inc.) $3,250 £1,923

A good reproduction Charles II two handled porringer and cover, engraved with chinoiserie birds and foliage, 22.5cm. high overall, by Messrs. D. & J. Welby, 1912, 42oz. (Phillips London)
                          $1,272 £800

A porringer by William Simpkins, Boston, 1730–1770, with a pierced keyhole handle engraved with block initials, 8in. long, 7 oz. 10 dwt.
(Christie's) $1980   £1245

A porringer by Jonathan Otis, Newport, circa 1750–1765, with a pierced keyhole handle engraved 'S. Coggeshall', 8in. long, 8 oz. 10 dwt.
(Christie's) $2860   £1799

A porringer by John Hancock, Boston, circa 1750–1765, with a pierced keyhole handle, 8¹/₄in. long, 8 oz.
(Christie's) $2420   £1522

SALTS & PEPPERS

A pair of salts by Tiffany & Co., New York, 1870–1875, with a die-rolled guilloche border and three cast ram's-head feet, 3in. diam, 4 oz.
(Christie's) $770   £458

A salt cellar by Gorham, Providence, 1872, with a bail handle attached to angular handles, on four flaring cylindrical raking legs, 3in. high, 2 oz.
(Christie's) $660   £415

Crichton Brothers, a pair of Britannia standard trencher salt cellars, 3¹/₂in. diam., London, 1909, 10oz.
(Bonhams) $429   £260

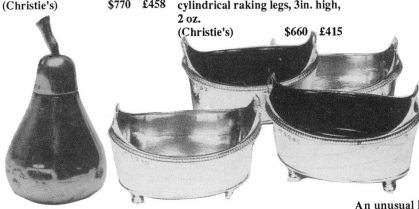

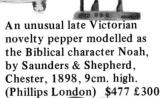

An Edwardian novelty silver salt caster as a pear, Chester marks, 3in. high.
(Spencer's) $181   £110

A set of four George IV silver salt cellars of oval tub shape, London 1802 and 1821, maker Richard Cooke, 16oz.
(Phillips) $1815   £1100

An unusual late Victorian novelty pepper modelled as the Biblical character Noah, by Saunders & Shepherd, Chester, 1898, 9cm. high.
(Phillips London) $477 £300

A pair of George III salt cellars, 4in. diam., with reeded borders, London, 1792, by William Fountain and Daniel Pontifex, 5 oz.
(Bonhams) $495   £300

A pair of novelty pepperettes in the form of busts in suits of armour, the hinged visor opening to reveal hollow interior, Birmingham, 1906, by George Unite.
(Bonhams) $528   £320

A pair of Victorian salt cellars, 3¹/₂in., oval with waived gadrooned borders and ovolo pierced sides, London 1853, by W. R. Smily, 5oz.
(Bonhams) $528   £320

SAUCE BOATS

A George V large sauce boat in the early Georgian style, of baluster form with acanthus leaf sheathed high scrolling and re-scrolling handle, London 1935, 302 grammes.
(Spencer's) $313   £190

A George III sauceboat with shaped gadroon border and shell pad feet, London 1761, 13oz. (Tennants) $967 £620

Kirk Repousse sterling sauce boat, Baltimore, 1903-07, chased floral design, 8⁵/₈in. long, approximately 9 troy oz.
(Skinner Inc.) $400   £244

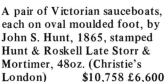

A pair of George IV gadrooned sauce boats on shell and scroll feet, Richard Sibley, London 1825, 8in., 32oz.
(Christie's S. Ken.)
          $4356   £2640

A pair of Victorian sauceboats, each on oval moulded foot, by John S. Hunt, 1865, stamped Hunt & Roskell Late Storr & Mortimer, 48oz. (Christie's London) $10,758 £6,600

A pair of George II sauceboats with shaped rims and foliate-chased elaborate scroll handles, Robert Tyrrill, London 1744 or 1746, 7¹/₂in. 33.25oz.
(Christie's S. Ken.)
          $4537   £2750

A George II Irish shaped-oval sauceboat, on moulded base with leaf-capped scroll handle, Dublin, circa 1735, maker's mark probably that of John Williamson, 9in. long, 22oz.
(Christie's) $3128   £1980

An elegant George III sauce boat, the oval boat with high looped spur handle, London 1790, probably by Hester Bateman, 224 grammes.
(Spencer's) $412   £250

A good quality George I sauce-boat, the sides flat chased with C-scrolls, scalework and leaves, London 1718, by Robert Pilkington, 20.4cm., 14.5oz.
(Bonhams) $945 £580

713

SNUFF BOXES

A Victorian table snuff box, the cover engraved with a view of St Michael's Mount, Penzance, by Edward Edwards, 1846, 7.25oz. (Phillips London) $986 £620

A George III rectangular snuff box with overall reeded decoration, 1813 by John Linnit and William Atkinson, 8.4cm. (Lawrence) $454 £275

A Russian rectangular gilt lined snuff box, the lid nielloed with an extensive townscape, Moscow, 1891, 2.3in. (Christie's S. Ken) $336 £198

A Victorian shaped rectangular pocket snuff box, Birmingham 1844 by Nathaniel Mills, 5.5.cm. (Lawrence) $399 £242

A William IV cartouche shaped gilt lined snuff box, applied with an engraved tortoiseshell plaque, Nathaniel Mills, 1833, 3¼in. (Christie's S. Ken) $887 £572

An early Victorian Castle Top snuff box by Nathaniel Mills, with a view of Newstead Abbey, Birmingham 1837, 6cm. wide. (Henry Spencer) $1,000 £625

An early 19th century Stobwasser circular papier mache snuff box lid, painted with the portrait of a young woman, the reverse inscribed *La Douceur*, 3¾in. diam. (Christie's S. Ken) $858 £550

A George III gold-mounted cowrie shell snuff-box, with reeded mounts, circa 1765, maker's mark probably that of Robert Tyrill, 2⅞in. long (Christie's) $3010 £1870

An early 19th century circular papier mache snuff box, the cover painted with a miser counting money, 4in. diam. (Christie's S. Ken) $206 £132

A Russian rectangular snuff box, one side nielloed with scrolling foliage, 3.1in. (Christie's S. Ken) $486 £286

A continental early 19th century oval horn snuff box, the hinged cover inlaid with three colour gold and silver flowers, 2¾in. (Christie's S. Ken.) $635 £385

A Russian rectangular gilt lined snuff box, the lid nielloed with figures on a gilt matted ground, 3in. (Christie's S. Ken) $1,028 £605

SNUFF BOXES

An early Victorian rectangular snuff box, engraved overall, 1841 by Edward Edwards, 7.8cm. (Lawrence) $690 £418

A Russian rectangular silver gilt snuff box, the base, sides and lid nielloed with townscapes, Moscow 1834, 3.2in. (Christie's S. Ken) $654 £385

A George IV rectangular snuff box, the cover chased with a view of Newstead Abbey, by Joseph Willmore, Birmingham, 1825, 7.2cm. long, 3.75oz. (Phillips London) $509 £320

A 19th century gilt lined China Trades snuff box, the lid and sides cast with various Oriental scenes, 2¾in. (Christie's S. Ken) $831 £495

A good and rare George III fox head snuff box, by Phipps & Robinson, 1795, 9.5cm. high, 5.25oz. (Phillips London) $3,498 £2,200

An 18th century cartouche shaped gilt lined snuff box, the lid inset with a brown mottled agate, 2¾in. wide. (Christie's S. Ken) $245 £154

An attractive French Vernis Martin style snuff box, painted with a miniature portrait of an 18th century lady, 8cm. diam. (Henry Spencer) $1,512 £900

A Victorian rectangular gilt lined snuff box, with a cast view in high relief of the Burns Memorial within a heavy scroll work border, F.M., Birmingham, 1861, 3¼in. (Christie's S. Ken) $808 £528

A Louis XV cartouche-shaped silver-mounted tortoiseshell snuff-box, the hinged cover inlaid in mother-of-pearl and repoussé, Paris, 1738-44, 3in. wide (Christie's) $885 £550

An early Victorian casket-shape snuff box, with an engine turned base, Joseph Willmore, Birmingham 1842, 4oz. (Woolley & Wallis) $680 £400

A George III Scottish snuff mull with engraved silver mounts, the hinged cover with initials having original chain with tools, circa 1800. (Woolley & Wallis) $510 £300

A Chinese export silver gift oblong snuff box, chased overall with fruiting vine on a matted ground, 19th century, 10.4cm. (Lawrence) $526 £319

TANKARDS

An unusual mid-19th century China Trades topographical tapering pint tankard with applied sinuous dragon scroll handle and moulded rim, circa 1850, 5in. (Christie's S. Ken) $924 £550

A late George II plain baluster pint tankard on a rising circular foot, John Langlands, Newcastle, 1757, 5in., 10oz. (Christie's S. Ken) $682 £440

A George III plain tapering tankard on a skirted foot, with a moulded body band, John Langlands, Newcastle, 1772, 5½in., 14.75oz. (Christie's S. Ken) $1,458 £858

A Victorian spouted lidded plain tapering quart tankard in the mid-18th century taste, Daniel and Charles Houle, London, 1877, 7in., 27¼oz. (Christie's S. Ken) $1,705 £1,100

A trophy tankard by Tiffany & Co., New York, circa 1890, with a low circular cover and scrolled handle, 10¼in. high, 47 oz. (Christie's) $4400 £2618

A George III gilt lined baluster pint tankard on a chased spreading circular foot, T. W., London, 1770, 4½in., 10.25oz. (Christie's S. Ken) $748 £440

A late George II baluster lidded tankard later chased with rising foliage, lion's masks and laurel swags, William Shaw and William Priest, London 1757, 7½in., 23.50oz. (Christie's S. Ken)$2,609 £1,705

Silver tankard, Benjamin Hurd, maker, 1739-1781, Boston, Massachusetts, circa 1760, 9in. high, approximately 30 troy oz. (Skinner Inc.) $2,300 £1,411

A George III, lidded tapering quart tankard on a skirted foot, Langlands and Robertson, Newcastle, 1785, 29oz. (Christie's S. Ken) $3,410 £2,200

TEA & COFFEE SETS

A Chinese 19th century three piece compressed spherical tea service applied with chased sinuous dragons and engraved with monograms, with bamboo style handles, 45.75oz. (Christie's S. Ken) $887 £528

A silver tea set, embellished with curvi-linear motifs and supported on a circular spreading base, stamped *G.R.J.,* maker's marks, Birmingham, 1947. (Phillips London) $1,222 £750

A Christofle five piece electroplated tea and coffee service designed by Henri Bouilhet, stamped mark *Christofle France Coll. Gallia.* (Christie's London) $2,152 £1,320

An American 19th century four-piece tapering moulded circular medallion tea service, Ball, Black and Co., circa. 1880, height of teapot 6in., 32.25oz. (Christie's S. Ken.) $817 £495

Dominick & Haff three-piece sterling tea set, chased with Renaissance-style panels with swags, floral bouquets and laurel wreath borders, approximately 44 troy oz. (Skinner Inc) $1300 £844

A Danish 19th century three piece coffee service on stylised foliate capped pad feet, each chased with rococo flowers, 41.75oz. gross. (Christie's S. Ken) $874 £550

TEA & COFFEE SETS

A Walker & Hall four piece hammered electroplated tea and coffee service, decorated with hammered rectangular panels, with short spout and wooden handle, 22cm. height of coffee pot. (Christie's London) $591 £352

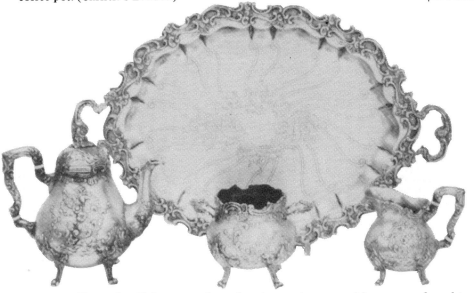

An Austro-Hungarian 19th century four piece tea service, comprising: a pear shaped tea-pot, milk jug and two handled sugar basin and a two handled shaped oval tray chased with a rococo scroll rim, length of tray 19¾in., the teapot 7¾in., 70oz. (Christie's S. Ken) $1,683 £990

An Austro-Hungarian 19th century spiral fluted four piece part tea and coffee service, comprising: a compressed spherical teapot with matching milk jug and a pear shaped coffee pot with matching pitcher, height of coffee pot 9in., 68.50oz. gross. (Christie's S. Ken) $1,589 £935

TEA & COFFEE SETS

A four piece tea service, three pieces marked *Jones, Ball & Co.,* teapot marked *Jones, Shreve, Brown & Co., Boston,* circa 1854, the spouts and handles cast in the rustic style, gross weight 73oz. (Christie's New York) $2,860 £1,798

A James Dixon & Sons electroplated three piece tea service, designed by Dr Christopher Dresser, of everted conical form with angular spout and handle, 1880, 10.3cm. height of tea pot. (Christie's London) $18,480 £11,000

A six piece tea service, by Ball, Tompkins & Black, New York, 1839-1851, the scrolled handles with insulating rings, the domed lids with floral finials, each marked, kettle 14½in. high, gross weight 177oz. (Christie's New York) $4,950 £3,113

TEA CADDIES

An oval tea caddy, the plain body with reeded rims, Chester 1929 Stokes and Ireland Ltd., 9.4cm.
(Lawrence) $544   £330

An Edwardian tea caddy, Sheffield 1903 by Richard Martin and Ebenezer Hall of Martin, Hall and Co., 9.3cm.
(Lawrence) $436   £264

An Edwardian tea caddy in the form of a Georgian knife box, Birmingham 1905 by William Hutton and Sons Ltd., 8.8cm.
(Lawrence) $544   £330

A George III oval tea caddy with domed cover and leaf finial, engraved with two bands of starbursts and leaves, 14cm. high, by Peter and Anne Bateman, 1788, 14oz.
(Phillips London)
    $1,908 £1,200

An Edwardian tea caddy, the oval body with vertical lobes, 1907 by William Hutton and Sons Ltd., 13cm.
(Lawrence) $363   £220

A George II chinoiserie caddy decorated in relief with a woman and boy boiling a pot of tea, maker's mark apparently overstruck by that of Abraham Portal, 1754, 14cm. high, 15.75oz. (Phillips London) $6,042 £3,800

An Edwardian tea caddy in the form of a Georgian knife box, Chester 1907 by S. Blanckensee and Sons Ltd., the caddy spoon by Benoni Stephens, 8.8cm.
(Lawrence) $581   £352

A late Victorian tea caddy, Birmingham 1900 by T. Hayes, the cap Birmingham 1896, 10.6cm.
(Lawrence) $363   £220

A George III tea caddy, of plain rectangular form, engraved with a shield of arms, 1770 maker's mark ED in script, 12.5cm., 11.1oz.
(Lawrence) $3448   £2090

TEA KETTLES

A kettle on stand and a teapot, by Tiffany & Co., New York, 1876-1891, each globular, kettle 13in. high, gross weight 85oz. (Christie's New York) $1,870 £1,176

A good Victorian large silver tea kettle, stand and burner, 16½in., fully marked, London 1851, maker George John Richards, 75½oz. (Phillips) $2557 £1550

A Victorian tea kettle in the George II style, on a stand with central burner and three scroll supports, 1879 by Robert Harper, 35cm. overall height, 46.1oz.(Lawrence) $1906 £1155

An Edwardian part fluted compressed tea kettle applied with a shell and foliate rim, James Dixon & Son, Sheffield, 1908, 12in., 48oz. gross. (Christie's S. Ken) $1,016 £605

A large Victorian Louis Quatorze pattern tea kettle, with central burner, Sheffield, 1854, by Martin, Hall and Co., 43.5cm., 81.5oz. (Lawrence Fine Arts) $6,349 £4,070

Dominick and Haff sterling kettle and lamp stand, circa 1880, the hammered globular body decorated in the Japanese taste, 11½in. high, approximately 37 troy oz.(Skinner Inc.) $4600 £2806

A George II inverted pear-shaped tea-kettle, stand and lamp, by Samuel Courtauld, 1758, 15in. high, gross 79oz. (Christie's) $6198 £3850

A fine tea kettle and stand by Tiffany & Co., New York, 1881–1891, in the Japanese taste, 12¾in. high, 467 oz. (Christie's) $12100 £7198

A Victorian tea kettle on stand, the compressed spherical body engraved with a wide band of scroll foliage, 1855 maker's mark JA, 36cm., 48.1oz. (Lawrence) $1996 £1210

TEAPOTS

A George IV silver teapot of compressed circular form, with florette finial, foliate claw and ball panel feet, London 1823, 25³/₄oz.
(Phillips) $594   £360

A George III bright-cut moulded oblong teapot with rising curved spout, Dorothy Langlands, Newcastle probably 1805, height of teapot 5¹/₂in., 19.75oz. gross.
(Christie's S. Ken.) $1543   £935

A George IV Irish teapot and cover, of compressed slightly melon fluted globular form, Dublin 1824, by Samuel Beere, 587gr. gross. (Henry Spencer) $672 £400

A good Victorian silver teapot of octagonal form with scrolling spout, London 1856, maker's mark WS, 24³/₄oz.
(Phillips) $792   £480

George III silver teapot, Peter, Anne and Wm. Bateman, London, 1803–04, 7in. high., approximately 15 troy oz.
(Skinner Inc.) $1000   £610

A Victorian compressed pear shaped teapot on scrolling foliate feet, E. & J. Barnard, London, 1856, 6³/₄in., 23.25oz. (Christie's S. Ken)
    $785 £462

A William IV plain pear shaped teapot, with partly fluted curved spout and domed cover, by Paul Storr, 1831, stamped *Storr & Mortimer,* gross 30oz.
(Christie's London)
    $2,331 £1,430

Japanese silver teapot, Arthur & Bond, Yokohama, late 19th century, globular body with long neck modelled in high relief with two dragons, approximately 15¹/₂ troy oz. (Skinner Inc) $1000 £621

A teapot, by Joseph Richard son, Sr., Philadelphia, 1745-1765, the spout with a scallop shell and drop, with later wood finial, 8½in. long, overall, gross weight 16oz. (Christie's New York) $9,350 £5,880

A George III teapot and stand, the concave panelled and oval body with an upper and lower bright cut draped frieze, 18cm. high, by Peter & Anne Bateman, 1791, 21oz.
(Phillips London) $2,226 £1,400

A George I Irish plain bullet teapot, on rim foot and with tapering angular spout, by Phillip Kinnersly, Dublin, 1719, 5in. high, gross 17oz. (Christie's London) $21,516 £13,200

A George III oval silver teapot with wood scroll handle and ivory finial, London 1804, maker John Emes, 19¹/₄oz.
(Phillips) $837   £530

SILVER

TEAPOTS

A silver teapot and cover modelled as a pomegranate, the chased details realistically rendered, its leafy branches forming a handle rendered in ivory, late 19th century, 12.8cm. long. (Christie's London) $3,823 £2,420

A George III tea pot, the straight sided oval body engraved with script initials within a shield, 1780 by Thomas Daniell, 25.5cm. across, 13oz. all in. (Lawrence) $1724   £1045

A George III oblong silver teapot, part fluted and with bands of anthemions, London 1812, marks rubbed, 21¼oz. (Phillips) $412   £250

George III Teapot, Peter, Anne & William Bateman, London, 1789–9, with bright-cut banded borders, (minor repairs, dents), 6½in. high, approximately 230 troy oz.
(Skinner Inc) $950   £616

A fine teapot by John Hurt, Boston, 1735–1745, the flat circular cover with a bell-shaped finial, 5in. high, 9¼in. long overall, 16 oz.
(Christie's) $770   £4581

A George III oblong silver teapot with wooden handle and finial, Sheffield 1806, maker Thomas Law, 16½oz.
(Phillips) $528   £320

A Hutton & Sons silver teapot, of broad cylindrical shape with angular spout, wickered loop handle and flat cover, Sheffield 1909, 16.5cm. high.
(Phillips) $544   £340

A rare teapot, New York, circa 1740–1760, the domed hinged cover with gadrooning and a turned finial, 8¼in. high, 24 oz. 10 dwt.
(Christie's) $16500   £10,377

Round silver teapot, moulded with floral medallions and knopped lid and black wooden handle on round base with shell relief and ball feet, lower Saxony, Hamburg, mid-19th century, 22cm. high.
(Kunsthaus am Museum)
                $757 £435

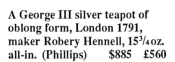

A George III silver teapot of oblong form, London 1791, maker Robery Hennell, 15¾oz. all-in. (Phillips) $885   £560

A Victorian silver teapot of compressed circular form, London 1841, makers Charles Thomas Fox and George Fox, 23¼oz. (Phillips) $379   £230

A George III teapot, of cushioned oval form, the domed cover with ebony finial, London 1801, by Charles Chesterman, 528 grammes gross. (Henry Spencer)
                $1,020 £600

TOAST RACKS

A Hukin & Heath electroplated toastrack designed by Dr. Christopher Dresser, with registration mark for 9th May 1881.
(Phillips) $480 £300

A novelty five bar toast rack in the form of a swan, 7in. long.
(Spencer's) $99 £60

A Hukin & Heath electroplated toastrack designed by Dr. Christopher Dresser, with registration mark for 9th October 1878, 12cm. high.
(Phillips) $4320 £2700

Fine large late Victorian silver toast rack in Gothic taste, standing on four ball feet, Sheffield 1901, 10oz.
(G.A. Key) $190 £115

A good William IV seven bar toast rack, on four anthemion and scroll supports, 1835, by Joseph and John Angell, 18.7cm., 14.2oz. (Lawrence Fine Arts) $652 £418

A Hukin and Heath electroplated toast rack, the wirework frame with seven supports, on a convex base, stamped *H & H*, 12cm. high. (Christie's London) $370 £220

A late Victorian small five bar toast rack, the arched upright on a wrythen fluted 'shell' base, Sheffield 1900, 103 grammes, 5in. long.
(Spencer's) $115 £70

A late George III seven bar toast rack, with acanthus leaf sheathed ring handle, London 1817, by Rebecca Emes and Edward Barnard, 335 grammes, 17cm. wide.
(Spencer's) $313 £190

London & North Eastern Railway ornate toast rack with coat of arms. (Onslow's) $180 £110

TRAYS & SALVERS

Japanese sterling two handled tray, early 20th century, impressed *Arthur & Bond Yokohama,* applied with irises in relief, 30in. long to handles, approx. 118 troy oz. (Skinner Inc.) $4,000 £2,454

A large George III shaped circular salver with plain centre, 1776 by John Carter II, 43.7cm., 61oz.
(Lawrence) $2541 £1540

Tiffany & Co. Sterling Tray, New York, early 20th century, 20in. long., approximately 74 troy oz.
(Skinner Inc) $1800 £1233

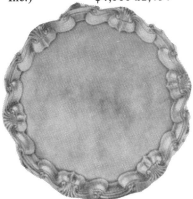

A George II shaped circular salver, with an applied shell and scroll rim and plain ground, Hugh Mills, London, 1748, 12¼in., 33oz. (Christie's S. Ken) $1,960 £1,210

Continental white metal pin tray, stamped *Silver,* with fluted border. (G. A. Key) $163 £105

A George II shaped circular salver, of exceptional quality and gauge, 32cm. diam., by Thomas Gilpin, 1748, 45oz. (Phillips London) $8,745 £5,500

Set of Twelve Schofield Co. Sterling Dinner Plates, Baltimore, 20th century, in the Baltimore Rose pattern, 10½in. diam, approximately 242 troy oz. (Skinner Inc) $8000 £5194

A Hukin & Heath electroplated tray, designed by Dr Christopher Dresser, with plain gallery rim and ebonised bar handles, 48.6cm. wide. (Christie's London) $1,478 £880

An Edwardian dressing table tray of rectangular form, Chester 1901, by John and William Deakin of James Deakin and Sons., 30.5cm., 12.4oz. (Lawrence) $617 £374

725

TRAYS & SALVERS

A rectangular tea tray, the raised gadroon rim with shell motifs at the angles, Sheffield, 1936 by Emile Viner of Viner and Co., 62cm., 89.4oz. (Lawrence Fine Arts)
$1,802 £1,155

A mid 18th century style shaped circular salver on hoof feet, with a moulded rim and plain ground, Elkington & Co., 12in. 26oz. (Christie's S. Ken)
$654 £385

Tiffany sterling silver butler's tray, rectangular, stylised foliate border, 21in. wide. (Skinner Inc.) $13,000 £8,280

A Regency gadrooned shaped circular salver on foliate and floral capped pad feet, Paul Storr, London, 1814, 12in., 26oz. (Christie's S. Ken)
$1,159 £682

Fine and heavy George III silver salver, with acanthus edge, London 1800, 16in. diam. 68oz., probably by William Burwash. (G. A. Key)
$2,210 £1,300

A George III circular salver, the raised rim with a reeded border and on three similar splayed supports, 1796, by Peter and Ann Bateman, 41.1cm., 42oz. (Lawrence Fine Arts) $2,659 £1,705

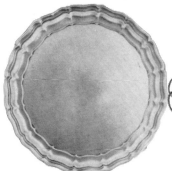

An attractive salver, with moulded border, on three scroll chased bracket feet, Sheffield 1939, by Gladwin Ltd., 35.6cm. diam., 51oz. (Bonhams) $848 £520

A Georg Jensen circular tray, designed by Johan Rohde, the handles cast with interlocking scrolls, 13in. diam. (Christie's S. Ken) $1,125 £660

A George III shaped circular salver with shell border, London 1763, 12¼in. diam., 26½oz. (Tennants)
$1,170 £750

TRAYS & SALVERS

An 18th century Maltese shaped oval tray, embossed with shells and foliage, maker's mark MX, probably Michele Xicluna, circa 1770, 27.7cm. long, 7oz. (Phillips London) $1,193 £750

A Victorian salver, of hexagonal form, Sheffield 1854, by Henry Wilkinson and Co., 817 grammes, 32cm. wide. (Henry Spencer) $832 £520

A good quality tea tray, the centre engraved with strap-work oval roundels, by Barnards, London 1845, 76.2cm. diam., 168oz. (Bonhams) $5,661 £3,700

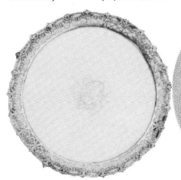

An early George III circular salver, 1763, maker's mark script WT., possibly for William Turner, 35.5cm., 38.5oz. (Lawrence Fine Arts) $3,089 £1,980

A waiter, by Gorham, Providence, 1881, the surface engraved with swallows and cattails, above a raised and chased folded damask napkin, marked, 6in. diam., 5oz. (Christie's New York) $1,430 £899

A Victorian shaped circular salver, the diaper flat chased rim with a scroll and matted leaf border, 1862 by Stephen Smith and William Nicholson, 26.6cm., 19.6oz. (Lawrence Fine Arts) $686 £440

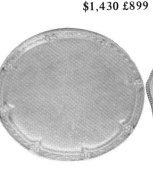

A Queen Anne tazza, of good gauge, the plain circular surface engraved with a finely executed contemporary coat-of-arms, by David Willaume I, 1702, 34oz. (Phillips London) $31,800 £20,000

A spot hammered circular salver on leafy pad feet, with flower capped wavy border, 21.5cm. diam., 1925, 11.75oz. (Phillips London) $1,431 £900

A Victorian shaped circular salver, the centre engraved with a crest, 1871, by Henry Holland of Holland, Aldwinckle and Slater, 41.3cm., 55.5oz. (Lawrence Fine Arts) $1,544 £990

SILVER

A French covered tureen, with two scroll foliate loop handles, post-1838, guarantee and purity marks for .950, maker's mark EP, 25.5cm. across handles, 1189g. (Lawrence Fine Arts) $1,458 £935

A Victorian soup tureen, cover and liner, of bellied oval form, 39cm. long, by John Mortimer & John Samuel Hunt, 1840, 126.5oz. (Phillips London)
$6,360 £4,000

A Continental 19th century moulded circular sauce tureen and cover chased with arabesques, 9in. overall, 19¼oz. (Christie's S. Ken) $767 £495

An Old Sheffield plate shaped oval, two handled soup tureen and cover, on four foliate scroll feet, circa 1820, 16¾in. long overall. (Christie's London)
$1,613 £990

A pair of small sauce tureens and covers on stand, the tureens of two handled wrythen fluted globular form, 25cm. long. (Henry Spencer) $330   £200

A George III sauce tureen, on pedestal base, the domed part-fluted cover with leaf mounted loop handle, London 1804, by Richard Sibley I, 23.5cm. diam., 26oz. (Bonhams)
$1,467 £900

A covered soup tureen by William Gale, Jr., New York; retailed by Ford & Tupper, circa 1860, with a cast steer finial above repoussé and chased grass, 11¾in. high, 90 oz. (Christie's) $8250   £5188

A covered tureen, by Samuel Kirk & Son, Baltimore, 1880-1890, the low domed cover with a pineapple finial, marked, 10in. high, 57oz. (Christie's New York) $2,200 £1,383

A Regency gadrooned compressed sauce tureen, with eagle crest finial, William Bruce, London, 1818, 8¼in., 31oz. (Christie's S. Ken)
$1,194 £770

URNS

Victorian silver plated hot water urn, 19th century, with stag's head handles, on a square base shaped by C-scrolls, 15½in. high. (Skinner Inc.) $275 £169

George III silver plated hot water urn, late 18th century, with bell flower swags, on square base with ball feet, 21½in. high. (Skinner Inc.) $425 £261

A plated tea urn, by Gorham, Providence, 2nd half 19th century, on four angular supports each surmounted by a figure of a seated Chinese man, marked, 14¾in. high. (Christie's New York) $1,650 £1,037

A Puiforcat silver urn, of shouldered ovoid form, tapering to an everted scalloped rim, with domed cover and carved ivory finial, 34.5cm. high. (Christie's London) $1,434 £880

A rare tea urn, attributed to Edward and Samuel S. Rockwell, New York, circa 1825, on a shaped square base with four lion's paw feet, the spigot in the form of a dolphin, 16in. high, 139oz. (Christie's New York) $5,500 £3,459

A tea urn, by Gorham, Providence, 1890-1910, the conical cover with an ivory urn finial, marked, 17½in. high, gross weight 94oz. (Christie's New York) $2,200 £1,383

A sugar urn, by Joseph Richardson, Jr., Philadelphia, circa 1790-1810, the cover and foot with beaded borders, marked, 9½in. high, 17oz. (Christie's New York) $2,860 £1,798

A late Victorian tea urn in the George III style, with ebonised knop to the spigot handle, Sheffield 1896, 1927gr. total gross, 41cm. high. (Henry Spencer) $1,377 £820

A sugar urn, by Christian Wiltberger, Philadelphia, 1793-1817, with a conical cover, urn finial, and a flaring cylindrical stem on a square foot, marked, 9¾in. high, 12oz. (Christie's New York) $1,320 £830

VASES

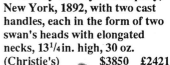

An attractive vase, part gilt Classical form, by Frederick Elkington, Birmingham 1875, 29.8cm. high, 23oz. (Bonhams) $949 £620

A pierced vase by Tiffany & Co., New York, 1902–1907, with fluted sides, scalloped rim, scrolling handles and a repoussé foliate base, 11½ in. high, 51 oz. 10 dwt.
(Christie's) $4400 £2618

A Vase by Tiffany & Company, New York, 1892, with two cast handles, each in the form of two swan's heads with elongated necks, 13¼ in. high, 30 oz.
(Christie's) $3850 £2421

A cut glass and silver vase by Gorham, Providence; glass by Hawkes, circa 1912, 15in. high.
(Christie's) $1760 £1107

A pair of Liberty & Co. 'Cymric' silver and enamelled vases designed by Archibald Knox, Birmingham marks for 1903, 12.5cm. high.
(Phillips) $5760 £3600

A trophy vase by Whiting Manufacturing Co., New York, 1887, with a flaring scalloped rim, the sides etched with mermaids riding seahorses, 15½ in. high, 37 oz. 10 dwt.
(Christie's) $4950 £2945

A rare presentation vase by W. K. Vanderslice, San Francisco, circa 1876, with a flaring rim and two scrolling handles enclosing pierced and chased oak leaves and acorns, 11⅝ in. high, 31 oz. 10 dwt.
(Christie's) $3410 £2145

An enamelled vase by Gorham, Providence, 1897, with a flaring square rim and foot, the front and back cast with a pond and lilypads, 7¾ in. high, 16 oz.
(Christie's) $2420 £1440

A vase by Towle, Newburyport, circa 1910, with a moulded circular rim and footrim, 9⅝ in. high, 30 oz.
(Christie's) $1100 £654

VINAIGRETTES

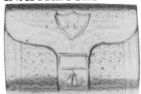

A George III gilt lined vinaigrette in the form of a handbag, John Shaw, Birmingham 1817, 1¼in. (Christie's S. Ken) $299 £176

A Victorian parcel-gilt vinaigrette, the cover cast in relief with Windsor Castle, by Gervase Wheeler, Birmingham, 1840, 1⅝in. long. (Christie's) $920 £572

A gold rectangular vinaigrette, the slightly sloped lid inset with a garnet and engraved with flowerheads, circa 1840, 1.4in. (Christie's S. Ken) $710 £418

A Swiss gold rectangular vinaigrette in the form of a book, the covers with rayed engine-turning, circa 1840, 1¼in. (Christie's S. Ken) $897 £528

A French gold scalloped shaped vinaigrette chased at the hinge with foliage and shells, Paris, 1809-19, 1¾in. long. (Christie's) $2125 £1320

A Victorian gilt lined vinaigrette in the form of a book, the 'covers' engraved with foliage, Joseph Wilmore, Birmingham, 1841, 1½in. (Christie's S. Ken) $406 £242

A Victorian bag shaped gilt lined vinaigrette, the lid cast with a view of Windsor Castle, J. T., Birmingham, 1846, 1¼in. (Christie's S. Ken) $682 £440

A Victorian shaped rectangular gilt lined vinaigrette, the lid engraved with a study of the Burns Memorial in Edinburgh, Nathanial Mills, Birmingham, 1849, 2in. (Christie's S. Ken) $351 £209

A William IV gilt lined vinaigrette in the form of a book, Taylor & Perry, Birmingham 1835, 1in., with chain attached. (Christie's S. Ken) $205 £121

A George III silver-gilt vinaigrette, the cover cast with a shepherd piping beneath a tree with goats and cows, by Joseph Wilmore, Birmingham, 1813, 2in. long. (Christie's) $1416 £880

A Victorian Scottish thistle-shaped vinaigrette, on matted stem with naturalistically chased flower, Edinburgh, 1881, maker's mark A F, 1⅞in. long (Christie's) $1239 £770

A Victorian gilt lined rectangular vinaigrette, the lid chased with a view of Abbotsford House, Edward Smith Birmingham 1840, 1½in. (Christie's S. Ken) $785 £462

WINE COOLERS

An attractive pair of Old Sheffield plate wine coolers, 11½in. high, vase-form with two leaf mounted side handles, circa 1860.
(Bonhams) $2970   £1800

An Old Sheffield plate campana shaped wine cooler on a rising circular base, with a detachable collar and liner, engraved with a crest, 10in. (Christie's S. Ken)
                    $707 £462

A pair of William IV style two-handled Warwick vase wine coolers on square bases, 10¼in., 231.50oz.
(Christie's S. Ken.)
                    $7623   £4620

A pair of fine George III silver-gilt two-handled campana-shaped wine coolers, stands, collars and liners, by Benjamin Smith, 1807, 11in. high, 348oz.
(Christie's) $258390   £159500

A Regency two-handled campana-shaped wine cooler on a rising circular foot, William Burwash, London 1813, fitted with a metal liner, 75.25oz. free. (Christie's S. Ken.)
                    $5082   £3080

A pair of old Sheffield plate two-handled campana-shaped wine coolers, each on spreading circular base, circa 1830, 10¾in. high
(Christie's) $3896   £2420

A pair of two-handled spool-shaped wine coolers, chased with fluting and applied with vine tendrils between tendril scroll handles, by James Dixon & Sons, Sheffield, circa 1835, 10¾in. high. (Christie's) $3476 £2200

A pair of tapering cylindrical wine coolers, each in the form of a bucket, by Garrard & Co. Ltd., 1973, 7¼in. high, 118oz. (Christie's) $8500   £5280

A pair of George IV Sheffield plate wine coolers, having fruiting vine handles and borders, detachable liners, 10in., circa 1825.
(Woolley & Wallis)
                    $2722   £1650

WINE FUNNELS

A George III wine funnel, crested within a scroll cartouche and chased with scrolls and foliage, 5.5in. long, Thomas Wallis and Jonathan Hayne, London 1818, 182gms., 5.8oz. (Bearne's) $1023 £620

A George III reeded wine funnel with curved spigot and shaped clip, Peter and Ann Bateman, London 1792, 4¾in. (Christie's) $976 £638

A good George IV floral and foliate-chased and part-fluted wine funnel with curved spigot, Rebecca Emes and Edward Barnard, London 1827, 6in., 7oz. (Christie's S. Ken.) $1906 £1155

A George III silver wine funnel, London 1810, makers Peter and William Bateman, 4½oz. (Phillips) $511 £310

A George III/IV silver wine funnel of conventional form, 4³/₄in., London 1820, makers Rebecca Emes and Edward Barnard, 4¹/₄oz. (Phillips) $544 £330

A good George III silver wine funnel, the rounded bowl with a part fluted and curved spout, London 1805, maker William Allen III, 6¹/₄oz. (Phillips) $759 £460

A George III silver wine funnel and stand by James Le Bass, Dublin 1822, 4oz. (Riddetts) $231 £140

A George III silver wine funnel with gadrooned edge, 4¹/₄in., marks rubbed, 1³/₄oz. (Phillips) $165 £100

A William IV melon-fluted wine funnel with shaped rim, curved spigot and shell clip, John & Henry Lias, London 1836, 5¾in. (Christie's) $925 £605

A jade snuff bottle, carved as a bag tied with ribbons and a monkey and butterfly around the sides, 1750-1820.
(Bonhams) $660   £400

Early snuff bottle with original label, *Lori Lards Maccoboy Snuff,* olive green, sheared lip, pontil scar, 4½in., New England, 1845-1860. (Robt. W. Skinner Inc.) $75 £47

A pale celadon jade snuff bottle, carved with a wickerwork pattern, a narrow rope border around the neck, 1750-1820.
(Bonhams) $462   £280

A glass overlay seal type snuff bottle, Yangzhou School, overlaid in black with a cat by a potted plant, circa 1880.
(Bonhams) $907   £550

An agate snuff bottle, carved in deep relief with a cat below a butterfly, 1800-1860.
(Bonhams) $495   £300

A rare porcelain snuff bottle, painted with dragons on each side, jadeite stopper, Daoguang two character mark.
(Bonhams) $990   £600

A glass overlay and inside painted snuff bottle, painted with a fisherwoman, the reverse with a landscape, 19th century.
(Bonhams) $49   £30

A chalcedony snuff bottle, carved in deep relief with an eagle perched on a rock, 1800-1860.
(Bonhams) $528   £320

An agate snuff bottle, of ovoid form with russet thumb print patterns, 1800-1860.
(Bonhams) $363   £220

A reticulated porcelain snuff bottle, decorated on each side with a central floral medallion, enclosed by bats and a Shou character, 1820-1860.
(Bonhams) $82 £50

A Sardonyx double snuff bottle, carved with branches of prunus in pink and white tones, 1800-1860.
(Bonhams) $792 £480

A jade snuff bottle, of ovoid form, jadeite stopper, 1750-1820.
(Bonhams) $594 £360

A porcelain snuff bottle, painted in famille verte enamels on either side with a dragon and flaming pearl.
(Bonhams) $165 £100

A chalcedony snuff bottle, carved in deep relief with a camel, monkey and lynx, yellow metal and jadeite stopper, 1800-1860.
(Bonhams) $1155 £700

An enamelled glass snuff bottle, painted in coloured enamels on each side with insects amongst flowering plants and rockwork, 1820-1880.
(Bonhams) $264 £160

A chalcedony snuff bottle, carved in high relief with an Immortal with his stag and bat, gold and jadeite stopper, 1820-1880.
(Bonhams) $792 £480

A glass overlay seal type snuff bottle, Yangzhou School, overlaid in red with a farmer holding a bird, circa 1880.
(Bonhams) $907 £550

A large amethyst snuff bottle, carved in high relief with a man on a buffalo, late 19th century.
(Bonhams) $148 £90

A rare mid-18th century rosewood charcoal burner of canted square form, the lid with flame finial, 12in. wide.
(Bonhams) $2475   £1500

Cast iron Franklin stove, America, 19th century, marked *Wilson & Co., Patent,* 56in. high. (Skinner Inc.)
          $1,500 £888

The American Heating No. 12 light oven with glimmer glass to all sides and urn finial, 143cm. high, circa 1900. (Auction Team Koeln)
          $1,706 £1,053

A Danish Hess Vejle room stove with warming facility, 1925. (Auction Team Koeln)
          $643 £407

A French cast iron and enamelled Caloria 252 cooking oven, 1915. (Auction Team Koeln)
          $496 £314

An Art Nouveau Amalienhuette Nr 121 room stove, circa 1910. (Auction Team Koeln)
          $643 £407

A German Art Nouveau room stove Amalienhuette Nr 182-184, 1905. (Auction Team Koeln) $1,577 £998

A Flamme Bleue paraffin stove, Paris, 73cm. high, circa 1900. (Auction Team Koeln) $47 £29

An Art Nouveau column Bjerrings stove, with warming compartment, Danish, 1900. (Auction Team Koeln)
          $730 £462

A Flemish enamel stove with regulating baking oven, 1925. (Auction Team Koeln) $496 £314

A French tiled stove with expansion joint, circa 1920. (Auction Team Koeln) $935 £592

A decorative French cast iron oven with keep warm facility and towel rails on both sides, 85cm. wide, circa 1905. (Auction Team Koeln) $536 £331

A German room stove with warming facility, 1925. (Auction Team Koeln) $278 £176

An American Heating No. 14 luminous stove with smoke circulation and warming compartment, 1900. (Auction Team Koeln) $1,869 £1,183

An Art Nouveau tiled stove Le Lion 426 by Pied-Selle Fumay, Ardennes, 1910. (Auction Team Koeln) $702 £444

An American Heating No. 44 decorative luminous stove, with smoke circulation system and warming compartment, 1890. (Auction Team Koeln) $1,081 £684

A salesman's cast iron demonstration model of *Smith and Wellstood's celebrated kitchener, The Sovereign Range,* made by the Bonnybridge Foundry, Scotland. (Christie's S. Ken) $1,255 £770

A Norwegian Eidsfor Verk 154 room stove, 1925. (Auction Team Koeln) $468 £296

A Flemish tapestry fragment woven with a man and woman running through a wooded landscape, 17th century, 58 x 81in. (Christie's London) $7,436 £4,400

A Flemish verdure tapestry woven with a hawk and its kill in the foreground, 17th century, restorations, 8ft. 5in. x 13ft. 2in. (Christie's London) $16,511 £10,450

An 18th century English tapestry depicting Elymas the Sorcerer appearing before Sergius Paulus, 2.68 x 2.22m. (Phillips London) $9,945 £6,500

Brussels tapestry, 18th century, scene depicting two boys with rifle and girl in plumed hat, heavy weave, 7ft. x 5ft.3in. (Skinner Inc.) $5,000 £3,185

An Aubusson tapestry woven in silks and wools with a parrot, a heron and another bird with webbed feet in a landscape, 18th century, 9ft.2in. x 6ft. 8in. (Christie's) $11368 £7150

Flemish verdure tapestry fragment, circa 17th century, depicting birds among trees, floral and ribbon border, 92in. high, 80in. wide. (Skinner Inc.) $3,000 £1,840

A Norwegian tapestry carriage cushion, late 18th/early 19th century, woven in wool on a linen warp, depicting a young man and a girl with a dog and a deer, 75cm. x 1.52m. (Phillips London) $1,224 £800

A Brussels Verdure tapestry woven in wools and silks depicting a farmyard with pigs, duck and other animals with two soldiers talking in a wooded landscape, Brussels town mark, late 16th century, 21ft. 3in. x 5ft. 10½in. (Christie's) $34980 £22000

A Mortlake tapestry woven in red, blue and brown wools and silks, depicting a scene from the life of Diogenes with a Philosopher, late 17th century, 107in. x 71½in. (Christie's) $20113 £12650

A Flemish tapestry woven in silks and wools with a girl on a swing in a wood escorted by two gallants with a sheep and fruiting shrubs in the foreground, mid-18th century, 8ft. 11 in. x 6ft. 11in. (Christie's) $13117 £8250

A Flemish tapestry woven in wools with courtly figures, a monkey and birds amid fruiting shrubs, 5ft. x 5ft. 7in. (Christie's) $2886 £1815

A Flemish tapestry woven in silks and wools with four figures seated at dinner with a dog, 17th century, 8ft. 9in. x 6ft.11in. (Christie's London) $13,035 £8,250

A long blonde plush covered teddy bear, with small hump, large feet and growler, 20in. high. (Christie's S. Ken) **$608 £385**

An early 20th century German gold plush teddy bear with black boot button eyes, stitched muzzle, felt paws, hump and growl box, probably Steiff, 38cm. high. (Spencer's) **$107   £65**

An early 20th century golden plush Steiff teddy bear, with Steiff metal button in the ear, swivel joints with felt pads, 51cm. high. (Henry Spencer) **$1980   £1200**

A beige plush covered teddy bear with felt pads, hump and squeeze growler, small blank Steiff button in ear, circa 1903-4, 10in. high. (Christie's S. Ken.) **$998 £605**

A pale golden plush covered teddy bear with boot button eyes, wide apart ears, elongated limbs, hump, cut muzzle, stitched nose with four claws, felt pads and growler, with Steiff button in ear, circa 1911, 28in. high.(Christie's S. Ken.) **$3448 £2090**

Edwardian gold plush teddy bear with black stitched snout, black and brown glass eyes, partly straw filled with squeaker, 19in. high (Hobbs & Chambers) **$478   £290**

A rare 'laughing Roosevelt teddy bear', with dark golden mohair plush, glass eyes, jointed arms and legs, by Columbia Teddy Bears Manufacturers, circa 1907, 23in. high. (Christie's S. Ken.) **$817   £495**

A cotton plush covered teddy bear, with clear glass eyes, felt pads and embroidered claws, 13½in. high, circa 1917. (Christie's S. Ken) **$535 £330**

A dark golden plush covered teddy handbag, with black button eyes, pronounced snout, and moveable joints, 8in. long, pads replaced, possibly by Schuco. (Christie's S. Ken.) **$1270   £770**

A cinnamon plush covered teddy bear, with boot button eyes, wide apart ears, elongated limbs, hump and cut muzzle, with Steiff button in ear, 13in. high. (Christie's S. Ken) $3,476 £2,200

An early golden plush covered teddy bear, with boot button eyes, hump, excelsior stuffing and elongated limbs, wearing tortoiseshell rimmed spectacles, with small blank Steiff button in ear, circa 1903/4, 20in. high. (Christie's S. Ken) $608 £385

A long plush mohair covered teddy bear, with boot button eyes, wide apart ears, hump and elongated limbs, 22in. high. (pads replaced) (Christie's S. Ken) $4,171 £2,640

A good early golden plush Steiff teddy bear, with black boot button eyes, pointed brown stitched snout, rounded pricked ears, back hump, swivel joints, felt pads and a growl box, 38.5cm. long. (Henry Spencer) $3,978 £2,600

A Steiff gold plush teddy bear, circa 1912, with black boot button eyes, rounded pricked ears, hump back, swivel joints, and growl box, 68cm. long. (Henry Spencer) $627 £380

An early 20th century German blond plush large teddy bear, with black wooden eyes, stitched pointed snout, hump back and moving arms, 52cm. high, probably Steiff. (Spencer's) $1980 £1200

Noel, a rare black plush covered teddy bear, with boot button eyes mounted by red felt, elongated limbs and wide apart ears, by Steiff, circa 1910, 20½in. high. (Christie's S. Ken) $4,518 £2,860

A golden short plush covered teddy bear with boot button eyes, hump, low set ears, horizontally stitched nose, felt pads, firm stuffing and long straight legs, probably early American, 29in. high. (Christie's S. Ken.) $1452 £880

A rare central seam golden plush covered teddy bear, with boot button eyes, wide apart ears, elongated limbs, hump and pronounced snout, by Steiff, circa 1905, 20in. high. (Christie's S. Ken) $1,564 £990

A Bell Telephone Mfg. Comp., Antwerp, desk telephone, circa 1930. (Auction Team Koeln) $70 £43

A Praezisions Telephone, the first model by Siemens & Halske after Bell's patent, with wooden earpiece and leather covered stem, circa 1880. (Auction Team Koeln) $2,629 £1,664

A line dial Le Parisien desk telephone by Unis France, with bakelite casing and handle, circa 1930. (Auction Team Koeln) $33 £20

A highly decorative L.M. Ericsson & Co. desk telephone, circa 1910. (Auction Team Koeln) $1,092 £670

A Norwegian wall telephone, with decorative cast iron back plate, and simulated intarsia tin 'desk' surface, by Aktieselskabet Elektrisk Bureau Kristiania, Oslo, circa 1890. (Auction Team Koeln) $1722 £1031

A German Reichspost OB 05 telephone with crank, by Rudolf Krueger, 1907. (Auction Team Koeln) $186 £114

An American Candlestick desk telephone by Stromberg-Carlson, circa 1920. (Auction Team Koeln) $321 £197

A desk top coin telephone by Merk of Munich, with key, 1938. (Auction Team Koeln) $64 £39

A French desk telephone by Ch. Ventroux Paris, wooden base and stand, receiver and extra receiver marked P. Jacquesson Paris, circa 1920. (Auction Team Koeln) $258 £158

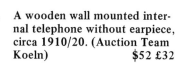

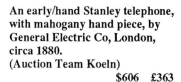

An early/hand Stanley telephone, with mahogany hand piece, by General Electric Co, London, circa 1880. (Auction Team Koeln)

$606   £363

A Bell System hand telephone, with so-called Bell mahogany receiver for speaking and listening, circa 1880. (Auction Team Koeln)

$530   £317

A wooden wall mounted internal telephone without earpiece, circa 1910/20. (Auction Team Koeln) $52 £32

A decorative Tax table telephone with magneto, by L M Ericsson, circa 1900. (Auction Team Koeln)

$1149   £688

A French Citophone internal desk telephone, receiver with call button, circa 1920. (Auction Team Koeln)

$116 £71

A Thomson-Houston Paris desk telephone, circa 1920. (Auction Team Koeln) $96 £59

A German iron army telephone by Siemens & Halske, 1912/13. (Auction Team Koeln)$160 £98

An OB wall telephone by Siedle & Soehne, Schwenningen, with wooden housing and with crank, circa 1910. (Auction Team Koeln) $179 £110

The Praezisions telephone, the first telephone by Siemens & Halske after Bell's patent (1876), with wooden ear piece and leather covered handle, circa 1880. (Auction Team Koeln)

$2,054   £1,260

A terracotta group of three amorini, adorned with fruiting vines, the base signed indistinctly, possibly Belgian, 20in. high. (Christie's S. Ken) $710 £418

A pair of painted terracotta busts, in Arab costume. (Phillips) $1320 £800

French terracotta bust of a young woman, Charles Eugene Breton, dated 1916, smiling with long tresses bound at the back, 22in. high. (Skinner Inc.) $650 £396

A 19th century French terra cotta bust of Rouget de l'Isle, by David d'Angers, signed and dated *David 1835,* 45.5cm. high. (Christie's London) $13,282 £8,250

Pair of Empire terracotta urns, second quarter 19th century, campagna form, 20in. high. (Skinner Inc.) $1,200 £736

A pair of terracotta chimney pots of Gothic design, the octagonal tops above cylindrical bodies, 43in. (Christie's) $1089 £660

A terracotta bust of an Art Nouveau maiden, with long flowing hair, embellished with large trailing poppies in a green patination, 42cm. high. (Phillips) $660 £400

A pair of Continental poly-chrome terracotta figures of Arab tribesmen, each robed and holding staffs, 18½in. high. (Christie's S. Ken) $772 £495

A 19th century French terra-cotta group of a Bacchante, in the manner of Clodion, an infant satyr at her side, 15½in. high. (Christie's S. Ken) $1,122 £660

Quill work picture, England, late 17th/early 18th century, exuberant basket of flowers, 21.6 x 27cm. (Skinner Inc.) $1,900 £1,166

One of a pair of cushions, incorporating 17th century verdure tapestry panels, depicting figures among pillars and arches, 26 x 16in. (Christie's London) Two $1,328 £825

A mid-19th century needlework picture worked in pastel wool threads, designed with cottages by a country church, 30 x 42cm. (Phillips West Two) $736 £460

A late 18th century purse of knitted silk threads, designed with applied pansies and carnations. (Phillips West Two) $544 £320

One of a pair of collage cloth and velvet figures by G. Smart, Frant, near Tunbridge Wells, Mr Bright the Postman and The Goose Woman of Erridge Castle, 10½ x 8½in. (Christie's S. Ken) Two $2,574 £1,650

An embroidered bag, worked in coloured silks with a swan and a lyre among flowers, the embroidery circa 1840, 8 x 6in. (Christie's S. Ken) $140 £83

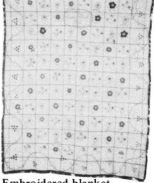

Peacock and Dragon, a pair of Morris & Co. woven twill curtains, 166 x 275cm. (Christie's London) $1,757 £1,078

Needlework and watercolour picture, America, early 19th century, depicting a young lady seated under a tree, 5½in. (Skinner Inc.) $600 £368

Embroidered blanket, *Lucretia Brush Busti, 1831*, probably New York, each square of white and blue checked wool, 6ft.4in. x 7ft.4in. (Skinner Inc.) $3,000 £1,840

TEXTILES

A commemorative linen cloth with cutwork and embroidered decoration, designed with fruit and foliage around a central field, 93cm. x 1.16m. (Phillips West Two) $448 £280

A pair of crewelwork curtains, embroidered in shades of green, blue, brown and red wool, 18th century, in 17th century style, 82 x 34in. (Christie's S. Ken) $1,870 £1,100

A hairwork picture, embroidered in black and pale yellow silk, depicting Christ and the Woman of Samaria at the well, circa 1800, 16 x 22in. (Christie's S. Ken) $365 £220

Swivel, two pairs of Morris & Co. loose woven silk and wool curtains, beige, navy blue and pale blue, 200 x 140cm, 138 x 112.5cm. (Christie's London) $1,478 £880

A Lord Chancellor's bourse, of honey coloured velvet, worked with metallic threads and sequins, with the royal coat of arms and motto, Victorian, 17in. square. (Christie's S. Ken.) $1543 £935

Le Tennis, a crepe handkerchief, printed in green with figures playing tennis, signed *Raoul Dufy*, 15in. square, circa 1918-1924. (Christie's S. Ken) $1,533 £935

Arsenal Football Club, Season 1930-31. Holders of the English Cup, a commemorative cotton handkerchief, 15 x 15in. (Christie's S. Ken) $223 £143

Two cotton window curtains, each lined, the first in rose red moreen, the second in rose red, cream and green stripes, approximately 65in. long. (Christie's) $242 £151

Grenfell hooked mat, Grenfell Industries, Newfoundland or Labrador, 20th century, 13ft. 14in. x 11ft. 8in. (Skinner Inc.) $550 £335

Yarn sewn rug, New England, mid-19th century, worked with clipped cotton and wool yarns, 31 x 50in. (Skinner Inc.) $600 £355

A fine handkerchief of ivory silk, edged with Valenciennes lace, embroidered with a royal crown. (Christie's S. Ken) $358 £220

Grenfell hooked mat, Grenfell Labrador Industries, Newfoundland and Labrador, early 20th century, 39¼ x 26in. (Skinner Inc.) $700 £414

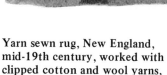

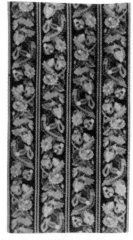

A white tablecloth with scalloped edge decorated with embroidery, drawnthread work and filet insertion of flowers, 1.80 x 3m. (Phillips West Two) $374 £220

A white linen tablecover with cutwork, embroidered decoration and lace insertions, 3.20 x 2.08m. (Phillips West Two) $442 £260

A Napoleon III needlework panel with garlands of flowers embroidered in multi-coloured wools, 1.93 x 1.09m. (Phillips London) $1,377 £900

Pictorial hooked rug, America, dated '1934', worked in colourful yarns depicting the cruise ship 'Morro Castle', 30in. x 35in. (Skinner Inc.) $550 £335

A 19th century cotton handkerchief printed in black and red depicting four children playing lawn tennis, 13½ x 14in. (Christie's S. Ken) $721 £462

Joe Fletcher, 9st.6lb, Champion of England Matched with Johnny Summers, For £320 at the N.S.C., March 25 1907, a commemorative silk handkerchief, 28½ x 30½in. (Christie's S. Ken) $112 £72

Painted and decorated tin bread tray, America, 19th century, shallow rectangular form with bowed ends, 13in. long. (Skinner Inc.) $800 £491

Large presentation tin and wood foot warmer, America, early 19th century, heavy wooden frame with turned corner posts, 9in. high. (Skinner Inc.) $1,700 £1,043

Painted tin panel, Pennsylvania, circa 1870, depicting an American eagle with outspread wings grasping a banner inscribed *Rainbow Fire Company,* 9½ x 13½in. (Skinner Inc.) $1,500 £920

Painted and decorated tin coffee pot, America, 19th century, of flaring conical form with straight spout and strap handle, 21.3cm. high. (Skinner Inc.) $800 £491

Painted Tin Trade sign, America, 19th century, painted ochre and green (paint loss), 8in. high. (Skinner Inc.) $1,100 £651

A red and gilt tole plate warmer with dome shape top, bow-front door, 31in. high. (Lawrence Fine Art) $998 £605

Painted and decorated tin document box, America, early 19th century, asphaltum ground decorated with yellow swags, 8in. wide. (Skinner Inc.) $300 £183

Painted and decorated tin coffee pot, America, 19th century, hinged domed lid above flaring conical form, 8½in. high. (Skinner Inc.) $1,300 £798

Painted and decorated tin tray, 19th century, stencilled and free hand decoration in green, yellow, red and brown, 65.7 x 48.3cm. (Skinner Inc.) $950 £562

A French blue and white painted tole and wire jardiniere of oval form, mid-19th century, 19in. wide. (Christie's London) $717 £440

Pair of tin whale oil chamber lamps, America, 19th century, 11in. high. (Skinner Inc.) $375 £229

A scarlet and gilt japanned tole tray, the central oval painted with a child releasing a parrot watched by a woman, 19th century, 30in. wide. (Christie's London) $807 £495

Painted and decorated tin coffee pot, America, first half 19th century, with polychrome floral roundels and yellow stylised leaves, 10½in. high. (Skinner Inc.) $1,000 £614

Rare pair of painted and decorated tin wall sconces, New England, circa 1830, each with crimped circular crest, 13½in. high. (Skinner Inc.) $1,800 £1,104

A painted and decorated toleware document box, probably Massachusetts, early 19th century, 9¾in. wide. (Christie's) $495 £310

Painted and decorated tin bread tray, America, 19th century, having flowerheads and buds in red, green, and yellow, 12¾in. long. (Skinner Inc.) $650 £399

An early Victorian black japanned tole basket decorated in gilt with chinoiseries, with swing handle, 11in. (Christie's London) $448 £275

A Regency painted tole tray, the central oval painted with a scene depicting the death of General Wolfe at Quebec after Benjamin West, 28½in. wide. (Christie's London)$1,201 £770

An Elem four slice rotary toaster, unused, 1958. (Auction Team Koeln) $87 £55

A rare very early Dix single slice flat toaster with single heating coil, 1919/20. (Auction Team Koeln) $321 £203

A very rare early Pyramid cooking appliance for toasting on an open flame, circa 1890. (Auction Team Koeln) $139 £86

An early Belgian Kalorik

The first electric toaster, the Eclipse, with ceramic handle and base, patented 1893. (Auction Team Koeln) $2119 £1269

The Universal Model E 947 toaster, a rare American two sided swing toaster designed by Alonzo Warner, 1922. (Auction Team Koeln)$190 £117

An early Belgian Kalorik toaster with turned wooden handles, circa 1925. (Auction Team Koeln) $196 £121

A Mitrella toaster with bakelite base, 1935. (Auction Team Koeln) $44 £27

A Siemens Munich 1972 Olympics souvenir toaster. (Auction Team Koeln) $28 £17

An Omega chromium toaster, circa 1935. (Auction Team Koeln) $47 £29

A Steiff golden velvet bulldog, with black stitched muzzle, orange felt tongue and glass eyes, 9.5cm. high. (Henry Spencer) $321 £210

A 'The Designoscope' kaleidoscopic toy, contained in maker's original box bearing the legend *The Designoscope. An endless source of artistic pleasure.* (Christie's S. Ken) $82 £50

A German painted tinplate clockwork pigeon, with nodding head and call, circa 1910, 21cm. long. (Christie's S. Ken) $321 £198

An Edwardian table racing game with folding mahogany board painted in green with a race track with baize centre, and a mahogany box containing ten lead horses and riders, dice, tumblers and ivory markers, 60in. long. (Christie's London) $1,303 £825

A good hand cranked cardboard *JWB Patent. Excursion to London,* moving panorama. (Christie's S. Ken) $598 £352

A 7in. diam. 'Spin-E-Ma' zoetrope with three picture strips each labelled *Kay. Made in England. Copyright.* (Christie's S. Ken) $394 £242

A hand cranked cardboard *The Royal Illuminated Panorama,* with rear mounted candle holder and internal paper strip of views. (Christie's S. Ken) $561 £330

Dinky Supertoys No. 918
Guy van, advertising Ever
Ready, in original box.
(Christie's S. Ken)$330 £209

An early wood/composition
base toy of a Dreadnought
with three funnels, 12.5cm.,
circa 1905. (Phillips West Two)
$76 £50

A painted tinplate pool player,
with clockwork mechanism
and seven numbered pockets at
far end, probably by Gunter-
mann, circa 1910, 28cm. long.
(Christie's S. Ken) $891 £550

An early 20th century stock
tin plate clockwork four
wheel gocart, driven by a uni-
formed school boy, 12.75cm.
long. (Henry Spencer)
$379 £240

Schuco tinplate Donald Duck,
right foot fatigued, boxed,
with label. (Phillips West Two)
$745 £460

Dinky, 701 Shetland Flying
Boat. (Phillips West Two)
$291 £180

Dinky Supertoys, No. 957
Ruston Bucyrus Excavator, in
original box. (Christie's S. Ken)
$246 £154

Carette, a lithographed tinplate
flywheel driven carpet toy
sailing vessel, with eccentric
rocking action and lithographed
card sail (lacks flywheel), circa
1905, 24cm. long. (Christie's
S. Ken) $392 £242

Dinky Supertoys No. 930
Bedford Pallet Jekta van, in
original box. (Christie's S. Ken)
$282 £176

A wooden toy grocer's shop, stencilled and lined in brown, with printed paper labelled drawers, 21¼in. wide, German circa 1930s. (Christie's S. Ken) $802 £495

Dinky, 922, Avro Vulcan Delta Wing Bomber. (Phillips West Two) $2,025 £1,250

Hornby Speed Boat No. 2 'Hawk', green and white, in original box, circa 1936, 9¼in. long. (Christie's S. Ken) $141 £88

A twelve inch diameter black painted Zoetrope and a quantity of picture strips each with a printed title and *Entered at Stationer's Hall*. (Christie's S. Ken) $524 £308

Horikawa: Rotate-o-Matic Super Giant Robot, with automatic action, swing open door, blinking and shooting gun, in original box. (Christie's S. Ken) $160 £99

An interesting Victorian child's horsedrawn carriage, the wicker seat lined with buttoned leatherette cushions, 150cm. long. (Henry Spencer) $2,601 £1,700

Dinky Supertoys No. 923 Big Bedford Van, advertising 'Heinz Tomato Sauce', in original box. (Christie's S. Ken) $968 £605

Well's Big Chief mechanical motor cycle, with Indian Chief rider, clockwork mechanism, in original box, 1930s, 7½in. long. (Christie's S. Ken) $869 £550

Distler Electro Matic 7500, lithographed and painted battery operated Porsche car, with telesteering control, in original box, circa 1955, 9¾in. long. (Christie's S. Ken) $608 £385

Hide covered rocking horse, attributed to Whitney Reed Corporation, Leominster, Massachusetts, 19th century, covered with dapple-brown hide, 43in. high. (Skinner Inc.) $4,800 £2,945

Dinky Supertoys, No. 514 Guy van, advertising Lyons Swiss Rolls, in original box. (Christie's S. Ken)$729 £462

Fighting boxers, with clock-work mechanism, in original paintwork, by Einfalt, circa 1935, 9½in. long. (Christie's S. Ken) $382 £242

Oh My, a lithographed tinplate dancing negro, with hand-cranked clockwork mechanism, by Lehman, circa 1912, 9¾in. high. (Christie's S. Ken) $608 £385

A bisque headed clown acro-batic toy, the white face with painted blue and red cap, grey tufts of hair and clown maquillage, impressed *138 3 3*, German, late 19th century, 16½in. high. (Christie's S. Ken) $695 £440

A plated and tinplate child's live steam kitchen stove, with five burners, three ovens, adjustable rings, Bing, circa 1920, 19in. wide. (Christie's S. Ken) $729 £462

Charlie Chaplin, with clockwork mechanism, in original clothing, walking stick and bowler hat, by Schuco, circa 1933, 6¾in. high. (Christie's S. Ken) $521 £330

A painted wood Noah's Ark, the flat bottom vessel with twenty-three pairs of animals, three others, six members of the Noah family, German, probably Erzgebirge, late 19th century, 12¾in. long. (Christie's S. Ken) $608 £385

Marx, electric robot and son, finished in grey, gold and maroon, 43.5cm. high. (Phillips West Two) $306 £200

An early Structo constructional two seater racing car, with hand cranked clockwork mechanism, USA, circa 1910, marked *Iwafame,* 9½in. long. (Christie's S. Ken) $486 £308

Kadi, a printed and painted teabox with two Chinese coolies, clockwork mechanism concealed in box, by Lehmann, circa 1910, 7in. long. (Christie's S. Ken) $660 £418

A repainted tinplate limousine, with clockwork mechanism driving rear axle, possibly by H. Fischer & Co., circa 1912, 13in. long. (Christie's S. Ken) $382 £242

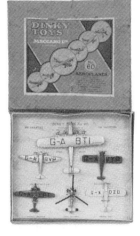

A bisque headed moving clown toy, the white face with painted hat and features, the wood and wire body with wooden hands and feet, the head impressed *1720,* German, late 19th century, 10in. high. (Christie's S. Ken) $695 £440

Dinky pre-war set No. 60 Aeroplanes (2nd Issue), with markings and instructions, in original box. (Christie's S. Ken) $729 £462

Li La hansom cab, driver, two lady passengers and a dog, by Lehmann, circa 1910, 5¼in. (Christie's S. Ken) $1,477 £935

Donald Duck, a felt covered and painted tinplate toy, with clockwork mechanism, by Schuco, circa 1936, 6in. high. (Christie's S. Ken) $382 £242

A large carved wood Noah's Ark, with twenty-two pairs of carved wood animals and two members of the Noah family, German, probably Erzegbirge, circa 1880. (Christie's S. Ken) $1,042 £660

Marx, electric robot and son, finished in black, red and silver, 43.5cm. high. (Phillips West Two) $245 £160

Ernst Plank, a large hand painted battleship with guns, handrails, finished in grey with red lining, 60cm. (Phillips West Two) $3,060 £2,000

A Shackleton clockwork blue and red painted Foden flat truck with rubber tyres, 31cm. long. (Henry Spencer) $253 £160

C.I.J., an Alfa Romeo P2 racing car, painted tinplate, finished in blue, with cloverleaf insignia, early type, circa 1926. (Christie's S. Ken)$3,029 £1,870

Corgi, 262, Lincoln Continental, in rare colour scheme, blue/tan. (Phillips West Two) $229 £150

French Hornby 'O' gauge electric loco S.N.C.F.BB 8051, c1950's. (James of Norwich) $119 £70

Hornby 'O' gauge No 2 breakdown crane, boxed. (James of Norwich) $68   £40

Miniature painted Windsor rocking armchair and a miniature peg wooden doll, 4½in. high. (Skinner Inc.) $800 £491

Dinky No 955/555 fire engine with extending ladder. (James of Norwich) $65   £38

A Chad Valley lithographed tinplate clockwork Delivery Van, in original box, 1940's, 10in. long. (Christie's S. Ken.) $1180   £715

A Bing repainted Third Series ocean liner, with clockwork mechanism, circa 1920, 41cm. long. (Christie's S. Ken) $417 £264

Painted rocking horse, America, late 19th century, painted white with dapple grey spots having applied horse hair tail, 54½in. high. (Skinner Inc.) $2,200 £1,419

Chein tin roller coaster and car, original paint and stencilling, key wind, 19in. x 9½in. (Du Mouchelles) $155   £96

Hindenburg, a rare printed and painted tinplate airship, with clockwork mechanism, in original paintwork with swastikas, German, 10in. long. (Christie's S. Ken)$729 £462

Dinky Gift Set No. 699 Military Vehicles, in original box. (Christie's S. Ken) $422 £264

A German painted tinplate steam riverboat, finished in red and white, blue and red lined, and yellow funnel with red star, circa 1905, 30cm. long. (Christie's S. Ken) $624 £385

Pre-war 33R, railway mechanical horse and trailer van, 'LNER' (chipped). (Christie's S. Ken) $299 £187

Britain's Set No. 1470 The State Coach, in original box, circa 1937. (Christie's S. Ken)
$264 £165

Meccano No 2 special model aeroplane constructor outfit complete & good order, play damage to paintwork, pilot missing, c1939, (James of Norwich) $357 £210

A model house and garden in a boxed scene, with balconies and balustrading to the first floor and simulated slate roof, circa 1850, 19in. wide. (Christie's S. Ken.) $690   £418

Miniature paint decorated Windsor armchair, America, last half of 19th century, the black ground painted with floral decoration, 8¼in. high. (Skinner Inc.) $700 £429

Peepshow — hand coloured peepshow of the Palais Royal, extending to 492mm. in 5 sections, 128 x 189mm., Paris (?), circa 1820. (Phillips London) $672 £420

Dinky pre-war Set No. 60 Aeroplanes (2nd issue), in original box. (Christie's S. Ken)
$845 £528

Dinky Supertoys, No. 948 Foden 14-ton tanker Regent, in original box. (Christie's S. Ken) $451 £286

A well built approx. ¼ scale model of the Scammell timber tractor, Reg. No. HDW471, built by K. Bryan, Nottingham, 42 x 77in. (Christie's S. Ken)
$9,861   £6,050

Cunard Line 'Quickest Route New York to London and the Continent via Fishguard', by Odin Rosenvinge. (Onslow's) $1,690 £1,000

Leslie Carr, 'The World's Greatest Liners Use Southampton Docks RMS Queen Mary and SS Normandie', published by SR, quad royal, 1936. (Onslow's) $896 £550

Lewitt-Him, 'Welcome To Paris Imperial Airways British Airways', 50 x 32cm. (Onslow's) $139 £85

Frank H. Mason, 'SS Arnhem New Luxury Ship Harwich-Hook of Holland Service', published by LNER, quad royal. (Onslow's) $155 £95

Lionel Edwards, 'Come To Britain For Racing', published by The Travel Association, double crown on linen. (Onslow's) $978 £600

H. G. Gawthorn, 'Lowestoft', published by LNER, quad royal. (Onslow's) $1,141 £700

John Vickery, 'Tasmania Australia', double royal. (Onslow's) $489 £300

Charles Pears, 'Lytham St Annes Sea Sunshine and Sport', published by LMS, quad royal. (Onslow's) $1,304 £800

Michael, 'Scarborough', published by LNER, double royal. (Onslow's) $326 £200

'I'm taking an early holiday', published by SR, double royal, 1936. (Onslow's) $734 £450

P. Irwin Brown, 'Your Continental Holiday', published by the big four railway companies, quad royal, 1932. (Onslow's) $1,174 £720

Odin Rosenvinge, 'Royal Line from Bristol Fastest To Canada' (Royal Edward), double royal. (Onslow's) $407 £250

'Jaffa', EMB RBA 5, double crown. (Onslow's) $90 £55

Jo Roux, 'Les Lainages Bisanne, on linen, 120 x 80cm. (Onslow's) $717 £440

'The Wye Valley', published by GWR. (Onslow's) $179 £110

Frank H. Mason, 'The Bait Gatherers', published by LNER, double royal. (Onslow's) $98 £60

'South Devon', published by GWR/SR. (Onslow's) $179 £110

Brien, 'Silloth on the Solway Finest Seaside Golf', published by LNER, double royal. (Onslow's) $1,206 £740

'Holland America Line Southampton to New York' (Statendam), by G. H. Davis. (Onslow's) $974 £580

'Cunard Europe America' (Aquitania), by Odin Rosenvinge, with loss to right margin. (Onslow's) $706 £420

'United States Lines to America Safety Courtesy Comfort and Speed'. (Onslow's) $168 £100

S. R. Badmin, 'Come and Explore Britain', published by The Travel Association, double crown on linen. (Onslow's) $489 £300

'Cunard Europe America' (Berengaria), by Odin Rosenvinge. (Onslow's) $1,428 £850

'Cunard Line to All Parts of the World' (Lusitania). (Onslow's) $1,210 £720

'Cunard Line to All Parts of the World' (Mauretania). (Onslow's) $2,100 £1,250

'Cunard USA and Canada', by Frank H. Mason. (Onslow's) $4,200 £2,500

E. McKnight Kauffer, 'Spring', published by LT, double royal, 1938. (Onslow's) $277 £170

'Cunard Line to New York', by
Charles Pears, loss to right
margin. (Onslow's) $907 £540

C. Bellaigne, 'Fly By Air Union
and Get There First', 40 x 30cm.
published January 1926.
(Onslow's) $179 £110

'Cunard The Connecting Link
Europe America'. (Onslow's)
$1,294 £770

'Cunard USA—Canada', extensive loss to right side.
(Onslow's) $202 £120

'Cunard Line A Cunarder In
Fishguard Harbour Quickest
Route New York to London',
by Odin Rosenvinge. (Onslow's)
$739 £440

'Grand Trunk Railway System
to Canada'. (Onslow's)$336 £200

'Cunard Line Europe—America',
by Kenneth D. Shoesmith.
(Onslow's) $4,704 £2,800

'White Star Line Canada's Call
to Women'. (Onslow's)
$420 £250

'Cunard Europe—America', by
W. S. Bylitipolis. (Onslow's)
$1,176 £700

'Cunard Line To All Parts of the World' (Mauretania), double royal. (Onslow's) $1,402 £860

'Edgware by Tram', double crown, 1929. (Onslow's) $122 £75

Odin Rosenvinge, ,Cunard Europe America' (Berengaria), double royal. (Onslow's) $570 £350

'The Golfing Girl Well Out On The True Line', by The Caledonian Railway, 102 x 76cm. (Onslow's) $5,542 £3,400

Ellis Silas, 'Orient Line To Australia', double royal. (Onslow's) $799 £490

L. C. Mitchell, 'Mount Cook New Zealand', double royal. (Onslow's) $375 £230

Montague B. Black, 'American Line Liverpool and Queenstown to Philadelphia', double royal. (Onslow's) $505 £310

Harold McCready, 'Imperial Airways City of Wellington', double crown, April 1929. (Onslow's) $978 £600

Severin, 'Imperial Airways Through Africa In Days Instead of Weeks', double royal, 1939. (Onslow's) $1,011 £620

Guy Lipscombe, 'LBSCR Southsea', double royal. (Onslow's) $848 £520

Jack Roussau, 'Chemins de Fer de L'Etat de Brighton Paris A Londres' (Thames punting), double royal on linen. (Onslow's) $244 £150

Roger Soubie, 'Vichy', 106 x 76cm. (Onslow's) $1,369 £840

H. Cassiers, 'Red Star Line' (Belgenland), double royal. (Onslow's) $212 £130

Anita Parkhurst, 'The Friendly Road', published by YWCA, on linen, 69 x 52cm. (Onslow's) $733 £450

'East Coast Types No. 5 The Deck-Chair Man'. (Onslow's) $212 £130

'Oriend Line Cruises', double royal. (Onslow's) $139 £85

'Imperial Airways The British Airline Weekly Service Between Africa India Egypt and England', double royal. (Onslow's) $815 £500

Montague B. Black, 'White Star Line Europe To America' (Olympic), double royal. (Onslow's) $1,141 £700

TUNBRIDGE WARE

Brush. (Derek Roberts Antiques) $41 £25

Candle holder. (Derek Roberts Antiques) $232 £140

Cribbage board. (Derek Roberts Antiques) $199 £120

Handkerchief box. (Derek Roberts Antiques) $664 £400

Book ends with Penshurst Place. (Derek Roberts Antiques) $664 £400

Shaped double caddy with Netley Abbey. (Derek Roberts Antiques) $1,245 £750

Single caddy of cube design. (Derek Roberts Antiques) $747 £450

Cigar table by Barton. (Derek Roberts Antiques) $3,320 £2,000

Correspondence box. (Derek Roberts Antiques) $996 £600

Stationery box by Nye. (Derek Roberts Antiques) $1,494 £900

Picture frame. (Derek Roberts Antiques) $249 £150

Work box with castle. (Derek Roberts Antiques) $1,660 £1,000

Trinket box. (Derek Roberts Antiques) $124 £75

Simple cribbage board. (Derek Roberts Antiques) $124 £75

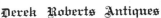

Double caddy. (Derek Roberts Antiques) $913 £550

Rare desk set. (Derek Roberts Antiques) $1,826 £1,100

Work box showing Tunbridge Castle. (Derek Roberts Antiques) $1,079 £650

Games Table. (Derek Roberts Antiques) $3,320 £2,000

Games box with Bayham Abbey. (Derek Roberts Antiques) $1,826 £1,100

Large fine double caddy with Eridge. (Derek Roberts Antiques) $1,660 £1,000

Handkerchief box with stag. (Derek Roberts Antiques) $581   £350

Octagonal games box. (Derek Roberts Antiques) $1,660 £1,000

A three tier Williams No. 2 American type bar machine with 'grasshopper' mechanism, 1897. (Auction Team Koeln) $706 £433

An unusual Burnett American typewriter with slanting type basket and streamlined shape, one of only four models known, 1907. (Auction Team Koeln) $8,988 £5,514

A very early American Granville Automatic fender machine with two carriage return handles, by Mossberg & Granville Mfg. Co., Providence, Rhode Island, USA, 1896. (Auction Team Koeln) $2,499 £1,533

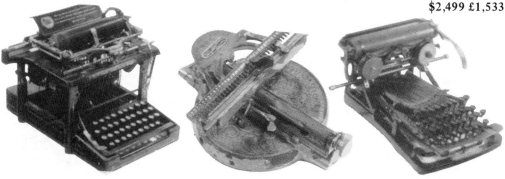

An early American Remington No. 2 upstrike machine with special carriage return lever, *WH Jayne patent applied for,* 1879. (Auction Team Koeln) $513 £315

An Odell No. 4 decorative American dial typewriter, nickel badly rubbed, 1889. (Auction Team Koeln) $963 £591

A rare Daugherty American type bar machine, low serial no. 1871, 1890. (Auction Team Koeln) $1,798 £1,103

A rare Buckner Lino-Typewriter keyboard machine for typesetters, adapted for Smith Premier 1 Model for practice purposes, circa 1896. (Auction Team Koeln) $1,798 £1,103

An 1889 Victor type wheel typewriter, the first of its kind in the world. (Auction Team Koeln) $3,081 £1,890

A robust American Densmore No. 4 upstrike typewriter without cylinder turning buttons, 1902. (Auction Team Koeln) $481 £295

American Standard Folding portable typewriter with fold over case, 1907. (Auction Team Koeln) $417 £256

A very rare Salter No. 5 improved model of the English type bar typewriter, with three row circular keyboard, 1892. (Auction Team Koeln)
$4,173 £2,560

A very rare Crown American type wheel machine with controls by Byron A. Brooks, New York, 1894. (Auction Team Koeln) $15,407 £9,452

A Rem-Sho Bronze American understrike typewriter with shift and copper coloured housing, 1896. (Auction Team Koeln) $1,540 £945

A Commercial Visible 'wasp waist' type bar machine with reverse hammer strike, in original wooden box, 1898. (Auction Team Koeln)
$3,531 £2,166

A Salter Improved No.5 typewriter, No. 2164, with gilt transfers and wood baseboard (bright parts corroded). (Christie's S. Ken)
$4,330 £2,640

A fine replica model of the first Mitterhofer typewriter (1867), with needle type. (Auction Team Koeln)
$2,407 £1,477

A red Mignon Model 2 typewriter, with Danish type-sleeve and index (paint scratched on paper support plate). (Christie's S. Ken)
$1,984 £1,210

A rare Bar-Lock Model 1b typewriter by Columbia Type Writer Co New York with highly ornate cast iron type basket. (Auction Team Koeln)
$5395   £3230

German Bing No. 2 type bar
typewriter, 1925. (Auction
Team Koeln) $179 £110

A rare Morris index typewriter,
American, circa 1885.
(Auction Team Koeln)
                    $21854   £13086

An Emerson No. 3 typewriter
with unusual type bar arrangement, 1907. (Auction Team
Koeln) $898 £551

A Sholes Visible No. 4 (Meiselbach) typewriter with amazing
type bar arrangement to permit
visible typing, 1901. (Auction
Team Koeln) $3,402 £2,087

Early American World Model 1
pointer typewriter with small
type segment, 1885. (Auction
Team Koeln) $610 £374

A Mignon Model 3 typewriter
with wooden case, 1913.
(Auction Team Koeln)
                       $175 £111

A North's typewriter with
original metal case, a rare over-
strike machine with reverse
type bar arrangement, 1892.
(Auction Team Koeln)
            $5,258 £3,328

A Columbia Bar-lock No. 11,
American full keyboard typewriter with decorative type
basket, two keys missing, 1900.
(Auction Team Koeln) $245 £150

A very rare Sholes Visible
(Meiselbach), typewriter of
unusual design, 1901. (Auction
Team Koeln) $3,209 £1,969

American Index pointer typewriter with semi-circular
control scale, 1893. (Auction
Team Koeln) $546 £335

A German Schubert variable
wheel typewriter, circa 1925.
(Auction Team Koeln)$103 £63

Japanese Nikkei typewriter,
circa 1958. (Auction Team
Koeln) $643 £407

A rare Czechoslovakian Tip Tip
typewriter, 1936. (Auction
Team Koeln) $642 £394

An early Daugherty US type
bar typewriter, with open type
basket, 1890. (Auction Team
Koeln) $1,798 £1,103

American Chicago cylinder
type machine, 1898. (Auction
Team Koeln) $577 £354

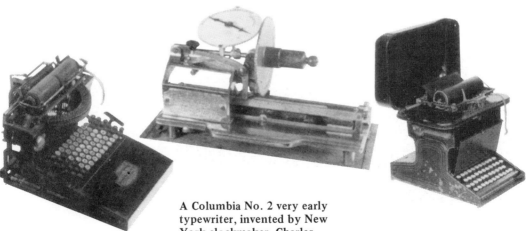

A Caligraph No. 4 American
full case typewriter, 1883.
(Auction Team Koeln)
      $437 £268

A Columbia No. 2 very early
typewriter, invented by New
York clockmaker Charles
Spiro, with large type wheel
for large and small lettering, in
fine mahogany case, 1884.
(Auction Team Koeln)
      $4,173 £2,560

A Sholes & Glidden typewriter
with blue and gold line decoration and rare fully detachable
hood, 1873. (Auction Team
Koeln) $6,420 £3,938

A French Virotyp pointer typewriter with table base, 1914. (Auction Team Koeln) $963 £591

An Odell No. 2 typewriter, re-plated but all parts original, in perfect condition, 1891. (Auction Team Koeln) $1,412 £866

A curious hammond type-writer, with folding key board, 1921. (Auction Team Koeln) $292 £172

A German black painted Mignon AGE typewriter, with English type and spare German key plate and type cylinder. (Spencer's) $132 £80

An English Imperial Model B. type bar typewriter with Russian keyboard and very broad shape, lacking space bar, in wooden case, 1914. (Auction Team Koeln) $262 £166

An early American Densmore No. 5 understrike typewriter with ball bearing carriage, 1907. (Auction Team Koeln)$161 £99

The Fox No 23, decorative American front strike machine, 1906. (Auction Team Koeln) $328 £207

An American Bennett type bar typewriter, (silver), 1907, in 'coat pocket' format. (Auction Team Koeln) $360£228

A Titania front strike machine with tin case, Berlin 1910. (Auction Team Koeln)$131 £83

VACUUM CLEANERS

A German Vorwerk Kobold Model 34 110v electric vacuum cleaner with tools such as hairdrier and duster, 1934. (Auction Team Koeln) $70 £44

An Abner's Sonderklasse carpet sweeper, German, circa 1910. (Auction Team Koeln) $11 £7

A German Vorwerk Kobold Model S vacuum cleaner, with bakelite housing, electric, circa 1935. (Auction Team Koeln) $11 £7

A Vorwerk Kobold Model S electric vacuum cleaner, with bakelite housing, 1945. (Auction Team Koeln) $57 £35

An Electrostar Type 558 vacuum cleaner with complete set of tools, in original box, 1935. (Auction Team Koeln) $73 £44

A Daisy wooden vacuum cleaner/wheel machine, without hose, 1908. (Auction Team Koeln) $128 £81

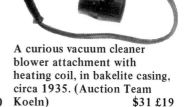

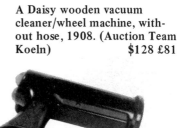

A Mercedes Model PM1 electric vacuum cleaner with bakelite housing, in original box with tools, circa 1955. (Auction Team Koeln) $19 £12

A Matador Junior electric vacuum cleaner with tools, by H. Schmidt, Chemnitz, circa 1950. (Auction Team Koeln) $32 £20

A curious vacuum cleaner blower attachment with heating coil, in bakelite casing, circa 1935. (Auction Team Koeln) $31 £19

VEHICLE REGISTRATION MARKS

100 PR	ANN 1E	C1 DER
$9,438 £6,050	$49,764 £31,900	$27,456 £17,600
GEM 1	TON 1C	2 TWO
$41,184 £26,400	$24,024 £15,400	$13,728 £8,800
10 ANT	FRY 1T	4 US
$6,349 £4,070	$16,302 £10,450	$14,586 £9,350
PUP 1L	1000 RS	MED 1A
$11,154 £7,150	$17,160 £11,000	$39,468 £25,300
4 PUT	10 TON	SHE 1K
$13,728 £8,800	$8,580 £5,500	$36,036 £23,100
10 LBW	F1 FTY	147 MAX
$4,118 £2,640	$12,870 £8,250	$10,639 £6,820
BRA 1N	8 TS	180 TOP
$27,456 £17,600	$15,444 £9,900	$13,728 £8,800
8 EEN	10 CC	100 UFO
$12,012 £7,700	$18,876 £12,100	$8,580 £5,500
ORB 1T	100 MCC	1 A
$16,302 £10,450	$7,722 £4,950	$274,560 £176,000
1 NN	BUY 1T	1 OLD
$44,616 £28,600	$46,332 £29,700	$24,024 £15,400
F1 LLY	99 OK	FRU 1T
$46,332 £29,700	$13,728 £8,800	$20,592 £13,200
C1 GAR	333 EEE	1 HMS
$24,024 £15,400	$7,207 £4,620	$30,030 £19,250

(Christie's)

VEHICLE REGISTRATION MARKS

MUS 1C	**F1 RST**	**D1 NKY**
$111,540 £71,500	$56,628 £36,300	$25,740 £16,500
E1 GHT	**10 TEN**	**4 PAS**
$27,456 £17,600	$15,444 £9,900	$7,722 £4,950
1 T	**999 JO**	**560 SEC**
$96,096 £61,600	$11,154 £7,150	$18,876 £12,100
900 MAC	**B10 PSY**	**XJS 777**
$6,864 £4,400	$7,722 £4,950	$10,296 £6,600
500 SL	**1 OFF**	**1 SOV**
$63,492 £40,700	$44,616 £28,600	$18,876 £12,100
ALF 1E	**18 PAM**	**928 S**
$29,172 £18,700	$17,160 £11,000	$21,450 £13,750
22 RR	**99 MG**	**21 ROB**
$22,308 £14,300	$13,728 £8,800	$12,012 £7,700
MAR 10N	**911 POR**	**B1 LLY**
$44,616 £28,600	$42,900 £27,500	$61,776 £39,600
JUL 1E	**1990 RR**	**100 JAG**
$58,344 £37,400	$12,870 £8,250	$30,030 £19,250
10 JR	**F1 GHT**	**LUV 1T**
$14,586 £9,350	$17,160 £11,000	$28,314 £18,150
G1 LTS	**1 RON**	**1 OU**
$20,592 £13,200	$42,900 £27,500	$44,616 £28,600
ART 1C	**1 SUE**	**ACT 10N**
$12,870 £8,250	$53,196 £34,100	$30,888 £19,800

(Christie's)

500 MER	**FEL 1X**	**11 JB**
$13,360 £8,000	$70,140 £42,000	$33,400 £20,000
1 XM	**LAL 1T**	**8 JC**
$43,420 £26,000	$33,400 £20,000	$19,205 £11,500
ALB 10N	**D 1 PAK**	**125 JD**
$31,730 £19,000	$38,911 £23,000	$15,865 £9,500
1 GR	**NEV 1N**	**1 JM**
$46,760 £28,000	$12,525 £7,500	$65,130 £39,000
1 GC	**SAL 1M**	**18 JR**
$41,750 £25,000	$60,120 £36,000	$20,040 £12,000
88 AS	**SUN IL**	**73 JS**
$16,700 £10,000	$60,120 £36,000	$11,022 £6,600
999 DR	**ADK 1N**	**10 PS**
$11,690 £7,000	$16,700 £10,000	$21,710 £13,000
123 EK	**1 VOR**	**100 SB**
$4,342 £2,600	$50,100 £30,000	$13,026 £7,800
G 1 LLY	**A 735 BMW**	**4 TC**
$116,900 £70,000	$19,038 £11,400	$20,875 £12,500
ART 1E	**10 GC**	**1 TES**
$33,400 £20,000	$25,050 £15,000	$21,710 £13,000
WYL 1E	**1 GE**	**APR 1L**
$23,380 £14,000	$31,730 £19,000	$77,655 £46,500
LEV 1T	**D 1 NAH**	**KAR 1M**
$51,770 £31,000	$23,380 £14,000	$56,780 £34,000

(Central Motor Auctions PLC)

VEHICLE REGISTRATION MARKS

UNW 1N	**MAG 1E**	**B 1 FFS**
$21,710 £13,000	$76,820 £46,000	$20,040 £12,000
ELW 1N	**A 1 LSA**	**1 LL**
$15,364 £9,200	$21,710 £13,000	$30,060 £18,000
D 1 NES	**B 1 BBY**	**CLA 1M**
$12,692 £7,600	$18,370 £11,000	$61,790 £37,000
F 1 RTH	**DUG 1E**	**4 WON**
$38,410 £23,000	$33,400 £20,000	$7,014 £4,200
HEW 1T	**LEW 1S**	**TRA 1L**
$28,390 £17,000	$60,120 £36,000	$18,370 £11,000
ELS 1E	**DAV 1S**	**D 1 ETS**
$25,050 £15,000	$60,120 £36,000	$18,370 £11,000
NAD 1A	**JUD 1E**	**1 AM**
$36,740 £22,000	$31,730 £19,000	$83,500 £50,000
D 1 XON	**SEW 1T**	**AGA 1N**
$59,285 £35,500	$13,360 £8,000	$20,040 £12,000
D 1 GBY	**RAD 1A**	**1 1 MR**
$25,050 £15,000	$26,720 £16,000	$35,070 £21,000
FOX 1E	**D 1 ALS**	**1 PM**
$37,575 £22,500	$8,350 £5,000	$93,520 £56,000
COW 1E	**ALL 1N**	**B 1 RDY**
$21,710 £13,000	$13,360 £8,000	$25,050 £15,000
BLA 1R	**B 1 MBO**	**G 1 ANT**
$35,070 £21,000	$30,060 £18,000	$25,050 £15,000

(Central Motor Auctions PLC)

'Spitfire In Action', stock version, double crown. (Onslow's) $288 £180

'Care of Arms is Care of Life Mud Snow Ice in your rifle muzzle cause burst barrel', 38 x 25cm. (Onslow's) $49 £30

'See How Your Salvage Helps A Bomber', double crown. (Onslow's) $23 £14

John Gilroy, 'We Want Your Kitchen Waste', double crown. (Onslow's) $272 £170

J. C. Leyendecker, 'USA Bonds Third Liberty Loan Campaign Boy Scouts of America', double crown. (Onslow's) $256 £160

Eric Kennington, 'Aspectos da Guerra', double crown. (Onslow's) $29 £18

'An Appeal To You', 98 x 63cm. (Onslow's) $72 £45

'Don't Forget That Walls Have Ears!' by Fougasse. (Onslow's) $560 £350

'Zec, Women of Britain Come Into the Factories', double crown. (Onslow's) $480 £300

H. M. Bateman, 'Coughs and Sneezes Spread Diseases', canteen, double crown. (Onslow's) $768 £480

E. Kealey, 'Women of Britain Say Go!' double crown. (Onslow's) $384 £240

Saville Lumley, 'Daddy What Did You Do In The Great War?' double crown. (Onslow's) $505 £310

Marc Stone, 'The Downfall of the Dictators is Assured', double crown. (Onslow's) $112 £70

Abram Games: 'Join the ATS', signed by the artist and model and dated 1941, double crown, together with a scrap book of photocopies and cuttings concerning the famous poster. (Onslow's) $4,800 £3,000

'El Hombre del Momento', double crown. (Onslow's) $192 £120

'When? — It's Up To Us!' double crown. (Onslow's) $208 £130

'Tylko Z Polska', published Poland, double royal. (Onslow's) $73 £45

Henry Raleigh, 'Halt The Hun! Buy US Government Bonds Third Liberty Loan', double crown. (Onslow's) $26 £16

Cast zinc and moulded copper weathervane, H. Howard & Co., West Bridgewater, Massachusetts, 1854-1867. 34in. long. (Skinner Inc.) $8,000 £4,908

A zinc weather vane formed as a figure of a running fox, 28½in. wide. (Christie's) $440 £275

A painted sheet iron small weathervane in the form of an Indian, American, late 19th/early 20th century, with feather headdress, traces of original paint, 15½in. high overall. (Christie's New York) $2,420 £1,522

Moulded copper weathervane, America, 19th century, flattened full bodied figure of 'Colonel Patchen', with an applied cast zinc head, 26½in. long. (Skinner Inc.) $1,700 £1,097

A gilt copper weather vane with fleur-de-lys finial, pierced with a winged dragon, 21in. high.(Christie's) $616 £385

Moulded copper weathervane, America, 19th century, the full bodied American eagle with outspread wings and a tilted head, wing span 24in. (Skinner Inc.) $500 £323

Moulded copper weathervane, possibly Cushing & White, Waltham, Massachusetts, 19th century, full bodied jockey astride a full bodied running horse, 26¼in. long. (Skinner Inc.) $2,400 £1,548

A moulded and gilded copper horse weathervane, by J. Howard & Co., Bridgewater, Massachusetts, third quarter 19th century, modelled in the form of a full bodied walking horse. (Christie's New York) $6,050 £3,805

Moulded copper gilded weathervane, America, late 19th century, in the form of strutting rooster with applied sheet copper tail, 19½in. high. (Skinner Inc.) $1,200 £736

Moulded copper weathervane, New England, 19th century, full bodied figure of a codfish with moulded scales 36in. long. (Skinner Inc.) $5,500 £3,374

A cast moulded and gilt pig weathervane, American, 19th century, the standing pig with applied ears and cast zinc curlique tail, 16in. high, 26in. long. (Christie's New York) $8,800 £5,534

A 19th century iron weather vane formed as an Indian on horseback, 36½in. wide. (Christie's) $492 £308

Sheet iron weathervane, America, 19th century, silhouette of a prancing horse, supported with iron bracing (bullet holes), 34in. long. (Skinner Inc.) $800 £516

Moulded copper weathervane, attributed to Harris & Co., Boston, 19th century, the flattened full bodied figure of a stag leaping over a flower covered log (regilt), 32½in. long. (Skinner Inc.) $10,000 £6,452

Moulded copper weathervane, attributed to Harris & Co., Boston, 19th century, flattened full bodied figure of a trotting horse pulling a sulky with a jockey, 33in. long. (Skinner Inc.) $800 £516

A moulded and gilt trotting horse weathervane, New England, 19th century, the fully extended trotting horse with cast zinc head, 42in. long, 21½in. high. (Christie's New York) $6,600 £4,150

Carved and painted horse and sulky with driver, early 20th century, mounted above a shaped wooden stand (imperfections), 11¾in. long. (Skinner Inc.) $1,600 £982

An early 20th century African carved wood mortar of waisted and panelled cylindrical form, 33.5cm. high. (Henry Spencer) $97 £60

A Florentine silvered carved wood headboard, the pierced acanthus C-scrolling and fruit festooned cresting in high relief, part 19th century, 65 x 61in. (Christie's S. Ken) $797 £495

A carved and painted wood figure, American, 19th century, in the form of a man wearing a tailcoat, 31cm. high. (Christie's New York) $660 £415

A carved walnut cakeboard, stamped *J. L. Watkins, N.Y.*, circa 1850, centring a mounted soldier enclosed by a foliate medallion, 10¾ x 10¾in. (Christie's New York) $825 £518

Carved wooden gingerbread mould, probably Continental, late 18th century, one side with the caricatured figure of a gentleman wearing a wig, 27in. high. (Skinner Inc.) $1,100 £675

Carved polychrome wooden cigar store figure, America, circa 1900, of a seated man carved in the full round, 52in. high. (Skinner Inc.) $700 £452

Pair of swan decoys, attributed to Thomas Langedon, New York, 20th century, each hollow carved with inletted curving necks, 46in. long. (Skinner Inc.) $1,200 £774

A yew wood treadle lathe with screw adjustable, stone counter-balanced yew flywheel, 37in. wide. (Christie's S. Ken) $1,564 £990

A good early 18th century lignum vitae wassail bowl and cover, the multiple turned body on short stem and circular foot, 38cm. high. (Phillips London) $10,710 £7,000

A 19th century carved oak coat rack, with a dog's head surmount, inset with glass eyes, 34½in. wide. (Christie's S. Ken) $739 £440

Carved and painted wall box, America, 19th century, shaped crest with diamond cut out over scallop edge, 8¼in. high. (Skinner Inc.) $2,400 £1,472

Carved and painted parrot with metal hoop, possibly Canada, late 19th century (paint wear), 18½in. high. (Skinner Inc.) $2,800 £1,718

A pair of 18th century French boxwood and ivory figures of a lady and gentleman in elegant costume, 6in. high. (Christie's S. Ken) $1,716 £1,100

An Austro-Hungarian mid 19th century covered bowl fashioned from an unpolished coconut shell, date indistinct, possibly 1845, 7in. (Christie's S. Ken) $523 £308

A carved and painted pine parrot by William Schimmel, Cumberland Valley, Pennsylvania, 1865-1890, painted yellow, green, red and black, 10¼in. high. (Christie's New York) $7,700 £4,842

Walnut pastry mould, S. Y. Watkins, New York, first half of 19th century, carved with an American eagle, 10¾ x 11¼in. (Skinner Inc.) $1,300 £798

An Italian polychrome carved wood reliquary statuette of St Ferdinand, 1914, Stuflesser, robed in vestments, 48in. high overall. (Christie's S. Ken) $858 £550

WOOD

A Galle marquetry oval tray, inlaid in various woods with stylised chrysanthemums, 60cm. long, signed. (Phillips London) $293 £180

A pair of Venetian painted, gilt and ebonised blackamoor torcheres, each with gadrooned tazza supported on the head, 64in. high. (Christie's London) $11,511 £7,150

Painted pine fireboard, possibly Central Massachusetts, circa 1815, depicting fruit and flowering boughs in a vase, 37½in. wide. (Skinner Inc.) $26,000 £15,951

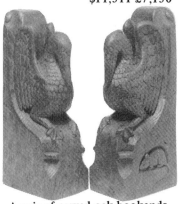

Motherhood, a carved oak figure by James Woodford, carved *JW* monogram and inscribed paper label *No.3, Motherhood, English Oak, James Woodford, 19 St Peter's Sq., W6,* 90cm. high. (Christie's London) $2,957 £1,760

A pair of carved oak bookends, by Robert Thompson of Kilburn, known as the Mouseman, each carved with a large bird, 25.6cm. high. (Phillips London) $782 £480

One of a pair of limed oak corner posts carved with heraldic atlantes, early 16th century, 126in. high. (Christie's S. Ken) Two $4,303 £2,640

A fine okimono in lightly stained boxwood depicting Gama Sennin seated with a large toad on his shoulders, signed *Hokyudo Itsumin,* mid-19th century, 12.7cm. high. (Christie's London) $3,476 £2,200

A Buddhist travelling shrine of gilded wood with metal fittings, the Divinity wearing loose and partially covering vestments, late Edo period, 41cm. high. (Christie's London) $1,390 £880

A carved oak figure of St James standing with a pilgrim staff in his right hand, carved in full relief on new base, possibly Belgian, Antwerp, 16th century, 36cm. high. (Kunsthaus am Museum) $2,053 £1,180

A stylish carved rosewood model of an antelope, designed by Jacques Adnet, modelled as the spirited creature caught leaping through stylised zig-zag foliage, 25cm. high. (Phillips London) $1,271 £780

Large burl bowl, New England, 19th century, of deep circular form, 12¼in. diam. (Skinner Inc.) $850 £503

Italian Gilt and Polychromed Wood Coat-of-Arms of the House of Savoy, 18th century, 24½in. high. (Skinner Inc) $1300 £844

A 19th century Continental ebonised photograph frame, the spandrels inlaid in pietra dura with sprays of flowers, 13in. high. (Christie's S. Ken) $430 £264

A pair of carved oak figures of Roman soldiers, each standing on a shaped rectangular base and holding up a shield, 38in. and 40in. high. (Christie's London) $2,302 £1,430

A fine lignum wassail, the base with three brass taps and moulded circular plinth, 18th century, possibly associated, 20in. high. (Christie's London) $2,656 £1,650

Japanese lacquered wood figure of Kwannon, 17th century, standing in flowing robes, 21in. high. (Skinner Inc.) $400 £250

A Scandinavian treen tankard and cover, the turned lid carved with a lion, the handle incised with foliage, 17th century, 10¼in. high. (Christie's London) $3,542 £2,200

German carved walnut planter, mid-19th century, in the form of a wicker basket heavily carved with birds and fruits, 28½in. high. (Skinner Inc.) $1,800 £1,104

Miniature carved and painted squirrel, America, early 20th century, 3½in. high.
(Skinner Inc.) $150   £91

Carved gilt and painted wall plaque, attributed to John Haley Bellamy (1836–1914), Kittery Point, Maine, 28in. long.
(Skinner Inc.) $2800   £1708

A carved mahogany wood figure, American, 20th century, in the form of a mermaid with fish-scale details, 42in. long.
(Christie's) $1870   £1171

A late 17th century carved oak and painted coat of arms of His Majesty King William III, 19in. high.
(Andrew Hartley Fine Arts) $3230   £1900

A mid-19th century Mauchline fernware tulip shaped vase, with a transfer cameo, 14in. high. (Christie's S. Ken) $168 £110

Egyptian polychrome Sarcophagus mask, 26th dynasty, painted on a layer of gesso and linen over wood, 19in. high.
(Skinner Inc.) $2000   £1220

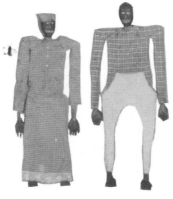

Ancient Egyptian wood figural plaque, Late period, striding female carved in low relief, traces of gesso and pigment, 16in. high.
(Skinner Inc) $850   £527

Two large carved and painted articulated dancing dolls, American, early 20th century, 43½in., 41in. high respectively.
(Christie's) $1650   £1038

An early 18th century Italian carved giltwood and polychrome figure of the Virgin Annunciate, 11in. high.
(Christie's S. Ken.) $690   £418

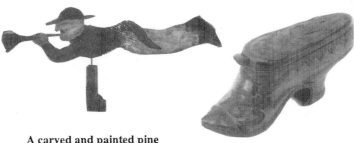

Carved and painted eagle, America, early 20th century, the stlised figure painted in naturalistic colour, 13³/₄in. high.
(Skinner Inc.) $1300 £793

A carved and painted pine sailor's Angel Gabriel weathervane, American, 19th century, 41¹/₂in. long.
(Christie's) $2860 £1798

An 18th century treen shoe snuff box, inlaid in pewter with a figure of a man and foliage, bearing the date 1762, 6in. long.
(Christie's S. Ken.) $218 £132

Automated wood and brass horse and sulky with driver, America, first half 20th century, the carved and painted driver, articulated horse with leather tack, 24in. long.
(Skinner Inc.) $3500 £2135

Pair of carved limewood figures of a travelling Chinaman and his wife and child, each approximately 20in.
(G.A. Key) $74 £45

An 18th century Neapolitan carved giltwood and polychrome group of the Archangel Michael, 16¹/₂in. high, on a stepped cut corner base.
(Christie's S. Ken.)
$3085 £1870

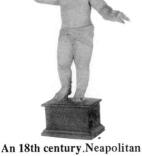

An 18th century Neapolitan polychrome carved wood figure of The Christ Child, with inset glass eyes, 20¹/₂in. high.
(Christie's S. Ken.) $635 £385

A pair of 18th century Neapolitan carved polchrome, giltwood and gesso figures, each holding a cornucopiae of flowers, 22in. high
(Christie's S. Ken.)
$5082 £3080

A carved and painted Toll Gate, English, 19th century, with carved inscription 'Molwich Side Gate, Table of Tolls' and a table of fees, 62³/₄in. x 26¹/₂in.
(Christie's) $6050 £3805

A wood sculpture depicting Sugawara No Michizani wearing a courtier's eboshi, his court costume decorated with umemon, early 19th century, 33.5cm. high. (Christie's London) $3,476 £2,200

Italian Painted and Parcel Gilt Ornament, in the form of a sun god, 18th century, 76in. high. (Skinner Inc) $3300 £2142

A 19th century polychrome carved wood altar candlestick, the tapering shaft supported by a robed saint, 21in. high. (Christie's S. Ken) $480 £308

The Offering, signed and dated *William Fuller Curtis MCMII*, in carved wood relief with gilt highlights, 29 x 5ft.8in. (Skinner Inc.) $10,000 £6,173

A Chokwe wood mask, the light brown stained head with coffee bean eyes pierced below the arching brows, 12in. high. (Spencer's) $1610 £1000

Pair of Brant decoys, South-eastern Massachusetts, late 19th century, each with incised bill, metal tack eyes, 17in. long. (Skinner Inc.) $2,700 £1,598

Italian Polychromed Wood Figure of the Madonna, 18th century, with arms folded across the chest, (flaking, losses), 21in. high. (Skinner Inc) $650 £422

INDEX

INDEX